CCNP ISCW
Official Exam
Certification Guide

Brian Morgan, CCIE No. 4865
Neil Lovering, CCIE No. 1772

PEARSON
Education

About the Authors

Brian Morgan, CCIE No. 4865, is a consulting systems engineer for Cisco, specializing in Unified Communications technologies. He services a number of Fortune 500 companies in architectural, design, and support roles. With more than 15 years in the networking industry, he has served as director of engineering for a large telecommunications company, is a certified Cisco instructor teaching at all levels, from basic routing and switching to CCIE lab preparation, and spent a number of years with IBM Network Services serving many of IBM's largest clients. He is a former member of the ATM Forum and a long-time member of the IEEE.

Neil Lovering, CCIE No. 1772, works as a design consultant for Cisco. Neil has been with Cisco for more than three years and works on large-scale government networking solutions projects. Prior to Cisco, Neil was a network consultant and instructor for more than eight years and worked on various routing, switching, remote connectivity, and security projects for many customers all over North America.

Contributing Author

Mark Newcomb, CCNP, CCDP, is a retired network security engineer. Mark has more than 20 years of experience in the networking industry, focusing on the financial and medical industries. Mark is a frequent contributor and reviewer for Cisco Press books. Mark also served as a technical reviewer for this book.

About the Technical Reviewer

Sean Walberg is a network engineer from Winnipeg, Canada. He has worked in ISP, healthcare, and corporate environments, designing and supporting LANs, WANs, and Internet hosting. Sean is the author of *CCSA Exam Cram 2* and many articles about UNIX, Linux, and VoIP. He holds a bachelor's degree in computer engineering and is a registered Professional Engineer.

Dedications

To Beth, Amanda, and Emma: Thank you for your love and support. You make life worth living.

—Brian Morgan

This book is dedicated to my wife, Jody, and my children, Kevin and Michelle, who together give me the inspiration to learn more and dream bigger.

—Neil Lovering

Acknowledgments

First and foremost, we would like to acknowledge the sacrifices made by our families in allowing us to make the time to write this book. Without their support, it would not have been possible.

Thanks to our friends who were not shy about stepping in for a bit of motivational correction when timelines were slipping.

As always, a huge thank you goes to the production team. Mary Beth, Chris, and Tonya suffered no end of frustration throughout this writing. They never fully gave up on it, and for that, we are in their debt.

Contents at a Glance

Contents

Icons Used in This Book

 PC

 Workstation

 Video over IP

 Optical Switch

 Optical Transport

 NAT/PAT Device

 DSLAM

 Cisco IP Phone

 File Server

 Web Server

 Multilayer Switch

 Voice-Enabled Router

 ATM/FastGB Etherswitch

 ATM Switch

 Router

 Broadband Router

 Router with Firewall

 Switch

 Modem

 Phone 2

 CallManager

 Multi-Fabric Server Switch

 Server Switch

 Firewall

 Cell Phone

 NetRanger

 Firewall Services Module (FWSM)

 Route/Switch Processor

 Satellite

 Satellite dish

 Network Management Appliance

 Network Cloud

 Lightweight Single Radio Access Point

 Line: Ethernet

 Line: Serial

Wireless Connection

Command Syntax Conventions

The conventions used to present command syntax in this book are the same conventions used in the IOS Command Reference. The Command Reference describes these conventions as follows:

- **Boldface** indicates commands and keywords that are entered literally as shown. In actual configuration examples and output (not general command syntax), boldface indicates commands that are manually input by the user (such as a **show** command).

- *Italics* indicate arguments for which you supply actual values.

- Vertical bars (|) separate alternative, mutually exclusive elements.

- Square brackets [ ] indicate optional elements.

- Braces { } indicate a required choice.

- Braces within brackets [{ }] indicate a required choice within an optional element.

Foreword

CCNP ISCW Official Exam Certification Guide is an excellent self-study resource for the CCNP ISCW exam. Passing the exam validates the knowledge, skills, and understanding needed to master the features used in larger corporate remote-access facilities and Internet service provider (ISP) operations. It is one of several exams required to attain the CCNP certification.

Gaining certification in Cisco technology is key to the continuing educational development of today's networking professional. Through certification programs, Cisco validates the skills and expertise required to effectively manage the modern enterprise network.

Cisco Press Exam Certification Guides and preparation materials offer exceptional—and flexible—access to the knowledge and information required to stay current in your field of expertise, or to gain new skills. Whether used as a supplement to more traditional training or as a primary source of learning, these materials offer users the information and knowledge validation required to gain new understanding and proficiencies.

Developed in conjunction with the Cisco certifications and training team, Cisco Press books are the only self-study books authorized by Cisco. Cisco Press books offer students a series of exam practice tools and resource materials to help ensure that they fully grasp the concepts and information presented.

Additional instructor-led courses, e-learning, labs, and simulations authorized by Cisco are available exclusively from Cisco Learning Solutions Partners worldwide. To learn more, visit www.cisco.com/go/training.

I hope that you will find this guide to be an enriching and useful part of your exam preparation.

Erik Ullanderson
Manager, Global Certifications
Learning@Cisco
February, 2007

Introduction

Professional certifications have been an important part of the computing industry for many years and will continue to become more important. Many reasons exist for these certifications, but the most popularly cited reason is that of credibility. All other considerations held equal, the certified employee/consultant/job candidate is considered more valuable than one who is not.

Goals and Methods

The most important and somewhat obvious goal of this book is to help you pass the ISCW exam (642-825). In fact, if the primary objective of this book were different, the book's title would be misleading; however, the methods used in this book to help you pass the CCNP ISCW exam are designed to also make you much more knowledgeable about how to do your job. Although this book and the accompanying CD-ROM together provide more than enough questions to help you prepare for the actual exam, the method in which they are used is not to simply make you memorize as many questions and answers as you possibly can.

One key methodology used in this book is to help you discover the exam topics that you need to review in more depth, to help you fully understand and remember those details, and to help you prove to yourself that you have retained your knowledge of those topics. So this book helps you pass the exam not by memorization, but by truly learning and understanding the topics. Although the ISCW exam is just one of the foundation areas for the CCNP certification, you should not consider yourself a truly skilled routing and switching engineer or specialist until you have demonstrated that you understand the material covered on the exam. This book would do you a disservice if it did not attempt to help you learn the material. To that end, the book uses the following methods to help you pass the ISCW exam:

- Helps you discover which test topics you have not mastered
- Provides explanations and information to fill in your knowledge gaps
- Supplies exercises and scenarios that enhance your ability to recall and deduce the answers to test questions
- Provides practice exercises on the topics and the testing process via test questions on the CD-ROM

Who Should Read This Book?

This book is not designed to be a general networking topics book, although it can be used for that purpose. This book is intended to tremendously increase your chances of passing the CCNP ISCW exam. Although other objectives can be achieved from using this book, the book is written with one goal in mind: to help you pass the exam.

So why should you want to pass the CCNP ISCW exam? Because it is one of the milestones toward getting the CCNP certification; no small feat in itself. And many reasons exist for getting CCNP certification. You might want to enhance your resume, demonstrate that you are serious about continuing the learning process, or help your reseller-employer obtain a higher discount from Cisco by having more certified employees. Or perhaps it would mean a raise, a promotion, or greater recognition.

Strategies for Exam Preparation

The strategy you use to prepare for the CCNP ISCW exam might be slightly different from strategies used by other readers, mainly based on the skills, knowledge, and experience you already have obtained. For instance, if you have attended the ISCW course, you might take a different approach from that taken by someone who has learned switching via on-the-job training. The section "How to Use This Book to Pass the Exam," later in this introduction, includes various preparation strategies that are tailored to match differing reader backgrounds.

Regardless of the strategy you use or the background you have, the book is designed to help you get to the point that you can pass the exam with the least amount of time required. For instance, there is no need for you to practice or read about IP addressing and subnetting if you fully understand it already. However, many people like to make sure that they truly know a topic and thus read over material that they already know. Several book features help you gain the confidence that you know some material already and also help you know what topics you need to study more.

Although this book can be read cover to cover, it is designed to be flexible and allow you to easily move between chapters and sections of chapters to cover just the material that you need more work with. If you intend to read all chapters, the order in the book is an excellent sequence to use.

The chapters cover the following topics:

- **Chapter 1, "Describing Network Requirements"**—This chapter describes the basic framework for network evolution using the Service-Oriented Network Architecture (SONA) framework to build an Intelligent Information Network (IIN).

- **Chapter 2, "Topologies for Teleworker Connectivity"**—This chapter describes connectivity and security requirements for teleworker access to a central site.

- **Chapter 3, "Using Cable to Access a Central Site"**—This chapter describes cable access and the underlying technologies that make it a viable connectivity option for SOHO and teleworkers.

- **Chapter 4, "Using DSL to Access a Central Site"**—This chapter describes DSL access and the underlying technologies that make it a viable connectivity option for SOHO and teleworkers.

- **Chapter 5, "Configuring DSL Access with PPPoE"**—This chapter discusses the PPPoE technology and its use in SOHO and teleworker deployments.

- **Chapter 6, "Configuring DSL Access with PPPoA"**—This chapter discusses the PPPoA technology and its use in SOHO and teleworker deployments.

- **Chapter 7, "Troubleshooting DSL Access"**—This chapter discusses some basic DSL troubleshooting techniques specific to DSL in a SOHO or teleworker deployment.

- **Chapter 8, "The MPLS Conceptual Model"**—This chapter discusses the basic switching technologies and concepts in MPLS networks.

- **Chapter 9, "MPLS Architecture"**—This chapter discusses the manner in which routing and label switching take place in an MPLS network.

- **Chapter 10, "Configuring Frame Mode MPLS"**—This chapter discusses the configuration of MPLS technologies on Cisco routers.

- **Chapter 11, "MPLS VPN Technologies"**—This chapter describes MPLS VPN architecture and how it improves upon traditional VPN models.

- **Chapter 12, "IPsec Overview"**—This chapter describes the concepts used to secure network connections today with IPsec. The various protocols and concepts are covered.

- **Chapter 13, "Site-to-Site VPN Operations"**—This chapter discusses the purpose and use of site-to-site VPNs. It shows configuration of site-to-site VPNs via both the CLI and SDM.

- **Chapter 14, "GRE Tunneling over IPsec"**—This chapter discusses the use of GRE over IPsec to permit dynamic routing over VPN connections. Once again, both CLI and SDM configurations are discussed.

- **Chapter 15, "IPsec High Availability Options"**—This chapter discusses how failures in a network can occur and what steps can be taken to mitigate the risks of failure.

- **Chapter 16, "Configuring Cisco Easy VPN"**—This chapter examines the use of the Cisco Easy VPN solution to simplify the deployment of VPN connections to remote offices.

- **Chapter 17, "Implementing the Cisco VPN Client"**—This chapter discusses the installation, configuration, and use of the Cisco VPN Client for individual VPN connections.

- **Chapter 18, "Cisco Device Hardening"**—This chapter discusses the various vulnerabilities that exist in network devices and explains steps to secure the devices from compromise.

- **Chapter 19, "Securing Administrative Access"**—This chapter discusses the various ways to restrict administrative access to Cisco devices.

- **Chapter 20, "Using AAA to Scale Access Control"**—This chapter examines how to quickly configure and maintain a system that uses AAA with either Remote Authentication Dial-In User Service (RADIUS) or Terminal Access Controller Access Control System Plus (TACACS+) as part of its security strategy

- **Chapter 21, "Cisco IOS Threat Defense Features"**—This chapter examines the advantages, concepts, and strategy behind the Cisco IOS firewall offerings, how the Cisco IOS firewall operates, and the differences between packet filters, application layer gateways (ALG), and stateful packet filters. All these concepts contribute to the overall security strategy as implemented by the administrator to create greater flexibility in access control to prevent security breaches.

- **Chapter 22, "Implementing Cisco IOS Firewalls"**—This chapter explores how to quickly set up, configure, and monitor a firewall using Cisco IOS Software features in order to secure your network.

- **Chapter 23, "Implementing Cisco IDS and IPS"**—This chapter discusses the concepts of both IPS and IDS systems, and how to configure the Cisco IOS IPS solution via both the CLI and SDM.

Sample test questions and the testing engine on the CD-ROM allow simulated exams for final practice.

Each of these chapters uses several features to help you make best use of your time in that chapter. The features are as follows:

- **"Do I Know This Already?" quiz**—Each chapter begins with a quiz that helps you determine the amount of time you need to spend studying that chapter. The quiz is broken into subdivisions, each of which corresponds to a section of the chapter. Following the directions at the beginning of each chapter, the "Do I Know This Already?" quiz will direct you to study all or particular parts of the chapter.

- **Foundation Topics**—This is the core section of each chapter that explains the protocols, concepts, and configuration for the topics in the chapter.

- **Foundation Summary**—Near the end of each chapter, this section collects the most important tables and figures from the chapter. This section is designed to help you review the key concepts in the chapter and is an excellent tool for last-minute review.

- **Q&A**—These end-of-the-chapter questions, based on the topics covered in the "Foundation Topics" section, challenge your recall of the key topics covered in the chapter.

- **CD-ROM-based practice exam**—The companion CD-ROM contains a large number of questions that are not included in the text of the book. You can answer these questions by using the simulated exam feature or by using the topical review feature. This is the best tool for helping you prepare for the test-taking process.

Pedagogical Approach

Retention and recall are the two features of human memory most closely related to performance on tests. This exam preparation guide focuses on increasing both retention and recall of the topics on the exam. The other human characteristic involved in successfully passing the exam is intelligence; this book does not address that issue.

Adult retention is typically less than that of children. For example, it is common for 4-year-olds to pick up basic language skills in a new country faster than their parents. Children retain facts as an end unto itself; adults typically either need a stronger reason to remember a fact or must have a reason to think about that fact several times to retain it in memory. For these reasons, a student who attends a typical Cisco course and retains 50 percent of the material is actually quite an amazing student.

Memory recall is based on connectors to the information that needs to be recalled—the greater the number of connectors to a piece of information, the better chance and better speed of recall.

Recall and retention work together. If you do not retain the knowledge, it will be difficult to recall it. This book is designed with features to help you increase retention and recall. It does this in the following ways:

- By providing succinct and complete methods of helping you decide what you recall easily and what you do not recall at all.
- By giving references to the exact passages in the book that review those concepts you did not recall so that you can quickly be reminded about a fact or concept. Repeating information that connects to another concept helps retention, and describing the same concept in several ways throughout a chapter increases the number of connectors to the same pieces of information.
- By including exercise questions that supply fewer connectors than multiple-choice questions. This helps you exercise recall and avoids giving you a false sense of confidence, as an exercise with only multiple-choice questions might do. For example, fill-in-the-blank questions require you to have better recall than multiple-choice questions.

Finally, accompanying this book is a CD-ROM that has exam-like, multiple-choice questions. These are useful for you to practice taking the exam and to get accustomed to the time restrictions imposed during the exam.

How This Book Can Help You Pass the CCNP ISCW Exam

The primary focus of this book is not to teach material in the detail that is covered by an instructor in a 5-day class with hands-on labs. Instead, we tried to capture the essence of each topic and to present questions and scenarios that push the envelope on each topic that is covered for the ISCW exam.

The audience for this book includes both candidates who have successfully completed the ISCW class and candidates who have not taken the ISCW class but have a breadth of experience in this area. The **show** and **debug** commands from that class are fair game for questions within the ISCW exam, and hands-on work is the best way to commit those to memory.

If you have not taken the ISCW course, the quizzes and scenarios in this book should give you a good idea of whether you are sufficiently prepared to skip the class and test out based on your experience. On the flip side, however, you should know that although having the knowledge from just a classroom setting can be enough to pass the exam, some questions assume a CCNA level of internetworking knowledge.

How to Use This Book to Pass the Exam

There are four sections in each chapter: a short pre-assessment quiz, the main topics of the chapter, a summary of the key points of the chapter, and a test to ensure that you have mastered the topics in the chapter.

Each chapter begins with a "Do I Know This Already?" quiz, which maps to the major topic headings in the chapter. If you get a high score on this quiz, you might want to review the "Foundation Summary" section at the end of the chapter and then take the chapter test. If you score high on the test, you should review the summary to see if anything else should be added to your crib notes for a final run-through before taking the live test.

The "Foundation Summary" section in each chapter provides a set of "crib notes" that can be reviewed prior to the exam. These notes are not designed to teach, but merely to remind the reader what was in the chapter. Each "Foundation Summary" section consists of charts and raw data that complement an understanding of the chapter information.

All "Do I Know This Already?" and "Q&A" questions, with answers, are in Appendix A, "Answers to the 'Do I Know This Already?' Quizzes and Q&A Sections." These conveniently located questions can be read and reviewed quickly prior to taking the live test. The CD-ROM has testing software, as well as many additional questions similar to the format of the ISCW exam. These questions should be a valuable resource when making final preparations for the exam.

Anyone preparing for the ISCW exam can use the guidelines at the beginning of each chapter to guide their study. However, if you would like some additional guidance, the final parts of this chapter give additional strategies for study, based on how you have prepared before buying this book. So, find the section that most closely matches your background in the next few pages, and then read some additional ideas to help you prepare. There is a section for the reader who has passed other CCNP exams and is ready for the ISCW exam, one for the reader who has passed the CCNA and is starting the CCNP track, and one for the reader who has no Cisco certifications and is starting the CCNP track.

You Have Passed Other CCNP Exams and Are Preparing for the ISCW Exam

Scenario 1: You Have Taken the ISCW Course

Because you have taken other Cisco exams and have taken the ISCW course, you know what you are up against in the test experience. The ISCW exam is like all the others. The questions and answer selections are sometimes confusing if you read too much into them.

The best approach with this book is to take each chapter's "Do I Know This Already?" quiz and focus on the parts for which you draw a blank. It is best not to jump to the final exam until you have given yourself a chance to review the entire book. Save the final exam to test your knowledge after you have mentally checked each section to verify that you have an idea of what the whole test could cover. Remember that the CD-ROM testing engine spools out a sampling of questions and might not give you a good picture the first time you use it; the test engine could spool a test that is easy for you, or it could spool one that is very difficult.

Before the test, make your own notes using the "Foundation Summary" sections and your own handwritten notes. Writing something down, even if you are copying it, makes it easier to remember. Once you have your bank of notes, study them, and then take the final exam three or four times. Each time you take the test, force yourself to read each question and each answer, even if you have seen them before. Again, repetition is a super memory aid.

Scenario 2: You Have Not Taken the ISCW Course

Because you have taken other Cisco exams, you know what you are up against in the test experience. The ISCW exam is like all the others. The questions and answer selections are sometimes confusing if you read too much into them.

The best approach with this book, because you have not taken the class, is to take each chapter's "Do I Know This Already?" quiz as an aid for what to look for as you read the chapter. Once you have completed a chapter, take the end-of-chapter test to see how well you have assimilated the material.

After you complete each chapter, you should use the CD-ROM testing engine to find out how well you know the material.

Before the test, make notes using the "Foundation Summary" sections and your own additions. Writing something down, even if you are copying it, makes it easier to remember. Once you have your bank of notes, study them, and then take the final practice exam on the CD-ROM testing engine three or four times. Each time you take the test, force yourself to read each question and each answer, even if you have seen them before. Again, repetition is a super memory aid.

You Have Passed the CCNA and Are Preparing for the ISCW Exam

Scenario 1: You Have Taken the ISCW Course

Because you have taken other Cisco exams and have taken the ISCW course, you know what you are up against in the test experience. The ISCW exam is like all the others. The questions and the answer selections are sometimes confusing if you read too much into them.

The best approach with this book is to take each chapter's "Do I Know This Already?" quiz and focus on the parts for which you draw a blank. It is best not to jump to the final exam until you have given yourself a chance to review the entire book. Save the final exam to test your knowledge after you have mentally checked each section to verify that you have an idea of what the whole test could cover. The CD-ROM testing engine spools out a sampling of questions and might not give you a good picture the first time you use it; the test engine could spool a test that is easy for you, or it could spool one that is very difficult.

Before the test, make your own notes using the "Foundation Summary" sections and your own additions. Writing something down, even if you are copying it, makes it easier to remember. Once you have your bank of notes, study them, and then take the final practice exam on the CD-ROM testing engine three or four times. Each time you take the test, force yourself to read each question and each answer, even if you have seen them before. Again, repetition is a super memory aid.

Scenario 2: You Have Not Taken the ISCW Course

Because you have taken other Cisco exams, you know what you are up against in the test experience. The ISCW exam is like all the others. The questions and answer selections are sometimes confusing if you read too much into them.

The best approach with this book, because you have not taken the class, is to take each chapter's "Do I Know This Already?" quiz to determine what to look for as you read the chapter. Once you have completed a chapter, take the end-of-chapter test to see how well you have assimilated the material.

After you complete each chapter, you should use the CD-ROM testing engine to find out how well you know the material.

Before the test, make your own notes using the "Foundation Summary" sections and your own additions. Writing something down, even if you are copying it, makes it easier to remember. Once you have your bank of notes, study them, and then take the final practice exam on the CD-ROM testing engine three or four times. Each time you take the test, force yourself to read each question and each answer, even if you have seen them before. Again, repetition is a super memory aid.

You Have Experience and Want to Skip the Classroom Experience and Take the ISCW Exam

Scenario 1: You Have CCNA Certification

Because you have taken other Cisco exams, you know what you are up against in the test experience. The ISCW exam is like the others. The questions and the answer selections are sometimes confusing if you read too much into them.

The best approach with this book, because you have not taken the course, is to take each chapter's "Do I Know This Already?" quiz to determine what to look for as you read the chapter. Once you have completed a chapter, take the end-of-chapter test to see how well you have assimilated the material.

After you complete each chapter, you should use the CD-ROM testing engine to find out how well you know the material.

Before the test, make your own notes using the "Foundation Summary" sections and your own additions. Writing something down, even if you are copying it, makes it easier to remember. Once you have your bank of notes, study them, and then take the final practice exam on the CD-ROM testing engine three or four times. Each time you take the test, force yourself to read each question and each answer, even if you have seen them before. Again, repetition is a super memory aid.

Scenario 2: You Do Not Have a CCNA Certification

Why don't you have the certification? The prerequisite for the CCNP certification is to be certified as a CCNA, so you really should pursue your CCNA certification before tackling the CCNP certification. Beginning with the ISCW exam gives you a skewed view of what is needed for the Cisco Professional certification track.

That being said, if you *must* pursue the certifications out of order, follow the spirit of the book. Read each chapter and then do the quiz at the front of the chapter to see if you caught the major points. Once that is done, try the test on the CD-ROM and pay particular attention to the VUE/Thomson Prometric-way of testing so that you are prepared for the live test.

One Final Word of Advice

The "Foundation Summary" section and your notes are your "crib note" knowledge of ISCW. These pieces of paper are valuable when you are studying for the CCIE or Cisco recertification exam. You should take the time to organize them so that they become part of your paper "long-term memory."

Reviewing information that you actually wrote in your own handwriting is the easiest data to put back into your brain RAM. Gaining a certification but losing the knowledge is of no value. For most people, maintaining the knowledge is as simple as writing it down. Good luck to all!

This part of the book covers the following ISCW exam topics:

Implement basic teleworker services.

- Describe Cable (HFC) technologies.
- Describe xDSL technologies.
- Configure ADSL (i.e., PPPoE or PPPoA).
- Verify basic teleworker configurations.

Part I: Remote Connectivity Best Practices

Part I: Remote Connectivity
Best Practices

Exam Topic List

This chapter covers the following topics that you need to master for the CCNP ISCW exam:

- **Describing Network Requirements**—This section discusses the basic vision of an IIN.

- **Intelligent Information Network**—This section discusses the evolutionary path of the network as the platform for next-generation services and applications.

- **SONA**—This section discusses the template for enterprise networks on the path to becoming an IIN.

- **Cisco Network Models**—This section discusses the Cisco architectural templates for common enterprise network deployment scenarios.

- **Remote Connection Requirements in a Converged Network**—This section discusses integrated services and applications needs for enterprise sites.

CHAPTER 1

Describing Network Requirements

Throughout the history of networking, individuals, companies, and other organizations have made it their goals to better use technology. Where a technology did not exist, new ones sprang to life. The process of topological development and evolution in the industry has been nothing short of astounding. Technology has advanced immeasurably in a relatively short period of time. However, the network has always been viewed as just another tool to facilitate connectivity between the user community and the server platforms on which applications run and data is stored. The network has always held the role of a simple transport mechanism.

That role changes now. With the introduction of its vision of the network as the platform, Cisco has brought about a change in the way enterprise networks are designed, built, and deployed.

Network infrastructure needs of the current day dictate an exceedingly high service and availability level. With this, new demands in ever-increasing amounts are being placed on the network. This increased demand is not isolated solely to wired or office-based access. End users are demanding more access to their day-to-day applications and services from remote and mobile devices. The demand is simple: one experience no matter the method of access.

"Do I Know This Already?" Quiz

The purpose of the "Do I Know This Already?" quiz is to help you decide whether you really need to read the entire chapter. If you already intend to read the entire chapter, you do not necessarily need to answer these questions now.

The 8-question quiz, derived from the major sections in the "Foundation Topics" portion of the chapter, helps you to determine how to spend your limited study time.

Table 1-1 outlines the major topics discussed in this chapter and the "Do I Know This Already?" quiz questions that correspond to those topics.

Table 1-1 *"Do I Know This Already?" Foundation Topics Section-to-Question Mapping*

Foundation Topics Section	Questions Covered in This Section	Score
Intelligent Information Network	1-2	
SONA	3-4	
Cisco Network Models	5-6	
Remote Connection Requirements in a Converged Network	7-8	
Total Score		

> **CAUTION** The goal of self-assessment is to gauge your mastery of the topics in this chapter. If you do not know the answer to a question or are only partially sure of the answer, you should mark this question wrong for purposes of self-assessment. Giving yourself credit for an answer that you correctly guess skews your self-assessment results and might provide you with a false sense of security.

1. The construction of an IIN relies on which of the following (select all that apply)?

   a. Integrated services

   b. Integrated transport

   c. Integrated applications

   d. IP telephony

   e. Data compression

2. The goal of an IIN includes which of the following?

   a. Increased complexity

   b. Intelligent, adaptive network

   c. Multivendor network

   d. Multiprotocol network

3. Which layer of the SONA model is geared toward virtualization of resources in the network?

   a. Application Layer

   b. Interactive Services Layer

   c. Networked Infrastructure Layer

   d. Access Layer

4. Which of the following best defines SONA?

   a. A compression algorithm

   b. A queuing mechanism

   c. A conceptual model geared toward service-provider networks

   d. A conceptual framework to provide a network evolutionary path to the IIN state

5. Which Cisco network model is geared toward integration of applications and services within an enterprise corporate headquarters?

   a. Cisco Branch Network Architecture

   b. Cisco Data Center Architecture

   c. Cisco WAN/MAN Architecture

   d. Cisco Campus Network Architecture

6. Which Cisco network model focuses on interconnectivity between public and/or partner sites and the enterprise network?

   a. Cisco Enterprise Edge Architecture

   b. Cisco WAN/MAN Architecture

   c. Cisco Campus Network Architecture

   d. Cisco Teleworker Architecture

7. Which of the following eases the deployment of integrated services and applications to branch and/or satellite offices?

   a. Cisco Integrated Services Routers

   b. Cisco Content Delivery Modules

   c. Cisco SONA

   d. Cisco LAN switches

8. Which of the following is/are available technology/technologies for remote and branch office sites (select all that apply)?

   a. DSL

   b. Cable modem

   c. Metropolitan wireless

   d. Satellite

The answers to the "Do I Know This Already?" quiz are found in Appendix A, "Answers to the 'Do I Know This Already?' Quizzes and Q&A Sections." The suggested choices for your next step are as follows:

- **4 or fewer overall score**—Read the entire chapter. This includes the "Foundation Topics," "Foundation Summary," and "Q&A" sections.

- **5 or 6 overall score**—Begin with the "Foundation Summary" section, and then go to the "Q&A" section.

- **7 or more overall score**—If you want more review on these topics, skip to the "Foundation Summary" section and then go to the "Q&A" section. Otherwise, move to the next chapter.

Foundation Topics

Describing Network Requirements

Through the introduction of two concepts known as the Intelligent Information Network (IIN) and Service-Oriented Network Architecture (SONA), Cisco has made new recommendations for the way networks are designed and implemented based on the particular size and business need to be met.

The IIN concept provides a means of articulating the evolving role of the network in enabling all components of an Information Technology (IT) infrastructure. The network is the common denominator that brings all the pieces together. This new view of the network's role in today's business models provides a means of reclassifying that role from mere transport into a service- and application-oriented role. SONA provides an underlying foundation (or framework) encompassing all technologies, applications, and services, combining them into a single entity focused on becoming an IIN.

In support of this, Cisco has released the Cisco Enterprise Architecture (CEA). The CEA is an enterprise-wide model that allows companies to protect, optimize, and grow their infrastructures as business needs dictate. The CEA provides a comprehensive design and implementation resource for a wide range of service offerings required in the typical network infrastructure today and into the future, including Campus, Data Center, Branch, Teleworker, and WAN architectures.

Intelligent Information Network

The Intelligent Information Network (IIN) offers companies an understanding of how the role of the network is evolving to meet business needs. The IIN vision is essentially the concept of network simplification through the alignment of technology and business priorities. Beyond evolution, the role of the network is expanding as more and more services become available network offerings. Cisco has established four technological roadmaps specific to the individual business needs of its customers. Each of the four roadmaps defines the IIN vision for a particular market segment or business type. These architectures are meant to show businesses how to look forward three to five years in planning network expansion. These four technological roadmaps are as follows:

■ Service-Oriented Network Architecture (SONA)

■ Service Provider Architecture (IP Next-Generation-Networks or IP-NGN)

■ Commercial Architecture

■ Consumer Architecture

Together these comprise the foundation of the IIN. The goal of the IIN is to build intelligence across multiple protocols and infrastructure layers to allow the network to be more aware of the needs of its users and respond efficiently to those needs by allocating needed resources and/or applications regardless of the nature of the connected device. The network aligns itself with the business priorities of an organization through services, availability, adaptivity, and resilience. The Cisco vision of the IIN composition includes these features:

- **Network resource and information asset integration into the network**—Includes video, voice, and data integration into the network infrastructure

- **Cross-platform/cross-product intelligence spanning all layers of infrastructure**— Network-wide extension of that intelligence to permit end-to-end connectivity and a common user experience regardless of access device or method

- **A network that actively participates in the delivery of services and applications**— Proactive allocation of network resources as needs demand for a particular application, service, or user

IIN is beyond the traditional concept of basic network connectivity, bandwidth allocation, and access to applications. A true IIN offers end-to-end functionality that adaptively shapes the user experience on-the-fly and promotes true business transparency and agility.

The evolutionary approach of the IIN technology model consists of the following three essential phases. In each phase, the opportunity exists to further augment the applications and services available to meet the business need.

- **Integrated transport phase**—The network is a common pathway for all traffic types. Each traffic type is classified according to the identified business priorities and/or the nature and sensitivity of the traffic to latency, jitter, and other assorted network conditions. This permits the network architect to present a modular functionality that can be customized by organizations or individual departments according to their individual needs. Network convergence also lays the foundation for a new class of IP-enabled applications delivered through Cisco IP Communications solutions.

- **Integrated services phase**—With full network convergence, IT resources can be pooled and personnel can be cross-trained and utilized more efficiently. This remedies the age-old issue of having only one "go-to" person in IT. Each IT staff member becomes a "go-to" person. Diverse resources required by individual organizations and personnel can be virtualized and moved into the network so that a new degree of flexibility can become reality. This flexibility comes into reality by using the network as the platform—a single resource capable of providing common services to all applications. Rather than having hundreds or thousands of mission-specific servers, the network becomes the platform. The servers are moved into the network as virtual services, thereby providing immense savings in hardware, power consumption, and real estate usage in the data center. Business continuity is also enhanced because shared resources across the IIN provide services in the event of a local systems failure.

■ **Integrated applications phase**—The third phase of the IIN evolution is known as Application-Oriented Networking (AON). This is where the plans come to fruition. The network reaches an "application-aware" state that allows it to optimize application performance and more efficiently deliver networked applications to the end-user community. Additional capabilities, such as content caching, load balancing, and application-level security, allow the infrastructure to add intelligence through simplification of the overall network infrastructure.

Of particular interest in this book is the technical roadmap focused on enterprise networks known as SONA. SONA is the framework that provides the evolutionary path for an enterprise network to become an IIN. While the remaining three architectures are critical for their respective market segments, they are beyond the scope of this book. They are mentioned here to illustrate that concepts similar to those discussed here are laid out for service provider (SP), small/medium business (SMB), and small office/home office (SOHO) networks.

SONA

The path of evolution for business services and applications is emerging into a more efficient, flexible, and dynamic model. This is the IIN. The network is the platform. Individual resources can be allocated dynamically, as needed by resource-hungry applications or services. Resources such as CPU, memory, and storage can be added and/or removed on-the-fly and without impact on other processes. Even better, the cost of such a model is reduced through shared resource utilization. No longer are dedicated resources needed for mission-specific applications. Instead, the network maintains resource pools that provide dynamic allocation of resources on demand.

For enterprise networks, SONA provides the architectural framework necessary to build an IIN. SONA leverages the network to allow interactive services to be added to it. This provides the additional benefit of allowing loosely connected services and/or applications to communicate, yet remain independent of each other. This collaborative capability permits provisioning of a new level of service, allowing an enterprise to offer its user community the same network experience, including applications, services, and capabilities, regardless of their location or choice of network-endpoint device.

As previously mentioned, the SONA vision is built around the enterprise network. The architecture itself is further subdivided into layers so that each can be implemented properly to support the next. SONA is the architectural framework that leads enterprise network evolutionary processes, allowing a network to reach the IIN state in order to accelerate applications, business processes, and, most importantly, profitability. Figure 1-1 illustrates the breakdown of the SONA layers.

Figure 1-1 *Cisco SONA*

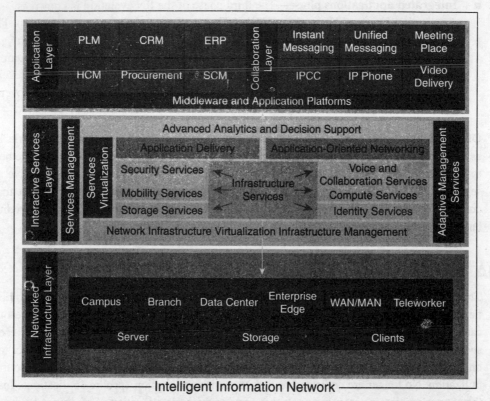

SONA makes extensive use of Cisco product lines and business partners to accomplish its goal of providing secure, flexible, adaptive, and converged network infrastructures. To aid the comprehension and to promote understanding of individual technology roles in the architecture, a layered model was created. Unlike the OSI Model, the SONA layered model consists only of three layers. As shown in Figure 1-1, these are as follows (from the bottom up):

- Networked Infrastructure Layer

- Interactive Services Layer

- Application Layer

Service integration is a key concept in the overall SONA picture. This allows common services to be provided from a single point within the infrastructure. Keeping these services in loosely coupled relationships with other services (for example, web services, XML, and so on) allows a single service or resource to be shared among multiple applications. This simplifies support, reduces maintenance costs, and potentially provides licensing savings on some applications.

Each layer has its form and function in the construction of an IIN. The sections that follow provide a brief discussion of that form and function at each layer.

Networked Infrastructure Layer

The lowest of the three SONA layers provides the point of interconnection between various IT resources. The Networked Infrastructure Layer encompasses servers, storage, and network-connected endpoints. These resources exist in various volumes and geographies throughout the network. The Networked Infrastructure Layer provides the common transport and connectivity between required services such as CPU cycles, storage, memory, and I/O. Rather than using individual, dedicated (or mission-specific) resources, SONA sees these elements simply as resource pools.

The SONA model reaches out across network geographies to pull all resources into a single, logical entity. The architecture includes specifications on the construction of all of these geographies, including the campus, branch, data center, WAN/MAN, and teleworkers. Each is addressed individually in the SONA model as each is crucial to the creation of an IIN capable of providing a common user experience anytime, anywhere and from any device.

As you might expect, TCP/IP becomes the pervasive network protocol and the network provides the shared transport for all business application traffic. This is known as *convergence*. This allows the network infrastructure to become *service ready*, allowing the offloading of application functions away from application resources through service integration.

Interactive Services Layer

A significant cause of inefficiency within an IT organization is the presence of "silos"; that is, application-specific hardware and software that cannot be reused or shared. As more and more businesses begin to rely on collaborative services, the need to more closely align IT resources and computing platforms becomes more crucial.

The Infrastructure Services Layer (ISL) pools these resources in a process known as virtualization. These resources include both the Networked Infrastructure Layer and Infrastructure Services.

The Infrastructure Services Layer sees these as resource pools as well. However, in addition, SONA sees the network infrastructure as simply one more element in a resource pool to be managed and shared.

By virtualizing these resources and defining their use through adaptive management capabilities, the business transformation becomes more dynamic and, more importantly, more simplified. By keeping these resources loosely coupled, they remain modular. That is, they can be added, removed, upgraded, and maintained individually with no impact whatsoever on other resources in the pool.

No longer are individual servers dedicated to mission-specific roles. They become part of a bigger picture and a shared resource. Flexibility is achieved when virtual resources are available on an as-needed basis over a shared infrastructure without having to make any change to the underlying network architecture. As silos are removed and hardware/software investments further leveraged as shared resources, individual components can no longer negatively impact business operations in the event of maintenance, failure, or another service-impacting event.

As resources become part of the larger shared (or virtualized) entity, the lines between the application and the network begin to blur as the network is the transport and is providing access dynamically to needed services and associated resources seamlessly.

One function of the ISL deals specifically with application networking services. Application networking refers to a set of services consisting of network-embedded technologies that improve the deployment of applications in a distributed model without impacting the responsiveness of the application and resulting user experience (as the experience will vary depending on the location of the user versus that of the resource). The goal is to remove location dependency while maintaining comparable functionality.

Breaking the location dependency is possible in the architecture through delivery of high application throughput, reduced latency, encryption, compression, and optimization of communications between client and application resources.

Examples of these resources and services include

- Voice and collaboration services
- Device mobility services
- Security and identity services
- Storage services
- Computer services
- Application networking services
- Network infrastructure virtualization

- Services management

- Adaptive management services

- Advanced analytics services

- Infrastructure management services

The list goes on, but the services identified here should provide some idea of the concept of resource virtualization.

Application Layer

The Application Layer contains the business and collaborative applications that use interactive services to function more efficiently. The interactive services allow the applications to grow dynamically, thus allowing more rapid and efficient deployment while keeping integration costs down. When a new user base, department, or branch site is added, the application can simply be allocated a larger share of the resource pools dynamically to compensate for the increased use.

The Application Layer is most concerned with two application categories:

- **Business applications**—Include those applications that are mission-specific to a business or department and are crucial to that organization's function. For example, a procurement or human resources application would be used only by the respective departmental personnel. Yet, those personnel would require use of the shared resources at all three layers.

- **Collaboration applications**—Include Instant Messaging (IM), Unified Messaging (UM), IP Contact Center (IPCC), IP Phones, and Video delivery. These are the tools that allow people to interact in the manner and time of their own choosing. The use of presence technologies allows an individual to choose the manner in which they wish to be contacted at a given time and on which device that contact should be made. The experience and functionality will be similar (for a given application type) regardless of the access device.

Cisco Network Models

Now that the basic concepts of SONA, the road to the creation of an IIN, are somewhat clearer, some discussion of network models is needed. Network models vary based on the technology being implemented; however, the goal of the models is still the same—convergence and enabling service integration.

As mentioned previously, Cisco has created a visionary architecture for its customer market segments. For the enterprise network, SONA is the architecture. At the Networked Infrastructure Layer exists a rather wide array of technologies and possibilities. These were touched upon briefly in the "Describing Network Requirements" section and are expanded upon in this section.

Typically, six distinct geographies exist in an end-to-end network architecture. These are contained within the Networked Infrastructure Layer of SONA. Refer to Figure 1-1 for an illustrated view.

■ **Campus network**—Provides network access to campus-wide resources

■ **Branch network**—Provides network access to remote resources

■ **Data Center**—Provides access to and interconnectivity between servers and storage resources

■ **Enterprise Edge**—Provides secure access to and from public and partner networks

■ **WAN/MAN**—Provides connectivity between branch offices, campuses, and/or data centers

■ **Teleworker**—Provides connectivity to the corporate network for home-based employees

As is readily apparent, all of these are somewhat interdependent, yet very different in terms of resource and architectural needs.

Cisco Hierarchical Network Model

Prior to any discussion of the architecture models proposed in the IIN vision, it is necessary to step back to a discussion of a somewhat older model advocated for network scalability, the Cisco Hierarchical Network Model. Figure 1-2 illustrates the model for purposes of discussion.

Figure 1-2   *Cisco Hierarchical Network Model*

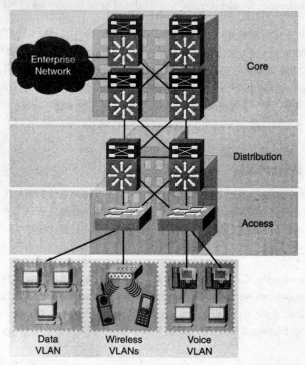

As is evident in the figure, the essential layers of the network are divided into three layers: Core, Distribution, and Access. This provides a repeatable, or "cookie-cutter," model that is easily reproduced site to site. The model also has the benefit of being scalable from hundreds to thousands of devices in a campus network. Additionally, this model supports the integration of SONA Interactive Services Layer applications and services, facilitating an improved experience in the interaction between the clients and applications/services provided by the network.

Each layer has its prescribed function, as described here:

- **Access Layer**—Devices deployed throughout the network with the express purpose of providing user access to the network, generally through switch port access. Access layer switches are generally located near the user populous they serve.

- **Distribution Layer**—Devices deployed as aggregation points for Access layer devices. Distribution layer devices can be used to segment workgroups or departments in a campus environment. The Distribution layer devices also provide for WAN aggregation connectivity at the Campus Edge and provide policy-based connectivity.

- **Core Layer (a.k.a. Backbone Layer)**—Devices that carry the weight of the network. They are designed to switch packets as fast as possible. The Core layer must be highly available and redundant to ensure that no loss or degradation of service is experienced in the event of a network outage.

This model can be applied to any network of any size regardless of the technologies and connectivity options it presents. This includes LAN, WAN, MAN, wireless, VPN, and other networks. In smaller networks, it is feasible that one or more of these layers might be combined into a multi-functional layer. In the discussions to follow, and throughout nearly any networking technology-related book, these three layers are referenced quite frequently.

Campus Network Architecture

Campus network architecture has evolved rapidly over the last decade or more. The number of services supported in a campus environment has evolved just as quickly, if not more so. The basic infrastructure has traditionally been summed up under the Cisco Hierarchical Network Model mentioned in the previous section.

This remains the case because that model scales very well. The role has expanded somewhat on its own to include technologies such as quality of service (QoS), Multiprotocol Label Switching Virtual Private Networks (MPLS VPN), IPsec VPN, Hot Standby Router Protocol (HSRP), and more. Shifting topological ideology has seen a dramatic increase in the number of enterprise networks shifting from traditional Layer 2 switching to Layer 3 switching at the Access and Distribution layers. The campus network architecture is meant to provide enterprise corporate headquarters sites (which might mean a single building or multiple buildings in a common geography) with a means of consolidating and simplifying network support and administration while increasing service and application offerings to the user community. Figure 1-3 illustrates the campus network architecture.

Figure 1-3 *Campus Network Architecture*

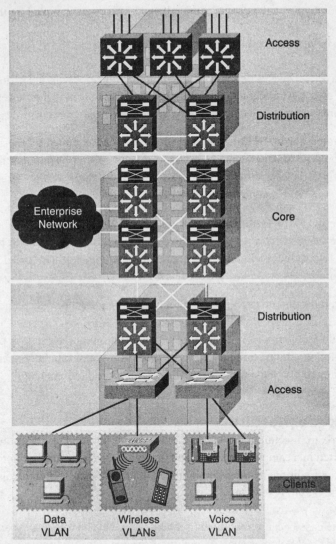

Campus services are changing in nature from traditional stateless (connection and/or session unaware and packet switching) to stateful services requiring highly available, redundant devices to track sessions and connections at all times. Meeting this need requires changes in the basic networking paradigm.

For example, a wireless client roaming throughout a wireless-enabled campus using both a laptop and a Cisco 7920 802.11b IP Phone would need to have the ability to seamlessly home from access point to access point with no interruption in service. This is especially true of voice calls in progress. The presence of voice and data together would necessitate a fully QoS-enabled network for both wired and wireless connected devices. An access point would be required to be able to exchange session state information and user/device credentials with no user interaction.

This poses only a single example of the need for campus evolution to accommodate dynamic needs of users and devices. Also, as the evolution progresses and more devices become network-dependent, the need to eliminate any/all single points of failure becomes more and more critical as a factor to success.

Branch Network Architecture

Branch network architecture provides an integrated, multiservice environment that provides connectivity to its users who are working in remote or satellite offices rather than in the primary corporate headquarters or campus. This provision requires both hardware- and software-specific integration considerations to provide the applications and services required for the users to properly perform their job functions.

The SONA branch architecture allows an enterprise to extend campus-like services and applications to the remote branch site while maintaining proper service levels and responsiveness. Advanced services such as Cisco Unified Communications, security, and more can be offered at branch sites, a traditionally unavailable option for some services due to inadequate connectivity and reachability. Figure 1-4 illustrates the branch network architecture.

Figure 1-4 *Branch Network Architecture*

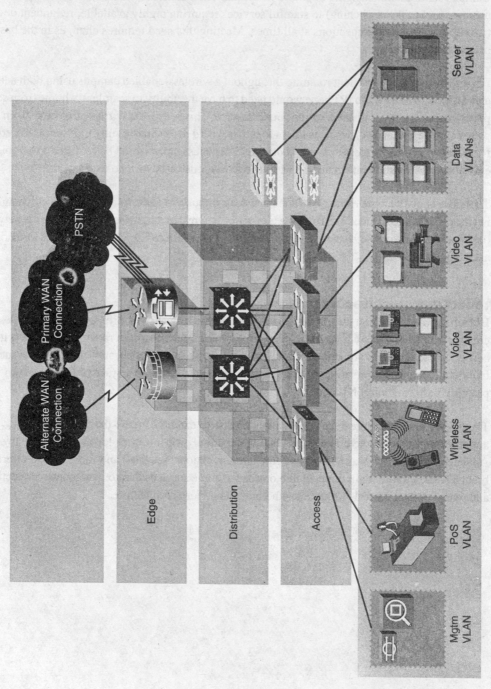

Cisco integrates security, switching, network analysis, content caching, and converged voice/ video services into a series of products known as integrated services routers (ISRs). Aside from filling the role of traditional router platforms, these devices are multitalented and designed for performance. ISRs are affectionately known as "branch-in-a-box" routers. They very effectively stand up to that name. Key individual services, such as voice and security, are built into the motherboard as standard components. Additional modules provide voice messaging and content services that easily install into the same chassis.

This solution provides for local access to key services and/or applications without reliance on a WAN link or other connectivity. Call control, security, VPN connectivity, and more are simply built into the same router chassis. Configuration is also simplified through the addition of the Security Device Manager (SDM). The SDM provides an intuitive graphical, web-based interface that can be used to configure firewall services, routing, VPN, and more.

Data Center Architecture

The data center is a key point in the evolution of the network. It is rapidly evolving to take in more and more service-oriented functions. The move toward a dynamic, demand-based service offering dictates that the network be aware of server and application health at all times. This health information is then used to take appropriate action, making incremental increases in service resources that are available to a particular application or service. This can be the addition of virtual servers, application instances, or dynamic network configuration changes needed to bring newly added resources online to support increasing needs.

Resources can be provisioned for server OS needs, Layer 2 functionality (for example, switch port mode, VLAN assignment), Layer 3 functionality (for example, routing, HSRP, multicast, and so on), and services for Layers 4 through 7. Figure 1-5 illustrates the data center architecture.

Figure 1-5 *Data Center Architecture*

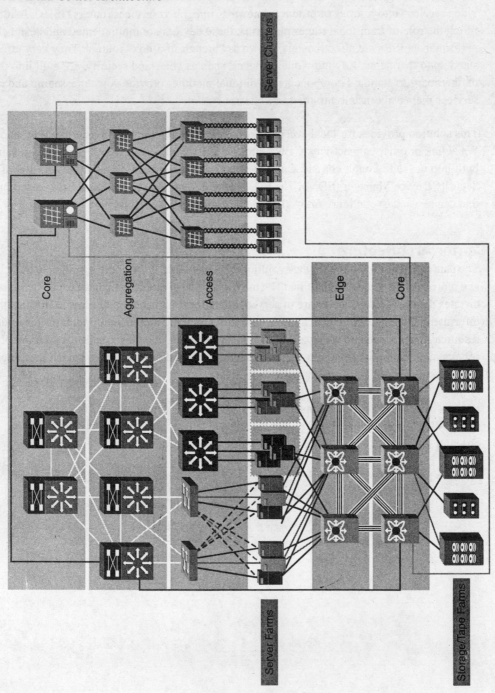

This architecture provides a cohesive, adaptive network that allows for consolidation of resources while increasing availability and business continuance. Enabling service-oriented architectures, virtualization, and on-demand services to provide a dynamic network environment for all users in all locations leads to streamlined management and reporting and more effective use of capital. This solution allows the network to scale to a significant degree without infrastructure changes that would traditionally be needed to support a diverse and varied user base.

Enterprise Edge Architecture

The enterprise edge is evolving with the need to provide more and higher-level security features as a first line of defense for the network. This is true of both internal- and external-facing server farms and services. Figure 1-6 illustrates the enterprise edge architecture.

Figure 1-6 *Enterprise Edge Architecture*

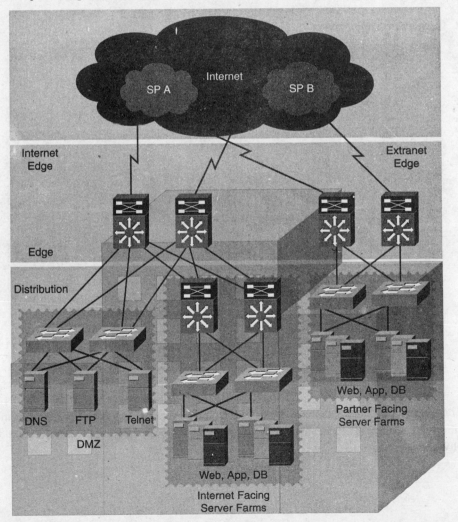

A number of server farms may be supported, each varying in function from demilitarized zone (DMZ) functions for internal or external users (DNS, FTP, web, Telnet, and so on) to Internet services or partner-access servers hosting applications shared with business partners and their employees.

Teleworker Architecture

Increasingly, due to space, real estate, employee accommodation, workforce diversification, and other factors, the population of the home-based workforce is increasing at an exceedingly high rate. Call center remote agents with access to features and functionality identical to their in-office counterparts are taking customer calls from home offices. Salespeople are making deals and booking them via VPN connections back to the corporate site. Most of these workers are using IP telephony to place their office desk phone on their home desk. Figure 1-7 illustrates the teleworker architecture.

Figure 1-7   *Teleworker Architecture*

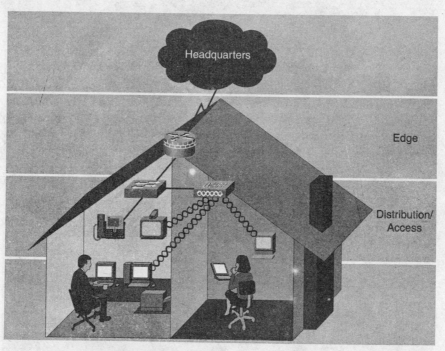

These and many other examples are out there in the world. Cisco is a very big proponent of the enterprise teleworker model and using an ISR platform to provide all the comforts, and access, of physically being in the office.

This architecture dictates the delivery of secure voice and data services to remote small or home office sites over standard, widely available broadband connections (cable, DSL, fiber optic services [FiOS], and so on). This allows for centralized management of devices and standardized application and service availability identical to that of campus-based employees. This includes "always-on" connectivity, security, and, in most cases, wireless connectivity and audio/video conferencing capabilities.

All these applications and services must be provided over "nailed-up" (always on) VPN links that are QoS enabled for the various traffic types used throughout the architecture.

WAN/MAN Architecture

With all the discussion of service-enabled networking, convergence, QoS, and more, the focus tends to be somewhat removed from an equally crucial component of the bigger picture. The design and construction of the wide-area network (WAN) and (where utilized) metropolitan-area network (MAN) can make or break the overall architectural vision.

The transport services necessary for end-to-end connectivity as viewed from the SONA perspective are somewhat different from the traditional view of "just enough bandwidth to make it function properly and no more." Equally dangerous to the vision is the outdated (and far from true) assertion that QoS can be avoided by provisioning "a big, fat pipe." Figure 1-8 illustrates the WAN/MAN architecture.

Geography and function play large roles in deciding the method and speed of connectivity between various sites. Figure 1-8 shows the various possibilities for connecting Site A to Site B.

Whether the connection is traditional Frame Relay WAN connectivity or provided via a service provider MPLS network providing full Layer 3 connectivity from end to end, the needs of the business and the costs involved have a great deal to do with connectivity selection. If sites are very close in relation to each other; for example, in adjacent or nearby buildings, a Metro Ethernet connection might be feasible. Where sites are large and business-critical, requiring high availability, a Synchronous Optical Network (SONET) ring might be the chosen connection type. Whatever the needs of the business and the users at a given site, a means of connecting those sites is available.

Figure 1-8   *WAN/MAN Architecture*

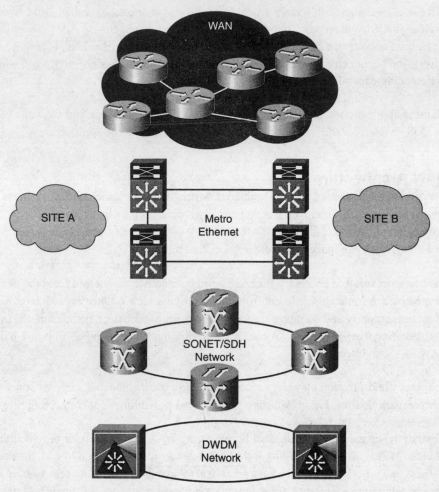

The convergence of voice, video, and data over a single IP network requires a significant degree of forethought and consideration to properly provide services over potentially large geographical areas. QoS, granular service levels, and security factor into the equation as well, to provide secure delivery of various supported traffic types. Emerging trends have seen the deployment of WAN/MAN environments to provide path isolation for traffic between clients and their destination devices, which is a requirement of traffic segmentation over shared infrastructure. Technologies supporting such deployments include MPLS, generic routing encapsulation (GRE), Virtual Routing and Forwarding (VRF), and IPsec.

Remote Connection Requirements in a Converged Network

In the process of evaluating factors and details necessary to effectively design and deploy a central site, branch office, or SOHO site, the most basic requirement is that the site must work effectively for the personnel who staff it. While that factor should be rather obvious and up-front, that is not always the case. Poor site selection can make or break a business, depending on the type of business and needs of that business.

Central Site

A central site must be capable of providing needed services and applications to its user community. Many of these services need to be scalable and flexible, as discussed in the SONA portion of this chapter. Typically, the central site is the largest site in terms of size and population. It could be a corporate headquarters site or a dedicated IT site for larger enterprise networks.

Because all users will access resources at the central site, it is crucial that proper network management practices be in place. This includes planning, design, implementation, and change control practices, to name a few. This site will also accommodate the hub of WAN connectivity, providing access to other sites, branch offices, and teleworkers. Regardless of the geographical disposition of the user population, the network should be designed to provide a consistent user experience across all sites and platforms.

Branch Office

Branch offices vary in size and purpose according to the business needs. A decision must be made about how the branch office network will be designed and what services will be provided locally versus what services will be offered via a WAN connection to the central site. Providing applications and services from the central site is typically most effective in providing a consistent experience for the users. More importantly, the central site is then well positioned to leverage a more complete business picture based on real-time information gathered from those centrally housed applications and services. The process of gathering and processing information from multiple branch office networks with locally provided applications and services can be time consuming and inefficient.

Branch offices can benefit from high-speed WAN links to the central site as well as to the Internet. When branch sites have their own locally provisioned Internet connectivity they also need locally provisioned security resources such as firewalls and content engines.

In cases where sites have only an Internet connection and no dedicated WAN connection to the central site, VPN connections can be "nailed-up" via an Internet connection to ensure a more secure connection back to the central site.

Branch offices of significant size can provide local service and applications to local teleworkers needing access to company resources from a home or satellite branch site. QoS is a concern at all points in the architecture, especially if voice and video services are being provided from the central site to remote employees.

SOHO Site

SOHO sites typically are single-user sites but may include several employees. In any event, these are the smallest sites. A smaller size does not equate to a smaller need for access to applications and services. Although providing those services from a central or branch office site to the SOHO site might be more challenging, doing so is still a crucial factor in ensuring business success.

SOHO sites will likely access resources at multiple other sites including branch offices and the central site. This presents some challenges in figuring out just how the SOHO sites will access all of these resources independently and simultaneously. Here again is the argument for centralized or virtualized applications and resources for all sites being based and hosted from the central site. The need to access resources at multiple branch offices is eliminated.

SOHO site users typically require VPN connectivity back to the central site. This access may be accomplished through a VPN client installed on a company-provided laptop or via small VPN-capable router placed at the user's home. The connectivity back to the central site will vary based on the local service provider offerings available in the user's home area. The connectivity options are relatively wide-ranging and include DSL, cable modem, satellite, and other technologies. A small router (for example, Cisco 871) will make a permanent VPN connection back to a VPN aggregator at the central site to provide access to needed services and applications. This provides the needed security as well as connectivity over which to pass voice, video, and data traffic.

Integrated Services for Secure Remote Access

The cost of providing voice and data services to all users who require them has traditionally been exceedingly high. This has made the business case for opening branch offices a rather difficult one to make. The office required a small PBX or key system to provide telephony and a router to provide data connectivity. This often required two separate departments to maintain services at a single branch office. Add to that equation the need for a third department for support and maintenance of user PCs and laptops and things could get quickly out of hand.

This is no longer the case. With SONA, the applications and services, including voice, data, and essential PC maintenance needed to support users at all sites, are built into the single platform that is the network. No longer is a PBX or key system needed at each branch site. The Cisco ISR platforms provide fallback call control when a centralized call-control model is in use. Alternately, the Cisco ISR platform can provide primary call control on a site-by-site basis. No changes are needed in hardware or software on the router to affect the change between the centralized and distributed call-control models.

Along with voice capabilities, the ISR can also provide native security functions such as VPN connectivity to the central site and firewall capabilities for the local site should they have a local Internet connection. Figure 1-4, in the "Branch Network Architecture" section, illustrates a good reference point for such a deployment. The single Cisco ISR provides a single point of administration for LAN/WAN, PSTN, call control, and security services provided to the branch. The model is most typically used to provide virtualized services at the central site with failover capabilities for each service at the branch site should the WAN connection(s) become unavailable. This provides a significant step forward over traditional telephony because there is typically no redundancy built into smaller PBXs and/or key systems.

A remote office might make use of local broadband connectivity for both Internet and VPN access back to a central site resource pool. Bandwidth, as always, is a primary consideration. With SOHO users, the residential broadband solutions include technologies such as DSL, cable modem, satellite, and fiber optic solutions such as that recently made available to residential customers by local service providers. All of these solutions are relatively affordable and easily installed.

For office sites, the solutions are not always so well laid out. Business-class DSL, traditional Frame Relay, or, in more modern terms and in line with SONA, MPLS VPN connectivity have all become viable solutions for home and office. Many cities, corporations, and even housing subdivisions have begun to offer metropolitan-area wireless connectivity to their tenants/residents. Public reaction and marketing viability will certainly dictate the course of this type of network in the next few years. MPLS will be discussed in more detail in Chapter 8, "The MPLS Conceptual Model." For now, suffice to say that the carrier MPLS networks are Layer 3 end-to-end networks and can be QoS enabled for varied traffic types, unlike traditional WAN connectivity technologies.

Foundation Summary

The next three to five years will see a significant change in the way organizations view the network as an entity. Currently, many of the services and applications providing businesses with the means to function in their respective industries reside on dedicated hardware platforms, using dedicated resources. As these businesses grow, so does the resource demand on these dedicated platforms. Eventually, the demand outpaces the platform's ability to keep up with the needs of the business. The cycle is reset and the process repeated. This evolution to obsolescence is inefficient and needlessly costly.

SONA details various architectures common in enterprise networks, including campus, data center, enterprise edge, branch, and teleworker architectures. These individual architectures allow the IT personnel to lay out a modular path for each of the various deployments common in today's networks.

Cisco has provided a new routing platform in support of the SONA vision of integrated applications and services. The ISR line of routers is specifically positioned to provide capabilities needed in edge, branch, and teleworker architectures to match those offerings present in campus and data center architectures. The ISRs provide local call control, call-control fallback for centralized call-control models, content caching, and security and VPN capabilities, among others.

Q&A

The questions and scenarios in this book are designed to be challenging and to make sure that you know the answer. Rather than allowing you to derive the answers from clues hidden inside the questions themselves, the questions challenge your understanding and recall of the subject.

Hopefully, mastering these questions will help you limit the number of exam questions on which you narrow your choices to two options, and then guess.

You can find the answers to these questions in Appendix A. For more practice with exam-like question formats, use the exam engine on the CD-ROM.

1. In the SONA model, collaboration services are offered in which layer?

2. Corporate resources are often allocated and deployed in silo-like models. While these resources are dedicated to a department or group within the company, are there any resources they might have in common?

3. Which architecture would typically be associated with a remote user based in a residential office integration solution?

4. List the architectures addressed at the SONA networked infrastructure layer.

5. A branch site housing 50 users needs to access services and applications housed in the central site data center. Consider a solution that would allow these services and applications to be provided to duplicate the experience of central site users accessing the same resources.

6. List at least five services provided at the SONA integrated services layer.

7. Virtualization of resources for dynamic allocation provides a compelling business case in support of a SONA model. Which types of resources can be virtualized?

8. What is the difference between SONA and IIN?

Exam Topic List

This chapter covers the following topics that you need to master for the CCNP ISCW exam:

- **Facilitating Remote Connections**— Describes how to facilitate remote connections that an enterprise network has to support

- **Challenges of Connecting Teleworkers**— Describes the challenges faced in connecting teleworkers to the enterprise network, and the solutions that exist to address these challenges

CHAPTER 2

Topologies for Teleworker Connectivity

A revolution is in the works with regard to the workplace for well over half of the United States workforce. According to a September 2005 Gartner research publication, by 2008 41 million full-time corporate employees will fall into the telecommuter classification, also known by the more correct term, teleworkers. The term *commuter* gives the impression of changing locations or moving from one place to another for a particular purpose. Teleworkers have the luxury of taking that early morning conference call in their pajamas.

Cisco Service-Oriented Network Architecture (SONA) addresses the teleworker with its own full architecture solution, rather than a cursory glance and a wave in passing. In fact, the teleworker has spawned a number of leading-edge technologies and augmentations to existing technologies. Among these are virtual private network (VPN) solutions, customer premises equipment (CPE) choices for the home, and a Cisco Solutions Reference Network Design (SRND) detailing teleworker best practices. The needs of the teleworker are simple: make the experience exactly as if he or she were sitting in the office (without the bathrobe, of course).

This chapter serves the purpose of providing a high-level overview of some challenges and solutions available to meet the needs of the business-ready teleworker.

"Do I Know This Already?" Quiz

The purpose of the "Do I Know This Already?" quiz is to help you decide whether you really need to read the entire chapter. If you already intend to read the entire chapter, you do not necessarily need to answer these questions now.

The 8-question quiz, derived from the major sections in the "Foundation Topics" portion of the chapter, helps you to determine how to spend your limited study time.

Table 2-1 outlines the major topics discussed in this chapter and the "Do I Know This Already?" quiz questions that correspond to those topics.

Table 2-1   *"Do I Know This Already?" Foundation Topics Section-to-Question Mapping*

Foundation Topics Section	Questions Covered in This Section	Score
Facilitating Remote Connections	1-6	
Challenges of Connecting Teleworkers	7-8	
Total Score		

> **CAUTION**   The goal of self-assessment is to gauge your mastery of the topics in this chapter. If you do not know the answer to a question or are only partially sure of the answer, you should mark this question wrong for purposes of self-assessment. Giving yourself credit for an answer that you correctly guess skews your self-assessment results and might provide you with a false sense of security.

1.   The guidelines for deploying a teleworker solution are part of the SONA vision and defined in detail by which of the following?

   a.   RFC

   b.   IEEE

   c.   SRND

   d.   RSVP

2.   The teleworker architecture is defined in which layer of the SONA framework?

   a.   Application Layer

   b.   Interactive Services Layer

   c.   Networked Infrastructure Layer

3.   Which of the following are goals for the teleworker architecture?

   a.   Rapid convergence

   b.   Safe boundaries for the solution

   c.   Dial-on-demand routing

   d.   Free home network equipment for personal use

   e.   Internet connectivity

4.   Which remote connectivity option is the most viable for teleworker connections?

   a.   MPLS VPN

   b.   Frame Relay

   c.   ATM

   d.   IPsec VPN

5. Which connectivity option provides a Layer 3, fully meshed solution?

   a. MPLS VPN

   b. Frame Relay

   c. ATM

   d. IPsec VPN

6. What is the difference between an IPsec VPN and a remote-access VPN?

   a. A remote-access VPN is an on-demand connection whereas an IPsec VPN is an always-on connection.

   b. A remote-access VPN is an always-on connection whereas an IPsec VPN is an on-demand connection.

   c. A remote-access VPN is a dialup-only connection whereas an IPsec VPN is dialup or LAN access connection.

7. Among the components typically deployed for a campus to support teleworkers is which of the following?

   a. IP Phone, webcam, laptop, or desktop computer

   b. Firewall and remote VPN router

   c. VPN Concentrator and headend router

   d. Fax machine and analog telephone

8. Among the components typically deployed for a teleworker solution are which of the following?

   a. Remote VPN router

   b. VPN Concentrator

   c. ASA

   d. CallManager

The answers to the "Do I Know This Already?" quiz are found in Appendix A, "Answers to the 'Do I Know This Already?' Quizzes and Q&A Sections." The suggested choices for your next step are as follows:

■ **4 or fewer overall score**—Read the entire chapter. This includes the "Foundation Topics," "Foundation Summary," and "Q&A" sections.

■ **5 or 6 overall score**—Begin with the "Foundation Summary" section, and then go to the "Q&A" section.

■ **7 or more overall score**—If you want more review on these topics, skip to the "Foundation Summary" section and then go to the "Q&A" section. Otherwise, move to the next chapter.

Foundation Topics

Facilitating Remote Connections

In Chapter 1, the discussion centered, very briefly, on teleworker architectures. Now that you are familiar with some of the available options, it is an appropriate opportunity to explore the concept further. Throughout the discussions to follow, SONA will continue to guide the overall path of the subject matter. For in-depth details regarding the various available technologies and methodologies regarding teleworkers, Cisco has published the "Business-Ready Teleworker" SRND document, available at http://www.cisco.com/go/srnd.

To the outside observer, it might be quite easy to settle on the idea that the role of the teleworker, as compared to an all-out campus architecture, is a detail scribbled in the margin down near the legend on a map of the way to some grandiose treasure. Interestingly enough, the plight of the teleworker has brought about a revolution in the way businesses operate and, obviously, from where they do that business.

IIN and the Teleworker

The idea of the Intelligent Information Network (IIN) brings into focus the idea that a network should be dynamic, flexible, and, above all, consistent in the experience offered to its user community. The IIN will provide service integration and allow the shared resource pools to maximize the business productivity. Intelligent networks make it possible to merge dissimilar networks (that is, traditional data, voice, and video networks) into a single, converged network. By building in the intelligence to adapt to changing resource needs and overcome resource silos by merging multiple mission-specific networks into a single entity, a tool is forged that is greater than the sum of its parts.

How is the IIN a greater tool? It does everything that its predecessors could do and more. More importantly, it can do those tasks at reduced cost due to simplification and virtualization. Cost reductions flow from having only one network to maintain and support rather than several. Value is added because applications and services require no additional infrastructure above what is already part of the IIN.

Teleworker connectivity is, by definition, a wide-area network (WAN) connectivity scenario. It contains many of the same needs and requirements as a branch office or other remote site. The connection must be secure, reliable, and capable of protecting critical traffic types such as voice and video.

Enterprise Architecture Framework

SONA was assembled to address the needs of today's enterprise networks and provide a map of how they can evolve into an IIN. To maintain the SONA mindset, Figure 2-1 repeats the illustration of the SONA model from Chapter 1.

Figure 2-1 *Cisco SONA*

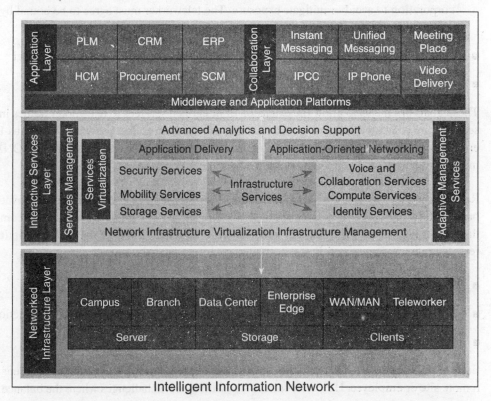

As is evident in Figure 2-1, SONA encompasses a number of architectures at the networked infrastructure layer, including campus, data center, branch, edge, WAN/MAN, and teleworker architectures. The focus of this chapter is on the teleworker portion of that framework—more specifically, the home office portion of the SOHO deployment. This chapter will not spend additional time restating a significant amount of information regarding the various architectures, so please refer to Chapter 1 for a more in-depth review.

Remote Connection Options

The enterprise architecture framework, and therefore the Cisco SRND for teleworkers, emphasizes a few ideas for the overall solution. These ideas are the primary goals of the solution:

- Defining safe boundaries within which the solution may be deployed (facilitated by proper expectation setting). That is, the solution must maintain the security standards of the corporation to avoid or mitigate exposure. The teleworker must agree to be bound by corporate security policies in the residential office.

- Providing hardware and software recommendations for a given deployment model

- Including or referencing performance and configuration information

These goals are meant to allow the extension of integrated services to teleworker homes in a safe, secure manner while maintaining a comparable service level to that provided to campus-based employees. The overall goal is similar to that of the other architectures put forth by SONA, including protection, cost reduction, and scalable growth potential.

Remote connectivity is not without its challenges, obviously. For each challenge, innovation has brought forth new possibilities for connectivity. Regardless of the chosen option, the common theme still rings true, "Design today with tomorrow in mind." Some of the available options for remote connectivity are as follows:

- Traditional Layer 2 technologies such as Frame Relay, ATM, or leased lines

- Service provider MPLS VPNs offering scalable, flexible, and fully meshed connections

- Site-to-site and remote-access IPsec VPNs over the public Internet

Each of these options could easily be selected and expected to fully serve the basic needs of the remote site or employee. However, each comes with its own challenges where the balance of cost versus security is concerned.

Traditional Layer 2 Connections

Traditional Layer 2 connections such as Frame Relay and ATM are, most importantly, not available to residential premises (typically). Also, the nature of a Layer 2 connection does not provide much in the way of QoS configuration beyond basic traffic shaping over the link. This aspect alone might be enough to disqualify it as an option if it were available to the teleworker premise. However, these technologies tend to be quite secure, even if there is near-total reliance on the service provider for that security.

Service Provider MPLS VPN

MPLS VPNs, as a technology, tend to be the preferred method of the day. The nature of the technology is to provide Layer 3, any-to-any connectivity throughout the network in a secure manner. A similar Layer 2 deployment would prove to be cost prohibitive simply due to the number of circuits required. This is where MPLS shines. A single circuit provides the needed connectivity for all sites. MPLS networks allow the extension of enterprise QoS across the service provider network and the honoring of service levels dictated therein. This alone is a tremendous step forward in the quest for the IIN. There is a bit of confusion associated with VPNs however.

The confusion comes in the service provider's specific implementation. At what point is the traffic flow being tagged and protected according to established QoS policies? This is a bit of a sticking point because it varies from provider to provider. At the time of this writing, the majority of providers are still backhauling traffic to their core prior to any tagging or traffic classification. The chapters in Part II, "Implementing Frame Mode MPLS," discuss this in more detail. For now, suffice to say that, prior to selecting a service provider, you should take precautions and ask in-depth questions regarding QoS policies.

NOTE   MPLS, being a Layer 3 technology, still requires a Layer 2 technology for connectivity at the local loop. This is most often accomplished with a Frame Relay connection from the CPE to the provider ingress edge.

Site-to-Site VPN over Public Internet

This solution tends to be the most prevalent for teleworker solutions, because the Layer 2 and Layer 3 technologies previously mentioned are more appropriate for campus-to-branch connectivity and typically are not available to a residence (due to cost and/or availability). The site-to-site VPN solution tends to have the highest volume of security-related considerations as well, due to its contact with the public Internet.

The use of the Internet as a transport for VPN connections back to the campus or central site is likely the most feasible and cost effective due to the widespread broadband capabilities available (and already installed) in most homes. This allows the corporation to avoid taking on the actual cost of the connection, if so desired, while enabling it to easily provide secure connectivity back to the central site.

The manner in which that is accomplished, however, is open to debate based on the needs of the user and the nature of the connection. Is the connection to be transparent to the user in the form of a nailed-up VPN connection established by a router placed in the home? Or, is that connection going to be one established by the use of a VPN client launched from a laptop on an as-needed basis? Each is a viable solution.

Challenges of Connecting Teleworkers

In maintaining position on the path to IIN, it should be noted that some sections of the map are more mature and well-traveled than others, meaning that there is greater detail available. The industry experience with providing multiple enhanced functions to teleworker devices is at a relatively early stage. The enterprise teleworker solution provides an always-on (potentially), secure, and centrally managed connection to business resources and services. In keeping with established goals, this should provide services and applications identical to those available to users based in campus and/or branch sites. In doing so, a number of requirements spring forth:

■ Continuity of operation in case of loss of access to the workplace network (that is, home broadband connection outage)

■ Comparable network application responsiveness across geographical, functional, business, and/or decision-making boundaries—or, more to the point, one experience regardless of locale

■ Secure, reliable access to critical applications and services necessary for job function fulfillment

■ Cost-effective extension of data, voice, video, and real-time applications and services over a common (and sometimes best-effort) network connection

■ Increased employee productivity, satisfaction, and retention

Recommended practice dictates that targeted pilots be used to streamline the solution and document the process of its implementation to a very high degree. In all honesty, the use of network administration personnel as guinea pigs is advocated and applauded in such cases.

Consider the fact that the corporate network is being extended to co-exist with the user's home network. The corporation has no control whatsoever over the traffic flow habits in the home network. A careless teleworker can easily compromise the security of a corporate network infrastructure. In that, there are associated risks and potential for breach of security. This is the case for both wired and wireless home networks.

All functionality to be deployed at the home should be thoroughly tested before deployment. This includes security, data connectivity, and, most importantly, voice and video quality. This will allow the tweaking of the solution for improved quality of each prior to wide-scale deployment. Most network applications will perform well over the network within the corporate office. These same applications might not do quite so well in a teleworker deployment, however, due to the simple, yet chaotic, nature of the Internet. In any intrinsically latent network, you must take care to thoroughly test any proposed solution.

Infrastructure Options

Consider the number of applications used daily by the typical network user. It doesn't take long for the application count to get into double-digits. That said, now consider those applications and services that are actually relevant to the business at hand for a given job position or function, specifically those applications and services that are critical for one to do the job for which they were hired. Once again, it remains rather easy to get to a significant number of items on the list.

What options are available that will allow these applications and services to be accessed from varying degrees of connectivity? For purposes of discussion, keep the idea of "varying degrees of connectivity" limited to those available to the home. The plight of the road warrior is a discussion, though no less important, for a later time.

One of the early considerations in constructing a solution must be the access methodology and bandwidth afforded by said methodology. Three somewhat prevalent methods come to mind as having the widest availability currently:

- Cable

- DSL

- Fiber optic access

Each offers relatively high bandwidth capabilities to the user community. By far, fiber optic solutions offer the highest bandwidth (ranging from 5 to 30 Mbps downstream, 2 to 5 Mbps upstream and climbing), dwarfing cable and DSL capabilities. Cable and DSL are in heavy competition, providing nearly equivalent bandwidth (1.5 to 10 Mbps downstream; upstream varies) in most markets. The typical mid-range fiber optic offering is roughly equivalent in price to the high-end price of DSL and cable at 5 to 6 Mbps. However, it should be said that cable has excellent prospects for future development. Some providers are offering 25 Mbps downstream speeds in early 2007 with 100+ Mbps offerings on the horizon.

While no further discussion of the fiber optic solution is included in this book, there are further discussions of both cable and DSL as the more widely available options for connectivity. Metropolitan wireless networks are emerging with mixed reviews. However, it is only a very small matter of time and evolution before wireless broadband is a viable reality for the teleworker. Notably absent from the array of options is the traditional dialup modem. There is simply too much lacking in available bandwidth and reliability for such an option to be viable.

Infrastructure Services

Once the access solution for the teleworker's basic connectivity has been addressed and a solution decided upon, you need to consider the choice of infrastructure services to be provided. This is not to be confused with the applications and services necessary for job performance. This discussion revolves around the architecture necessary to provide secure, reliable access to those applications and services.

Typically, a router, such as a Cisco 800 series router, will be placed at the teleworker home. This router provides the necessary technologies for the connection back to the central site. The 800 series routers vary in technological capability. Therefore, some research into the proper model will be necessary. The "Business-Ready Teleworker" SRND contains much of this information.

From an infrastructure services point of view, some of the options to consider include

- **IPsec VPN**—Establishes a secure tunnel over the public Internet to provide an always-on, secure connection to the central site. This is typical of an 800 series router "nailed-up" connection.

- **Remote Access VPN**—Establishes a secure connection on-demand using a VPN software client.

- **Security**—Safeguards for the corporate network to prevent backdoor access to the central site network via a teleworker home network. This involves firewall, intrusion protection services (IPS), and web filtering at the teleworker premises.

- **Authentication**—Verification of the identity of those accessing network resources. This involves identity-based network services, authentication, authorization, and accounting (AAA) service, and 802.1x authentication services for port-based access control. Cisco security and trust agents can also play an integral role in protecting the network.

- **QoS**—Establishing traffic classification to ensure application or service availability and behavior. QoS mechanisms must be in place to regulate priority traffic flow and optimize the use of WAN bandwidth for critical applications and services.

- **Management**—Practice and policy describing the support of remote resources even in those circumstances where there might be loss of corporate control of remote devices. Teleworker solutions should be centrally administered and managed to enable application and security updates to be pushed to company assets at will. This also allows the monitoring of compliance with service level agreements (SLA) for various solutions, including teleworker deployments.

Teleworker Components

Teleworker solutions present a number of challenges in terms of deployment and support. The deployment must be almost entirely automated, thereby limiting user involvement. It also must be supportable and manageable from a corporate IT policy standpoint. The solution comprises three distinct components:

- Home office components

- Corporate components

- IP telephony/video components

Not every solution will include components for IP telephony and video from day one. However, in the evolution of the network as well as keeping on the path to the IIN, these services will need to be included at some point. Figure 2-2 illustrates the basic connectivity of the teleworker solution.

The requirement for home office components includes the access methodology, remote VPN router with QoS capabilities, and the desktop or laptop computer to be used by the teleworker. Optionally, the components may include a Cisco IP Phone, Cisco Unified Video Advantage (CUVA) camera for video, a wireless LAN access point (separate or integrated into the 800 series router), and possibly a laptop docking station.

The corporate components include a VPN headend router, a multifunction security appliance (such as the Cisco Adaptive Security Appliance [ASA]), management services, AAA services, and devices capable of providing resilient termination of IPsec VPN tunnels.

In support of IP telephony components and services, there must be a call-control facility such as Cisco Unified Communications Manager (formerly Cisco Unified CallManager [CUCM]) or Cisco Unified Communications Manager Express (formerly Cisco Unified CallManager Express [CME]). CME would be used only if the teleworker were connecting back to a smaller branch site with its own local call-control functionality such as that seen in a distributed dial plan scenario. Such services allow the teleworker IP Phone to be viewed as simply another extension of the corporate telephone system. Just as any other extension on the network, the teleworker phone would be able to use the PSTN connectivity of the central site and place or receive calls as if located physically at the central site. Available services would include such capabilities as Unified Messaging (UM) or basic Voice Messaging (VM) as well as the ability to log in as a call center agent.

Figure 2-2   *Cisco Teleworker Components*

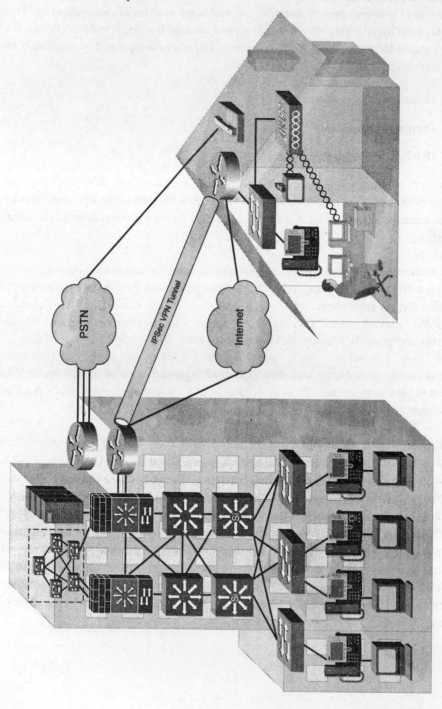

Traditional Teleworker versus Business-Ready Teleworker

So how does the business-ready teleworker differ from the teleworker or, in the traditional sense, the telecommuter? The simplest answer is—evolution.

The telecommuter was simply connected however and whenever necessary. There was no thought of "one experience regardless of device or locale." There was no concept of SLA for the teleworker. The ability for a full-time employee to perform all job functions from home was a novelty rather than a compelling business case for cost reduction with increased productivity.

Every service offered to the telecommuter of yesterday was best-effort, if it could even be thought of to that level. The construction of a corporate solution, security policy, and all-out elevation to an actual executive-accepted business solution was beyond the extent of most lines of thought.

The advent of higher-speed broadband solutions available to residential areas is likely one of the most significant drivers of the solution as well as one of the most relevant contributors to the viability of the teleworker solution of today. With legacy dialup services, the connectivity was a challenge. Providing the services and applications or necessary infrastructure to make a remotely connected user feel as though they were sitting in the office was totally out of the question. Fortunately, advances in security technologies, remote management, and control utilities have greatly enhanced the viability of the teleworker solution.

Essentially, it comes down to the fact that the network was simply not ready to handle such challenges as those presented by remotely connected offices and users. That is, until now. With the teleworker architecture, applications and services can be delivered to home-based users, providing a network experience similar to that of corporate office-based users.

Foundation Summary

SONA provides the pathway to the Intelligent Information Network. The teleworker architecture is a key part of the SONA framework at the networked infrastructure layer. Technologies have been evolving over the past decade to allow for integrated services and applications to be provided to the teleworker in a manner not previously possible.

Connection speeds and technologies available to the home office provide much needed bandwidth, security, and services that enable one network experience regardless of locale. The "Business-Ready Teleworker" SRND provides detailed guidance on the deployment of these technologies. Table 2-2 lists connection types and bandwidths typically available (bandwidth speeds are typical offerings, not minimum and maximum limits of the respective technology).

Table 2-2 *Remote Connectivity Access Methodologies*

Technology	Upstream Bandwidth	Downstream Bandwidth	Availability
DSL	256 to 1024 kbps	1.5 to 6 Mbps	Nearly every local telephone provider offers service
Cable	2 to 6 Mbps	4 to 6 Mbps	Offered by cable TV providers who are promising speeds of 25 Mbps to 100+ Mbps in the not-so-distant future
Fiber optic	2 to 5 Mbps	5 to 30 Mbps	Limited offering by select providers

Once the access methodology is in place, the access options to be provided to teleworkers must be decided upon. Table 2-3 lists typical options.

Table 2-3 *Remote Connectivity Options*

Technology	Connection Type	Connection Device
Remote-access VPN	On-demand using a VPN client	Laptop or desktop computer connection via software VPN client
IPsec VPN	Always-on or nailed-up VPN connection	Remote router connection to VPN Concentrator

With the connection access methodology and options in place, QoS-protected services and applications can be offered to teleworkers in a secure and robust manner.

Q&A

The questions and scenarios in this book are designed to be challenging and to make sure that you know the answer. Rather than allowing you to derive the answers from clues hidden inside the questions themselves, the questions challenge your understanding and recall of the subject.

Hopefully, mastering these questions will help you limit the number of exam questions on which you narrow your choices to two options, and then guess.

You can find the answers to these questions in Appendix A. For more practice with exam-like question formats, use the exam engine on the CD-ROM.

1. Consider teleworker access options as discussed in the chapter. Compare IPsec VPN connections with remote-access VPN connections and illustrate a viable case for each.

2. Consider a typical network implementation. List some tasks that must be completed and components that must be acquired to support a business-ready teleworker environment.

3. Among the remote-connection topologies discussed in this chapter, describe a viable solution or need that can be served by each. Those discussed include MPLS, Frame Relay/ATM, and site-to-site VPN.

4. List at least three technologies that have evolved to a degree that has made it possible for the teleworker of the 1990s to become the teleworker of today.

5. What are some risks associated with teleworker deployments?

6. How might some of the risks brought about by teleworker access be mitigated?

7. Among the solutions discussed in the chapter for teleworker connectivity are DSL, cable, and fiber. Obviously, these do not encompass all the possible connection options for the teleworker. What are some other possibilities?

8. Where is the best source of information and case studies for teleworker solutions documentation?

Exam Topic List

This chapter covers the following topics that you need to master for the CCNP ISCW exam:

- **Cable Access Technologies**—Defines basic terminology and standards relevant to cable technology, the components of a cable system that provide data services, and features of cable technology

- **Radio Frequency Signals**—Describes digital cable use of radio frequency bands for signal transmission

- **Data over Cable**—Describes how data over cable services can be delivered using an HFC architecture

- **Cable Technology Issues**—Describes the combination of technologies necessary for cable systems to function

- **Provisioning Cable Modems**—Describes the cable provisioning process in a customer network

CHAPTER 3

Using Cable to Connect to a Central Site

Chapter 2, "Topologies for Teleworker Connectivity," discussed some of the options available for teleworker connectivity. Among these options is cable modem access. Heavy competition has been building in recent years among cable providers and telephone companies in the broadband services market. The companies offering these services are benefiting greatly from both the Internet generation's demand for high-speed access and the corporate move toward teleworker deployments.

This chapter discusses, in more detail, the terminology, capabilities, and technologies surrounding cable access as a teleworker access methodology.

"Do I Know This Already?" Quiz

The purpose of the "Do I Know This Already?" quiz is to help you decide whether you really need to read the entire chapter. If you already intend to read the entire chapter, you do not necessarily need to answer these questions now.

The 18-question quiz, derived from the major sections in the "Foundation Topics" portion of the chapter, helps you to determine how to spend your limited study time.

Table 3-1 outlines the major topics discussed in this chapter and the "Do I Know This Already?" quiz questions that correspond to those topics.

Table 3-1 *"Do I Know This Already?" Foundation Topics Section-to-Question Mapping*

Foundation Topics Section	Questions Covered in This Section	Score
Cable Access Technologies	1–8	
Radio Frequency Signals	9–12	
Data over Cable	13–16	
Provisioning Cable Modems	17–18	
Total Score		

> **CAUTION**   The goal of self-assessment is to gauge your mastery of the topics in this chapter. If you do not know the answer to a question or are only partially sure of the answer, you should mark this question wrong for purposes of self-assessment. Giving yourself credit for an answer that you correctly guess skews your self-assessment results and might provide you with a false sense of security.

1. Which of the following would be found in a cable subscriber's home?

    a. Feeder network

    b. Transportation network

    c. Tap

    d. Amplifier

2. Which of the following terms describes RF signals transmitted from the headend to the subscriber?

    a. Upstream

    b. Downstream

    c. HFC

    d. CATV

3. Which of the following terms refers to a mixture of coaxial and fiber optic cable in the network?

    a. HFC

    b. COAX

    c. DOCSIS

    d. NTSC

4. Which of the following cable components would provide signal processing, formatting, and distribution?

    a. Antenna site

    b. Headend

    c. Transportation network

    d. Distribution network

    e. Subscriber drop

5. The cable modem connects to the cable system network via which of the following components?

    a. Antenna site

    b. Headend

    c. Transportation network

    d. Distribution network

    e. Subscriber drop

6. Remote antenna sites are connected to the headend via which of the following cable components?

    a. Antenna site

    b. Headend

    c. Transportation network

    d. Distribution network

    e. Subscriber drop

7. A coaxial cable contains all but which of the following components?

    a. Copper conductor

    b. Foil shielding

    c. Braided wire shielding

    d. Optical core

8. Cable systems came about to solve which of the following problems?

    a. Poor-quality over-the-air transmissions

    b. RF bandwidth competition

    c. CATV regulations

    d. FCC mandate

9. Which of the following is the RF range of the electromagnetic spectrum?

    a. 1 MHz to 5 MHz

    b. 10 GHz to 50 GHz

    c. 5 MHz to 1 GHz

    d. 500 kHz to 1 MHz

10. Specifications for data service over cable are defined by which of the following?

    a. DOCSIS

    b. NTSC

    c. PAL

    d. SECAM

11. The definition of data signals to be used by cable operators is a function of which of the following OSI layers?

    a. Layer 1

    b. Layer 2

    c. Layer 3

    d. Layer 4

12. Which version of the DOCSIS document defines the use of channel bonding in cable networks?

    a. DOCSIS 1.0

    b. DOCSIS 1.1

    c. DOCSIS 2.0

    d. DOCSIS 3.0

13. Which of the following are driving forces behind the advent of HFC networks?

    a. Reduced signal degradation

    b. Invulnerability to outside electromagnetic interference

    c. Reduced service outages

    d. RF range density on fiber

14. Upon reaching the subscriber home, the signal strength must be at what minimum level to provide the necessary services?

    a. 50 dB

    b. 125 MHz

    c. 6 MHz

    d. 75 dB

15. The CMTS resides where in the cable system network infrastructure?

    a. Transportation network

    b. Headend

    c. Subscriber drop

    d. Feeder trunks

16. In the subscriber home, which device takes the received signal and passes it on to individual devices?

    a. Tap

    b. Splitter

    c. Television

    d. CM

17. During which step of the provisioning process does the CM find the pathway for data signals received from the headend?

    a. Upstream setup

    b. Downstream setup

    c. Layer 1 and 2 establishment

    d. DOCSIS configuration

18. The DOCSIS configuration file is provided to the CM from which of the following devices?

    a. DHCP server

    b. Headend

    c. TFTP server

    d. ToD server

The answers to the "Do I Know This Already?" quiz are found in Appendix A, "Answers to the 'Do I Know This Already?' Quizzes and Q&A Sections." The suggested choices for your next step are as follows:

■ **12 or fewer overall score**—Read the entire chapter. This includes the "Foundation Topics," "Foundation Summary," and "Q&A" sections.

■ **14 or 15 overall score**—Begin with the "Foundation Summary" section, and then go to the "Q&A" section.

■ **16 or more overall score**—If you want more review on these topics, skip to the "Foundation Summary" section and then go to the "Q&A" section. Otherwise, move to the next chapter.

Foundation Topics

Cable Access Technologies

Cable access is among the fastest growing technologies for home access to multiple services via a common connection. One connection to the cable company carries the television signal and Internet traffic. Most cable carriers are now getting into the voice market as well by providing voice services with unlimited long distance and other traditional services over the cable connection. The addition of teleworker functionality is a natural extension of this already multiservice connection technology.

Today, cable access is typically sold in bundles. These bundles offer a mix of services including television, Internet access, and voice. Most companies also offer a "build your own" bundle for services, to allow a customer to mix and match the solution to meet their needs.

Cable Internet access typically is available at speeds ranging from 2-Mbps to 6-Mbps downstream bandwidth (that is, from the Internet to the home) from the average carrier. The cost of this connection is typically bundled with the monthly cable television recurring charge at a discounted rate, as most companies seem to avoid offering Internet access without other services in the bundle, most importantly, television. The concern with downstream speeds versus upstream speeds is relevant simply because the bulk of the traffic load on the connection will be generated by small outbound (from the subscriber) requests returning large amounts of inbound (to the subscriber) data. For example, when a web browser is pointed to http://www.cisco.com, little in the way of traffic is generated by the request. However, a significant amount of information is generated by the reply and subsequent loading of images and information requested. For this reason, service providers have taken an asynchronous view of bandwidth allocation, preferring to focus on the speed of the connection toward the subscriber.

Cable Technology Terminology

In any discussion of relatively new or different technologies, a definition of terminology associated with that technology is necessary. This allows a more rapid familiarization with the technology. With cable access, the new terms are quite numerous compared with other networking technologies. The following are terms that will be referenced throughout this chapter:

- **Broadband**—Data transmission using a multiplexing methodology to provide more efficient use of available bandwidth. In cable, the term *broadband* refers to the frequency-division multiplexing (FDM) of multiple signals in a wide radio frequency (RF) bandwidth over a hybrid fiber-coaxial (HFC) network and the capability to handle large amounts of information. FDM is a means by which information from multiple channels or frequencies can be allocated bandwidth on a single wire.

- **Community Antenna Television (CATV)**—A broad term referring to cable television in general.

- **Coaxial cable**—The primary medium used in the construction of cable television systems. Coaxial cable (or coax) is used in the transmission of RF signals and has specific physical characteristics regarding signal attenuation. These characteristics include cable diameter, dielectric construction, ambient temperature, and operating frequency.

- **Tap**—A device used to divide the input signal RF power to support multiple outlets. Typically, cable operators deploy taps with two, four, or eight ports.

- **Amplifier**—A device that magnifies an input signal, thus producing a significantly larger output signal.

- **Hybrid fiber-coaxial (HFC)**—A mixed optical-coaxial network in which fiber optic cable is installed in place of some or all of the traditional trunk portion of the cable network.

- **Downstream**—An RF signal transmission traveling in the direction of the subscriber from the headend. Downstream is also called a *forward path* (viewed from the perspective of the cable provider).

- **Upstream**—An RF signal transmission traveling in the direction of the headend from the subscriber. Upstream is also called a *return* or *reverse path* (again, from the provider perspective).

As most of the general population has lived with cable television for a number of years, the coaxial cable associated with it is quite readily recognized. Obviously, there are many types of coaxial cable available in the marketplace at any given time. Each has differing characteristics and is utilized in a variety of manners and technologies. For example, Ethernet 10BASE2 and 10BASE5 networks used a coaxial cable but each had differing physical and electrical characteristics. Table 3-2 shows the physical differences in some coaxial cable types.

Table 3-2 *Coaxial Cable Types and Characteristics*

Specification	Cable Type	American Wire Gauge (AWG)
10BASE2 Ethernet	RG-58	20
10BASE5 Ethernet	RG-11	12
CATV cable	RG-6 or RG-59	18

Hopefully, the table establishes something of a point of reference for coaxial cable uses. CATV cable is somewhat thick and rigid in comparison to 10BASE2 or Thinnet cable. The 10BASE2 cable is quite flexible and, as the name "Thinnet" implies, quite small in diameter. In general, the thinner the cable, the shorter the functional distance. The use of an HFC network remedies much of the issue caused by cable distance limitations by introducing fiber optic cabling where needed.

Cable System Standards

Like any networking technology, cable systems have associated standards meant to loosely govern the manner in which the technologies evolve and the manner in which they are implemented by various hardware and software vendors. These standards include

- **National Television Standards Committee (NTSC)**—Created in 1941, and named after its authoring committee, NTSC defines technical standards for analog television systems (utilizing a 6-MHz modulated signal) used in North America.

- **Phase Alternating Line (PAL)**—A color coding system used in broadcast television throughout Europe, Asia, Africa, Australia, Brazil, and Argentina using a 6-, 7-, or 8-MHz modulated signal. Color differences signal an alternate phase at the horizontal line rate.

- **Système Electronic Couleur avec Memoire (SECAM)**—An analog color television system used in France and some other Eastern European countries using an 8-MHz modulated signal.

Modulation is the addition of information to an electronic or optical signal carrier. It can be applied to direct current (DC) by turning it on or off, to alternating current (AC), or to optical signals. Signal modulation is a process of varying a *waveform* to convey a message. The waveform can be changed in amplitude, frequency, phase, or some combination of any or all three to convey these messages.

Cable System Components

The description of the components associated with cable systems essentially equates to defining additional terminology. Typical components include:

- **Antenna site**—A location containing a cable provider's main receiving and satellite dish facilities. This site is chosen based on potential for optimal reception of transmissions over the air, via satellite, and via point-to-point communication.

- **Headend**—A master facility where signals are received, processed, formatted, and distributed over to the cable network. This includes both the transportation and distribution networks. This facility is typically heavily secured and sometimes "lights-out," meaning that it is not regularly staffed.

- **Transportation network**—The means and media by which remote antenna sites are connected to the headend facility. Alternately, this could be a headend facility connection to the distribution network. The transmission media may be microwave, coaxial supertrunk, or fiber optic.

- **Distribution network**—In typical cable system architectures, consists of trunk and feeder cables. The trunk is the backbone cable (usually 0.75-inch diameter) over which the primary connectivity is maintained. In many networks, the distribution network tends to be a hybrid fiber-coaxial network.

- **Node**—Performs optical-to-RF conversion of CATV signal as needed. Feeder cables (typically 0.5-inch diameter) originate from nodes that branch off into individual communities to provide services to anywhere between 100 and 2000 customers each.

- **Subscriber drop**—Connects the subscriber to the cable service network via a connection between the feeder portion of a distribution network and the subscriber terminal device (for example, TV set, VCR, high-definition TV set-top box, or cable modem). The subscriber drop components consist of the physical coaxial cabling, grounding and attachment hardware, passive devices, and a set-top box.

These components tend to be relatively easy to understand in concept. In practice, these are implemented in differing manners depending on the cable provider. Regardless of the chosen architecture, the concepts remain the same. Figure 3-1 illustrates typical cable provider architecture.

Figure 3-1 *Cable System Provider Architecture*

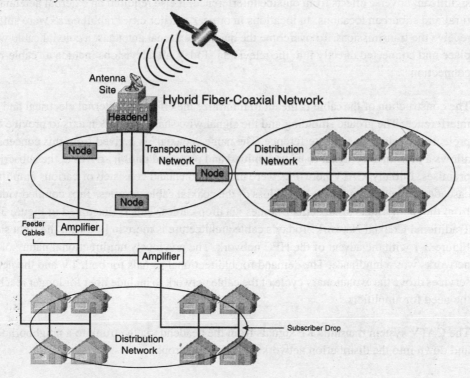

Cable Features

Cable systems use coaxial cable at the subscriber premises. The cable itself consists of a copper core surrounded by insulation and grounded shielding of braided wire. Figure 3-2 illustrates the basic anatomy of the coaxial cable.

Figure 3-2 *Coaxial Cable Anatomy*

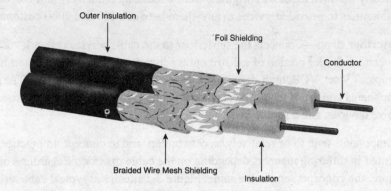

Traditional television signal transmitted over the air lacked in quality and was subject to significant adverse effects from outside interference. It also required an external antenna in many rural and suburban locations. In locations in or near a major city, "rabbit ears" were sufficient to receive the transmissions. To overcome the need for external antennas, a coaxial cable was put in place and connected directly into the television. Today, all televisions include a "cable-ready" connection.

The construction of the cable is meant to minimize the effects of external electrical and RF interference. The ground shielding and the signal wire share a common axis to provide better protection against outside interference. The name "coaxial" is derived from this concept. This allows a high-quality signal to be transmitted and protected until it arrives at the subscriber premises. Initially, CATV networks were unidirectional and consisted of various amplifiers in cascade compensating for the signal loss of the coaxial cable in series. Taps coupled video signal from the main trunks to subscriber homes via drop cables. This is illustrated in Figure 3-1 as the Traditional Coaxial Network. Today's cable architecture is more in line with the right side of Figure 3-1 with the advent of the HFC network. The previously unidirectional nature of cable networks was a hindrance. The demand for bidirectional signals for both TV and the newer data services drove the evolutionary cycle of the cable network to include fiber for longer reach without the need for amplifiers.

The CATV system transmits RF signals from the headend via the trunk to a neighborhood node and down into the distribution network to subscriber drops.

Cable System Benefits

The essential idea behind cable is to bring cost-effective television and services to a dense subscriber base while maintaining high-quality content. Traditionally, this content was limited simply to television channels ranging from "life-line" (local weather/news/information channels) to premium-channel content.

In recent years, additional services have been added to the mix, including voice, data, and digital television options. Over the next few years, all of the services offered by cable providers will leverage the IP network as a platform for integrated services. IP-based services will carry all data, voice, and video content to the subscriber premises. Set-top boxes currently using RF signal will be IP attached and capable of delivering content to any number of access devices, including IP phones, mobile phones, and more.

The more advanced capabilities offered by high-speed network access brought about a practice of placing equipment, including telephone switches and cable modem termination systems (CMTS), in a common facility so that services could be leveraged in a variety of manners. The resulting broadband Internet access offering presents corporations with cost-effective connectivity for teleworkers who connect back to a central site either through a IPsec VPN or remote-access VPN. Additionally, interactive television content and Public Switched Telephone Network (PSTN) voice access for voice and fax calls allow cable providers to offer VoIP services.

Radio Frequency Signals

The term *radio frequency* defines a relatively small portion of the known electromagnetic spectrum. Figure 3-3 shows a small portion of the electromagnetic spectrum.

The whole of the electromagnetic spectrum is significantly more wide-ranging in terms of frequencies than what is shown in the figure. Smaller still is the portion of the spectrum specifically associated with RF (5 MHz to 1 GHz).

Generally, *frequency* is defined as the rate at which a repeated event occurs over time. In terms of electromagnetism, that event is known as a *cycle*. One cycle per second is known as 1 hertz (Hz). RF is measured in number of cycles or "waves" per second. Other characteristics of interest include wavelength and amplitude. The wavelength is the distance between peaks or valleys in the wave cycle (that is, the length of one complete cycle) where the amplitude is the peak height or depth of the wave during the cycle. *Frequency* has an inverse relationship to wavelength. As frequency increases, the wavelength tends to decrease. Where f is frequency, c is the speed of light ($3 * 10^8$ meters per second), and Λ is wavelength:

$$f = c/\Lambda$$

Figure 3-3 *Partial Electromagnetic Spectrum*

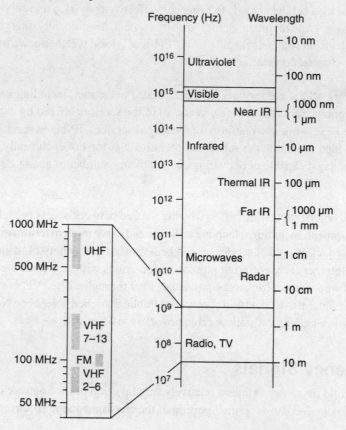

This calculation assumes a waveform moving through a vacuum. As the wave travels through different media types, the frequency is constant but the wavelength and speed change. The effect of various media types on a waveform is measured by a refractive index and would need to be factored into the discussion for a true representation. However, because the physics of waveform dynamics is outside the scope of the exam, further discussion will be put aside.

When tuning a radio or television, the tuner is finding individual frequencies in their respective ranges. When a frequency used by a radio station is tuned in, the transmission from that station is transformed into voltage that applies current of varying strength to a strong magnet in the speaker. The speaker's magnet becomes stronger with the application of that current. Metallic rings in the diaphragm of the speaker are attracted to the magnet, creating motion and vibration that our ears end up interpreting as sound.

In cable systems, a similar concept is applied. Rather than being transmitted over the air, the signals are sent across the cable provider's HFC to the subscriber. Televisions (high-definition or otherwise), set-top boxes, cable modems, and other equipment tune to various frequencies that allow them to interpret the signals to provide content.

In terms of over-the-air television broadcasts, there are traditionally very high frequency (VHF) and ultra-high frequency (UHF) channels. VHF utilizes the 30- to 300-MHz range and UHF the 300- to 3000-MHz range. The individual television channels utilize broadcast frequencies in their respective ranges.

The cable television industry defines the television spectrum only in the downstream path. The upstream path is not subject to a frequency plan. The frequencies can be monitored and upstream signals placed into "clean" areas free from interference and noise from other signals. Typically the range of 5 to 15 MHz tends to be noisy and difficult or impossible to utilize.

The cable network is able to transmit upstream and downstream simultaneously. For downstream signals, those directed toward subscribers, the frequency range includes 50 to 860 MHz. Alternately, upstream signals, those directed away from subscribers, utilize the range of 5 to 42 MHz.

The downstream range has been subdivided into smaller channels as defined by a standardized frequency plan. This plan places a "guard band" between the ranges for upstream and downstream transmissions. This is required due to the cutoff characteristics of high-pass and low-pass filters. Such filters are needed to ensure that there is no signal leakage into other frequency spectrums.

Digital Signals over RF Channels

Cable specifications are defined by a document known as Data-over-Cable Service Interface Specifications (DOCSIS). DOCSIS is an international standard developed by CableLabs, a nonprofit organization and development consortium dedicated to cable-related technologies. Founded in 1988, CableLabs is essentially charged with the testing and certification of cable technology access equipment such as cable modems and CMTS. The organization makes decisions on standardization and grants for DOCSIS certification and qualification.

The core of DOCSIS defines the manner in which individual components communicate in the cable network. The specification for data-over-cable defines high-speed data transfer over an existing CATV system. Cable operators use DOCSIS to implement Internet access over their existing HFC infrastructure.

Cable transmissions are highly similar to wireless transmissions, with the obvious exception of the presence or absence of copper. DOCSIS defines the frequency plan to be used as well (6 MHz for DOCSIS, 7 MHz and 8 MHz for Euro-DOCSIS). As discussed, cable transmission uses the RF bands. The RF band is composed of the frequencies above audio and below infrared.

Within DOCSIS are the OSI Layer 1 and Layer 2 requirements for connectivity between cable devices:

- **Physical layer (Layer 1)**—Definition of data signals to be used by cable operators. DOCSIS specifies bandwidths for each channel. These channel widths are 200 kHz, 400 kHz, 800 kHz, 1.6 MHz, 3.2 MHz, and 6.4 MHz. Additionally, DOCSIS defines the manner in which these signals are modulated.

- **MAC layer (Layer 2)**—Definition of a deterministic access method depending on DOCSIS version: time division multiple access (TDMA) for version 1.0, 1.1, and 2.0 or synchronous code division multiple access (S-CDMA) in version 2.0. The MAC layer protocol controls access to the return path. The DOCSIS MAC protocol uses a request/grant system for transmissions. This means that there is little or no use of contention for bandwidth as in Ethernet networks (and no collisions).

Like many other standards and specifications relating to technology, DOCSIS is evolving. DOCSIS version 1.0 was released in March 1997, followed by version 1.1 in April 1999. Version 2.0 came about in January 2002 as a result of increased demand for symmetric, real-time services and applications such as IP telephony. This release enhanced the technology by augmenting upstream speeds and putting QoS capabilities in place.

DOCSIS 3.0 was released in August 2006. Expected enhancements may include IPv6 support and channel bonding. Channel bonding allows the use of multiple downstream and upstream channels together, at the same time, by the same subscriber to increase overall bandwidth. In fact, through the use of the Wideband architecture pioneered by Cisco, current expectations would allow the offering of 100+ Mbps services to the subscriber. In fact, DOCSIS 3.0 expects capabilities reaching 160 Mbps downstream with 120 Mbps upstream.

With new products on the horizon from Cisco's Linksys and Scientific Atlanta business units, speeds and services will most likely continue to evolve well beyond current imagination.

More information regarding DOCSIS can be found at CableLabs' website: http://www.cablemodem.com/specifications/.

Data over Cable

Television, alone, simply doesn't meet the market demand anymore. Bruce Springsteen's song, "57 Channels (And Nothin' On)" says it well. While in need of an update to a number of channels placed well into triple-digits, it may well ring true for the foreseeable future. The Internet has changed the definition of what is considered entertainment.

Cable provider infrastructure has evolved somewhat from pure coaxial networks to HFC. The driving force behind this evolution to HFC is easily understandable. Simply put, the signal from the antenna degrades as it travels across the copper medium. This can be corrected to some degree by amplifiers in the path, roughly every 2000 feet. This ensures that the signal is delivered to the subscriber with adequate power to provide all of the channels within the spectrum for analog television, digital television, and cable modem services (the range of 50 to 860 MHz).

In a 20-mile plant, roughly 52 amplifiers would be required to maintain the necessary signal strength to serve all subscribers along the line. Unfortunately, as the signal degrades, it picks up noise or distortion, and that noise or distortion is amplified along with the signal. Eventually, what's left is an unusable mass of wasted voltage. The result is a disruption in service and unhappy customers.

To mitigate the risk of customer satisfaction issues, the network must implement infrastructure necessary to avoid the signal degradation and loss. Luckily, a suitable technological solution is available in the form of fiber optics.

Hybrid Fiber-Coaxial Networks

Fiber dramatically cuts the number of amplifiers needed in the distribution and transport networks. The degree to which fiber is installed varies from provider to provider. Some providers have opted to go entirely fiber into the subscriber premises. Fiber transports the signal using either laser or light emitting diode (LED) technologies depending on the type being deployed.

Fiber has a number of benefits over traditional cable. Fiber is thin and lightweight, able to cover longer distances with virtually no loss of signal or noise, and is immune to outside sources of electromagnetic interference. Because the number of amplifiers is reduced, there is some monetary benefit associated with support and equipment costs. There is some discussion as to which is easier to handle, cable or fiber. Essentially, that discussion comes down to preference. Cable tends to be rigid and sturdy whereas fiber is thin and somewhat pliable, requiring some advanced skills and care to properly terminate.

Fiber trunks have been used to replace trunk cables in the architecture. These carry downstream traffic from the headend to the neighborhood node where the signal is converted from light to electrical and forwarded on to the subscriber via copper coaxial cable at signal strength greater than 50 decibels (dBm). A *decibel* is a unit of measure for expressing ratios between two quantities. The prefix "deci-" follows the International System of Units (SI) unit designation, meaning 1/10, and is always lowercase. To further confuse the issue, the decibel merely follows the SI naming convention; it is not an SI unit. The "bel" portion of the word is derived from Alexander Graham Bell's name; therefore, it is capitalized. When discussing absolute power levels, such as the signal strength on a cable network when the signal reaches the subscriber, the power is given in relation to milliwatts. This is expressed as dBm.

The movement of the cable system infrastructure to the HFC network architecture is essentially the catalyst that allowed for more advanced services to be offered. Initially, this was limited to data over cable but has evolved significantly and will continue to do so. DOCSIS 3.0 and Cisco's Wideband channel bonding technology will push the services and applications offerings forward at an unimaginable pace. This, coupled with the integrated services and applications afforded to the teleworker by Service-Oriented Network Architecture (SONA), will reinvent the way in which we work, live, play, and learn. In the same manner that SONA provides the framework for enterprise evolution to an Intelligent Information Network (IIN), the service provider market has an IP-Next Generation Network (IP-NGN) architecture providing a path to a similar destination. Once both the enterprise and the service providers begin to reach the true IIN state, the goal of "one experience regardless of locale or access device" will evolve to encompass both networks. One user, any service, anywhere will be a realistic expectation.

Data Transmission

DOCSIS has a number of components that comprise its architecture. These include

- **Cable modem termination system (CMTS)**—The CMTS usually resides in the headend. The CMTS modulates the signal to the cable modem (CM) and demodulates the CM response.

- **Cable modem (CM)**—The CM is a CPE device that terminates as well as performs modulation and demodulation of signals to and from the CMTS. Typical transmission speeds for CMs range from 1.5 to 6 Mbps.

- **"Back office" services**—Services such as TFTP (for configuration file upload/download), DHCP (dynamic IP addressing), ToD (Time of Day for log timestamping), and others that provide vital tools for the maintenance of a CM installation.

Critical information for the configuration of CM hosts is carried in the DOCSIS configuration file. This is a file that contains information pertinent to all CM hosts attaching to the provider network.

The headend CMTS communicates with the CMs located in subscriber homes. The headend provides the systems necessary to provide Internet access for associated CMs. A typical network segment serves anywhere from 500 to 2000 active data connections sharing the upstream and downstream bandwidth. The cable network can support up to 40 Mbps downstream and 30 Mbps upstream under the DOCSIS 2.0 specification. DOCSIS 3.0 will increase capacity to 160 Mbps downstream and 120 Mbps upstream. However, the current service offerings vary based on cable provider architecture and provisioning practices—the typical range is 256 kbps to 6 Mbps for access speeds.

As the network grows through the provisioning of additional subscribers and services, the network infrastructure can be augmented with relative ease. This is accomplished by adding an additional television channel allocated to high-speed data, thus doubling available subscriber bandwidth. Alternatively, a reduced number of subscribers per network segment would have a similar effect of increased bandwidth per subscriber. This is done either by increasing the number of headends or by laying additional fiber infrastructure connections close to the subscriber base to be served.

Figure 3-4 serves the purpose of bringing together a more complete vision of the technologies discussed in this chapter.

Figure 3-4 *Cable Technology Architecture*

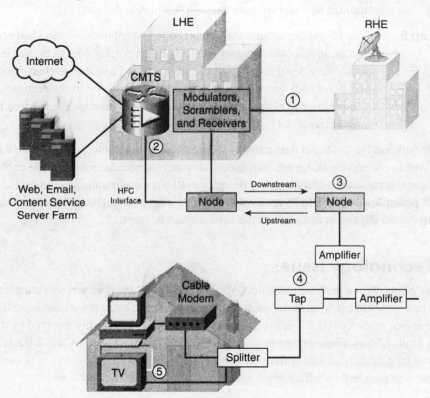

With much of the technology and terminology defined, Figure 3-4 provides a conceptual illustration of the operations of cable networks.

Step 1   In the downstream path, the local headend (LHE) receives television signals through the satellite dishes, antennas, analog and digital video servers, local programming, and other headends.

Step 2   The LHE distributes these television signals throughout a distribution network to subscribers. The signals are combined onto a coaxial cable, and then passed to a fiber transmitter in the headend.

Step 3   The headend fiber transmitter performs the signal conversion from RF to light. The signal is then passed across the network to a fiber node located relatively near the subscribers it serves, where a conversion from light back to RF is performed.

Step 4   The RF is passed via coaxial cable to the subscriber home where it passes through taps and splitters to reach destination devices.

Step 5   The RF splitter divides the combined RF signal into its individual service pieces, in this case data and video. The data portion goes to the cable modem while the video goes to the cable set-top box. The cable modem demodulates the signal back into digital data prior to passing it on to the destination end station (user workstation PC) over the LAN connection, be it wired Ethernet or wireless 802.11a/b/g.

For outbound or upstream data transmissions, the user's computer transmits the data via the available connection (Ethernet, wireless, and so on) to the cable modem. The cable modem modulates the digital data from the computer to RF signal and transmits the data at predefined RF and power levels. The CMTS receives the data RF channels and demodulates the data signal back into digital data for routing across the network and Internet.

Cable Technology Issues

The primary drawback for cable networks is the fact that the data services are using a shared infrastructure. That is, all of the subscribers on a cable carrier's network are essentially competing for scarce resources (in this case bandwidth). These issues are readily resolved by the cable carrier by limiting subscribers or by expanding available data channels. DOCSIS 3.0 has addressed this issue significantly as well with the concept of channel bonding. However, it is unclear how much time will pass before full adoption and deployment of the 3.0 capabilities.

The most compelling drawback to using shared bandwidth architectures is that privacy issues can potentially arise if the network is not properly secured. This can be addressed by encryption and other features specified in the DOCSIS standards.

As with any technology, oversubscription of a CMTS is a potential issue. This is a factor well out of control of the subscriber. Fortunately, the technological advances within DOCSIS are providing innovation with minimal incremental hardware costs. They are finding new ways to utilize the same resources more effectively.

Many of the support issues that arise surrounding cable installations end up having to do with the manner in which the cabling was installed in the subscriber home. The home must be grounded and bonded correctly for both safety and the elimination of ground loops. Ground loops can result in the introduction of significant noise on the wire. Coils, ferrite beads, and filters might be able to reduce noise on the wire. If the cable was tightly coiled before installation, the cable might experience some degradation of signal due to breaches in the cable sheath.

Provisioning Cable Modems

Cable modem provisioning can seem a bit daunting when compared with other technologies. There are several steps involved in the process. The headend CMTS must have operational provisioning servers such as DHCP and TFTP in order for IP addressing and configuration files to be provided. The steps defined by DOCSIS are as follows:

Step 1   **Downstream setup**—At power-on, the cable modem scans and locks the downstream path for the allocated RF data channel in order for physical and data link layers to be established.

Step 2   **Upstream setup**—The cable modem listens to the management messages arriving via the downstream path. These include information regarding how and when to communicate in the upstream path. These are used to establish the upstream physical and data link layers.

Step 3   **Layer 1 and 2 establishment**—Connection established from CM to CMTS to build physical and data link layers.

Step 4   **IP address allocation**—After Layer 1 and 2 are established, Layer 3 can be allocated as well. This is done by the DHCP server.

Step 5   **Getting DOCSIS configuration**—The CM requests the DOCSIS configuration file from the TFTP server. This is an ASCII file created by DOCSIS editors. A DOCSIS configuration file is a "binary file" and has the parameters for cable modems to come online in accordance to what the ISP is provisioning, such as maximum downstream and upstream rates, maximum upstream burst rate, class of service or baseline privacy, management information bases (MIBs), and many other parameters. This file can be loaded on the CM via TFTP or the CM can be manually configured.

Step 6   **Register QoS with CMTS**—The CM negotiates traffic types and QoS settings with the CMTS.

Step 7   **IP network initialization**—Once Layers 1, 2, and 3 are established and the configuration file is pulled from the TFTP server, the CM provides routing services for hosts on the subscriber side of the CM. It also performs some Network Address Translation (NAT) functions so that multiple hosts might be represented by a single public IP address.

As part of the initialization phase, the CM makes contact with a DHCP server on the provider's network. The DHCP server provides the following information to the CM:

- IP address
- Subnet mask
- Default gateway
- TFTP server
- DHCP relay agent
- The complete name of the DOCSIS configuration file
- Address of ToD server
- Syslog server address

Once this information is obtained, the CM can issue a request to the ToD server to set its clock to the correct time. This facilitates syslog timestamps. At this point, also, it can issue a TFTP request to the TFTP server for its DOCSIS configuration file.

To facilitate standardization of router software on client CMs, the Cisco IOS images desired for use with the CMs can be stored on the TFTP server. The Cisco IOS version and filename can be specified in the DOCSIS configuration file to be downloaded at each power-on of the router. This takes several minutes, but does provide some degree of control on the part of the service provider.

Additionally, the router configuration(s) can be stored on the TFTP server to be downloaded at each power-on as well.

These are additional steps, as the Cisco IOS image and configuration can be stored on the router as traditionally done in most routing environments. This makes the power-on sequence a much shorter process in the event of a router reload.

Critical information for the configuration of CM hosts is carried in the DOCSIS configuration file. This is a file that contains information pertinent to all CM hosts attaching to the provider network. All DOCSIS-compliant configuration files include the following information elements:

- Radio frequency information
    — Downstream frequency
    — Upstream channel ID
    — Network access configuration
- Class of service information
    — Class of service ID
    — Maximum downstream rate

- — Maximum upstream rate
- — Upstream channel priority
- — Minimum upstream rate
- — Maximum upstream channel burst
- — Class of service privacy enable
- Vendor-specific options
  - — Vendor ID
  - — Vendor-specific options
- SNMP management
  - — SNMP write-access control and SNMP MIB objects
- Baseline privacy interface configuration
  - — Authorize wait timeout
  - — Reauthorize wait timeout
  - — Authorization grace timeout
  - — Operational wait timeout
  - — Rekey wait timeout
  - — TEK grace time
  - — Authorize reject wait timeout
- Customer premises equipment
  - — Maximum number of CPEs
  - — CPE Ethernet MAC address
- Software upgrade
  - — TFTP software server IP address
  - — Software image filename
- Miscellaneous
  - — Concatenation support
  - — Use RFC 2104 HMAC-MD5
  - — CMTS authentication

After the CM has downloaded its configuration file, it can begin to communicate further on the network. Many options in the DOCSIS configuration file are unused for the bulk of CM provisioning.

Foundation Summary

Cable architecture will continue to evolve and grow to add more applications and services. Subscriber demand will drive the speed of that evolution. The needs of the teleworker will be no small part of that drive.

The term *cable* refers to the coaxial cable predominantly used in the cable provider's network. The cable system architecture provides a broadcast or shared media access method to subscribers. Table 3-3 lists the components in a cable system.

Table 3-3 *Cable System Components*

Component	Description
Antenna site	Location with primary receiving antennas and satellite dishes
Headend	Facility where signals are received, processed, formatted, and combined Transmits cable signal via distribution network to subscriber drops
Transportation network	Links an antenna site to a headend
Distribution network	Trunk and feeder cable infrastructure
Subscriber drop	Devices and components used to connect the subscriber home to the distribution network (for example, taps, splitters, and cable modem)

As with any technology, cable systems have numerous associated standards, as listed in Table 3-4.

Table 3-4 *Cable System Standards*

Standard	Description
NTSC	Technical standards for analog TV systems used in North America Uses a 6-MHz modulated signal
PAL	Color encoding system used in broadcast television systems in most of the world Uses 6-, 7-, or 8-MHz modulated signal
SECAM	Analog color TV system used in France and some other European countries Uses an 8-MHz modulated signal

DOCSIS provides the specification for data over cable. It is the data service interface standard for data carried over RF interfaces. DOCSIS also dictates the process by which CMs are provisioned. The DOCSIS CMTS uses differing channels to communicate upstream and downstream with the CM in the subscriber home. The RF range for the downstream flow will be specified while the upstream range will by allocated based on available bandwidth frequencies.

The HFC network allows providers to increase services offered while decreasing infrastructure cost. Fiber optic cable overcomes issues of coaxial cable relating to noise, electromagnetic interference, and relatively short distance limitations.

Q&A

The questions and scenarios in this book are designed to be challenging and to make sure that you know the answer. Rather than allowing you to derive the answers from clues hidden inside the questions themselves, the questions challenge your understanding and recall of the subject.

Hopefully, mastering these questions will help you limit the number of exam questions on which you narrow your choices to two options, and then guess.

You can find the answers to these questions in Appendix A. For more practice with exam-like question formats, use the exam engine on the CD-ROM.

1. Describe a situation in which a cable provider would benefit from the use of fiber over coaxial cable.

2. List at least three of the cable system components detailed in this chapter and their purpose.

3. Data over cable has enabled a number of advanced services and applications. List at least three, then consider two to three additional services that may be beneficial as a future offering.

4. Describe how the cable access technology fits in to the SONA framework.

5. Describe the provisioning process for a cable modem.

6. DOCSIS 3.0 promises some very interesting service offerings. Which technology innovation allows these promises to become reality?

7. With the release of DOCSIS 3.0, what are the advertised maximum upstream and downstream transmission speeds?

8. A DOCSIS configuration file contains a standard listing of information. List at least five of the items included in the file.

Exam Topic List

This chapter covers the following topics that you need to master for the CCNP ISCW exam:

- **DSL Features**—Describes the features of DSL

- **DSL Limitations**—Describes the limitations of DSL technology

- **DSL Variants**—Describes the various implementations of DSL, including symmetric and asymmetric DSL types

- **ADSL Basics**—Describes the basics of ADSL technology

- **ADSL Modulation**—Describes ADSL modulation technologies

- **Data Transmission over ADSL**—Describes data transmission over ADSL

- **PPP over Ethernet**—Describes the architecture and deployment models of PPPoE

- **PPP over ATM**—Describes the architecture and deployment models of PPPoA

CHAPTER 4

Using DSL to Connect to a Central Site

Chapter 2, "Topologies for Teleworker Connectivity," discussed some of the options available for teleworker connectivity. Among these was digital subscriber line (DSL) access. Heavy competition has been building in recent years among telephone companies in the broadband services market. The companies offering these services are benefiting greatly from both the Internet generation's demand for high-speed access and the corporate move toward teleworker deployments.

This chapter discusses, in more detail, the terminology, capabilities, and technologies surrounding DSL access as a teleworker access methodology.

"Do I Know This Already?" Quiz

The purpose of the "Do I Know This Already?" quiz is to help you decide whether you really need to read the entire chapter. If you already intend to read the entire chapter, you do not necessarily need to answer these questions now.

The 21-question quiz, derived from the major sections in the "Foundation Topics" portion of the chapter, helps you to determine how to spend your limited study time.

Table 4-1 outlines the major topics discussed in this chapter and the "Do I Know This Already?" quiz questions that correspond to those topics.

Table 4-1 *"Do I Know This Already?" Foundation Topics Section-to-Question Mapping*

Foundation Topics Section	Questions Covered in This Section	Score
DSL Features	1–4	
DSL Limitations	5–7	
DSL Variants	8–10	
ADSL Basics	11–12	
ADSL Modulation	13–14	
Data Transmission over ADSL	15–17	
PPP over Ethernet	18–19	
PPP over ATM	20–21	
Total Score		

> **NOTE** The goal of self-assessment is to gauge your mastery of the topics in this chapter. If you do not know the answer to a question or are only partially sure of the answer, you should mark this question wrong for purposes of self-assessment. Giving yourself credit for an answer that you correctly guess skews your self-assessment results and might provide you with a false sense of security.

1. The frequency range within which voice typically exists (not that which is set aside for it on the line) is which of the following?

   a. 0 Hz to 4 kHz

   b. 300 Hz to 3 kHz

   c. 50 Hz to 3000 kHz

   d. 3 kHz to 1.1 MHz

2. Which device makes it possible for ADSL data traffic to coexist with analog voice service?

   a. Microfilter

   b. DSL modem

   c. VPN

   d. CPE router

3. The range of 0 Hz to 4 kHz is reserved for analog voice traffic. ADSL occupies frequencies above that range. What is the upper boundary for current ADSL implementations?

   a. 3 kHz

   b. 4 kHz

   c. 1.1 MHz

   d. 40 kHz

4. The technique used to represent digital signals transported over a copper wire is known as what?

   a. Framing

   b. Line code

   c. Splitter

   d. Wavelength

5. Interference between two wires in a bundle is known as which of the following?

   a. Crosstalk

   b. Impedance mismatch

   c. AM radio interference

   d. Signal attenuation

6. Inductors used to extend signal range of a local loop, but which badly distort DSL frequencies are known as which of the following?

   a. Bridge taps

   b. Load coils

   c. Wire gauge

   d. Fiber optic cable

7. Extensions between the CPE and CO that cause noise and signal reduction are known as which of the following?

   a. Bridge taps

   b. Load coils

   c. Crosstalk

   d. Wire gauge

8. Which DSL variant offers coexistence of voice and data on a single line and throughput capabilities of 1 Mbps upstream and 8 Mbps downstream?

   a. SDSL

   b. S.SHDSL

   c. ADSL

   d. IDSL

9. Which DSL variant is known as splitterless ADSL?

   a. VDSL

   b. G.Lite

   c. HDSL

   d. RADSL

10. Which DSL variant provides only 144 kbps upstream and downstream?

   a. IDSL

   b. ADSL

   c. HDSL

   d. G.SHDSL

11. The DSL modem at the CPE is known as which of the following?

   a. ATU-R

   b. ATU-C

   c. DSLAM

   d. Last mile

12. The DSL modem at the CO side of a DSL link is known as which of the following?

   a. ATU-R

   b. ATU-C

   c. Splitter

   d. CPE

13. Which of the following DSL modulation methods uses a single channel for all downstream transmission?

   a. CAP

   b. DMT

   c. DSL

   d. AMI

14. How many channels does DMT use for downstream transmission?

   a. 128

   b. 224

   c. 512

   d. 1024

15. Which of the following devices terminates the provider side of the DSL connection?

   a. CPE

   b. DSLAM

   c. ATM

   d. PPP

16. IP connectivity originating at the CPE will use which of the following devices as its next logical hop device?

   a. DSLAM

   b. ATU-R

   c. ATU-C

   d. Aggregation router

17. Which three methodologies are used to facilitate ADSL connectivity to subscribers?

   a. PPPoE

   b. VoIPoFR

   c. PPPoA

   d. RFC 1483/2684 bridging

18. PPP authentication takes place after which of the following phases?

   a. Discovery

   b. Session

   c. Callback

   d. Call setup

19. In a PPPoE call initiation, what are the two phases of the setup?

   a. Session

   b. Setup

   c. Discovery

   d. Transport

20. Which VCI is the first available for use in ATM end-user configurations?

   a. 5

   b. 16

   c. 32

   d. 18

21. What are functions of the ATM SAR process?

   a. Payload fragmentation and defragmentation

   b. Add an 8-byte SAR trailer as a checksum

   c. Cell switching

   d. Cell header creation and removal

The answers to the "Do I Know This Already?" quiz are found in Appendix A, "Answers to the 'Do I Know This Already?' Quizzes and Q&A Sections." The suggested choices for your next step are as follows:

- **15 or fewer overall score**—Read the entire chapter. This includes the "Foundation Topics," "Foundation Summary," and "Q&A" sections.

- **16 or 17 overall score**—Begin with the "Foundation Summary" section, and then go to the "Q&A" section.

- **18 or more overall score**—If you want more review on these topics, skip to the "Foundation Summary" section and then go to the "Q&A" section. Otherwise, move to the next chapter.

Foundation Topics

Like cable, digital subscriber line (DSL) is a commonly offered broadband access methodology. DSL is a technology created to coexist with the existing telephone infrastructure found in most homes today through the use of varied frequency bands available on the analog local loop between the subscriber home (known as the customer premises equipment [CPE]) and the local telephone company central office (CO). For this reason, DSL is known as a "last-mile" technology. It has the capability to allow voice and high-speed data to be sent simultaneously over the same copper pair. The service provides an always-on connection, so the user does not have to dial in or wait for call setup prior to launching network applications.

Unlike cable, DSL has a number of variations in deployment. The bandwidth options available from DSL providers are nearly as varied as the ways in which it can be utilized.

While this chapter will mention a number of DSL variants, the primary focus will be asymmetric digital subscriber line (ADSL), as it is the most commonly used in the teleworker architecture.

DSL Features

To provide a point of reference throughout the discussions in the chapter, Figure 4-1 illustrates the basic teleworker architecture using DSL.

During the course of a phone conversation, a great deal of potential bandwidth is simply not utilized. A wide range of frequencies can coexist on a single copper pair such as is used in an analog phone line. Voice conversations use only a small portion of that available range, usually within the bounds of 300 Hz to 3 kHz. Above that 3 kHz boundary is simply unused space.

Figure 4-1 *DSL Teleworker Architecture*

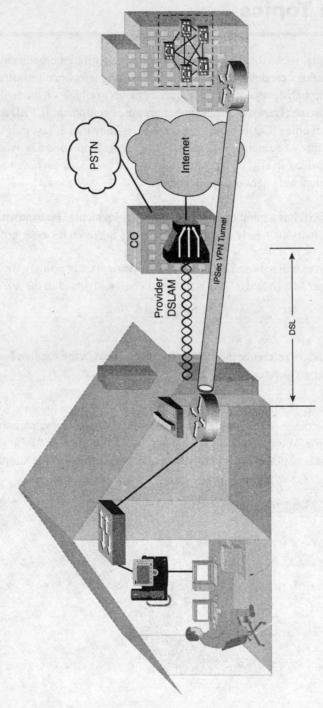

POTS Coexistence

Plain old telephone service (POTS) has evolved greatly over the years. When Bell invented the telephone in 1876, he had no idea of the profound effect it would have on the world. In fact, few people initially thought of the invention as having any commercial value. Even the media was more than a little skeptical, stating that well-informed people know that it is impossible to transmit voice over wires. Obviously, they were not so well informed.

The telephone has undergone countless changes in both form and function since its rather humble, but highly competitive, beginning. Significant evolutionary steps have come rapidly for the telephone. The related technologies spawned in response, both directly and indirectly, have pushed the imaginations of engineers across the globe. What was once a social status symbol available to relatively few is now as much a part of daily life as clothing and cars.

The need for newer, faster, and more effective means of communication along with the demands placed on the industry by the Internet community has driven technologies in new directions. It has also driven a number of very viable inventions into the ground due to cost of implementation or simply being too innovative and ahead of its time. Lessons learned in these types of situations bode well for DSL. The capability of DSL to make use of existing infrastructure while requiring comparatively little in the way of incremental costs is what has allowed it to survive in today's market.

This shared infrastructure has presented challenges to which the engineering and standards bodies have stepped up. The use of existing telephone wiring and varied modulation of signals to allow voice and data to coexist is the very basis of DSL technology.

The modulation methods employed in bringing DSL to the CPE router simply exploit existing wires, making use of the untapped frequencies by setting aside channels or carriers for use by downstream and upstream data transfers.

A slight change in the way the local loop is provisioned can allow for the previously unused space in the range of 3 kHz to 1.1 MHz to be used for high-speed data service offerings to phone company subscribers. Very little, if any, additional wiring is necessary on the CPE side of the connection. Splitters at both the customer and CO sides of the connection are in charge of combining or dividing the signals as needed based on the direction of the traffic flow. As shown in Figure 4-1, a splitter at the CO redirects the voice traffic to the PSTN switch and out. The data traffic is passed to a DSL access multiplexer (DSLAM). Once the DSLAM receives the signal, it passes the data traffic on to the provider router to traverse the network to which it is connected, in this case, the Internet.

To define DSL, it is necessary to be familiar with the terminology used in dealing with it and its associated technological variations. Along with the following terms, some additional attention is given to relevant waveform properties.

- **Amplitude**—A measure of the magnitude of the oscillation of a waveform. This essentially is the peak height or depth of a wave peak or valley, in relation to the horizontal axis of a graph, during one cycle.

- **ATU-C**—ADSL Transmission Unit–central office, a subscriber-facing DSL modem in the provider's CO.

- **ATU-R**—ADSL Transmission Unit–remote, a provider-facing DSL modem in the subscriber home. This could be a DSL-capable router or DSL modem.

- **Downstream**—Transmissions from a CO toward a subscriber.

- **DSLAM**—A single chassis containing multiple ATU-C units.

- **Frequency**—A measure of the number of cycles of a waveform over a given time (typically cycles per second or hertz). Frequency has an inverse relationship to wavelength. As frequency increases, wavelength decreases:

Frequency (f) = speed (v) ÷ wavelength (λ)

NOTE In cases where the waveform is moving through a vacuum, then speed (v) = speed , the speed of light. Moving from one medium (for example, air to vacuum or vice versa) to another, frequency remains constant but wavelength (λ) and speed (v/c) change to some degree, hence the differentiation in speed variables.

- **Line code**—Technique used to represent the digital signals to be transported, over a copper twisted pair, by an amplitude-discreet and time-discreet signal that allows a receiving device to synchronize to the phase of signals transmitted.

- **Maximum data rate**—Maximum transmission speed possible for a particular variant of DSL.

- **Microfilter**—A passive low-pass filter, connected to a subscriber telephone wall-jack (RJ-11), into which analog end stations (analog phones, analog faxes, modems, and so on) are plugged. These are necessary to maintain voice quality on analog devices when DSL and traditional voice service are coexistent on a single line. Microfilters allow only frequencies in the 0 to 4 kHz range to pass to the connected analog device(s).

- **Modulation**—The process of varying a periodic waveform in order to use that signal to convey a message.

- **Nature**—The relationship between downstream and upstream speeds (asynchronous or synchronous).

- **Network interface device (NID)**—The CPE device providing the termination point of the local loop.

- **Phase**—A measure of the relative position over time of two waveforms with identical frequency. For example, a sine wave and cosine wave of identical frequency are said to be 90 degrees (or π radians) out of phase and will cancel each other out entirely.

- **Splitter**—Also known as a POTS splitter, a passive device used to separate DSL data traffic from voice traffic. POTS splitters are inserted into the network at both CO and CPE sides of the local loop. Today, microfilters typically replace the splitter at the CPE side of the local loop.

- **Upstream**—Transmissions from a subscriber toward a CO.

- **Wavelength**—A measure of the distance between repeating units of a wave pattern. The measurement is taken from wave peak to the next wave peak:

  Wavelength (λ) = Frequency (f) ÷ speed (v)

DSL Limitations

DSL is a relatively distance-sensitive technology. As the distance between the subscriber and their local CO increases, the signal quality and connection speeds decrease. ADSL service is limited to a maximum distance of 18,000 feet (5460 m) between the DSL CPE and the DSLAM, although many ADSL providers place an even lower limit on the distance to ensure quality.

The 18,000-foot distance limitation for ADSL is not a limitation for voice telephone calls, but for data transmission. Telephone companies use small amplifiers, called *load coils*, to boost voice signals. Load coils have a rather nasty tendency to disrupt DSL data signals. This means that if there are load coils in the loop between the CPE and CO, those subscribers are likely not within an area that can receive DSL service.

Table 4-2 outlines the distance limitations of some common DSL data-rate offerings.

Table 4-2   *DSL Distance Limitations*

DSL Technology	Data Rate Downstream/Upstream	Maximum Distance
ADSL	8 Mbps/1 Mbps	18,000 ft
VDSL	55 Mbps/13 Mbps	4,500 ft
IDSL	144 kbps/144 kbps	18,000 ft
SDSL	768 kbps/768 kbps	22,000 ft
G.SHDSL	2.3 Mbps/2.3 Mbps	28,000 ft

As is evident from the table, DSL is offered in a wide range of transfer rates. The table does not represent all available rates. In theory, the maximum throughput potential of any first-generation ADSL technology is 8.448 Mbps. However, that would require a subscriber to be very close (within a few hundred feet) to the local CO.

In 2004, the second generation ADSL, known as ADSL2 (ITU G.992 3/4), was created to offer 12 Mbps downstream at distances less than or equal to 8000 feet. Additionally, ADSL2+ (ITU G.992.5) was created to provide up to 24 Mbps for distances less than 5000 feet.

Throughput capacity and subscriber distance from the CO are inversely proportional in nature. As distance increases, maximum upstream and downstream speeds decrease. Additionally, other impairments or conditions may contribute to reduced functionality. These include the following:

- **AM radio interference**—AM radio frequencies can interfere with DSL signal quality, causing throughput reduction. This is particularly problematic with in-house wiring using low-quality cabling (untwisted or poorly twisted-pair wiring).

- **Bridge taps**—These are extensions between the CPE and the CO. Essentially, bridge taps are an additional wire with an unterminated cable end that is connected to the local loop. This causes noise, reflections, and potential for power bleed that reduces signal strength (and therefore throughput)

- **Crosstalk**—Crosstalk is interference between two wires in a bundle as a result of electromagnetic interference. Crosstalk occurs when there is frequency overlap between channels.

- **Fiber optic cable**—ADSL signals cannot pass through the conversion from analog to digital to analog that occurs if a portion of the telephone circuit traverses fiber optic cable in transit.

- **Impedance mismatch**—Impedance mismatch in the local loop causes echo, resulting in noise. The mismatch can be caused by changes in wire gauge, splices, or corrosion.

- **Load coils**—Load coils are used to extend the range of a local loop for voice operations. They are intended to function as inductors to compensate for parallel capacitance on the line. Essentially, they are inductors that act like a low-pass filter, disallowing higher frequency signals. Because of this, load coils significantly distort DSL frequencies and must be removed for any DSL operation. They are often found within loops extending farther than 12,000 ft.

- **Signal attenuation**—Attenuation is the loss or degradation of signal strength (energy) over distance. Attenuation varies with the distance between subscriber and CO.

- **Wire gauge**—Variations in wire thickness can affect throughput by introducing impedance mismatches. Also, the use of thicker wire in the local loop can improve signal strength and improve throughput.

DSL Variants

DSL is available in a number of so-called flavors. Though different in practice or deployment, each of these flavors inevitably falls into one of the following classifications of DSL service:

- **Asymmetrical DSL (ADSL)**—Communication in which differing transmission speeds are used for downstream and upstream signals. Typically, downstream speeds tend to be higher than upstream speeds.

- **Symmetrical DSL (SDSL)**—Communication in which identical transmission speeds are used for downstream and upstream signals.

Overall, the various implementations of DSL are grouped under a single, quite general term, xDSL. The following sections describe the implementations of DSL that are classified as either ADSL or SDSL.

Asymmetric DSL Types

ADSL is most commonly deployed in the current broadband market where DSL is offered. The following are the different flavors of DSL currently available:

- **ADSL**—The full-rate offering of ADSL, which can be configured to deliver from 1.5 to 8 Mbps downstream and 16 kbps to 1 Mbps upstream over a local loop up to 18,000 feet in length. ADSL enables voice and high-speed data to be sent simultaneously over the existing telephone line. ITU-T Recommendation G.992.1 and ANSI Standard T1.413-1998 specify full-rate ADSL.

- **G.Lite ADSL**—Known as splitterless ADSL, an ITU standard specifically developed to meet the "plug-and-play" requirements of the consumer market segment. G.Lite is a medium-bandwidth version of ADSL that allows up to 1.5 Mbps downstream and up to 512 kbps upstream, and allows voice and data to coexist on the wire without the use of splitters. G.Lite is a globally standardized (ITU-T G.992.2) interoperable ADSL system. Typical telco implementations currently provide 1.5 Mbps downstream and 512 kbps upstream.

- **RADSL (rate-adaptive DSL)**—A nonstandard version of ADSL that automatically adjusts the connection speed to adjust for the quality of the telephone line. This allows RADSL to function over longer distances than ADSL. Note, however, that standard ADSL also permits the ADSL modem to adapt speeds of data transfer.

- **VDSL (very-high-bit-rate DSL)**—Provides 13 to 55 Mbps, over distances up to 4500 feet on short loops, such as from fiber to the curb. In most cases, VDSL lines are served from neighborhood cabinets that link to a central office via optical fiber. VDSL can also be configured in symmetric mode. Cisco Long Reach Ethernet (LRE) is based on VDSL technologies.

Symmetric DSL Types

Although SDSL methodologies are not as widespread as those in the ADSL offerings, they are just as viable as broadband technologies. SDSL is available in the following forms:

- **SDSL (symmetric DSL)**—Provides identical transfer rates, both downstream and upstream, ranging from as slow as 128 kbps to as fast as 2.32 Mbps. The most typical implementation is 768 kbps. SDSL is a rather general term that encompasses a number of varying vendor implementations providing variable rates of service over a single copper pair. SDSL has a distance limit of 21,000 feet.

- **G.SHDSL (symmetric high-data-rate DSL)**—An industry-standard SDSL offering. SHDSL equipment conforms to the ITU-T Recommendation G.991.2. G.SHDSL outperforms older SDSL versions with a better loop reach (26,000 feet) and less crosstalk into other transmission systems in the same cable, and promises vendor interoperability. G.SHDSL systems operate in a range of transfer rates from 192 kbps to 2.3 Mbps. SHDSL is best suited to data-only applications that require higher upstream transfer rates than those typically available in DSL implementations.

- **HDSL (high-data-rate DSL)**—Created in the late 1980s, this technology is meant to deliver symmetric service at upstream and downstream transfer rates up to 768 kbps in each direction (for a total of 1.544 Mbps). It is available in 1.544 Mbps (T1) as described or 2.048 Mbps (E1) depending on the country in which it is deployed. This symmetric fixed-rate service does not allow for standard telephone service over the same copper pair.

- **HDSL2 (second-generation HDSL)**—Evolution of HDSL that allows 1.5 Mbps downstream and upstream transfer rates while still enabling the support of voice (Voice over IP), data, and video using either ATM or other technology over the same copper pair. HDSL2 does not provide standard POTS voice telephone service on the same wire pair. HDSL2 differs from HDSL in that HDSL2 uses one pair of wires to convey 1.5 Mbps, whereas ANSI HDSL uses two wire pairs.

- **IDSL (ISDN DSL)**—Supports downstream and upstream transfer rates of up to 144 kbps (two 64-kbps channels plus one 16-kbps D channel for signaling) using existing phone lines. IDSL supports a local loop length of 18,000 feet but can be augmented to 45,000 feet using repeaters. It is unique in that it has the ability to deliver services through a digital loop carrier (DLC), a remote device that is typically located in remote terminals placed in newer housing developments to simplify the distribution of wiring from the telco. IDSL differs from traditional ISDN in that it is an always-available service rather than a dialup service. It is, however, capable of using the same terminal adapter (TA) used in traditional ISDN installations. IDSL is a data-only service and does not support traditional voice services.

ADSL Basics

The nature of DSL and its coexistence with POTS telephone service has been the subject of some discussion in both the industry at large and within xDSL circles. With terminology and limitations well in-hand, some additional depth regarding ADSL and how it is positioned in the teleworker architecture is in order.

As mentioned, DSL is a local loop or "last-mile" service. The CPE might be a DSL modem or a DSL-capable router. Both are very common depending on the type of access required or, more importantly, the number of hosts in the subscriber's home needing access to the Internet. The subscriber access device, be it a modem or a router with the modem functionality built in, is known as an ADSL Transmission Unit–remote (ATU-R). The ATU-R goes through a training process, similar in concept to that of a traditional modem, with the provider's modem—the ADSL Transmission Unit–central office (ATU-C). Multiple ATU-C units are bundled into a single chassis known as a DSLAM.

ADSL utilizes three distinct channels within the local loop. Each of these channels has a bit of buffer space between it and the adjacent channel. The manner in which the channels are utilized depends on the modulation type used for the particular ADSL deployment.

The modulation methods employed in bringing DSL to the CPE router simply exploit existing wires, making use of the untapped frequencies by setting aside channels or carriers for use by downstream and upstream data transfers.

ADSL Modulation

Modulation, as defined earlier in the chapter, is the process of varying a periodic waveform to use that signal to convey a message. The ANSI standards for DSL define two modulation types:

- Carrierless Amplitude Phase (CAP)
- Discrete Multi-Tone (DMT)

Line code represents a means of transmitting bits by increasing or decreasing (pulsing) voltage on the wire to represent a bit value of 1 in binary. A zero is represented with no alteration in voltage. The line-coding techniques associated with DSL technologies include a single-carrier method (CAP) as well as multicarrier methods (DMT and G.Lite). Until the advent and standardization of DMT, CAP was the more widely used modulation type. DMT's flexibility, coupled with the fact that it is an accepted industry standard, has allowed it to surpass CAP in today's market. The modulation method choice is, of course, made by the provider of the service.

CAP

CAP is a single-carrier modulation technique that divides the available space into three bands:

- The range from 0 to 4 kHz is allocated for POTS transmission.

- The range of 25 kHz to 160 kHz is allocated for upstream data traffic.

- The range of 240 kHz to 1.1 MHz is allocated for downstream data traffic.

These ranges may vary slightly based on environmental factors and implementations. Figure 4-2 illustrates the channels on the wire.

Figure 4-2 *CAP Modulation*

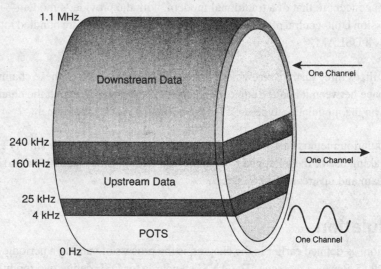

This figure effectively shows how the voice and downstream/upstream data are separated on the wire. Note that the range of frequencies available to downstream data is significantly wider than that available to upstream data or voice.

CAP is a variation of quadrature amplitude modulation (QAM). QAM conveys data by changing the amplitude of two carrier waves that are 90 degrees out of phase from one another (for example, sine vs. cosine wave forms), hence the name quadrature carriers. The changes (modulations) in the wave represent the data signal.

CAP is used only in legacy ADSL implementations. This is primarily because it offers significantly inferior performance, albeit at a reduced cost, compared to DMT. Unlike DMT, CAP is not an industry standard. CAP was, however, the de facto standard for xDSL deployments (deployed in 97 percent of xDSL installs) up until 1996; therefore, it is still commonly encountered.

With the advent of DMT, CAP is rarely, if at all, used today in ADSL service offerings.

DMT

DMT describes a version of multicarrier DSL modulation in which incoming data is collected and then distributed over a large number of small individual carriers, each of which uses a form of QAM modulation. DMT is a form of orthogonal frequency-division multiplexing (OFDM) called coded OFDM. This is essentially a very technical name for the use of multiple, independent subchannels within a larger channel (RF range), which can be brought up or taken down dynamically with no effect whatsoever on other existing channels.

NOTE   As an interesting bit of trivia, Orthogonal Discreet Multitone Modulation was invented by Paul Baran. Mr. Baran founded a company called Telebit to market this technology. His marketing efforts worked quite well, as Cisco acquired Telebit in 1996. Mr. Baran is also credited with the invention of the doorway metal detector such as is used in airports, government buildings, and a number of schools. Among his incredible accomplishments, the most significant is the invention of packet switching. As we all know, packet switching is the very reason for the existence of not only internetworking as we know it, but also the Internet itself. While Mr. Baran's deeds are not covered in the exam objectives, it is proper, at this point, to add a brief statement of recognition and a polite nod of thanks.

The word *orthogonal* is synonymous with the word *perpendicular*, if a set of wave forms can be thought of as being perpendicular. When waveforms are described as orthogonal, they are said to be occupying the same or similar space, yet in a manner that keeps them from overlapping. In the context of straight lines, being perpendicular means that they are at right angles (90 degrees) to each other. In terms of waveforms, this can be the case as well, but the relationship between the waveforms is phase rather than a right angle. By shifting the amplitude, frequency, and/or phase of a waveform, a particular binary bit pattern can be conveyed. In the case of DSL, orthogonality means that there is no interference between subchannels. Interference is often frequency-specific. So, when interference is detected, the channels in question or being compromised can be dynamically reallocated to other frequencies and away from the interference.

Most of the ADSL equipment installed today uses DMT. DMT divides what was, in CAP, a single upstream or downstream channel into 256 separate subchannels (aka carriers), each of which is 4.312 kHz wide. In other words, the available bandwidth on the line is divided into 256 (numbered 0–255) equally sized channels (also known as bins), which can be used independently of each other. These channels can be individually modulated with a maximum of 15 bps/Hz (or bits per cycle). Each channel is monitored constantly. Should the quality become overly impaired, the signal will be relocated to another channel. Signals are constantly reallocated in the search for the best-quality channels for transmission. Figure 4-3 illustrates the concept of DMT channel utilization as well as the orthogonal nature of the upstream and downstream channels. They can coexist without interfering with each other.

Figure 4-3   *DMT Modulation*

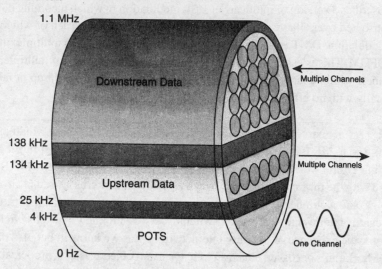

The DMT line code, as defined in ANSI T1.413-1998, divides the useful bandwidth of the standard two-wire copper medium used in the PSTN, which is 0 to 1,104 kHz, into 256 separate 4.3125 kHz–wide bins called subcarriers. Each subcarrier is associated with a discrete frequency, or tone, indicated by 4.3125kHz * n, where n = 1 to 256, and is essentially a single distinct data channel.

A maximum of 255 subcarriers can be used to modulate data in the downstream direction. Subcarrier 256, the downstream Nyquist frequency, and subcarrier 64, the downstream pilot frequency, are not available for user data, thus limiting the total number of available downstream subcarriers to 254. Each of these 254 subcarriers can support the modulation of 0 to 15 bits. Similarly, 31 low-frequency subcarriers are used for upstream transmissions.

The lower frequency subcarriers will handle upstream transmissions, while the higher frequency subcarriers handle downstream transmissions. Typically, a small number of channels are unused to allow for buffer space between the upstream and downstream channels as well as between the upstream and voice channels. The channels used for this buffer are not defined by the ITU specification, but rather are vendor-specific implementations. When voice and data are coexistent on the line, the lowest channel used by ADSL is seven. The spectrum of each channel overlaps that of its adjacent neighboring channels. Orthogonality of the channels is what makes this possible.

DMT has the capability to step up or down in 32-kbps increments to maintain quality, although the improved quality sometimes comes at the sacrifice of speed. This capability to adjust speed, correct errors, reallocate channels, and so on generates a significantly higher rate of power consumption to maintain it all, thus increasing power draw of both the ATU-C and ATU-R.

DMT is more complex than CAP because of the processes and resources involved in monitoring and allocating information on the individual channels, coupled with the constant monitoring of the quality of all channels; however, DMT allows more flexibility than CAP. Until recently, the resources necessary to make DMT viable were cost prohibitive. Advances in technology and dropping prices have made DMT feasible.

Data Transmission over ADSL

The discussion up to this point has dealt with Layer 1 of the OSI reference model entirely. The technologies surrounding the actual transmission of bit patterns through manipulation of voltage, frequency, amplitude, phase, and so on tend to have the ability to numb the sharpest mind. The migraine-inducing mathematical equations that make it all work are necessary to understanding, at very least in concept. To simply state, "Trust me, it works. Please don't put both wires in your mouth at once." would not provide an adequate technological base upon which to build knowledge for the exam.

From a Layer 2 perspective, the discussion is somewhat simpler because it involves only a limited number of technologies. The discussion also focuses, now, entirely on the data transmission side of the technology. In the realm of ADSL, the Point-to-Point Protocol (PPP) is the protocol of choice for data link connectivity, although not entirely. Ethernet framing and Asynchronous Transfer Mode (ATM) framing (which admittedly involves slicing and dicing of the payload; more to come on that topic) are also put into the mix, though not at the same instant.

DSL provides the Layer 1 resources for the connectivity. Architecturally, a DSLAM is an ATM switch housing DSL interface cards (ATU-Cs). The DSLAM exists solely to terminate the CO side of the DSL link and move the data payload from the subscriber one step closer to its ultimate destination, which is typically an ATM switch fabric co-housed in the DSLAM chassis. The payload is cell-switched across the ATM network, however far that might be in the provider's network, finally ending up at an aggregation router on the provider's Internet-facing egress.

This is the first point in the payload's journey that actually understands Layer 3. Figure 4-4 provides a conceptual view of this architecture.

Figure 4-4 *Data over DSL*

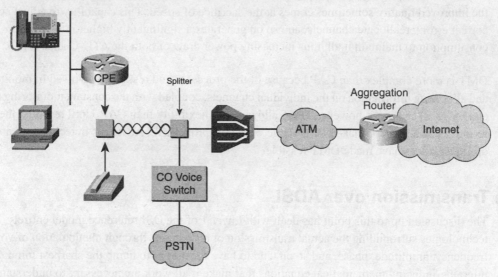

There are three ways in which data is encapsulated and transported from the CPE to the aggregation router:

- **RFC 1483/2684 bridging**—Defines multiprotocol data encapsulation (AAL5SNAP) over ATM circuits. This is essentially traditional bridging of subscriber Ethernet frames over an ATM network.

- **PPP over Ethernet**—Uses traditional Ethernet framing to encapsulate and transport PPP frames.

- **PPP over ATM**—Uses ATM cells to encapsulate and transport PPP frames.

RFC 1483/2684 Bridging

RFC 2684 defines the transport of multiple protocols over a single ATM virtual circuit. RFC 2684 also defines the transport of individual protocols over individual circuits. Of primary interest, however, is the multiprotocol capabilities defined therein. The RFC leverages the traditional 802.3 LLC encapsulation mechanisms used in transporting multiple protocols over Ethernet networks. ATM as a technology will be discussed in greater detail later in this chapter.

Most providers offer various Internet access packages. These include access capabilities for one host or many hosts on the subscriber's home network. Typical packages that are focused on a single host in the subscriber home would include a DSL modem rather than a CPE DSL router. This DSL modem is simply a bridge with DSL capabilities.

The benefit to this solution is simplicity. It is relatively simple to automate and requires only minimal configuration of the CPE, if any. The drawbacks include reduced security and very low density of users supported at the customer premises.

Cisco DSL routers in bridging mode can be configured for integrated routing and bridging (IRB) capabilities to get a bit of both Layer 2 and 3 benefits. However, this does not tend to offset the rather large holes in feature richness, security, and scalability.

PPP Background

PPP (RFC 1661) provides a standard method of encapsulating higher-layer protocols across point-to-point connections. It extends the High-Level Data Link Control (HDLC) packet structure with a 16-bit protocol identifier that contains information about the content of the packet.

The packet contains the following:

- **Link Control Protocol (LCP)**—Negotiates link parameters, packet size, or type of authentication

- **Network Control Protocol (NCP)**—Contains information about higher-layer protocols

- **Data frames**—Contain user data

PPP has a relatively simple function. RFC 1661 sets down the rules for it in quite a concise fashion. Point-to-point links can be used in establishing ISDN connections, dialup connections, serial connections, and now DSL connections. The essential mechanics of PPP are as follows:

1. To establish communications, each end of the PPP link must first send LCP packets to configure and test the data link.

2. After the link has been established and optional facilities have been negotiated as needed, PPP must send NCP packets to choose and configure one or more network layer protocols.

3. Once each of the chosen network layer protocols has been configured, traffic from each network layer protocol can be sent over the link.

4. The link remains configured for communications until explicit LCP or NCP packets close the link down, or until some external event occurs (such as the expiration of an inactivity timer or the intervention of a network administrator). In other words, PPP is a pathway that is opened for multiple protocols simultaneously.

PPP was originally developed with IP in mind; however, it functions independently of the Layer 3 protocol that is traversing the link. Each of the Layer 3 protocols that is to traverse the link will have an open NCP. For IP, there is an IP Control Protocol (IPCP) that must be established for IP to flow properly.

PPP over Ethernet

Point-to-Point Protocol over Ethernet (PPPoE) is, obviously, a twist on traditional PPP implementations. It is essentially a bridging architecture. Typical bridging implementations include wide-ranging security holes. Adding PPP architecture (using PAP or CHAP authentication) on top of this Ethernet bridging function alleviates the security holes and provides a well-known, robust platform.

PPPoE, as defined in RFC 2516, provides the ability to connect a network of hosts over a simple bridging access device to a remote access concentrator, or in this discussion, an aggregation router. Figure 4-5 shows the connectivity between the subscriber host and the aggregation router.

Figure 4-5 *PPPoE Topology*

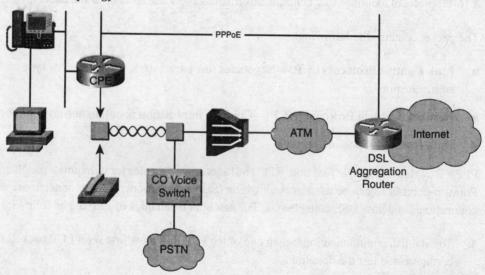

The DSLAM terminates the Layer 1 DSL connection and pushes the payload out the other side to ride the chosen media type (copper/fiber, and so on) across the ATM network. From CPE router to aggregation router, the only OSI layers used are Layers 1 and 2. The first Layer 3 function occurs once PPP negotiation has completed between the CPE and the aggregation router.

It should be pointed out that either a DSL-capable CPE router or a subscriber PC running PPPoE-capable client software may provide the subscriber side of the PPPoE connection. In either event, PPP frames are encapsulated inside of Ethernet frames for transport across the network. IP address allocation is handled by a provider DHCP server once the IPCP portion of the PPP connection is established.

With this model, each router uses its own PPP stack and the user is presented with a familiar user interface. Access control, billing, and provision of service can be performed on a per-user, rather than a per-site, basis.

To provide point-to-point connections over Ethernet, each PPP session must learn the MAC address of the remote peer and establish a unique session identifier. PPPoE includes a discovery protocol that provides this function.

As with traditional dialup PPP sessions, the link must be created and initialized. The PPPoE initialization process has added two additional phases:

■   Discovery

■   PPP Session

Discovery Phase

To initiate a PPPoE session, the CPE router must first perform Discovery to identify the MAC address of the device to which it must build a peer relationship. It must establish a PPPoE SESSION_ID. The Discovery process is inherently a client/server relationship. During Discovery, a router discovers the provider access concentrator. Discovery allows the CPE router to discover all available aggregation resources, and then select one. Upon successful completion, both the CPE router and the selected access concentrator have the information they will use to build their connection.

The Discovery stage remains stateless until a PPP session is established. Once a PPP session is established, both the CPE router and the access concentrator *must* allocate the resources for a PPP virtual interface. Now, the access concentrator can perform its role as aggregation router. The virtual interface on the aggregation router will act as the default gateway for the CPE router.

There are four basic steps in the Discovery phase:

1.   The PPPoE client sends a PPPoE Active Discovery Initiation (PADI) packet requesting service. The destination MAC address is set to broadcast.

2.   The aggregation router responds with a PPPoE Active Discovery Offer (PADO) packet describing offered service(s). The destination MAC address is unicast to the originating client.

3.   The PPPoE client sends a unicast PPPoE Active Discovery Request (PADR) to the aggregation router. The request is to move on to the Session phase.

4.   The aggregation router sends a unicast PPPoE Active Discovery Session-Confirmation to the client. This assigns a Session-ID and confirms progression to the Session phase.

As might be expected, the conversation takes place within the confines of an Ethernet frame payload. The structure of the Ethernet frame is typical for frames in LAN environments. For purposes of review and further discussion, Figure 4-6 illustrates the Ethernet frame structure.

Figure 4-6 *PPPoE Frame Structure*

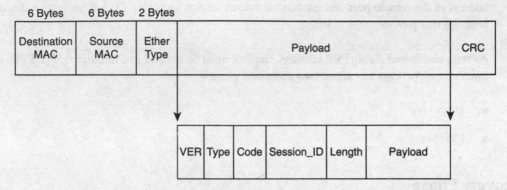

The destination MAC address during Discovery is FF.FF.FF.FF.FF.FF, which is the Ethernet broadcast address. In contrast, the source MAC address is that of the CPE router. The ETHER_TYPE field is set to either 0x8863 (PPPoE control frames during Discovery phase) or 0x8864 (PPPoE data frames during PPP Session phase).

Within the Ethernet frame payload rides the PPPoE structure. PPPoE requires the use of additional information, which is contained within a subheader and breaks down as follows:

■ The VER field is 4 bits and *must* be set to 0x1 for this version of the PPPoE specification.

■ The TYPE field (not to be confused with the ETHER_TYPE field in the Ethernet header) is 4 bits and *must* be set to 0x1 for this version of the PPPoE specification.

■ The CODE field is 8 bits. The value, during Discovery, is variable based on a given stage of the Discovery process. The PPPoE CODE field *must* be set to 0x00 during the Session phase.

■ The SESSION_ID field is 16 bits. It is an unsigned value in network byte order. Its value is variable based on a given stage of the Discovery process. The value, however, is fixed for a given PPP Session (it must use the value assigned during Discovery) and, in fact, defines a PPP session along with the Ethernet SOURCE_ADDR and DESTINATION_ADDR. A value of 0xffff is reserved for future use and *must not* be used.

■ The LENGTH field is 16 bits. The value, in network byte order, indicates the length of the PPPoE payload. It does not include the length of the Ethernet or PPPoE headers.

During the Discovery phase, the CODE and SESSION_ID values will change based on the chain of events. The Discovery phase encompasses Initiation, Offer, Request, Session-confirmation, and Termination operations. Both values will be constant during the Session phase.

PPP Session Phase

Once the PPPoE Session phase begins, PPP data is sent as in any other PPP encapsulation. That is to say that the LCP negotiation takes place and NCPs are opened as needed. All Ethernet frames are unicast between the aggregation router and PPPoE client at this point.

RFC 2516 specifies a Maximum Receivable Unit (MRU) for PPPoE negotiated payload size at 1492 bytes. The PPPoE header is 6 bytes in length with a Protocol-ID field of 2 bytes. This keeps PPPoE in line with Ethernet's 1500-byte maximum payload.

The ETHER_TYPE field, in the Ethernet header, is set to 0x8864. The PPPoE CODE field *must* be set to 0x00. The SESSION_ID field *must not* change for that PPPoE Session and *must* be the value assigned in the Discovery stage. The PPPoE payload contains a PPP frame. The frame begins with the PPP Protocol-ID (PID).

Once the Session stage is complete, the PPP LCP options can engage. As mentioned previously, the Session is stateless until the PPP connection is negotiated, including authentication, and any additionally or optionally configured LCP options.

PPPoE Session Variables

The needs of the subscriber community served by a particular service provider are nearly as diverse as the population itself. With that in mind, flexibility is a key benefit in the marketplace. It is crucial that a balance be struck in the offered options and the ease of support. Allowing too much hardware and configuration diversity will affect the provider's ability to support the solution when need arises. Typically, three options are made available in some form or fashion to the subscriber:

- **Placing a DSL-capable router at the subscriber home**—This router will have an integrated DSL modem and built-in PPPoE client capabilities, allowing the router to be configured in an always-on service offering. No additional software is needed on the subscriber computer. It also remedies the need to have a subscriber install PPPoE client software on all machines that wish to be connected to the network. This router will provide DHCP, NAT/PAT, and other relevant services to the subscriber home network.

- **Placing a non-DSL-capable router at the subscriber home**—This requires the additional placement of an external DSL modem at the subscriber premises to terminate the DSL connection. The router should have PPPoE client capabilities in order to provide the always-on service. This router, too, will provide DHCP, NAT, and PAT services.

■ **Placing an external DSL modem at the subscriber home to terminate the DSL connection**—PPPoE client software is installed on the subscriber hosts wishing to connect to the network.

Optimizing PPPoE MTU

This brief discussion is meant to add a bit of additional value to the overall picture. Perhaps some additional comprehension will result as well because many of the pieces of the PPPoE puzzle must be considered. However, this information does not fall under the category of Exam Objective.

Discussions of payload sizing typically end in the assumption that bigger is better. If the MTU is as large as it can be, then the throughput must be optimal as well. Unfortunately, that is not the case. To show the case, it is necessary to break down the components of the puzzle. Table 4-3 lists the relevant pieces.

Table 4-3 *PPPoE Framing Components*

Component	Size (in bytes)
Data payload	1–1452
TCP header	20
IP header	20
PPP header	2
PPPoE header	6
Ethernet header	18
AAL5 trailer	8 bytes + 1–40 bytes padding
ATM cell header	5 bytes per cell
ATM cell payload	48 bytes per cell

The data payload, TCP header, and IP header make up the PPP payload and therefore combine to reach the 1492-byte maximum for PPPoE. The PPP, PPPoE, and Ethernet headers are outside the requirement and add additional overhead:

$$1492 + 2 + 6 + 18 = 1518 \text{ bytes}$$

ATM adaptation layer 5 (AAL5) adds an 8-byte trailer to the whole of the frame and then adds padding to reach the next 48-byte multiple. Every ATM cell has a 48-byte payload and a 5-byte header, without exception:

$$(1518 \div 48) = (31 \text{ cells} + 30 \text{ bytes}) \text{ or } 32 \text{ cells}$$

The 8-byte AAL5 trailer is added to the ending 30 bytes and then 10 bytes padding follows to reach a 48-byte count. Finally, add 5 bytes per cell for ATM cell headers:

32 cells * 5 byte header = 160 bytes

Finally, the entire payload and overhead can be calculated using total frame size, AAL5 trailer, padding, and cell header sizes:

1518 + 8 + 10 + 160 = 1696 bytes

1696 bytes are transmitted for 1452 bytes (1492 less the 40 bytes of TCP and IP overhead) of actual payload. To put it into percentages:

$100(1696 \div 1452) = 116.80\% - 100\% = 16.80\%$ overhead

Dropping the MTU to 1454 kicks out the 10-byte overhead by pulling the payload to an even 48-byte multiple. Recalculating the numbers, adding PPP, PPPoE, and Ethernet overhead to the payload:

1454 + 2 + 6 + 18 = 1480 bytes
$(1480 \div 48)$ = (30 cells + 40 bytes) or 31 cells

The 8-byte AAL5 trailer is added to complete the final cell payload, with no padding needed. ATM headers are also attached to each cell:

31 cells * 5-byte header = 155 bytes

Assembling entire payload and overhead:

1480 + 8 + 155 = 1643 bytes

1643 bytes are transmitted for 1414 (1454 less 40-byte TCP and IP overhead) bytes of actual payload. To put it into a percentage:

$100(1643 \div 1414) = 116.20\% - 100\% = 16.20\%$ overhead

In the end, the efficiency seems very similar with only a difference of 0.6 percent. However, it represents a net reduction in overhead of 3.6 percent per frame. The end result is slightly faster and more efficient transmission. At 1.544 Mbps, the net gain is 9.3 kbps. At 3 Mbps, the net gain is 36 kbps.

PPP over ATM

PPPoA is similar in operation to PPPoE. In fact, both implementations use RFC 1483/2684 functions. Unlike RFC 1483/2684 bridging, PPPoA is a routed solution. PPPoA uses ATM adaptation layer 5 (AAL5) framing along with Logical Link Control/Subnetwork Access Protocol

(LLC/SNAP) encapsulation on virtual circuits. Both permanent virtual circuits (PVC) and switched virtual circuits (SVC) are possible in PPPoA installations; however, only PVC implementations are addressed at this time.

An overall discussion of ATM would seem out of place in this chapter, and rightly so. However, it is prudent to take a look at some of the basics behind ATM.

ATM uses a 53-byte cell as its framing structure; 5 bytes are header and the remaining 48 bytes constitute the payload. Every cell is 53 bytes. The fact that it is a fixed length is the reason it is called a cell rather than a frame. As seen in the MTU discussion, if a cell payload falls short of the 48-byte mandate for payload, padding will be added. Padding is simply filler with no use otherwise. Figure 4-7 illustrates the encapsulation process for ATM cell production.

Figure 4-7 *PPPoA Cell Structure*

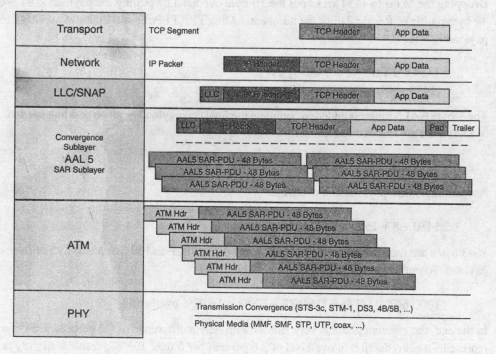

As Figure 4-7 shows, ATM is simply another method of Layer 2 encapsulation. The only real difference is the added step of segmentation and reassembly (SAR). SAR is simply a nice way to communicate the idea of chopping something up into small pieces, and then hoping it can be put back together on the other end. Prior to the slicing and dicing, an 8-byte SAR trailer is added to ensure that the reassembly results in the same information that was transmitted. Occasionally, a cell will be lost or dropped. Once the segmentation is complete, ATM headers can be added to the newly created SAR PDUs to complete the creation of ATM cells.

ATM uses virtual circuits that are identified by unique connection identifiers. Each connection identifier is a pair of numbers denoting both a virtual path identifier (VPI) and a virtual circuit identifier (VCI). Valid VPI/VCI pairs vary based on the equipment in use. The valid range of VPIs, supported by the ATM cell header, is 0–255. The valid range of VCIs supported by the User-Network Interface (UNI) cell header is 0–65535. VCIs 0–15 are reserved for use by the ITU and 16–31 are reserved for use by the ATM Forum (the ATM standards body). Therefore, 32 is the first valid VCI for end-user configurations. The service provider will specify the VPI and VCI for each virtual circuit to be provisioned.

Otherwise, the process is relatively similar to what was done with PPPoE. The PPP Discover and Session phases must still be performed to establish the connection to the aggregation router at the far end. PPPoA, as is the case with PPPoE, simply carries additional overhead to facilitate the PPP connectivity. A CPE device encapsulates the PPP session based on RFC 2684 for transport across the ADSL loop and the DSLAM.

Foundation Summary

DSL is a well-established technology and certainly a viable broadband solution for the teleworker. Cisco 800 series routers, as listed in the "Business-Ready Teleworker" SRND, are configurable for PPPoE, PPPoA, or RFC 1483/2684 bridging. Cisco ISR platforms contain VPN functionality built-in along with firewall capabilities as well. These features combine to facilitate the SONA model in a number of the network infrastructure architectures.

The key benefit of DSL is its native capability to coexist with existing home telephone wiring. Splitters in the home have been replaced by the microfilter, which is connected between each analog end station (phone/fax/modem) and the RJ-11 wall-jack. If traditional telephony coexistence is not adequate as a benefit for DSL, add to that the current and future data rate capabilities while maintaining the same coexistence. In the near future, DSL will be on a level playing field with the fiber optic offerings of some providers as well as cable data service providers. Table 4-4 provides a review of the DSL variants discussed in this chapter.

Table 4-4 *DSL Variants*

Variant	Downstream/Upstream Data Rate	Distance Limit	Voice Coexist?
ADSL	8 Mbps/1 Mbps	18,000 ft	Yes
VDSL	55 Mbps/13 Mbps	4,500 ft	No
IDSL	144 kbps/144 kbps	18,000 ft	No
SDSL	768 kbps/768 kbps	22,000 ft	No
G.SHDSL	2.3 Mbps/2.3 Mbps	28,000 ft	No
HDSL (T1)	768 kbps/768 kbps	10,000 ft	No
HDSL2	1.5 Mbps/1.5 Mbps	10,000 ft	No

As with any technology, DSL and the related technologies discussed in this chapter have numerous associated standards. Table 4-5 lists some of those standards.

Table 4-5 *DSL-Related Standards*

Standard	Description
ITU-T 992.1/ANSI T1.413-1998	Defines ADSL using DMT
ITU-T G.991.2	Defines G.SHDSL
RFC 1483/RFC 2684	Multiprotocol encapsulation over AAL5
RFC 1661	PPP
RFC 2516	PPPoE
RFC 2364	PPPoA
IEEE 802.2	Logical Link Control (SNAP)
ISO 7495-1	OSI reference model

Q&A

The questions and scenarios in this book are more difficult than what you will experience on the actual exam. The questions do not attempt to cover more breadth or depth than the exam, but they are designed to make sure that you know the answer. Rather than enabling you to derive the answer from clues hidden inside the question itself, the questions challenge your understanding and recall of the subject.

Hopefully, mastering these questions will help you limit the number of exam questions on which you narrow your choices to two options, and then guess.

The answers to these questions can be found in Appendix A.

1. What are three things that can adversely affect DSL signals?

2. CAP modulation divides voice from upstream and downstream data transmission. List the ranges of frequency for each of the three traffic types.

3. DMT modulation divides the signals into how many separate channels?

4. If there is signal degradation or other quality impairments on the line, what will DMT do to correct the situation?

5. What are the two general categories of DSL implementations and what is the basic difference between them?

6. What is the range of bandwidths available with ADSL offerings?

7. What is G.Lite and what are its advantages?

8. In the establishment of a PPPoE session, what options are typically implemented to overcome the security issues brought about in a traditional bridged environment?

9. In the PPP architecture, which portion of the protocol stack deals with link negotiation, packet size, and authentication?

10. What is the purpose of the Discovery phase in PPPoE session initiation?

11. During the Discovery phase, what is the address in the Destination MAC Address field of the PPPoE frame?

12. PPPoA uses what RFC to define operations for VC encapsulation?

Exam Topic List

This chapter covers the following topics that you need to master for the CCNP ISCW exam:

- **Configure a Cisco Router as a PPPoE Client**—Describes the steps for configuring a Cisco router for PPPoE connectivity

- **Configure an Ethernet/ATM Interface for PPPoE**—Describes the information required for configuring an Ethernet or ATM interface for PPPoE

- **Configure the PPPoE DSL Dialer Interface**—Describes the use of a dialer interface for PPPoE configurations

- **Configure Port Address Translation (PAT)**—Describes the configuration of PAT with PPPoE configurations

- **Configure DHCP for DSL Router Users**—Describes the configuration of DHCP with PPPoE

- **Configure Static Default Route on a DSL Router**—Describes the configuration of a static default route with PPPoE

CHAPTER 5

Configuring DSL Access with PPPoE

DSL access has become an overwhelmingly popular access methodology for homes and home offices. Along with this surge in popularity comes a host of additional possible application and service offerings. These applications and services may be provided by a service provider or offered by a corporation deploying a teleworker architecture.

This chapter builds upon the topics discussed in Chapter 4, "Using DSL to Connect to a Central Site." Configuring a Cisco router for PPPoE access, like other technologies, is not a difficult process. However, there are some not-so-subtle differences that must be addressed.

"Do I Know This Already?" Quiz

The purpose of the "Do I Know This Already?" quiz is to help you decide whether you really need to read the entire chapter. If you already intend to read the entire chapter, you do not necessarily need to answer these questions now.

The 12-question quiz, derived from the major sections in the "Foundation Topics" portion of the chapter, helps you to determine how to spend your limited study time.

Table 5-1 outlines the major topics discussed in this chapter and the "Do I Know This Already?" quiz questions that correspond to those topics.

Table 5-1 *"Do I Know This Already?" Foundation Topics Section-to-Question Mapping*

Foundation Topics Section	Questions Covered in This Section	Score
Configure a Cisco Router as a PPPoE client	1–2	
Configure an Ethernet/ATM Interface for PPPoE	3–4	
Configure the PPPoE DSL Dialer Interface	5–6	
Configure Port Address Translation (PAT)	7–8	
Configure DHCP for DSL Router Users	9–10	
Configure Static Default Route on a DSL Router	11–12	
Total Score		

CAUTION The goal of self-assessment is to gauge your mastery of the topics in this chapter. If you do not know the answer to a question or are only partially sure of the answer, you should mark this question wrong for purposes of self-assessment. Giving yourself credit for an answer that you correctly guess skews your self-assessment results and might provide you with a false sense of security.

---

1. DSL operates at which layer of the OSI reference model?

   a. Layer 1

   b. Layer 2

   c. Layer 3

   d. Layer 4

2. Layer 3 connectivity will be established between the CPE and which device in the provider network?

   a. DSLAM

   b. Splitter

   c. Aggregation router

   d. Headend

3. In DSL installations using Ethernet interfaces for both subscriber-facing and provider-facing connectivity, which of the following is true?

   a. The subscriber-facing Ethernet interface is configured with an IP address while the provider-facing Ethernet interface is not. A dialer interface will be configured for IP connectivity.

   b. The provider-facing Ethernet interface is configured with an IP address while the subscriber-facing Ethernet interface is not. A dialer interface will be configured for IP connectivity.

   c. Both the subscriber-facing and provider-facing Ethernet interfaces must have an IP address configured.

   d. Neither the subscriber-facing Ethernet interface nor the provider-facing Ethernet interface needs an IP address. A dialer interface will be configured for IP connectivity.

4. In configuring an ATM interface for PPPoE connectivity, which commands are necessary? Choose all that apply.

   a. **atm pvc 0/32 encapsulation aal5snap**

   b. **dsl operating-mode auto**

   c. **pppoe-client dial-pool-number 1**

   d. **atm map ip 172.16.0.2 pvc 0/32**

5. The dialer interface controls which physical interface? Choose all that apply.

   a. Subscriber-facing Ethernet

   b. Provider-facing Ethernet

   c. Provider-facing ATM

   d. Subscriber-facing ATM

6. A logical dialer interface is bound to a physical interface by what?

   a. Dialer group number on the physical interface that matches the dialer pool number on the dialer interface

   b. Dial pool number on the physical interface that matches the dialer pool number on the dialer interface

   c. DDR interesting traffic

   d. Dialer idle-timeout

7. Port Address Translation is dependent on the configuration of which technology in order to function?

   a. NAT

   b. LAT

   c. DDR

   d. DHCP

8. PAT allows which of the following?

   a. One-to-one IP address translation through the CPE router

   b. Many-to-one IP address translation through the CPE router

   c. Application-specific port numbers to be manually configured for translation

   d. Static IP address translations

9. DHCP configuration must include which of the following? Choose all that apply.

   a. IP address range

   b. DNS server(s)

   c. Subnet mask

   d. WINS server(s)

   e. TFTP server(s)

10. To avoid an address or range of addresses from being assigned to network hosts, which of the following should be configured?

    a. **dhcp reservation**

    b. **ip dhcp excluded-address**

    c. **import all**

    d. **DNS reverse-lookup**

11. Which of the following are good reasons to use a static default route? Choose all that apply.

    a. Decision made to disallow routing protocols at the teleworker sites

    b. Single entry/exit point (stub network) at the CPE site

    c. Limited router resources (CPU/memory)

    d. Desire to avoid full static routing definition

12. Which of the following properly defines a static default route?

    a. **ip route 0.0.0.0 255.255.255.255 dialer0**

    b. **ip route 0.0.0.0 0.0.0.0 dialer0**

    c. **ip default-gateway 0.0.0.0**

    d. **ip default-network 0.0.0.0**

The answers to the "Do I Know This Already?" quiz are found in Appendix A, "Answers to the 'Do I Know This Already?' Quizzes and Q&A Sections." The suggested choices for your next step are as follows:

■ **8 or fewer overall score**—Read the entire chapter. This includes the "Foundation Topics," "Foundation Summary," and "Q&A" sections.

■ **9 or 10 overall score**—Begin with the "Foundation Summary" section, and then go to the "Q&A" section.

■ **11 or more overall score**—If you want more review on these topics, skip to the "Foundation Summary" section, and then go to the "Q&A" section. Otherwise, move to the next chapter.

Foundation Topics

Configure a Cisco Router as a PPPoE Client

Configuration of a home router for DSL connectivity includes a number of pieces and parts that must be assembled properly in order for the solution to function properly. As discussed in Chapter 4, Asynchronous Transfer Mode (ATM) is DSL's underlying technology. As the PPPoE name implies, Point-to-Point Protocol (PPP) and Ethernet both play a significant role as well.

DSL is a Layer 1 access methodology that relies on multiple Layer 2 protocols in order to function properly. The Layer 1 connection exists across the local loop between the customer premises equipment (CPE) and the DSL access multiplexer (DSLAM). Layer 3 connectivity is established between the CPE and an aggregation router located somewhere beyond the DSLAM. For purposes of review and to provide a point of reference for discussion topics in this chapter, Figure 5-1 provides a topological view.

Figure 5-1 *DSL Topology*

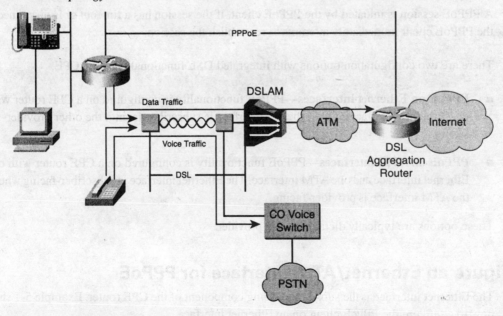

The figure shows the connectivity between the CPE and the Internet. The data traffic must traverse the local loop to the DSLAM and then go across the ATM network to the aggregation router.

There are multiple ways in which PPPoE can be configured. The configuration options will be decided upon by the provider. The example discussed here will be one using a dial-on-demand configuration option. Among the tasks necessary to configure PPPoE are the following:

- Ethernet/ATM interface configuration

- Dialer interface configuration

- PAT configuration

- DHCP server services configuration

- Static default route configuration

Each of these tasks must be completed before the data connectivity will function properly. Fortunately, they are fairly uncomplicated.

There are basically two relevant physical interfaces on any router, the ingress (inbound) and the egress (outbound). What takes place inside the router is mystical smoke-and-mirrors to the typical user. The definition of ingress and egress are subject to the direction of the traffic flow. So, to avoid confusion, the interfaces on the CPE will be called *subscriber-facing* and *provider-facing*.

A PPPoE session is initiated by the PPPoE client. If the session has a timeout or is disconnected, the PPPoE client immediately attempts to reestablish the session.

There are two configuration options with integrated DSL functionality in the CPE:

- **PPPoE on Ethernet interfaces**—PPPoE functionality is configured on a CPE router with two Ethernet interfaces. One Ethernet interface is subscriber-facing, the other provider-facing.

- **PPPoE on ATM interfaces**—PPPoE functionality is configured on a CPE router with one Ethernet interface and one ATM interface. The Ethernet interface is subscriber-facing whereas the ATM interface is provider-facing.

These options are typically dictated by the provider.

Configure an Ethernet/ATM Interface for PPPoE

The Ethernet interface is the subscriber-facing component of the CPE router. Example 5-1 shows how to configure the PPPoE client on an Ethernet interface.

Example 5-1 *Configuring the PPPoE Client on an Ethernet Interface*

```
!
interface Ethernet0/0
 ip address 172.16.0.1 255.255.0.0
!
interface Ethernet0/1
 no ip address
 pppoe enable
 pppoe-client dial-pool-number 1
!
```

This portion of the configuration enables the PPPoE functionality on the interface as well as assigning it to a dialer pool. This configuration element is required when using PPPoE over an Ethernet interface. Interface Ethernet 0/1 is bound to the logical dialer interface and an ATM permanent virtual circuit (PVC) is automatically provisioned across it.

> **NOTE**   As of Cisco IOS Software Release 12.2(13)T and later, the PPPoE client functionality was separated from the VPDN functionality, resulting in changes to the PPPoE client configuration. The configuration examples in this chapter are post-12.2(13)T examples.

For cases in which an ATM interface (ATM0/0 in this case) is used rather than the Ethernet 0/1 interface, you would use the configuration in Example 5-2.

Example 5-2 *Configuring the PPPoE Client on an ATM Interface*

```
!
interface Ethernet0/0
 ip address 172.16.0.1 255.255.0.0
!
interface ATM0/0
 no ip address
 dsl operating-mode auto
 pvc 8/35
 pppoe-client dial-pool-number 1
!
```

Configure the PPPoE DSL Dialer Interface

The dialer interface is the DSL provider-facing component of the CPE router. Example 5-3 demonstrates how to configure the basic elements of the dialer interface.

Example 5-3 *Configuring the Dialer Interface*

```
!
interface Dialer0
 ip address negotiated
 ip mtu 1492
 encapsulation ppp
 dialer pool 1
!
```

This configuration specifies that the dialer interface should get its IP address from the provider's DHCP server while specifying the upstream MTU and setting the interface encapsulation to PPP. Finally, the **dialer pool** command associates the dialer back to the **pppoe-client** command issued on the Ethernet interface. The pool numbers must match on the dialer and Ethernet interfaces in order for the configuration to function.

If PPP negotiation fails or the PPP line protocol is brought down for any reason, the PPPoE session and the virtual access will be brought down. When the PPPoE session is brought down, the client waits for a predetermined number of seconds before trying again to establish a PPPoE.

Configure Port Address Translation

Port Address Translation (PAT) is an extension of Network Address Translation (NAT). PAT adds a unique identifier to the outside translation entry of each inside host. Using PAT allows many inside IP addresses to use a single outside IP address because the outside address has a unique port number mapped to each inside host. NAT allows IP addresses to be changed as they pass through a router in order to be properly routed on another network. For NAT to work properly, some additional information and planning is necessary. Inside and outside interfaces must be defined.

Inside interfaces are those that exist on the internal, private network. In this case, inside interfaces are those with IP addresses on the subscriber's home network. This is typically a nonroutable address as defined by RFC 1918:

- **Inside local**—Configured IP address assigned to a host on the inside network

- **Inside global**—The IP address of an inside host as it appears to the outside network

Outside interfaces are those that exist on the external provider network and/or public Internet. Depending on the implementation, this may be a nonroutable RFC 1918 address or a public routable address:

- **Outside local**—The IP address of an outside host as it appears to the inside network

- **Outside global**—The configured IP address assigned to a host in the outside network

Figure 5-2 illustrates the concepts of NAT with PAT.

Figure 5-2 *NAT with PAT*

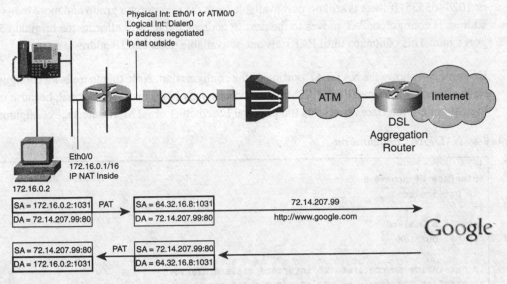

Figure 5-2 shows the subscriber host (inside local address) sending a web request to www.google.com. A DNS lookup resolves the host name in the URL to its public IP address. The resolved address is then placed in the Destination IP Address field (inside global address). In this example, NAT is performed in only one direction. Additional subscriber hosts would have a unique inside local address but be assigned the same inside global address and a unique port number. The coupling of an IP address with a port number is known as a *socket*.

> **NOTE**   The process can be performed bidirectionally to translate addresses inbound and outbound. This is one method for dealing with overlapping address space in merged, acquired, or mismanaged networks by effectively concealing outside addresses from inside hosts.
>
> For bidirectional NAT to work, DNS must be configured internally to map outside hosts to the proper inside addresses (that is, outside local addresses). The NAT process will translate the outside local address to its actual address (that is, the outside global address).

With NAT alone, each subscriber host inside local address would be translated to an individual, unique inside global address (one-to-one). With PAT, each subscriber inside local address is translated to a single inside global address (many-to-one) to conserve IP address space utilization. To keep the individual hosts organized and pass the proper traffic flows to and from each host, the source port number is attached to the IP address. In theory, up to 65,535 inside addresses can be translated to a single outside address. However, in practice, this might not be the best theory to test on a router not designed for very high user density.

PAT uses unique source port numbers on the inside global IP address to distinguish between translations. PAT attempts to preserve the original source port. If the source port is already in use, PAT attempts to use the first available port from the appropriate port group 0–5111, 5112–1023, or 1024–65535. If there is still no port available from the appropriate group and more than one IP address is configured, PAT moves to the next IP address and tries to allocate the original source port again. This continues until PAT runs out of available ports and IP addresses.

Example 5-4 shows the NAT/PAT portion of the configuration. Note that there is no configuration on the Interface Ethernet0/1 (or ATM0/0 as the case may be). This is intentional, because the logical dialer0 interface represents the physical Ethernet0/1 or ATM0/0 interface configuration.

Example 5-4   *NAT/PAT Configuration*

```
!
interface Ethernet0/0
 ip nat inside
!
interface Dialer0
 ip nat outside
!
ip nat inside source list 100 interface dialer0 overload
access-list 100 permit ip 172.16.0.0 0.0.255.255 any
!
```

This configuration is added to the examples presented to this point, so the IP addresses and so on are not shown. In the example, the Ethernet interface is defined as *inside* while the dialer interface is *outside*. The access list defines hosts that are eligible for translation, in this case all 172.16.X.X source addresses. The NAT definition uses access-list 100 as the "inside source" list and maps it to dialer0. The **overload** parameter enables PAT on the interface. The configuration then uses the provider-assigned address of dialer0 as the outside address for traffic flow. For this reason, no NAT pool is necessary. Without the **overload** parameter, a NAT pool would be defined for one-to-one translations.

Configure DHCP for DSL Router Users

The CPE router can function as a Cisco IOS–based DHCP server for subscriber network hosts. Address pools are configured for each subnet to be serviced. The address of the Ethernet interface should be excluded from the address range defined for the DHCP server. This is also the case for any other statically assigned host addresses on the subscriber's network such as print servers. The Cisco IOS DHCP functionality has been enhanced to support centralized DHCP services and administration. The pool definition(s) can be imported from centralized servers if desired.

Example 5-5 can be added to the CPE router configuration discussed up to this point to enable DHCP services for the subscriber network.

Example 5-5 *DHCP Services Configuration*

```
!
ip dhcp excluded-address 172.16.0.1 172.16.0.9
!
ip dhcp pool PCLAN
   import all
   network 172.16.0.0 255.255.0.0
   default-router 172.16.0.1
!
```

The **dhcp excluded-address** command specifies that no addresses in the defined range should be allocated. Because of this, the first address available for host allocation is 172.16.0.10. Technically, the 172.16.0.1 address need not be included in the exclusion because the local router already has this address assigned, but it was included for clarity's sake. The **import all** option will dynamically populate any DNS server, WINS server, or other options, such as TFTP server, into the database so that they can be provided to hosts on the subscriber network.

If multiple VLANs are defined, each VLAN interface will provide addresses from the pool that shares its IP subnet. When a router receives a DHCP request, it checks all configured DHCP pools for a network match. If a match is found, an address will be assigned from the appropriate pool. If no match is found, no DHCP offer is made. To service the request, the router would require an additional pool configuration matching the network in question. Alternatively, if no pool is sharing its subnet, an IP helper address must be configured to forward the DHCP request to the appropriate server or no address will be allocated.

Configure Static Default Route on a DSL Router

Because the teleworker home network is typically a stub network, there is no need to enable routing protocols to maintain connectivity. This simply adds unneeded overhead to the router and WAN link. A static default route will suffice to send all nonlocal traffic to the next logical hop router and out to the Internet or enterprise network, as the case may be. Example 5-6 shows the configuration of the static default route.

Example 5-6 *Static Default Route Configuration*

```
!
ip route 0.0.0.0 0.0.0.0 interface dialer0
!
```

Any traffic destined for non-172.16.0.0 addresses will be sent via dialer0 to the next-hop router where another routing decision will be made based on the destination IP address.

The Overall CPE Router Configuration

Overall, the configuration of the CPE router is relatively uncomplicated, although the preceding sections have discussed the interface-specific and routing-specific dependencies. Example 5-7 assembles the configuration options detailed in this chapter to render the basic CPE router configuration.

Example 5-7 *CPE Router Configuration*

```
no service pad
service timestamps debug datetime msec localtime show-timezone
service timestamps log datetime msec localtime show-timezone
service password-encryption
!
hostname PPPoE-CPE
!
memory-size iomem 5
enable secret 5 [removed]
!
username Emma privilege 15 secret 5 [removed]
username Amanda privilege 15 secret 5 [removed]
clock timezone est -6
clock summer-time cdt recurring
no aaa new-model
ip subnet-zero
no ip domain lookup
ip domain name mydomain.com
ip name-server 4.2.2.1
!
ip dhcp excluded-address 172.16.0.1 172.16.0.9
! Configures DHCP Exclusions
!
ip dhcp pool PCLAN
! Creates DHCP Pool
   import all
   network 172.16.0.0 255.255.0.0
   default-router 172.16.0.1
!
interface Ethernet0/0
 description ***Internal Private Network***
 ip address 172.16.0.1 255.255.0.0
 ip nat inside
! Specifies NAT role
!
```

Example 5-7 *CPE Router Configuration (Continued)*

```
interface ATM0/0
 description ***physical interface bound to dialer0***
 no ip address
 dsl operating-mode auto
 pvc 8/35
! Creates ATM PVC
 pppoe-client dial-pool-number 1
! Assigns dial pool
!
interface Dialer0
 description ***External Provider Network***
 ip address negotiated
 ip mtu 1492
! Configures MTU
 ip nat outside
! Specifies NAT role
 encapsulation ppp
 dialer pool 1
! Dialer association
!
ip classless
ip route 0.0.0.0 0.0.0.0 interface dialer0
! Sets static default
no ip http server
no ip http secure-server
ip nat inside source list 100 interface dialer0 overload
! Configures NAT/PAT
!
access-list 100 permit ip 172.16.0.0 0.0.255.255 any
! Specifies addresses to NAT
!
line con 0
 exec-timeout 0 0
 login local
line aux 0
line vty 0 4
 exec-timeout 240 0
 login local
!
scheduler max-task-time 5000
ntp peer 172.16.1.50
ntp server XXX.118.25.3 prefer
!
End
```

Example 5-8 shows the output confirming a successfully negotiated PPPoE session.

Example 5-8 *Confirming a Successfully Negotiated PPPoE Session*

```
PPPoE-CPE#show pppoe session all
%No active L2TP tunnels
%No active L2F tunnels
PPPoE Session Information Total tunnels 1 sessions 1

Session count: 1

PPPoE Session Information
SID  RemMAC            LocMAC          Intf   Vast   OIntf   VP/VC
1    0050.7359.35b7    0001.96a4.84ac  Vi1    UP     ATM0    8/35
```

In this example, you can see that the SID is a non-zero number, and that both the RemMAC and LocMAC fields are populated. The other field of interest is Vast, which indicates whether PPP has been successfully negotiated and authenticated.

Foundation Summary

Configuration of PPPoE is similar to most other LAN/WAN configurations in that it requires multiple, dependent pieces to be assembled. Only the most basic configuration parameters are discussed in this chapter. Options such as PPP authentication, VPN options, quality of service (QoS), network management, and security are all still on the to-do list with regard to teleworker solution deployments and can be found in detail in the Business Ready Teleworker SRND found at http://www.cisco.com/go/srnd.

Table 5-2 is provided to review the basic configuration elements.

Table 5-2 *PPPoE Configuration Elements*

Element	Description
Ethernet interface	Physical interface, typically subscriber-facing but may be both subscriber- and provider-facing if two exist.
ATM interface	Physical interface, typically provider-facing and carries data traffic to the DSLAM then on to the aggregation router.
Dialer interface	Logical interface bound to a physical interface (usually ATM or second Ethernet) to establish PPPoE session to aggregation router.
NAT/PAT	Services allowing one-to-one and one-to-many IP address translation capabilities in the CPE router. PAT is also known as NAT with Overload.
Inside local address	Configured IP address assigned to a host on the inside network.
Inside global address	The IP address of an inside host as it appears to the outside network.
Outside local address	The IP address of an outside host as it appears to the inside network.
Outside global address	The configured IP address assigned to a host in the outside network.
DHCP server	Service configured to allocate IP address, gateway, and other relevant information to IP hosts on a particular subnet.
Static default route	A route to a gateway of last resort. In teleworker deployments, no routing protocol is necessary because there is typically only a single subnet. The static default route takes any traffic destined to nonlocal destinations and directs it to the aggregation router.

Q&A

The questions and scenarios in this book are designed to be challenging and to make sure that you know the answer. Rather than allowing you to derive the answers from clues hidden inside the questions themselves, the questions challenge your understanding and recall of the subject.

Hopefully, mastering these questions will help you limit the number of exam questions on which you narrow your choices to two options, and then guess.

You can find the answers to these questions in Appendix A. For more practice with exam-like question formats, use the exam engine on the CD-ROM.

1. Which solutions discussed in this chapter would be relevant to the typical teleworker?

2. In a teleworker solution, is there ever a case for using a routing protocol rather than a static default route?

3. Consider a scenario in which NAT is configured at a teleworker site. Are there circumstances that might warrant the use of NAT without PAT?

4. Explain the use of the **import all** parameter in a DHCP pool configuration.

5. When using a dialer interface, how are physical interfaces bound or associated with the dialer interface?

6. List the tasks that must be completed to configure an interface for PPPoE or PPPoA.

7. Which command should be issued to view the status of the PPPoE connection?

8. How does a router determine whether it can service a DHCP request it receives on any given interface?

Exam Topic List

This chapter covers the following topics that you need to master for the CCNP ISCW exam:

- **Configure a Cisco Router as a PPPoA Client**—Describes the requirements of configuring a PPPoA connection

- **Configure an ATM Interface for PPPoA**—Describe the tasks involved in configuring a PPPoA connection

- **Configure the PPPoA Dialer and Virtual-Template Interfaces**—Describes interface-specific requirements for PPPoA

- **Configure Additional PPPoA Elements**—Describes additional configuration requirements for PPPoA

CHAPTER 6

Configuring DSL Access with PPPoA

With the discussion of PPPoE covered in Chapter 5, some of the information presented here is redundant. This is to be expected with two fairly similar technologies. However, in the interest of reducing the amount of page turning, some of the covered information is offered once again as review.

PPPoA is a technology based on the ability of the customer premises equipment (CPE) to offer a native Asynchronous Transfer Mode (ATM)-capable interface as the provider-facing interface. As with PPPoE, the configuration is contingent on a number of additional elements being put in place.

"Do I Know This Already?" Quiz

The purpose of the "Do I Know This Already?" quiz is to help you decide whether you really need to read the entire chapter. If you already intend to read the entire chapter, you do not necessarily need to answer these questions now.

The 7-question quiz, derived from the major sections in the "Foundation Topics" portion of the chapter, helps you to determine how to spend your limited study time.

Table 6-1 outlines the major topics discussed in this chapter and the "Do I Know This Already?" quiz questions that correspond to those topics.

Table 6-1 *"Do I Know This Already?" Foundation Topics Section-to-Question Mapping*

Foundation Topics Section	Questions Covered in This Section	Score
Configure a Cisco Router as a PPPoA Client	1–3	
Configure an ATM Interface for PPPoA	4–5	
Configure the PPPoA DSL Dialer and Virtual-Template Interfaces	6–7	
Total Score		

> **CAUTION** The goal of self-assessment is to gauge your mastery of the topics in this chapter. If you do not know the answer to a question or are only partially sure of the answer, you should mark this question wrong for purposes of self-assessment. Giving yourself credit for an answer that you correctly guess skews your self-assessment results and might provide you with a false sense of security.

1. ATM connections are formed through the use of which of the following?

   a. PVC

   b. SVC

   c. PVP

   d. SVP

2. To configure an ATM interface to carry a single protocol per virtual circuit, which encapsulation should be used?

   a. **aal5snap**

   b. **aal5mux**

   c. **aal5cisco**

   d. **aal1**

3. Which field in the LLC header contains protocol information?

   a. DSAP

   b. SSAP

   c. OUI

   d. NLPID

4. If not specified, what is the default encapsulation used for an ATM PVC?

   a. **aal5mux**

   b. **aal5snap**

   c. **aal5cisco**

   d. **aal34smds**

5. Which two types of logical interfaces may be used in a PPPoA configuration?

   a. Loopback

   b. Dialer

   c. BVI

   d. Virtual-template

6. Which command set is properly associating a logical interface with the interface to be placed under its control?

   a.

   ```
   interface Ethernet0/1
    dialer pool 1
   !
   interface Dialer0
    dialer pool-member 1
   ```

   b.

   ```
   interface Ethernet0/1
    dialer pool-member 1
   !
   interface dialer0
    dialer pool 1
   ```

   c.

   ```
   interface ATM0/0
    dialer-pool-member 1
   !
   interface virtual-template 1
    encapsulation ppp
   ```

   d.

   ```
   interface ATM0/0
     pvc 0/35
     dialer pool-member 1
   !
   interface dialer0
    dialer 1
   ```

7. To automatically configure the type DSL implementation on the interface, which command is necessary?

   a. **dsl operating-mode auto**

   b. **dialer 1**

   c. **dialer pool-member 1**

   d. **interface virtual-template 1**

The answers to the "Do I Know This Already?" quiz are found in Appendix A, "Answers to the 'Do I Know This Already?' Quizzes and Q&A Sections." The suggested choices for your next step are as follows:

■ **3 or fewer overall score**—Read the entire chapter. This includes the "Foundation Topics," "Foundation Summary," and "Q&A" sections.

■ **4 or 5 overall score**—Begin with the "Foundation Summary" section, and then go to the "Q&A" section.

■ **6 or more overall score**—If you want more review on these topics, skip to the "Foundation Summary" section, and then go to the "Q&A" section. Otherwise, move to the next chapter.

Foundation Topics

Configure a Cisco Router as a PPPoA Client

To clear up a rather widespread misconception, PPPoA is defined in RFC 2364 as *PPP over AAL5*. However, it is commonly referred to simply as *PPP over ATM*. Chapter 5, "Configuring DSL Access with PPPoE," covered the configuration of PPPoE on a home router for DSL connectivity in some detail. The relative technology behind PPPoA is identical in nature to PPPoE. However, there are some significant differences that exist on the provider-facing side of the configuration, primarily:

- The handling of the ATM interface

- The configuration of the ATM permanent virtual circuit (PVC) or switched virtual circuit (SVC)

DSL is a Layer 1 access methodology. The Layer 1 connection exists across the local loop between the CPE and the DSL access multiplexer (DSLAM). Layer 2 connectivity is provided by ATM from the CPE to the DSLAM and beyond. Layer 3 connectivity is established between the CPE and an aggregation router located somewhere beyond the DSLAM. For purposes of review and to provide a point of reference for discussion topics in this chapter, Figure 6-1 provides a topological view. It shows the connectivity between the CPE and the Internet. The data traffic must traverse the local loop to the DSLAM and then go across the ATM network to the aggregation router.

Although similar to PPPoE, PPPoA is its own technology. It does present several configuration differences (due to the needs of an ATM interface versus an Ethernet interface) when compared to PPPoE. The principal difference in PPPoA is that the CPE router is now using RFC 1483/2684 encapsulation to transport PPP frames across the local loop inside of ATM cells. In other words, it actually gets to be a router this time, rather than a bridge.

Like PPPoE, a logical interface is used for managing the PPP connection. This interface is known as a virtual access interface. It will be associated with the ATM PVCs configured on the ATM interface. This configuration encapsulates each PPP connection into a separate PVC or SVC to allow each session to appear as if it is being terminated on a traditional PPP serial interface. To facilitate these connections, a virtual interface template is created to provide configuration details when the virtual circuit is created.

Figure 6-1 *PPPoA DSL Topology*

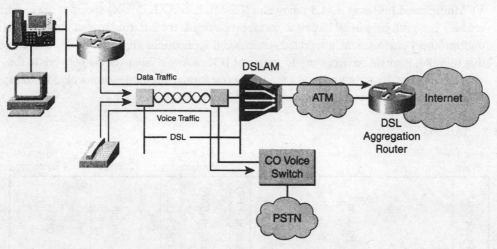

PPP over AAL5 Connections

Three separate types of connectivity options are offered under the PPPoA banner:

■   Virtual circuit multiplexed PPP over AAL5 (AAL5VCMUX)

■   LLC encapsulated PPP over AAL5 (AAL5SNAP)

■   Cisco PPP over ATM (PPPoA)

RFC 2364 defines the AAL5VCMUX and AAL5SNAP options. Cisco PPPoA, as the name implies, is a Cisco proprietary implementation. The sections that follow describe these three different connectivity options in greater detail.

> **NOTE**   As a general rule, Cisco implements its own proprietary solutions in situations where underlying technologies are not progressing quickly enough to meet market demand. Cisco continues to use the proprietary methodology until a standardized equivalent is made available to the industry. For example, consider Power over Ethernet (PoE). Well ahead of the IEEE 802.3af standard release, Cisco provided PoE capabilities to its customers in March 2000. It came in the form of a proprietary PoE known as "pre-standard power". Even in the absence of a standardized method of providing PoE, an extremely large volume of customers were requesting the capability. In response, Cisco implemented its proprietary solution. This allowed the deployment of PoE switches and technologies well ahead of a published standard. The IEEE standard was finally released in 2003. Cisco quickly converted its products to support both its pre-standard power and the standard 802.3af power.

VCMultiplexed PPP over AAL5

VCMultiplexed PPP over AAL5 (known as VC-MUX or AAL5MUX) specifies the capability to create a per-protocol virtual circuit to transport payloads for differing routed protocols. In a multiprotocol environment, integrated services and applications might not be IP-compatible. With that in mind, it might be necessary to transport IPX or AppleTalk over the network to the teleworker site. This solution allows the use of one virtual circuit per protocol to be transported. Figure 6-2 shows the framing structure for AAL5MUX.

Figure 6-2 *AAL5MUX*

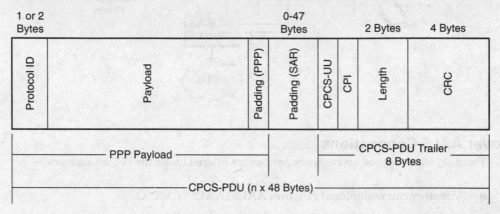

Because there is only one protocol per virtual circuit, the Protocol ID field in the frame suffices to adequately point to the upper-layer protocol encapsulated in the payload. The PPP padding is meant only to maintain the Minimum Transmittable Unit requirements of PPP.

LLC Encapsulated PPP over AAL5

Also defined in RFC 2364, this methodology uses a single virtual circuit to transport all protocols. In support of this, additional information is required to be carried in the ATM Common Part Convergence Sublayer-Protocol Data Unit (CPCS-PDU). To that end, this option specifies the use of Logical Link Control (LLC) encapsulation. Figure 6-3 shows the framing structure for AAL encapsulated PPP.

Within this specification is a detailed structure of an LLC encapsulated PPP frame. When using the LLC encapsulation technique, the payload's protocol type is explicitly identified on a per-Protocol Data Unit (PDU) basis by an in-band LLC header, followed by the payload data.

Figure 6-3 *LLC Encapsulated PPP*

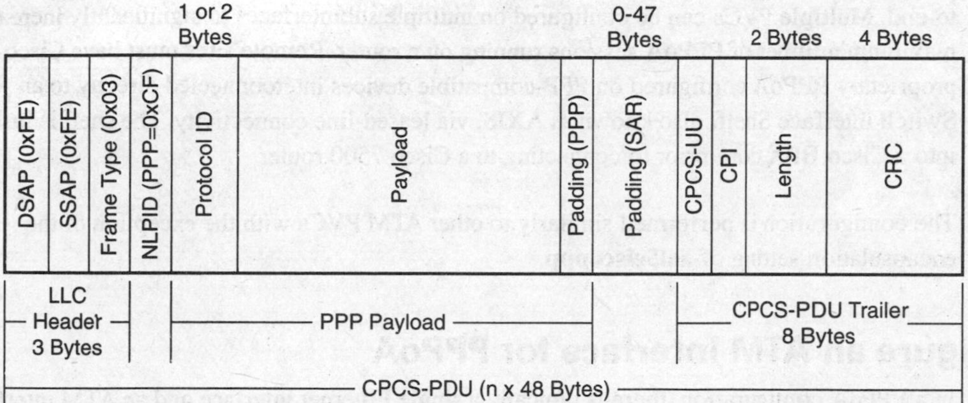

The LLC encapsulation technique provides a means to define a protocol number inside the LLC header, which allows the payload to be identified as containing a particular protocol. The LLC header contains the following information:

- **Destination service access point (DSAP)**—Destination network endpoint identifier used for OSI network layer protocols such as Connectionless Network Service (CLNS). In SNAP encapsulation, it is set to 0xFE.

- **Source service access point (SSAP)**—Source network endpoint identifier used for OSI network layer protocols. In SNAP encapsulation, it is set to 0xFE.

- **Frame Type**—This field denotes the type of frame in use and therefore its structure. This field is also known as Control (Ctrl) and is set to 0x03 (unnumbered information).

The Network Layer Protocol Independent (NLPID) field is not part of the LLC header. Typically, it is associated with the Sub-Network Access Point (SNAP) header. The SNAP Header contains an Organizationally Unique Identifier (OUI) field as well as the NLPID. This is not the case with the LLC Encapsulated PPP frame structure. The NLPID field is set to 0xCF in the LLC encapsulation technique to identify PPP as the encapsulated protocol.

The cell stream is sent from CPE to DSLAM. Once it arrives at the DSLAM, the cells are switched and forwarded across to the aggregation router. With PPPoA, the overhead created by the existence of the Ethernet frame structure is eliminated because the CPE simply uses ATM as the encapsulation rather than bridging the Ethernet frame across the network, as with PPPoE.

Cisco PPPoA

Cisco's proprietary PPP over ATM PVC technology is one dependent on Cisco infrastructure end-to-end. Multiple PVCs can be configured on multiple subinterfaces to significantly increase the maximum number of PPPoA sessions running on a router. Remote sites must have Cisco-proprietary PPPoA configured on PPP-compatible devices interconnected directly to an ATM Switch Interface Shelf, also known as AXIS, via leased-line connectivity. The shelf is installed into a Cisco BPX core prior to connecting to a Cisco 7500 router.

The configuration is performed similarly to other ATM PVCs with the exception of the encapsulation setting of **aal5ciscoppp**.

Configure an ATM Interface for PPPoA

In a PPPoA configuration, there is typically a single Ethernet interface and an ATM interface on the CPE router. The Ethernet interface is the subscriber-facing component of the CPE router. Example 6-1 shows how to configure an Ethernet interface.

Example 6-1 *Subscriber-Facing Ethernet Interface Configuration*

```
!
interface Ethernet0/0
 description ****Inside Private Network****
 ip address 172.16.0.1 255.255.0.0
!
```

Once the Layer 1 connection is established, the router's PPP subsystem will initialize and send PPP configuration requests to the aggregation router. If the router's PPP subsystem does not receive a response, it will fall back into "listen" mode to wait for an inbound configuration request. After a brief timeout period, the router will again attempt to make contact with the aggregation router. Example 6-2 demonstrates an AAL5MUX configuration.

Example 6-2 *AAL5MUX Configuration*

```
!
interface Ethernet0/0
 ip address 172.16.0.1 255.255.0.0
!
interface ATM0/0
 no ip address
 dsl operating-mode auto
 pvc 8/35
  encapsulation aal5mux ppp dialer
  dialer pool-member 1
!
```

Example 6-3 demonstrates a similar configuration but uses the LLC encapsulated PPP technique. Note that this is, in fact, accomplished by using the **encapsulation aal5snap** command. While the **encapsulation aal5snap** command has been included in this example, it is the default setting if no encapsulation is specified.

Also configured on the ATM interface is the **dsl operating-mode auto** command. This sets the interface to auto-detect the DSL modulation method to be used rather than having to define it specifically.

Example 6-3 *AAL5SNAP Configuration*

```
!
interface ATM0/0
 no ip address
 dsl operating-mode auto
interface ATM0/0.1 multipoint
 class-int ppp-default
 pvc 8/35
!
vc-class atm ppp-default
 encapsulation aal5snap
 protocol ppp virtual-template 1
 ubr 256
!
```

This example shows the use of the virtual-template interface rather than the dialer interface. The section that follows discusses the virtual-template configuration in greater detail.

Configure the PPPoA DSL Dialer and Virtual-Template Interfaces

The dialer interface is the DSL provider-facing component of the CPE router. Example 6-4 shows how to configure the basic elements of the dialer interface.

Example 6-4 *Dialer Interface Configuration*

```
!
interface ATM0/0
 no ip address
 dsl operating-mode auto
 pvc 8/35
 pppoe-client dial-pool-number 1
!
interface Dialer0
 ip address negotiated
 ip mtu 1492
 encapsulation ppp
 dialer pool 1
!
```

This configuration specifies that the dialer interface should get its IP address from the provider's DHCP server while specifying the upstream MTU and setting the interface encapsulation to PPP. Finally, the **dialer pool** command associates the dialer back to the ATM interface where the **pppoe-client dial-pool-number** command was issued. This is similar to the PPPoE configuration discussed in Chapter 5, "Configuring DSL Access with PPPoE." The pool numbers must match on the dialer and ATM interfaces in order for the configuration to function.

Virtual templates are logical interfaces that provide characteristics to physical interfaces under their control. This function is similar to the dialer interface in that regard. Like the dialer interface, the virtual-template interface is configured with all relevant PPP characteristics and parameters. Example 6-5 demonstrates the configuration for a virtual template that would function with AAL5SNAP as configured in Example 6-3.

Example 6-5 *Virtual-Template Configuration*

```
!
interface virtual-template1
 encapsulation ppp
 ip address negotiated
 ip nat outside
 ppp authentication chap
 ppp chap hostname cpe_router@cisco.com
 ppp chap password 0 cisco
!
```

The PPP CHAP options in Example 6-5 are simply added for demonstrative purposes. They are required only at the discretion of the provider. Note that NAT has also been included in the configuration. This is for demonstrative purposes to show that the virtual-template interface should be treated like any other outside interface.

Configure Additional PPPoA Elements

The information regarding additional PPPoA elements is identical to that discussed in Chapter 5 with PPPoE. For that reason, as well as to save a tree or two, the information will not be revisited here. Please refer to Chapter 5 for information on NAT/PAT, DHCP, and static default route configuration.

The Overall CPE Router Configuration

The configuration of the CPE router is relatively uncomplicated overall. Example 6-6 assembles the configuration options detailed in this chapter to render the basic CPE router configuration.

Example 6-6 *CPE Router Configuration for DSL Access with PPPoA*

```
no service pad
service timestamps debug datetime msec localtime show-timezone
service timestamps log datetime msec localtime show-timezone
service password-encryption
!
hostname PPPoA-CPE
!
memory-size iomem 5
enable secret 5 [removed]
!
username Emma privilege 15 secret 5 [removed]
username Amanda privilege 15 secret 5 [removed]
clock timezone est -6
clock summer-time cdt recurring
no aaa new-model
ip subnet-zero
no ip domain lookup
ip domain name mydomain.com
ip name-server 4.2.2.1
!
ip dhcp excluded-address 172.16.0.1 172.16.0.9
!
ip dhcp pool PCLAN
   import all
   network 172.16.0.0 255.255.0.0
   default-router 172.16.0.1
!
interface Ethernet0/0
 description ***Internal Private Network***
 ip address 172.16.0.1 255.255.0.0
 ip nat inside
!
interface ATM0/0
 no ip address
 dsl operating-mode auto
! Auto detect Modulation method
!
interface ATM0/0.1 multipoint
 class-int ppp-default
! Configure interface characteristics
 pvc 8/35
!
interface virtual-template1
! Configures virtual-template
 encapsulation ppp
 ip address negotiated
 ip nat outside
```

continues

Example 6-6 *CPE Router Configuration for DSL Access with PPPoA (Continued)*

```
!
vc-class atm ppp-default
! Class sets circuit characteristics
 encapsulation aal5snap
 protocol ppp virtual-template1
! Ties circuit to virtual-template
 ubr 256
!
ip classless
ip route 0.0.0.0 0.0.0.0 interface virtual-template1
no ip http server
no ip http secure-server
ip nat inside source list 100 interface virtual-template1 overload
!
access-list 100 permit ip 172.16.0.0 0.0.255.255 any
!
line con 0
 exec-timeout 0 0
 login local
line aux 0
line vty 0 4
 exec-timeout 240 0
 login local
!
scheduler max-task-time 5000
ntp peer 172.16.1.50
ntp server XXX.118.25.3 prefer
!
End
```

Alternatively, the configuration options may use AAL5MUX and a dialer interface. Example 6-7 illustrates the configuration.

Example 6-7 *AAL5MUX Configuration*

```
no service pad
service timestamps debug datetime msec localtime show-timezone
service timestamps log datetime msec localtime show-timezone
service password-encryption
!
hostname PPPoA-837
!
boot-start-marker
boot-end-marker
!
memory-size iomem 5
```

Example 6-7   *AAL5MUX Configuration (Continued)*

```
logging buffered 65536 debugging
enable secret 5 [removed]
!
username Emma privilege 15 secret 5 [removed]
username Amanada privilege 15 secret 5 [removed]
clock timezone est -6
clock summer-time cdt recurring
no aaa new-model
ip subnet-zero
no ip domain lookup
ip domain name mydomain.com
ip name-server 4.2.2.1
!
ip dhcp excluded-address 172.16.0.1 172.16.0.9
!
ip dhcp pool LAN_HOSTS
 import all
 network 172.16.0.0 255.255.0.0
 default-router 172.16.0.1
 dns-server 4.2.2.1
 domain-name mydomain.com
 option 150 ip xx.xxx.2.93
 netbios-name-server xxx.68.235.228 xxx.68.235.229
!
ip cef
!
interface Ethernet0
 description ****Internal Private Network****
 ip address 172.16.0.1 255.255.0.0
 ip nat inside
!
interface ATM0
 no ip address
 ip route-cache flow
 no ip mroute-cache
 load-interval 30
 no atm ilmi-keepalive
 dsl operating-mode auto
!
interface ATM0.35 point-to-point
 description ****ATM Subinterface for DSL Access****
 no ip mroute-cache
 pvc dsl 0/35
  encapsulation aal5mux ppp dialer
  dialer pool-member 1
!
interface Dialer1
```

continues

Example 6-7 *AAL5MUX Configuration (Continued)*

```
  description ****Logical Outside Interface****
  ip address negotiated
  ip nat outside
  ip mtu 1492
  encapsulation ppp
  ip tcp adjust-mss 542
  dialer pool 1
  ppp authentication pap callin
  ppp chap refuse
  ppp pap sent-username csconerd@mydomain.com password 7 [removed]
!
ip classless
ip route 0.0.0.0 0.0.0.0 Dialer1
no ip http server
no ip http secure-server
ip nat inside source list 100 interface dialer1 overload
!
access-list 100 permit ip 172.16.0.0 0.0.255.255 any
!
control-plane
!
rtr responder
banner motd ^C
C i s c o S y s t e m s

UNAUTHORIZED ACCESS TO THIS NETWORK DEVICE IS PROHIBITED.
You must have explicit permission to access or configure this
device. All activities performed on this device are logged and
violations of this policy may result in disciplinary action.
^C
!
line con 0
 exec-timeout 0 0
 login local
line aux 0
line vty 0 4
 exec-timeout 240 0
 login local
!
exception memory minimum 786432
scheduler max-task-time 5000
sntp server xxx.5.41.41
sntp server xxx.5.41.40
sntp server xxx.210.169.40
!
end
```

Foundation Summary

Configuration of PPPoA is similar to PPPoE. However, the options are somewhat different and admittedly a bit difficult to understand initially. Only the most basic configuration parameters are discussed in this chapter. The AAL5SNAP and AAL5MUX options are the overwhelmingly more dominant choices in the market today. The Cisco-proprietary PPPoA option works very well in "Cisco-on-Cisco" environments.

Table 6-2 provides a review of the basic configuration elements.

Table 6-2 *PPPoA Configuration Elements*

Element	Description
Ethernet interface	Physical interface providing service to the subscriber's home network.
ATM interface	Physical interface, provider-facing and encapsulates PPP frames inside ATM cells via native ATM functionality in the CPE router.
Dialer interface	Logical interface bound to a physical interface (usually ATM) to establish PPPoA session to aggregation router. PPP and NAT options are configured on this interface.
Virtual-template	Logical interface bound to an ATM interface via a vc-class configuration. PPP and NAT options are configured on this interface.
NAT/PAT	Services allowing one-to-one and one-to-many IP address translation capabilities in the CPE router. PAT is also known as NAT with Overload.
Inside local address	Configured IP address assigned to a host on the inside network.
Inside global address	The IP address of an inside host as it appears to the outside network.
Outside local address	The IP address of an outside host as it appears to the inside network.
Outside global address	The configured IP address assigned to a host in the outside network.
DHCP server	Service configured to allocate IP address, gateway, and other relevant information to IP hosts on a particular subnet.
Static default route	A route to a gateway of last resort. The static default route takes any traffic destined to nonlocal destinations and directs it to the aggregation router.

Q&A

The questions and scenarios in this book are designed to be challenging and to make sure that you know the answer. Rather than allowing you to derive the answers from clues hidden inside the questions themselves, the questions challenge your understanding and recall of the subject.

Hopefully, mastering these questions will help you limit the number of exam questions on which you narrow your choices to two options, and then guess.

You can find the answers to these questions in Appendix A. For more practice with exam-like question formats, use the exam engine on the CD-ROM.

1. In ATM interface configurations, what is the first usable VCI available for user-defined virtual circuits?

2. What is the purpose of the **dsl operating-mode auto** command?

3. What purpose does the LLC header serve in the LLC encapsulated technique for PPPoA?

4. Consider a situation in which you want each routed protocol to use a different virtual circuit for transport across the network. Which encapsulation would allow this, and what might be accomplished by such a configuration?

5. In the following example, what is the IP address assigned to the provider-facing interface?

```
interface Ethernet0/0
 ip address 172.16.0.1 255.255.0.0
 ip nat inside
!
interface ATM0/0
 no ip address
 dsl operating-mode auto
!
interface ATM0/0.1 multipoint
 class-int ppp-default
 pvc 8/35
!
interface virtual-template1
 encapsulation ppp
 ip address negotiated
 ip nat outside
!
vc-class atm ppp-default
 encapsulation aal5snap
 protocol ppp virtual-template1
 ubr 256
!
```

6. List one alternative to the use of a static default route.

7. Is there a time when a router using a dynamic routing protocol might also benefit from a static default route? If so, when?

8. If a source address does not match a defined access list for a NAT definition, what is the result?

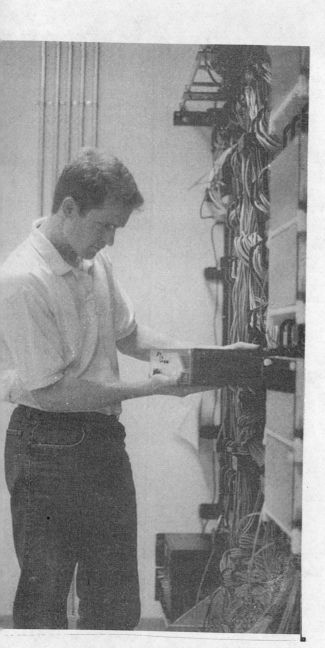

Exam Topic List

This chapter covers the following topics that you need to master for the CCNP ISCW exam:

- **DSL Connection Troubleshooting—** Describes basic DSL troubleshooting principles

- **Isolating Physical Layer Issues—**Describes how to diagnose Layer 1 issues

- **Isolating Data Link Layer Issues—** Describes how to diagnose Layer 2 issues

CHAPTER 7

Verifying and Troubleshooting ADSL Configurations

Verification of proper functionality is relatively simple when everything functions as designed on the initial configuration attempt. In reality, however, many things can and will go wrong. This chapter deals with some of the more common issues associated with ADSL in particular.

Over the course of this chapter, Layers 1 and 2 (physical and data link layers) of the OSI reference model will be discussed individually, along with potential issues and resolutions. The network layer and associated connectivity issues, from the DSL standpoint, are in the hands of the provider. The assignment of IP addressing and routing functionality are directly impacted by the provider's implementation. As such, the issues surrounding the network layer will not be discussed in this chapter.

"Do I Know This Already?" Quiz

The purpose of the "Do I Know This Already?" quiz is to help you decide whether you really need to read the entire chapter. If you already intend to read the entire chapter, you do not necessarily need to answer these questions now.

The 10-question quiz, derived from the major sections in the "Foundation Topics" portion of the chapter, helps you to determine how to spend your limited study time.

Table 7-1 outlines the major topics discussed in this chapter and the "Do I Know This Already?" quiz questions that correspond to those topics.

Table 7-1 *"Do I Know This Already?" Foundation Topics Section-to-Question Mapping*

Foundation Topics Section	Questions Covered in This Section	Score
DSL Connection Troubleshooting	1	
Isolating Physical Layer Issues	2–8	
Isolating Data Link Layer Issues	9–10	
Total Score		

> **CAUTION** The goal of self-assessment is to gauge your mastery of the topics in this chapter. If you do not know the answer to a question or are only partially sure of the answer, you should mark this question wrong for purposes of self-assessment. Giving yourself credit for an answer that you correctly guess skews your self-assessment results and might provide you with a false sense of security.

1. Which of the following is the troubleshooting methodology most effective in resolving DSL connection issues?

   a. Bottom-down

   b. Ladder

   c. Bottom-up

   d. Top-down

2. In the physical layer, there are two distinct sublayers. Which are they?

   a. Media access control sublayer

   b. Transmission convergence sublayer

   c. Physical medium dependent sublayer

   d. Voltage regulation sublayer

3. The term "line code" refers to what function?

   a. Physical transmission of bits

   b. Placing bits in order for transmission

   c. Ethernet framing

   d. Control protocol negotiation

4. Which command provides the most useful physical layer information of all interfaces?

   a. **debug ppp negotiation**

   b. **debug atm packets**

   c. **show ip interface brief**

   d. **show diag**

5. On a 6-pin RJ-11 connector, which pins are used by the DSL connection?

   a. 1 and 2

   b. 3 and 4

   c. 5 and 6

   d. 2 and 5

6. On a 4-pin RJ-11 connector, which pins are used by the DSL connection?

   a. 1 and 2

   b. 3 and 4

   c. 1 and 4

   d. 2 and 3

7. To enable automatic negotiation of the DSL modulation mode, which command should be entered on the interface?

   a. line code auto

   b. dsl operating-mode auto

   c. dsl line-modulation auto

   d. dsl line-mode auto

8. Which of the following modulation types will not be negotiated by auto-negotiation?

   a. ANSI-DMT

   b. CAP

   c. ITU-DMT

   d. Splitterless

9. To ascertain the VPI/VCI of the ATM PVC provisioned from the DSLAM to the customer premises, which command should be used?

   a. debug atm events

   b. debug atm packets

   c. debug atm pvc

   d. debug atm all

10. To isolate issues relating to username and password entry, which command is best used to display this information?

   a. debug ppp chap

   b. debug ppp authentication

   c. debug ppp negotiation

   d. debug ppp events

The answers to the "Do I Know This Already?" quiz are found in Appendix A, "Answers to the 'Do I Know This Already?' Quizzes and Q&A Sections." The suggested choices for your next step are as follows:

- **5 or fewer overall score**—Read the entire chapter. This includes the "Foundation Topics," "Foundation Summary," and "Q&A" sections.

- **6 or 8 overall score**—Begin with the "Foundation Summary" section, and then go to the "Q&A" section.

- **9 or more overall score**—If you want more review on these topics, skip to the "Foundation Summary" section, and then go to the "Q&A" section. Otherwise, move to the next chapter.

Foundation Topics

DSL Connection Troubleshooting

In the internetworking industry, it seems that there are more problems to be addressed than there are technologies to cause them. At times, it may be that correcting one problem simply gives rise to another.

With proper monitoring and proactive network management practices in place, the vast majority of network problems can be addressed and resolved before they ever become anything one might classify as a problem. This gives the IT staff the ability to reduce downtime and/or service-impacting outages. This type of management requires proper resources and tools to be effective. To many companies, the cost of those resources in employee hours, facilities, and so on are difficult to justify when coupled with the cost of the tools necessary to do the job correctly.

These same companies are the first to complain loudly that there should have been some way to avoid the issues and service-impacting outages experienced. Suddenly, the cost of the outage is well beyond what the resources and tools would have cost. Sadly, it usually requires a similar event to get the funding for those resources and tools. There also tends to be some fallout aimed squarely at the individual who decided against those resources and tools based on cost, and said individual is demoted from Hero to Zero rather quickly.

Layers of Trouble to Shoot

The preferred method of troubleshooting is known as "bottom-up" troubleshooting. The bottom-up approach to troubleshooting is a direct reference to the OSI reference model. As with the planning, design, and implementation steps involved in building a network infrastructure, the OSI reference model plays a very important part in troubleshooting issues that arise. Troubleshooting is a game of layers and logic. Different people are capable of exercising varying degrees of ability with both. It is said by many that there was a law enacted that dictates the placement of an OSI reference model graphic in every book relating to networking technologies. While this is doubtful at best, it is prudent to add such a graphic for reference purposes. Figure 7-1 serves to satisfy mythical and sarcastic legalities.

Figure 7-1 *The OSI Model*

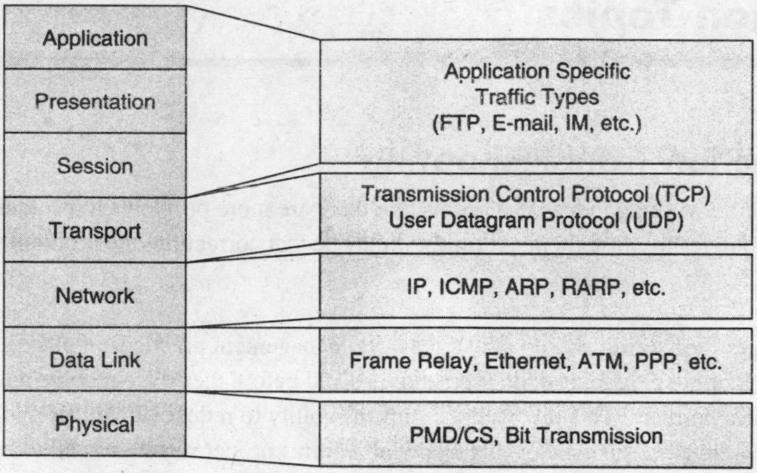

The ability to troubleshoot is a talent that many in the industry have developed over some years of experience and no small amount of pain. Many have learned the value of the bottom-down approach (which amounts to keeping one's bottom down and covered). There is some debate about whether the instinctive ability to stare at a complex network problem and pick the root cause out of the mix is something that can be taught. In any event, a process can be taught that may lead to the development of this ability over time.

Obviously, the focus of this chapter will turn to specific issues surrounding ADSL. With that in mind, the job becomes somewhat simpler in that the bottom pair of layers (physical and data link) of the OSI reference model are all that need be addressed.

Isolating Physical Layer Issues

The OSI reference model was created in layers so that it would be modular and more easily implemented. In essence, it boils down to a simple assembly-line function. Each layer is responsible only for its own little job function. This function includes a means of passing the payload to the layer above, below, or adjacent. The adjacent layer is its twin on the remote host. With that in mind, it stands to reason that no higher layer may function unless the layer below it is functioning fully and properly.

Layer 1, the physical layer, is no different. It has a seemingly simple task of moving light or electrons, as the case may be, along to the destination. It seems simple, but in reality it is anything but simple. Without a happy Layer 1, there is no network connectivity. The six higher layers cannot function.

Layer 1 Anatomy

There are typically two distinct functions performed at Layer 1. These usually include some form of transmission convergence (TC) sublayer and a physical medium dependent (PMD) sublayer. They sound quite technical but all they really mean is that the bits have to be placed in a particular order as per protocol between the endpoints and that the bits must be transmitted.

The process of placing the bits in a formalized, predetermined order is known as *framing*. The process of actually transmitting the bits is known as *line coding*. Both are somewhat generic terms and significantly factor into the overall functionality of Layer 1. When all is said and done, the job of the TC and PMD sublayers is to line up bits and kick them out the interface. If the bits are lined up incorrectly, they will arrive incorrectly and not be understood at the far end. If they are sent incorrectly, they will be seen as errors and dropped.

ADSL Physical Connectivity

With regard to ADSL, there are a number of points at which there can be a physical issue. Figure 7-2 provides a reference point for the physical connectivity of ADSL.

Figure 7-2 *ADSL Physical Connectivity*

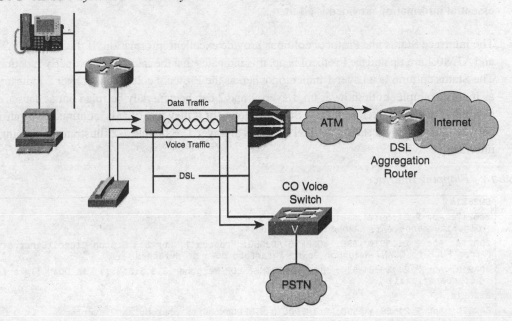

The physical connectivity relies on a number of individual segments in order to function properly for a DSL connection. Each time another device is encountered, the PMD and TC sublayers must perform their "line up the bits and kick them out the interface" function once again. However, each egress interface may use varied media types (copper, fiber, air, and so on). So, the job of the PMD and TC sublayers will vary along with variations in media types. Any physical wiring fault between the subscriber and the DSL access multiplexer (DSLAM) will result in the DSL modem being unable to train to the DSLAM, resulting in the failure of the Point-to-Point Protocol (PPP) connection and subsequently IP connectivity.

Where to Begin

The easiest way to determine which layer you should begin to troubleshoot is to issue the command **show ip interface brief**, as demonstrated in Example 7-1.

Example 7-1   **show ip interface brief** *Command Output Helps You Discern at Which OSI Layer the Problem Originate*

```
Router#show ip interface brief
Interface     IP-Address     OK?     Method     Status     Protocol
ATM0          unassigned     YES     manual     up         up
ATM0.1        unassigned     YES     unset      up         up
Ethernet0     10.10.10.1     YES     manual     up         up
```

The output of this command differs slightly depending on your configuration. However, the essential information provided is all there.

The interface Status and Protocol columns provide excellent information. If the status of ATM0 and ATM0.1 are up and the Protocol is up, this indicates that the interface is properly functioning. The Status column is a Layer 1 indicator, whereas the Protocol column is a Layer 2 indicator. If, as in this example, both show as up, Layers 1 and 2 can be generally be ruled out as causes of trouble. If the ATM interfaces show Status as down, or if they flap (that is, continuously transition between up and down state), the likely issue is at Layer 1. Example 7-2 illustrates a flapping interface.

Example 7-2   *Flapping Interface*

```
BM2821#
000217: Apr 2 21:59:01.536: %LINEPROTO-5-UPDOWN: Line protocol on Interface
  GigabitEthernet0/1, changed state to down
000218: Apr 2 21:59:01.536: %OSPF-5-ADJCHG: Process 1, Nbr 3.3.3.3 on GigabitEthernet0/1
  from FULL to DOWN, Neighbor Down: Interface down or detached
000219: Apr 2 21:59:01.544: %LDP-5-NBRCHG: LDP Neighbor 3.3.3.3:0 (1) is DOWN (Interface
  not operational)
BM2821#
000220: Apr 2 21:59:11.536: %LINEPROTO-5-UPDOWN: Line protocol on Interface
  GigabitEthernet0/1, changed state to up
BM2821#
000221: Apr 2 21:59:21.536: %OSPF-5-ADJCHG: Process 1, Nbr 3.3.3.3 on GigabitEthernet0/1
  from INIT to DOWN, Neighbor Down: Interface down or detached
000222: Apr 2 21:59:21.536: %LINEPROTO-5-UPDOWN: Line protocol on Interface
  GigabitEthernet0/1, changed state to down
```

Example 7-2 *Flapping Interface (Continued)*

```
BM2821#
000223: Apr 2 21:59:31.536: %LINEPROTO-5-UPDOWN: Line protocol on Interface
  GigabitEthernet0/1, changed state to up
BM2821#
```

In Example 7-2, the interface state changes are logged to the console by default or some other configured logging facility.

Obviously, a Status of down will be accompanied by Protocol down. If Layer 1 is down, Layer 2 cannot be up. However, there are cases where Status can be up and Protocol is down. This is indicative of a Layer 2 problem.

If the status shows the interface to be administratively down, the interface has been manually placed in a shutdown state, as demonstrated here:

```
Router#show interface atm 0
ATM0 is administratively down, line protocol is down
<output omitted>
```

To remedy this issue, you must enter the **no shutdown** command in the router's interface configuration for the interface in question:

```
Router#configure terminal
Enter configuration commands, one per line. End with CNTL/Z.
Router(config)#interface atm 0
Router(configif)#no shutdown
```

Once this is completed, check the status of the interface once again by reissuing the **show interface** command:

```
Router#show interface atm 0
ATM0 is up, line protocol is up
   Hardware is PQUICC_SAR (with Alcatel ADSL Module)
```

Now issue the **show dsl interface atm0** command and check to ensure that the status shows "Showtime," which indicates successful training, as demonstrated in Example 7-3.

Example 7-3 **show dsl interface interface** *Command Output Verifies Successful Training*

```
Router#show dsl int atm 0
                ATU-R (DS)                      ATU-C (US)
Modem Status:   Showtime (DMTDSL_SHOWTIME)
DSL Mode:       ITU G.992.1 (G.DMT)
! Output omitted for brevity
```

Playing with Colors

Another logical starting point is with the most useful troubleshooting tool ever created, the trusty old light emitting diode (LED). Look at the front of the DSL modem or router and check the LED states. Many hours of troubleshooting have been avoided by the mantra of the network technician, "Green is good!" That is to say that on the front of the DSL router or modem, there should be a Carrier Detect (CD) LED. When training, it may flash, but when connected properly, it will be solid and green. If the LED is amber or red, a thorough checking of the cable connections is in order. Obviously, DSL hardware will vary from time to time, so it is likely best to refer to the documentation provided for a particular piece of hardware.

Tangled Wires

If the DSL connection will not train up, there are some items to be checked prior to placing the call to the provider's help desk. A high percentage of DSL customers maintain multiple phone lines. There is one in place to provide traditional phone services (long distance calling, international calling, call waiting, and so on). The other line is typically dedicated to DSL and inbound/outbound fax. Of course, this varies, and the splitting of the call capabilities in this manner is unnecessary because it can all coexist on a single line. However, it does tend to happen in a high number of cases. In the event of physical layer issues in this type of environment, step one in troubleshooting must be to ensure that the DSL router is connected to the phone line with the DSL service.

A very common issue arises when a microfilter is connected to the wall-jack, which is then connected to the cable leading to the DSL interface on the router or modem. This will stop the device from training up and establishing the DSL connection. The microfilter should be used only with analog end devices such as fax machines, modems, and telephones. In most cases, the microfilter is a dongle-like device, usually about 6 inches in length, which has a female RJ-11 jack on one end and a male RJ-11 connector on the other. The male end connects to the wall-jack while the female end receives the phone line from the analog device itself. If the microfilter is not attached between the wall and phone, anyone lifting the handset will be presented with loud static. The dial tone may or may not be heard along with the static.

Keeping the Head on Straight

There is also the rare occurrence of a cable pinout issue. If the phone cable has been incorrectly terminated or the cable head crimped with wires in the wrong order, no connection will be established. An RJ-11 standard connector is a 6-pin connector. A typical phone cord uses only four wires, sometimes only two. The wires on a typical 4-wire phone cord use a different color for each wire (red, green, black, and yellow). Typically, red/green are the inner pair and black/yellow are the outer pair.

Each pair of wires has one wire designated as "tip" and one designated as "ring." The tip and ring wires for xDSL connections are pins 3 and 4, respectively, on the 6-pin connector, or 2 and 3 on a 4-pin connector. Figure 7-3 illustrates this concept.

Figure 7-3 *RJ-11 Connector*

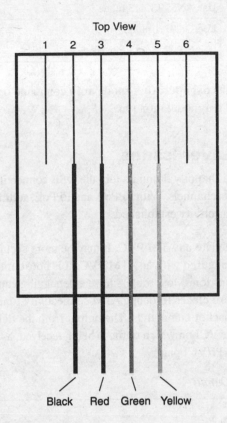

When in doubt, replace the cable with a known-good cable, to rule it out as an issue contributing to the problem.

DSL Operating Mode

If the DSL modulation is set incorrectly, the connection cannot train up. The service provider should be consulted to determine whether or not the chipset (Alcatel, for example) contained in the DSL router or modem is supported. The modulation type should be configured according to that used by the provider. Table 7-2 shows the supported types.

Table 7-2 *Supported DSL Operating Modes*

Operating Mode	Description
auto	Automatic negotiation of the modulation type with the DSLAM
ansi-dmt	Use ANSI T1.413 mode
itu-dmt	Use G.992.1 mode
splitterless	Use G.992.2 or G.Lite mode

On Cisco DSL routers, the **dsl operating-mode auto** command on the interface will allow the automatic negotiation of the modulation type.

Isolating Data Link Layer Issues

Once the physical layer is happily doing its job, the DSL connection will train up and negotiate upstream and downstream channels. With PPPoA and PPPoE, additional functions must take place at Layer 2 to get the connectivity established.

The DSL router will negotiate an ATM PVC. It may be more accurate to say that the DSL router will be automatically configured with an ATM PVC. It is not so much a negotiation function, but simply a provisioning function. Most routers have a debugging capability that can be used in watching this function take place. To debug ATM connectivity functions, use the **debug atm events** and **debug atm packet** commands. The output from the **debug atm events** command shows the current VPI and VCI on which traffic is being received, as demonstrated in Example 7-4. In this case, 8/35 is the VPI/VCI pair.

Example 7-4 **debug atm events** *Output*

```
Router#debug atm events
ATM events debugging is on
2d18h: RX interrupt: conid = 0, rxBd = 0x80C7EF74 length=52
2d18h: Data Cell received on vpi = 8. vci = 35
2d18h: RX interrupt: conid = 0, rxBd = 0x80C7EEC0 length=52
2d18h: Data Cell received on vpi = 8 vci = 35
```

The output from the **debug atm packet** command shows the current state of ATM traffic hitting the interface and the encapsulation type. In Example 7-5, the highlighted line shows that the SAP is AAAA. This is both DSAP (AA) and SSAP (AA). CTL is set to 03 and OUI to 0080C2. From previous discussions of ATM, this is readily recognizable as LLC SNAP encapsulation (also known as AAL5SNAP encapsulation). This means that there is the potential for multiple protocols to be transported over this ATM circuit.

Example 7-5 **debug atm packet** *Output*

```
Router#debug atm packet
03:21:32: ATM0(I):
VCD:0x2 VPI:0x1 VCI:0x1 Type:0x0 SAP:AAAA CTL:03 OUI:0080C2 TYPE:0007 Length:0x30
03:21:32: 0000 0050 7359 35B7 0001 96A4 84AC 8864 1100 0001 000E C021 09AB 000C 0235
03:21:32: 279F 0000 0000
03:21:32:
```

If the VPI and VCI are received and the circuit looks good and is trained up, the connectivity of the local ATM segment can be tested through the use of an ATM ping, as demonstrated in Example 7-6. This is an additional extension to the Cisco Extended Ping capability and is specific to ATM interfaces.

Example 7-6 *ATM Ping Results*

```
Router#ping atm interface atm 0/1 8 35 seg-loopback
Type escape sequence to abort.
Sending Seg-Loopback 5, 53-byte OAM Echoes to a neighbor, timeout is 5 seconds:
!!!!!
Success rate is 100 percent (5/5)
```

The segment loopback sends ATM Operation, Administration, and Maintenance (OAM) cells across the circuit to the next ATM device encountered and then the cells are looped back to return in the same manner. This verifies the configuration of the local PVC.

PPP Negotiation

The Point-to-Point Protocol (PPP) is key to the success of the connectivity for DSL. If the ATM configuration and encapsulation have been found to be properly configured and trained, the PPP connectivity is the next item on the troubleshooting list. PPP connections go through three distinct phases during negotiation:

■ **Link Control Protocol (LCP) phase**—Parameters related to establishing, configuring, and testing the connection are negotiated. This phase is mandatory.

■ **Authentication phase**—User authentication is performed according to the methodology negotiated in the LCP phase. This phase is optional.

■ **Network Control Protocol (NCP) phase**—Network layer protocol negotiation is performed to set up individual control protocols for each Layer 3 protocol to be transported. This phase is mandatory.

The most useful commands in monitoring these phases include **debug ppp negotiation** and **debug ppp authentication**. In the output in Example 7-7, both commands are used in tandem for a more complete picture.

Example 7-7 *Monitoring PPP Negotiation Phases*

```
Router#debug ppp negotiation
PPP protocol negotiation debugging is on
Router#debug ppp authentication
PPP authentication debugging is on
06:36:03: ATM0 PPP: Treating connection as a callout
06:36:03: ATM0 PPP: Phase is ESTABLISHING, Active Open [0 sess, 1 load]
06:36:03: ATM0 PPP: No remote authentication for call-out
06:36:03: ATM0 LCP: O CONFREQ [Closed] id 1 len 10
!-- "O" indicates an outbound packet; in this, case a request.
06:36:03: ATM0 LCP:    MagicNumber 0x03013D43 (0x050603013D43)
06:36:03: ATM0 LCP: I CONFACK [REQsent] id 1 len 10
!-- "I" indicates an inbound packet; in this case, an acknowledgement.
06:36:03: ATM0 LCP:    MagicNumber 0x03013D43 (0x050603013D43)
06:36:05: ATM0 LCP: I CONFREQ [ACKrcvd] id 2 len 15
06:36:05: ATM0 LCP:    AuthProto CHAP (0x0305C22305)
!-- Authentication protocol is CHAP
06:36:05: ATM0 LCP:    MagicNumber 0x65E315E5 (0x050665E315E5)
06:36:05: ATM0 LCP: O CONFACK [ACKrcvd] id 2 len 15
06:36:05: ATM0 LCP:    AuthProto CHAP (0x0305C22305)
06:36:05: ATM0 LCP:    MagicNumber 0x65E315E5 (0x050665E315E5)
06:36:05: ATM0 LCP: State is Open
!-- PPP Successfully negotiated because state is "Open"
06:36:05: ATM0 PPP: Phase is AUTHENTICATING, by the peer [0 sess, 1 load]
06:36:05: ATM0 CHAP: I CHALLENGE id 9 len 26 from "nrp-b"
06:36:05: ATM0 CHAP: Using alternate hostname client1
06:36:05: ATM0 CHAP: Username nrp-b not found
!-- Router hostname (nrp-b) is not the CHAP username; client1 is the CHAP username
06:36:05: ATM0 CHAP: Using default password
06:36:05: ATM0 CHAP: O RESPONSE id 9 len 28 from "client1"
06:36:05: ATM0 CHAP: I SUCCESS id 9 len 4
!-- Authentication succeeds
06:36:05: ATM0 PPP: Phase is FORWARDING [0 sess, 1 load]
06:36:05: ATM0 PPP: Phase is AUTHENTICATING [0 sess, 1 load]
06:36:05: ATM0 PPP: Phase is UP [0 sess, 1 load]
06:36:05: ATM0 IPCP: O CONFREQ [Closed] id 1 len 10
!-- Outbound request for IP Control Protocol initialization
06:36:05: ATM0 IPCP:    Address 0.0.0.0 (0x030600000000)
06:36:05: ATM0 CDPCP: O CONFREQ [Closed] id 1 len 4
!-- Outbound request for CDP Control Protocol initialization
06:36:05: ATM0 IPCP: I CONFREQ [REQsent] id 1 len 10
06:36:05: ATM0 IPCP:    Address 8.8.8.1 (0x030608080801)
06:36:05: ATM0 IPCP:    Address 8.8.8.1 (0x030608080801)
```

Example 7-7 *Monitoring PPP Negotiation Phases (Continued)*

```
06:36:05: ATM0 IPCP:    Address 9.9.9.2 (0x030609090902)
06:36:05: ATM0 IPCP: O CONFREQ [ACKsent] id 2 len 10
06:36:05: ATM0 IPCP:    Address 9.9.9.2 (0x030609090902)
06:36:05: ATM0 LCP: I PROTREJ [Open] id 3 len 10 protocol CDPCP (0x820701010004)
06:36:05: ATM0 CDPCP: State is Closed
06:36:05: ATM0 IPCP: I CONFACK [ACKsent] id 2 len 10
06:36:05: ATM0 IPCP:    Address 9.9.9.2 (0x030609090902)
06:36:05: ATM0 IPCP: State is Open
06:36:05: ATM0 IPCP: Install negotiated IP interface address 9.9.9.2
06:36:05: ATM0 IPCP: Install route to 8.8.8.1
!-- IP Address assigned and default route installed
06:36:06. %LINEPROTO-5-UPDOWN: Line protocol on Interface ATM0, changed state to up
```

As evident from the output, the connectivity begins with an establishing phase as part of the negotiation. In the negotiation, the decision of which authentication type to be used can be seen.

In the authentication phase, the negotiated type is used and user-specific information is exchanged. With successful completion of authentication, the IP Control Protocol (IPCP) and CDP Control Protocol (CDPCP) can be seen initializing. An IP address is negotiated with the far-end server and a default route is established to provide routing connectivity for off-net traffic. Key lines of the output are highlighted for clarity.

At times, the authentication will fail. Whether by misconfiguration of the username or the password, the result is a failed connection. In Example 7-7, the name **nrp-b** was attempted but failed. Then the name of **client1** was attempted and succeeded. In the next example, there is no entry for **client1**. Example 7-8 shows an example of the authentication failure. This output is from the authenticating router rather than the router requesting a connection.

Example 7-8 *PPP Authentication Failure at the Provider Router*

```
ATM0 CHAP: I RESPONSE id 18 len 33 from "npr-b"
! -- Incoming CHAP response to our challenge.
! -- The username used in the response is npr-b.
ATM0 CHAP: Unable to validate Response.  Username npr-b not found
! -- The username supplied by the peer is not configured on the router.
ATM0 CHAP: O FAILURE id 18 len 26 msg is "Authentication failure"
! -- Outgoing CHAP failure message.
ATM0 PPP: Phase is TERMINATING [0 sess, 0 load]
```

In the example, the configured hostname was not found or was mistyped. A username mismatch is the result of one the following:

- The peer did not supply the username expected by the target router or authentication server.

- The target router or authentication server does not have a username configured for the subscriber.

In either event, the provider should be engaged to assist in sorting out the username and password issues associated with the authentication failure.

If the ATM circuit is up, it is reasonable to assume that the router configuration is correct. If PPP still cannot establish a connection, the provider will need to be engaged to find the particular issue causing the failure.

Once the IPCP is open and the IP address is assigned, initiate a ping to the router's next-hop gateway, in this case the aggregation router. If the ping is successful, but no traffic goes beyond it on subsequent pings to Internet locations, initiate a traceroute to ensure that the lack of response is not due to the destination being specifically configured to ignore ICMP Echo Request packets. Many providers and companies today are disabling ICMP functions on their Internet-facing devices.

If the trace does not go beyond the aggregation router, once again the provider must be engaged for troubleshooting purposes.

Foundation Summary

While it can be somewhat involved, general troubleshooting is not a difficult process most of the time. It can, however, be a long process. Considering the full connectivity picture and ascertaining a logical starting point for troubleshooting can save hours. Through logic and a thorough understanding of cause/effect relationships between network devices, a big service impact can be turned into a small one.

Begin at the bottom and work up layer by layer, verifying functionality at each step. Have a process in mind and do not be afraid to engage additional resources to get the problem resolved. Also, keep in mind that one of the most effective, and underutilized, troubleshooting tools is a short break every so often. The benefit of viewing a problem from a fresh perspective often aids in rapid resolution. Table 7-3 reviews the bottom-up troubleshooting methodology and Table 7-4 reviews the troubleshooting commands discussed in this chapter.

Table 7-3 *Bottom-up Troubleshooting*

Layer	Components	Dependency
Network layer	Routed and routing protocol information	Layer 1 Active Layer 2 Active
Data link layer	Media-specific framing information and addressing	Layer 1 Active
Physical layer	PMD and TC sublayers for bit ordering and transmission	Framing and line code mechanisms

Table 7-4 *Troubleshooting **debug** Commands*

Command	Purpose
debug atm events	Verification of ATM VPI/VCI configuration
debug atm packets	Verification of ATM encapsulation and circuit protocol
debug ppp negotiation	Verification of PPP LCP option negotiation
debug ppp authentication	Verification of PPP authentication

Q&A

The questions and scenarios in this book are designed to be challenging and to make sure that you know the answer. Rather than allowing you to derive the answers from clues hidden inside the questions themselves, the questions challenge your understanding and recall of the subject.

Hopefully, mastering these questions will help you limit the number of exam questions on which you narrow your choices to two options, and then guess.

You can find the answers to these questions in Appendix A. For more practice with exam-like question formats, use the exam engine on the CD-ROM.

1. Describe the purpose of the PMD and TC sublayers as well as their relation to each other.

2. A teleworker contacts the IT help desk with an issue regarding their connection back to the corporate headquarters. This link had worked previously and has suddenly stopped. Consider a course of action in troubleshooting the issue.

3. Consider the following example and provide feedback regarding the GigabitEthernet0/0 interface.

```
BM2821#show ip interface brief
Interface            IP-Address    OK? Method Status                 Protocol
GigabitEthernet0/0   unassigned    YES NVRAM  administratively down  down
Service-Engine0/0    192.168.1.1   YES TFTP   up                     up
GigabitEthernet0/1   10.10.1.2     YES NVRAM  up                     up
FastEthernet0/1/0    unassigned    YES unset  up                     up
FastEthernet0/1/1    unassigned    YES unset  down                   down
FastEthernet0/1/2    unassigned    YES unset  up                     up
FastEthernet0/1/3    unassigned    YES unset  up                     up
FastEthernet0/1/4    unassigned    YES unset  up                     up
FastEthernet0/1/5    unassigned    YES unset  up                     up
FastEthernet0/1/6    unassigned    YES unset  up                     up
FastEthernet0/1/7    unassigned    YES unset  up                     up
FastEthernet0/1/8    unassigned    YES unset  up                     down
Vlan1                172.16.0.4    YES NVRAM  up                     up
Vlan100              192.168.1.1   YES NVRAM  up                     up
Loopback0            unassigned    YES NVRAM  up                     up
BM2821#
```

4. Once again, consider the output shown in question 3. What information is evident regarding the FastEthernet interfaces listed?

5. In troubleshooting physical layer issues regarding DSL cabling, it is necessary to understand the cable type and pinout required for proper operation. Describe the cable and pinout that can be used to connect the DSL interface on the router to the provider network.

This part of the book covers the following ISCW exam topics:

Implement Frame-Mode MPLS.

- Describe the components and operation of Frame-Mode MPLS (e.g., packet-based MPLS VPNs).
- Configure and verify Frame-Mode MPLS.

Part II: Implementing Frame Mode MPLS

Exam Topic List

This chapter covers the following topics that you need to master for the CCNP ISCW exam:

- **Introducing MPLS Networks**—Describe MPLS as an overall technology and how it relates to legacy WAN options

- **Router Switching Mechanisms**—Describe MPLS label switching functionality

CHAPTER 8

The MPLS Conceptual Model

Traditionally, wide-area network (WAN) connectivity is deployed as a Layer 2 topology configured to transport Layer 3 traffic. The WAN has always been portrayed as a cloud in pictures, diagrams, and documentation. This is due to the fact that a third-party provider owns the network and decides how it is to be constructed, its traffic policies, and the manner in which it is managed.

Although most of this still rings true, today's WAN is somewhat different in operation and deployment. Architecturally, it is owned, managed, and maintained by a service provider. However, the service provider might just relinquish a bit of control to the end customer when it comes to traffic policy. This chapter discusses the technologies making this shift possible.

"Do I Know This Already?" Quiz

The purpose of the "Do I Know This Already?" quiz is to help you decide whether you really need to read the entire chapter. If you already intend to read the entire chapter, you do not necessarily need to answer these questions now.

The 8-question quiz, derived from the major sections in the "Foundation Topics" portion of the chapter, helps you to determine how to spend your limited study time.

Table 8-1 outlines the major topics discussed in this chapter and the "Do I Know This Already?" quiz questions that correspond to those topics.

Table 8-1 *"Do I Know This Already?" Foundation Topics Section-to-Question Mapping*

Foundation Topics Section	Questions Covered in This Section	Score
Introducing MPLS Conceptual Networks	1–5	
Router Switching Mechanisms	6–8	
Total Score		

CAUTION The goal of self-assessment is to gauge your mastery of the topics in this chapter. If you do not know the answer to a question or are only partially sure of the answer, you should mark this question wrong for purposes of self-assessment. Giving yourself credit for an answer that you correctly guess skews your self-assessment results and might provide you with a false sense of security.

1. Which is the most commonly used traditional WAN topology?

    a. Full mesh

    b. Partial mesh

    c. Hub-and-spoke

    d. Point-to-point

2. In a full mesh topology, how many individual circuits would need to be maintained to provide connectivity to 45 sites?

    a. 1000

    b. 990

    c. 435

    d. 45

3. MPLS networks rely on which of the following for switching throughout the network?

    a. Label swapping

    b. Process switching

    c. Fast switching

    d. LAN switching

4. In traditional routing, packets destined for the same next-hop router are grouped into classifications known as which of the following?

    a. Egress queues

    b. Reverse path verification

    c. Forwarding equivalence classes

    d. Classes of service

5. Which of the following would typically perform a routing table lookup?

    a. LSR

    b. LSP

    c. MPLS core router

    d. MPLS edge router

6. CEF is which type of switching mechanism?

   a. Process switching

   b. Fast switching

   c. Optimal switching

   d. Topology-driven switching

7. Which type of switching mechanism offers the least efficiency?

   a. Process switching

   b. Fast switching

   c. Optimal switching

   d. Topology-driven switching

8. The CEF FIB is updated by which of the following?

   a. Dynamic CEF keepalives

   b. CEF routing updates sent to all adjacent neighbors

   c. IP routing table updates processed by the routing protocol then copied by CEF

   d. Packet-triggered updates

The answers to the "Do I Know This Already?" quiz are found in Appendix A, "Answers to the 'Do I Know This Already?' Quizzes and Q&A Sections." The suggested choices for your next step are as follows:

- **4 or fewer overall score**—Read the entire chapter. This includes the "Foundation Topics," "Foundation Summary," and "Q&A" sections.

- **5 or 6 overall score**—Begin with the "Foundation Summary" section, and then go to the "Q&A" section.

- **7 or more overall score**—If you want more review on these topics, skip to the "Foundation Summary" section, and then go to the "Q&A" section. Otherwise, move to the next chapter.

Foundation Topics

Introducing MPLS Networks

Multiprotocol Label Switching (MPLS) is, as WAN technologies go, a new technology. RFC 3031 defines the MPLS architecture. Interestingly, the authors of the RFC were from Cisco Systems, Inc., Force10 Networks, and Juniper Networks. This goes to show that multiple vendors can work together when they need to do so or when the technology is just that intriguing (which is the case with MPLS).

Traditional WAN Connections

To know where one is going, one must know where one has been. In learning any relatively new technology, it is useful to begin on common or well-known ground and progress into the unknown from that point. MPLS is somewhat of a departure for WAN connections in a number of ways.

Traditional WAN connections are Layer 2 and classified as point-to-point or multipoint connections. These networks do not understand Layer 3 quality of service (QoS). At best, they understand traffic shaping. In really ornate cases, there can be some circuit prioritization done at the edges. However, across the WAN itself, there is little or no traffic protection.

Traditional WANs typically exist in a limited number of architectures based on the company size and budget for bandwidth between said sites. The most common architectural models include:

- Hub-and-spoke

- Partial mesh

- Full mesh

- Redundant hub-and-spoke

Each model or topology has its pros and cons. Most of those pros and cons come down to cost vs. connection in the end. As the number of connections and the bandwidth per connection increase, so does the cost; however, higher bandwidth and pathway diversity add to the resilience and flexibility of the network, especially in times of need such as hurricanes, tsunamis, or other less than desirable situations.

Figure 8-1 illustrates the hub-and-spoke network model.

Figure 8-1 *Hub-and-Spoke Topology*

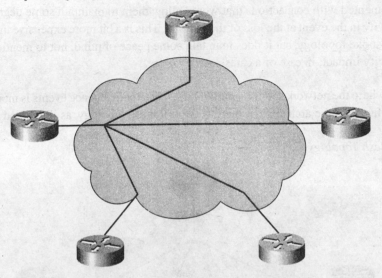

As is evident in Figure 8-1, there is a central, or "hub," site to which all other sites are connected. For any "spoke" site to pass traffic to another "spoke" site, it must send that traffic via the hub site. This topology is by far the most commonly used model because it offers the lowest cost overall. However, it is the least redundant topology. Should the router at the hub site be lost or damaged, the entire network is effectively unavailable. To augment the topology with minimal incremental costs, you could use a partial mesh topology, as illustrated in Figure 8-2.

Figure 8-2 *Partial Mesh Topology*

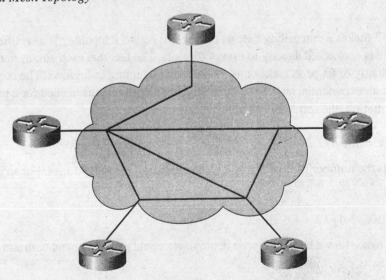

In Figure 8-2, the original hub-and-spoke topology is still evident; however, critical sites have been augmented with connections that would allow them to maintain some degree of network connectivity in the event of the loss of the hub site. This is a bit more expensive than the traditional hub-and-spoke topology, but it does maintain some peace of mind, not to mention minimal connectivity impact, in case of a catastrophic failure.

In cases where the network and its capability to react to convergence events is more important than cost as a factor in the architecture, there is the full mesh topology, as illustrated in Figure 8-3.

Figure 8-3   *Full Mesh Topology*

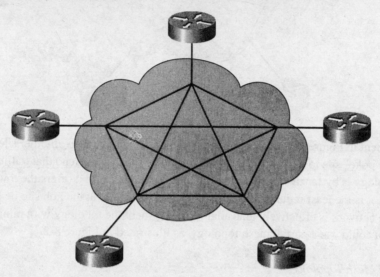

Figure 8-3 makes a compelling case as to why this network topology is as resilient as it is costly. Every site is connected directly to every other site. The fact that each circuit must be maintained independently of its peers makes this model rather daunting as it grows. The cost begins to grow almost at an exponential rate. To calculate the number of circuits needed for a given implementation, the formula is as follows:

$$c = n(n-1)/2$$

where c is the number of circuits and n is the number of networked sites. For an installation of 30 sites:

$$30(30-1)/2 = 435 \text{ circuits}$$

It is easy to see how a large enterprise deployment could get out of hand both administratively and monetarily.

The full mesh model has the benefit of allowing minimal latency and maximum redundancy for the network. Additional steps might be taken at key sites to terminate redundant circuits on separate router chassis for added redundancy.

In recent years, as these models began to evolve out of the architectural picture as new technologies started to become available (namely MPLS), another model became quite common as a compromise between redundancy, latency, and cost. This topology has been known by a few names such as redundant hub-and-spoke, multihub-and-spoke, dual-hub-and-spoke, and so on. Figure 8-4 illustrates the concept behind this topology.

Figure 8-4   *Redundant Hub-and-Spoke Topology*

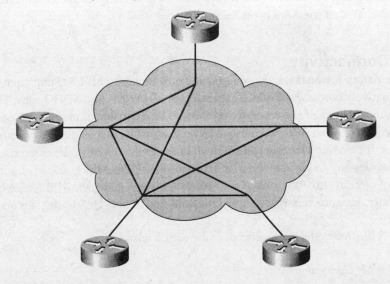

From Figure 8-4, it becomes clearer as to why it might have a number of names. This figure illustrates a dual-hub model. There are two designated hub sites. As more hubs are added, it becomes a multihub model, and so on. In some cases, there are dual connections between the hub sites. Again, it all comes down to the delicate balancing act of cost vs. resilience. The cost-saving hero can quickly find a hostile environment when things go wrong.

Architecturally, any network designer is going to prefer the maximum amount of redundancy available, regardless of cost. The architect's job is to build it right. Someone else will have to worry about cost. Build the network design with the end in mind. Make the network modular so that there is room for certain "modules" or pieces of it to be deferred, not cut, to reduce immediate cost of implementation. This allows for the construction to be pushed out across a longer period of time, thus distributing the cost impact.

Alternatively, equipment leases have become a very cost-attractive way of procuring equipment with little or no upfront costs. In recent years, Cisco Capital (the financial entity of Cisco) has put forth a number of financing options with this in mind. It is finding a wide acceptance with CFO-level executives when engaged to discuss cost justification of a network design. While this does sound like something of an advertisement for Cisco Capital, it is meant to provide an additional, and little known, tool in cost-justifying an all-at-once network implementation. In other words, the creative financial exercises in which network architects find themselves embroiled are removed and their designs are implemented with all the pieces or "modules" intact from day one. If Total Cost of Ownership (TCO) and Return on Investment (ROI) reports could be generated in binary and/or hexadecimal, network staff might be better suited to prepare them. As this is not the case, this option provides a means of leaving the financials to the financial teams. Sanity and peace of mind ensue, at least for the network team.

MPLS WAN Connectivity

With the history lesson done, the conversation now moves to MPLS. Simply put, MPLS extends Layer 3 natively across the distance between central, branch, and SOHO sites. The MPLS network, though owned by the service provider, is an extension of the enterprise network. Picture the entire WAN, which was previously a Layer 2 obstacle, as a single router with multiple interfaces. It contains a routing table with all of the route entries of the enterprise network. The WAN provides any-to-any connectivity between sites without the hassle of administering a large number of circuits. Like any routed network with diverse paths, the MPLS network converges dynamically, supports multiple routing protocols, and honors QoS traffic tags and policies.

Figure 8-5 illustrates the basic concept of the MPLS network.

Figure 8-5 *MPLS WAN Concept*

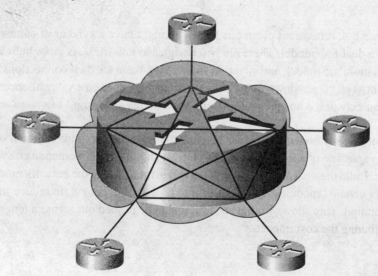

Each site requires only one connection to the service provider network. This connection will most likely be Frame Relay or a similar technology at the local loop; however, that is where the similarity stops with traditional WAN technologies.

MPLS Terminology

To fully appreciate and understand the technology behind MPLS, it is necessary to have a grasp on associated terminology. These terms are addressed throughout this chapter and are merely offered here for reference. Some of the common MPLS terms defined in RFC 3031 are as follows:

- **Label**—A short, fixed-length, physically contiguous identifier used to identify a group of networks sharing a common destination, usually of local significance.

- **Label stack**—An ordered set of labels attached to a packet header. Each label in the stack is independent of the others.

- **Label swap**—The basic forwarding operation, which consists of looking up an incoming label to determine the outgoing label, encapsulation, port, and other data-handling information.

- **Label-switched hop (LSH)**—The hop between two MPLS nodes, on which forwarding is done using labels.

- **Label-switched path (LSP)**—The path through one or more LSRs at one level of the hierarchy followed by a packet in a particular FEC.

- **Label switching router (LSR)**—An MPLS node that is capable of forwarding labeled packets.

- **MPLS domain**—A contiguous set of nodes performing MPLS routing and forwarding. These are typically in one routing or administrative domain.

- **MPLS edge node**—An MPLS node that connects to a neighboring node outside of its MPLS domain.

- **MPLS egress node**—An MPLS edge node that handles traffic leaving an MPLS domain.

- **MPLS ingress node**—An MPLS edge node that handles traffic entering an MPLS domain.

- **MPLS label**—A label that is carried in a packet header and represents the packet's FEC.

- **MPLS node**—A node running MPLS. An MPLS node is aware of MPLS control protocols, operates one or more Layer 3 routing protocols, and is capable of forwarding packets based on labels. Optionally, an MPLS node can also forward native Layer 3 packets.

MPLS Features

As the name denotes, MPLS is a switching mechanism. The process of switching MPLS packets includes the analysis of a label. This label contains the forwarding information needed to perform a path switch of the packet inside the LSR. It is possible that forwarding is performed by devices that are capable of doing label lookup and replacement but incapable either of analyzing network layer headers or of analyzing them at adequate speed. In other words, LSRs need not be capable of performing native Layer 3 routing.

Labels usually correspond, in some manner, to destination networks similar to traditional routing protocol operations. However, they can correspond to other variables such as the Layer 3 VPN destination, Layer 2 virtual circuit, egress interface, QoS, or a source address. These options are configurable on a per-device basis. The reason for this is that MPLS was not necessarily designed to forward only IP packets. Certainly, IP is at the forefront, as is IPv6, of the architectural vision.

As packets traverse the network from router to router, the role of each router is simply to make a forwarding decision, perform a path switch, and dispatch the packets to the next-hop router. Essentially, this process amounts to a high-speed and high-tech game of "pass the buck." This game is played based on information contained in the label imposed on the packet, whatever the Layer 3 protocol might be.

The architects of MPLS as a technology hold to the simple idea that the Layer 3 header contains significantly more information than is necessary to perform the forwarding functions. An idea behind MPLS is to build a Layer 3 routing protocol that functions in the absence of unnecessary information and without dependence on individual Layer 3 routed protocols. The basic principals of routing apply to MPLS just as do to any other routing protocol.

Essentially, the choice of a next-hop device, regardless of the nature of the underlying routing process, is one that can be broken into two basic functions:

- Sort entire sets of possible packets into classes based on the destination address of each known as forwarding equivalence classes (FEC).

- Map each FEC to a next-hop address.

It should be noted that packets assigned to the same FEC are indistinguishable when it comes to forwarding decisions. All packets in a particular FEC will follow the same pathway as the path is associated with the FEC, not the individual packets.

In traditional IP routing, a router considers two packets to belong to the same FEC if they contain a destination address matching the same "longest match" prefix entry in the routing table. This could be a prefix of any length. Obviously, an 8-bit prefix has the potential to match a very large number of packets, whereas a 32-bit prefix would match comparatively fewer packets. As packets are forwarded on to next-hop devices in the pathway, each is re-examined and assigned to an FEC based on that individual router's view of the network. So, it is entirely conceivable that packets sorted into the same FEC at one router will be sorted into separate FECs at another router down the line.

In MPLS, there is only one examination of the packet and only one assignment to an FEC. This is done at the MPLS ingress node. The FEC is encoded as a short, fixed-length value known as a *label*. When a packet is sent to a next-hop device, the FEC is sent with it. In other words, packets are labeled prior to being forwarded. At subsequent hops, only the FEC or label is examined. There is no routing table lookup. The ingress label is used as an index to allow the choice of an egress label identifying the next-hop device. The ingress label is then discarded by the device and replaced with an appropriate new label that will get it to the next-hop. The packet is then forwarded on to the next-hop device, where the process is repeated.

More simply put, in MPLS networks, only the edge LSRs perform the routing table lookup, in the process-switching sense. All non-edge LSRs perform their forwarding processes based on the label only, not on the Layer 3 header information. This allows for decreased latency through the network path (that is, faster packet forwarding).

Service providers use MPLS technologies to allow each customer's routing information to be isolated from every other customer's routing information within the provider cloud. For this reason, MPLS networks are called MPLS VPNs. The addition of the VPN designation denotes a secure and reliable transport. This is the case with an MPLS VPN. The routes advertised within an enterprise network are advertised to the MPLS network, which are then redistributed into what amounts to a customer-specific instance of BGP configured throughout the provider network. Routes are tagged with a specific Route Descriptor (RD) that keeps them unique and separate from another company's routes inside the provider cloud.

MPLS Concepts

The concept of switching should not be foreign to anyone contemplating taking the ISCW exam by any means. MPLS is simply another methodology for switching paths of traffic. Rather than looking into Layer 3 headers, the MPLS devices need only look at labels. This gives MPLS Layer 3 protocol independence. The label on an inbound packet is examined and compared to a label database. Based on the information therein, a new label is attached and the packet is transmitted out the appropriate interface. Figure 8-6 illustrates this concept.

Figure 8-6   *MPLS Label Switching*

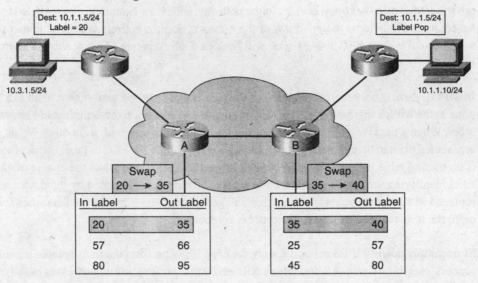

Figure 8-6 shows a pair of core routers labeled A and B. Two additional routers exist on the edges of the MPLS cloud. The traffic flow is sourced from the host on the far left and destined for the host on the far right. Each router builds a label database that ties destination subnets to a label tag. There is an inbound and an outbound label entry in the table associated with each destination. For this reason, they are called Label Switching Routers (LSRs).

As Figure 8-6 shows, the core routers do not participate in the routing table lookup. The initial edge router performs the routing lookup and attaches the egress label. Once the packet is dispatched, it travels from device to device where a forwarding decision is made solely on the basis of the label. The LSRs in the core see only the ingress label and replace it with an appropriate egress label prior to forwarding the packet to the next-hop device. The final edge router "pops" (removes) the label from the packet and performs a new routing table lookup prior to forwarding the packet on to its destination.

At times, an LSR immediately prior to the destination edge router will pop the label before sending the packet to the final edge LSR or node. This is known as a *penultimate hop pop* of the label. This is advantageous at times, because the final edge device does not need to perform both a label lookup and a network layer routing lookup once it figures out that it is the last hop prior to the destination.

Router Switching Mechanisms

The underlying mechanism for MPLS switching is provided in Cisco IOS Software by Cisco Express Forwarding (CEF). To understand the evolution of CEF, a short discussion of other IOS switching mechanisms is in order:

- **Process switching**—Each packet is processed individually and a full routing table lookup is performed prior to packet dispatch. This is the slowest and most resource-intensive method of packet forwarding.

- **Cache-driven switching**—Packet destinations are stored in memory and used for packet forwarding. For a particular destination, the first packet is process switched and an entry is made in a fast-switching cache in router memory so that the routing table may be bypassed for packets with identical destination addresses.

- **Topology-driven switching**—A prebuilt Forwarding Information Base (FIB) is assembled and used for high-speed switching operations at Layer 3.

Standard IP Switching

In terms of process and cache-driven switching, the routing process is relatively straightforward. Within the enterprise network, an Interior Gateway Protocol (IGP) will be used. To connect to an external autonomous system (AS), an Exterior Gateway Protocol (EGP) is used. In most cases, the selected EGP is the Border Gateway Protocol (BGP). To advertise reachability to enterprise prefixes, routes are redistributed between the two entities, so long as the routes in question are outside the scopes defined by RFC 1918. That is, the routes must be considered publicly routable if advertised into the Internet.

For a route to be added into the BGP routing table, the routing table of the IGP must know about that route first. Otherwise, BGP will not see it as a valid route, even though it will be listed in the table.

When BGP receives an update from a neighbor advertising a new prefix, an entry is made in the BGP table if it is selected as the best route, or equal to the best route, to that destination based on metric calculations.

When, for the first time, a packet arrives destined for a network associated with the newly added prefix, the router searches the fast-switching cache to see if an entry already exists. Not finding one, the router performs a routing table lookup to find the egress interface and next-hop address. The packet is then dispatched and a new entry is added to the fast-switching cache reflecting the new destination.

Subsequent packets destined for that same destination will be spared the delay associated with a recursive routing table lookup needed for process switching. The fast-switching cache will contain the entry associating the outbound interface and next-hop address. The fast-switching process occurs in interrupt code, which means the packet is processed immediately. The appropriate Layer 2 encapsulation type is assembled from a pre-generated header that already contains the appropriate Layer 2 source and destination addresses. No Address Resolution Protocol (ARP) request or ARP cache lookup need be performed, as that information was obtained for the first packet and stored in the fast-switching cache as well. For this reason, however, fast switching has a difficult time dealing effectively with load-balanced link situations.

Entries in the fast-switching cache are not maintained for unlimited amounts of time. They do age out after 60 seconds. If an entry is not used and ages out, the next packet destined for the destination network in question will need to be process switched so that the information can be reacquired.

CEF Switching

CEF is a topology-driven technology and makes use of a FIB. The FIB is basically a mirror image of the IP routing table. When topological changes occur, the FIB is updated based on the updates in the IP routing table. The FIB maintains next-hop address information based on information provided by the protocol routing table. Because CEF maintains a one-to-one listing of routes in the IP routing table, the need for constant maintenance of FIB entries is eliminated because that function is provided by the Layer 3 routing protocol. CEF simply cheats and copies its work.

Updates to the CEF FIB are not packet-triggered. They are change-triggered. As the IP routing table converges, the CEF FIB is also updated. This update mechanism is dependent upon, but separate from, the algorithm used by the routing protocol for update maintenance whether the protocol is link-state or distance vector.

The FIB differs from a fast-switching cache in that it does not contain information regarding the egress interface and corresponding Layer 2 encapsulation information. CEF maintains an adjacency table for this purpose. Nodes are said to be *adjacent* if they are able to make contact across a single Layer 2 connection. Adjacencies are built at Layer 2 and linked to the FIB, thereby eliminating any need for ARP requests. As adjacencies are discovered, the adjacency table is updated along with pertinent information regarding the adjacent device.

Enabling CEF on Internet-facing devices is not a decision to be taken lightly if the Internet routing table is to be redistributed into that router, due to the sheer size of the job. The Internet routing table is well in excess of 200,000 routes and 24,000 autonomous systems at the time of this writing. The amount of processing and memory it takes to maintain the routing table is enormous.

On high-end routers, CEF can be run in distributed mode. This allows routers such as the Cisco 12000 GSR router to run independent CEF instances on each blade, thereby increasing the independence of the blade and reducing load on the central routing table and FIB. This provides a faster, more efficient switching environment.

Foundation Summary

MPLS provides a Layer 3 WAN alternative to traditional Layer 2 WAN technologies. It allows a secure, dynamic extension of an enterprise network across a service provider network. It also provides the network team in charge of the enterprise network some control over traffic classifications and prioritizations. This allows for preferential treatment of critical and time-sensitive traffic over the WAN. Table 8-2 provides a brief review of traditional WAN topologies.

Table 8-2 *Traditional WAN Topologies*

Topology	Pros	Cons
Hub-and-spoke	Low-cost connectivity to all sites	Single point of failure at hub site can impact network service dramatically
Partial mesh	Moderate cost balanced with some redundancy in connectivity	Potential for significant service impact due to outages at key sites
Full mesh	Fully redundant; no site dependent on any other for connectivity	High cost
Redundant hub-and-spoke	More redundant than traditional hub-and-spoke with moderate incremental cost	Like a partial mesh, there is significant potential for service impact with the loss of key sites

Table 8-3 provides a brief review of the switching mechanisms in Cisco IOS Software.

Table 8-3 *Cisco IOS Switching Mechanisms*

Switching Mechanism	Pros	Cons
Process switching	Recursive routing lookup. Up-to-date information at all times.	Slow and inefficient repetition of lookups.
Fast switching (a.k.a cache-driven)	Interrupt code driven and significantly faster than process switching.	First packet is process switched. Difficulty with load balancing.
CEF switching (a.k.a topology-driven)	Full load balancing capable on per-packet basis or based on source address, destination address, or other characteristics.	High memory and CPU utilization. Should not be enabled on routers with insufficient horsepower.

Q&A

The questions and scenarios in this book are designed to be challenging and to make sure that you know the answer. Rather than allowing you to derive the answers from clues hidden inside the questions themselves, the questions challenge your understanding and recall of the subject.

Hopefully, mastering these questions will help you limit the number of exam questions on which you narrow your choices to two options, and then guess.

You can find the answers to these questions in Appendix A. For more practice with exam-like question formats, use the exam engine on the CD-ROM.

1. Describe, generically, the process of process switching a packet.

2. How is process switching different from fast switching?

3. Describe the process of packet switching with CEF as opposed to process switching and/or fast switching.

4. What is an MPLS label stack?

5. Describe the concept of a PHP.

6. Consider a network deployed using a full-mesh topology with Frame Relay versus one deployed using MPLS. Both provide any-to-any connectivity. What is the benefit of MPLS over Frame Relay in this regard?

7. In MPLS networks, where are full routing table lookups performed for packets in transit?

8. When is a CEF-FIB updated?

Exam Topic List

This chapter covers the following topics that you need to master for the CCNP ISCW exam:

- **MPLS Components**—Describes the basic, underlying architecture of MPLS

- **MPLS Labels**—Describes label format and use

- **Label Switching Routers**—Describes the role of LSRs in an MPLS network

- **Label Allocation in Frame Mode MPLS Networks**—Explains how label information is constructed in the router

- **Label Distribution**—Describes the process of label propagation

CHAPTER 9

MPLS Architecture

Multiprotocol Label Switching (MPLS) is growing in popularity as a technological replacement for traditional WAN deployments. MPLS provides a fully Layer 3 environment and the ability to fully mesh sites across WAN connections. This is an immense advance in terms of latency reduction and topological resilience. MPLS extends the reach of the enterprise network across the provider network. This includes routing information as well as quality of service (QoS) protection of critical network traffic types and the possibility of numerous "in the cloud" services offered by service providers such as VPN remote access, firewall, and content-filtering services.

"Do I Know This Already?" Quiz

The purpose of the "Do I Know This Already?" quiz is to help you decide whether you really need to read the entire chapter. If you already intend to read the entire chapter, you do not necessarily need to answer these questions now.

The 14-question quiz, derived from the major sections in the "Foundation Topics" portion of the chapter, helps you to determine how to spend your limited study time.

Table 9-1 outlines the major topics discussed in this chapter and the "Do I Know This Already?" quiz questions that correspond to those topics.

Table 9-1 *"Do I Know This Already?" Foundation Topics Section-to-Question Mapping*

Foundation Topics Section	Questions Covered in This Section	Score
MPLS Components	1–3	
MPLS Labels	4–5	
Label Switching Routers	6–7	
Label Allocation in Frame Mode MPLS Networks	8–10	
Label Distribution	11–14	
Total Score		

> **CAUTION** The goal of self-assessment is to gauge your mastery of the topics in this chapter. If you do not know the answer to a question or are only partially sure of the answer, you should mark this question wrong for purposes of self-assessment. Giving yourself credit for an answer that you correctly guess skews your self-assessment results and might provide you with a false sense of security.

1. Which of the following is the underlying architectural component of MPLS that deals with maintaining routing information and label exchange?

    a. FIB

    b. LFIB

    c. Control plane

    d. Data plane

2. Which of the following is the underlying architectural component of MPLS that deals with traffic forwarding based on destination address or label?

    a. FIB

    b. LFIB

    c. Control plane

    d. Data plane

3. Which of the following MPLS architectural components would deal with protocols such as OSPF and RSVP?

    a. Control plane

    b. Data plane

    c. LIB

    d. MPLS TE

4. MPLS labels are associated with which of the following to more efficiently forward packets?

    a. FEC

    b. FECN

    c. LDP

    d. FIB

5. In number of bits, how long is an MPLS label?

    a. 20 bits

    b. 3 bits

    c. 32 bits

    d. 8 bits

6. An MPLS node that is capable of performing a label lookup and replacement is known as which of the following?

   a. LSP

   b. LSR

   c. CE

   d. PE

7. Which of the following is a device that adds or removes labels in the course of its normal operation?

   a. LSP

   b. Edge LSR

   c. CE

   d. PHP

8. Which MPLS table exists in the control plane and provides the database of label information learned from neighbors?

   a. LIB

   b. LFIB

   c. FIB

   d. FLIB

9. Which of the following is populated from the IGP routing table and used in forwarding labeled packets?

   a. LIB

   b. FIB

   c. LFIB

   d. LDP

10. Which of the following is used in forwarding unlabeled packets?

    a. LIB

    b. FIB

    c. LFIB

    d. LDP

11. MPLS architecture allows for two ways of propagating label information. Which are they?

    a. Extension of existing protocol functionality

    b. Static routes

    c. Creation of new protocols designed for label exchange

    d. Reconfiguration of network devices to manually input label information

12. The decision to assign a label to a particular FEC is made by which of the following?

    a. LSR

    b. PE

    c. CE

    d. MP-BGP

13. When no label exists on a packet traversing the network and individual LSRs find that they must forward the packet based solely on FIB lookup, this is known as which of the following?

    a. Interim packet propagation

    b. Packet propagation

    c. Penultimate hop popping

    d. Label allocation

14. When a path exists between a particular source and destination and all LSRs in the path have label entries for that source and destination, a tunnel is created known as which of the following?

    a. LSP

    b. LSR

    c. MPLS-LDP

    d. MPLS-TE

The answers to the "Do I Know This Already?" quiz are found in Appendix A, "Answers to the 'Do I Know This Already?' Quizzes and Q&A Sections." The suggested choices for your next step are as follows:

- **9 or fewer overall score**—Read the entire chapter. This includes the "Foundation Topics," "Foundation Summary," and "Q&A" sections.

- **10 or 11 overall score**—Begin with the "Foundation Summary" section, and then go to the "Q&A" section.

- **12 or more overall score**—If you want more review on these topics, skip to the "Foundation Summary" section, and then go to the "Q&A" section. Otherwise, move to the next chapter.

Foundation Topics

MPLS Components

Chapter 8 covered most of the terminology involved with MPLS. However, not all of the concepts were touched upon. It is doubtful that any one or two chapters could cover MPLS technology completely and remain within the scope of the exam topic coverage.

In terms of underlying architecture, MPLS has separated traditional routing mechanisms into two major components:

- **Control plane**—Maintains routing and label information exchange between adjacent devices

- **Data plane**—Forwards traffic based on destination addresses or labels (also known as the forwarding plane)

The control plane deals with the complexities of routing in general. It includes routing protocols such as Open Shortest Path First (OSPF), Enhanced Interior Gateway Routing Protocol (EIGRP), Intermediate System-to-Intermediate System (IS-IS) Protocol, Border Gateway Protocol (BGP), and so on.

Aside from typical routing protocols, there are label-based routing protocol equivalents known as Tag Distribution Protocol (TDP) and Label Distribution Protocol (LDP). TDP is an early predecessor of LDP. The typical practice of Cisco is to create a solution to a technological problem when there is no accepted standard methodology or solution. Once a standardized solution is available, Cisco adopts it, abandoning its proprietary or interim solution. Such is the case with TDP. TDP is an early Cisco proprietary protocol that was put in place in the absence of an approved or adopted standard protocol. When LDP was ratified, Cisco dropped TDP altogether.

Resource Reservation Protocol (RSVP) is used by MPLS to provide an MPLS Traffic Engineering (MPLS TE) mechanism that allows reservation of bandwidth throughout the MPLS network. RSVP allocates bandwidth on demand, if available, for a requesting entity. This is typically used for voice traffic or other highly critical or time-sensitive traffic definition.

The data plane exists for the sole purpose of forwarding traffic based on information gleaned from the routing protocol or LDP. A Label Forwarding Information Base (LFIB) is created to store label information for use by the forwarding engine in dispatching packets toward their destinations. The LFIB is built by information from sources including LDP, BGP, and RSVP, or some combination thereof.

To aid comprehension of the relationship between the two planes, some discussion of the label itself is in order, as covered in the section that follows.

MPLS Labels

MPLS, like traditional routing, is destination-based in nature. MPLS labels function to separate forwarding operations from Layer 3 destinations contained in packet headers. By associating a label with a forwarding equivalence class (FEC), labels become a highly efficient source of forwarding information.

As discussed in Chapter 8, an FEC is a group of IP packets that are forwarded in the same manner, over the same path, and with the same forwarding treatment per-hop. An FEC might correspond to a destination IP network or to any traffic class that the LSR considers significant. Each LSR in an LSP will sort packets into FECs and assign labels to those packets accordingly.

Labels define destination, certainly. However, they also define service level. Various traffic types can be classified based on a service level agreement (SLA) per traffic type. These SLAs can be negotiated with service providers. The service provider has the benefit of being able to build the MPLS network once, and then sell its services over and over again. It is to their benefit, ultimately, to engineer it properly and negotiate sane, achievable SLAs.

Labels are added to packets by edge LSRs. In many cases, the provider edge (PE) router is the edge LSR that adds the label. However, this is not always the case. The provider's architecture determines the location of the edge LSRs. Figure 9-1 illustrates the placement of MPLS routers in the network.

PE routers interface directly with customer edge (CE) routers, which are typically customer premises equipment (CPE). CE routers are usually configured with a Frame Relay local loop to reach the PE router, but the Frame Relay stops there. The connection from CE to PE is a Layer 3 exchange simply using Frame Relay as a Layer 2 transport. The whole of the path from the ingress PE to the egress PE is known as the label-switched path (LSP).

The MPLS Label provides a mechanism by which packets can be sorted into their various FECs without the need for examination of the Layer 3 header. Each LSP along the path uses the label to make forwarding decisions for each packet. The label is inserted (or imposed) between the Layer 2 header and the Layer 3 header. This is known as *frame mode MPLS*. Figure 9-2 shows the structure of an MPLS label.

Figure 9-1 *MPLS Routers*

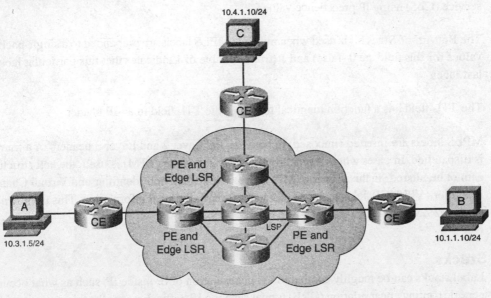

Figure 9-2 *MPLS Label Structure*

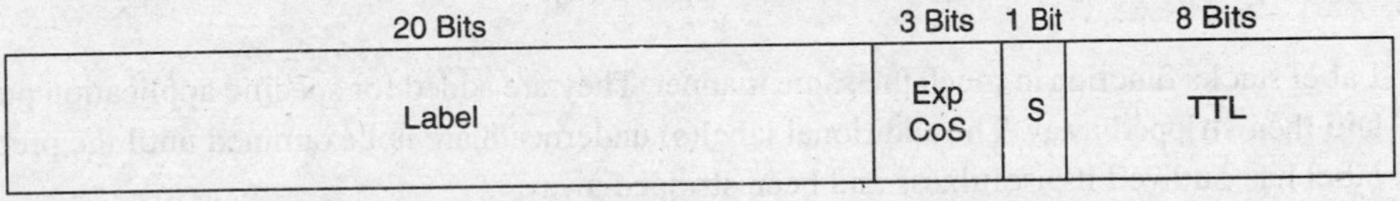

20 Bits	3 Bits	1 Bit	8 Bits
Label	Exp CoS	S	TTL

As evident in the figure, the label has a simple structure. The goal of MPLS was to reduce the amount of information needed to forward packets while eliminating a dependence on knowing the Layer 3 header information. This allows Layer 3 protocol independence.

The label itself is a four-octet (32-bit) structure, including the following fields:

- Label—20 bits

- Experimental CoS—3 bits

- Bottom of Stack Indicator—1 bit

- Time To Live (TTL)—8 bits

The Label field itself can contain values between 0 and 1,048,575; however, the values from 0 to 15 are reserved for future use. Therefore, 16 is the first available Label value.

The use of the Experimental CoS field is undefined in RFC 3031. Cisco uses this field for class of service (CoS) using IP precedence values.

The Bottom-of-Stack bit is used when multiple MPLS labels are prepended to a single packet. The values for this field are 0 (false) and 1 (true). A value of 1 indicates that this particular label is the last label.

The TTL field has a function identical to that of the TTL field in an IP header.

MPLS labels are inserted (imposed) in between the Layer 2 and Layer 3 headers of a frame as it is dispatched. In cases where Asynchronous Transfer Mode (ATM) is used, the cell structure cannot be altered. In this scenario, MPLS uses the Virtual Path Identifier and Virtual Channel Identifier (VPI/VCI) fields in the ATM header to carry the label information. This is known as *cell mode MPLS*.

Label Stacks

Label stacks can be roughly compared to encapsulation of IP inside IP, such as what occurs in a generic routing encapsulation (GRE) tunnel carrying IP traffic. Essentially, this amounts to IP over IP. For each packet in the tunnel, there are two IP headers, yet only the first one is used in making routing decisions—that is, until the packet reaches the tunnel destination. At that point, the extra IP header is no longer of any use and is stripped away.

Label stacks function in much the same manner. They are added for specific application purposes and then stripped away. The additional label(s) underneath are not examined until the preceding label has outlived its usefulness and been stripped away.

The use of labels is relatively straightforward in a typical MPLS design. It is possible that some scenarios would include the use of multiple labels to accomplish a particular purpose. Some of the most common of these scenarios are as follows:

■ **MPLS VPNs**—Multiprotocol BGP (MPBGP) is used to propagate label information relevant to a second label added to packets that identifies a particular VPN. This second label is imposed along with the initial MPLS label.

■ **MPLS TE**—MPLS Traffic Engineering (TE) uses RSVP to establish LSP tunnels. RSVP propagates additional label information relevant to labels used to identify the LSP tunnels. These labels are imposed in a label stack on top of the primary MPLS label.

■ **MPLS VPNs with MPLS TE**—Three (or more) labels are imposed into a frame. These include the primary MPLS label, a VPN label, and an LSP label.

- A received labeled packet is forwarded based on the label; however, the LFIB shows that this edge LSR is the egress MPLS edge. Therefore the label is popped and the packet routed normally.

If a received labeled packet is dropped, this is symptomatic of a lack of an LFIB entry, even if the destination exists in the routing table.

Similarly, a received IP packet might be dropped if there is no routing entry in the routing table even if the entry does exist in the LFIB for the destination.

Label Allocation in Frame Mode MPLS Networks

Over the course of Chapter 8 and a good portion of this chapter, the forwarding process has been discussed. In each discussion, a new facet of information has been added to the overall discussion to expand comprehension. This section serves to bring together the concepts discussed up to this point.

The traditional functions of both routed and routing protocols are leveraged in an MPLS environment. While it should be understood that MPLS is Layer 3 protocol independent, the discussions herein will focus on IP as the protocol of choice.

When all routers in an internetwork have built a routing table, which includes all destinations within that internetwork, it is said that *convergence* has occurred. Convergence is temperamental at best and is measured differently by different routing protocols. An event that causes the devices in an internetwork to reconverge can have far-reaching effects with regard to network reachability. If critical resources become unreachable due to unstable network conditions, there may be considerable business impact.

LIB, LFIB, and FIB

The LIB, LFIB, and FIB are designations that have nothing to do with political beliefs or untruths, large or small. Neither are they evolutionary results of each other. Well, not in the Darwinian sense, anyway. They are somewhat interconnected and interdependent, however. This is mentioned simply because these are among the most common responses to the introduction of the concepts of all three.

Proper configuration of an advanced routing protocol can limit the effects of convergence on the internetwork. This is desirable simply due to the fact that while a router is processing routing protocol update information, it is not routing traffic. This tends to project negativity into the minds of many regarding the state of the internetwork in general.

MPLS depends on the underlying routing protocol to glean the information it requires to construct the LFIB. The LFIB is essentially the label routing table. Labels are shared through distribution protocols, but the information is built based on the IP routing table information. If the IP network experiences convergence issues or other types of instability, the MPLS network will be affected in a like manner.

Once the IP routing table is built and the network is converged, each LSR assigns labels to each network destination represented in the routing table. These assigned labels are only locally significant and stored in a Label Information Base (LIB). The LSR then announces its assigned labels to its adjacent peers, who, in turn, propagate the information to their peers. Peers use received label information to associate next-hop label information with network destinations. This information is stored in the Forwarding Information Base (FIB) and Label Forwarding Information Base (LFIB). Each LSR builds its LIB, LFIB, and FIB based on received labels.

It is worth noting that only service provider networks will experience label allocation, imposition, swapping, and/or popping. A typical enterprise network has no need to see the labels.

The LIB is part of the control plane and provides the database used by LDP for label distribution. This is where IP prefixes are associated with their local and next-hop label entries learned from downstream peers. The LIB maintains the mapping between the IP prefix, the assigned label, and the assigning label.

The LFIB is part of the data plane and provides the database used in forwarding labeled packets. The IGP is used to populate the routing tables in all MPLS routers throughout the network. Based on information shared in IGP routing updates, each router determines the path with the most attractive metric for a given network destination.

Locally generated labels previously advertised to upstream peers are mapped to labels for those destinations received from upstream peers. This provides both ingress and egress labels for traffic flowing bidirectionally between a particular source and destination. It is modified to contain the local label mapped to the forwarding action or interface. If the destination is untagged, there is no label for the particular destination. Therefore, the packet will be routed rather than label switched. Example 9-1 provides a brief example of an LFIB received from a downstream peer.

Example 9-1 *LFIB Example*

```
BM2821#show mpls forwarding-table
Local   Outgoing     Prefix         Bytes tag   Outgoing     Next Hop
tag     tag or VC    or Tunnel Id   switched    interface
16      Pop tag      1.1.1.1/32     0           Gi0/1        10.10.1.1
17      Pop tag      2.2.2.2/32     0           Gi0/1        10.10.1.1
18      Pop tag      3.3.3.3/32     0           Gi0/1        10.10.1.1
BM2821#
```

In Example 9-1, the highlighted text shows the information relevant to the tag switch. In this case, the output shows that the inbound tag is 16 while the outbound is Pop tag. This indicates that the LSR in question is to remove the tag altogether. Also shown in the output is the destination network, outbound interface, and next-hop IP address.

The FIB is also part of the data plane and provides the database used in forwarding unlabeled IP packets. This essentially amounts to the IP routing table itself. If a next-hop destination is reached via a non-MPLS-enabled outbound interface, the FIB information is used, ignoring the LIB and LFIB information. Figure 9-4 revisits the concept of label switching.

Figure 9-4 *Label Switching*

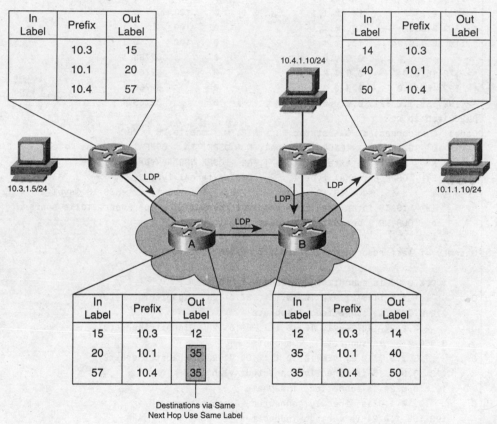

In all routers in Figure 9-4, the IP routing protocol has reached a state of convergence. The LIB, LFIB, and FIB are all properly constructed through routing protocol and LDP updates. The routing protocol advertises IP subnet destinations while the LSRs construct label information for each learned destination. Example 9-2 demonstrates the BGP and OSPF FIBs.

Example 9-2 *BGP and OSPF FIBs*

```
BM2821#sh ip bgp
BGP table version is 11, local router ID is 192.168.1.1
Status codes: s suppressed, d damped, h history, * valid, > best, i - internal,
              r RIB-failure, S Stale
Origin codes: i - IGP, e - EGP, ? - incomplete

   Network          Next Hop           Metric LocPrf Weight Path
*>i1.1.1.1/32       10.10.1.1               0    100      0 i
*>i2.2.2.2/32       10.10.1.1               0    100      0 i
*>i3.3.3.3/32       10.10.1.1               0    100      0 i
* i10.10.1.0/24     10.10.1.1               0    100      0 i
*>                  0.0.0.0                 0         32768 i
*> 172.16.0.0       0.0.0.0                 0         32768 i
*> 192.168.1.0      0.0.0.0                 0         32768 i
*> 192.168.1.2/32   0.0.0.0                 0         32768 ?
BM2821#sh ip ro
Codes: C - connected, S - static, R - RIP, M - mobile, B - BGP
       D - EIGRP, EX - EIGRP external, O - OSPF, IA - OSPF inter area
       N1 - OSPF NSSA external type 1, N2 - OSPF NSSA external type 2
       E1 - OSPF external type 1, E2 - OSPF external type 2
       i - IS-IS, su - IS-IS summary, L1 - IS-IS level-1, L2 - IS-IS level-2
       ia - IS-IS inter area, * - candidate default, U - per-user static route
       o - ODR, P - periodic downloaded static route

Gateway of last resort is 172.16.0.1 to network 0.0.0.0

     1.0.0.0/32 is subnetted, 1 subnets
O       1.1.1.1 [110/2] via 10.10.1.1, 00:01:23, GigabitEthernet0/1
     2.0.0.0/32 is subnetted, 1 subnets
O       2.2.2.2 [110/2] via 10.10.1.1, 00:01:23, GigabitEthernet0/1
     3.0.0.0/32 is subnetted, 1 subnets
O       3.3.3.3 [110/2] via 10.10.1.1, 00:01:23, GigabitEthernet0/1
C    172.16.0.0/16 is directly connected, Vlan1
     10.0.0.0/24 is subnetted, 1 subnets
C       10.10.1.0 is directly connected, GigabitEthernet0/1
     192.168.1.0/24 is variably subnetted, 2 subnets, 2 masks
C       192.168.1.0/24 is directly connected, Vlan100
S       192.168.1.2/32 is directly connected, Service-Engine0/0
S*   0.0.0.0/0 [1/0] via 172.16.0.1
BM2821#
```

As shown in Example 9-2, the BGP routing table and the OSPF routing table are in agreement regarding the reachable subnets. This information is used to build the LFIB used by MPLS. The highlighted portion of the example is consistent with the **show mpls forwarding-table** command in Example 9-1.

Label Distribution

By now, it is clear that the processes of label switching and distribution are shockingly similar to routing in a traditional sense. This is true with the significant exception that label switching and distribution do not have any need to analyze network layer information. When the edge LSR adds the label, the packet is predestined to arrive at its appropriate end. This greatly increases the efficiency of the routing process overall.

MPLS does add overhead in the form of additional communication between adjacent routers. Aside from routing prefix propagation, the added functions of maintaining the LIB and LFIB along with an adjacency table can use significant resources. In terms of memory utilization, for example, BGP uses approximately 72 MB of router memory for every 100,000 prefixes. With the Internet routing table at roughly 215,000 prefixes at the time of this writing, it is conceivable that the BGP table alone might use around 150 MB of memory. When CEF, LDP, and other processes are added to that, it is easy to see how a resource shortage might come into being for a given router. This also reflects a compelling case for being careful when enabling the propagation of Internet routes.

Label distribution is performed by a label distribution protocol. In fact, whether due to lack of originality or simply a love of the Keep It Simple Stupid (KISS) principal, the protocol is aptly named MPLS Label Distribution Protocol (MPLS-LDP). The assumption should be made from this point forward that the term "LDP" is meant to refer to MPLS-LDP. This clarification is necessary because a number of other methodologies of label propagation are being explored. For example, MP-BGP can piggyback labels on BGP routing updates due to standards extensions made to the BGP structure. With that in mind, it is important to mention that MPLS architecture does allow for two ways of propagating the needed additional information:

■ Extend functionality of existing protocols

■ Create a new protocol or protocols dedicated to the task of label exchange

Extending the functionality of an existing protocol requires a great deal of time and effort. This is especially true for protocols such as BGP and OSPF, both of which already have a multiprotocol version. However, the wide adoption of both protocols prior to the extensions would require that the new version be implemented throughout an internetwork in order to introduce label exchange. This would require a great deal of work and testing before, during, and after the upgrade.

The Internet Engineering Taskforce (IETF) has taken the second approach to the matter. LDP is implemented in the control plane and exchanges labels with neighbors, storing the results in the LIB.

In the MPLS architecture, the decision to assign a particular label to a particular FEC is made by the LSR at each hop along the way. The downstream LSR informs the upstream LSR of its decided label for that FEC. Essentially, this implies that labels are downstream-assigned as route entries come from the downstream side. So, traffic flow is a factor in the decision. It should be noted that upstream and downstream are subjective terms relating to the direction of traffic flow. Assuming that traffic flows bidirectionally, labels will be propagating in both directions. Also, the concept behind split horizon is in play as well because labels are distributed only in the downstream direction. This will have the effect of a label not being advertised to the neighbor from whom it was learned. The FIB is subject to split horizon from a pure routing perspective, therefore the LIB and LFIB will be subject to split horizon as well by default. The two LSRs that happen to be label distribution peers are said to have a *label distribution adjacency* between them.

Label distribution can occur in two basic manners: unsolicited downstream and downstream-on-demand. The names are essentially what they denote. An MPLS neighbor can receive an update due to a convergence event (unsolicited) or it can request an update from a neighbor. This might occur when a label is not present for a particular FEC. Advanced routing protocols, such as EIGRP, will request a route for a destination for which it does not have an entry when a packet arrives destined for said destination.

Packet Propagation

An inbound packet may be forwarded in a number of ways, including with and without label imposition.

Incoming labeled packets are forwarded by the LFIB and sent out as labeled packets. The far-end edge LSR will pop the label unless PHP has been implemented. The section "Further Label Allocation" discusses PHP in more detail.

An unlabeled packet can be labeled and forwarded by an edge LSR. There are exceptions to this during network convergence or other conditions that result in incomplete destination information. This exception is dealt with by interim packet propagation.

Interim Packet Propagation

When a packet arrives at an LSR prior to said LSR knowing of a label associated with the necessary FEC to get the packet out, the packet is forwarded based on information stored in the FIB. The packet is, of course, forwarded to the next-hop router listed in the FIB. The receiving downstream router performs a lookup and determines whether it has a label associated with the needed FEC. If so, the receiving downstream router imposes the label and sends the packet on its way. If not, the process repeats itself. It is conceivable, though unlikely, that the router might be CEF switched all the way across the network.

The reasoning behind this functionality is to allow packet forwarding in times of convergence or other situations where MPLS routers have no labels for a particular FEC.

Further Label Allocation

Routers are routers. They route and they switch and they forward. It seems that these terms have evolved into synonyms of a sort in recent years. The job of a router is to find paths and make use of them.

When MPLS has a path from point A to point B, a label-switched path (LSP) is created. The LSP is essentially a tunnel between source and destination for a particular FEC. Zooming out, it would look more like a tunnel with many forks in the road, because it is feasible for two FECs to share a label at one point, then diverge at another. For a given destination or FEC, however, the end-to-end path is built. LSRs from edge to edge will contain labels for a particular FEC. This allows the implementation of a penultimate hop popping (PHP) of the label.

PHP is a relatively simple feature that was implemented with efficiency in mind. On an egress edge LSR, an LFIB lookup is performed on an inbound labeled packet. If the destination network is a directly connected network, there will not be a label defined for the destination. Therefore, the label is popped and a FIB table lookup is initiated. This redundant lookup is cumbersome.

PHP allows the LSR immediately prior to the edge LSR to pop the label; hence the term penultimate hop pop.

When the downstream router realizes that it is the second-to-last node in the LSP, it can distribute a label value of 3 to the upstream router. As a reminder, label values of 0–15 are reserved. This type of operation and other similar features will use these label values.

When the upstream router makes the next hop determination and sees that the label value is 3, it will remove the label and forward the packet normally. The LIB in the upstream router will read as imp-null in such a case rather than a value of 3 actually showing up in the table itself. The value of 3 is assumed with imp-null. Example 9-3 demonstrates how that would look in the router.

Example 9-3 *The MPLS LIB*

```
BM2821#show mpls ip binding
  0.0.0.0/0
        in label:      imp-null
  1.1.1.1/32
        in label:      16
        out label:     imp-null  lsr: 10.10.1.1:0        inuse
  2.2.2.2/32
        in label:      17
        out label:     imp-null  lsr: 10.10.1.1:0        inuse
  3.3.3.3/32
        in label:      18
        out label:     imp-null  lsr: 10.10.1.1:0        inuse
  10.10.1.0/24
        in label:      imp-null
        out label:     imp-null  lsr: 10.10.1.1:0
  172.16.0.0/16
        in label:      imp-null
        out label:     16        lsr: 10.10.1.1:0
  192.168.1.0/24
        in label:      imp-null
        out label:     17        lsr: 10.10.1.1:0
  192.168.1.2/32
        in label:      imp-null
        out label:     18        lsr: 10.10.1.1:0
BM2821#
```

Foundation Summary

MPLS is not a difficult subject to grasp conceptually. It amounts to essentially another routing process without all the overhead or useless information. It should be noted that said useless information is only useless to devices whose sole wish is to forward things regardless of what they contain. All that matters is label-in, FEC, and label-out.

MPLS essentially breaks into two components, as outlined in Table 9-2.

Table 9-2 *MPLS Planes*

Plane	Purpose
Control plane	Exchange routing information and labels
Data plane	Forward packets based on labels

Several tables are constructed in the MPLS architectures. Table 9-3 provides some review of those tables.

Table 9-3 *MPLS Information Bases*

Table	Built By	Contains	Purpose
FIB	IGP routing processes	Known destination prefixes, outbound interfaces, and next-hop addresses	Maps destination networks to next-hop address and outbound interface. Also forwards unlabeled packets.
LIB	LDP or other label distribution method	Local labels, FEC, LDP information	Associate local labels with FECs. Also performs label distribution to adjacent peers.
LFIB	IGP and LDP information	Label-in, FEC, out-interface, label-out	Database used to forward labeled packets to next-hop addresses.
Adjacency table	Forming of neighbor relationship	Out-Interface and encapsulation along with neighbor ARP information	Maintain needed layer 2 information as well as LDP exchange capabilities.

Q&A

The questions and scenarios in this book are more difficult than what you will experience on the actual exam. The questions do not attempt to cover more breadth or depth than the exam, but they are designed to make sure that you know the answer. Rather than enabling you to derive the answer from clues hidden inside the question itself, the questions challenge your understanding and recall of the subject.

Hopefully, mastering these questions will help you limit the number of exam questions on which you narrow your choices to two options, and then guess.

The answers to these questions can be found in Appendix A.

1. Describe the purpose of the control plane as it relates to routing as a process.

2. Describe the purpose of the data plane as it relates to routing as a process.

3. The process of packet forwarding in MPLS is particularly important to understand prior to any implementation. Explain the essential process of a packet traversing an LSR.

4. Explain the concept of a label stack and where it might be used.

5. Describe the structure of the label itself and the purpose of each field therein.

6. A LIB of an LSR references an entry as having a label of imp-null. What does this denote?

7. What is meant by the term frame mode MPLS?

8. List the possible actions that can be taken by an edge-LSR in making a forwarding decision.

9. Why is MPLS considered to be protocol-independent?

Exam Topic List

This chapter covers the following topics that you need to master for the CCNP ISCW exam:

- **Configuring CEF**—Describes the requirements and process for configuring CEF

- **Configuring MPLS on a Frame Mode Interface**—Describes the process of configuring Frame Mode MPLS on an interface

- **Configuring MTU Size**—Describes the process of configuring a proper MTU size on an MPLS-enabled interface

CHAPTER 10

Configuring Frame Mode MPLS

Multiprotocol Label Switching (MPLS) is experiencing a rapid expansion in deployment throughout the service provider and enterprise networking industries. The move to a Layer 3 WAN has allowed the offering of applications and services thought impossible up to now. This fits well with the Service-Oriented Network Architecture (SONA) framework in that the same applications and services offered at central or headquarters sites can now be easily extended to the branch office, the home office, and even the mobile client. The goal of creating a single network experience regardless of method of accessing the network is now a step closer.

Chapters 8 and 9 provided a fairly detailed description of MPLS architecture. Having addressed the basics of the technology, this chapter focuses on the basics of MPLS implementation.

"Do I Know This Already?" Quiz

The purpose of the "Do I Know This Already?" quiz is to help you decide whether you really need to read the entire chapter. If you already intend to read the entire chapter, you do not necessarily need to answer these questions now.

The 6-question quiz, derived from the major sections in the "Foundation Topics" portion of the chapter, helps you to determine how to spend your limited study time.

Table 10-1 outlines the major topics discussed in this chapter and the "Do I Know This Already?" quiz questions that correspond to those topics.

Table 10-1 *"Do I Know This Already?" Foundation Topics Section-to-Question Mapping*

Foundation Topics Section	Questions Covered in This Section	Score
Configuring CEF	1–2	
Configuring MPLS on a Frame Mode Interface	3–4	
Configuring MTU Size	5–6	
Total Score		

> **CAUTION** The goal of self-assessment is to gauge your mastery of the topics in this chapter. If you do not know the answer to a question or are only partially sure of the answer, you should mark this question wrong for purposes of self-assessment. Giving yourself credit for an answer that you correctly guess skews your self-assessment results and might provide you with a false sense of security.

1. CEF is configurable in central mode or what other mode?

   a. Distributed

   b. MPLS

   c. Fast

   d. Process

2. CEF uses which table in monitoring network destinations?

   a. LIB

   b. FIB

   c. LFIB

   d. Adjacency

3. To enable MPLS on an interface, which command should be entered at the interface configuration mode?

   a. **mpls ip**

   b. **mpls label protocol ldp**

   c. **mpls mtu 1504**

   d. **ip cef**

4. Which command would enable support for TDP and LDP on a single MPLS interface?

   a. **mpls ip**

   b. **mpls label protocol both**

   c. **mpls mtu 1504**

   d. **ip cef**

5. The alteration of the MTU on MPLS interfaces is meant to avoid issues relating to which of the following?

   a. Runts

   b. Jumbo frames

   c. Label distribution

   d. The LFIB

6. Which command is used in altering the MTU size on an MPLS interface to accommodate a two-label stack?

   a. **mtu 1508**

   b. **mpls mtu 1508**

   c. **mtu 1504**

   d. **mpls mtu 1504**

The answers to the "Do I Know This Already?" quiz are found in Appendix A, "Answers to the 'Do I Know This Already?' Quizzes and Q&A Sections." The suggested choices for your next step are as follows:

■ **2 or fewer overall score**—Read the entire chapter. This includes the "Foundation Topics," "Foundation Summary," and "Q&A" sections.

■ **3 or 4 overall score**—Begin with the "Foundation Summary" section, and then go to the "Q&A" section.

■ **5 or more overall score**—If you want more review on these topics, skip to the "Foundation Summary" section, and then go to the "Q&A" section. Otherwise, move to the next chapter.

Foundation Topics

The configuration of MPLS on a per-router basis is relatively straightforward. That is, the basic configuration is straightforward. There are a number of considerations that must be taken into account. These include the size of the network and the number of prefixes to be propagated.

MPLS and its associated overhead may be a significant hit to the resources of a router. In a typical service provider model, the router should expect to hold the full Internet routing table, which is well in excess of 200,000 prefixes. Typically the service provider runs an Interior Gateway Protocol (IGP) such as Intermediate System-to-Intermediate System (IS-IS) and an Exterior Gateway Protocol (EGP) such as Border Gateway Protocol (BGP). Each protocol will maintain a number of prefixes. BGP will contain all of the publicly advertised prefixes while the IGP will contain the internal destinations of the service provider network. This is a daunting amount of information to keep current. Add to that the need for Cisco Express Forwarding (CEF) information and the MPLS required Forwarding Information Base (FIB), Label Information Base (LIB), and Label Forwarding Information Base (LFIB), along with adjacency information required for IGP, EGP, and MPLS, and it is easy to see where the router may become rather overloaded.

MPLS is typically enabled on an interface-by-interface basis. There are global commands as well, certainly. The idea behind frame mode MPLS is to impose labels between the Layer 2 and Layer 3 headers. This can cause problems in large packets. The addition of four additional bytes of information might cause the frame size to exceed the Maximum Transmission Unit (MTU) defined for the interface. This will preclude such frames from traversing the router.

The procedure for enabling MPLS consists of only a few steps:

Step 1   **Configure CEF**—CEF must be enabled as a prerequisite to enabling MPLS.

Step 2   **Configure MPLS on a Frame Mode Interface**—MPLS backbone interfaces should be MPLS enabled.

Step 3   **Configure MTU sizes as needed**—To prevent frames from exceeding MTU size on the interface, the MTU should be manually adjusted in MPLS-enabled interfaces.

Configuring CEF

A Cisco proprietary switching mechanism, CEF is extremely fast and efficient. CEF is an advanced Layer 3 switching technology that optimizes the performance and stability of networks with large, dynamic traffic patterns. CEF switching is less CPU intensive than process switching or fast switching, allowing more CPU time to be allocated to services and applications.

CEF can be run in central mode or distributed mode. In central mode, only one instance of CEF is running on the router. Distributed mode CEF (called dCEF) is designed to run on high-end routers. This allows each blade in a router to run its own instance of CEF and maintain its own switching cache. This allows the ability for some percentage of traffic to be same-blade switched if source and destination interfaces are on the same blade.

As discussed in previous chapters, the FIB is a mirror copy of the routing table, containing all known routing prefixes from the routing table. CEF uses the FIB rather than a route cache to eliminate cache maintenance and fast/process switching of packets.

The FIB and adjacency tables provide the operational base for CEF. CEF uses the FIB to make IP destination switching decisions. The adjacency table keeps a database of Layer 2 information, including Layer 2 next-hop information. CEF uses the adjacency table to prepend Layer 2 information to outbound traffic. This avoids any need for Address Resolution Protocol (ARP) or other Layer 2/3 resolution processes.

CEF is enabled at the global configuration command prompt in the router. The command is as follows:

```
BM2851(config)#ip cef
```

Optionally, the command can be entered to enable CEF for distributed mode by entering

```
BM2851(config)#ip cef distributed
```

Distributed mode CEF should be used only when the router's line cards are capable of performing express forwarding. This allows the route processor (RP) on the blade to handle the switching functions.

To enable CEF operation on a particular interface, use the following command:

```
BM2851(config-if)#ip route-cache cef
```

There are no configuration options for this command. This is useful simply because the enabling of CEF in global configuration mode enables CEF on all CEF-capable interfaces. To disable CEF on interfaces where it is not desired or needed, issue the **no** form of the command.

Additional options available for CEF configuration include the following:

- **CEF load balancing**—Can be configured for per-destination or per-packet load balancing.

- **CEF network accounting**—Allows collecting of traffic statistics such as packets and bytes switched to a particular prefix.

- **CEF distributed tunnel switching**—Enabled automatically with CEF, this option allows the switching of tunnels such as GRE tunnels. This option is not configurable.

To monitor and view CEF statistics, you can use the **show ip cef** command; to view more detailed information, enter the **detail** keyword. Example 10-1 displays the resulting output from the **show ip cef detail** command.

Example 10-1 show ip cef detail *Command Output*

```
BM2851#show ip cef detail
IP CEF with switching (Table Version 21), flags=0x0
  16 routes, 0 reresolve, 0 unresolved (0 old, 0 new), peak 0
  16 leaves, 24 nodes, 27392 bytes, 29 inserts, 13 invalidations
  0 load sharing elements, 0 bytes, 0 references
  universal per-destination load sharing algorithm, id CB41AB75
  3(0) CEF resets, 0 revisions of existing leaves
  Resolution Timer: Exponential (currently 1s, peak 1s)
  0 in-place/0 aborted modifications
  refcounts:  6433 leaf, 6400 node

  Table epoch: 0 (16 entries at this epoch)


Adjacency Table has 2 adjacencies
0.0.0.0/0, version 0, epoch 0, attached, default route handler
0 packets, 0 bytes
  via 0.0.0.0, 0 dependencies
    valid no route adjacency
0.0.0.0/32, version 1, epoch 0, receive
1.1.1.1/32, version 18, epoch 0, connected, receive
  tag information set
    local tag: implicit-null
2.2.2.2/32, version 19, epoch 0, connected, receive
  tag information set
    local tag: implicit-null
3.3.3.3/32, version 20, epoch 0, connected, receive
  tag information set
    local tag: implicit-null
10.10.1.0/24, version 13, epoch 0, attached, connected
0 packets, 0 bytes
  tag information set
    local tag: implicit-null
```

Example 10-1   **show ip cef detail** *Command Output (Continued)*

```
   via GigabitEthernet0/1, 0 dependencies
     valid glean adjacency
10.10.1.0/32, version 11, epoch 0, receive
10.10.1.1/32, version 10, epoch 0, receive
10.10.1.2/32, version 14, epoch 0, connected, cached adjacency 10.10.1.2
0 packets, 0 bytes
  via 10.10.1.2, GigabitEthernet0/1, 0 dependencies
    next hop 10.10.1.2, GigabitEthernet0/1
    valid cached adjacency
10.10.1.255/32, version 12, epoch 0, receive
172.16.0.0/16, version 15, epoch 0, cached adjacency 10.10.1.2
0 packets, 0 bytes
  tag information set
    local tag: 16
  via 10.10.1.2, GigabitEthernet0/1, 0 dependencies
    next hop 10.10.1.2, GigabitEthernet0/1
    valid cached adjacency
    tag rewrite with Gi0/1, 10.10.1.2, tags imposed: {}
192.168.1.0/24, version 16, epoch 0, cached adjacency 10.10.1.2
0 packets, 0 bytes
  tag information set
    local tag: 17
  via 10.10.1.2, GigabitEthernet0/1, 0 dependencies
    next hop 10.10.1.2, GigabitEthernet0/1
    valid cached adjacency
    tag rewrite with Gi0/1, 10.10.1.2, tags imposed: {}
192.168.1.2/32, version 17, epoch 0, cached adjacency 10.10.1.2
0 packets, 0 bytes
  tag information set
    local tag: 18
  via 10.10.1.2, GigabitEthernet0/1, 0 dependencies
    next hop 10.10.1.2, GigabitEthernet0/1
    valid cached adjacency
    tag rewrite with Gi0/1, 10.10.1.2, tags imposed: {}
224.0.0.0/4, version 7, epoch 0
0 packets, 0 bytes
  via 0.0.0.0, 0 dependencies
    next hop 0.0.0.0
    valid drop adjacency
224.0.0.0/24, version 3, epoch 0, receive
255.255.255.255/32, version 2, epoch 0, receive
BM2851#
```

The **show ip cef detail** command displays summary information residing in the FIB. Each known prefix is represented along with next-hop information. Table 10-2 lists other possible parameters of the **show ip cef** command.

Table 10-2 **show ip cef** *Command Parameters*

Parameter	Description
unresolved	Displays unresolved FIB entries
summary	Displays a FIB summary
adjacency	Displays FIB entries known via a particular interface and next-hop address
A.B.C.D	Displays a FIB entry for a specific destination network
A.B.C.D A.B.C.D	Displays a FIB entry for a specific destination network and mask
longer-prefixes	Displays a FIB entry for all specified destinations
detail	Displays detailed FIB information
type number	Displays interface-specific FIB entries

Among the many commands available to monitor the CEF processes, a few other important ones are added here to provide a more complete picture.

There are times when the network becomes unstable or a single router finds itself in duress and unable to properly maintain the juggling act imposed upon it. In such circumstances, commands such as **clear adjacency**, **clear ip cef inconsistency**, and **clear cef interface** will become the friend of the network administrator. In monitoring real-time events of CEF on a particular router, **debug ip cef** and **debug ip cef events** are useful commands.

Configuring MPLS on a Frame Mode Interface

The second step of MPLS configuration entails the setting of interface parameters. This means that a label distribution protocol needs to be configured so that label information exchange can being. In some environments, the Cisco proprietary Tag Distribution Protocol (TDP) is used. TDP was used prior to the existence of a standardized label exchange mechanism. TDP is not typically used at this time. Instead, the Label Distribution Protocol (LDP) is used in most deployments.

To enable MPLS support on a router, enter the **mpls ip** command at the global configuration mode prompt. With that done, the process should be repeated on interfaces on which MPLS will run.

By default, MPLS support is enabled in Cisco routers. This can be disabled by using the **no mpls ip** command at the global configuration mode prompt. MPLS must be configured individually on a per-interface basis on interfaces that will be participating in the MPLS environment. After enabling MPLS on the interface, the label distribution protocols also must be enabled by using the **mpls label protocol** command. As has been mentioned, the Label Distribution Protocol (LDP) is responsible for the construction of the Label Information Base (LIB). Table 10-3 shows the parameters available with the **mpls label protocol** command.

Table 10-3 **mpls label protocol** *Command Parameters*

Parameter	Description
both	Use LDP or TDP (adapt to peer on multiaccess interface)
ldp	Use LDP
tdp	Use TDP

The LDP should be explicitly defined once MPLS is enabled on the interface. In older versions of Cisco IOS, the label protocol-related commands will show up as **tag-switching** commands. Many of the **tag-switching** commands are still available for backward compatibility with existing configurations. However, this will not be the case in years to come.

If no protocol is selected, LDP is set as the default protocol for label exchange. This default behavior was added in Cisco IOS Software Release 12.4(3). In prior releases, the default was set to TDP. To avoid confusion or, worse, embarrassment before network colleagues, it is best to explicitly define the protocol on the interface.

As a best practice, non-MPLS interfaces typically have access lists applied to them that block TDP and/or LDP traffic. TDP uses TCP port 711, while LDP uses UDP port 646. This is simply a precaution and reinforces the idea that this interface is not wanted in the MPLS architecture. Without the **mpls ip** command on the interface, no adjacency will form. However, it is sometimes desirable to add such commands to more strongly communicate a distinct message to colleagues who might enter the router to view the configuration once it is completed that MPLS is intentionally not enabled on the interface (and was not simply overlooked in configuration).

In a multivendor MPLS environment, should one exist, it would be prudent to ensure that TDP is not used anywhere in the network. As might be obvious, TDP is not supportable in a multivendor deployment. When in doubt, the **both** parameter is a viable alternative when enabling the label protocol.

Example 10-2 demonstrates a sample configuration of the commands addressed thus far. Portions of the configuration that are not relevant to the information addressed herein have been removed for the sake of brevity.

Example 10-2 *MPLS Sample Configuration*

```
BM2851#show running-config
Building configuration...

version 12.4
no service pad
service timestamps debug datetime msec
service timestamps log datetime msec
service password-encryption
service sequence-numbers
!
hostname BM2851
!
no logging buffered
enable secret <output removed>
!
clock timezone CST -6
clock summer-time CDT recurring
!
!
ip cef
!
interface GigabitEthernet0/1
 ip address 10.10.1.1 255.255.255.0
 duplex full
 speed 1000
 mpls label protocol ldp
 mpls ip
!
line con 0
 logging synchronous
 login local
line aux 0
line vty 0 4
 login local
 transport input telnet ssh
line vty 5 15
 login local
 transport input telnet ssh
end
BM2851#
```

Note the absence of the **mpls ip** command from the global configuration in Example 10-2. This command does, however, appear in the interface configuration. As a rule, Cisco configurations do not print commands enabled by default in the configuration. This avoids needless clutter in the configuration output.

Configuring MTU Size

As mentioned previously in this chapter, the addition of one or more labels to a packet traversing an MPLS network might cause the violation of the MTU size parameter. This is one of the most common issues experienced in MPLS deployments and should not be taken lightly by any means. The introduction of jumbo frames, giants, or baby giants, however one might wish to name them, into a LAN environment can have far-reaching effects.

This is typically only an issue on LAN interfaces where the MTU size is usually around 1500 bytes. Most WAN types today have much larger MTU sizes by default, with many of them taking on a dynamic ability to adjust.

The MTU size must be increased by a value equal to or greater than the additional byte count of the imposed label stack. Given that a label is 4 bytes in length, an MTU of 1504 may be feasible so long as only a single label is imposed. When MPLS Traffic Engineering (MPLS-TE) or MPLS VPNs have been deployed, additional size is needed. In cases where both are in use, an MTU size of 1512 is needed.

The alteration of the MTU is simple, though not typical of an MTU change. This MTU change is MPLS specific. At interface configuration mode, enter

```
BM2851(config-if)#mpls mtu 1512
```

This command sets an MTU on the interface that is specific to label switching rather than setting it for all traffic types. The valid range of MTU sizes is 64 to 65,535 bytes.

With the MTU modified, the configuration example previously presented has obviously changed. The interface configuration itself now looks like what Example 10-3 shows.

Example 10-3 *MTU Configuration*

```
!
interface GigabitEthernet0/1
 ip address 10.10.1.1 255.255.255.0
 duplex full
 speed 1000
 mpls label protocol ldp
 mpls ip
 mpls mtu 1512
!
```

Figure 10-1 provides some additional clarity in the setting of the MTU size.

Figure 10-1 *MPLS MTU Configuration Requirements*

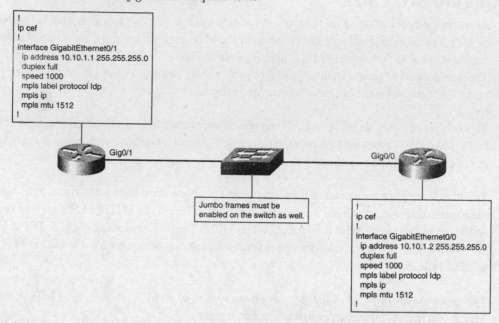

As evident in Figure 10-1, the typical MPLS configuration that has been discussed up to this point is entered on both MPLS routers. However, the switch must also be configured for jumbo frames. The command set that needs to be entered into the configuration depends on whether the switch runs CatOS or IOS software.

To ensure that LDP adjacencies have been established, the **show mpls ldp neighbor** command can be entered. Example 10-4 shows sample output from this command.

Example 10-4 **show mpls ldp neighbor** *Command Output*

```
BM2851#sh mpls ldp neighbor
    Peer LDP Ident: 192.168.1.1:0; Local LDP Ident 3.3.3.3:0
        TCP connection: 192.168.1.1.17080 - 3.3.3.3.646
        State: Oper; Msgs sent/rcvd: 17/18; Downstream
        Up time: 00:07:01
        LDP discovery sources:
          GigabitEthernet0/1, Src IP addr: 10.10.1.2
        Addresses bound to peer LDP Ident:
          172.16.0.4       192.168.1.1     10.10.1.2
BM2851#
```

In the example, only a single peer is established. The output shows that the state of the connection is operational. Also shown are the peer LDP identifiers for the remote peer.

If it becomes necessary to monitor the label exchange in real time, the **debug mpls ldp bindings** command is available. Example 10-5 provides sample output from this command.

Example 10-5 debug mpls ldp bindings *Command Output*

```
BM2851#debug mpls ldp bindings
LDP Label Information Base (LIB) changes debugging is on
BM2851#
000049: Apr 20 19:18:33.271: tib: find route tags: 10.10.1.0/24, Gi0/1, nh 0.0.0.0, res nh
  0.0.0.0
000050: Apr 20 19:18:33.271: tagcon: announce labels for: 10.10.1.0/24; nh 0.0.0.0, Gi0/
  1, inlabel imp-null, outlabel unknown (from 0.0.0.0:0), find route tags
000051: Apr 20 19:18:33.271: tagcon: tc_iprouting_table_change: 10.10.1.0/255.255.255.0,
  event 0x1
000052: Apr 20 19:18:33.271: tagcon: rib change: 10.10.1.0/255.255.255.0; event 0x1; ndb
  attrflags 0x1000220; ndb->pdb_index 0x0
000053: Apr 20 19:18:33.271: tib: find route tags: 1.1.1.1/32, Lo1, nh 0.0.0.0, res nh
  0.0.0.0
000054: Apr 20 19:18:33.271: tagcon: announce labels for: 1.1.1.1/32; nh 0.0.0.0, Lo1,
  inlabel imp-null, outlabel unknown (from 0.0.0.0:0), find route tags
000055: Apr 20 19:18:33.271: tagcon: tc_iprouting_table_change: 1.1.1.1/255.255.255.255,
  event 0x1
000056: Apr 20 19:18:33.271: tagcon: rib change: 1.1.1.1/255.255.255.255; event 0x1; ndb
  attrflags 0x1000220; ndb->pdb_index 0x0
000057: Apr 20 19:18:33.271: tib: find route tags: 2.2.2.2/32, Lo2, nh 0.0.0.0, res nh
  0.0.0.0
000058: Apr 20 19:18:33.271: tagcon: announce labels for: 2.2.2.2/32; nh 0.0.0.0, Lo2,
  inlabel imp-null, outlabel unknown (from 0.0.0.0:0), find route tags
000059: Apr 20 19:18:33.271: tagcon: tc_iprouting_table_change: 2.2.2.2/255.255.255.255,
  event 0x1
000060: Apr 20 19:18:33.271: tagcon: rib change: 2.2.2.2/255.255.255.255; event 0x1; ndb
  attrflags 0x1000220; ndb->pdb_index 0x0
000061: Apr 20 19:18:33.271: tib: find route tags: 3.3.3.3/32, Lo3, nh 0.0.0.0, res nh
  0.0.0.0
000062: Apr 20 19:18:33.271: tagcon: announce labels for: 3.3.3.3/32; nh 0.0.0.0, Lo3,
  inlabel imp-null, outlabel unknown (from 0.0.0.0:0), find route tags
000063: Apr 20 19:18:33.271: tagcon: tc_iprouting_table_change: 3.3.3.3/255.255.255.255,
  event 0x1
000064: Apr 20 19:18:33.275: tagcon: rib change: 3.3.3.3/255.255.255.255; event 0x1; ndb
  attrflags 0x1000220; ndb->pdb_index 0x0
000065: Apr 20 19:18:33.275: tib: find route tags: 172.16.0.0/16, Gi0/1, nh 10.10.1.2, res
  nh 10.10.1.2
000066: Apr 20 19:18:33.275: tagcon: announce labels for: 172.16.0.0/16; nh 10.10.1.2, Gi0/
  1, inlabel 16, outlabel imp-null (from 192.168.1.1:0), find route tags
000067: Apr 20 19:18:33.275: tagcon: tc_iprouting_table_change: 172.16.0.0/255.255.0.0,
  event 0x1
000068: Apr 20 19:18:33.275: tagcon: rib change: 172.16.0.0/255.255.0.0; event 0x1; ndb
  attrflags 0x0; ndb->pdb_index 0x2
000069: Apr 20 19:18:33.275: tib: find route tags: 192.168.1.0/24, Gi0/1, nh 10.10.1.2,
  res nh 10.10.1.2
000070: Apr 20 19:18:33.275: tagcon: announce labels for: 192.168.1.0/24; nh 10.10.1.2,
  Gi0/1, inlabel 17, outlabel imp-null (from 192.168.1.1:0), find route tags
000071: Apr 20 19:18:33.275: tagcon: tc_iprouting_table_change: 192.168.1.0/255.255.255.0,
  event 0x1
```

continues

Example 10-5 **debug mpls ldp bindings** *Command Output (Continued)*

```
000072: Apr 20 19:18:33.275: tagcon: rib change: 192.168.1.0/255.255.255.0; event 0x1; ndb
  attrflags 0x1000000; ndb->pdb_index 0x2
000073: Apr 20 19:18:33.279: tib: find route tags: 192.168.1.2/32, Gi0/1, nh 10.10.1.2,
  res nh 10.10.1.2
000074: Apr 20 19:18:33.279: tagcon: announce labels for: 192.168.1.2/32; nh 10.10.1.2,
  Gi0/1, inlabel 18, outlabel imp-null (from 192.168.1.1:0), find route tags
000075: Apr 20 19:18:33.279: tagcon: tc_iprouting_table_change: 192.168.1.2/
  255.255.255.255, event 0x1
000076: Apr 20 19:18:33.279: tagcon: rib change: 192.168.1.2/255.255.255.255; event 0x1;
  ndb attrflags 0x1000000; ndb->pdb_index 0x2
BM2851#
```

The output shows the exchange of label information regarding each network prefix in the routing table. The highlighted portion shows an **inlabel** of **17** and an **outlabel** of **imp-null** (value = 3). This signifies that the label should be popped.

Foundation Summary

In general, the MPLS configuration is relatively simple. It can, however, become more complex as advanced protocols and features are introduced.

Table 10-4 provides a review of the steps in configuring frame mode MPLS.

Table 10-4 *MPLS Configuration Steps*

Configure	Command	Configuration Mode	Parameters
CEF	ip cef	Global	distributed
MPLS	mpls ip	Global	default-route propagate-ttl ttl-expiration
MPLS	mpls ip	Interface	encapsulate
LDP or TDP	mpls label protocol	Interface	both, tdp, ldp
MTU	mpls mtu	Interface	64–65535

Q&A

The questions and scenarios in this book are designed to be challenging and to make sure that you know the answer. Rather than allowing you to derive the answers from clues hidden inside the questions themselves, the questions challenge your understanding and recall of the subject.

Hopefully, mastering these questions will help you limit the number of exam questions on which you narrow your choices to two options, and then guess.

You can find the answers to these questions in Appendix A. For more practice with exam-like question formats, use the exam engine on the CD-ROM.

1. Describe CEF and some of the characteristics that make it a more efficient switching mechanism than fast switching or process switching.

2. When might a mixed LDP/TDP environment be encountered and what are some ways to deal with such a scenario?

3. Altering the MTU properly is crucial to proper operation of any MPLS network. Where must the MTU be adjusted?

4. In the LDP table, an outlabel value of 3 has what significance?

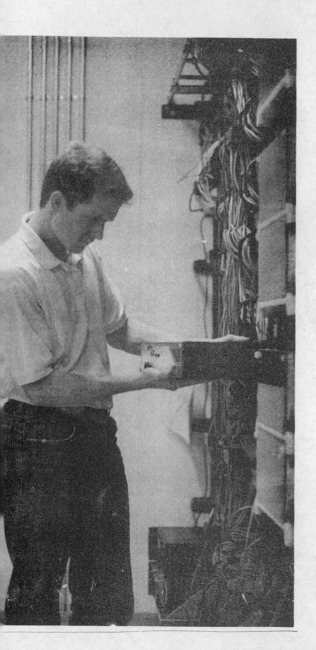

Exam Topic List

This chapter covers the following topics that you need to master for the CCNP ISCW exam:

- **MPLS VPN Architecture**—Describes the basic architecture behind MPLS VPNs

- **Traditional VPNs**—Describes traditional VPN implementations

- **Peer-to-Peer VPNs**—Describes peer-to-peer VPN connectivity

- **MPLS VPNs**—Describes the characteristics of MPLS VPNs

CHAPTER 11

MPLS VPN Technologies

Chapter 2 provided some brief discussion of Virtual Private Network (VPN) architecture with respect to connectivity options for teleworkers. Remote-access VPNs and IPsec VPNs were both discussed along with some key differences between the two. Among the items discussed was the fact that a remote-access VPN is an on-demand connection, whereas an IPsec VPN is an always-on connection. Each has its particular place in the bigger picture of the Intelligent Information Network (IIN).

The Service-Oriented Network Architecture (SONA) framework encourages the offering of applications and services to all network users so that they may have the same network experience regardless of how they access the network. The Multiprotocol Label Switching (MPLS) VPN is another piece of the SONA framework that allows those applications and services to be offered to remote branch offices and small office/home office (SOHO) sites. With MPLS VPNs, two key pieces of the framework fall into place: the teleworker and, now, the branch office sites. For SOHO sites, any of the three VPN options is viable depending on the implementation.

"Do I Know This Already?" Quiz

The purpose of the "Do I Know This Already?" quiz is to help you decide whether you really need to read the entire chapter. If you already intend to read the entire chapter, you do not necessarily need to answer these questions now.

The 12-question quiz, derived from the major sections in the "Foundation Topics" portion of the chapter, helps you to determine how to spend your limited study time.

Table 11-1 outlines the major topics discussed in this chapter and the "Do I Know This Already?" quiz questions that correspond to those topics.

Table 11-1 *"Do I Know This Already?" Foundation Topics Section-to-Question Mapping*

Foundation Topics Section	Questions Covered in This Section	Score
MPLS VPN Architecture	1–2	
Traditional VPNs	3	
Peer-to-Peer VPNs	4	
MPLS VPNs	5–12	
Total Score		

> **CAUTION** The goal of self-assessment is to gauge your mastery of the topics in this chapter. If you do not know the answer to a question or are only partially sure of the answer, you should mark this question wrong for purposes of self-assessment. Giving yourself credit for an answer that you correctly guess skews your self-assessment results and might provide you with a false sense of security.

1. Which type of VPN does not require any participation by the service provider in the routing functionality?

   a. Overlay VPN

   b. Peer-to-peer VPN

   c. Overlay-to-overlay VPN

   d. MPLS VPN

2. Which of the following is implemented with routers, ACLs, and dedicated routers per customer?

   a. Overlay VPNs

   b. Peer-to-peer VPNs

   c. Overlay-to-overlay VPNs

   d. MPLS VPNs

3. In a Layer 2 overlay VPN model, how is redundancy achieved?

   a. It is automatic due to routing protocol convergence.

   b. By provisioning additional circuits between critical sites.

   c. Only through the hub router.

   d. Redundancy is the responsibility of the provider.

4. Which is a characteristic of a peer-to-peer VPN?

    a. Dedicated PE router per customer

    b. Shared PE routers

    c. MPLS VPNs

    d. Lack of dynamic routing

5. Which of the following comprise all or part of the LSP?

    a. C network

    b. CE router

    c. P router

    d. PHP

6. Which of the following is prepended to a customer route?

    a. VPNv4 address

    b. RD

    c. RT

    d. LDP

7. Which of the following is appended to a customer route to indicate VPN membership?

    a. VPNv4 address

    b. RD

    c. RT

    d. LDP

8. Which protocol runs in the P network with the express purpose of propagating customer routes between PE routers?

    a. BGP

    b. OSPF

    c. MPBGP

    d. MPOSPF

9. Where would an import RT most likely be used?

    a. Ingress PE

    b. Egress PE

    c. P router

    d. CE router

10. Customer routes from a VRF are exported as VPNv4 routes into what?

   a. LDP

   b. Egress PE

   c. MPBGP

   d. CE router

11. PE routers use a label stack consisting of how many labels in a typical MPLS VPN?

   a. 1

   b. 2

   c. 3

   d. 4

12. When the final P router in an LSP removes the top label in the stack, this is known as?

   a. Label unstacking

   b. Penultimate hop popping

   c. VRF export

   d. VPN label

The answers to the "Do I Know This Already?" quiz are found in Appendix A, "Answers to the 'Do I Know This Already?' Quizzes and Q&A Sections." The suggested choices for your next step are as follows:

■ **7 or fewer overall score**—Read the entire chapter. This includes the "Foundation Topics," "Foundation Summary," and "Q&A" sections.

■ **8 or 9 overall score**—Begin with the "Foundation Summary" section, and then go to the "Q&A" section.

■ **10 or more overall score**—If you want more review on these topics, skip to the "Foundation Summary" section, and then go to the "Q&A" section. Otherwise, move to the next chapter.

Foundation Topics

MPLS VPN Architecture

To properly understand MPLS VPNs as a solution, it is important to understand the problem. MPLS VPNs are a Layer 3 WAN solution to an age-old Layer 2 WAN problem—that is, the quest to provide any-to-any connectivity among sites in a cost-efficient manner. In the past, WAN architects struggled with topological design principals that amounted to choosing the least of all evils. A full mesh topology was too expensive but most robust. A hub-and-spoke topology was least expensive but least robust. A failure at the hub site would have a severe network impact. Partial mesh topologies created a balance of pain created by leveraging cost against connectivity.

MPLS is the answer to the problem. With MPLS, it is possible to have a fully meshed network, but beyond that, it is a Layer 3–capable, fully meshed network. The possibilities for architecting a WAN solution are greatly expanded with little or no incremental cost over traditional Layer 2 circuits.

The idea of a VPN brings to mind the concepts of security and privacy. These things have always been an enterprise solution that had to be implemented by knowledgeable individuals within a particular company or by an outside consultant brought in for just such a deployment. The term VPN still brings to mind, for most people, the IPsec and remote-access VPNs discussed in Chapter 2.

All-in-all, the term VPN has become rather wide reaching. Figure 11-1 illustrates this fact in detailing what VPN has come to mean in a wider sense.

Figure 11-1 *VPN Taxonomy*

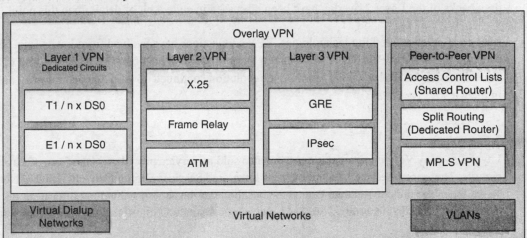

In essence, Figure 11-1 shows an evolutionary path of the VPN and how it has come to encompass a very different set of technologies depending on how it is to be deployed.

Virtual local-area networks (VLAN) allow the isolation of traffic on a per-subnet basis across a common physical infrastructure.

Virtual private dialup networks (VPDN) allow the use of dialup infrastructure via private implementation or as a service offered by a service provider.

VPNs allow the use of a shared infrastructure offered by a service provider to implement private networks. The degree of security is, of course, subject to negotiation. Many service provider offerings now include a "firewall in the cloud" offering to filter traffic to and from an Internet connection or other network. Also available are managed voice, content caching, and content filtering services. It all depends on the negotiated package.

From a typical VPN implementation standpoint, there are essentially two models:

- **Overlay VPNs**—Include older technologies such as X.25, Frame Relay, and Asynchronous Transfer Mode (ATM) for Layer 2 overlay VPNs as well as generic routing encapsulation (GRE) tunnels and IPsec for Layer 3 overlay VPNs

- **Peer-to-peer VPNs**—Implemented with shared service provider router infrastructure using access control lists (ACL) and providing separate routers per customer

Traditional VPNs

Traditional VPNs, or overlay VPNs, are essentially what has been considered a WAN solution for the past few decades and then some. These are based on a Layer 2 overlay model in which a service provider sells permanent virtual circuits (PVC) and/or switched virtual circuits (SVC). The drawbacks of the Layer 2 overlay have been discussed in quite a bit of detail up to this point.

Like most other networking technologies, VPN connections have evolved from Layer 1 up. The concept of Overlay VPNs began years ago in the form of dedicated circuits primarily used for Time-Division Multiplex (TDM) traffic. This evolution continued upward to reach Layers 2 and 3 in their respective forms.

Layer 1 Overlay

Layer 1 overlay VPN implementations were also sold by service providers in the form of Layer 1 circuits. These included such technologies as Integrated Services Digital Network (ISDN). Not to be excluded are the circuits that formed the backbone of the access technology offerings, the digital service (DS) hierarchy, DS0, DS1, and so on. A single DS0 offers 64 kbps of bandwidth but when time-division multiplexing (TDM) implementations grouped 24 DS0s together, a DS1 was the result, offering 1.544 Mbps of bandwidth or what is more commonly referred to as a T1 line. In Europe and other locales around the globe, service providers would group 30 DS0s into a bundle, use an additional DS0 for framing operations, and use yet another DS0 for signaling. This 32 DS0 implementation, known as E1, offers 2.048 Mbps of bandwidth.

Other higher-speed technologies such as Synchronous Optical Network (SONET) and Synchronous Digital Hierarchy (SDH) were brought about by the ever-present need for more speed.

Service providers delivered the Layer 1 and the customer was responsible for applying a Layer 2 and any other features that might be appropriate. Today's market calls for much more on the part of the service provider.

Layer 2 Overlay

Layer 2 VPN overlay, as mentioned, is more along the lines of what most network administrators and IT staff think of as a traditional WAN service. This includes X.25, Frame Relay, ATM, High-Level Data Link Control (HDLC), Synchronous Data Link Control (SDLC), and Switched Multimegabit Data Service (SMDS), to name a few. At this point, the service provider is delivering Layer 1 and Layer 2, leaving the higher-level services at the discretion of the customer. Again, today's market demands yet more from the service provider as protection of applications and services traffic becomes more significant across the WAN. The momentum behind this is driven by the ideas expressed in the SONA framework and the desire to deliver a single experience for all users, regardless of location or access method. Figure 11-2 illustrates a classic example of a Layer 2 overlay VPN.

In Figure 11-2, a headquarters site is connected via Layer 2 virtual circuits (VCs) in a hub-and-spoke topology. The Layer 3 connectivity is unknown to the provider's network and routing updates must be sent across the VCs to each site. All traffic between the remote sites traverses the hub router at the headquarters site. Should the router at the headquarters site experience a failure, there will be considerable impact on the other remote sites.

In such scenarios, enterprise network administrators implement such backup features as dial-backup to facilitate data flow between sites in the event of a primary WAN link failure.

Figure 11-2 *Layer 2 Overlay VPN*

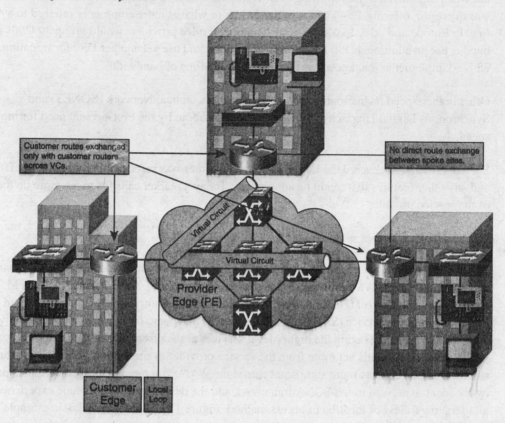

Layer 3 Overlay

Traditional WAN connectivity would entail the configuration of Layer 3 options manually to send routing information via WAN circuits. For example, the use of the **broadcast** keyword when configuring **frame-relay map** statements when mapping a next-hop IP address to a local data-link connection identifier (DLCI) would complete a necessary Layer 2 to Layer 3 address mapping, allowing routing updates to be transmitted across the link.

Even with such a configuration in place, there is no real Layer 3 capability to adapt to changes brought about by routing protocol updates. Each circuit is still a point-to-point connection in every sense of the concept. While Layer 3 protocols may flow across the links, the links are not Layer 3 aware. Customer routes flow directly between customer routers across the WAN connection.

Peer-to-Peer VPNs

The introduction of a peer-to-peer VPN causes the service provider to take a more active role in the routing operations of its customer base. This means that the service provider will be maintaining customer routing information stored in a separate routing instance within its network. The customer edge (CE) router exchanges routing information not with the far-end CE router, but with the local, provider edge (PE) router. These routes are conveyed across the provider network to other CE routers.

This connection to and sharing of routing information with the service provider facilitates the concept of a peer-to-peer VPN. This evolutionary step forward allows the WAN to be Layer 3 aware rather than simply a Layer 3 transport. Figure 11-3 illustrates this concept.

Figure 11-3 *Peer-to-Peer VPN*

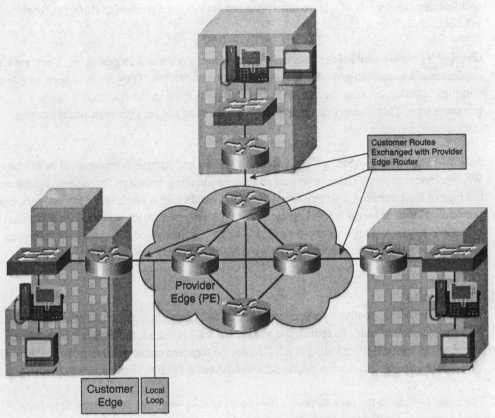

With a peer-to-peer network, the provider is handing off a Layer 1, Layer 2, and Layer 3 connection. Typically, the Layer 2 is still Frame Relay simply because most network administrators are comfortable with it. However, the next-hop addresses are those of the PE router. Most providers allow the customer to choose the routing protocol that is used across the local loop. Once the routes hit the PE, they are redistributed into the provider's Border Gateway Protocol (BGP) table.

Even though the local loop has not changed, the essence of the network has changed. The provider is now part of the customer routing infrastructure. A full mesh topology is accomplished through a single link to the provider network. The added benefits of a full mesh network come to bear. The network is more resilient because it is simply an extension of the existing customer routing infrastructure.

VPN Benefits

As access technologies advance, options become more numerous. The choices made for connectivity will be driven primarily by the needs of the business constructing the network architecture. The needs of a large enterprise network will be somewhat different from those of a small business.

Overlay VPNs are well known and have gone down in price to a large degree. They are easily implemented from both provider and customer points of view. They are now seen as a less-complex solution because the provider does not participate in the customer's routing infrastructure. This means that route redistribution need not be a concern when passing information between sites.

Peer-to-peer VPNs provide optimal routing solutions and full mesh topological redundancy for WAN-connected sites. There is no real additional planning or design for the implementation on the part of the customer. The provider will have already traffic engineered the network based on services offered and service level agreements (SLA) negotiated. Provisioning of additional sites is as simple as placing a router and dropping a local loop into place. The configuration does not require the creation of multiple VCs to provide the full mesh capabilities.

VPN Drawbacks

The cost and administrative overhead associated with a large enterprise full mesh Layer 2 topology is daunting on any scale. To reduce the number of VCs required, redundancy is sacrificed. Each site requires manual provisioning of a VC to get the required connectivity and traffic flow. Overlay VPNs also incur encapsulation overhead when IPsec or GRE tunneling is involved.

The chief benefit in the peer-to-peer VPN model is also, at times, its greatest drawback. The provider is involved in the customer routing process. Routing information is redistributed at CE and PE routers to be passed into or out of each respective network. Route filters should be placed on each interface to protect both parties from route floods sometimes caused by convergence events. The customer now must place additional trust in the capabilities of the service provider to properly configure and maintain their routing infrastructure. This can be problematic at times.

At critical sites with redundant routers and connections to the service provider network, care should be taken to ensure diversity in the connection so that both circuits do not land on the same PE router. The goal is to eliminate any single point of failure. Figure 11-4 illustrates this concept.

Figure 11-4 *Redundant Connections*

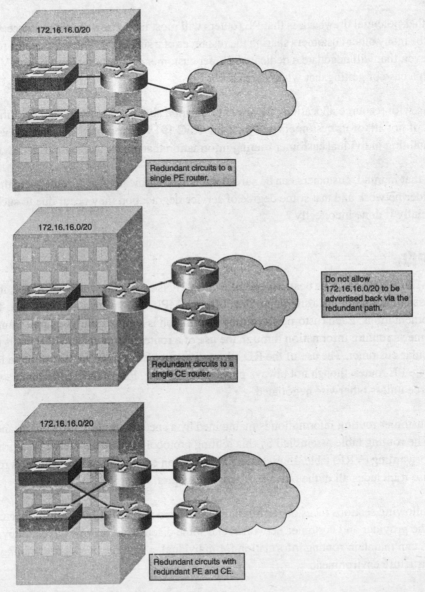

As Figure 11-4 points out, it is also necessary to ensure that routes advertised via one circuit are not redistributed out to the PE and then right back in via the redundant circuit to the CE. This will cause a significant routing loop. Split horizon will not stop it, because the update is not received via the interface through which it was initially sent. Suddenly the routers have an erroneously valid path to the 172.16.16.0/20 subnet via a PE router. A simple inbound route filter blocking 172.16.16.0/20 on both CE routers or, more preferably, an outbound route filter on both PE routers will remedy the situation.

Another potential drawback is that PE routers will most likely be a shared resource. That is, there may be many other customers sharing the resources of a single PE. There are quite a few providers, however, that will negotiate a dedicated PE per customer connection. Peer-to-peer VPNs are very much a case of getting that which is paid for.

Along with resource allocation, the provider must be able to effectively deal with the fact that most, if not all, of its customers will be using RFC 1918 addressing. This makes the job of maintaining individual customer routing information that much more important.

With that in mind, customers can be sure that there is significant use of route filters throughout the provider network and that some degree of service degradation may occur due to such filtering, especially if done incorrectly.

MPLS VPNs

The MPLS VPN takes the best aspects of overlay VPNs and the best aspects of peer-to-peer VPNs and assembles them into a single product offering. MPLS VPNs are essentially peer-to-peer VPN implementations. Each customer's routing information is kept securely separate from every other customer's routing information through the use of a route distinguisher (RD) that is unique to a particular customer. The use of the RD allows the provider to give each customer a logically separate PE router, though not always physically separate. PE routers will remain a shared resource unless otherwise negotiated.

The customer routing information is maintained by a specific routing protocol instance tied to its RD. The routing table assembled by this routing protocol instance is known as a virtual routing and forwarding (VRF) table. In essence, it is simply an extension of the customer's routing table, because it includes all of the customer's advertised prefixes.

The following sections focus on terminology associated with MPLS VPNs, architectural needs of both the provider and customer networks, and some discussion on how a technology such as MPLS can maintain routing information for individual customers in a shared routing infrastructure environment.

MPLS VPN Terminology

Much of the terminology of MPLS VPNs has been discussed at one point or another in previous chapters. It is prudent to touch on it once more at this point to ensure that all of the terms associated with the technology are in the forefront of the mind while taking in the information in the remainder of the chapter.

- **C network**—The customer-controlled internal network.

- **CE router**—The customer edge router (also known as customer premises equipment, or CPE), which connects to a PE router.

- **Label-switched path (LSP)**—The pathway established for use by a label-switched packet through a P network in transit to a particular destination.

- **P network**—The service provider–controlled internal network comprised of core routers providing transport across the provider backbone but carrying no customer routing information.

- **P router**—A service provider MPLS core or backbone router with no customer-facing interfaces and carrying no VPN routes.

- **PE router**—A provider edge MPLS router containing customer-facing interface(s) and connecting to CE router(s) for the purpose of customer routing information exchange.

- **Penultimate hop pop (PHP)**—The final P router in the P network pops the label prior to the packet's arrival at the egress PE router.

- **PoP**—Service provider point of presence.

- **Route distinguisher (RD)**—A 64-bit identifier prepended to an IPv4 address to make it a globally unique VPNv4 address.

- **Route target (RT)**—An attribute appended to a VPNv4 BGP route to indicate VPN membership.

- **Virtual routing and forwarding (VRF) table**—A customer-specific routing table instance.

CE Router Architecture

Over the course of the discussions of the technologies involved in this chapter, the CE router will play an important role. Regardless of what designation is applied to it, the CE router is a router. It runs an IGP (available protocols include BGP, OSPF, EIGRP, RIP, or static routing) and exchanges routes with a neighboring router discovered through whatever routing protocol process the chosen protocol uses.

The CE router is not MPLS aware and does not participate in the MPLS architecture in any way other than the sending and receiving of customer routing information. The provider's MPLS P routers are similarly invisible to CE routers. The MPLS architecture simply appears to be an extension of an intra-company BGP routing implementation between WAN sites with little or no visibility beyond the customer-facing PE router interface.

All redistribution and MPLS-related manipulation will be done on the PE router and will remain transparent to the CE routers at each site. A CE router will be no different, architecturally or functionally, from any other router in the C network.

PE Router Architecture

The architecture of the PE routers in a provider's network is similar to that of a typical PoP in a dedicated peer-to-peer model. The major difference is that the architecture is compressed into a single device. The PE routers are usually relatively high-end routers such as the Cisco 7200VXR router.

Each customer is assigned its own RD and VRF table dedicated to maintaining routing information within the provider infrastructure. Routing across the provider backbone is performed by yet another routing process meant to bring some sense of simplification back into the picture in the form of a global IP routing table. The PE is managed as a single router but runs multiple instances of a routing protocol to maintain customer-specific routes and redistribute them into the global IP routing table. Figure 11-5 illustrates the concept of the PE router architecture.

Figure 11-5 *PE Router Architecture*

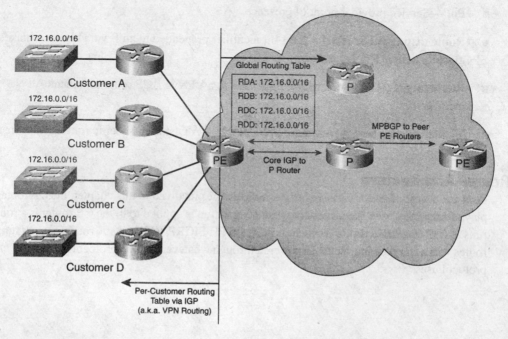

As Figure 11-5 shows, the VRF provides isolation between customer routes. The information from these routing tables still must be exchanged between various PE routers. Therefore, a routing protocol is needed that will allow the transport of all customer routes across the P network while allowing the continued independence of each customer's address space.

The decision was made that a single routing protocol be run between PE routers that will exchange customer routes without the involvement of the P routers. The PE routers that connect to a given customer network will be peered to each other and routes will be exchanged. With this model, the number of routing protocols between PE routers need not increase in proportion to the number of customers served.

This also has the added benefit of keeping the customer routes off of the P routers as they are unicast from peer to peer.

The number of prefixes advertised by each customer, when added to those P network routes already in existence, can combine to create an excessively large routing table overall. BGP is the only protocol with the scalability to handle these types of operations while giving the most flexibility in manipulation of routing and traffic flow in general. BGP neighbor relationships are configured between PE routers directly so that prefixes can be exchanged for a given customer. The global IP routing table in the P network need not actually carry any of the actual customer routes.

P Router Architecture

P routers make up the backbone of the P network. They do not carry VPN routes and do not participate in MPLS routing. They do provide transport for traffic between PEs but that is essentially where their job stops. They run a routing protocol such as IS-IS, OSPF, or BGP across the provider backbone and carry only P network routing information in their routing tables. They interface with PE routers to facilitate the transport of BGP peering information across to remote PE routers.

BGP is typically the protocol of choice for P networks due to its scalability and functionality, not for any MPLS-related need or requirement.

Route Distinguishers

On PE routers, there is obviously a need to deal with the fact that most, if not all, customers will be using RFC 1918 addressing and that all that common space will be allocated in varying manners. So, there is a need to be able to keep individual customer routes separate and distinct so that each network is reachable. One customer's 10.1.1.0/24 subnet will likely co-exist with another customer's 10.1.1.0/24 subnet, for example. These will obviously have differing outbound interfaces.

An RD allows these prefixes to be kept unique. The RD is a 64-bit identifier that is tacked on to the front of the IPv4 address. These VPNv4 addresses are advertised between BGP peers on PE routers. The BGP implementation known as Multiprotocol BGP (MPBGP) supports address families other than IPv4 addressing. This creates a 96-bit entity known as a VPNv4 address. Figure 11-6 illustrates the mechanics involved.

Figure 11-6 *PE Peers*

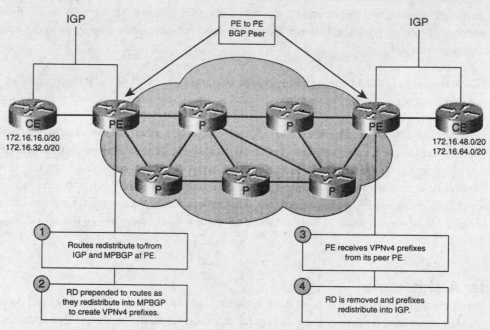

An IGP running across the local loop serves to move customer routing information between the PE and CE routers. This routing information is redistributed into MPBGP where the prefixes are converted to VPNv4 addresses. The PE routers are peered directly to each other via an Interior BGP (IBGP) peering so that they exchange routes directly with one another. Once the neighbor PE receives VPNv4 information from its peer, the RD is removed so that routes can be redistributed back into the customer IGP and sent to the CE router for propagation through the enterprise.

RD values have no real specific meaning. They are only meant to allow the routing architecture to deal with overlapping address space. So long as each is unique within the P network, there should be no risk of route overlap. Because there has to be a unique mapping between the RD and the VRF, the RD can be viewed as the VRF identifier in Cisco implementations.

Usually, each customer has a single RD assigned to its prefixes. There are times, however, when customers will want to protect interdepartmental routing information or business-to-business.

connectivity via an MPLS VPN. A single RD per customer would preclude some scenarios and create a need for a more versatile form of management. On the surface, this would seem to require the use of multiple RDs and redistribution of the desired routes between the VRFs. This is indeed the case.

Consider a deployment of an enterprise Voice over IP (VoIP) solution managed by the provider, similar to that shown in Figure 11-7.

Figure 11-7 *VoIP Service Example*

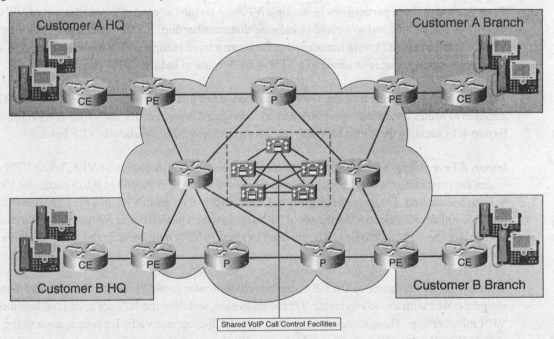

Shared VoIP Call Control Facilities

The provider would be responsible for all call control for both customer-internal calling between sites and PSTN calling. The provider would also have particular designs for calling between customers across the network. These calls are no different from typical Public Switched Telephone Network (PSTN) calls to each customer, but the traffic need never leave the provider's network if both are MPLS VPN customers.

Because some or all customers would share a common call-control facility, certain routing changes would be necessary to ensure that all customers can reach this common point inside the provider network. A single RD would preclude this capability. In some cases, the provider would institute a specific voice RD for reachability to the shared call-control and PSTN gateway devices. Firewalls, ACLs, and more would be necessary to ensure security of all signaling and media traffic so that no unauthorized traffic would be able to traverse the alternate RDs.

In such an example, both Customer A and B sites would be participating in their own customer-specific VPN as well as the shared voice VPN. To mitigate the possibility for unauthorized access or activity, the Customer A and B branch sites may route in hub-and-spoke fashion via the HQ site to place and receive voice calls. This would mean that the branch sites would participate only in the customer-specific VPNs, leaving the HQ sites as the sole point of contact with any shared infrastructure.

Route Targets

To indicate that a site participates in multiple VPNs, a method is needed in which a set of VPN identifiers can be attached to a route to indicate that membership. An RD is adequate for a single VPN. Route targets (RT) were introduced to facilitate a more complex VPN topology. An RT is an additional attribute that is attached to a VPNv4 BGP route to indicate VPN membership.

The RT is appended at the time the IPv4 route is converted to a VPNv4 route by the PE router. RTs attached to routes are called *export RTs* and are configured separately for each VRF in a PE router. Export RTs identify the VPNs to which the sites associated with a particular VRF belong.

Import RTs are those RTs that specify the routes associated with a particular VRF. When VPNv4 routes are propagated to neighboring PE routers, routes meant to be imported into a particular VRF need to be selected. This is accomplished based on import RTs. Each VRF in a PE router can have multiple import RTs identifying the set of VPNs from which the VRF is accepting routes. In cases of overlapping VPN topologies, RTs are used to identify VPN membership and allow for more complex scenarios.

With this implementation, as the CE router advertises routes to the PE router, the inbound routes are prepended with the RD to create VPNv4 addresses, and then the RTs are appended based on VPN membership. These routes are exported into the appropriate VRFs for propagation to the remote PEs. Routes will be imported by remote PEs based on import RT values and redistributed to the remote CE routers.

End-to-End Routing Update Flow

Now that all of the pertinent pieces of the MPLS VPN puzzle have been introduced, a final walk through the routing update flow is in order. Figure 11-8 provides a visual aid for the flow of the discussion.

Figure 11-8 *End-to-End Routing Updates*

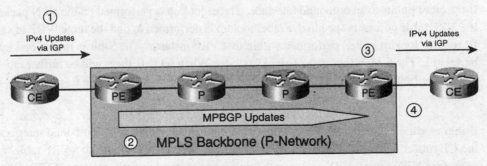

In Figure 11-8, there are four designated steps in the routing update process:

Step 1   PE routers receive IPv4 routing updates from the CE router via a configured common IGP. These routes are installed in the appropriate VRF table.

Step 2   Customer routes from the VRF are exported as VPNv4 routes into the MPBGP instance and propagated to other PE routers. To become VPNv4 routes, RDs must be prepended to the route entries. To be exported, export RTs are appended to specify VPN membership.

Step 3   The PE routers receiving MPBGP updates import the incoming VPNv4 routes into the appropriate VRFs according to the values specified by the import RTs attached to the routes and the individual VRF tables.

Step 4   The VPNv4 routes installed in the VRF table(s) are redistributed into the IGP instance running between PE and CE and then propagated to the CE and into the C network.

From the CE standpoint on both sides of the P network, the P network simply looks like any other routing instance. The CE routers have no visibility to the MPLS network or its structure. Once routing updates are successfully flowing, end-user traffic can begin to flow as well.

MPLS VPN Packet Forwarding

PE routers use a two-label stack to label the VPN packets for forwarding across the P network. The label stack is imposed by the ingress PE router.

The top label in the stack will be used by LDP for P network traversal along an LSP that will get it to the egress PE router. The S-bit in the top label will be set to 0.

The second label will be assigned by the egress PE router. Remember, the label values are downstream-assigned. The purpose of the second label is to tell the router how to forward the incoming VPN packet. This label could point to a particular outbound interface or to a VRF table. If the label points to an outbound interface, a label lookup is performed on the VPN packet itself. If a VRF table pointer is specified, a label lookup is performed to find the target VRF instance. An IP routing lookup is then performed within that VRF instance. The S-bit in the second label will be set to 1. The S-bit is the "end-of-stack" pointer. When set to 0, there will be further labels in the stack. The bottom label in the stack will have the S-bit set to 1, indicating its position as the last label.

Either method is acceptable. The second label in the stack points to an outbound interface when the CE router is the next hop in the VPN route. The second label points to a VRF table for aggregate VPN routes, VPN routes to the null interface, and directly connected VPN interfaces.

The P routers perform label switching based only on the top label. They never see the second label because they do not analyze the structure any further than the first label.

The egress PE performs a label switch on the second label because the first one has been popped. It will then forward the packet according to the parameters of the packet, which point it to a VRF or an outbound interface.

MPLS VPN PHP

It seems rather inefficient for the egress PE to deal with both labels. The use of PHP allows the final P router in the LSP to pop the label, thereby relieving the egress PE router of the need to do so. This allows the egress PE router to simply perform its function using only the VPN label in the stack. Once that label is removed, an IP routing lookup can take place and the packet can be forwarded.

Foundation Summary

MPLS VPNs are somewhat of a departure from traditional WAN technologies. However, the benefits of being able to deploy a fully Layer 3–aware WAN topology with built-in redundancy is very alluring. The possibilities for service and application offerings by both providers and enterprise customers are exceedingly diverse.

Service provider offerings such as firewall-in-the-cloud and managed voice service are just the beginning of what is possible with a creative architect.

A great deal of information has been covered in a short span in this chapter. The information that follows serves to summarize the key points discussed herein. Table 11-2 revisits the roles of routers in MPLS VPN architectures.

Table 11-2 *MPLS VPN Router Roles*

Router	Location	Purpose	Description
C router	C network, internal	Maintains C network routes and forwards traffic	A router internal to the customer-controlled network
CE router	C network, edge	Exchanges C network routes with a PE router	A customer-controlled router that interfaces and exchanges routing information with a PE router
P router	P network, internal	Maintains P network routes and forwards traffic	A router internal to the provider-controlled network, usually an LSR
PE router	P network, edge	Exchanges VPN routes with CE router	A provider-controlled router that interfaces and exchanges routing information with a CE router

Various protocols are present in MPLS VPN architectures. Table 11-3 provides a snapshot review of them as they pertain to the MPLS technologies.

Table 11-3 *MPLS VPN Related Protocols*

Protocol	Where	Description
Customer IGP	C network and CE-PE router connection	The customer internal routing protocol used to maintain routing information throughout the enterprise
Provider IGP	P network	The provider internal routing protocol used to maintain routing information, usually BGP, IS-IS, and/or OSPF
MPBGP	PE-to-PE peering	Multiprotocol BGP maintaining peer connections between PE routers for the express purpose of propagating C network routing information

Q&A

The questions and scenarios in this book are designed to be challenging and to make sure that you know the answer. Rather than allowing you to derive the answers from clues hidden inside the questions themselves, the questions challenge your understanding and recall of the subject.

Hopefully, mastering these questions will help you limit the number of exam questions on which you narrow your choices to two options, and then guess.

You can find the answers to these questions in Appendix A. For more practice with exam-like question formats, use the exam engine on the CD-ROM.

1. Consider a traditional Layer 2 overlay VPN. List some technologies and possible topologies that are available for such implementations.

2. What is the primary benefit of a peer-to-peer VPN over a Layer 2 overlay VPN?

3. When using redundant connections at a single site, what are some pitfalls that should be avoided?

4. Consider Figure 11-9. The routing entry for 192.168.1.0/24 needs to make its way to the routing table of Router B. Trace its path from left to right, explaining the process.

Figure 11-9 *MPLS Routing Information Flow*

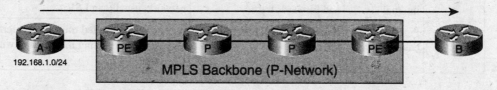

5. Consider Figure 11-10. Now that the 192.168.1.0/24 network is known in Router B, the host at 192.168.5.3 would like to ping the host at 192.168.1.5. Trace the path of the first ICMP echo-request packet from 192.168.5.3 to 192.168.1.5 from CE to CE. Assume that any and all address resolution activities have been successfully completed and that full routing convergence has been reached.

Figure 11-10 *End-to-End Traffic Flow Over MPLS*

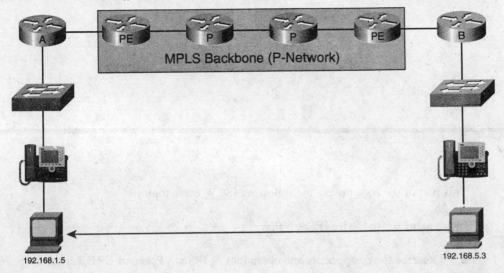

This part of the book covers the following ISCW exam topics:

Implement a site-to-site IPSec VPN.

- Describe the components and operations of IPSec VPNs and GRE Tunnels.
- Configure a site-to-site IPSec VPN/GRE Tunnel with SDM (i.e., preshared key).
- Verify IPSec/GRE Tunnel configurations (i.e., IOS CLI configurations).
- Describe, configure, and verify VPN backup interfaces.
- Describe and configure Cisco Easy VPN solutions using SDM.

Part III: IPsec VPNs

Part III: IPsec VPNs

Exam Topic List

This chapter covers the following topics that you need to master for the CCNP ISCW exam:

- **IPsec**—Internet Protocol Security (IPsec) is a suite of protocols that can provide data confidentiality, data integrity, and data origin authentication to IP packets.

- **Internet Key Exchange (IKE)**—A framework used to exchange security parameters and authentication keys between IPsec endpoints.

- **Encryption Algorithms**—Mathematical algorithms (and the associated keys) used to make data unreadable to everyone except those who have the proper keying material.

- **Public Key Infrastructure**—A hierarchical framework for managing the security attributes for devices that engage in secure communications across a network.

CHAPTER 12

IPsec Overview

IP Security, or IPsec, has been in use for a number of years now to protect sensitive data as it flows from one location to another. The evolution of corporate communications has changed the way that private data is exchanged and maintained. Most companies have distributed resources and personnel. It is important that corporate data remains private during transit. IPsec offers a standards-based mechanism to provide such secure data transmission.

Typically, IPsec is associated with Virtual Private Networks (VPN). A VPN creates a private connection, or network, between two endpoints. This is a virtual connection because the physical means of connectivity is indifferent to the safety of the data involved. IPsec adds a layer of protection to the data that travels across the VPN.

Many years ago, wide-area network (WAN) connections between branch offices was accomplished with point-to-point (p2p) circuits. A single port of a router at one site would connect, via a provider, to a single port of a router at a remote site. The introduction of X.25, ATM, and Frame Relay introduced the virtual circuit. With this technology, one router interface could have many virtual circuits, or connections, to many other sites.

Today, practically every site has Internet connectivity. Rather than lease a p2p or virtual circuit between sites across a carrier's network, most sites simply lease access to the Internet. The ability to send data packets from one location to another is simply a matter of knowing the destination IP address.

However, due to the "open" nature of the Internet, it is not considered safe to simply send packets from one site to another. IPsec is used as a means of safeguarding IP data as it travels from one site to another. Note that IPsec can be used on any type of connectivity—not just Internet links. But IPsec is predominantly used on data that traverses insecure or untrusted networks, such as the Internet.

"Do I Know This Already?" Quiz

The purpose of the "Do I Know This Already?" quiz is to help you decide whether you really need to read the entire chapter. If you already intend to read the entire chapter, you do not necessarily need to answer these questions now.

The 14-question quiz, derived from the major sections in the "Foundation Topics" portion of the chapter, helps you to determine how to spend your limited study time.

Table 12-1 outlines the major topics discussed in this chapter and the "Do I Know This Already?" quiz questions that correspond to those topics.

Table 12-1 *"Do I Know This Already?" Foundation Topics Section-to-Question Mapping*

Foundation Topics Section	Questions Covered in This Section	Score
IPsec	1–4	
Internet Key Exchange (IKE)	5–8	
Encryption Algorithms	9–12	
PKI	13–14	
Total Score		

CAUTION   The goal of self-assessment is to gauge your mastery of the topics in this chapter. If you do not know the answer to a question or are only partially sure of the answer, you should mark this question wrong for purposes of self-assessment. Giving yourself credit for an answer that you correctly guess skews your self-assessment results and might provide you with a false sense of security.

1. Which layers of the OSI model can IPsec protect (select all that apply)?

    a. Layer 1—physical

    b. Layer 2—data link

    c. Layer 3—network

    d. Layer 4—transport

    e. Layer 5—session

2. In IPsec, what does data confidentiality mean?

    a. Identity validation of the remote peer

    b. Encryption of the link layer and up

    c. Encryption following the outer IP header

    d. Preventing the ability to replay or resend packets

    e. Ensuring that the packet's contents have not been read during transit

3. Which of the following are IPsec protocols (select all that apply)?

   a. IKE

   b. UDP

   c. AH

   d. ESP

   e. TCP

4. Which of the following are hash algorithms (select all that apply)?

   a. MD5

   b. DES

   c. 3DES

   d. AES

   e. SHA

5. How many phases does IKE consist of?

   a. One required phase and one optional phase

   b. One required phase and two optional phases

   c. Two required phases and one optional phase

   d. Two required phases and two optional phases

   e. Three required phases

6. Which of the following modes occur during IKE phase 1 (select all that apply)?

   a. Quick mode

   b. Fast mode

   c. Main mode

   d. Aggressive mode

   e. Short mode

7. Which of the following functions occur during IKE phase 1 (select all that apply)?

   a. Establish a bidirectional SA

   b. Establish unidirectional SAs

   c. Perform user authentication

   d. Negotiate IKE parameters

   e. Run quick mode

8. For NAT traversal, when are NAT support and NAT existence determined?

   a. NAT support is determined during IKE phase 1, while NAT existence is determined during IKE phase 2.

   b. Both NAT support and NAT existence are determined during IKE phase 1.

   c. NAT existence is determined during IKE phase 1, while NAT support is determined during IKE phase 2.

   d. Both NAT support and NAT existence are determined during IKE phase 2.

   e. NAT support and NAT existence are really the same feature, and their determination occur during IKE phase 2.

9. Which of the following IPsec protocols provide authentication and integrity checks (select all that apply)?

   a. IKE

   b. MD5

   c. AH

   d. ESP

   e. SHA

10. Which HMAC hash algorithm creates a 160-bit output?

    a. IKE

    b. MD5

    c. AH

    d. ESP

    e. SHA

11. Which of the following encrypting algorithms are considered symmetrical (select all that apply)?

    a. DES

    b. 3DES

    c. Diffie-Hellman

    d. RSA

    e. AES

12. Which of the following algorithms uses a public/private structure to generate a shared secret?

   a. DES

   b. 3DES

   c. Diffie-Hellman

   d. MD5

   e. AES

13. Which PKI element contains information to uniquely identify a peer?

   a. CA

   b. Digital certificate

   c. RA

   d. Neighbor

   e. Distribution mechanism

14. What is the first step in the PKI message exchange process?

   a. The CA sends its public key to the end host.

   b. The end host saves the certificate to some nonvolatile storage area.

   c. An end host generates an RSA key pair.

   d. The CA signs the certificate request with its private key.

   e. The end host generates a certificate request.

The answers to the "Do I Know This Already?" quiz are found in Appendix A, "Answers to the 'Do I Know This Already?' Quizzes and Q&A Sections." The suggested choices for your next step are as follows:

- **10 or fewer overall score**—Read the entire chapter. This includes the "Foundation Topics," "Foundation Summary," and "Q&A" sections.

- **11 or 12 overall score**—Begin with the "Foundation Summary" section, and then go to the "Q&A" section.

- **13 or more overall score**—If you want more review on these topics, skip to the "Foundation Summary" section, and then go to the "Q&A" section. Otherwise, move to the next chapter.

Foundation Topics

IPsec

IPsec is best thought of as a set of features that protects IP data as it travels from one location to another. The locations involved in the VPN typically define the type of VPN. A location could be an end client (such as a PC), a small remote office, a large branch office, a corporate headquarters, a data center, or even a service provider. The combination of any two of these locations determines the type of VPN in use. For example, a small remote office connecting to a corporate headquarters would be a site-to-site VPN.

It is important to remember that IPsec can protect only the IP layer and up (transport layer and user data). IPsec cannot extend its services to the data link layer. If protection of the data link layer is needed, then some form of link encryption is needed. Such encryption is typically performed within a trusted infrastructure, where the security of the link can be assured. Such encryption is not feasible in the Internet because intermediate links are not controlled by the end users.

Often, the use of encryption is assumed to be a requirement of IPsec. In reality, encryption, or data confidentiality, is an optional (although heavily implemented) feature of IPsec. IPsec consists of the following features, which are further explained later in this chapter:

- Data confidentiality

- Data integrity

- Data origin authentication

- Anti-replay

The features, or services, of IPsec are implemented by a series of standards-based protocols. It is important that the implementation of IPsec is based on open standards to ensure interoperability between vendors. The IPsec protocols do not specify any particular authentication, encryption algorithms, key generation techniques, or security association (SA) mechanisms. The three main protocols that are used by IPsec are as follows:

- Internet Key Exchange (IKE)

- Encapsulating Security Payload (ESP)

- Authentication Header (AH)

These protocols are detailed a bit later in this chapter in the section "IPsec Protocols." It is important to understand that these protocols are based on open standards. IPsec uses the preceding protocols to establish the rules for authentication and encryption, and existing standards-based algorithms provide the actual means of authentication, encryption, and key management.

Remember that IPsec is used to protect the flow of data through a VPN. However, a VPN does not necessarily imply that the contents are protected. A VPN can simply be a tunnel, or link, between two endpoints. As such, a new outer header or tag may be applied, but the internal contents are still available for inspection to anyone between the endpoints. So, an IPsec VPN can be considered safe and protected, while other types of VPNs might not share this luxury.

IPsec Features

As noted earlier, the primary features of IPsec consist of the following:

- Data confidentiality

- Data integrity

- Data origin authentication (peer authentication)

- Anti-replay

It is important to understand the meaning of each of these features. The protocols that implement these features are covered later in this chapter.

Data confidentiality involves keeping the data within the IPsec VPN private between the participants of the VPN. As noted earlier, most VPNs are used across the public Internet. As such, it is possible for data to be intercepted and examined. In reality, any data in transit is subject to examination, so the Internet should not be viewed as the only insecure media.

Data confidentiality involves the use of encryption to scramble the data in transit. Encrypted packets cannot be easily, if ever, understood by anyone other than the intended recipient. The use of encryption involves the selection of an encryption algorithm and a means of distributing encryption keys to those involved. IPsec encryption algorithms are covered later in this chapter.

Data confidentiality, or encryption, is not required for IPsec VPNs. More often than not, packets are encrypted as they pass through the VPN. But data confidentiality is an optional feature for IPsec.

Data integrity is a guarantee that the data was not modified or altered during transit through the IPsec VPN. Data integrity itself does not provide data confidentiality. Data integrity typically uses a hash algorithm to check if data within the packet was modified between endpoints. Packets that are determined to have been changed are not accepted.

Data origin authentication validates the source of the IPsec VPN. This feature is performed by each end of the VPN to ensure that the other end is exactly who you want to be connected to. Note that the use of the data origin authentication feature is dependent upon the data integrity service. Data origin authentication cannot exist on its own.

Anti-replay ensures that no packets are duplicated within the VPN. This is accomplished through the use of sequence numbers in the packets and a sliding window on the receiver. The sequence number is compared to the sliding window and helps detect packets that are late. Such late packets are considered duplicates, and are dropped. Like data confidentiality, anti-replay is considered an optional IPsec feature.

IPsec Protocols

IPsec consists of three primary protocols to help implement the overall IPsec architecture:

- Internet Key Exchange (IKE)

- Encapsulating Security Payload (ESP)

- Authentication Header (AH)

Together, these three protocols offer the various IPsec features mentioned earlier. Every IPsec VPN uses some combination of these protocols to provide the desired features for the VPN.

IKE

Internet Key Exchange (IKE) is a framework for the negotiation and exchange of security parameters and authentication keys. The IPsec security parameters will be examined later in the "Internet Key Exchange (IKE)" section. For now, it is important to understand that there are a variety of possible options between two IPsec VPN endpoints. The secure negotiation of these parameters used to establish the IPsec VPN characteristics is performed by IKE.

IKE also exchanges keys used for the symmetrical encryption algorithms within an IPsec VPN. Compared to other encryption algorithms, symmetrical algorithms tend to be more efficient and easier to implement in hardware. The use of such algorithms requires appropriate key material, and IKE provides the mechanism to exchange the keys.

ESP

Encapsulating Security Payload (ESP) provides the framework for the data confidentiality, data integrity, data origin authentication, and optional anti-replay features of IPsec. While ESP is the only IPsec protocol that provides data encryption, it also can provide all of the IPsec features mentioned earlier. Because of this, ESP is primarily used in IPsec VPNs today. The following encryption methods are available to IPsec ESP:

- **Data Encryption Standard (DES)**—An older method of encrypting information that has enjoyed widespread use.

- **Triple Data Encryption Standard (3DES)**—A block cipher that uses DES three times.

- **Advanced Encryption Standard (AES)**—One of the most popular symmetric key algorithms used today.

AH

Authentication Header (AH) provides the framework for the data integrity, data origin authentication, and optional anti-replay features of IPsec. Note that data confidentiality is not provided by AH. AH ensures that the data has not been modified or tampered with, but does not hide the data from inquisitive eyes during transit. As such, the use of AH alone in today's networks has faded in favor of ESP. Both AH and ESP use a Hash-based Message Authentication Code (HMAC) as the authentication and integrity check. Table 12-2 shows the HMAC hash algorithms in IPsec.

Table 12-2   *Hash Algorithms*

Hash Algorithm	Input	Output	Used by IPsec
Message Digest 5 (MD5)	Variable	128 bits	128 bits
Secure Hash Algorithm (SHA-1)	Variable	160 bits	First 96 bits

Both MD5 and SHA-1 use a shared secret key for both the calculation and verification of the message authentication values. The cryptographic strength of the HMAC is dependent upon the properties of the underlying hash function. Both MD5 and SHA-1 take variable-length input data and create a fixed-length hash. The difference is the size and strength of the hash created. Although IPsec uses only the first 96 bits of the 160-bit SHA-1 hash, it is considered more secure than MD5 (although SHA-1 is computationally slower than MD5).

IPsec Modes

IPsec defines two modes that determine the extent of protection offered to the original IP packet. Remember that the IPsec header follows an IP header, because it is referenced by an IP protocol number. As such, encryption and integrity services can be offered only beyond the IP header. The two IPsec modes are tunnel mode and transport mode.

When IPsec headers are simply inserted in an IP packet (after the IP header), it is called transport mode. In transport mode, the original IP header is exposed and unprotected. Data at the transport layer and higher layers benefits from the implemented IPsec features. Another way to think of this is that transport mode protects the transport layer and up. As such, when the IPsec packet travels across an untrusted network, all of the data within the packet is safe (based on the IPsec services selected). Devices in the untrusted network can see only the actual IP addresses of the IPsec participants.

IPsec offers a second mode called tunnel mode. In tunnel mode, the actual IP addresses of the original IP header, along with all the data within the packet, are protected. Tunnel mode creates a new external IP header that contains the IP addresses of the tunnel endpoints (such as routers or VPN Concentrators). The exposed IP addresses are the tunnel endpoints, not the device IP addresses that sit behind the tunnel end points. Figure 12-1 shows the two IPsec modes compared to a "normal" IP packet.

Figure 12-1 *IPsec Modes*

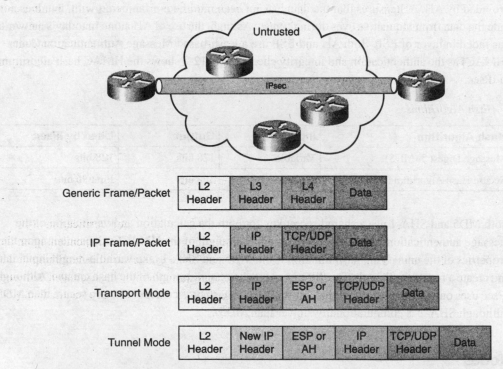

As mentioned earlier, the endpoints of the IPsec tunnel can be any device. Figure 12-1 shows routers as endpoints, which might be used for site-to-site VPNs (explained in Chapter 13, "Site-to-Site VPN Operations"). It is also important to remember that the concept of a *VPN tunnel* is used with both VPN modes—transport and tunnel. In transport mode, the packet contents are protected between the VPN endpoints, whereas in tunnel mode, the entire original IP packet is protected.

IPsec Headers

Both AH and ESP are implemented by adding headers to the original IP packet. The IPsec VPN uses AH or ESP, or both (but the use of AH along with ESP has no appreciable benefit). Remember that ESP implements all of the IPsec features mentioned earlier, while AH offers all features except data confidentiality. Both AH and ESP are recognized by their particular IP protocol numbers, which makes each a transport layer protocol. AH and ESP are recognized by their respective IP protocol numbers (51 and 50).

The placement of these headers means that the IPsec features that they provide (confidentiality and integrity) can only be for portions of the IP packet that follow the AH or ESP header.

Figure 12-2 shows how the ESP and AH headers are applied to an existing IP packet. Both transport and tunnel modes are shown for comparison.

Figure 12-2 *AH and ESP Headers*

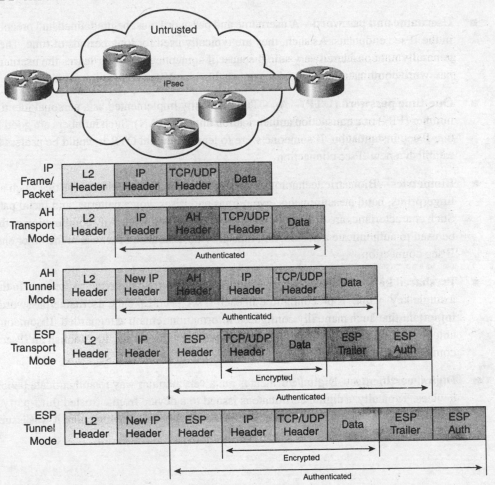

As shown in Figure 12-2, AH authenticates the entire packet after the Layer 2 header. If ESP authentication is used, the outer IP header is not authenticated. Also note that if ESP performs both encryption and authentication, encryption occurs first, and then the encrypted contents along with the ESP headers are authenticated.

Peer Authentication

As described thus far, IPsec has the capability to protect data in transit. It can encrypt the data to prevent those in the middle from seeing it (data confidentiality), and it can ensure that the data has not been modified while in flight (data integrity). However, these functions lose their appeal if one VPN endpoint is not sure of whom the other endpoint truly is. IPsec can secure the data transfer, but before such services are employed, the endpoints of the IPsec VPN must be validated.

The concept of peer authentication certifies that the remote IPsec endpoint is truly who it says it is. There are five different methods to authenticate an IPsec peer:

- **Username and password**—A username and password must be predefined and preconfigured in the IPsec endpoints. As such, they are typically used for long periods of time. They are generally not considered very safe, because if someone guesses or learns the username/ password combination, that person can establish an IPsec connection with you.

- **One-time password (OTP)**—An OTP is typically implemented as a personal identification number (PIN) or a transaction authentication number (TAN). Such numbers are good for only one IPsec instantiation. If someone were to learn of an old OTP, it would be useless to establish a new IPsec connection.

- **Biometrics**—Biometric technologies analyze physical human characteristics, such as fingerprints, hand measurements, eye retinas and irises, voice patterns, and facial patterns. Such characteristics are difficult, if not impossible, to duplicate. Any combination of these can be used to authenticate a person, and thus provide assurance of who is at the other end of the IPsec connection.

- **Preshared keys**—Preshared keys are similar to the username/password concept. In this case, a single key (value) is preconfigured in each IPsec peer. Like the username/password, it is important that such manually configured information remain safeguarded. If someone were able to determine the preshared key, they would have the ability to establish an IPsec connection with you.

- **Digital certificates**—Digital certificates are a very popular way to authenticate people and devices. Typically, a digital certificate is issued to a device from a trusted third-party certification authority (CA). This certificate is only good for the machine it was issued to.

When that device needs to authenticate, it presents its certificate, which is then validated against the third-party CA. If another device attempts to use the certificate, the authentication will fail.

Internet Key Exchange (IKE)

A secure IPsec connection between two devices can initially be established by configuring encryption keys in both devices. However, the failure to periodically change these keys makes the network susceptible to brute-force password attacks. The need to manually change the IPsec keys every hour or every day can prove troublesome. If dozens or hundreds of IPsec connections are in use, manual key maintenance can be a nightmare.

IKE Protocols

The IKE protocol, as described earlier, is a means of dynamically exchanging IPsec parameters and keys. IKE makes IPsec scalable by automating the key exchange/update process needed to repel password attacks against the IPsec sessions. IKE helps to automatically establish security associations (SAs) between two IPsec endpoints. An SA is an agreement of IPsec parameters between two peers.

IKE actually uses other protocols to perform peer authentication and key generation:

- **ISAKMP**—The Internet Security Association and Key Management Protocol defines procedures on how to establish, negotiate, modify, and delete SAs. All parameter negotiation is handled through ISAKMP, such as header authentication and payload encapsulation (headers and modes were discussed earlier). ISAKMP performs peer authentication, but it does not involve key exchange.

- **Oakley**—The Oakley protocol uses the Diffie-Hellman algorithm to manage key exchanges across IPsec SAs. Diffie-Hellman is a cryptographic protocol that permits two end points to exchange a shared secret over an insecure channel.

IKE Phases

The IKE protocol/process is broken into two phases, which create a secure communications channel between two IPsec endpoints. Although there are two primary and mandatory IKE phases, there is an optional third phase. The three phases are described here:

- IKE phase 1 is one of the mandatory IKE phases. A bidirectional SA is established between IPsec peers in phase 1. This means that data sent between the end devices uses the same key material. Phase 1 may also perform peer authentication to validate the identity of the IPsec endpoints. There are two IKE modes available for IKE phase 1 to establish the bidirectional

SA: main mode and aggressive mode. IKE modes are described in the next section. Phase 1 consists of parameter negotiation, such as hash methods and transform sets. The two IPsec peers must agree on these parameters or the IPsec connection cannot be established.

■ IKE phase 1.5 is an optional IKE phase. Phase 1.5 provides an additional layer of authentication, called Xauth, or Extended Authentication. IPsec authentication provided in Phase 1 authenticates the devices or endpoints used to establish the IPsec connection. However, there is no means of validating the users behind the devices. A preconfigured IPsec device can be used by both friends and foes. Xauth forces the user to authenticate before use of the IPsec connection is granted.

■ IKE phase 2 is the second mandatory IKE phase. Phase 2 implements unidirectional SAs between the IPsec endpoints using the parameters agreed upon in Phase 1. The use of unidirectional SAs means that separate keying material is needed for each direction. Phase 2 uses IKE quick mode to establish each of the unidirectional SAs.

IKE Modes

IKE consists of three different modes. As mentioned earlier, IKE phase 1 has a choice of two modes (main or aggressive), while IKE phase 2 always uses the same mode (quick). For one IPsec session between two devices, either main or aggressive mode is used for IKE phase 1, and quick mode is always used for IKE phase 2. The IKE modes are described in the sections that follow. The third optional IKE mode is phase 1.5, which is optionally used for extended authentication.

IKE Main Mode

Main mode consists of six messages exchanged between the IPsec peers. If main mode is selected, aggressive mode is not used. Quick mode always follows main mode. These six messages of main mode are broken into three pairs:

■ **IPsec parameters and security policy**—The initiator sends one or more proposals, and the responder selects the appropriate one.

■ **Diffie-Hellman public key exchange**—Public keys are sent between the two IPsec endpoints.

■ **ISAKMP session authentication**—Each end is authenticated by the other.

IKE Aggressive Mode

Aggressive mode is an abbreviated version of main mode. If aggressive mode is selected, main mode is not used. Quick mode always follows aggressive mode. The six packets of main mode are condensed into three:

- The initiator sends all data, including IPsec parameters, security policies, and Diffie-Hellman public keys.

- The responder authenticates the packet and sends the parameter proposal, key material, and identification back.

- The initiator authenticates the packet.

IKE Quick Mode

Quick mode is used during IKE phase 2. The negotiation of quick mode is protected by the IKE SA negotiated in Phase 1. Such an option is not available during main or aggressive modes, because their function is to establish the first SA. Quick mode negotiates the SAs used for data encryption across the IPsec connection. It also manages the key exchange for those SAs.

Other IKE Functions

Thus far, IKE has been shown as a protocol that exchanges IPsec parameters and keys. However, it does perform other functions that are important to the setup and maintenance of the IPsec connections. These functions include:

- Dead peer detection (DPD)

- NAT traversal

- Mode configuration

- Xauth

Dead peer detection is accomplished by sending periodic keepalive (or hello) timers between IPsec peers. To be effective, the timer should be fairly repetitive (such as every 10 seconds). That way, the failure of the IPsec connection is quickly recognized by the loss of hello packets. One downside to DPD is the additional traffic that must be sent across the IPsec session.

NAT traversal solves one problem that Network Address Translation/Port Address Translation (NAT/PAT) introduces. Remember that PAT translates both IP addresses and ports typically to permit multiple "inside" devices to share a single or fewer "outside" IP addresses. To translate from one port number to another, the port numbers must be available in the transport layer headers. However, IPsec typically encrypts all data above Layer 3.

NAT traversal is solved using both IKE phase 1 and phase 2. During phase 1 (before quick mode), it is determined whether NAT is supported (NAT support) and whether NAT exists (NAT existence) along the path of the proposed IPsec connection. IKE phase 2 (quick mode) decides whether the IPsec peers will use NAT traversal. The negotiation of NAT traversal occurs via the quick mode SA that is established.

NAT traversal is accomplished by inserting a UDP header before the ESP header in the IPsec packet. This new transport layer header has unencrypted port information that can be stored in PAT tables, and thus the PAT translation process can successfully occur. Figure 12-3 shows a normal IPsec packet compared to one that has been modified for NAT traversal. As mentioned earlier, IPsec end devices can be routers (as shown) or other network devices, such as workstations, servers, or VPN Concentrators.

Figure 12-3 *NAT Traversal*

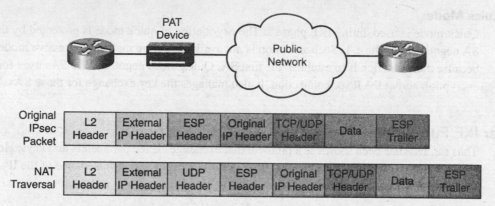

IKE mode configuration is simply a means of pushing all the IPsec attributes out to the remote IPsec client. Such attributes include the IP address to be used for the IPsec connection, and the DNS and NetBIOS name servers to be used across the IPsec connection. Because these and other attributes can be pushed down to the IPsec client, the required configuration on the client is minimized.

The Cisco Easy VPN solution is an example of such a push model. The server, which runs on Cisco routers, Cisco VPN Concentrators, and Cisco PIX Firewalls, pushes the necessary security policies and parameters out to the remote client, which can be another Cisco router, Cisco VPN Concentrator, Cisco PIX Firewall, or Cisco VPN Client on a workstation.

IKE extended authentication (Xauth), as already mentioned, is a way to authenticate a user of an IPsec connection. Remember that IKE itself provides for device authentication. Xauth adds an additional layer of authentication that a user must validate by means of a username/password combination, Challenge Handshake Authentication Protocol (CHAP), one-time passwords (OTP), or secure key (S/KEY).

Encryption Algorithms

Encryption is simply a mathematical algorithm and a key applied to data to make the contents unreadable to everyone except those who have the ability to decrypt it. Ideally, encrypted data can be decrypted only with the proper key. Thus, the strength of the cipher text (encrypted data) is based on the complexity of the encryption algorithm, and the size of the key used to encrypt the data. There are two types of encryption algorithms available: symmetric and asymmetric.

Symmetric Encryption

Symmetric encryption algorithms are also called secret key cryptography. As the name implies, there is a single, secret key that is used to both encrypt and decrypt the data. It is very important that the secret key remain a secret. Anyone who manages to get the key can decrypt any messages encrypted with it. This was the only type of encryption available through the mid-1970s. Symmetric algorithms tend to be computationally easier to implement, and are useful for large, bulk encryption requirements.

Today, DES, 3DES, and AES are examples of symmetric encryption algorithms:

- DES, with its 56-bit key, has been broken in less than 24 hours using modern computers.

- 3DES applies three different 56-bit keys (DES encrypt, DES decrypt, DES encrypt) to create the cipher text. It has not yet been broken, but has theoretical flaws.

- AES is considered the symmetric encryption choice today. It originally was called Rijndael. Both AES and Rijndael use the same encryption algorithm and support keys ranging from 128 bits to 256 bits. The difference between the two is that AES uses 64-bit increments, while Rijndael uses multiples of 32. AES is the only public symmetric encryption algorithm adopted by the National Security Agency for use in top-secret networks.

Asymmetric Encryption

Asymmetric encryption algorithms use different keys for encryption and decryption. In fact, the key used to encrypt data cannot be used to decrypt it. The encryption key is called the *public key*, while the decryption key is called the *private key*. It is possible, and expected, to widely distribute the public key. This key can be used only to encrypt messages that will eventually be decrypted with the associated private key.

For digital signatures, the use of the two keys is reversed. The private key is used to sign a hash of the message, while the public key decrypts and validates the signature. In all cases, the private key should be kept secret, similar to the shared secret keys used with symmetric encryption algorithms.

RSA (named after its designers—Rivest, Shamir, and Adleman) is an asymmetric encryption algorithm. It was also the first algorithm that could be used for both signing and encrypting. RSA key lengths start at 1024 bits and get longer (typically by doubling the key length). Full decryption of an RSA key is thought to be impossible due to the difficulty in factoring large prime integers (which is the basic premise of the RSA cryptosystem), although this has not been mathematically proven. Unlike symmetric algorithms, asymmetric algorithms tend to be computationally expensive to implement, and are not well suited for continuous, bulk encryption jobs.

It was mentioned earlier that symmetric encryption algorithms use the same secret key for encrypting and decrypting. The trick is to keep the secret key covert. Asymmetric encryption algorithms use different keys for encryption and decryption. Asymmetric key exchange algorithms can be used to safely deliver shared secret keys across an insecure network, which can then be use for bulk encryption via symmetric algorithms across that same network.

Diffie-Hellman is the primary asymmetric key exchange algorithm used in IPsec for the exchange of shared secret keys. Table 12-3 outlines the Diffie-Hellman exchange process, which occurs in parallel between two IPsec peers—A and B.

Table 12-3 *The Diffie-Hellman Key Exchange*

Step	What Peer A Does	What Peer A Knows	What Peer B Does	What Peer B Knows
1	Generates a large prime integer → P_A. Sends P_A to peer B. Receives the prime integer generated by peer B → P_B. Generates a primitive root of P_A and P_B → R.	P_A P_B R	Generates a large prime integer → P_B. Sends P_B to peer A. Receives the prime integer generated by peer A → P_A. Generates a primitive root of P_A and P_B → R.	P_A P_B R
2	Generates its private key → X_A.	P_A P_B R X_A	Generates its private key → X_B.	P_A P_B R X_B
3	Generates a public key for peer B → $Y_A = R \char`\^ X_A \bmod P_A$.	P_A P_B R X_A Y_A	Generates a public key for peer A → $Y_B = R \char`\^ X_B \bmod P_B$.	P_A P_B R X_B Y_B

Table 12-3   *The Diffie-Hellman Key Exchange (Continued)*

Step	What Peer A Does	What Peer A Knows	What Peer B Does	What Peer B Knows
4	Sends Y_A to peer B. Receives the public key from peer B → Y_B.	P_A P_B R X_A Y_A Y_B	Sends Y_B to peer A. Receives the public key from peer A → Y_A.	P_A P_B R X_B Y_A Y_B
5	Generates a shared secret number → $Z = Y_B \wedge X_A \bmod P_A$.	P_A P_B R X_A Y_A Y_B Z	Generates a shared secret number → $Z = Y_A \wedge X_B \bmod P_A$.	P_A P_B R X_B Y_A Y_B Z
6	Generates a shared secret key from Z → SS (for DES, 3DES, or AES).	P_A P_B R X_A Y_A Y_B Z SS	Generates a shared secret key from Z → SS (for DES, 3DES, or AES).	P_A P_B R X_B Y_A Y_B Z SS

The large prime number that is used as a seed of the whole process is determined by the Diffie-Hellman group that the two IPsec endpoints agreed upon. Diffie-Hellman consists of seven different groups (1–7). Each group defines a unique modular exponentiation (MODP) algorithm and key size. The base key is a large prime integer that is used to calculate the public/private key pairs (as shown in Table 12-3).

The mathematical exponentiation in steps 3 and 5 is computationally challenging. The respective public keys are generated in step 3 and exchanged in step 4. As mentioned before, the interception of a public key does not cause any security concerns for an asymmetrical encryption algorithm. Note that the private keys (X_A and X_B) are never exchanged.

Public Key Infrastructure

A public key infrastructure (PKI) is the progression of the key exchange and maintenance concepts discussed throughout this chapter. A PKI provides a hierarchical framework for managing the security attributes of entities who engage in secure communications across a network. Such entities can be all of the IPsec devices mentioned throughout this chapter, as well as the people who use those devices.

The PKI consists of a number of elements, which are also network entities:

- **Peers**—Devices and people who securely communicate across a network. Also known as end hosts.

- **Certification authority (CA)**—Grants and maintains digital certificates. Also known as a trusted entity or a trust point.

- **Digital certificate**—Contains information to uniquely identify a peer, a signed copy of the public encryption key used for secure communications, certificate validity data, and the signature of the CA that issued the certificate. X.509v3 is the current version of digital certificate.

- **Registration authority (RA)**—An optional entity that can handle enrollment requests (obtaining a certificate) for the CA.

- **Distribution mechanism**—A means to distribute certificate revocation lists (CRLs) across the network. LDAP and HTTP are examples.

Through PKI, every network entity who wishes to participate in secure communications receives a digital certificate, which contains a public/private key pair, and has their identity validated by a CA. When peers need to establish a secure communications channel, they exchange certificates.

Certificates can be validated by CAs, and the enclosed keys can be used to secure the channel. Table 12-4 details the PKI message exchange process.

Table 12-4 *The PKI Message Exchange Process*

Step	Action
1	An end host generates an RSA key pair (public/private) and requests the public key of its CA.
2	The CA sends its public key to the end host.
3	The end host generates a certificate request.
	Depending on the network configuration, either the request is automatically sent to the CA or manual intervention is needed to approve the request.
	The certificate request is sent to either the CA or the optional RA (if present).
	The CA or RA receives the certificate request.
4	Once approved, the CA signs the certificate request with its private key.
	The CA returns the completed certificate to the end host.
5	The end host saves the certificate to some nonvolatile storage area, such as disk, USB smart card (eToken), or NVRAM.
6	The end host uses the validated certificate to establish secure communications with other end hosts that have accomplished these steps.

Foundation Summary

The concept of IPsec often centers on the use of VPN tunnels to encrypt data between endpoints. The use of VPNs is ubiquitous today. The use of IPsec VPNs over the Internet has replaced many of the older point-to-point or virtual circuit–based shared WAN connections. A good understanding of how IPsec operates helps hasten successful deployments.

IPsec offers data confidentiality, data integrity, data origin authentication, and optional anti-replay. Confidentiality is provided through symmetric encryption algorithms such as DES, 3DES, and AES. Data integrity and origin authentication are provided by HMAC algorithms like MD5 and SHA-1.

IPsec can offer integrity and authentication services via AH or add confidentiality to integrity and authentication with ESP. The use of these two protocols can be implemented in either transport mode (only the IP data is protected) or tunnel mode (where the IP header and data are protected). IKE is the third IPsec protocol used to safely exchange keys for symmetric encryption and IPsec security parameters for proper IPsec connection establishment.

Q&A

The questions and scenarios in this book are more difficult than what you will experience on the actual exam. The questions do not attempt to cover more breadth or depth than the exam, but they are designed to make sure that you know the answer. Rather than enabling you to derive the answer from clues hidden inside the question itself, the questions challenge your understanding and recall of the subject.

Hopefully, mastering these questions will help you limit the number of exam questions on which you narrow your choices to two options, and then guess.

The answers to these questions can be found in Appendix A.

1. What are the features of IPsec?

2. What are the three main protocols specified by IPsec?

3. Describe the differences between data confidentiality and data integrity.

4. Which IPsec features are performed by an HMAC?

5. How does IPsec tunnel mode differ from IPsec transport mode?

6. Describe the port or protocol numbers used for AH, ESP, and IKE.

7. Define one-time passwords.

8. Which peer authentication methods require the use of predefined and/or preconfigured information into the IPsec endpoints?

9. What problem does IKE solve for IPsec?

10. Which IKE phase is responsible for extended authentication?

11. IKE creates a number of SAs. What is the purpose of a bidirectional SA?

12. Describe the three IKE modes.

13. What are some of the additional features of IKE?

14. What are the features of symmetric encryption?

15. Which algorithms are considered asymmetric?

16. Which optional PKI component can handle enrollment requests?

17. X.509v3 is considered the current version of which security mechanism?

18. Within the PKI, what are LDAP and HTTP examples of?

Exam Topic List

This chapter covers the following topics that you need to master for the CCNP ISCW exam:

- **Site-to-Site VPN Overview**—Describes how a single VPN between sites permits various devices to have secure communications.

- **Creating a Site-to-Site IPsec VPN**—Describes what is needed to create a site-to-site VPN.

- **Site-to-Site IPsec Configuration Steps**—Covers the steps needed to create a site-to-site VPN.

- **Security Device Manager Features and Interface**—Describes how SDM is used to configure a Cisco IOS device.

- **Configuring a Site-to-Site VPN in SDM**—Explains the specific steps within SDM to create a site-to-site VPN.

- **Monitoring the IPsec VPN Tunnel**—Describes how to examine and monitor the VPN tunnel after it has been created.

CHAPTER 13

Site-to-Site VPN Operations

The growth of the Internet has spawned the use of site-to-site VPNs. Prior to widespread adoption of the Internet, remote sites were connected to each other or back to a central location via point-to-point connections or virtual circuits. Because virtually every location has an Internet connection today, connectivity to virtually anywhere is possible. Secure connectivity is achieved through the use of IPsec VPNs.

Site-to-site VPNs are typically used to connect a remote office back to the central facility. Typically, more than one end device at one site needs to securely communicate with more than one end device at the other location. If only a single device is connecting to a network, then a VPN client on the workstation is sufficient.

A site-to-site VPN eliminates the need for each device to establish its own secure path to the remote location. A single IPsec VPN is used to securely carry all packets between sites.

"Do I Know This Already?" Quiz

The purpose of the "Do I Know This Already?" quiz is to help you decide whether you really need to read the entire chapter. If you already intend to read the entire chapter, you do not necessarily need to answer these questions now.

The 24-question quiz, derived from the major sections in the "Foundation Topics" portion of the chapter, helps you to determine how to spend your limited study time.

Table 13-1 outlines the major topics discussed in this chapter and the "Do I Know This Already?" quiz questions that correspond to those topics.

Table 13-1 *"Do I Know This Already?" Foundation Topics Section-to-Question Mapping*

Foundation Topics Section	Questions Covered in This Section	Score
Creating a Site-to-Site IPsec VPN	1–6	
Site-to-Site IPsec Configuration Steps	7–13	
Security Device Manager Features and Interface	14	
Configuring a Site-to-Site VPN in SDM	15–22	
Monitoring the IPsec VPN Tunnel	23–24	
Total Score		

CAUTION The goal of self-assessment is to gauge your mastery of the topics in this chapter. If you do not know the answer to a question or are only partially sure of the answer, you should mark this question wrong for purposes of self-assessment. Giving yourself credit for an answer that you correctly guess skews your self-assessment results and might provide you with a false sense of security.

---

1. In IPsec, what does interesting traffic refer to?

   a. Traffic that creates but does not travel through an IPsec tunnel

   b. Traffic that does not create but travels through an IPsec tunnel

   c. Traffic that both creates and travels through an IPsec tunnel

   d. Traffic that causes an IPsec tunnel to be torn down

   e. Traffic that causes a new set of IPsec keys to be exchanged

2. What are the two databases that are used to track IPsec SAs (select two)?

   a. Security Association Policy Database (SAPD)

   b. Security Association Database (SAD)

   c. Security Policy Database (SPD)

   d. Security Association Security Database (SASD)

   e. Security Association Security Database (SAS)

3. How are IKE transform sets used (select all that apply)?

   a. There is one transform set for each IKE parameter.

   b. There is one transform set for each IKE neighbor.

   c. There is one transform set for each unique group of IKE parameters.

   d. There may be multiple transform sets that are used for a single IKE neighbor.

   e. One transform set may be used for multiple IKE neighbors.

4. How many secure tunnels are created for a typical IPsec connection?

    a. One bidirectional IKE tunnel and two unidirectional IPsec SAs

    b. Two unidirectional IKE tunnels and one bidirectional IPsec SA

    c. One bidirectional IKE tunnel and one bidirectional IPsec SA

    d. Two unidirectional IKE tunnels and two bidirectional IPsec SAs

    e. One bidirectional tunnel for both IKE and IPsec traffic

5. What is the SA lifetime used for?

    a. Determines at what time an IPsec SA must be created

    b. Determines at what time an IPsec SA must be torn down

    c. Determines at what time an IKE SA must be created

    d. Defines the conditions when an IKE SA must be torn down

    e. Defines how long an IPsec SA can operate before it must be torn down

6. Which of the seven different Diffie-Hellman versions are supported by Cisco (select all that apply)?

    a. 1

    b. 2

    c. 4

    d. 5

    e. 7

7. The *configure ISAKMP policy* IPsec configuration step maps to which generic IPsec step?

    a. Specify interesting traffic

    b. IKE phase 1

    c. IKE phase 2

    d. Secure data transfer

    e. IPsec tunnel termination

8. The *configure IPsec transform sets* IPsec configuration step maps to which generic IPsec step?

    a. Specify interesting traffic

    b. IKE phase 1

    c. IKE phase 2

    d. Secure data transfer

    e. IPsec tunnel termination

9. Which of the following IKE parameters are configured within the **crypto isakmp policy** command (select all that apply)?

   a. Encryption algorithm

   b. Hash algorithm

   c. Authentication method

   d. Diffie-Hellman group

   e. IKE tunnel lifetime

10. Which of the following transform types are configured with the **crypto ipsec transform-set** command (select all that apply)?

    a. AH transform

    b. AH-ESP transform

    c. ESP encryption transform

    d. ESP authentication transform

    e. AH authentication transform

11. When configuring the ESP encryption transform, which key lengths are available for AES (select all that apply)?

    a. 64 bits

    b. 128 bits

    c. 192 bits

    d. 256 bits

    e. 512 bits

12. Which of the following is the correct interface command to apply the crypto map "test"?

    a. **crypto map test in**

    b. **crypto-map test in**

    c. **crypto map test out**

    d. **crypto-map test out**

    e. **crypto map test**

13. Which protocols/ports must be permitted so that IPsec VPNs can be created (select all that apply)?

   a. Protocol AHP

   b. Protocol ESP

   c. Protocol ISAKMP

   d. UDP port ESP

   e. UDP port AHP

14. Which SDM page is used to access the Site-to-Site VPN Wizard?

   a. Home

   b. Configure

   c. Monitor

   d. Refresh

   e. Save

15. Which options are offered at the start of the Site-to-Site VPN Wizard (select all that apply)?

   a. Create a Site to Site GRE Tunnel

   b. Create a Secure GRE Tunnel

   c. Create a Site to Site VPN

   d. Create a Secure VPN Tunnel

   e. Create an IPsec VPN Tunnel

16. The first step of the Site-to-Site VPN Wizard is to select a configuration option. Which of the following are available choices (select all that apply)?

   a. Quick Setup

   b. Instant Setup

   c. Step by Step Setup

   d. Step by Step Wizard

   e. Manual Setup

17. In the Quick Setup portion of the Site-to-Site VPN Wizard, what configuration options are possible (select all that apply)?

   a. Source interface

   b. IPsec peer IP address

   c. IKE policy

   d. IPsec transform set

   e. Destination subnet for the interesting traffic

18. Which window in the step-by-step setup of the Site-to-Site VPN Wizard is used to configure the tunnel mode?

   a. Connection Settings

   b. IKE Proposals

   c. IPSec Transform Sets

   d. Traffic to Protect

   e. Summary

19. Which IKE lifetime options are available in SDM (select all that apply)?

   a. Hours

   b. Minutes

   c. Seconds

   d. Bytes

   e. Kilobytes

20. On the IPsec Transform Sets screen, how many IPsec transform sets can be displayed at a time?

   a. All transform sets

   b. Only the active transform sets

   c. Only the transform sets applied to this IPsec VPN

   d. Only the transform set displayed in the pull-down menu

   e. Only the transform sets that are selected in the pull-down menu

21. When defining interesting traffic in the Quick Setup window, which options are available (select all that apply)?

   a. Source IP address

   b. Source IP subnet

   c. Destination IP address

   d. Destination IP subnet

   e. ACLs for multiple subnets

22. When completing the configuration of the site-to-site VPN tunnel in the Summary window, which options are available (select all that apply)?

    a. Return to the configuration with the **<Back** button

    b. Advance to the next summary screen with the **Next>** button

    c. Complete the configuration with the Finish button

    d. Edit the configuration with the Edit button

    e. Abort the configuration with the Cancel button.

23. Which SDM page allows you to view the status of various VPN configurations?

    a. Home page

    b. Configure page

    c. Monitor page

    d. VPN page

    e. Security page

24. In the IOS, what command displays the results of successful IKE phase II negotiations?

    a. **show crypto isakmp sa**

    b. **show crypto ipsec sa**

    c. **show crypto ipsec established**

    d. **show crypto ike negotiated**

    e. **show crypto isakmp established**

The answers to the "Do I Know This Already?" quiz are found in Appendix A, "Answers to the 'Do I Know This Already?' Quizzes and Q&A Sections." The suggested choices for your next step are as follows:

- **16 or fewer overall score**—Read the entire chapter. This includes the "Foundation Topics," "Foundation Summary," and "Q&A" sections.

- **18 or 20 overall score**—Begin with the "Foundation Summary" section, and then go to the "Q&A" section.

- **21 or more overall score**—If you want more review on these topics, skip to the "Foundation Summary" section, and then go to the "Q&A" section. Otherwise, move to the next chapter.

Foundation Topics

Site-to-Site VPN Overview

Even before the remarkable growth of the Internet, corporations had deployed remote offices, disbursed data centers, and establish global operations. Before the Internet was embraced as a trusted conduit to fulfill such corporate communications requirements, however, carriers were called upon to provide local, regional, national, and international conduits between locations. Figure 13-1 shows two corporate sites connected "the old way."

Figure 13-1 *Carrier-Provided Circuits*

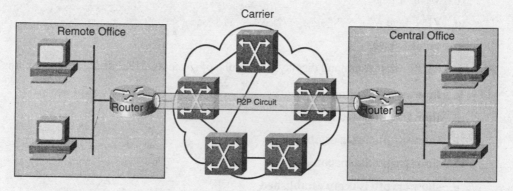

Before the Internet became the ubiquitous means of global connectivity that it is today, various carriers created enormous networks and provided connectivity services for a fee. Corporations often tried to use a single carrier to provide connections between the various remote offices. This is depicted in Figure 13-1. However, the use of a single carrier was often not possible due to the location of remote offices outside the carrier presence.

The circuit-based connections provided by the carriers can be thought of as the first site-to-site VPNs. They were indeed private connections between endpoints. Whether they were "nailed-up" permanent virtual circuits (PVC) or "create as needed" switched virtual circuits (SVC), the carriers ensured that the data was delivered as promised between the sites. PVCs tended to offer fixed-sized pipes across the carrier's network, while SVCs had fixed minimum data rates with burst capabilities.

When the Internet grew beyond its academic beginnings, corporations started to experiment with using it to transport data. Soon, the same carriers who offered VC services became Internet service providers (ISP) and offered Internet connectivity. The difference was that instead of providing end-to-end connections, they simply provided access—access to the entire Internet. It is difficult to provide throughput guarantees across the Internet due to its open and shared nature.

The need to create private, secure communications channels between sites saw the rise of site-to-site IPsec VPNs. Figure 13-2 shows such a connection.

Figure 13-2 *Site-to-Site IPsec VPN*

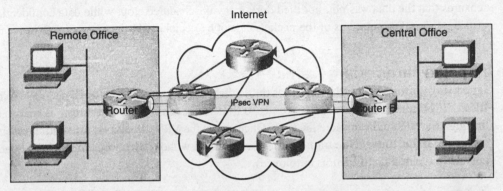

The networks depicted in both Figure 13-1 and Figure 13-2 are similar, and for a reason. The corporate sites shown have not changed all that much from the days of the carriers. Back then, a remote site had connectivity only back to the main campus or to some other central location. In today's networks, a remote site can use its generic Internet connectivity to get anywhere in the Internet (as depicted by the arrows to the great beyond) and use its IPsec VPN to securely communicate with the main campus.

Creating a Site-to-Site IPsec VPN

There are five generic steps in the lifecycle of any IPsec VPN. The steps described here are applied specifically to site-to-site VPNs, but these steps are true whenever any two endpoints wish to establish an IPsec VPN between them. The five steps in the life of an IPsec VPN are as follows:

Step 1   Specify interesting traffic.

Step 2   IKE phase 1.

Step 3   IKE phase 2.

Step 4   Secure data transfer.

Step 5   IPsec tunnel termination.

Each of these steps is detailed in the following sections. Some of these steps should be familiar from Chapter 12, "IPsec Overview," where IKE was a primary ingredient. In this chapter, IKE is moved from the explanation to the implementation.

The name "VPN tunnel" is somewhat of a misnomer to some. There is no tunnel that the packets are locked inside of as they transit the Internet (or some insecure network). All the IPsec VPN packets are subject to interception and capture at any point during their travels. Data integrity ensures that the data was not modified during any unscheduled stop, while data confidentiality guarantees that the contents of the packets cannot be deciphered by any unwanted inspectors.

Step 1: Specify Interesting Traffic

Interesting traffic is better thought of as traffic that must be protected by the IPsec VPN. When an IPsec VPN tunnel exists between two sites, traffic that is considered "interesting" is sent securely through the VPN to the remote location. Once inside the VPN, the data is safe until it reaches the other end of the tunnel. The traffic cannot be modified without detection, nor can it be read by anyone in the middle (if ESP is employed).

In fact, such traffic can only travel to the other end of the VPN tunnel. It cannot "escape" from the VPN tunnel and travel to some unintended destination. Only the predetermined VPN endpoint has the capability to validate and decrypt such packets.

This concept of interesting traffic also implies that packets that are not interesting do not enjoy the benefits of the IPsec VPN. They are not encrypted or protected in any way. They may travel to any destination, including the remote destination where the VPN tunnel terminates.

An extended access control list (ACL) is used to specify interesting traffic. Traffic that is permitted by this ACL has the appropriate security policy applied to it and the packets then enter the IPsec VPN tunnel. However, if the tunnel does not yet exist, then the arrival of the first interesting packet triggers the events needed to create the tunnel.

The five steps in the lifecycle of an IPsec VPN (explained here) assume that the tunnel does not yet exist and must be built upon the receipt of interesting traffic. It takes only one interesting packet to trigger the IPsec VPN tunnel process. If the IPsec tunnel already exists, then the traffic that is considered interesting (Step 1) is sent through the tunnel (Step 4).

Step 2: IKE Phase 1

Once the first packet deemed interesting arrives, the process of creating the site-to-site IPsec VPN tunnel commences. As already discussed in Chapter 12, IKE exchanges the security parameters and symmetric encryption keys used to create the IPsec tunnels that the data will eventually flow in. The second step in an IPsec VPN is the first phase of IKE.

Remember that IKE phase 1 has two possible modes: main mode or aggressive mode. The basic purpose of either mode is identical, but the number of messages exchanged is greatly reduced in aggressive mode. Figure 13-3 graphically shows IKE phase 1 main mode.

Figure 13-3 *IKE Phase 1, Main Mode*

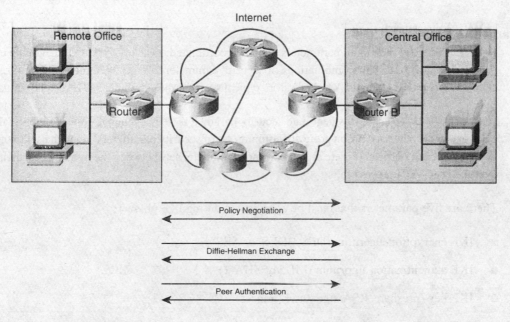

In main mode, the first two exchanges negotiate the security parameters used to establish the IKE tunnel. The two endpoints exchange proposals in the form of transform sets. The use of transform sets is explained later in this chapter.

The second pair of packets exchanges the Diffie-Hellman public keys needed to create the secure IKE tunnel. This tunnel is used later for the exchange of keys for the IPsec security associations (SA).

The final pair of packets performs peer authentication. Remember that a hash function is used to confirm identity and ensure that no rogue devices are permitted to establish a secure communications channel to your site.

Aggressive mode reduces the IKE phase 1 exchange to three packets:

■ The first packet goes from the initiator to the receiver. It sends security policy proposals, the Diffie-Hellman public key, a nonce (which is signed and returned for identity validation), and a means to perform authentication.

- The second packet goes from the receiver back to the initiator. It contains the accepted security policy proposal, its Diffie-Hellman public key, and the signed nonce for authentication.

- The final packet is a confirmation from the initiator to the receiver.

IKE Transform Sets

In IKE, numerous individual parameters must be coordinated. Instead of trying to negotiate each one individually, different combinations of security parameters are grouped into transform sets, also known as IKE policies. Administrators typically create these policies on IPsec endpoints.

Anytime two IPsec endpoints negotiate security parameters, they exchange IKE policies. If the pair of devices have a common policy (a common set of security parameters), then the setup of the IPsec VPN can continue. If there are no common parameter sets between the two devices, then the overall IPsec VPN process fails.

There are five parameters that must be coordinated during IKE phase 1:

- IKE encryption algorithm (DES, 3DES, or AES)

- IKE authentication algorithm (MD5 or SHA-1)

- IKE key (preshare, RSA signatures, nonces)

- Diffie-Hellman version (1, 2, or 5)

- IKE tunnel lifetime (time and/or byte count)

Figure 13-4 shows how the two IPsec endpoints use IKE transform sets to coordinate the IKE tunnel.

In Figure 13-4, Router A and Router B are attempting to negotiate an IKE tunnel. Assume that Router A starts the IKE negotiation process. Router A sends its two IKE policies, 10 and 20, to Router B. The change of a single parameter makes an entirely new IKE policy. It is possible to use the same IKE policy for multiple sites. However, different policies and parameters may dictate that unique IKE policies be used for each site.

When Router B receives the two transform sets, it compares the contents of each to any transform sets that it has. This comparison is done in sequence of the local IKE policies. The first match found becomes the policy that is used (which implies that there could be multiple policies with identical parameters). The policy number merely determines the comparison priority (sequence) and is not one of the parameters.

Figure 13-4 *IKE Transform Sets*

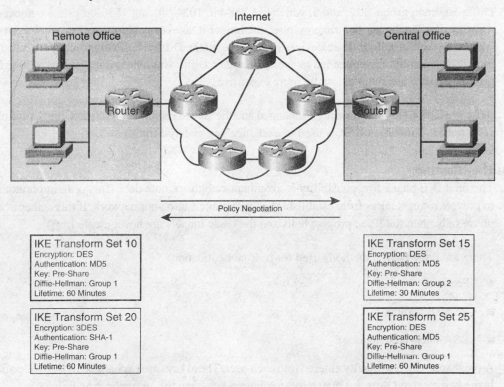

In this example, the contents of IKE policy 10 from Router A match those in IKE policy 25 in Router B. Router B responds to Router A that it accepts policy 10 and the IKE SA is created. If Router B could not find any exact parameter matches between the transform sets, then the IKE tunnel would not be constructed and the IPsec process would fail. Router A and Router B have found a common IKE policy, however, so an IKE SA can be established.

A remote site that creates only a single IPsec connection to one remote location needs only one IKE transform set. Multiple transform sets are needed if one location establishes many IPsec connections to different destinations and each uses different IKE parameters. It is possible to use a single transform set for multiple IKE connections, as long as each site uses the same security parameters.

Diffie-Hellman Key Exchange

After the IKE policies have been agreed to, the DH protocol is used to exchange the key material that will be used in Phase 1. Remember that DH allows two parties to share a secret key over an insecure channel. Because this key forms the basis of the rest of the VPN, it is essential that the key be kept secret.

Although there are seven different Diffie-Hellman groups (1–7), Cisco VPN devices support only Diffie-Hellman groups 1, 2, and 5, which use 768-bit, 1024-bit, and 1536-bit prime numbers, respectively. The larger the prime number, the longer it takes to generate the keys, but the more secure the keys are. Both IPsec devices must agree on the Diffie-Hellman group in the transform sets. It is generally recommended to avoid the use of Diffie-Hellman group 1 today, although groups 2 and 5 are computationally more expensive.

After the Diffie-Hellman keys are exchanged and the shared secret is established, the SA for phase 1 is created. This phase 1 SA is used to exchange key material for phase 2.

Peer Authentication

The final IKE phase 1 responsibility is to authenticate the remote peer. This is an important step to prevent rogue devices from establishing secure tunnels into your network. If this authentication phase fails, then the IPsec process halts and the IPsec tunnels are never created.

There are three typical methods used for peer authentication:

- Preshared keys

- RSA signatures

- RSA-encrypted nonces

A preshared key is manually entered into each peer. These keys are exchanged in the IKE policies. If the key received does not match the configured key, then the authentication fails.

RSA signatures use digital certificates to authenticate peers. Each peer is issued a certificate, and this certificate is passed in the transform set. The IPsec endpoint ensures that the certificate has been signed/validated by a known CA. If so, the peer is authenticated. RSA signatures are an instantiation of PKI.

A nonce is a number that is used only once. Think of it as a form of one-time password (OTP). A nonce is a "nonsense" random number generated by each peer, encrypted and sent to the other.

Step 3: IKE Phase 2

The actual IPsec tunnels are established in IKE phase 2. IKE phase 1 creates a very secure communications channel (its own SAs) so that the IPsec tunnels (SAs) can be created for data encryption and transport. IPsec parameters are negotiated via the IKE SAs.

The following functions are performed in IKE phase 2:

- Negotiation of IPsec security parameters via IPsec transform sets

- Establishment of IPsec SAs (unidirectional IPsec tunnels)

- Periodic renegotiation of IPsec SAs to ensure security

- An additional Diffie-Hellman exchange (optional)

Remember that IKE phase 2 has a single mode, called quick mode. Assuming phase 1 is successful (main or aggressive mode), quick mode is used in phase 2. Quick mode encompasses the entire process that occurs in IKE phase 2.

First, each IPsec peer must negotiate the IPsec parameters that are used to create the IPsec tunnels. Similar to IKE phase 1 (which uses IKE policies), IPsec transform sets are used during this process.

Once the IPsec parameters are agreed upon (discussed in the next section), the IPsec SAs can be created. IPsec SAs are unidirectional. Thus, two SAs are needed to have secure, bidirectional communication between two peers. Quick mode uses nonces to generate new key material for the shared secrets and to prevent replay attacks. Because a nonce is used only one time, the reuse of one would indicate a bogus SA attempt.

Quick mode also monitors the expiration of SAs and establishes new ones when needed. An SA should never stay up indefinitely, to prevent the encryption keys from ultimately being determined and compromised. When an SA nears expiration, a new one is created so that there is no loss of protected data flow.

Quick mode can also optionally perform additional Diffie-Hellman exchanges. Such exchanges would generate new public/private keys between the IPsec peers. This happens when the Diffie-Hellman keys expire, due to exceeding time or data allocations.

IPsec Transform Sets

A transform set, as described in the context of IKE policies, is a group of attributes that are exchanged together, which eliminates the need to coordinate and negotiate individual parameters. The difference between an IKE policy and an IPsec transform set are the attributes that are exchanged. Five parameters must be coordinated during quick mode between IPsec peers:

- IPsec protocol (ESP or AH)

- IPsec encryption type (DES, 3DES, or AES)

- IPsec authentication (MD5 or SHA-1)

- IPsec mode (tunnel or transport)

- IPsec SA lifetime (seconds or kilobytes)

Figure 13-5 shows how the two IPsec endpoints use IPsec transform sets to coordinate the IPsec SAs.

Figure 13-5 *IPsec Transform Sets*

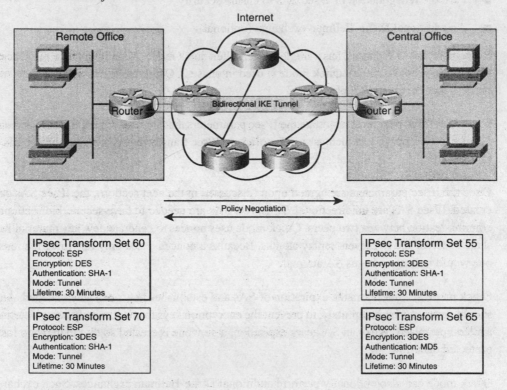

In Figure 13-5, Router A and Router B are attempting to negotiate parameters for IPsec SAs. Assume that Router A starts the IKE phase 2 negotiation process. Router A sends to Router B its two IPsec transform sets, 60 and 70. A single variation in any parameter makes the entire transform set different. The same IPsec transform set can be used for SAs to many destinations, so there is no need to create an identical transform set for each IPsec endpoint.

When Router B receives the two IPsec transform sets, it sequentially compares the contents of each to any transform sets that it has. The local IPsec transform set numbers determine the comparison priority or sequence. These numbers are not actual parameters in the transform set. The values of the security parameters are the important parts.

In this example, the contents of IPsec transform set 70 from Router A match those in IPsec transform set 55 in Router B. Router B responds to Router A that it accepts IPsec transform set 70 and the IPsec SAs are built. If Router B could not find any exact parameter matches between the IPsec transform sets, then the IPsec SAs would not be constructed and the IPsec process would fail.

A remote site that creates only a single IPsec connection to one location needs only one IPsec transform set. Multiple IPsec transform sets may be needed if one location establishes many IPsec connections to different destinations. It is possible to use a single IPsec transform set for SAs to multiple locations. Multiple IPsec transform sets would be needed if each IPsec connection used different security parameters.

Security Associations

A security association (SA) is a group of security services (parameters) agreed upon between two IPsec peers. As discussed earlier, these security parameters are exchanged during IKE phase 2 in transform sets. Once each IPsec endpoint agrees upon the common services to use, the IPsec SAs are constructed.

Each IPsec SA is a one-way connection between two IPsec peers. In most cases, effective network communications requires bidirectional traffic flow. Thus, a complete IPsec connection between two endpoints consists of two IPsec SAs—one incoming and one outgoing. Each of these SAs uses the same security parameters agreed upon in the IPsec transform sets. However, each SA is tracked and maintained separately.

Each SA is referenced by a Security Parameter Index (SPI). The SPI travels with each IPsec packet and is used to reference and confirm the security parameters upon arrival at the far end. The use of the SPI eliminates the need to send the security parameters with each IPsec packet.

Each IPsec client uses an SA Database (SAD) to track each of the SAs that the client participates in. Remember that for any remote client, there will be two SAs. The SAD contains the following information about each IPsec connection (SA):

- Destination IP address

- SPI number

- IPsec protocol (ESP or AH)

A second database, the Security Policy Database (SPD), contains the security parameters that were agreed upon for each SA (in the transform sets). For each SA, this database contains:

- Encryption algorithm (DES, 3DES, or AES)

- Authentication algorithm (MD5 or SHA-1)

- IPsec mode (tunnel or transport)

- Key lifetime (seconds or kilobytes)

The use of both the SAD and the SPD allows any IPsec client to quickly track IPsec attributes for any incoming or outgoing packets to any remote client.

SA Lifetime

One of the security parameters that must be agreed upon in the IPsec transform sets is the key lifetime. The IPsec tunnel must not use the same key indefinitely, due to the possibility of compromise. IPsec forces the keys to expire either after a predetermined amount of time (measured in seconds) or after a predetermined amount of data has been transferred (measured in kilobytes).

If data continues to flow through the IPsec connection as the key expiration approaches, new keys are exchanged, new tunnels are built, and the data stream is switched over to the new SAs. All of this typically occurs without any loss of data through the IPsec connection and without knowledge of the users involved.

The lifetime values must not be too excessive, to ensure that the security of the tunnel is not exposed or compromised. On the other hand, short lifetime values cause the two IPsec endpoints to continually generate and exchange new keys. Configuration of these values is described in the "Configure the IPsec Transform Sets" section later in this chapter.

Step 4: Secure Data Transfer

After the IPsec transform sets have been agreed upon by the two endpoints and the SAD and SPD have been updated at each end (which implies that the SAs have been built), traffic can flow through the IPsec tunnel. Remember that not all traffic is permitted through the tunnel. Only the interesting traffic that caused the tunnel to be created is permitted to use the tunnel. All other traffic continues to flow through the interface, but not through the IPsec VPN tunnel.

Step 5: IPsec Tunnel Termination

There are two events that can cause an IPsec tunnel to be terminated. As mentioned earlier, if the SA lifetime expires (time and/or byte count), then the tunnel must be torn down. However, if secure transfer is still needed between the two endpoints, then a new pair of SAs is normally created before the old set is retired.

It is also possible to manually delete an IPsec tunnel. This is typically done by an administrator at either end of the IPsec connection. In most cases, the automatic termination of the tunnel (due to excessive time or kilobyte usage) is sufficient and an administrator never needs to get involved.

Upon tunnel termination, all information about an SA is removed from both the SAD and SPD, regardless of the cause. The security parameters may be copied to a new SPI as the secure data exchange continues, but the actual entries in the database are deleted.

Site-to-Site IPsec Configuration Steps

Now that the components of a site-to-site IPsec VPN are understood, it is time to configure the secure connection using the Cisco IOS. There are five steps in the IPsec lifecycle (interesting traffic, IKE phase 1, IKE phase 2, secure data transfer, tunnel termination). However, not all of those steps require configuration. Thus, there cannot be a direct 1:1 map between IPsec steps and configuration steps. The six steps necessary to configure a site-to-site IPsec VPN are as follows:

Step 1   Configure the ISAKMP policy (IKE phase 1).

Step 2   Configure the IPsec transform sets (IKE phase 2, tunnel termination).

Step 3   Configure the crypto ACL (interesting traffic, secure data transfer).

Step 4   Configure the crypto map (IKE phase 2).

Step 5   Apply the crypto map to the interface (IKE phase 2).

Step 6   Configure the interface ACL.

> **NOTE**   A mapping to the generic IPsec steps is given to further understand the process. Each of these steps is explained with IOS CLI configurations in this chapter. Note that the sequence of the generic IPsec steps does not match the configuration sequence. And some configuration steps cover multiple generic IPsec steps.

Step 1: Configure the ISAKMP Policy

Configuration of the ISAKMP policy basically maps to IKE phase 1, described earlier. Remember that IKE phase 1 establishes a secure bidirectional tunnel that is used to exchange IPsec keys for the SAs. The following list is a reminder of the IKE phase 1 parameters:

- IKE encryption algorithm (DES, 3DES, or AES)

- IKE authentication algorithm (MD5 or SHA-1)

- IKE key (preshared, RSA signatures, nonces)

- Diffie-Hellman version (1, 2, or 5)

- IKE tunnel lifetime (time and/or byte count)

Figure 13-6 shows the configuration of ISAKMP parameters.

Figure 13-6 *ISAKMP Parameter Configuration*

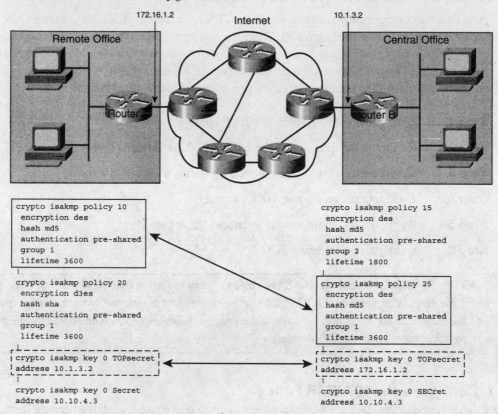

As shown earlier, IKE exchanges security parameters using IKE transform sets. The generic IKE parameters that were shown in Figure 13-4 are now configured in Figure 13-6. Each router has two ISAKMP policies configured. Because preshared keys are used, ISAKMP keys must be defined. These policies are exchanged during IKE phase 1. Policy 10 on Router A matches policy 25 on Router B and the appropriate key (TOPsecret) between the two peers also matches. Thus, the secure IKE tunnel is created using those attributes.

In reality, stronger IKE policies should be configured first (that is, with lower policy numbers). Remember that the IKE policies are examined top down, from the lowest policy number to the largest. If a weaker policy is matched due to a lower policy number, then stronger policies that appear later in the policy list are never used. This could potentially compromise the secure IPsec tunnel.

Step 2: Configure the IPsec Transform Sets

The configuration of the IPsec transform sets actually covers three of the IPsec configuration steps mentioned earlier. The IPsec transform set, crypto ACL, and crypto map are tightly woven together. It is difficult to talk about one of them without mentioning the other two. Thus, this section covers all three together.

The following list is a reminder of the IPsec security parameters that are negotiated between peers:

- IPsec protocol (ESP or AH)

- IPsec encryption type (DES, 3DES, or AES)

- IPsec authentication (MD5 or SHA-1)

- IPsec mode (tunnel or transport)

- IPsec SA lifetime (seconds or kilobytes)

Figure 13-7 shows how these IPsec parameters are configured.

Figure 13-7   *IPsec Transform Set Configuration*

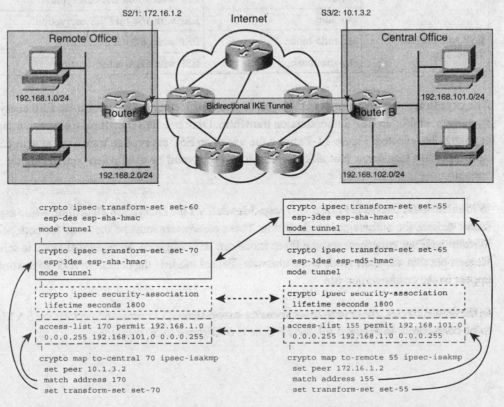

Earlier, Figure 13-5 showed the generic IPsec transform set attributes. Figure 13-7 now shows how each of those parameters is configured in Cisco IOS.

Each IPsec endpoint defines one or more IPsec transform sets. In this case, set-60, set-70, set-55, and set-65 can be compared to the IPsec transform sets shown earlier in Figure 13-5. These names only have local significance to the IPsec peering process. The IPsec transform set defines all of the IPsec security parameters mentioned above. The terms **esp-3des** and **esp-sha-hmac** define ESP as the IPsec protocol, versus AH. Table 13-2 displays the relevant IPsec transform sets for this certification.

Table 13-2 *IPsec Transform Sets*

Transform Type	IOS Transform	Description
AH Transform	ah-md5-hmac	AH with MD5 authentication
	ah-sha-hmac	AH with SHA authentication
ESP Encryption Transform	esp-aes	ESP with 128-bit AES encryption
	esp-aes 192	ESP with 192-bit AES encryption
	esp-aes 256	ESP with 256-bit AES encryption
	esp-des	ESP with 56-bit DES encryption
	esp-3des	ESP with 168-bit DES encryption
ESP Authentication Transform	esp-md5-hmac	ESP with MD5 authentication
	esp-sha-hmac	ESP with SHA authentication

The **crypto ipsec transform-set** command is used to select an AH transform, an ESP encryption transform, and/or an ESP authentication transform. Only one IOS transform from each transform type may be selected. Figure 13-7 shows the use of an ESP encryption transform and an ESP authentication transform. Not all three transform types must be used when configuring the IPsec tunnel.

Within the solid circles in Figure 13-7, **esp-3des** defines the encryption algorithm, while **esp-sha-hmac** defines the authentication algorithm. These parameters must be the same for both peers. Within the IPsec transform set, the IPsec mode can be configured. Here, tunnel mode is selected. Remember that transport mode is the alternate. Tunnel mode is the default in IOS, so it would not appear in the configuration file.

In the dotted circles, the **crypto ipsec security-association** CLI command permits the SA lifetime to be configured. In Figure 13-7, the lifetime is configured to 30 minutes.

Step 3: Configure the Crypto ACL

An extended access list is used to determine interesting traffic. The access lists are shown in the dashed circles. At the remote office, the access list is number 170, while at the central office, the list is number 155. Each list defines the source and destination addresses of traffic that will travel through the IPsec tunnels.

Usually, it is very important that the two lists be mirror images of each other. The source address in one list must be the destination address in the other and vice versa. A standard access list cannot be used for identifying interesting traffic because it does not have the ability to specify destination addresses.

It is also possible to simply have one site (say a remote site) send everything through an IPsec VPN tunnel to the main site, yet the main site only sends traffic destined for that remote site through the VPN. This makes the configuration at the remote site fairly simple, and isolates the more advanced configuration to the main site.

> **NOTE** Crypto access lists are sometimes called mirrored access lists. Each IPsec peer must have an extended access list that indicates interesting traffic. At a minimum, this interesting traffic must specify both source and destination IP addresses and can add protocols and ports for additional detail.
>
> From an IP addressing perspective, what is interesting to one site (source/destination) is exactly opposite to the other site (destination/source). If one side indicates source/destination subnets as interesting, then the other site must reverse the source/destination subnets for its interesting traffic configuration. If one end uses subnets in the crypto ACL for source/destination and the other end uses individual IP addresses for source/destination, the interesting traffic is not mirrored and the IPsec tunnel will not work.

In Figure 13-7, one subnet from each site is considered interesting (due to the ACLs) and will be protected through the IPsec VPN tunnel. The remaining subnets cannot take advantage of the IPsec configuration.

Step 4: Configure the Crypto Map

The final configuration is the crypto map, which ties the transform set and access list together and points them to a remote peer. The numbers 70 and 55 in each of the crypto maps are line numbers. Each map could have multiple lines, and the lines are referenced numerically from the lowest to the highest number. If a router has only a single interface, yet multiple remote VPN clients, a single crypto map must be used with a unique entry for each peer.

At the remote office, the crypto map to-central creates an SA to peer 10.1.3.2 and protects any traffic matching extended access list 170 (interesting traffic) using the IPsec security parameters defined in transform set set-70. The crypto map at the central office can be deciphered in a similar fashion.

Step 5: Apply the Crypto Map to the Interface

After the crypto map is successfully configured, it must be applied to an interface to be operational. Remember that the crypto map is a collection of the IP address of the remote peer, the interesting traffic that will flow through the IPsec tunnel, and the IPsec security parameters (transform set) that will be used to protect the data. Figure 13-8 shows the application of the crypto map to an interface.

Figure 13-8 *IPsec Interface Configuration*

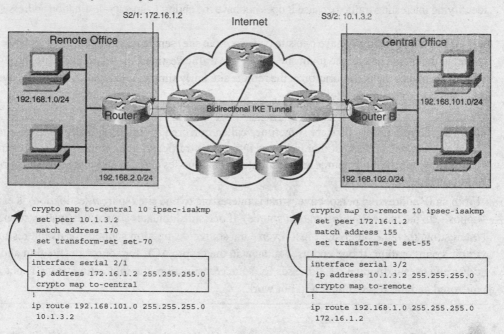

In Figure 13-8, the respective **crypto map** commands remain to compare two items. Notice that the command **crypto map** is used both globally to create the map and locally on the interface to apply it. It is important to note that the name used to create the map must be used when the map is applied to the interface. The remote office applies the crypto map to-central to its serial interface, while the central office applies the crypto map to-remote to the serial interface that connects to the remote office. Crypto maps are typically applied to outbound interfaces, and the IP address on that interface becomes the source address of the IPsec VPN.

One other necessary configuration on each side is a manual addition to the routing table. From the remote office, the intent is that all devices on the 192.168.1.0/24 subnet communicate across the IPsec VPN to the 192.168.101.0/24 devices. However, Router A knows nothing about the 192.168.101.0/24 subnet, because that subnet is not being advertised to the Internet from the central office. So a static route is added to each router to detail where the remote subnet is located.

For the remote office, subnet 192.168.101.0/24 can be found at gateway 10.1.3.2. A similar configuration is seen on Router B to reach the remote office.

Step 6: Configure the Interface ACL

In the examples shown thus far, the router connected to the Internet also served as the IPsec peer. It is likely that such an Internet-connected device would be a firewall in today's networks, although this is more of a guideline than a rule. In either case, it is important to permit IPsec packets so that IKE and IPsec SAs can be established. Typical Internet-facing devices block most packets that come toward them, unless the stream was initiated on the inside. Site-to-site IPsec VPN tunnels can be between Internet-facing devices.

In the case of site-to-site VPNs, the source IP address of the incoming IPsec packets is known. Most sites employ some type of static IP address to the Internet, and such addresses do not change very often, if ever. Thus, when creating an access list to permit IPsec, it is not necessary to permit IPsec packets from all Internet sources. It is possible to be selective and thus more secure, with extended access lists.

Figure 13-9 shows a partial access list that is used to permit IPsec packets in the interface. In the figure, the previous interface configurations remain to show continuity.

Figure 13-9   *Site-to-Site Interface Configuration*

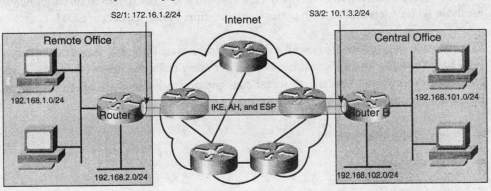

```
access-list 110 permit ahp host
  10.1.3.2 host 172.16.1.2
access-list 110 permit esp host
  10.1.3.2 host 172.16.1.2
access-list 110 permit udp host
  10.1.3.2 host 172.16.1.2 eq isakmp
!
interface serial 2/1
 ip address 172.16.1.2 255.255.255.0
 crypto map to-central
 ip access-group 110 in
```

```
access-list 120 permit ahp host
  172.16.1.2 host 10.1.3.2
access-list 120 permit esp host
  172.16.1.2 host 10.1.3.2
access-list 120 permit udp host
  172.16.1.2 host 10.1.3.2 eq isakmp
!
interface serial 3/2
 ip address 10.1.3.2 255.255.255.0
 crypto map to-remote
 ip access-group 120 in
```

The Internet-facing access list could be quite large or may simply deny everything unless it is already established. In either case, the three statements shown in Figure 13-9 represent the addition of AH, ESP, and IKE to the already-existing access list. These three lines in the access list also are very particular about the source and destination IP addresses that such traffic is permitted through the interface.

Security Device Manager Features and Interface

Cisco has a web-based configuration tool that permits virtually all IOS features to be configured without accessing the command-line interface (CLI). This tool is called the Cisco Router and Security Device Manager (SDM). This section provides an overview of the SDM tool, and the section that follows explains how to configure site-to-site IPsec VPNs using the tool.

SDM is embedded within a variety of IOS-based routers. The 800 through 3800 series routers benefit from this free tool, which is loaded into flash memory. SDM permits secure browser-based configuration and management of the applicable routers.

Although SDM does permit many individual IOS options to be configured, the true power of SDM is exhibited through its wizards. These intelligent modules enable rapid configuration of select Cisco access routers. SDM allows network administrators with little or no CLI experience to accurately configure the router. SDM is also useful to more advanced users. It enables them to edit ACLs and crypto maps (tasks not easily performed in IOS). The tool even offers an IOS preview for those who understand IOS yet prefer to use the time-saving aspects of SDM.

SDM provides the administrator with a variety of features that simplify the configuration of Cisco IOS–based routers. Smart wizards can be used for many tasks that might otherwise require complicated IOS input. Virtually all router configuration tasks have wizards to simplify the installation process, including:

- Initial router configuration

- Firewall setup

- Site-to-site VPN

- Router lockdown

- Security audit

The security audit actually uses both Cisco Technical Assistance Center (TAC) and Internet Computer Security Association (ICSA) recommended security configurations as a means to validate the effectiveness of the configured security policy.

When you first connect to the SDM interface using a web browser, you see the SDM home page. The top of each SDM window has a common set of buttons to control the active page. Figure 13-10 shows the SDM home page (note the indented Home button) and the common buttons across the top of every SDM page.

Figure 13-10 *SDM Home Page*

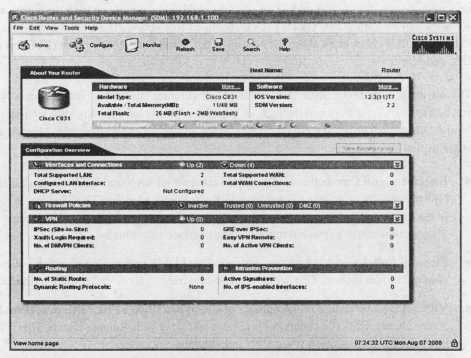

The selection buttons at the top of each SDM page serve the following purposes:

- **Home**—Displays the hardware, software, and configuration overview page

- **Configure**—Provides options to create and edit all router parameters and features

- **Monitor**—Displays configuration and operational status

- **Refresh**—Refreshes the current web page

- **Save**—Saves the current SDM configuration to the router

- **Search**—Allows you to search for key SDM words and features

- **Help**—Provides assistance on how to use SDM

The home page displays two sets of information, which allows you to view a complete capabilities summary of your router.

The first section, located on the upper portion of the home page, is labeled About Your Router. This section displays information about the hardware and software of your router. The hardware information includes the model, available and total memory (RAM), and total flash. The software information includes the IOS and SDM versions. Additional details on both the hardware and software can be retrieved by clicking the respective More option. The available features are also indicated with a check mark along the bottom of the About Your Router panel (IP, Firewall, VPN, IPS, and NAC).

The second section of the home screen is the Configuration Overview. This section only allows you to view configured options throughout the router, not actually modify such options. Modifications are permitted from the SDM Configure page. The Configuration Overview section contains five components:

- **Interfaces and Connections**—Displays a count of all LAN and WAN interfaces, as well as how many of them are actually configured. It also shows whether a DHCP server is configured in the router and that the router is acting as a DHCP server (which is typical in access routers). This section can be expanded to show each interface individually.

- **Firewall Policies**—Shows trusted, untrusted, and DMZ interfaces and which policies are configured and applied. This section can be expanded to show each policy individually.

- **VPN**—Displays a count of the number of site-to-site IPsec VPNs, GRE over IPsec tunnels, Xauth clients, DMVPN clients, VPN clients, and Easy VPN Remote clients. This section can be expanded to show each IPsec VPN individually.

- **Routing**—Displays a count of the number of static routes and dynamic routing protocols (if any) configured.

- **Intrusion Prevention**—Shows how many signatures the router is aware of and the number of interfaces that IPS is configured on.

Click the View Running Config button to retrieve a current read-only copy of the CLI configuration. This can be used to learn the appropriate CLI configurations as they are applied through the SDM interface.

As noted earlier, the home page offers a static snapshot of current capabilities and configurations in the router. Modifications to the configuration, as well as robust monitoring tools, are available on other SDM pages.

Configuring a Site-to-Site VPN in SDM

To configure site-to-site VPNs in SDM, start by clicking the Configure button at the top of the screen to display the Configure page, shown in Figure 13-11. On the left side of this window is the Tasks bar, which lists all the configuration options, described next:

Figure 13-11 *SDM Configure Page*

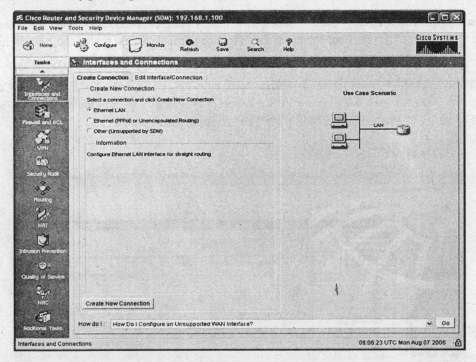

- **Interfaces and Connections**—Used to create and edit interfaces on the router.

- **Firewall and ACL**—Used to create and edit basic (inside and outside) and advanced (inside, outside, and DMZ) firewall configurations in the router.

- **VPN**—Used to create and edit IPsec VPNs, DMVPN, and the Easy VPN Remote and Server functions. This is the only task explored in this chapter.

- **Security Audit**—Used to perform a security audit of your router, and permits a one-step lockdown process to secure the router.

- **Routing**—Used to configure RIP, OSPF, and EIGRP on the router.

- **NAT**—Used to configure basic NAT (inside and outside) as well as advanced NAT (inside, outside, and DMZ).

- **Intrusion Prevention**—Used to apply network-based intrusion prevention rules to the router and edit them.

- **Quality of Service**—Used to configure LLQ QoS policies for outgoing traffic on both WAN interfaces and IPsec tunnels.

- **NAC**—Used to create and edit Network Access Control (NAC) policies on the router.

- **Additional Tasks**—Used to configure a variety of other router tasks, such as Router Properties (name, logging, date/time, and so on), Router Access (user accounts, vty lines, and so on), DHCP, DNS, ACL Editor, and AAA.

To access the VPN configuration options, click the VPN option in the Tasks bar on the Configure page. The following five primary VPN configuration options appear to the right of the Tasks bar. Figure 13-12 shows various VPN wizard and configuration options.

Figure 13-12 *SDM VPN Configuration Options*

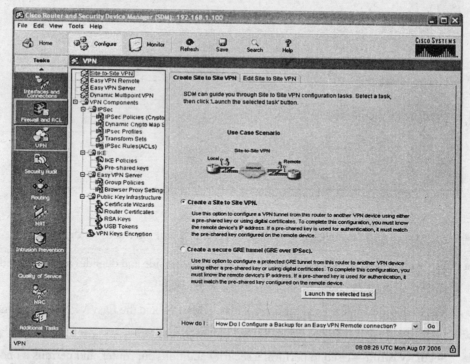

- **Site to Site VPN**—Launches the Site-to-Site VPN Wizard.

- **Easy VPN Remote**—Launches the Easy VPN Remote Wizard.

- **Easy VPN Server**—Launches the Easy VPN Server Wizard.

- **Dynamic Multipoint VPN**—Launches the Dynamic Multipoint VPN Wizard.

- **VPN Components**—Opens a list of individual options for IPsec VPN configuration, including IPsec, IKE, Easy VPN Server, PKI, and VPN Keys Encryption. Note that the VPN Keys Encryption option appears only if the Cisco IOS Software version supports Type 6 encryption.

The VPN wizards actually use preconfigured VPN options as well as user input gathered during the wizard execution. The preconfigured options could be default components in SDM, such as IKE policies or IPsec transform sets. The user can also create components in addition to the defaults provided, such as additional IKE or IPsec policies or PKI parameters.

The VPN wizards are used to quickly and easily configure VPN parameters in the router. The individual configuration options are used to correct an error from a wizard, to modify a setting configured by a wizard, or to manually set up the entire IPsec VPN process.

Site-to-Site VPN Wizard

The Site-to-Site VPN Wizard is launched by clicking the Site-to-Site VPN option at the top of the list to the right of the Tasks bar on the SDM Configure page. This option is available only if you previously clicked the Configure button at the top of the SDM screen and selected the VPN option from the Tasks bar.

Figure 13-12 shows the initial screen of the Site-to-Site VPN Wizard. This wizard has two tabs at the top of the window:

- **Create Site to Site VPN**—Used to create either a new site-to-site VPN or a new GRE over IPsec tunnel

- **Edit Site to Site VPN**—Used to modify and test an existing site-to-site VPN or GRE over IPsec tunnel

The Create Site to Site VPN tab of the wizard has two options:

- **Create a Site to Site VPN**—Used to configure an IPsec VPN tunnel from this router to another device

- **Create a secure GRE tunnel (GRE over IPsec)**—Used to configure a protected GRE tunnel from this router to another device

This chapter explores only the site-to-site VPN option. Chapter 14, "GRE Tunneling over IPsec," covers GRE over IPsec tunnels in greater detail.

On the **Create Site to Site VPN** tab, click the **Create a Site to Site VPN** radio button and click the **Launch the selected task** button near the bottom of the screen. The Site-to-Site VPN Wizard window appears and another choice is offered:

■ **Quick Setup**—Requires minimal information to set up a new IPsec VPN tunnel. Clicking the View Defaults button displays the noneditable defaults that are used.

■ **Step by Step Wizard**—Permits the use of either a default configuration or a customized configuration for the IPsec VPN tunnel.

Both of these options are explored in this chapter.

Quick Setup

From the Site-to-Site VPN Wizard window, click the **Quick Setup** radio button and click the **Next>** button at the bottom of the window.

The Quick Setup option is appropriately named. There is only one configuration screen, followed by a summary screen. Only basic IPsec VPN configuration is possible via the Quick Setup screen. If you need or want additional parameters, you must use the Step-by-Step wizard. Figure 13-13 shows the VPN Quick Setup configuration window.

Figure 13-13 *SDM VPN Quick Setup Window*

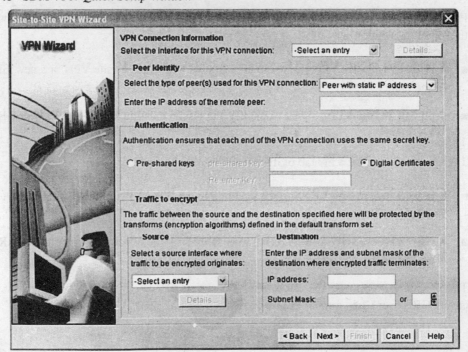

The Quick Setup window offers the following configuration options:

- **VPN Connection Information**—Specify the interface that is the source of the IPsec VPN from this router. This is an "outside" or "WAN" interface on the router. Select an appropriate interface from the pull-down menu.

- **Peer Identity**—Specify the type of IP address of the remote peer (the other end of the IPsec VPN tunnel) with the pull-down menu. If you choose Peer with static IP address, you must enter the IP address of the remote peer. If you choose Peer with dynamic IP address, the remote peer IP address option is removed.

- **Authentication**—Click either **Pre-shared keys** or **Digital Certificates** for IKE authentication. If preshared keys are used, you must enter the key twice for validation.

- **Traffic to encrypt**—Specify which traffic is encrypted and travels through the IPsec VPN, and which travels outside the VPN.

  — **Source**—Specify the interface where the encrypted traffic originates. This is typically the same router or WAN interface selected earlier.

  — **Destination**—Specify an IP address or IP subnet at the remote end of the IPsec VPN connection. The subnet mask or number of subnet bits is used to specify the range of destination IP addresses.

When you are finished with this short screen, click the **Next>** button at the bottom to proceed to the summary screen. The configured options are displayed. The interface, peer, IKE authentication, and interesting traffic options are repeated from the previous screen. Note that the source of the interesting traffic is the LAN subnet on the router. Other IPsec parameters, such as IKE policies and IPsec transform sets, are selected from the default or preconfigured options.

Click the **Finish** button at the bottom of the screen to apply the parameters and complete the configuration. The IPsec VPN configuration is pushed to the router. Click the **OK** button to continue. You are returned to the Edit Site to Site VPN tab of the Site-to-Site VPN Wizard.

Step-by-Step Setup

From the Site-to-Site VPN Wizard window, click the **Step by Step Wizard** radio button to select the wizard and click the **Next** button at the bottom of the window to proceed into the wizard.

The quick setup makes use of preconfigured parameters to simplify the VPN setup. However, the use of such default options limits the ability to select specific IKE policies or IPsec transforms or create a more robust collection of IP addresses and subnets for interesting traffic.

There are four primary tasks in the Step-by-Step wizard:

- **Define connection settings**—Identify the outside interface, peer address, and IKE authentication credentials

- **Define IKE proposals**—Specify priority, encryption algorithm (DES, 3DES, or AES), HMAC (MD5 or SHA-1), Diffie-Hellman group (1, 2, or 5), and lifetime (time)

- **Define IPsec transform sets**—Specify encryption algorithm (DES, 3DES, or AES), HMAC (MD5 or SHA-1), mode, and optional compression

- **Define traffic to protect**—Specify source and destination subnets or use ACLs to include a variety of IP addresses and subnets for the interesting traffic

Define Connection Settings

The first task in the Step-by-Step wizard is to define the connection settings. The information in this screen is very similar to the Quick Setup window and is shown in Figure 13-14.

Figure 13-14 *SDM Connection Settings*

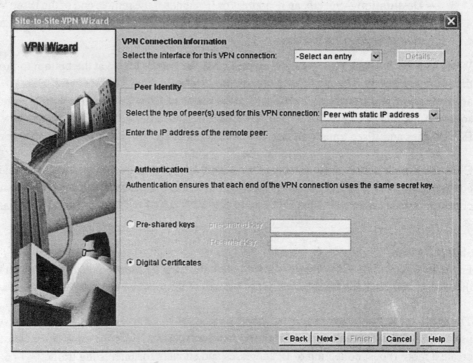

Similar to the Quick Setup window, the following configuration options are presented:

- **VPN Connection Information**—Specify the interface that is the source of the IPsec VPN from this router. This is an outside or WAN interface on the router. Select an appropriate interface from the pull-down menu.

- **Peer Identity**—Specify the type of IP address of the remote peer (the other end of the IPsec VPN tunnel) by choosing it from the pull-down menu. If you choose Peer with static IP address, you must enter the IP address of the remote peer. If you choose Peer with dynamic IP address, the remote peer IP address option is removed.

- **Authentication**—Click either **Pre-shared keys** or **Digital Certificates** for IKE authentication. If preshared keys are used, you must enter the key twice for validation.

When you are finished with the appropriate connection information, click the **Next>** button at the bottom of the screen.

Define IKE Proposals

The second task in the step-by-step setup is to configure the IKE proposals. Only one IKE proposal is needed, but the IPsec remote peer must have a duplicate proposal for IKE phase 1 to be successful. Multiple proposals are typically configured at a central site where many remote locations are peering. Figure 13-15 shows the IKE Proposals screen.

Figure 13-15 *SDM IKE Proposals*

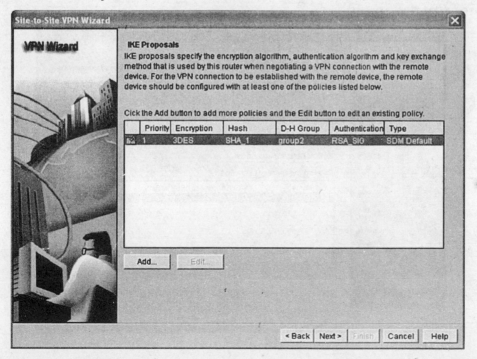

The IKE Proposals screen displays all SDM default IKE proposals and any IKE proposals configured individually. You can select a proposal from this list, or create a new one by clicking the Add button. If you click the **Add** button, the Add IKE Policy window appears, where you must configure the following:

- **Priority**—Determines how this new IKE policy is sequenced with existing ones.

- **Encryption**—Select the appropriate encryption algorithm (DES, 3DES, or AES).

- **Hash**—Select the appropriate hash algorithm (MD5 or SHA-1).

- **D-H Group**—Select the appropriate Diffie-Hellman group (group1, group2, or group5).

- **Authentication**—Select the authentication method (preshared keys or RSA signatures).

- **Lifetime**—Enter hours, minutes, and seconds for the IKE lifetime.

When you are finished with the new parameters, click the **OK** button and the new IKE proposal appears sequenced according to its priority number. You can highlight and edit any user-defined IKE proposals here if needed (the default IKE proposal cannot be edited). When you are done with IKE proposals, click the **Next>** button at the bottom of the screen.

Define IPsec Transform Sets

The third task in the step-by-step setup is to configure the IPsec transform sets. As with IKE proposals, only one IPsec transform set is needed, but the IPsec peer must have a duplicate transform set for IKE phase 2 to be successful. Multiple transform sets are typically configured at a central site where many remote locations are peering. Figure 13-16 shows the Transform Set screen.

Figure 13-16 *SDM IPsec Transform Set*

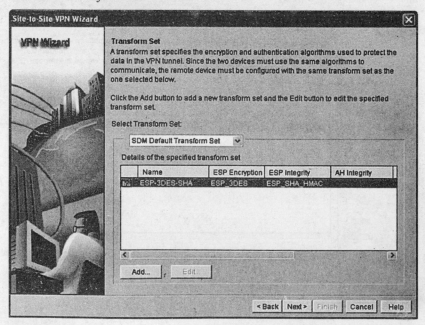

The IPsec Transform Set screen displays the selected transform set that is used with this IPsec VPN. The pull-down menu allows you to access all SDM default IPsec transform sets and any IPsec transform sets configured individually. You can select a transform set from this list or create a new one by clicking the Add button. If you click the **Add** button, the Add Transform Set window appears, where you must configure the following:

- **Name**—Provide a local name for this transform set that is inserted into the crypto map.

- **Data Integrity with Encryption (ESP)**—Check this box if you wish to use ESP. You then must select an identity algorithm (an authentication HMAC, either MD5 or SHA-1) and an encryption algorithm (DES, 3DES, or AES).

- **Data and Address Integrity Without Encryption (AH)**—Check this box if you wish to use AH. You then must select an identity algorithm (an authentication HMAC, either MD5 or SHA-1).

- **Mode**—Select either Tunnel (which protects both the data and the IP header) or Transport (which protects only the data).

- **IP Compression**—Check this box if you optionally want to use Comp-LZS compression through the IPsec VPN.

When you are finished with the new parameters, click the **OK** button and the new IPsec transform set appears in the list. When you are done with IPsec transform sets, click the **Next>** button at the bottom of the screen. The selected transform set is applied to this IPsec connection.

Define the Traffic to Protect

The fourth and final task in the step-by-step setup is to configure the interesting traffic. You can either match a single IP address/subnet on each end of the IPsec VPN (similar to Quick Setup) or use an access list to perform more advanced interesting traffic matches. Figure 13-17 shows the Traffic to Protect screen.

Figure 13-17 *SDM Traffic to Protect*

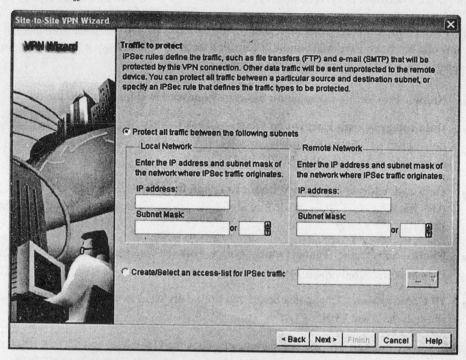

From this screen, you can either protect traffic between a single subnet on each side of the IPsec VPN or use an access list for more advanced interesting traffic options.

Protect a Single IP Address or Subnet

If you need to protect only a single IP address or subnet on both ends of the IPsec VPN, then click the **Protect all traffic between the following subnets** radio button. Enter an IP address or subnet and associated subnet mask in the Local Network portion of the screen. This is typically a subnet directly attached to the router, but does not have to be. Also enter an appropriate IP address or subnet with subnet mask in the Remote Network portion of the screen. This is some subnet that is behind the remote IPsec peer. When finished, click the **Next** button at the bottom of the screen to view the summary page.

Protect Multiple Subnets Using ACLs

To use an ACL to specify interesting traffic for the IPsec VPN, click the **Create/Select an access-list for IPSec traffic** radio button. This option has two different fulfillment paths. One is to select an existing ACL, and the second is to create a new ACL from scratch.

To select an existing ACL, click the **...** pull-down button and choose the **Select an existing rule (ACL)** option. On the Select a Rule screen, highlight an existing ACL and click **OK** at the bottom of that window to return to the Traffic to Protect screen.

To create a new ACL, click the **...** pull-down button and choose the **Create a new rule (ACL)** option. This action launches the Add a Rule window. Here, you must enter a name or number for the new ACL. Remember that interesting traffic must use an extended access list, so the number should be between 100 and 199, inclusive. The name can be any alphanumeric combination you desire. You can also optionally enter a description for this new ACL. Once you are done with these values, click the **Add** button to add new rules to this ACL.

The Add an Extended Rule Entry window appears. Each entry for this new access list is created with this window. If you have five different subnets that are to be protected via the IPsec VPN, you must visit this screen five times. Each time, you add a new line from the Add a Rule window.

In the Add an Extended Rule Entry window, the Action determines whether to "Protect the traffic" or "Do not protect" the traffic by the IPsec VPN. You might have a rule that does not protect a very specific subnet, and a second rule that does protect a more generic subnet that encompasses the one that is not protected. The end result would be that all traffic from the larger subnet except that from the specific subnet would be protected by the IPsec VPN.

As with all ACLs, you must first configure specific subnets and hosts, and configure more generic subnets later. Because ACLs are processed top-down, the statements earlier in the ACL are seen first. A generic statement at the start of the ACL would nullify any specific statements that fell under the umbrella of the generic statement but came later in the ACL.

You can also optionally add a description to each line of the ACL. Next, enter the source and destination hosts, subnets, or any traffic. Remember that ACLs use wildcard masks, and not normal subnet masks. The final process on this screen is to optionally select all IP packets, specific IP protocols, or specific ports within a particular IP protocol. One final option is to check the box that indicates you want to log packets that match this line of the ACL.

When you are finished with this one rule of the ACL, click the **OK** button to return to the Add a Rule window. As mentioned before, you can add as many rules to the ACL as necessary. Each one is created using the same process detailed above. When the entire access list has been created, you can use the **Move Up** and **Move Down** buttons to change the sequence of the ACL, the **Delete** button to remove a rule, or the **Edit** button to modify a rule. When the ACL is complete, click the **OK** button at the bottom of the window.

Complete the Configuration

All four tasks of the step-by-step site-to-site IPsec VPN setup are now complete. The configuration that was just created is displayed. The Summary screen has the same format as the one displayed after the Quick Setup. However, you have the choice to modify the options during the step-by-step setup. You likely need to use the scrollbar on the side of the window to view the entire configuration. If you notice a configuration error, you can navigate back (using the **<Back** button) to the appropriate portion of the wizard to correct the mistake, and then use the **Next>** button to return to the summary.

When the configuration appears complete and correct, click the **Finish** button. The IPsec VPN configuration is pushed to the router. Click the **OK** button to continue. You are returned to the Edit Site to Site VPN tab of the Site-to-Site VPN Wizard.

Testing the IPsec VPN Tunnel

When the IPsec VPN tunnel is configured, you are returned to the first page of the Site to Site VPN window. To test the new IPsec VPN, click the **Edit Site to Site VPN** tab at the top of the window (if you are not already there). The new IPsec VPN should appear. If there are multiple VPNs in the window, click the new one to select it.

If the remote peer is configured for an IPsec VPN with this router, click the **Test Tunnel** button at the bottom of this screen. If all of the parameters are correct on both sides, the tunnel should become active. Remember that an IPsec VPN does not normally become active until some interesting traffic appears. The Test Tunnel option forces the tunnel negotiation process to start.

There is also a **Generate Mirror** button at the bottom of this screen. This is used to create an IOS configuration that is an appropriate mirror of the IPsec VPN tunnel that is highlighted. This configuration can then be added to the remote router for proper IPsec VPN operation. This option is useful if the remote router does not have SDM installed.

Monitoring the IPsec VPN Tunnel

There are a variety of ways to monitor an IPsec VPN tunnel in a Cisco router. This section explores how to accomplish this both from SDM and with the IOS CLI.

In SDM, all monitor options are performed from the Monitor page. Click the Monitor button at the top of any SDM screen to enter this page. Figure 13-18 shows the Monitor page.

Figure 13-18 *SDM Monitor Page*

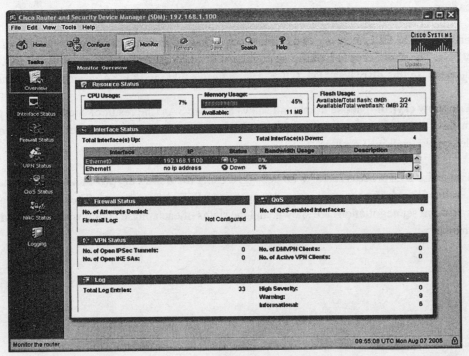

The Tasks bar options on the left of the screen change to the following:

- **Overview**—Displays a generic status of the router, including CPU and memory usage, as well as an overview of the interfaces, firewall, QoS, VPN, and logs

- **Interface Status**—Allows the ability to monitor live traffic or test the interfaces

- **Firewall Status**—Displays a log of packets denied by the firewall

- **VPN Status**—Displays a status of IPsec tunnels, DMVPN tunnels, the Easy VPN Server, and IKE SAs

- **QoS Status**—Displays the effects of the QoS interface configuration

- **NAC Status**—Displays the number of NAC sessions for both the router and the interfaces

- **Logging**—Displays the buffered log of the router

Click the **VPN Status** button in the Tasks bar of the Monitor page to display the VPN Status screen. This screen shows the current status of each IPsec VPN and a count of all packets that have navigated each VPN. The Test Tunnel button on the screen has the same functionality as described earlier.

From the IOS CLI, there are two primary commands to monitor the current status of all IPsec VPNs. The **show crypto isakmp sa** command displays all active IKE sessions (all IKE phase 1 tunnels). In this display, a QM_IDLE state indicates that the IKE SA is active and operational.

The **show crypto ipsec sa** command shows all IPsec SAs (the result of successful IKE phase 2). In this display, a successful IPsec SA is indicated by non-zero counts of encrypted (outgoing) and decrypted (arriving) packets.

The entire IKE process can also be debugged using the **debug crypto isakmp** command. The results of this debug are most active during the two IKE phases, 1 and 2. The IKE profile and IPsec transform set negotiations are shown, and the status of each phase, along with error conditions, is shown.

Foundation Summary

There are five generic steps in the lifecycle of any IPsec VPN:

Step 1   Specify interesting traffic.

Step 2   IKE phase 1.

Step 3   IKE phase 2.

Step 4   Secure data transfer.

Step 5   IPsec tunnel termination.

Interesting traffic is better thought of as traffic that must be protected by the IPsec VPN. When an IPsec VPN tunnel exists between two sites, traffic that is considered "interesting" is sent securely through the VPN to the remote location.

IKE phase 1 has two possible modes: main mode or aggressive mode. The basic purpose of either mode is identical, but the number of messages exchanged is greatly reduced in aggressive mode.

In main mode, the first two exchanges negotiate the security parameters used to establish the IKE tunnel. The second pair of packets exchanges the Diffie-Hellman public keys needed to create the IKE SAs. The final pair of packets performs peer authentication.

Aggressive mode reduces the IKE phase 1 exchange to three packets. The first packet sends security policy proposals, the Diffie-Hellman public key, a nonce (which is signed and returned for identity validation), and a means to perform authentication. The second packet contains the accepted security policy proposal, its Diffie-Hellman public key, and the signed nonce for authentication. The final packet is a confirmation from the initiator to the receiver.

Five parameters must be coordinated during IKE phase 1:

- IKE encryption algorithm (DES, 3DES, or AES)

- IKE authentication algorithm (MD5 or SHA-1)

- IKE key (preshare, RSA signatures, nonces)

- Diffie-Hellman version (1, 2, or 5)

- IKE tunnel lifetime (time and/or byte count)

There are seven different Diffie-Hellman groups (1–7), and Cisco VPN devices support groups 1, 2, and 5, which use 768-bit, 1024-bit, and 1536-bit prime numbers, respectively.

There are three typical methods used for peer authentication:

■ Preshared keys

■ RSA signatures

■ RSA-encrypted nonces

The following functions are performed in IKE phase 2:

■ Negotiation of IPsec security parameters via IPsec transform sets

■ Establishment of IPsec SAs (unidirectional IPsec tunnels)

■ Periodic renegotiation of IPsec SAs to ensure security

■ An additional Diffie-Hellman exchange (optional)

Five parameters must be coordinated during quick mode between IPsec peers:

■ IPsec protocol (ESP or AH)

■ IPsec encryption type (DES, 3DES, or AES)

■ IPsec authentication (MD5 or SHA-1)

■ IPsec mode (tunnel or transport)

■ IPsec SA lifetime (seconds or kilobytes)

Each SA is referenced by a Security Parameter Index (SPI).

Each IPsec client uses an SA Database (SAD) to track each of the SAs that the client participates in. The SAD contains the following information about each IPsec connection (SA):

■ Destination IP address

■ SPI number

■ IPsec protocol (ESP or AH)

The Security Policy Database (SPD) contains the security parameters that were agreed upon for each SA (in the transform sets):

- Encryption algorithm (DES, 3DES, or AES)

- Authentication algorithm (MD5 or SHA-1)

- IPsec mode (tunnel or transport)

- Key lifetime (seconds or kilobytes)

One of the security parameters that must be agreed upon in the IPsec transform sets is the key lifetime. IPsec forces the keys to expire either after a predetermined amount of time (measured in seconds) or after a predetermined amount of data has been transferred (measured in kilobytes).

There are two events that can cause an IPsec tunnel to be terminated: if the SA lifetime expires (time and/or byte count) or if the tunnel is manually deleted.

The six steps necessary to configure a site-to-site IPsec VPN are as follows:

Step 1   Configure the ISAKMP policy (IKE phase 1).

Step 2   Configure the IPsec transform sets (IKE phase 2, tunnel termination).

Step 3   Configure the crypto ACL (interesting traffic, secure data transfer).

Step 4   Configure the crypto map (IKE phase 2).

Step 5   Apply the crypto map to the interface (IKE phase 2).

Step 6   Configure the interface ACL.

Table 13-3 displays the relevant IPsec transform sets for this certification.

Table 13-3   *IPsec Transform Sets*

Transform Type	IOS Transform	Description
AH Transform	ah-md5-hmac	AH with MD5 authentication
	ah-sha-hmac	AH with SHA authentication
ESP Encryption Transform	esp-aes	ESP with 128-bit AES encryption
	esp-aes 192	ESP with 192-bit AES encryption
	esp-aes 256	ESP with 256-bit AES encryption
	esp-des	ESP with 56-bit DES encryption
	esp-3des	ESP with 168-bit DES encryption
ESP Authentication Transform	esp-md5-hmac	ESP with MD5 authentication
	esp-sha-hmac	ESP with SHA authentication

Crypto access lists are sometimes called mirrored access lists. Each IPsec peer must have an extended access list that indicates interesting traffic. At a minimum, this interesting traffic must specify both source and destination IP addresses, and can add protocols and ports for additional detail.

The final configuration is the crypto map, which ties the transform set and access list together and points them to a remote peer. Once the crypto map is successfully configured, it must be applied to an interface to be operational.

An interface access list must permit IKE, AH, and ESP to ensure IPsec operations.

SDM provides the administrator with a variety of wizards that simplify the configuration of Cisco IOS-based routers, including

- Initial router configuration

- Firewall setup

- Site-to-site VPN

- Router lockdown

- Security audit

The selection buttons at the top of each SDM page serve the following purposes:

- **Home**—Displays the hardware, software, and configuration overview page

- **Configure**—Provides options to create and edit all router parameters and features

- **Monitor**—Displays configuration and operational status

- **Refresh**—Refreshes the current web page

- **Save**—Saves the current SDM configuration to the router

- **Search**—Allows you to search for key SDM words and features

- **Help**—Provides assistance on how to use SDM

To access the VPN configuration options, click the **VPN** option in the Tasks bar on the SDM Configure page. Five primary VPN configuration options appear to the right of the Tasks bar:

- **Site to Site VPN**—Launches the Site-to-Site VPN Wizard.

- **Easy VPN Remote**—Launches the Easy VPN Remote Wizard.

- **Easy VPN Server**—Launches the Easy VPN Server Wizard.

- **Dynamic Multipoint VPN**—Launches the Dynamic Multipoint VPN Wizard.

- **VPN Components**—Opens a list of individual options for IPsec VPN configuration, including IPsec, IKE, Easy VPN Server, PKI, and VPN Key Encryption. Note that the VPN Key Encryption option appears only if the Cisco IOS Software version supports Type 6 encryption.

The Site-to-Site VPN Wizard window offers two configuration options:

- **Quick Setup**—Requires minimal information to set up a new IPsec VPN tunnel. Click the **View Defaults** button to display the noneditable defaults that are used.

- **Step by Step Wizard**—Permits the use of either a default configuration or a customized configuration for the IPsec VPN tunnel.

The Quick Setup window offers five configuration options:

- VPN Connection Information

- Peer Identity

- Authentication

- Source Interface

- Destination Traffic to Encrypt

There are four primary tasks in the step-by-step setup wizard:

- Define connection settings

- Define IKE proposals

- Define IPsec transform sets

- Define traffic to protect

The Add IKE Policy window allows you to configure the following parameters:

- Priority

- Encryption

- Hash

- Authentication

- D-H Group

- Lifetime

The Add Transform Set window allows you to configure the following parameters:

- Name

- Data Integrity with Encryption (ESP)

- Data and Address Integrity Without Encryption (AH)

- Mode

- IP Compression

Q&A

The questions and scenarios in this book are designed to be challenging and to make sure that you know the answer. Rather than allowing you to derive the answers from clues hidden inside the questions themselves, the questions challenge your understanding and recall of the subject.

Hopefully, mastering these questions will help you limit the number of exam questions on which you narrow your choices to two options, and then guess.

You can find the answers to these questions in Appendix A. For more practice with exam-like question formats, use the exam engine on the CD-ROM.

1. In which generic IPsec step are the unidirectional SAs created?

2. For what reasons is an IPsec tunnel terminated?

3. What happens to noninteresting traffic as it leaves a VPN interface?

4. What type of ACL is used to specify interesting traffic?

5. How does aggressive mode differ from main mode?

6. What happens during IKE phase 1 if two IPsec peers cannot find an exact match between IKE policies?

7. Which generic IPsec step is responsible for the periodic renegotiation of IPsec SAs?

8. Which mode is used to negotiate IPsec parameters?

9. Where is either tunnel or transport mode selected during IPsec configuration?

10. Where is the preshared key configured for IKE phase 1?

11. Which security database holds the negotiated security parameters for each SA?

12. Can an IPsec tunnel expire even though traffic is flowing through it?

13. Why should stronger IKE transform sets be configured with lower policy numbers?

14. When configuring IPsec, where does ISAKMP policy fall when compared to the generic IPsec steps?

15. Which is the correct IOS configuration for an ESP IPsec transform set with AES-128 encryption and SHA authentication?

16. Which IPsec parameters are specified in the crypto map?

17. What is the appropriate mirror (opposite) of the crypto ACL **access-list 100 permit 10.1.2.0 0.0.255.255 172.16.5.0 0.0.0.255**?

18. A site has created a crypto map named "test." What is the IOS command to apply this map to an interface?

19. In an extended access list, what does protocol "ahp" refer to?

20. What are the common buttons at the top of every SDM page?

21. Which wizards are available from the VPN configuration options?

22. In the Quick Setup window, what VPN option is selected in the VPN Connection Information field?

23. When selecting an IKE authentication, what methods are available?

24. Why would you select the "do not protect" option when creating an interesting traffic ACL?

25. What happens to traffic that is not specified at all in the interesting traffic ACL?

26. In the **show crypto ipsec sa** IOS screen, how do you know if the IPsec VPN is actually working?

Exam Topic List

This chapter covers the following topics that you need to master for the CCNP ISCW exam:

- **GRE Characteristics**—Describes how generic routing encapsulation (GRE) can be used to encapsulate virtually any routed or routing protocol through an IP network

- **GRE Header**—Describes the GRE header that defines what is carried inside the GRE tunnel

- **Basic GRE Configuration**—Describes how to define the tunnel source, destination, mode, and contents

- **Secure GRE Tunnels**—Describes how GRE and IPsec complement each other across the network

- **Configure GRE over IPsec Using SDM**—Describes how SDM wizards permit easy configuration of GRE over IPsec

CHAPTER 14

GRE Tunneling over IPsec

Generic routing encapsulation (GRE) tunnels have been around for quite some time. GRE was first developed by Cisco as a means to carry other routed protocols across a predominantly IP network. Some network administrators tried to reduce the administrative overhead in the core of their networks by removing all protocols except IP as a transport. As such, non-IP protocols such as IPX and AppleTalk were tunneled through the IP core via GRE.

GRE adds a new GRE header to the existing packet. This concept is similar to IPsec tunnel mode. The original packet is carried through the IP network, and only the new outer header is used for forwarding. Once the GRE packet reaches the end of the GRE tunnel, the external header is removed, and the internal packet is again exposed.

Today, multiprotocol networks have mostly disappeared. It is difficult to find traces of the various protocols that used to be abundant throughout enterprise and core infrastructures. In a pure IP network, GRE was initially seen as a useless legacy protocol. But the growth of IPsec saw a rebirth in the use of GRE in IP networks. This chapter talks about the use of GRE in an IPsec environment.

"Do I Know This Already?" Quiz

The purpose of the "Do I Know This Already?" quiz is to help you decide whether you really need to read the entire chapter. If you already intend to read the entire chapter, you do not necessarily need to answer these questions now.

The 15-question quiz, derived from the major sections in the "Foundation Topics" portion of the chapter, helps you to determine how to spend your limited study time.

Table 14-1 outlines the major topics discussed in this chapter and the "Do I Know This Already?" quiz questions that correspond to those topics.

Table 14-1 *"Do I Know This Already?" Foundation Topics Section-to-Question Mapping*

Foundation Topics Section	Questions Covered in This Section	Score
GRE Characteristics	1	
GRE Header	2	
Basic GRE Configuration	3	
Secure GRE Tunnels	4–5	
Configure GRE over IPsec Using SDM	6–15	
Total Score		

CAUTION The goal of self-assessment is to gauge your mastery of the topics in this chapter. If you do not know the answer to a question or are only partially sure of the answer, you should mark this question wrong for purposes of self-assessment. Giving yourself credit for an answer that you correctly guess skews your self-assessment results and might provide you with a false sense of security.

1. What is the minimum amount of additional header that GRE adds to a packet?

    a. 16 bytes

    b. 20 bytes

    c. 24 bytes

    d. 36 bytes

    e. 48 bytes

2. Which of the following are valid options in a GRE header (select all that apply)?

    a. GRE Header Length

    b. Checksum Present

    c. Key Present

    d. External Encryption

    e. Protocol

3. What is the purpose of a GRE tunnel interface?

    a. It is always the tunnel source interface.

    b. It is always the tunnel destination interface.

    c. It is where the protocol that travels through the tunnel is configured.

    d. It is the interface that maps to the physical tunnel port.

    e. It is not used today.

4. When IPSec transport mode is used, how many IP headers are found in the GRE over IPsec packet?

    a. One—the original IP header is replicated when needed.

    b. Two—the original IP header and the GRE IP header.

    c. Two—the original IP header and the IPsec IP header.

    d. Three—the original IP header, the GRE IP header, and the IPsec IP header.

    e. Four—the original IP header, the GRE IP header, the IPsec IP header, and the outer IP header.

5. What feature does GRE introduce that cannot be accomplished with normal IPsec?

    a. GRE increases the packet size so that the minimum packet size is easily met.

    b. GRE adds robust encryption to protect the inner packet.

    c. GRE requires packet sequencing so that out-of-order packets can be reassembled correctly.

    d. GRE adds an additional IP header to further confuse packet-snooping devices.

    e. GRE permits dynamic routing between end sites.

6. What are the basic components within the Secure GRE Wizard (select all that apply)?

    a. Router interface configuration

    b. GRE tunnel configuration

    c. IPsec parameters configuration

    d. Router authentication configuration

    e. Routing protocols configuration

7. What is the IP address inside of the GRE tunnel used for?

    a. The GRE tunnel peering point.

    b. The IPsec tunnel peering point.

    c. The routing protocols peering point.

    d. The management interface of the router.

    e. There is no IP address inside of the GRE tunnel.

8. Which option must be configured if a backup secure GRE tunnel is configured?

    a. Source interface

    b. Source IP address

    c. Destination interface

    d. Destination IP address

    e. Destination router name

9. What methods are available for VPN authentication when used with a GRE tunnel (select all that apply)?

   a. Digital certificates

   b. Pre-shared keys

   c. Biometrics

   d. OTP

   e. KMA

10. When creating/selecting an IKE proposal, what does the Priority number indicate?

    a. The Priority number is a sequence number.

    b. The Priority number determines the encryption algorithm.

    c. The Priority number helps determine the authentication method.

    d. The Priority number is related to the Diffie-Hellman group.

    e. The Priority number is necessary to select the hash algorithm.

11. How are IPsec transform sets used in the Secure GRE Wizard?

    a. There must be a unique IPsec transform set for each VPN peer.

    b. There must be a unique IPsec transform set for each GRE tunnel.

    c. The two ends of a VPN must use the same IPsec transform set.

    d. The same IPsec transform set can be used for all VPN peers.

    e. Site-to-site IPsec VPN transform sets cannot be used for GRE over IPsec VPNs.

12. Which dynamic routing protocols can be configured in the GRE over IPsec tunnel (select all that apply)?

    a. RIP

    b. OSPF

    c. EIGRP

    d. BGP

    e. Static

13. Which routing options are appropriate when using both a primary and a backup GRE tunnel (select all that apply)?

    a. RIP

    b. OSPF

    c. EIGRP

    d. BGP

    e. Static

14. When using OSPF in the GRE over IPsec tunnel, what OSPF parameters must match so that the two peers establish an OSPF adjacency (select all that apply)?

   a. IP address of the GRE tunnel interface

   b. Subnet of the GRE tunnel interface

   c. OSPF area of the GRE tunnel interface

   d. OSPF process ID of each router

   e. Number of networks configured in OSPF on each router

15. In the Summary of the Configuration window, how can the displayed configuration be modified?

   a. Type changes directly into the scroll window and click the **Apply** button at the bottom of the window.

   b. Changes cannot be made from within any wizard.

   c. Click the **Modify** button to return to the configuration windows.

   d. Click the **Back** button to return to the configuration windows.

   e. Click the **Next** button to proceed to the Modify Configuration window.

The answers to the "Do I Know This Already?" quiz are found in Appendix A, "Answers to the 'Do I Know This Already?' Quizzes and Q&A Sections." The suggested choices for your next step are as follows:

■ **10 or fewer overall score**—Read the entire chapter. This includes the "Foundation Topics," "Foundation Summary," and "Q&A" sections.

■ **11 or 13 overall score**—Begin with the "Foundation Summary" section, and then go to the "Q&A" section.

■ **14 or more overall score**—If you want more review on these topics, skip to the "Foundation Summary" section, and then go to the "Q&A" section. Otherwise, move to the next chapter.

Foundation Topics

GRE Characteristics

The initial power of GRE was that anything could be encapsulated into it. The primary use of GRE was to carry non-IP packets through an IP network; however, GRE was also used to carry IP packets through an IP cloud. Used this way, the original IP header is buried inside of the GRE header and hidden from prying eyes. The generic characteristics of a GRE tunnel are as follows:

- A GRE tunnel is similar to an IPsec tunnel because the original packet is wrapped inside of an outer shell.

- GRE is stateless, and offers no flow control mechanisms.

- GRE adds at least 24 bytes of overhead, including the new 20-byte IP header.

- GRE is multiprotocol and can tunnel any OSI Layer 3 protocol.

- GRE permits routing protocols to travel through the tunnel.

- GRE was needed to carry IP multicast traffic until Cisco IOS Software Release 12.4(4)T.

- GRE has relatively weak security features.

The GRE tunnel itself is similar to an IPsec tunnel. The tunnel has two endpoints. Traffic enters one end of the tunnel and exits the other end. While in the tunnel, routers use the new outer header only to forward the packets.

The GRE tunnel is stateless. Unlike an IPsec tunnel, the endpoints do not coordinate any parameters before sending traffic through the tunnel. As long as the tunnel destination is routable, traffic can flow through it. Also, by default, GRE provides no reliability or sequencing. Such features are typically handled by upper-layer protocols.

GRE tunnels offer minimal security, whereas IPsec offers security by means of confidentiality, data authentication, and integrity assurance. GRE has a basic encryption mechanism, but the key is carried along with the packet, which somewhat defeats the purpose.

GRE does add an additional 24-byte header of overhead. This overhead contains a new 20-byte IP header, which indicates the source and destination IP addresses of the GRE tunnel. The remaining 4 bytes are the GRE header itself. Additional GRE options can increase the GRE header by up to another 12 bytes.

It is important to note that the larger packet size caused by the additional headers can have a detrimental effect on network performance. Because the additional headers are dynamically added, most users believe that nothing "bad" can happen as a result. If a packet is larger than the interface maximum transmission unit (MTU) permits, the router must fragment the packet into smaller pieces to fit. This fragmentation effort can add significant CPU overhead to a router, which can affect all packet forwarding.

GRE is a simple yet powerful tunneling tool. It can tunnel any OSI Layer 3 protocol over IP. As such, it is basically a point-to-point private connection. A private connection between two endpoints is the basic definition of a VPN.

Unlike IPsec, GRE permits routing protocols (such as OSPF and EIGRP) across the connection. This is not the case with typical IPsec tunnels. IPsec tunnels can send IP packets, but not routing protocols. Before the IP packets can travel through the IPsec tunnel, however, static routes are necessary on each IPsec endpoint for routing awareness of the opposite end. This additional configuration overhead does not scale well with a large number of IPsec tunnels.

Until Cisco IOS Software Release 12.4(4)T, IP multicast had to be sent over GRE. Prior to this IOS release, IPsec could not carry IP multicast traffic. Even though IOS 12.4(4)T now supports IP multicast traffic, GRE over IPsec still must be used to carry dynamic routing protocols.

GRE does not have any strong security features. The header provides an optional, albeit weak, security key mechanism. As a result, no strong confidentiality, data source authentication, or data integrity mechanisms exist in GRE. However, IPsec provides confidentiality (DES, 3DES, or AES), and source authentication and data integrity with MD5 or SHA-1 HMACs.

Thus, a GRE tunnel, which carries multicast and routing traffic, can be sent through an IPsec tunnel for enhanced security.

GRE Header

The GRE header itself contains 4 bytes, which represent the minimum size of GRE header with no added options. The first pair of bytes (bits 0 through 15) contains the flags that indicate the presence of GRE options. Such options, if active, add additional overhead to the GRE header. The second pair of bytes is the protocol field and indicates the type of data that is carried in the GRE tunnel. Table 14-2 describes the GRE header options.

Table 14-2 *GRE Header Options*

GRE Header Bit	Option	Description
0	Checksum Present	Adds a 4-byte checksum field to the GRE header after the protocol field if this bit is set to 1.
2	Key Present	Adds a 4-byte encryption key to the GRE header after the checksum field if this bit is set to 1.
3	Sequence Number Present	Adds a 4-byte sequence number to the GRE header after the key field if this bit is set to 1.
13–15	GRE Version	0 indicates basic GRE, while 1 is used for PPTP.

The Checksum Present option (bit 0) adds an optional 4-byte checksum field to the GRE header. This checksum appears after the protocol field in the GRE header only if the Checksum Present bit is set. Normally, this option is not needed because other upper-layer protocols provide checksum capabilities to detect packet corruption.

The Key Present option (bit 2) adds an optional 4-byte key field to the GRE header. This clear-text key follows the checksum field. The key is used to provide basic authentication where each GRE endpoint has the key. However, the key itself is exposed in the GRE header. Due to this vulnerability, GRE encryption is not typically used. However, the key value can be used to uniquely identify multiple tunnels between two endpoints. This would be similar to an IPsec SPI.

The Sequence Number option (bit 3) adds an optional 4-byte sequence number field to the GRE header. This sequence value follows the key option. This option is used to properly sequence GRE packets upon arrival. Similar to the checksum option, this is not typically used because upper-layer protocols also offer this functionality.

Bits 13–15 indicate the GRE version number. 0 represents basic GRE, while 1 shows that the Point-to-Point Tunneling Protocol (PPTP) is used. PPTP is not covered in this book.

The second 2 bytes of the GRE header represent the Protocol field. These 16 bits identify the type of packet that is carried inside the GRE tunnel. Ethertype 0x0800 indicates IP. Figure 14-1 shows a GRE packet with all options present added to an IP header and data.

Figure 14-1 *GRE Packet Format*

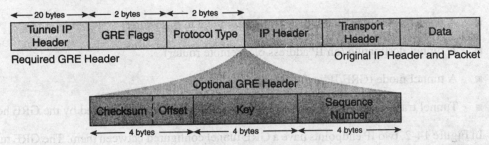

In Figure 14-1, only the required GRE header and original IP header and packet typically appear in GRE tunnel configurations. The GRE options are normally not used because upper-layer protocols provide similar functionality.

Basic GRE Configuration

A GRE tunnel carries some Layer 3 protocol between two IP endpoints. During the initial use of GRE tunnels, the tunnel contents were typically any protocol except IP. Today, GRE tunnels are used to carry IP data over an IP network. But the GRE tunnel itself can be sent through an IPsec tunnel for security. Figure 14-2 shows a basic GRE tunnel setup.

Figure 14-2 *GRE Tunnel Configuration*

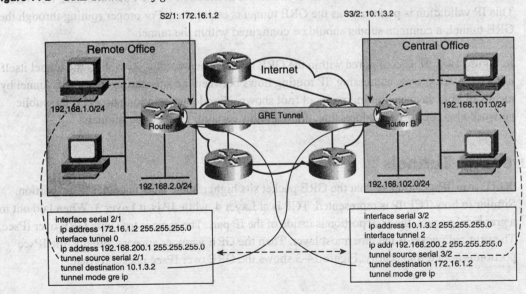

The basic configuration components of a GRE tunnel include

- A tunnel source (an interface or IP address local to this router)

- A tunnel destination (an IP address of a remote router)

- A tunnel mode (GRE/IP is the default)

- Tunnel traffic (data that travels through the tunnel, and is encapsulated by the GRE header)

In Figure 14-2, two IP endpoints have a GRE tunnel configured between them. The GRE tunnel is actually defined as an interface in each router. The GRE interface is what makes GRE multiprotocol. IPsec crypto maps can match only IP access lists. A router interface can be configured for, and thus transport, any protocol. The available protocols are dependent upon the Cisco IOS feature set installed.

> **TIP** The Cisco Software Advisor (http://tools.cisco.com/Support/Fusion/FusionHome.do) helps select the appropriate IOS feature set for any given Cisco router platform.

The tunnel source and destination are IP interfaces. Thus, the GRE travels across an IP network. The protocol configured on the GRE interfaces is the data that travels through the GRE tunnel.

The GRE tunnel source on one end must match the destination on the other end, and vice versa. This IP validation is performed as the GRE tunnel is established. For proper routing through the GRE tunnel, a common subnet should be configured within the tunnel.

In Figure 14-2, IP is configured within the GRE tunnel. The two sites, as well as the tunnel itself, use RFC 1918 private addressing. IP routing flows between the sites through the GRE tunnel by means of your favorite routing protocol (not shown). For documentation purposes, the public network also uses private addressing, although this certainly is not a requirement.

Secure GRE Tunnels

"GRE over IPsec" implies that the GRE packet sits higher in the stack than the IPsec portion. Similar to how TCP/IP is represented, TCP is at Layer 4, while IP is at Layer 3. When laid out in a graphical packet, the TCP portion is inside of the IP part. The same is true with GRE over IPsec. The original packet is the innermost layer. Then the GRE wrapper appears. Finally, the IPsec portion is added for security. Figure 14-3 shows the GRE over IPsec packet format.

Figure 14-3 *GRE over IPsec Packet Format*

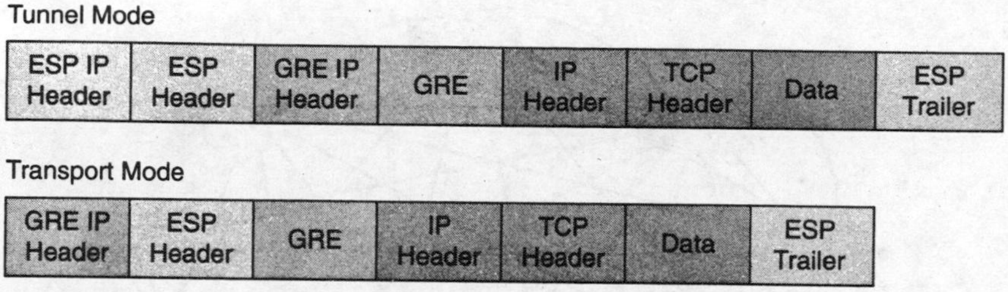

Tunnel Mode

ESP IP Header	ESP Header	GRE IP Header	GRE	IP Header	TCP Header	Data	ESP Trailer

Transport Mode

GRE IP Header	ESP Header	GRE	IP Header	TCP Header	Data	ESP Trailer

As Figure 14-3 shows, there are multiple IP layers in a GRE over IPsec packet. The innermost layer is the original IP packet. This represents data that is traveling between two devices, or two sites. The initial IP packet is wrapped in a GRE header to permit routing protocols to travel between in the GRE tunnel (something that IPsec alone cannot do). And IPsec is added as the outer layer to provide confidentiality and integrity (which is a shortcoming of GRE by itself). The end result is that two sites can securely exchange routing information and IP packets.

Figure 14-3 is also a reminder of the two IPsec modes: tunnel and transport. Transport mode is used if the original IP header can be exposed, while tunnel mode protects the original IP header within a new IPsec IP header. When using GRE over IPsec, transport mode is often sufficient, because the GRE and IPsec endpoints are often the same. Whether tunnel or transport mode is selected, the original IP header and packet are fully protected.

What might get lost in Figure 14-3 is the size of the new packets created due to the additional encapsulations. Each IP header adds 20 bytes to the packet size. This does not include overhead for ESP and GRE headers. For small IP packets, it is possible that the GRE over IPsec headers may be much larger than the original packet itself. Network efficiency can be determined by the ratio of actual data compared to the overhead associated with transporting the data. When there is more overhead (packet headers) than actual data, then the network is inherently less efficient.

Most GRE over IPsec implementations use a hub-and-spoke design. Although not a requirement, such a design minimizes the management overhead seen with managing a large number of IPsec tunnels. For example, if ten sites were fully meshed with GRE over IPsec tunnels, it would take 45 tunnels ([10 * 9]/2). In a hub-and-spoke design, full connectivity (via the hub) is accomplished with only nine tunnels. Figure 14-4 graphically compares a full mesh of tunnels versus a hub-and-spoke design.

Figure 14-4 *Full Mesh versus Hub-and-Spoke*

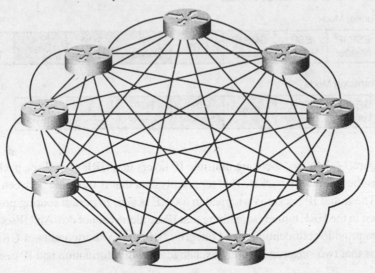

Full Mesh

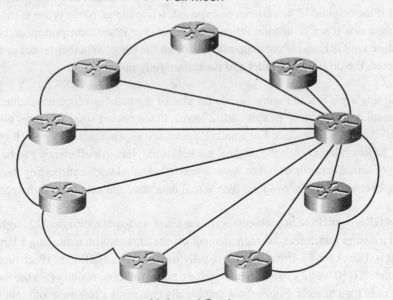

Hub and Spoke

In a normal IPsec tunnel, static routes are needed to direct IP packets into the IPsec VPN tunnel. Routing protocols can run inside the GRE tunnel, creating a dynamic routing topology. GRE provides the routing connectivity, while IPsec provides the confidentiality and integrity. With GRE, routing protocols can now run inside the IPsec tunnel.

Configure GRE over IPsec Using SDM

This chapter explores how to configure GRE over IPsec using the SDM tool. The previous chapter gave you the opportunity to create an IPsec tunnel in SDM, and get familiar with the SDM interface. This section expands upon previous navigation skills that you have learned.

Launch the GRE over IPsec Wizard

The GRE over IPsec wizard is accessed from the same window that started the Site-to-Site VPN wizard as seen in Chapter 13. Figure 14-5 shows how to access the GRE over IPsec wizard.

Figure 14-5 *GRE over IPsec Wizard*

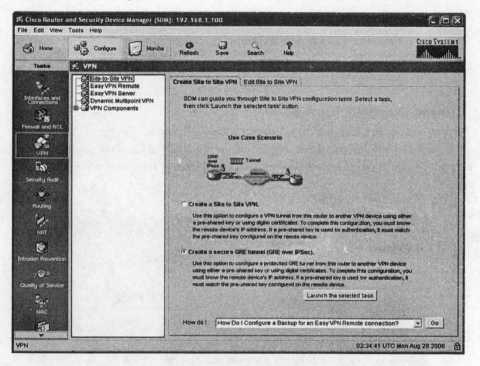

Similar to how the Site-to-Site VPN Wizard was initiated in Chapter 13, the GRE over IPsec wizard is accessed as follows:

Step 1   Click the **Configure** button at the top of the window.

Step 2   Click the **VPN** button in the Tasks bar on the left.

Step 3   Click the **Site-to-Site VPN** option at the top of the menu.

Step 4   Click the **Create Site to Site VPN** tab in the window.

Step 5   Click the **Create a secure GRE tunnel (GRE over IPSec)** radio button.

Step 6   Click the **Launch the selected task** button at the bottom of the window.

When you successfully accomplish these tasks, the Secure GRE Wizard starts. The Secure GRE Tunnel (GRE over IPsec) window reminds you of the capabilities and purpose of such a tunnel. The basic steps of the Secure GRE Wizard are as follows:

Step 1   Create the GRE tunnel.

Step 2   Create a backup GRE tunnel (optional).

Step 3   Select the IPsec VPN authentication method.

Step 4   Select the IPsec VPN IKE proposals.

Step 5   Select the IPsec VPN transform sets.

Step 6   Select the routing method for the GRE over IPsec tunnel.

Step 7   Validate the GRE over IPsec configuration.

To continue into the wizard, click **Next>** at the bottom of the window.

Step 1: Create the GRE Tunnel

The first part of the GRE over IPsec tunnel is the GRE tunnel. Figure 14-3 showed the various layers within the GRE over IPsec tunnel. The original IP packet is the innermost portion. Next comes the GRE layer. Figure 14-6 shows the GRE Tunnel Information window.

Figure 14-6 *GRE Tunnel Information*

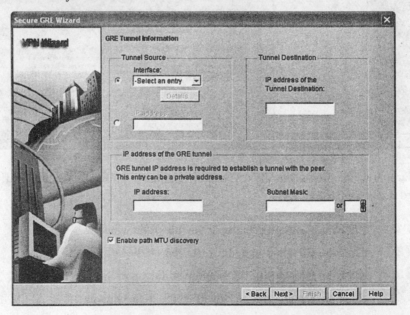

The GRE Tunnel Information window is the first configuration window of the Secure GRE Wizard. There are two sets of IP addresses that are applied to the GRE tunnel interface—the tunnel source and destination (at the top of the window) represent the GRE IP header (shown in Figure 14-3).

The tunnel source is either selected from a pull-down list of interfaces in this router or entered manually. If an interface is selected from the list, the IP address of the interface is automatically used as the GRE tunnel source. The tunnel destination is the IP address of the remote GRE peer and must be manually entered.

The IP address of the GRE tunnel is the IP subnet used within the tunnel itself. This subnet can be used for management (the other end can be pinged) or, more importantly, for routing protocol neighbors. The remote GRE peer must use a unique IP address on the same inner subnet.

Path MTU is enabled by default. Remember that GRE over IPsec considerably increases the IP packet size. Path MTU discovery uses Internet Control Message Protocol (ICMP) Unreachable messages to determine the maximum packet size possible between the GRE peers. If needed, fragmentation can then be performed by the GRE endpoints, versus en route, where it might not be performed at all.

When you are finished with the GRE Tunnel Information window, click **Next>** at the bottom of the window.

Step 2: Create a Backup GRE Tunnel

The Secure GRE Wizard offers the option to create a second GRE tunnel for survivability. If the GRE tunnel fails for any reason, then the IPsec tunnel that is carried within it fails also. A backup GRE tunnel provides stateless failover in the event of the loss of the primary GRE tunnel. Figure 14-7 shows the Backup GRE Tunnel Information window.

Because a backup GRE tunnel is an optional feature, you must check the **Create a backup secure GRE tunnel for resilience** box to activate this window. Once checked, the configuration options are very similar to those used to create the primary GRE tunnel.

The same tunnel source is used for both the primary and backup GRE tunnels, so there is no opportunity to select a tunnel source in the Backup window. Either an interface or a local IP address was entered earlier for the primary GRE tunnel. Simply enter the IP address of the alternate peer for this backup GRE tunnel. This IP address could be a different interface on the same peer router, or an entirely different device at the remote site.

Figure 14-7 *Backup GRE Tunnel Information*

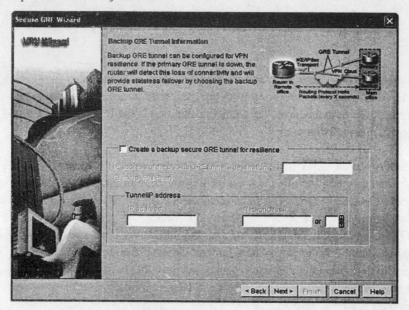

Similar to the primary GRE tunnel, you must create a unique IP address on a new IP subnet within this backup tunnel. The remote peer must use the same subnet with an exclusive IP address of its own. As with the primary GRE tunnel, the inner IP addresses are used to establish routing protocol neighbors.

When you are finished with the Backup GRE Tunnel Information window, click **Next>** at the bottom of the window.

Steps 3–5: IPsec VPN Information

The outermost layer of the GRE over IPsec tunnel is the IPsec VPN. The various windows used to enter the IPsec information are nearly identical to those used to create a site-to-site IPsec VPN discussed in Chapter 13, "Site-to-Site VPN Operations."

The first IPsec VPN task is to enter the VPN authentication information. Similar to Figure 13-14, either digital certificates or pre-shared keys can be used. If pre-shared keys are selected, the key must be entered twice to ensure accuracy.

The second IPsec VPN task is to select or create IKE proposals. This window is identical to the one shown in Figure 13-15, as are the procedures used to select an appropriate IKE proposal for this IPsec VPN. Remember that the remote IPsec peer must have an identical IKE proposal configured, and that the same IKE proposal can be used for many remote peers.

The third IPsec VPN task is to select or create IPsec transform sets. This window is identical to the one shown in Figure 13-16. From here, new transform sets can be created, and the appropriate transform set can be selected for use with this IPsec VPN. Remember that the remote IPsec peer must have an identical IPSec transform set configured, and that the same IPsec transform set can be used for many remote peers.

Step 6: Routing Information

Once both the GRE tunnel and the IPsec tunnels have been configured, the final step is to select a routing protocol to traverse the GRE tunnel. Remember that with a typical IPsec VPN, the only routing option is to configure static routes on each side. These static routes manually determine which prefixes are reachable through the IPsec VPN. Figure 14-8 shows the Select Routing Protocol window of the Secure GRE Wizard.

Figure 14-8 *Select Routing Protocol*

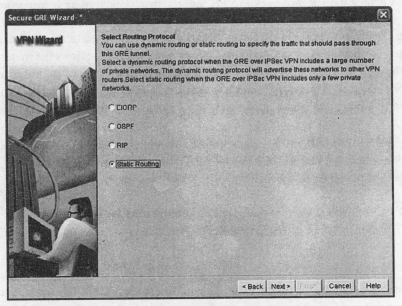

Static Routing is the default option (radio button) in the routing protocol selection process. There are four routing options supported within the GRE tunnel:

- EIGRP

- OSPF

- RIP

- Static routing

Each routing option uses the Routing Information window to configure individual options. Routes that are manually configured (static) or dynamically exchanged (RIP, OSPF, or EIGRP) through the GRE over IPsec tunnel become the "interesting traffic" described that decides which traffic is encrypted through the IPsec tunnel. Once you have selected a routing protocol, click **Next>** at the bottom of the window to proceed to the Routing Information window for the appropriate routing protocol.

When using the GRE over IPsec wizard, RIP is not an available dynamic routing option from the Select Routing Protocol window if a backup GRE tunnel was configured earlier. Only OSPF or EIGRP can be enabled when two GRE tunnels to the same remote location are used.

Static Routes

Static routing is typically used to support small stub sites that only have a single subnet. No dynamic routing information is exchanged between sites. If a site has multiple subnets that are to use the VPN, or if a site uses backup VPN tunnels, then static routing is inappropriate.

If static routing is selected in the Select Routing Protocol window of the wizard, the first choice presented is whether to do split tunneling or not. Split tunneling allows the router to send some traffic through the IPsec VPN to the remote side, and the remainder of the traffic unprotected into the public network. This is very similar to the definition of interesting traffic with IPsec VPNs. Enter an IP subnet and subnet mask that is to be protected in the VPN tunnel.

The wizard permits only a single static route to be configured within the split tunneling option. If split tunneling is not selected (the Tunnel All Traffic option), then a default route is added to the router that sends all traffic through the GRE over IPsec tunnel.

When you are finished with the static routing options, click **Next>** at the bottom of the window to advance to the Summary of the Configuration window.

RIP

The first RIP configuration option is the version. Select version 1 to use the older classful version of RIP, or version 2 for the more modern classless version that sends the subnet mask with the routing updates. Next, click the **Add...** button local networks to the RIP routing protocol. Remember that you can add only whole classful network numbers to RIP, and all subnets of that network number are included. You must add the IP subnet of the GRE interface for RIP to use the interface.

Routes that are not added to the RIP configuration are not exchanged through the GRE over IPsec tunnel. Only traffic in the exchanged routes is protected by the VPN. Traffic outside of the RIP routes avoids the VPN. It is important that the remote router also correctly configure RIP so routing neighbors can be formed.

When you are finished with the RIP options, click **Next>** at the bottom of the window to advance to the Summary of the Configuration window.

OSPF

The first OSPF task is to select or create an OSPF process ID. If OSPF is already operational in the router, you can select a process ID from the pull-down menu. If not, you must create a new OSPF process in the router. Once the process ID is configured, you must determine the OSPF area ID to be used in the GRE over IPsec tunnel.

Next, you must click the **Add...** button to add local networks to the OSPF routing protocol. In OSPF, you must enter a subnet number, a wildcard mask, and an area for each network. You must add the IP subnet/mask/area of the GRE interface for OSPF to use the interface.

Routes that are not added to the OSPF configuration are not exchanged through the GRE over IPsec tunnel. Only traffic in the exchanged routes is protected by the VPN. Traffic outside of the OSPF routes avoids the VPN. It is important that the remote router also correctly configure OSPF so routing adjacencies can be formed. For OSPF, this means that both peers use a common subnet and the same OSPF area.

When you are finished with the OSPF options, click **Next>** at the bottom of the window to advance to the Summary of the Configuration window.

EIGRP

The first EIGRP task is to select or create an EIGRP autonomous system (AS) number. If EIGRP is already operational in the router, you can select an AS number from the pull-down menu. If not, you must create a new EIGRP AS number in the router.

Then, you must click the **Add...** button to add local networks to the EIGRP routing protocol. In EIGRP, you must enter a subnet number and a wildcard mask for each network. You must add the IP subnet/mask of the GRE interface for EIGRP to use the interface.

Routes that are not added to the EIGRP configuration are not exchanged through the GRE over IPsec tunnel. Only traffic in the exchanged routes is protected by the VPN. Traffic outside of the EIGRP routes avoids the VPN. It is important that the remote router also correctly configure EIGRP so routing neighbors can be formed. For EIGRP, this means that both peers use a common subnet and the same EIGRP AS.

When you are finished with the EIGRP options, click **Next>** at the bottom of the window to advance to the Summary of the Configuration window.

Step 7: Validate the GRE over IPsec Configuration

Once you advance beyond either of the routing options (the appropriate Routing Information window), you reach the Summary of the Configuration window. You likely need to use the scrollbar to view the entire configuration created by the Secure GRE Wizard. This window is identical to the summary window at the end of the Site-to-Site VPN Wizard. The differences here are the additional configuration options of the GRE tunnel and the routing protocol (if one was configured).

As with the Site-to-Site VPN Wizard, you can either click Finish to end the wizard from this window or click **<Back** to go back into the wizard to modify any of the configurations shown.

Once the configuration is complete, the procedures to test and monitor the GRE over IPsec tunnel are identical to those for the site-to-site IPsec tunnel described in Chapter 13.

Foundation Summary

The generic characteristics of a GRE tunnel are as follows:

- A GRE tunnel is similar to an IPsec tunnel because the original packet is wrapped inside an outer shell.

- GRE is stateless and offers no flow control mechanisms.

- GRE adds at least 24 bytes of overhead, including the new 20-byte IP header.

- GRE is multiprotocol and can tunnel any OSI Layer 3 protocol.

- GRE permits routing protocols to travel through the tunnel.

- GRE was needed to carry IP multicast traffic until 12.4(4)T.

- GRE has relatively weak security features.

Table 14-3 describes the GRE header options.

Table 14-3 *GRE Options*

GRE Header Bit	Option	Description
0	Checksum Present	Adds a 4-byte checksum field to the GRE header after the protocol field if this bit is set to 1.
2	Key Present	Adds a 4-byte encryption key to the GRE header after the checksum field if this bit is set to 1.
3	Sequence Number Present	Adds a 4-byte sequence number to the GRE header after the key field if this bit is set to 1.
13–15	GRE Version	0 indicates basic GRE, while 1 is used for PPTP.

The basic configuration components of a GRE tunnel include

- A tunnel source (an interface or IP address local to this router)

- A tunnel destination (an IP address of a remote router)

- A tunnel mode (GRE/IP is the default)

- Tunnel traffic (data that travels through the tunnel, and is encapsulated by the GRE header)

GRE over IPsec uses the GRE tunnel to carry dynamic IP routing protocols, and uses IPsec to enforce confidentiality and integrity.

GRE over IPsec using tunnel mode has a total of three IP headers in the packet. GRE over IPsec using transport mode has only two IP headers in the packet.

Most GRE over IPsec implementations use a hub-and-spoke design to limit the number of IPsec tunnels required to secure the entire network.

The Secure GRE Wizard is accessed as follows:

Step 1   Click the **Configure** button at the top of the window.

Step 2   Click the **VPN** button in the Tasks bar on the left.

Step 3   Click the **Site-to-Site VPN** option at the top of the menu.

Step 4   Click the **Create Site to Site VPN** tab in the window.

Step 5   Click the **Create a secure GRE tunnel (GRE over IPSec)** radio button.

Step 6   Click the **Launch the selected task** button at the bottom of the window.

The basic steps of the Secure GRE Wizard include

Step 1   Create the GRE tunnel.

Step 2   Create a backup GRE tunnel (optional).

Step 3   Select the IPsec VPN authentication method.

Step 4   Select the IPsec VPN IKE proposals.

Step 5   Select the IPsec VPN transform sets.

Step 6   Select the routing method for the GRE over IPsec tunnel.

Step 7   Validate the GRE over IPsec configuration.

The GRE Tunnel Information window is where the GRE tunnel is configured in SDM. Configuration includes

■   Tunnel source (local interface or IP address)

■   Tunnel destination (remote IP address)

■   Interior tunnel IP address and subnet mask

■   Optional MTU path discovery to know if fragmentation must be performed on this router due to the larger packet size created by GRE over IPsec

The Backup GRE Tunnel Information window is where the backup GRE tunnel is configured in SDM. The backup GRE tunnel uses the same source as the primary GRE tunnel. Configuration includes

- Enable the backup tunnel
- Tunnel destination (remote IP address)
- Interior tunnel IP address and subnet mask

The IPsec VPN configuration has three phases, all of which are identical to those found in the site-to-site IPsec VPN configuration process:

1. VPN authentication
2. IKE proposals
3. IPsec transform sets

There are four routing options supported within the GRE tunnel:

- EIGRP
- OSPF
- RIP
- Static routing

Static routing can configure only one subnet and is not appropriate for sites with multiple subnets or for sites using two GRE tunnels.

RIP cannot be configured if a backup GRE tunnel is configured.

Both OSPF and EIGRP use inverse masks when adding subnets to the routing protocol.

Be sure to include the internal IP subnet of the GRE tunnel in the routing protocol configuration so that the configured protocol will use the GRE tunnel interface.

The Configuration Summary window allows you to view the configuration just created with the wizard. You can return to the wizard by clicking the **<Back** button to make changes, or you can finish the wizard by clicking the **Finish** button.

Q&A

The questions and scenarios in this book are designed to be challenging and to make sure that you know the answer. Rather than allowing you to derive the answers from clues hidden inside the questions themselves, the questions challenge your understanding and recall of the subject.

Hopefully, mastering these questions will help you limit the number of exam questions on which you narrow your choices to two options, and then guess.

You can find the answers to these questions in Appendix A. For more practice with exam-like question formats, use the exam engine on the CD-ROM.

1. What type of security features does GRE have natively?

2. What are the three optional headers possible with GRE?

3. What is the GRE encryption typically used for?

4. What is the relationship between the GRE source and destination addresses on the tunnel endpoints?

5. Which IPsec modes can be used with GRE over IPsec?

6. What is the primary driver to deploying GRE over IPsec?

7. What is the sequence to launch the Secure GRE Wizard in SDM?

8. Which options must be configured on the primary GRE tunnel in the Secure GRE Wizard?

9. Which GRE configuration option is not necessary when creating a backup GRE tunnel?

10. What are the three IPsec tasks that are configured in the Secure GRE Wizard?

11. Which routing options are available in the GRE over IPsec configuration?

12. How many static routes can be configured in the Secure GRE Wizard?

13. Which routing protocols must be used if a backup GRE tunnel is deployed?

14. What options are available in the Configuration Summary window?

Exam Topic List

This chapter covers the following topics that you need to master for the CCNP ISCW exam:

- **Sources of Failures**—Describes how to determine the source of a network failure in an IPsec VPN. Knowing where failures could occur can help you plan for quick recovery.

- **Failure Mitigation**—Describes how to avoid a failure, or how best to react when one occurs.

- **Failover Strategies**—Describes how alternative paths are used to continue the flow of data.

- **WAN Backed Up by an IPsec VPN**—Describes how a nonprotected link can use an established VPN to mitigate failure.

CHAPTER 15

IPsec High Availability Options

Redundancy is typically found at various spots throughout networks. Because any path or component has the potential to fail, an alternate solution ensures that data continues to flow from one point to another. However, redundancy does come with a price. The configuration of additional paths could imply that such paths must be procured from the provider, and such paths are not free. To avoid a hardware failure, additional hardware must be procured and installed. To avoid a cable cut catastrophe, alternate physical paths should be planned.

As the amount of equipment and the number of options increase, so do the complexity and cost of the network. This chapter explores how to offer high availability options to IPsec VPNs. Many of the best practice concepts for general redundancy and high availability apply to the IPsec VPN world. Such opportunities are highlighted when appropriate.

This chapter only discusses the CLI methodology for offering high availability solutions. Such configurations appear on the ISCW certification test.

"Do I Know This Already?" Quiz

The purpose of the "Do I Know This Already?" quiz is to help you decide whether you really need to read the entire chapter. If you already intend to read the entire chapter, you do not necessarily need to answer these questions now.

The 13-question quiz, derived from the major sections in the "Foundation Topics" portion of the chapter, helps you to determine how to spend your limited study time.

Table 15-1 outlines the major topics discussed in this chapter and the "Do I Know This Already?" quiz questions that correspond to those topics.

Table 15-1 *"Do I Know This Already?" Foundation Topics Section-to-Question Mapping*

Foundation Topics Section	Questions Covered in This Section	Score
Sources of Failures	1	
Failure Mitigation	2	
Failover Strategies	3–12	
WAN Backed Up by an IPsec VPN	13	
Total Score		

CAUTION The goal of self-assessment is to gauge your mastery of the topics in this chapter. If you do not know the answer to a question or are only partially sure of the answer, you should mark this question wrong for purposes of self-assessment. Giving yourself credit for an answer that you correctly guess skews your self-assessment results and might provide you with a false sense of security.

1. Which of the following are the primary failure sources (select all that apply)?

   a. Remote peer failure

   b. Local peer failure

   c. Access link failure

   d. Device failure

   e. Path failure

   f. Cable failure

2. Multiple interfaces or devices are a way to mitigate which of the following failures (select all that apply)?

   a. Access link failure

   b. Remote peer failure

   c. Local peer failure

   d. Device failure

   e. Path failure

3. Which of the following failover means are considered stateless (select all that apply)?

   a. DPD

   b. HSRP

   c. SSO

   d. IPC

   e. IGP in GRE over IPsec

4. Periodic DPD mode has which of the following characteristics (select all that apply)?

   a. It is the default mode in Cisco IOS devices.

   b. DPD keepalive messages are used only when there is a lull in tunnel traffic.

   c. DPD keepalive messages are never sent during idle tunnel moments.

   d. DPD keepalive messages are periodically sent between IPsec VPN peers.

   e. DPD keepalive messages are sent in addition to normal IPsec rekey messages.

5. How is the primary DPD peer configured in an IOS device?

   a. **set peer** *ip-address*

   b. **set peer** *ip-address* **default**

   c. **set dpd peer** *ip-address*

   d. **set dpd peer** *ip-address* **default**

   e. **set peer** *ip-address* **dpd default**

6. What IOS command determines the frequency of DPD keepalive messages?

   a. **dpd keepalive** *seconds* [*retries*]

   b. **set peer** *ip-address* **dpd-keepalive** *seconds*

   c. **set dpd keepalive** *seconds* [*retries*]

   d. **crypto isakmp keepalive** *seconds* [*retries*]

   e. **crypto isakmp dpd keepalive** *seconds* [*retries*]

7. Which dynamic routing protocols should be used within GRE over IPsec tunnels due to fast convergence (select all that apply)?

   a. RIPv2

   b. OSPF

   c. EIGRP

   d. BGP

   e. IS-IS

8. Which of the following terms best describes an HSRP active router?

   a. The router is properly configured and ready to participate in HSRP elections.

   b. The router is actively working on electing a primary HSRP router for the group.

   c. The router is the current primary forwarding router for the group.

   d. The router helps elect the next primary router if the current one fails.

   e. The router is alive but not the primary router in the group.

9. In HSRP, what is the purpose of the standby router?

    a. The router is next in line to be the active router of the group.

    b. The router is awaiting proper configuration.

    c. The router is forwarding traffic for only a small percentage of the group.

    d. The router is waiting for the group to become active.

    e. The router is waiting for permission from the primary router to become active.

10. What does the **preempt** command do in an HSRP router?

    a. Forces this router to be the active router in any condition

    b. Forces this router to be the active router only if it has the highest HSRP priority of the group

    c. Forces this router to be the active router only if it has the lowest HSRP priority of the group

    d. Prevents this router from becoming the active router of the group

    e. Prevents any other router from ever becoming active

11. What happens to an IPsec VPN that terminates on an HSRP group IP address when the active router fails?

    a. Nothing; the standby router assumes active status.

    b. The IPsec VPN is dynamically migrated to the standby router.

    c. The IPsec VPN drops, and is reestablished with the group IP address.

    d. The IPsec VPN drops, and is reestablished with the standby router IP address.

    e. Nothing, because all routers in the HSRP group terminated the IPsec VPN initially.

12. Which protocols are used to provide IPsec stateful failover (select all that apply)?

    a. OSPF

    b. HSRP

    c. EIGRP

    d. DPD

    e. SSO

13. How can an IPsec VPN be used to back up a typical WAN connection (select all that apply)?

    a. IPsec VPNs are not used for this type of backup.

    b. Use a floating static route with a high AD that becomes active only when the primary path fails.

    c. Use a floating static route with a low AD that becomes active only when the primary path fails.

    d. Use an IGP over the IPsec VPN, and make the VPN dynamic routes less favorable.

    e. Use an IGP over the GRE over IPsec VPN, and make the VPN dynamic routes less favorable.

The answers to the "Do I Know This Already?" quiz are found in Appendix A, "Answers to the 'Do I Know This Already?' Quizzes and Q&A Sections." The suggested choices for your next step are as follows:

■ **8 or fewer overall score**—Read the entire chapter. This includes the "Foundation Topics," "Foundation Summary," and "Q&A" sections.

■ **9 or 11 overall score**—Begin with the "Foundation Summary" section, and then go to the "Q&A" section.

■ **12 or more overall score**—If you want more review on these topics, skip to the "Foundation Summary" section, and then go to the "Q&A" section. Otherwise, move to the next chapter.

Foundation Topics

Sources of Failures

The network has a number of possible points vulnerable to failure. Remember that an IPsec VPN is an end-to-end connection. It typically travels across untrusted networks (such as the Internet), and through many different network devices. The loss of any one of these components can cause the IPsec VPN to fail. Such potential failure points include

- Access link failure

- Remote peer failure

- Device failure

- Path failure

An access link failure could include the failure of a physical interface on any transit network device (although *the* access link is typically seen at your end of the IPsec VPN), a module that contains many interfaces, or the "cable" (electrical, optical, or wireless) that provides transport.

Failure of the remote peer is typically attributed to "the other guy." Unless you have some network management reachability into the remote site, it is difficult to determine what the exact cause of the failure is.

A device failure is typically a failure of any device between, and including, the source and destination of the IPsec VPN. In many cases, these devices are beyond your administrative control, and the reason for failure cannot be determined.

A path failure could be a routing or circuit issue in a network between the two IPsec VPN endpoints. The failure is typically outside of your administrative reach, and cannot be easily determined.

The IPsec VPN design must consider all facets of potential network failure and implement redundancy accordingly to ensure that the secure traffic continues to flow from one site to another.

Failure Mitigation

Each of the failure sources mentioned earlier can be mitigated by employing one or more redundancy mechanisms. It is important to remember that the greater the level of high availability in the network, the greater the implementation cost. The primary failure points and some preventive solutions are as follows:

- **Access link failure**—To overcome the loss of an access link, multiple interfaces and devices can be used. A single IPsec VPN endpoint could have multiple interfaces, multiple interface cards, or multiple endpoint devices.

- **Remote peer failure**—Failure of the remote peer is mitigated in a similar manner to the way in which access link failure is mitigated. Multiple interfaces and devices can be used to survive a failure. Such duplication allows multiple IPsec VPN tunnels to securely connect the two sites, and each uses a different infrastructure.

- **Device failure**—Device failure comes in many flavors. As described for both the access link and remote peer, duplicate interfaces and devices can help overcome a local failure. However, a device failure outside of your administrative control is a challenge to correct. So rather than fix someone else's equipment, simply avoid it. Ensure that you have multiple diverse paths between endpoints in case a problem arises in the untrusted network.

- **Path failure**—A path failure is typically beyond your control. Path redundancy can be used to circumvent a path failure in an untrusted network.

It is important to consider what is truly required to achieve path redundancy. Any single point of failure should be removed from the path. Within your network, this would mean duplicate equipment and wiring. It would also imply separate and diverse paths into and out of the building. Many costly redundancy plans have been knocked out with a single swipe of a backhoe cutting the single physical path into the building.

The use of different ISPs ensures that the traffic starts in different pieces of the Internet. But it is difficult to ensure that a common circuit (from an upstream ISP) is not used "somewhere" between the source and destination points.

Failover Strategies

The best redundancy plans cannot be executed if the failure state cannot be recognized. There are two ways that IPsec failover can be executed:

- **Stateless**—In a stateless environment, redundant logical connections (IPsec VPN tunnels) are used to provide primary and backup paths. The use of the paths is determined by message exchanges between the peers, or a determination by the end devices on which path to use. The *state* of the IPsec VPN tunnels is not known. Traffic is sent across the backup tunnel if the end-to-end path has failed.

■ **Stateful**—To provide a stateful failover, redundant equipment is employed. The devices used to provide stateful failover are typically identical (configuration, interfaces, operating system, and so on). These devices also communicate with each other to determine which one is the current best device.

Most redundancy plans react to a failure and send traffic on an alternate path. The overall ability to provide timely redundancy begins with the detection of a failure.

IPsec Stateless Failover

There are three primary stateless means to detect and react to a fault. The ideal reaction to a detected fault is to automatically send traffic a different way. The three failure detection methods are as follows:

■ Dead peer detection (DPD)

■ An IGP within GRE over IPsec

■ Hot Standby Routing Protocol (HSRP) (or one of the related protocols)

The sections that follow discuss each of these methods in greater detail.

Dead Peer Detection

Dead peer detection is a configuration option during the IPsec VPN setup. DPD also offers a stateless failover from one VPN tunnel to another. This means that the routers are not keeping track of which VPN tunnels are currently alive. Instead, traffic flows through the primary tunnel until it fails, at which time a secondary tunnel is selected.

DPD has two operational modes: periodic mode and on-demand mode.

DPD periodic mode has the following characteristics:

■ DPD keepalive messages are periodically sent between IPsec VPN peers.

■ DPD keepalive messages are in addition to the normal IPsec rekey messages that also regularly traverse the tunnel.

■ DPD keepalive messages are not sent if user data is transmitted through the VPN tunnel.

■ DPD keepalive messages are used only when there is a lull in tunnel traffic.

One negative consequence of periodic DPD mode is the potentially excessive tunnel overhead. IKE already has a regular set of keepalive messages that pass through the tunnel. This keepalive mechanism is the IPsec SA rekeying messages that occur as the IPsec lifetime nears expiration.

Use of an IPsec VPN tunnel normally means that packets are encrypted at one end and decrypted at the other. The addition of DPD keepalive messages adds more encryption/decryption overhead to the VPN endpoints. However, the addition of these DPD keepalive messages provides more timely failure detection.

In contrast, DPD on-demand mode has the following attributes:

■ It is the default DPD mode in a Cisco IOS device.

■ DPD keepalive messages are sent only if the liveliness of the remote peer is in question. If traffic is sent to the peer, a response is expected. If such a response does not arrive, a DPD keepalive message is sent.

■ DPD keepalive messages are never sent during otherwise idle tunnel moments.

■ It is possible that a router might not discover a dead peer until the IKE or IPsec security association (SA) rekey is attempted.

The use of on-demand mode reduces the additional tunnel overhead that normal mode introduced. However, an alternate IPsec VPN tunnel might not be used immediately upon the failure of the primary one. This is not as bad as it may sound. If there is no traffic traveling through an IPsec VPN, and the VPN fails, there truly is no need to change to the alternate tunnel until user data arrives.

The configuration of DPD in a Cisco IOS device is simply a modification of an existing IPsec VPN setup. As already discussed, DPD uses keepalive messages to determine if the primary peer has failed, and then swaps over to a backup peer. Figure 15-1 shows a sample DPD configuration and topology.

Figure 15-1 shows how a remote site is configured with redundant IPsec VPN tunnels back to a central office using DPD. The two Cisco IOS commands that enable DPD are

```
crypto isakmp keepalive seconds [retries] [periodic ¦ on-demand]
set peer ip-address [default]
```

The **crypto isakmp keepalive** IOS command determines the mode and frequency of DPD. Remember that **periodic** mode sends DPD keepalive messages, which are continually sent to verify that the remote VPN peer is still alive. The default DPD mode is **on-demand**, which sends DPD messages only if the remote peer is believed to be dead. Default options do not appear in the configuration.

The **crypto isakmp keepalive** command has two timer options. The *seconds* option defines how often DPD keepalive messages are sent in periodic mode. The *retries* option defines how long to wait to resend DPD messages after the previous one has failed.

Figure 15-1 *DPD Configuration*

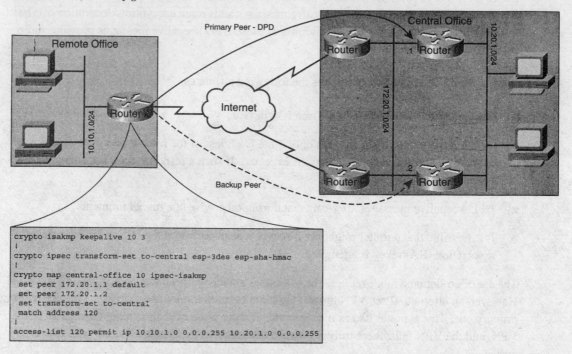

```
crypto isakmp keepalive 10 3
!
crypto ipsec transform-set to-central esp-3des esp-sha-hmac
!
crypto map central-office 10 ipsec-isakmp
 set peer 172.20.1.1 default
 set peer 172.20.1.2
 set transform-set to-central
 match address 120
!
access-list 120 permit ip 10.10.1.0 0.0.0.255 10.20.1.0 0.0.0.255
```

Figure 15-1 shows two peer configurations (with the set peer IOS commands). The primary peer (172.20.1.1) is indicated with the **default** option. This is the peer that is initially used between the remote and central offices. The secondary peer (172.20.1.2—the one without the **default** option) is not used until DPD determines that the primary peer has failed.

IGP Within a GRE over IPsec Tunnel

Chapter 14, "GRE Tunneling over IPsec," covered the use of GRE over IPsec. Remember that a normal IPsec VPN cannot transport dynamic routing protocols. A GRE tunnel is created for the routing protocol traffic, and then sent through the IPsec VPN for confidentiality and integrity.

OSPF and EIGRP have very fast convergence around failed links. The use of a backup GRE over IPsec VPN tunnel does provide redundancy, at the cost of additional IGP overhead in the VPN tunnel.

If two sites are connected with two or more GRE over IPsec tunnels, the IGP that runs across the tunnels can make very rapid routing decisions on alternative paths. Of course, it is important to create the tunnels such that there is no single point of failure in the paths. For example, if all the tunnels start on one router and end on a different router, the failure of either router eliminates all the tunnels.

HSRP

Most hosts are configured with a single gateway, or default, router. The address of this default router is typically delivered to the host during address acquisition via DHCP. However, if the gateway router fails, then all hosts that use it become isolated.

A good network design attempts to remove any single points of failure; however, such design options come at a price. The addition of a second gateway router not only costs money, but adds complexity to the network. The simple configuration of a second default gateway in the end hosts does not ensure a timely failover to the secondary gateway when needed.

It is possible to have the end hosts actually discover the gateways, or run routing protocols with the gateways. However, neither of these options is desirable for a number of reasons (administrative and processing overhead, feature support for some platforms, network security concerns).

HSRP offers the capability to use more than one router as a default gateway for end hosts. A group of routers form a logical gateway. This gateway IP address is used by the end hosts as their default gateway. A virtual MAC address is also used when the hosts broadcast (use ARP) for their default gateway.

Normally, the actual gateway IP address is configured on a single router. However, the HSRP group handles traffic destined for the logical gateway IP address. Within the group, the active router handles all packets destined for the logical IP address (and MAC address). A standby router exists to forward packets only if the active router fails.

Any number of routers can be in an HSRP group (although a large number quickly becomes impractical). There is only one active router per group (per gateway IP address). The remaining routers in the HSRP group elect the standby router. The active and standby routers periodically communicate with each other, which is how the standby router determines if the active router has failed. If the active router fails, the standby router takes control of the group and forwards traffic sent to the virtual group IP address. At this time, the remaining routers in the HSRP group elect a new standby router. Although the HSRP routers communicate with each other, this is still considered stateless VPN failover because the state of the IPsec VPN tunnels is unknown.

It is possible for one physical LAN to be home for multiple IP subnets. As such, each subnet would typically need a gateway router. With HSRP, each subnet would use a virtual standby group, where each standby group emulates a physical gateway router. HSRP groups can coexist and overlap on the same physical router. For example, one router could be the active router for one group and the standby router for another. In such a case, the router forwards traffic only for the active group. Another router forwards traffic for the other HSRP group.

Figure 15-2 shows a sample HSRP configuration and topology for the remote office. This actually shows the ultimate in redundancy, because there are two connections to the central office, and each uses a separate ISP. Because there are two physical connections, there are two different IPsec VPNs configured also. Not all remote sites are as fortunate.

Figure 15-2 *HSRP Configuration at the Remote Office*

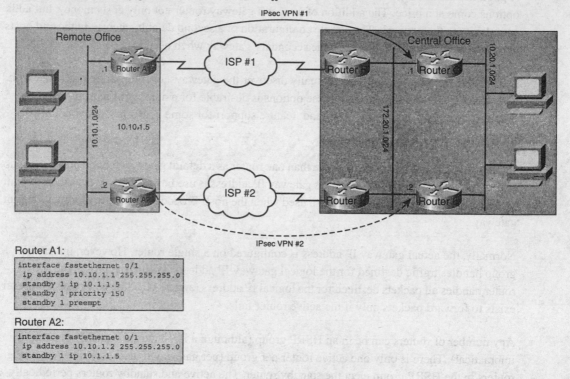

Router A1:
```
interface fastethernet 0/1
 ip address 10.10.1.1 255.255.255.0
 standby 1 ip 10.1.1.5
 standby 1 priority 150
 standby 1 preempt
```

Router A2:
```
interface fastethernet 0/1
 ip address 10.10.1.2 255.255.255.0
 standby 1 ip 10.1.1.5
```

The hosts at the remote site would use 10.10.1.5 as their default gateway. This is the HSRP group IP address (virtual IP address) between Routers A1 and A2. Router A1 is configured with a higher HSRP priority (the default is 100), which means that it will initially be the active router. The **preempt** command says that if it has a higher priority (and it does), it will regain active HSRP status if it ever fails and comes back to life.

The HSRP service provided to end hosts does not interact with the IPsec VPN configuration. For the hosts, and thus at the remote site, HSRP simply selects the active default gateway.

Figure 15-3 shows how HSRP can be used at the central office to terminate IPsec VPN connections from remote offices.

Figure 15-3 *HSRP Configuration at the Central Office*

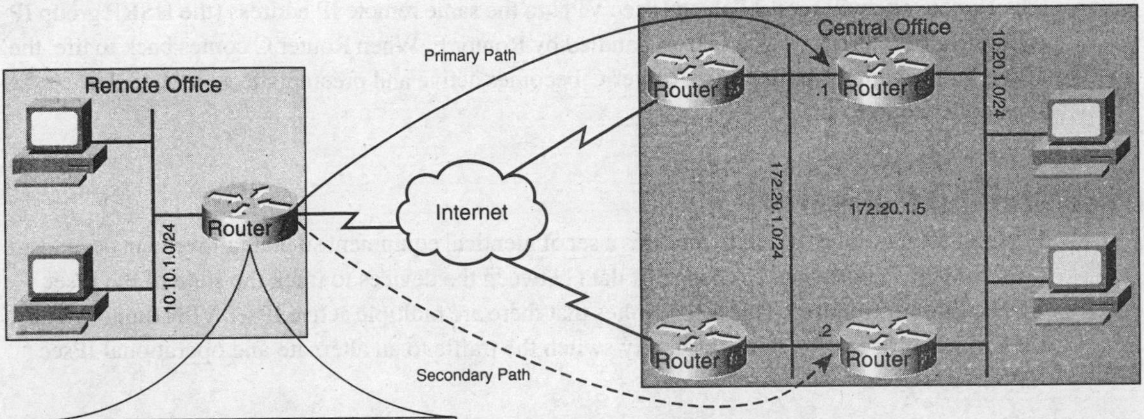

```
crypto map central-office 10 ipsec-isakmp
 set peer 172.20.1.5
```

Router C:

```
crypto dynamic-map from-remote 10
 set transform-set trans1
 reverse-route
!
crypto map central-office 10 dynamic from-remote
!
interface fastethernet 1/0
 ip address 172.20.1.1 255.255.255.0
 standby 1 ip 172.20.1.5
 standby 1 priority 150
 standby 1 preempt
 standby 1 name vpn-remote
 crypto map central-office redundancy vpn-remote
```

In this example, HSRP is configured between Routers C and E for the benefit of incoming IPsec VPN connections—not the hosts shown at the central office. These two routers represent the IPsec VPN headend for all remote sites. The 172.20.1.0/24 LAN is globally reachable. The remote site is configured to terminate its VPN connection to 172.20.1.5. At the central office, this IP address is actually a virtual group IP address between Routers C and E. In this example, the remote site does not benefit from as much redundancy as it does in Figure 15-2.

Figure 15-3 shows the HSRP configuration for Router C. The HSRP configuration for Router E would be very similar. A separate HSRP group can be configured between Router C and Router E to offer the hosts at the central office a redundant gateway. Such a configuration would be similar to the one shown in Figure 15-2.

The interface **crypto map** statement indicates that the HSRP group **vpn-remote** provides redundancy. This HSRP group name is defined on the interface. The central office is also configured with a dynamic crypto map. This means that any remote office (source IP address) can initiate a VPN connection with the central office. It is possible that remote offices that use DSL or cable connectivity to the Internet do not have fixed external IP addresses, and thus cannot be statically configured at the central office.

It is important to remember that if Router C is active and fails, the IPsec VPN to it will also drop. The remote site will reestablish an IPsec VPN to the same remote IP address (the HSRP group IP address—172.20.1.5), which is then handled by Router E. When Router C comes back to life, the IPsec VPN again drops (because Router C becomes active and preempts Router E) and is reestablished to Router C.

IPsec Stateful Failover

IPsec stateful failover typically requires a set of identical equipment so that failover can occur, and requires some continuous exchange of data between the devices to track the state of the IPsec VPNs (SA information). This also implies that there are multiple active IPsec VPN tunnels. Thus, the failure of one path can immediately switch the traffic to an alternate and operational IPsec VPN.

As described in the previous section on IPsec stateless failover, failover typically involves the creation of a new IPsec VPN tunnel when the first tunnel fails or becomes unreachable. Thus, there is a period of time during which secure connectivity does not exist. A stateful environment eliminates the temporary inability to communicate securely.

Stateful failover is accomplished through active (primary) and backup (secondary) devices. This concept is similar to how HSRP operates; however, SA information is also being maintained. The backup router automatically forwards traffic upon the failure (planned or unplanned) of the primary path. The switch from the primary to the backup is transparent to both the users and the remote IPsec VPN peer.

IPsec stateful failover uses two protocols for proper and continual operation:

- **HSRP**—Monitors both the inside and outside interfaces. If either goes down, the entire router is deemed unworthy and ownership of the IKE and IPsec SA processes is passed to the standby router. When this transition occurs, the standby router becomes the active HSRP router.

- **Stateful Switchover (SSO)**—Shares the IKE and IPsec SA information between the active and backup routers. At any time, either router knows enough to be the active IPsec VPN router.

There are some limitations/restrictions that exist when IPsec stateful failover is deployed. Some of the more important points to understand are as follows:

- Both the active and standby devices must run an identical Cisco IOS release.

- The active and standby devices must be connected via LAN ports, either directly or through a switch. WAN interfaces are not supported.

- Both the inside and outside interfaces must be connected via LAN ports.

- Only "box-to-box" failover is supported. Intrachassis (card-to-card) failover is not currently supported.

- Load balancing is not supported. Only one device in a redundancy group can be active at any time.

- IKE keepalive messages are not supported. DPD and periodic DPD are supported.

- Stateful failover of Layer 2 Tunneling Protocol (L2TP) is not supported.

- IPsec idle timers are not supported.

Because IPsec stateful failover uses HSRP and SSO, both protocols must be properly configured. Figure 15-4 shows the configuration necessary at the central office for the topology illustrated.

Figure 15-4 *IPsec Stateful Failover*

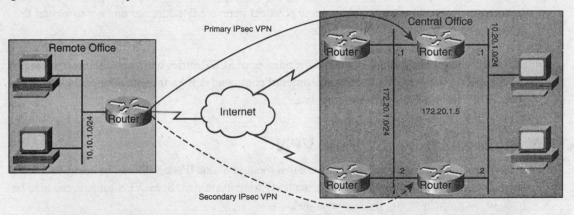

Router C:

```
crypto dynamic-map from-remote 10                    !
 set transform-set trans1                            redundancy inter-device
 reverse-route                                        scheme standby vpn-remote
!                                                    !
crypto map central-office 10 ipsec-isakmp dynamic from-remote   ipc zone default
!                                                     association 1
interface fastethernet 1/0                            protocol sctp
 ip address 172.20.1.1 255.255.255.0                   local-port 12321
 standby 1 ip 172.20.1.5                               local-ip 10.20.1.1
 standby 1 priority 150                                retransmit-timeout 300 10000
 standby 1 preempt                                     path-retransmit 10
 standby 1 name vpn-remote                             assoc-retransmit 20
 crypto map central-office redundancy vpn-remote stateful   remote-port 12321
                                                       remote-ip 10.20.1.2
```

The crypto map and interface configurations for Router C in Figure 15-4 are nearly identical to those from Figure 15-3. One minor addition is the term **stateful** to the crypto map on the interface. This permits the use of SSO to perform stateful failover. The HSRP configuration is the same as before. Router E would have a similar configuration as Router C to complete the stateful configuration.

The follow-on configuration box shows the IOS commands needed to enable SSO. The **redundancy inter-device** command configures redundancy and enters inter-device configuration mode. Currently, the only scheme supported is **standby**. Note that the name of the standby, *vpn-remote*, must match the standby group name defined with the crypto map on the interface.

The next block of commands configures the inter-device communication protocol (IPC) between the two gateways. The **ipc zone default** command initiates the communication link between active and standby routers. The subcommand **association** creates an association between the active and standby routers and uses the Stream Control Transmission Protocol (SCTP) as the transport protocol.

Within SCTP, the local and remote SCTP ports and IP addresses are defined. The *local-port* defined on this router must match the *remote-port* configured on the peer router. Also, the *local-ip* and *remote-ip* addresses should point to physical interface IP addresses and *not* to virtual IP addresses.

The **path-retransmit** command defines the number of SCTP retries before an attempt to create an SCTP session fails, and the **retransmit-timeout** command defines the maximum amount of time that SCTP waits before retransmitting data.

WAN Backed Up by an IPsec VPN

This chapter has focused on how to ensure that the loss of one IPsec VPN can be easily recovered by a second. Both stateful and stateless methods were examined. IPsec VPN tunnels can also be used to back up "normal" WAN connections.

Most of Part III, "IPsec VPNs," of this book deals with IPsec VPNs, which offer confidentiality to data as it passes from one site to another. A "normal" WAN connection is simply a PVC, such as a Frame Relay or ATM link between sites. No confidentiality or integrity is offered for such connections. However, if such a connection should fail, there is no reason that the traffic that does not expect protection cannot travel through the IPsec VPN.

The assumption is that both a "normal" WAN connection and an IPsec VPN link exist between two sites. The WAN connection is some sort of provider-based PVC, while the IPsec VPN travels across the untrusted Internet. As already explained in Chapter 13, an IPsec VPN can be statically configured to know which traffic is permitted to travel through it (interesting traffic). It has also been shown how to configure dynamic routing protocols across the IPsec VPN through the use of GRE over IPsec (refer to Chapter 14).

The "normal" WAN connection exchanges dynamic routing updates via OSPF or EIGRP. When this link fails, both sides realize the loss very quickly, due to the fast convergence time of both OSPF and EIGRP. There are two ways that routers on either end can decide to forward traffic over the IPsec VPN link.

The first solution is to ensure that the same dynamic routing protocol is also configured to run across the IPsec VPN, which is accomplished with GRE over IPsec. The IPsec VPN connection should be used only after the "normal" WAN connection fails. To ensure this, the EIGRP interface delay or OSPF cost can be adjusted to make the dynamic IPsec VPN routes less favorable than the "normal" WAN ones.

A second way to route traffic through the IPsec VPN upon WAN failure is to use floating static routes. A floating static route is a manually configured route with a high administrative distance (AD). Due to the high AD, the static route is not chosen as the best available path until the dynamic routes (with lower ADs) have evaporated. The loss of such dynamic routes occurs as a result of either path failure to the prefix or failure of the prefix itself.

With either of these solutions, the IPsec VPN is used primarily for specific traffic. Upon failure of the WAN connection, all traffic is permitted to temporarily travel through the VPN. When the primary WAN path has been reestablished, the normal WAN traffic returns to its desired connection.

Foundation Summary

Potential network failure points and some of the ways to mitigate them include:

- **Access link**—Use multiple interfaces and devices.

- **Remote peer**—Use multiple interfaces and devices.

- **Device failure**—Use duplicate interfaces and devices to help overcome a local failure. Having multiple diverse paths between endpoints helps avoid misbehaving devices beyond your administrative control.

- **Path failure**—Use path redundancy to circumvent a path failure in an untrusted network.

Two ways that IPsec failover can be executed are as follows:

- **Stateless**—In a stateless environment, redundant logical connections (IPsec VPN tunnels) are used to provide primary and backup paths. The use of the paths is determined by message exchanges between the peers, or a determination by the end devices on which path to use. The "state" of the IPsec VPN tunnels is not known. Traffic is sent across the backup tunnel if the end-to-end path has failed.

- **Stateful**—In a stateful environment, redundant equipment is employed. The devices used to provide stateful failover are typically identical (configuration, interfaces, operating system, and so on). These devices also communicate with each other to determine which one is the current best device.

Three primary stateless means to detect and react to a fault are as follows:

- Dead peer detection (DPD)

- An IGP within GRE over IPsec

- HSRP (or one of the related protocols)

DPD has two operational modes:

- DPD periodic mode, which has the following characteristics:

  — DPD keepalive messages are periodically sent between IPsec VPN peers.

  — DPD keepalive messages are in addition to the normal IKE keepalive messages that also regularly traverse the tunnel.

— DPD keepalive messages are not sent if user data is transmitted through the VPN tunnel.

— DPD keepalive messages are used only when there is a lull in tunnel traffic.

■ DPD on-demand mode, which has the following attributes:

— It is the default DPD mode in a Cisco IOS device.

— DPD keepalive messages are sent only if the liveliness of the remote peer is in question. If traffic is sent to the peer, a response is expected. If one does not arrive, then a DPD keepalive is sent.

— DPD keepalive messages are never sent during otherwise idle tunnel moments.

— It is possible that a router might not discover a dead peer until the IKE or IPsec SA rekey is attempted.

The two Cisco IOS commands that enable DPD are

```
crypto isakmp keepalive seconds [retries] [periodic ¦ on-demand]
set peer ip-address [default]
```

OSPF and EIGRP have very fast convergence around failed links. The use of a backup GRE over IPsec VPN tunnel does provide redundancy, but at the cost of additional IGP overhead in the VPN tunnel.

HSRP uses virtual MAC and IP addresses as default gateway addresses for end hosts.

An HSRP group consists of two or more routers. Each HSRP group is intended for one IP subnet.

One router can participate in more than one HSRP group.

In an HSRP group, there is only one active router and one standby router. Only the HSRP active router forwards traffic.

Typical host-based HSRP interface commands include

■ **standby** *group* **ip** *virtual-IP-address*—Defines the HSRP group ID and virtual IP address, which is the same for all group members.

■ **standby** *group* **priority** *priority-#*—Defines the HSRP priority for this router (the default is 100).

■ **standby** *group* **preempt**—Causes this router to regain active status if it has the highest priority.

Stateless IPsec VPN HSRP interface commands include

- **standby** *group* **name** *group-name*—Defines a name for the HSRP group that can be added to the crypto map.

- **crypto map** *map-name* **redundancy** *group-name*—Defines the HSRP group that provides redundancy for this crypto map.

IPsec stateful failover uses two protocols for proper and continual operation: HSRP and SSO.

Stateful IPsec VPN interface commands include

- **standby** *group* **ip** *virtual-IP-address*—Defines the HSRP group ID and virtual IP address, which is the same for all group members.

- **standby** *group* **priority** *priority-#*—Defines the HSRP priority for this router (the default is 100).

- **standby** *group* **preempt**—Causes this router to regain active status if it has the highest priority.

- **standby** *group* **name** *group-name*—Defines a name for the HSRP group that can be added to the crypto map.

- **crypto map** *map-name* **redundancy** *group-name* **stateful**—Defines the HSRP group that provides stateful redundancy for this crypto map.

SSO global commands include

- **redundancy inter-device**—Enables SSO.

- **scheme standby** *group-name*—Maps an HSRP group to the stateful failover.

- **ipc zone default**—Defines the inter-device communications protocol parameters for coordination between the active and standby routers. Local and remote ports and local and remote IP addresses must be defined on both routers.

There are two ways that an IPsec VPN link can be used to back up a typical WAN link: IGP via GRE over IPsec and floating static routes.

Q&A

The questions and scenarios in this book are designed to be challenging and to make sure that you know the answer. Rather than allowing you to derive the answers from clues hidden inside the questions themselves, the questions challenge your understanding and recall of the subject.

Hopefully, mastering these questions will help you limit the number of exam questions on which you narrow your choices to two options, and then guess.

You can find the answers to these questions in Appendix A. For more practice with exam-like question formats, use the exam engine on the CD-ROM.

1. What are the potential failure points in a network?

2. What are some of the ways to overcome an access link failure?

3. What are the three forms of stateless IPsec failover?

4. Which DPD mode is the default in a Cisco IOS device?

5. What is a negative consequence of periodic DPD mode?

6. What IOS command enables DPD?

7. Which routing protocols should be used within the GRE over IPsec tunnels to permit fast convergence around failed links?

8. How do the HSRP active and standby routers work together?

9. If an IPsec VPN terminates on an HSRP virtual IP address, and the active router fails, what happens to the VPN?

10. What two protocols are used to provide IPsec stateful failover?

11. If dynamic routing is used to permit an IPsec VPN to back up a normal WAN connection, what must be done?

12. What is a floating static route?

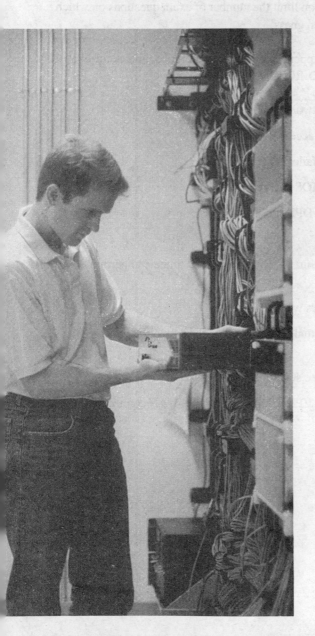

Exam Topic List

This chapter covers the following topics that you need to master for the CCNP ISCW exam:

- **Cisco Easy VPN Components**—Describes the constituent elements of the Easy VPN solution

- **Easy VPN Connection Establishment**—Describes the process of connecting to another site with Easy VPN

- **Easy VPN Server Configuration**—Describes the Easy VPN Server configuration process

- **Monitoring the Easy VPN Server**—Describes possible options available for connection monitoring with Easy VPN Server

- **Troubleshooting the Easy VPN Server**—Describes the basic process and options available in troubleshooting Easy VPN Server

CHAPTER 16

Configuring Cisco Easy VPN

Traditionally, Virtual Private Network (VPN) connectivity has been viewed as rather complex and requiring specialized resources to implement. While this is true from a hardware perspective, the same is not necessarily true from a software perspective. In fact, the advent of the Cisco Integrated Services Router has made VPN connectivity, well, easy.

"Do I Know This Already?" Quiz

The purpose of the "Do I Know This Already?" quiz is to help you decide whether you really need to read the entire chapter. If you already intend to read the entire chapter, you do not necessarily need to answer these questions now.

The 12-question quiz, derived from the major sections in the "Foundation Topics" portion of the chapter, helps you to determine how to spend your limited study time.

Table 16-1 outlines the major topics discussed in this chapter and the "Do I Know This Already?" quiz questions that correspond to those topics.

Table 16-1   *"Do I Know This Already?" Foundation Topics Section-to-Question Mapping*

Foundation Topics Section	Questions Covered in This Section	Score
Cisco Easy VPN Components	1–3	
Easy VPN Connection Establishment	4–6	
Easy VPN Server Configuration	7–9	
Monitoring the Easy VPN Server	10	
Troubleshooting the Easy VPN Server	11–12	
Total Score		

CAUTION   The goal of self-assessment is to gauge your mastery of the topics in this chapter. If you do not know the answer to a question or are only partially sure of the answer, you should mark this question wrong for purposes of self-assessment. Giving yourself credit for an answer that you correctly guess skews your self-assessment results and might provide you with a false sense of security.

1. Easy VPN Remote supports three modes of operation. These include Client mode, Network Extension mode, and which of the following?

   a. Network Extension Plus mode

   b. Peer-to-peer mode

   c. Overlay mode

   d. DMVPN mode

2. To implement Easy VPN Remote capabilities, which requirement must be met?

   a. The destination peer must be a Cisco Easy VPN Server or VPN Concentrator supporting Cisco Easy VPN Server.

   b. The source peer must be a Cisco Easy VPN Server or VPN Concentrator supporting Cisco Easy VPN Server.

   c. The destination peer must be a Cisco Easy VPN Remote device.

   d. The destination peer must support all available encryption and authentication types.

3. Easy VPN Servers must support Diffie-Hellman IKE negotiation using which group?

   a. Group 1

   b. Group 2

   c. Group 3

   d. Group 4

4. When establishing a VPN connection using an Easy VPN Remote Client, which of the following occurs immediately after the IKE phase 1 initialization?

   a. SA proposal acceptance

   b. ISAKMP SA establishment

   c. user authentication

   d. RRI

5. If not using a preshared key for authentication, which mode will IKE phase 1 initiate?

   a. Aggressive mode

   b. Main mode

   c. Authorization mode

   d. Configuration mode

6. The process of creating and redistributing a static route pointing to the client subnet is known as which of the following?

    a. Reverse Path Forward

    b. Reverse Route Injection

    c. Floating Static Route

    d. Route Dampening

7. To configure the Easy VPN Server using the SDM wizard, which of the following must be configured?

    a. TACACS

    b. A user account with privilege level 15

    c. DNS

    d. NTP

8. Group Lock and Saved Password capabilities are generally associated with the configuration of which of the following?

    a. RRI

    b. IKE

    c. Xauth

    d. ISAKMP SA

9. When configuring split tunneling capabilities, which of the following should also be configured?

    a. RRI

    b. Protected subnets

    c. Personal firewall

    d. Backup servers

10. Which command will allow an administrator to view the current status of a VPN Client ISAKMP SA?

    a. show crypto isakmp sa

    b. show ip isakmp sa

    c. show crypto ipsec sa

    d. show ip ipsec sa

11. Which command will allow a network administrator to view real-time information regarding ISAKMP connections on an Easy VPN Server?

    a. **debug crypto isakmp**

    b. **debug ip isakmp**

    c. **debug crypto ipsec**

    d. **debug ip ipsec**

12. In cases where AAA services are in use, which command will allow a network administrator to monitor activity related to username and password exchanges in real time?

    a. **debug crypto isakmp**

    b. **debug crypto ipsec**

    c. **debug aaa authentication**

    d. **debug aaa authorization**

The answers to the "Do I Know This Already?" quiz are found in Appendix A, "Answers to the 'Do I Know This Already?' Quizzes and Q&A Sections." The suggested choices for your next step are as follows:

■ **8 or fewer overall score**—Read the entire chapter. This includes the "Foundation Topics," "Foundation Summary," and "Q&A" sections.

■ **9 or 10 overall score**—Begin with the "Foundation Summary" section, and then go to the "Q&A" section.

■ **11 or more overall score**—If you want more review on these topics, skip to the "Foundation Summary" section, and then go to the "Q&A" section. Otherwise, move to the next chapter.

Foundation Topics

The growing move toward the Service-Oriented Network Architecture (SONA) is laying down a path of evolution that will enable clients of all types to access network resources, applications, and services available to those in the corporate headquarters site. This allows enterprise networks to move further toward the goal of providing a single experience to all users regardless of the method by which they access those applications and services.

The Cisco Easy VPN solution simplifies the deployment of remote offices and teleworkers. Teleworkers, on the whole, represent one of the fastest growth areas of network users. The availability of high bandwidth at low cost is spurring a great deal of industry evolution. Along with this growth in remote connection requests comes a similar, if not greater, growth in security needs of the network.

Cisco Easy VPN serves to simplify client configuration and allow for a centralized management model of VPN Clients. This client configuration can be dynamically pushed to remote clients. Cisco Easy VPN provides a quick, efficient, and, most importantly, secure means of configuring VPN services for remote users of all kinds. It consists of two primary components, Easy VPN Remote and Easy VPN Server.

Using Internet Key Exchange (IKE) Mode Config functionality to push configuration parameters to clients, the clients can be preconfigured to conform to a set of IKE policies and IPsec transform sets. This ensures that all clients are up to date with the latest policies in place prior to establishing connections.

Cisco Easy VPN Components

The Cisco Easy VPN solution consists of two components, Server and Remote. Cisco Easy VPN Server allows Cisco IOS Routers, Cisco PIX Security Appliances, and Cisco VPN 3000 Concentrators to act as VPN headend devices in site-to-site or remote-access VPN models. Easy VPN–enabled devices can terminate IPsec tunnels initiated by teleworkers using the Cisco VPN Client software on a PC. This makes it possible for mobile and remote workers to access corporate services and applications.

Easy VPN Remote

Cisco Easy VPN Remote enables Cisco IOS routers, Cisco PIX Firewalls, and Cisco VPN 3000 series hardware/software clients to act as remote VPN Clients. They receive security policies from an Easy VPN Server. This minimizes the need for manual configuration tasks. Easy VPN Remote provides for automated, centralized management of the following:

■ Tunnel parameter negotiation (addresses, algorithms, and duration)

■ Tunnel establishment according to set parameters

■ Automatic creation of Network Address Translation (NAT) and Port Address Translation (PAT) as well as any needed access control lists (ACL)

■ User authentication

■ Security key management for encryption and decryption

■ Tunneled data authentication, encryption, and decryption

Easy VPN Remote supports three modes of operation:

■ **Client**—Specifies that NAT or PAT be used so that end stations at the remote end of the VPN tunnel do not use IP addresses in the space of the destination server. The needed security associations (SA) are created automatically for IP addresses assigned to remote hosts.

■ **Network Extension**—Specifies that remote-end hosts use IP addresses that are fully routable and reachable by the destination network over the tunnel connection so that they form a single logical network. In such cases, PAT is not used, to allow remote-end PCs direct access to destination network services and applications.

■ **Network Extension Plus**—Identical to Network Extension mode with the additional capability of being able to request an IP address via mode configuration and automatically assign it to an available loopback interface. The IPsec SAs for this IP address are automatically created.

Client mode is relatively simple and is used on a regular basis in countless deployments. Figure 16-1 shows an example of the Easy VPN Client concept.

Figure 16-1 *Easy VPN Remote Client Mode*

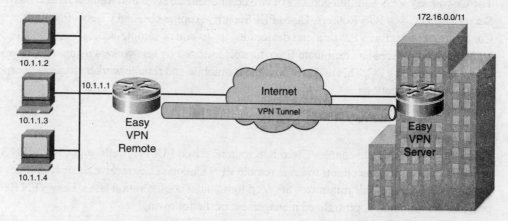

In the figure, the hosts at the teleworker's home are all addressed with RFC 1918 addresses, as are the destination resources at the corporate office site. RFC 1918 addresses are nonroutable addresses within the public Internet; however, NAT/PAT allow them to be translated and routed across. With the VPN connection running in Client mode, routing information can pass between the customer premises equipment (CPE) and the corporate office site.

Network Extension mode is very similar in concept to Client mode. So long as the addresses in the teleworker subnet are fully routable and unique within the corporate infrastructure, Figure 16-1 can also be said to be an example of Network Extension mode. If not, there will need to be a NAT/PAT operation performed at the VPN Server to pass traffic into the corporate network and back to the teleworker premises.

Easy VPN Server Requirements

To implement Easy VPN Remote capabilities, a number of prerequisite guidelines must be met. The Cisco Easy VPN Remote feature requires that the destination peer be a Cisco Easy VPN Server or VPN Concentrator that supports the Cisco Easy VPN Server feature. Essentially, the hardware and software feature sets must be those capable of performing the roles and functions of the Easy VPN solution. To that end, a minimum Cisco IOS version is required as follows:

- **Cisco 831, 836, 837, 851, 857, 871, 876, 877, and 878 Series Routers**—Cisco IOS Software Release 12.2(8)T or later (note that 800 series routers are not supported in Cisco IOS 12.3(7)XR but are supported in 12.3(7)XR2

- **Cisco 1700 Series Routers**—Cisco IOS Software Release 12.2(8)T or later

- **Cisco 2600 Series Routers**—Cisco IOS Software Release 12.2(8)T or later

- **Cisco 3600 Series Routers**—Cisco IOS Software Release 12.2(8)T or later

- **Cisco 7100 Series VPN Routers**—Cisco IOS Software Release 12.2(8)T or later

- **Cisco 7200 Series Routers**—Cisco IOS Software Release 12.2(8)T or later

- **Cisco 7500 Series Routers**—Cisco IOS Software Release 12.2(8)T or later

- **Cisco PIX 500 Series**—PIX OS Release 6.2 or later

- **Cisco VPN 3000 Series**—Software Release 3.11 or later

Additionally, requirements for Easy VPN Servers include the need for Internet Security Association and Key Management Protocol (ISAKMP) policies using Diffie-Hellman group 2 (1024-bit) IKE negotiation. This is necessary because the Cisco Unity protocol supports only ISAKMP policies using group 2 IKE. The Cisco Unity protocol refers to a methodology VPN clients use to determine the order of events when attempting a connection to a VPN server. The

Cisco Unity protocol operates based on the notion of a client group. A Unity client must identify and authenticate itself by group first and, if XAUTH enabled, by user later. The Easy VPN Server cannot be configured for ISAKMP group 1 or 5 when used with Easy VPN Clients.

To ensure secure tunnel connections, the Cisco Easy VPN Remote feature does not support transform sets providing encryption without authentication or those providing authentication without encryption. Both encryption and authentication must be represented.

The Cisco Unity protocol does not support Authentication Header (AH) authentication but it does support Encapsulation Security Payload (ESP).

Sometimes, a VPN connection might be used as a backup connection meant to be established and used when the primary link is unavailable. Various backup capabilities are available to meet such a need, including, but not limited to, dial backup. When using dial backup scenarios with Easy VPN, it should be understood that any backup method based on line status is not supported. This means that a primary interface in up/down state will not trigger the VPN connection establishment.

Also worthy of mention at this point is the fact that NAT interoperability is not supported in Client mode when split tunneling is enabled. This is because the client will be connected to both the central site and to the local LAN, with routing enabled to both networks per the split tunneling definition. Without split tunneling, the IP address assigned by the central site will become the address of the client interface. This avoids any possibility of address overlapping. When split tunneling is enabled, this cannot always be the case. When the connection is established and a route is injected into the central site network for remote site reachability, the route must be unique. Split tunneling allows the possibility for address overlap.

Easy VPN Connection Establishment

Easy VPN connectivity is relatively straightforward. The configuration and connection phases are subject to certain restrictions as listed in the previous section. The Cisco Easy VPN Remote feature supports a two-stage process for client/server authentication:

- Stage 1 is Group Level Authentication, which represents a portion of the channel creation process. During this stage, two types of authentication can be used, either preshared keys or digital certificates.

- Stage 2 of the authentication is known as Extended Authentication, or Xauth. The remote side of the connection submits a username and password to the central site VPN device. This is the same method that is used when a Cisco VPN Software Client is prompted for a username and password to activate a VPN tunnel. However, in this case, a user is not authenticated to the central site. Instead, the Easy VPN Remote Router, itself, is authenticated. Xauth, while optional, is typically used in order to improve security. Once the Xauth is successfully completed and the VPN tunnel is created, all PCs behind the Easy VPN Remote Router can use the connection.

The following list represents a step-by-step method used to establish Easy VPN Remote Client connectivity with an Easy VPN Server gateway:

Step 1   The VPN Client initiates IKE phase 1.

Step 2   The VPN Client establishes an ISAKMP SA.

Step 3   The Easy VPN Server accepts the SA proposal.

Step 4   The Easy VPN Server initiates user authentication.

Step 5   Mode configuration begins.

Step 6   The Reverse Route Injection (RRI) process begins.

Step 7   IPsec quick mode completes the connection.

At each step, decisions are made and/or information is exchanged. The following sections describe further details about each step in the process.

IKE Phase 1

During the initial step of the connection attempt, the IKE phase 1 process is initiated. There are two separate manners in which authentication can be performed when initiating IKE phase 1:

■ **Use of a preshared key for authentication**—The VPN Client initiates aggressive mode. Each peer is aware of the key of the other peer. Preshared keys are visible in the running-config of the router or VPN device on which they reside. With this in mind, an optional encrypted preshared key option is available. An accompanying group must be entered in the configuration of the VPN Client. This group name is used to identify the group profile associated with the VPN Client.

■ **Use of a digital certificate for authentication**—The VPN Client initiates main mode. Digital certificates use Rivest, Shamir, and Adelman (RSA) signatures on Easy VPN Remote devices. This support is provided by an RSA certificate stored in a central repository or on the remote device itself. With digital certificates, an organizational unit of a distinguished name is used to identify the group profile to be used. Cisco recommends a timeout of 40 seconds when using digital certificates with Easy VPN.

When using aggressive mode for connections, the identity of the Cisco IOS VPN device should be changed using the **crypto isakmp identity hostname** command. Changing the name will have no effect on the certificate authentication via IKE main mode. The **crypto isakmp identity** command allows the use of an address or a hostname. To set an address, use the following:

```
BM2821(config)#crypto isakmp identity address
BM2821(config)#crypto isakmp key sharedkeystring address 192.168.1.33
```

This effectively sets the ISAKMP identity to the specified IP address. To change it to use a hostname instead, use the following:

```
BM2821(config)#crypto isakmp identity hostname
BM2821(config)#crypto isakmp key sharedkeystring hostname RemoteRouter.example.com
BM2821(config)#ip host RemoteRouter.example.com 192.168.1.33
```

The two configurations essentially have identical results.

Establishing an ISAKMP SA

When a VPN Client attempts to establish an SA between peers, it sends multiple ISAKMP proposals to the Easy VPN Server. As mentioned previously, Easy VPN supports only group 2 ISAKMP policy.

The VPN Client attempts to establish an SA between the peer IP addresses through the transmission of multiple ISAKMP proposals to the Easy VPN Server.

To reduce the amount of manual configuration of devices necessary to implement and support the Easy VPN solution, ISAKMP proposals include multiple combinations of encryption and hash algorithms, authentication methods, and Diffie-Hellman group sizes.

SA Proposal Acceptance

Several proposals can compose an ISAKMP policy. When multiple proposals exist, the Easy VPN Server will make a choice by first match. For this reason, the most secure policies should be first in the list to ensure the most secure connectivity.

As mentioned, the VPN Client sends multiple proposals to the Easy VPN Server. Once a proposal is accepted (that is, the ISAKMP SA is established), the device is considered to be authenticated and user authentication begins.

Easy VPN User Authentication

Now that the SA is accepted and the device is authenticated, a challenge is issued according to the configured methodology. If the Easy VPN Server is configured (as is typical) for Xauth, the VPN Client will wait for a username/password challenge.

Obviously, some input from the user is required at this point. The username and password are entered upon receipt of the prompt. This information is checked against some authentication entity, be it local authentication or some combination of TACACS, RADIUS, and/or hard/soft token service.

Authentication, authorization, and accounting (AAA) policies define which users can perform which functions on a managed device and keeps track of the changes made. Chapter 20, "Using AAA to Scale Access Control," covers AAA in more depth.

All Easy VPN Servers should be configured to manage VPN Clients and enforce user authentication

Mode Configuration

Once the Easy VPN Server indicates a successful authentication, the VPN Client requests any remaining configuration parameters that may have been configured in the VPN Server. Mode configuration begins and parameters such as IP address, DNS, split tunneling information, and other available configuration options are downloaded to the client. The only mandatory component to be downloaded to the client is the IP addressing information. Other mentioned parameters are optional.

Reverse Route Injection

Reverse Route Injection (RRI) is the process of injecting a static route into the Interior Gateway Protocol (IGP) routing table. This static route points to the client's destination network. This is useful when per-client static IP addressing is used with VPN Clients rather than per-VPN address pools.

RRI should be enabled on the dynamic crypto map when per-user IP addresses are used in environments where multiple VPN Servers are used. The redistribution of the RRI ensures reachability to the client host(s).

IPsec Quick Mode

When all authentication is complete, the parameters provided from the VPN Server to the VPN Client, and the RRI is injected, IPsec quick mode is initiated to negotiate an IPsec SA establishment. This is the final step in the VPN connection establishment. Once the IPsec SA is created, the connection is complete and active.

Easy VPN Server Configuration

To configure the Easy VPN Server, some amount of information gathering is necessary. The information necessary includes the user's account information, any required enable secret passwords, AAA configuration (if not already done), and the configuration of the Easy VPN Server itself. The configuration can be done through the traditional command-line interface (CLI) or through the Security Device Manager (SDM) interface of the router itself.

SDM provides a graphical, web-based interface for configuring and monitoring an individual router. SDM also includes a number of wizards expressly for purposes of configuring common components of routing, firewall, intrusion detection/prevention, and VPN connectivity. One of the wizards associated with VPN connectivity is the Easy VPN Server Wizard. Figure 16-2 shows the home page of SDM running on a Cisco Integrated Services Router (ISR).

Figure 16-2   *Cisco SDM*

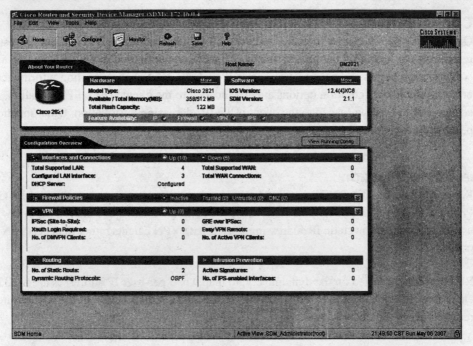

The SDM interface is quite straightforward and intuitive. The buttons across the top provide various options for configuration, monitoring, and saving configuration changes. By clicking the **Configure** button, the interface changes to the Configure page with the Tasks bar displayed down the left side of the screen. This is the primary configuration interface for the router. Figure 16-3 shows the Configure Tasks page.

By default, the SDM Configure page begins on the Interfaces and Connections page. This is where interface connectivity options and specific parameters are configured for each of the router's interfaces.

The third icon under the Tasks bar is VPN. Clicking this icon opens the page where the Easy VPN Server configuration is performed, as shown in Figure 16-4.

Figure 16-3 *SDM Configure Page*

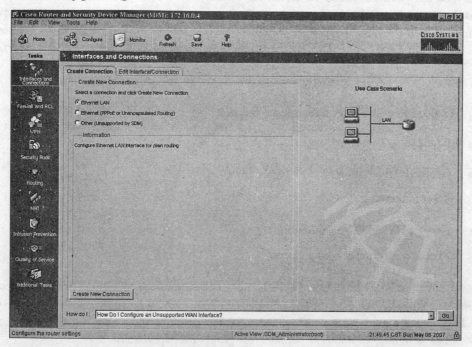

Figure 16-4 *SDM VPN Page*

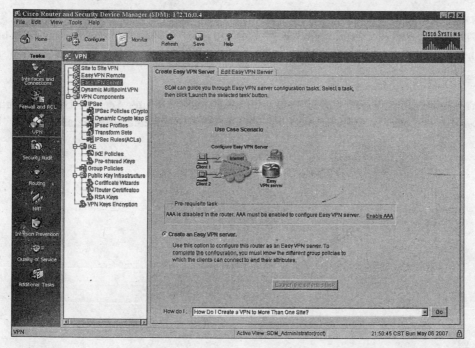

Several options are available on the left side of the page. Out-of-the-box, an ISR can support Site-to-Site VPN, Easy VPN Remote, Easy VPN Server, and Dynamic Multipoint VPN (DMVPN) functionality. Obviously, the desired connection type for this discussion is Easy VPN Server. Clicking the Easy VPN Server selection opens the first page of the Easy VPN Server Wizard.

The Easy VPN Server Wizard includes a number of tasks in the configuration:

- Selection of the IPsec termination interface

- IKE policy configuration

- Group policy lookup methodology configuration

- User authentication

- Local group policy configuration

- IPsec transform set configuration

Any and all services to be used by Easy VPN Clients should be configured prior to the Easy VPN Server configuration. This includes all services to be used by AAA (RADIUS/TACACS+), IP addressing and routing for client subnets, certification authorities (CA) as needed, and additional services such as DNS and NTP settings (for proper PKI operation).

User Configuration

The configuration of users via the SDM interface is performed via the Additional Tasks button at the bottom of the Tasks bar on the Configure page. Figure 16-5 shows the User Accounts/View screen.

The figure shows the result of clicking **Additional Tasks > Router Access > User Accounts/View > Add**. The options available allow the administrator to add, edit, or delete users.

Figure 16-5 *SDM User Configuration*

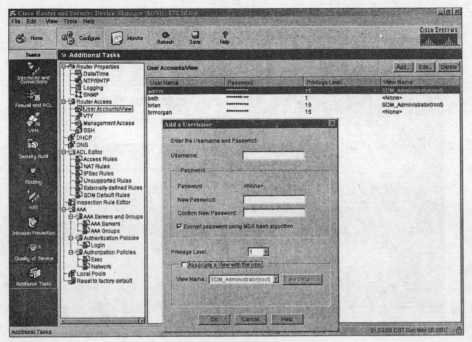

Easy VPN Server Wizard

Returning the discussion to the actual Easy VPN Server configuration, the Easy VPN Server Wizard is now ready to be run. AAA and necessary user information and privilege levels have been set. Click the **Launch the Selected Task** button on the Easy VPN Server screen to launch the wizard. The initial screen is a summary of tasks to be performed similar to that shown on the first page of the Easy VPN Server Wizard. If AAA has not already been configured, the wizard prompts you for the required AAA configuration information at this point. AAA must be enabled for Easy VPN Server to function properly. Additionally, at least one user must have privilege level 15 before enabling AAA on the device.

Click **Next** to open the Select an Interface screen, where you select the interface to be used with Easy VPN. This will be the interface through which all Easy VPN Clients connect. From the perspective of a NAT process, this is the outside interface. Figure 16-6 shows the Select an Interface screen of SDM.

Figure 16-6 *SDM Interface Selection*

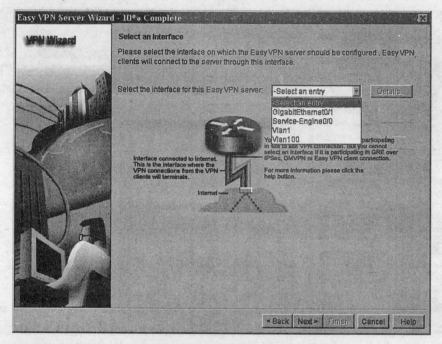

After you select the interface, click **Next** to move the wizard to the next step, where you can configure the needed IKE proposals.

You can use the default IKE proposals already configured by the wizard, or you can manually configure additional IKE proposals. Required parameters are as follows:

- IKE proposal priority

- Diffie-Hellman group (1, 2, or 5)

- Encryption algorithm (DES, 3DES, AES, or SEAL)

- HMAC (SHA-1 or MD5)

- IKE lifetime

Figure 16-7 shows the IKE Proposals page where a new proposal is being added to the list of available proposals.

Figure 16-7   *Easy VPN Server IKE Proposals*

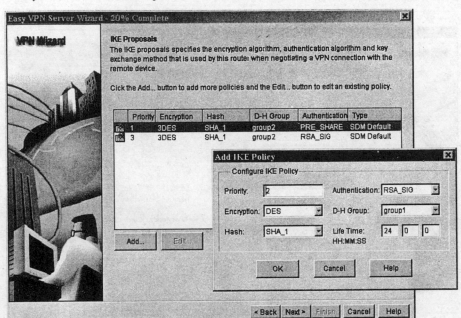

After you select all the appropriate options, click **Next** to move the wizard to the page where you can configure the transform sets.

As with IKE proposals, there is a default SDM transform set. The parameters for the transform set are as follows:

■   Transform set name

■   Encryption algorithm

■   HMAC

■   Compression (optional)

■   Mode of operation (tunnel or transport)

Figure 16-8 shows the Transform Set page where a new transform set is being added to the list of available transform sets.

Figure 16-8 *Easy VPN Server Transform Sets*

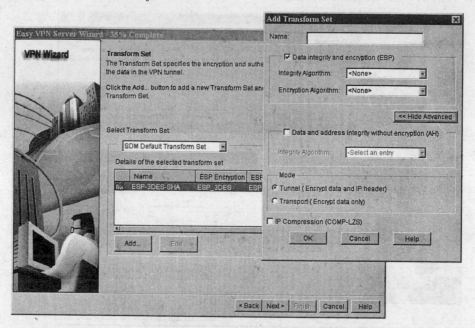

With transform sets completed, the next step is group authorization/policy configuration. This is used for groups of VPN Clients who use the same authentication and configuration information. You can configure the policies on the local Easy VPN Server, an external Radius/TACACS+ server, or both. The AAA method lists will be used in defining the order in which policies are searched.

If you select local authentication, you must configure the user accounts in the Router Access portion of SDM. If you select RADIUS or TACACS+, you must configure the appropriate servers using the appropriate drop-down boxes. Once you select the option in the Method Selection box, the adjacent button becomes active and you can configure servers.

The second portion of the configuration is the method for user authentication (Xauth). Xauth is an enhancement of the existing IKE protocol. Xauth allows all Cisco IOS AAA authentication methods to perform user authentication in a separate phase after the IKE phase 1 exchange. With Xauth, IKE can provide user authentication using the device. This is possible only after the device has been successfully authenticated during normal IKE authentication. Any AAA method can be configured to accomplish this.

Figure 16-9 shows the User Authentication configuration page of the Easy VPN Server Wizard.

Figure 16-9 *Easy VPN Server User Authentication Page*

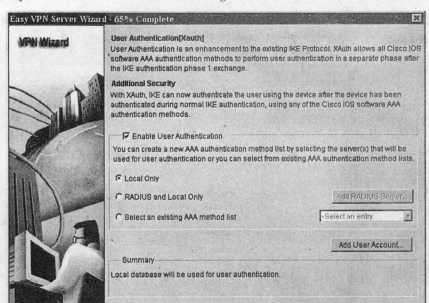

Note that this screen provides options to add new users should the need exist. Clicking the Add User Account button opens the same dialog box shown in Figure 16-5.

Click **Next** to move the wizard to the Group Authorization/User Group Policies page. This page allows you to configure groups of remote users who will be using Cisco VPN Clients and/or Easy VPN Remote Clients. Attributes configured on this page are downloaded through the client or device according to its group membership. Group names should be configured identically on both Remote Client and Device to ensure that the appropriate group attributes are downloaded to each.

Figure 16-10 shows the Group Authorization/User Group Policies page with the Add Group Policy dialog box open (accessed by clicking the **Add** button), which is used to insert a new group policy.

Figure 16-10 *Easy VPN Server Group Authorization/User Group Policies Page*

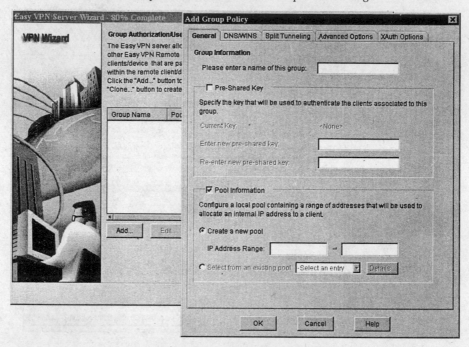

Note that the Add Group Policy dialog box has a collection of tabs across the top. These tabs can be used to configure options for all users within the group membership, including

- Group Name

- Pre-Shared Key

- Pool Information (IP addressing)

- DNS/WINS (DNA and WINS server information

- Split Tunneling (if enabled, configure accessible protected subnets as necessary and/or configure split tunneling ACLs)

- Backup Servers (additional VPN access concentrators)

- Personal Firewall Information

- Local LAN Access while connected (non-split tunneling)

- Maximum Number of Group Connections

■ Xauth Options such as Group Lock (adding group name to the Xauth username) and Saved
Password capability

■ Maximum Number of Logins Per User

After you enter the policy information and save it to the Group configuration, click the **Next** button
to access the wizard's configuration summary page. This page details all of the information
entered regarding the Easy VPN Server configuration prior to its upload to the router.

Also included on the summary page is an option to test the VPN connection after the configuration
is uploaded to the router. If this box is checked, the configuration will be uploaded and then a
simulated connection attempt will be made to the VPN Server to establish connectivity.

The commands relevant to the configuration entered via the wizard will be uploaded to the router
and a summary page will be displayed showing success or failure of the configuration commands
entry. With that done, the test can be initiated. Figure 16-11 shows the results of the VPN test for
the Easy VPN Server configured throughout this chapter.

Figure 16-11 *Easy VPN Server Connection Test*

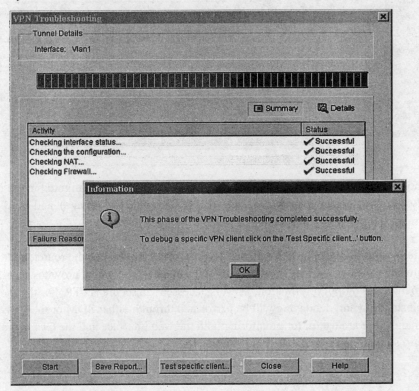

Monitoring the Easy VPN Server

At the top of the main SDM page is a row of buttons listed as Home, Configure, Monitor, Refresh, Save, and Help. The Home and Configure settings have been discussed in some detail in this chapter. This section discusses the monitoring of an Easy VPN Server. Figure 16-12 shows the Easy VPN Monitor page.

Figure 16-12 *Easy VPN Server Monitoring*

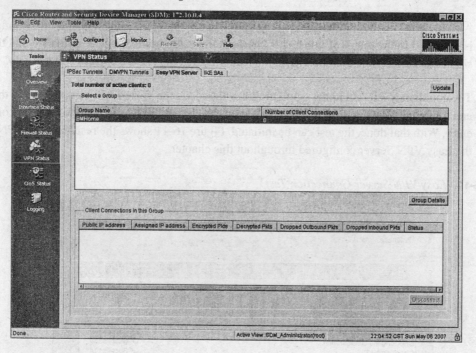

As shown in the figure, each individual Easy VPN Server group configured in the router will be monitored. Concurrent connections, addresses (both public and private), and encryption information are listed in the two panes of the Monitor window.

Although security best practice calls for disabling HTTP access to the router, additional monitoring can be performed via the traditional web interface, which provides access to Cisco IOS commands and output information. SDM is accessed via secure HTTP. For the most part, troubleshooting and debugging will be performed through either SDM or the CLI. Among the commands that are useful for monitoring both the web interface and the CLI is the **show crypto isakmp sa** command, as detailed in Example 16-1.

Example 16-1   show crypto isakmp sa *Command Output*

```
BM2821#show crypto isakmp sa
IPv4 Crypto ISAKMP SA
dst             src             state         conn-id slot status
172.16.0.4      172.16.1.40     QM_IDLE          1004     0 ACTIVE


IPv6 Crypto ISAKMP SA
```

The example shows the ISAKMP SA that has been proposed and accepted for the duration of the connection. The information shown includes the destination and source IP addresses, the state of the connection, a connection ID, the slot, and the status.

Also of particular use in monitoring and/or troubleshooting VPN connections is the **show crypt ipsec sa** command, as shown in Example 16-2.

Example 16-2   show crypto ipsec sa *Command Output*

```
BM2821#show crypto ipsec sa

interface: Vlan1
    Crypto map tag: SDM_CMAP_1, local addr 172.16.0.4

   protected vrf: (none)
   local  ident (addr/mask/prot/port): (0.0.0.0/0.0.0.0/0/0)
   remote ident (addr/mask/prot/port): (172.16.1.190/255.255.255.255/0/0)
   current_peer 172.16.1.40 port 500
     PERMIT, flags={}
    #pkts encaps: 22, #pkts encrypt: 22, #pkts digest: 22
    #pkts decaps: 32, #pkts decrypt: 32, #pkts verify: 32
    #pkts compressed: 0, #pkts decompressed: 0
    #pkts not compressed: 0, #pkts compr. failed: 0
    #pkts not decompressed: 0, #pkts decompress failed: 0
    #send errors 0, #recv errors 1

     local crypto endpt.: 172.16.0.4, remote crypto endpt.: 172.16.1.40
     path mtu 1500, ip mtu 1500
     current outbound spi: 0xD35124D3(3545310419)

     inbound esp sas:
      spi: 0x7783DD3C(2005130556)
        transform: esp-3des esp-sha-hmac ,
        in use settings ={Tunnel, }
        conn id: 2001, flow_id: NETGX:1, crypto map: SDM_CMAP_1
        sa timing: remaining key lifetime (k/sec): (4570709/3346)
        IV size: 8 bytes
        replay detection support: Y
        Status: ACTIVE
```

continues

Example 16-2 **show crypto ipsec sa** *Command Output (Continued)*

```
    inbound ah sas:

    inbound pcp sas:

    outbound esp sas:
     spi: 0xD35124D3(3545310419)
        transform: esp-3des esp-sha-hmac ,
        in use settings ={Tunnel, }
        conn id: 2002, flow_id: NETGX:2, crypto map: SDM_CMAP_1
        sa timing: remaining key lifetime (k/sec): (4570711/3346)
        IV size: 8 bytes
        replay detection support: Y
        Status: ACTIVE

    outbound ah sas:

    outbound pcp sas:
```

The command output shows information pertinent to the existing connection(s). The highlighted lines draw emphasis to the assigned IP address for the connection (inside) as well as the actual source and destination IP addresses (local VPN gateway and destination client). Also of note are the inbound and outbound transform sets configured by the VPN connection.

Troubleshooting the Easy VPN Server

Troubleshooting, like monitoring, can be performed from the SDM interface or the CLI; however, it is usually more useful to gather CLI debugging information from various available commands when working with Cisco's Technical Assistance Center (TAC). To that end, this section presents a few VPN troubleshooting commands for use in remedying VPN Server issues.

Example 16-3 shows the output from the **debug crypto isakmp** command. This command shows the IKE communication negotiation and associated details for a new VPN connection. While there is a great deal of output, the more important portions have been highlighted. Here is some background on the connection for the sake of clarity:

- VPN server address: 172.16.0.4

- Client actual address: 172.16.1.40

- Client VPN assigned address: 172.16.1.191

In the output in Example 16-3, all the major steps of the connection negotiation can be viewed as they occur. This is the output from an initial VPN connection request and negotiation.

Example 16-3   **debug crypto isakmp** *Command Output*

```
BM2821#debug crypto isakmp
BM2821#
000365: Mar 26 21:00:24.056: ISAKMP (0:0): received packet from 172.16.1.40 dport 500 sport
  500 Global (N) NEW SA
000366: Mar 26 21:00:24.056: ISAKMP: Created a peer struct for 172.16.1.40, peer port 500
000367: Mar 26 21:00:24.056: ISAKMP: New peer created peer = 0x47910754 peer_handle =
  0x80000006
000368: Mar 26 21:00:24.056: ISAKMP: Locking peer struct 0x47910754, refcount 1 for
  crypto_isakmp_process_block
000369: Mar 26 21:00:24.056: ISAKMP:(0):Setting client config settings 487F46E4
000370: Mar 26 21:00:24.056: ISAKMP:(0):(Re)Setting client xauth list  and state
000371: Mar 26 21:00:24.056: ISAKMP/xauth: initializing AAA request
! -- Beginning authentication process
000372: Mar 26 21:00:24.056: ISAKMP: local port 500, remote port 500
000373: Mar 26 21:00:24.056: ISAKMP: Find a dup sa in the avl tree during calling
  isadb_insert sa = 47E78440
000374: Mar 26 21:00:24.056: ISAKMP:(0): processing SA payload. message ID = 0
000375: Mar 26 21:00:24.056: ISAKMP:(0): processing ID payload. message ID = 0
000376: Mar 26 21:00:24.056: ISAKMP (0:0): ID payload
        next-payload : 13
        type         : 11
        group id     : BMHome
! - Configured Group ID
        protocol     : 17
        port         : 500
        length       : 14
000377: Mar 26 21:00:24.056: ISAKMP:(0):: peer matches *none* of the profiles
000378: Mar 26 21:00:24.056: ISAKMP:(0): processing vendor id payload
000379: Mar 26 21:00:24.056: ISAKMP:(0): vendor ID seems Unity/DPD but major 215 mismatch
000380: Mar 26 21:00:24.056: ISAKMP:(0): vendor ID is XAUTH
000381: Mar 26 21:00:24.056: ISAKMP:(0): processing vendor id payload
000382: Mar 26 21:00:24.056: ISAKMP:(0): vendor ID is DPD
000383: Mar 26 21:00:24.056: ISAKMP:(0): processing vendor id payload
000384: Mar 26 21:00:24.056: ISAKMP:(0): vendor ID seems Unity/DPD but major 123 mismatch
000385: Mar 26 21:00:24.056: ISAKMP:(0): vendor ID is NAT-T v2
000386: Mar 26 21:00:24.056: ISAKMP:(0): processing vendor id payload
000387: Mar 26 21:00:24.060: ISAKMP:(0): vendor ID seems Unity/DPD but major 194 mismatch
000388: Mar 26 21:00:24.060: ISAKMP:(0): processing vendor id payload
000389: Mar 26 21:00:24.060: ISAKMP:(0): vendor ID is Unity
000390: Mar 26 21:00:24.060: ISAKMP:(0): Authentication by xauth preshared
000391: Mar 26 21:00:24.060: ISAKMP:(0):Checking ISAKMP transform 1 against priority 1
  policy
! - Check ISAKMP against first transform set
000392: Mar 26 21:00:24.060: ISAKMP:      encryption AES-CBC
000393: Mar 26 21:00:24.060: ISAKMP:      hash SHA
```

continues

Example 16-3   debug crypto isakmp *Command Output (Continued)*

```
000394: Mar 26 21:00:24.060: ISAKMP:           default group 2
000395: Mar 26 21:00:24.060: ISAKMP:           auth XAUTHInitPreShared
000396: Mar 26 21:00:24.060: ISAKMP:           life type in seconds
000397: Mar 26 21:00:24.060: ISAKMP:           life duration (VPI) of  0x0 0x20 0xC4 0x9B
000398: Mar 26 21:00:24.060: ISAKMP:           keylength of 256
000399: Mar 26 21:00:24.060: ISAKMP:(0):Encryption algorithm offered does not match policy!
! - No match, go on to the next one.
000400: Mar 26 21:00:24.060: ISAKMP:(0):atts are not acceptable. Next payload is 3
000401: Mar 26 21:00:24.060: ISAKMP:(0):Checking ISAKMP transform 2 against priority 1
  policy
! - Check ISAKMP against second transform set
000402: Mar 26 21:00:24.060: ISAKMP:           encryption AES-CBC
000403: Mar 26 21:00:24.060: ISAKMP:           hash MD5
000404: Mar 26 21:00:24.060: ISAKMP:           default group 2
000405: Mar 26 21:00:24.060: ISAKMP:           auth XAUTHInitPreShared
000406: Mar 26 21:00:24.060: ISAKMP:           life type in seconds
000407: Mar 26 21:00:24.060: ISAKMP:           life duration (VPI) of  0x0 0x20 0xC4 0x9B
000408: Mar 26 21:00:24.060: ISAKMP:           keylength of 256
000409: Mar 26 21:00:24.060: ISAKMP:(0):Encryption algorithm offered does not match policy!
! - No match, go on to the next one.
000410: Mar 26 21:00:24.060: ISAKMP:(0):atts are not acceptable. Next payload is 3
! - Check ISAKMP against third transform set
000471: Mar 26 21:00:24.064: ISAKMP:(0):Checking ISAKMP transform 3 against priority 1
  policy
000472: Mar 26 21:00:24.064: ISAKMP:           encryption 3DES-CBC
000473: Mar 26 21:00:24.064: ISAKMP:           hash SHA
000474: Mar 26 21:00:24.064: ISAKMP:           default group 2
000475: Mar 26 21:00:24.064: ISAKMP:           auth XAUTHInitPreShared
000476: Mar 26 21:00:24.068: ISAKMP:           life type in seconds
000477: Mar 26 21:00:24.068: ISAKMP:           life duration (VPI) of  0x0 0x20 0xC4 0x9B
000478: Mar 26 21:00:24.068: ISAKMP:(0):atts are acceptable. Next payload is 3
000479: Mar 26 21:00:24.068: ISAKMP:(0): processing KE payload. message ID = 0
000480: Mar 26 21:00:24.096: ISAKMP:(0): processing NONCE payload. message ID = 0
000481: Mar 26 21:00:24.096: ISAKMP:(0): vendor ID is NAT-T v2
000482: Mar 26 21:00:24.096: ISAKMP:(0):Input = IKE_MESG_FROM_PEER, IKE_AM_EXCH
000483: Mar 26 21:00:24.096: ISAKMP:(0):Old State = IKE_READY  New State =
  IKE_R_AM_AAA_AWAIT

000484: Mar 26 21:00:24.100: ISAKMP:(1005): constructed NAT-T vendor-02 ID
000485: Mar 26 21:00:24.100: ISAKMP:(1005):SA is doing pre-shared key authentication plus
  XAUTH using id type ID_IPV4_ADDR
! - Match successful. Accept and begin parameter download
000486: Mar 26 21:00:24.100: ISAKMP (0:1005): ID payload
         next-payload : 10
         type         : 1
         address      : 172.16.0.4
         protocol     : 17
         port         : 0
```

Example 16-3 **debug crypto isakmp** *Command Output (Continued)*

```
              length      : 12
000487: Mar 26 21:00:24.100: ISAKMP:(1005):Total payload length: 12
000488: Mar 26 21:00:24.100: ISAKMP:(1005): sending packet to 172.16.1.40 my_port 500
  peer_port 500 (R) AG_INIT_EXCH
000489: Mar 26 21:00:24.100: ISAKMP:(1005):Input = IKE_MESG_FROM_AAA, PRESHARED_KEY_REPLY
000490: Mar 26 21:00:24.100: ISAKMP:(1005):Old State = IKE_R_AM_AAA_AWAIT  New State =
  IKE_R_AM2

000491: Mar 26 21:00:24.108: ISAKMP (0:1005): received packet from 172.16.1.40 dport 500
  sport 500 Global (R) AG_INIT_EXCH
000492: Mar 26 21:00:24.108: ISAKMP:(1005): processing HASH payload. message ID = 0
000493: Mar 26 21:00:24.108: ISAKMP:(1005): processing NOTIFY INITIAL_CONTACT protocol 1
        spi 0, message ID = 0, sa = 47E78440
000494: Mar 26 21:00:24.112: ISAKMP:received payload type 20
000495: Mar 26 21:00:24.112: ISAKMP:received payload type 20
000496: Mar 26 21:00:24.112: ISAKMP:(1005):SA authentication status:
        authenticated
000497: Mar 26 21:00:24.112: ISAKMP:(1005):SA has been authenticated with 172.16.1.40
000498: Mar 26 21:00:24.112: ISAKMP:(1005):SA authentication status:
        Authenticated
! - Authentication process complete.
000499: Mar 26 21:00:24.112: ISAKMP:(1005): Process initial contact,
bring down existing phase 1 and 2 SA's with local 172.16.0.4 remote 172.16.1.40 remote port
  500
000500: Mar 26 21:00:24.112: ISAKMP:(1005):returning IP addr to the address pool
000501: Mar 26 21:00:24.112: ISAKMP: Trying to insert a peer 172.16.0.4/172.16.1.40/500/,
  and inserted successfully 47910754.
000502: Mar 26 21:00:24.112: ISAKMP: set new node 1714588361 to CONF_XAUTH
000503: Mar 26 21:00:24.112: ISAKMP:(1005):Sending NOTIFY RESPONDER_LIFETIME protocol 1
        spi 1210114920, message ID = 1714588361
000504: Mar 26 21:00:24.112: ISAKMP:(1005): sending packet to 172.16.1.40 my_port 500
  peer_port 500 (R) QM_IDLE
000505: Mar 26 21:00:24.112: ISAKMP:(1005):purging node 1714588361
000506: Mar 26 21:00:24.112: ISAKMP: Sending phase 1 responder lifetime 86400

000507: Mar 26 21:00:24.112: ISAKMP:(1005):Input = IKE_MESG_FROM_PEER, IKE_AM_EXCH
000508: Mar 26 21:00:24.112: ISAKMP:(1005):Old State = IKE_R_AM2  New State =
  IKE_P1_COMPLETE

000509: Mar 26 21:00:24.112: ISAKMP:(1005):Need XAUTH
000510: Mar 26 21:00:24.112: ISAKMP: set new node -1119688077 to CONF_XAUTH
000511: Mar 26 21:00:24.112: ISAKMP/xauth: request attribute XAUTH_USER_NAME_V2
000512: Mar 26 21:00:24.112: ISAKMP/xauth: request attribute XAUTH_USER_PASSWORD_V2
000513: Mar 26 21:00:24.112: ISAKMP:(1005): initiating peer config to 172.16.1.40. ID = -
  1119688077
000514: Mar 26 21:00:24.112: ISAKMP:(1005): sending packet to 172.16.1.40 my_port 500
  peer_port 500 (R) CONF_XAUTH
000515: Mar 26 21:00:24.116: ISAKMP:(1005):Input = IKE_MESG_INTERNAL, IKE_PHASE1_COMPLETE
```

continues

Example 16-3 debug crypto isakmp *Command Output (Continued)*

```
000516: Mar 26 21:00:24.116: ISAKMP:(1005):Old State = IKE_P1_COMPLETE  New State =
  IKE_XAUTH_REQ_SENT


000517: Mar 26 21:00:28.836: ISAKMP (0:1005): received packet from 172.16.1.40 dport 500
  sport 500 Global (R) CONF_XAUTH
000518: Mar 26 21:00:28.836: ISAKMP:(1005):processing transaction payload from 172.16.1.40.
  message ID = -1119688077
000519: Mar 26 21:00:28.840: ISAKMP: Config payload REPLY
000520: Mar 26 21:00:28.840: ISAKMP/xauth: reply attribute XAUTH_USER_NAME_V2
000521: Mar 26 21:00:28.840: ISAKMP/xauth: reply attribute XAUTH_USER_PASSWORD_V2
000522: Mar 26 21:00:28.840: ISAKMP:(1005):deleting node -1119688077 error FALSE reason
  "Done with xauth request/reply exchange"
000523: Mar 26 21:00:28.840: ISAKMP:(1005):Input = IKE_MESG_FROM_PEER, IKE_CFG_REPLY
000524: Mar 26 21:00:28.840: ISAKMP:(1005):Old State = IKE_XAUTH_REQ_SENT  New State =
  IKE_XAUTH_AAA_CONT_LOGIN_AWAIT


000525: Mar 26 21:00:28.848: ISAKMP: set new node 375567395 to CONF_XAUTH
000526: Mar 26 21:00:28.848: ISAKMP:(1005): initiating peer config to 172.16.1.40. ID =
  375567395
000527: Mar 26 21:00:28.848: ISAKMP:(1005): sending packet to 172.16.1.40 my_port 500
  peer_port 500 (R) CONF_XAUTH
000528: Mar 26 21:00:28.848: ISAKMP:(1005):Input = IKE_MESG_FROM_AAA, IKE_AAA_CONT_LOGIN
000529: Mar 26 21:00:28.848: ISAKMP:(1005):Old State = IKE_XAUTH_AAA_CONT_LOGIN_AWAIT  New
  State = IKE_XAUTH_SET_SENT


000530: Mar 26 21:00:28.848: ISAKMP (0:1005): received packet from 172.16.1.40 dport 500
  sport 500 Global (R) CONF_XAUTH
000531: Mar 26 21:00:28.848: ISAKMP:(1005):processing transaction payload from 172.16.1.40.
  message ID = 375567395
000532: Mar 26 21:00:28.848: ISAKMP: Config payload ACK
000533: Mar 26 21:00:28.848: ISAKMP:(1005):        (blank) XAUTH ACK Processed
000534: Mar 26 21:00:28.848: ISAKMP:(1005):deleting node 375567395 error FALSE reason
  "Transaction mode done"
000535: Mar 26 21:00:28.848: ISAKMP:(1005):Input = IKE_MESG_FROM_PEER, IKE_CFG_ACK
000536: Mar 26 21:00:28.848: ISAKMP:(1005):Old State = IKE_XAUTH_SET_SENT  New State =
  IKE_P1_COMPLETE


000537: Mar 26 21:00:28.848: ISAKMP:(1005):Input = IKE_MESG_INTERNAL, IKE_PHASE1_COMPLETE
000538: Mar 26 21:00:28.848: ISAKMP:(1005):Old State = IKE_P1_COMPLETE  New State =
  IKE_P1_COMPLETE


000539: Mar 26 21:00:28.892: ISAKMP (0:1005): received packet from 172.16.1.40 dport 500
  sport 500 Global (R) QM_IDLE
000540: Mar 26 21:00:28.892: ISAKMP: set new node 893794532 to QM_IDLE
000541: Mar 26 21:00:28.892: ISAKMP:(1005):processing transaction payload from 172.16.1.40.
  message ID = 893794532
000542: Mar 26 21:00:28.892: ISAKMP: Config payload REQUEST
000543: Mar 26 21:00:28.892: ISAKMP:(1005):checking request:
000544: Mar 26 21:00:28.892: ISAKMP:    IP4_ADDRESS
000545: Mar 26 21:00:28.892: ISAKMP:    IP4_NETMASK
000546: Mar 26 21:00:28.892: ISAKMP:    IP4_DNS
```

Example 16-3 **debug crypto isakmp** *Command Output (Continued)*

```
000547: Mar 26 21:00:28.892: ISAKMP:      IP4_NBNS
000548: Mar 26 21:00:28.892: ISAKMP:      ADDRESS_EXPIRY
000549: Mar 26 21:00:28.892: ISAKMP:      MODECFG-BANNER
000550: Mar 26 21:00:28.892: ISAKMP:      MODECFG_SAVEPWD
000551: Mar 26 21:00:28.892: ISAKMP:      DEFAULT_DOMAIN
000552: Mar 26 21:00:28.892: ISAKMP:      SPLIT_INCLUDE
000553: Mar 26 21:00:28.892: ISAKMP:      SPLIT_DNS
000554: Mar 26 21:00:28.892: ISAKMP:      PFS
000555: Mar 26 21:00:28.892: ISAKMP:      BACKUP_SERVER
000556: Mar 26 21:00:28.896: ISAKMP:      APPLICATION_VERSION
000557: Mar 26 21:00:28.896: ISAKMP:      FW_RECORD
! - Request parameters
000558: Mar 26 21:00:28.896: ISAKMP:      CONFIG_MODE_UNKNOWN Unknown Attr: 0x700A
000559: Mar 26 21:00:28.896: ISAKMP:      CONFIG_MODE_UNKNOWN Unknown Attr: 0x7005
000560: Mar 26 21:00:28.896: ISAKMP/author: Author request for group BMHomesuccessfully
  sent to AAA
000561: Mar 26 21:00:28.896: ISAKMP:(1005):Input = IKE_MESG_FROM_PEER, IKE_CFG_REQUEST
000562: Mar 26 21:00:28.896: ISAKMP:(1005):Old State = IKE_P1_COMPLETE  New State =
  IKE_CONFIG_AUTHOR_AAA_AWAIT


000563: Mar 26 21:00:28.900: ISAKMP:(1005):attributes sent in message:
000564: Mar 26 21:00:28.900:          Address: 0.2.0.0
000565: Mar 26 21:00:28.900: ISAKMP:(1005):allocating address 172.16.1.191
000566: Mar 26 21:00:28.900: ISAKMP: Sending private address: 172.16.1.191
000567: Mar 26 21:00:28.900: ISAKMP: Sending subnet mask: 255.255.0.0
000568: Mar 26 21:00:28.900: ISAKMP: Sending IP4_DNS server address: 172.16.0.1
000569: Mar 26 21:00:28.900: ISAKMP: Sending IP4_DNS server address: 4.2.2.1
000570: Mar 26 21:00:28.900: ISAKMP: Sending ADDRESS_EXPIRY seconds left to use the address:
  86395
000571: Mar 26 21:00:28.900: ISAKMP: Sending save password reply value 1
000572: Mar 26 21:00:28.900: ISAKMP: Sending DEFAULT_DOMAIN default domain name:
  bmorgan.org
! - Assign requested parameters including IP address, default router, DNS servers, domain
  name, etc.
000573: Mar 26 21:00:28.900: ISAKMP: Sending APPLICATION_VERSION string: Cisco IOS
  Software, 2800 Software (C2800NM-ADVIPSERVICESK9-M), Version 12.4(4)XC6, RELEASE SOFTWARE
  (fc2)
Synched to technology version 12.4(5.13)T
Technical Support: http://www.cisco.com/techsupport
Copyright  1986-2007 by Cisco Systems, Inc.
Compiled Thu 15-Feb-07 02:54 by ealyon
000574: Mar 26 21:00:28.900: ISAKMP (0/1005): Unknown Attr: CONFIG_MODE_UNKNOWN (0x700A)
000575: Mar 26 21:00:28.900: ISAKMP (0/1005): Unknown Attr: CONFIG_MODE_UNKNOWN (0x7005)
000576: Mar 26 21:00:28.900: ISAKMP:(1005): responding to peer config from 172.16.1.40. ID
  = 893794532
000577: Mar 26 21:00:28.904: ISAKMP:(1005): sending packet to 172.16.1.40 my_port 500
  peer_port 500 (R) CONF_ADDR
000578: Mar 26 21:00:28.904: ISAKMP:(1005):deleting node 893794532 error FALSE reason "No
  Error"
```

continues

Example 16-3 debug crypto isakmp *Command Output (Continued)*

```
000579: Mar 26 21:00:28.904: ISAKMP:(1005):Input = IKE_MESG_FROM_AAA, IKE_AAA_GROUP_ATTR
000580: Mar 26 21:00:28.904: ISAKMP:(1005):Old State = IKE_CONFIG_AUTHOR_AAA_AWAIT  New
  State = IKE_P1_COMPLETE

000581: Mar 26 21:00:28.904: ISAKMP:(1005):Input = IKE_MESG_INTERNAL, IKE_PHASE1_COMPLETE
000582: Mar 26 21:00:28.904: ISAKMP:(1005):Old State = IKE_P1_COMPLETE  New State =
  IKE_P1_COMPLETE

000583: Mar 26 21:00:28.916: ISAKMP (0:1005): received packet from 172.16.1.40 dport 500
  sport 500 Global (R) QM_IDLE
000584: Mar 26 21:00:28.916: ISAKMP: set new node 1682961045 to QM_IDLE
000585: Mar 26 21:00:28.916: ISAKMP:(1005): processing HASH payload. message ID =
  1682961045
000586: Mar 26 21:00:28.916: ISAKMP:(1005): processing SA payload. message ID = 1682961045
000587: Mar 26 21:00:28.916: ISAKMP:(1005):Checking IPsec proposal 1
! - Begin IPSec process and check against proprosal 1
000588: Mar 26 21:00:28.916: ISAKMP: transform 1, ESP_AES
000589: Mar 26 21:00:28.916: ISAKMP:    attributes in transform:
000590: Mar 26 21:00:28.916: ISAKMP:        authenticator is HMAC-MD5
000591: Mar 26 21:00:28.916: ISAKMP:        key length is 256
000592: Mar 26 21:00:28.916: ISAKMP:        encaps is 1 (Tunnel)
000593: Mar 26 21:00:28.916: ISAKMP:        SA life type in seconds
000594: Mar 26 21:00:28.916: ISAKMP:        SA life duration (VPI) of  0x0 0x20 0xC4 0x9B
000595: Mar 26 21:00:28.916: ISAKMP:(1005):atts are acceptable.
000596: Mar 26 21:00:28.916: ISAKMP:(1005):Checking IPsec proposal 1
000597: Mar 26 21:00:28.916: ISAKMP:(1005):transform 1, IPPCP LZS
000598: Mar 26 21:00:28.916: ISAKMP:    attributes in transform:
000599: Mar 26 21:00:28.916: ISAKMP:        encaps is 1 (Tunnel)
000600: Mar 26 21:00:28.916: ISAKMP:        SA life type in seconds
000601: Mar 26 21:00:28.916: ISAKMP:        SA life duration (VPI) of  0x0 0x20 0xC4 0x9B
000602: Mar 26 21:00:28.916: ISAKMP:(1005):atts are acceptable.
000603: Mar 26 21:00:28.916: ISAKMP:(1005): IPsec policy invalidated proposal with error
  256
! - No match, check second proposal
000604: Mar 26 21:00:28.916: ISAKMP:(1005):Checking IPsec proposal 2
000605: Mar 26 21:00:28.916: ISAKMP: transform 1, ESP_AES
000606: Mar 26 21:00:28.916: ISAKMP:    attributes in transform:
000607: Mar 26 21:00:28.916: ISAKMP:        authenticator is HMAC-SHA
000608: Mar 26 21:00:28.916: ISAKMP:        key length is 256
000609: Mar 26 21:00:28.916: ISAKMP:        encaps is 1 (Tunnel)
000610: Mar 26 21:00:28.916: ISAKMP:        SA life type in seconds
000611: Mar 26 21:00:28.916: ISAKMP:        SA life duration (VPI) of  0x0 0x20 0xC4 0x9B
000612: Mar 26 21:00:28.916: ISAKMP:(1005):atts are acceptable.
000613: Mar 26 21:00:28.916: ISAKMP:(1005):Checking IPsec proposal 2
000614: Mar 26 21:00:28.916: ISAKMP:(1005):transform 1, IPPCP LZS
000615: Mar 26 21:00:28.916: ISAKMP:    attributes in transform:
000616: Mar 26 21:00:28.916: ISAKMP:        encaps is 1 (Tunnel)
000617: Mar 26 21:00:28.916: ISAKMP:        SA life type in seconds
```

Example 16-3 **debug crypto isakmp** *Command Output (Continued)*

```
000618: Mar 26 21:00:28.916: ISAKMP:      SA life duration (VPI) of  0x0 0x20 0xC4 0x9B
000619: Mar 26 21:00:28.916: ISAKMP:(1005):atts are acceptable.
000620: Mar 26 21:00:28.920: ISAKMP:(1005): IPsec policy invalidated proposal with error
   256
! - No match, check third proposal
000736: Mar 26 21:00:28.924: ISAKMP:(1005):Checking IPsec proposal 3
000737: Mar 26 21:00:28.924: ISAKMP: transform 1, ESP_3DES
000738: Mar 26 21:00:28.924: ISAKMP:   attributes in transform:
000739: Mar 26 21:00:28.924: ISAKMP:    authenticator is HMAC-SHA
000740: Mar 26 21:00:28.924: ISAKMP:    encaps is 1 (Tunnel)
000741: Mar 26 21:00:28.924: ISAKMP:    SA life type in seconds
000742: Mar 26 21:00:28.924: ISAKMP:    SA life duration (VPI) of  0x0 0x20 0xC4 0x9B
000743: Mar 26 21:00:28.924: ISAKMP:(1005):atts are acceptable.
! - Match.  Begin SA process.
000744: Mar 26 21:00:28.924: ISAKMP:(1005): processing NONCE payload. message ID =
   1682961045
000745: Mar 26 21:00:28.924: ISAKMP:(1005): processing ID payload. message ID = 1682961045
000746: Mar 26 21:00:28.924: ISAKMP:(1005): processing ID payload. message ID = 1682961045
000747: Mar 26 21:00:28.924: ISAKMP:(1005):QM Responder gets spi
000748: Mar 26 21:00:28.924: ISAKMP:(1005):Node 1682961045, Input = IKE_MESG_FROM_PEER,
   IKE_QM_EXCH
000749: Mar 26 21:00:28.924: ISAKMP:(1005):Old State = IKE_QM_READY  New State =
   IKE_QM_SPI_STARVE
000750: Mar 26 21:00:28.928: ISAKMP:(1005): Creating IPsec SAs
000751: Mar 26 21:00:28.928:      inbound SA from 172.16.1.40 to 172.16.0.4 (f/i)  0/ 0
         (proxy 172.16.1.191 to 0.0.0.0)
000752: Mar 26 21:00:28.928:       has spi 0xF38581A8 and conn_id 0
000753: Mar 26 21:00:28.928:       lifetime of 2147483 seconds
000754: Mar 26 21:00:28.928:      outbound SA from 172.16.0.4 to 172.16.1.40 (f/i) 0/0
         (proxy 0.0.0.0 to 172.16.1.191)
000755: Mar 26 21:00:28.928:       has spi  0x7065A45A and conn_id 0
000756: Mar 26 21:00:28.928:       lifetime of 2147483 seconds
000757: Mar 26 21:00:28.928: ISAKMP:(1005): sending packet to 172.16.1.40 my_port 500
   peer_port 500 (R) QM_IDLE
000758: Mar 26 21:00:28.928: ISAKMP:(1005):Node 1682961045, Input = IKE_MESG_INTERNAL,
   IKE_GOT_SPI
000759: Mar 26 21:00:28.928: ISAKMP:(1005):Old State = IKE_QM_SPI_STARVE  New State =
   IKE_QM_R_QM2
000760: Mar 26 21:00:28.932: ISAKMP (0:1005): received packet from 172.16.1.40 dport 500
   sport 500 Global (R) QM_IDLE
000761: Mar 26 21:00:28.932: ISAKMP:(1005):deleting node 1682961045 error FALSE reason "QM
   done (await)"
000762: Mar 26 21:00:28.936: ISAKMP:(1005):Node 1682961045, Input = IKE_MESG_FROM_PEER,
   IKE_QM_EXCH
000763: Mar 26 21:00:28.936: ISAKMP:(1005):Old State = IKE_QM_R_QM2  New State =
   IKE_QM_PHASE2_COMPLETE
000764: Mar 26 21:00:30.884: %CRYPTO-4-RECVD_PKT_INV_SPI: decaps: rec'd IPSEC packet has
   invalid spi for destaddr=172.16.0.4, prot=50, spi=0x94040000(2483290112),
   srcaddr=172.16.1.40
000765: Mar 26 21:00:30.888: ISAKMP: set new node -189570038 to QM_IDLE
```

continues

Example 16-3 **debug crypto isakmp** *Command Output (Continued)*

```
000766: Mar 26 21:00:30.888: ISAKMP:(1005): sending packet to 172.16.1.40 my_port 500
  peer_port 500 (R) QM_IDLE
000767: Mar 26 21:00:30.888: ISAKMP:(1005):purging node -189570038
000768: Mar 26 21:00:30.888: ISAKMP:(1005):Input = IKE_MESG_FROM_IPSEC, IKE_PHASE2_DEL
000769: Mar 26 21:00:30.888: %CRYPTO-4-RECVD_PKT_NOT_IPSEC: Rec'd packet not an IPSEC
  packet.
        (ip) vrf/dest_addr= /10.250.1.10, src_addr= 172.16.1.191, prot= 1
000770: Mar 26 21:00:30.888: ISAKMP:(1005):Old State = IKE_P1_COMPLETE  New State =
  IKE_P1_COMPLETE
```

The highlighted portions show that each policy is offered in hopes of finding one in common. The process continues until one is acceptable to both sides. Upon acceptance of the transform set, the connection parameters are uploaded to the client as shown by the highlighted text once again. Once those parameters are uploaded, the IPsec portion of the connection begins and, once again, policies are negotiated. It is clear that the order of input of the policies for both ISAKMP and IPsec can have some bearing on the processing and response time for the connection.

Example 16-3 was performed using only local authentication. In cases where RADIUS and TACACS+ servers are used, or any AAA model in fact, the process of authentication can be monitored using the appropriate command or combination of commands, as follows:

- **debug aaa authentication**

- **debug aaa authorization**

- **debug radius**

Foundation Summary

The Easy VPN Server functionality is, as the name implies, quite straightforward in its configuration and function. The polices, preshared keys, DNS/WINS servers, DNS domain(s), and IP address pools all need to be preconfigured in the group policy to facilitate VPN Client connections.

The Easy VPN Server provides a mechanism for IT organizations to better and more effectively support the teleworker in the small office/home office (SOHO) and on the road. This allows IT organizations to provide to teleworkers a common experience through access to identical applications and services as are available to those workers located in central and/or headquarters sites.

Table 16-2 revisits the aspects of VPN connectivity managed by Cisco Easy VPN.

Table 16-2 *Easy VPN Automated Tasks*

Task	Description
Tunnel parameter negotiation	Tunnel addresses, algorithms, and duration
Tunnel establishment	Creation of tunnel connection between its source and destination
NAT/PAT/ACL	Automatic creation of NAT and PAT tables as well as ACL generation
Security key management	Encryption and decryption key management
Tunneled data handling	Encryption, decryption, and authentication

Cisco Easy VPN Client functions in one of three modes, as summarized in Table 16-3.

Table 16-3 *Cisco Easy VPN Client Modes*

Mode	Description
Client	Specifies that NAT and/or PAT is used and that end stations on the client side of the connection do not use IP addressing from the address space of the VPN Server side
Network Extension	Client-side end stations use IP addressing from the address space of the VPN Server so that they form a single internetwork
Network Extension Plus	Similar to Network Extension mode with the added capability of being able to request an IP address via mode configuration and assign it to an available loopback interface

Q&A

The questions and scenarios in this book are designed to be challenging and to make sure that you know the answer. Rather than allowing you to derive the answers from clues hidden inside the questions themselves, the questions challenge your understanding and recall of the subject.

Hopefully, mastering these questions will help you limit the number of exam questions on which you narrow your choices to two options, and then guess.

You can find the answers to these questions in Appendix A. For more practice with exam-like question formats, use the exam engine on the CD-ROM.

1. Easy VPN Remote feature supports a two-stage process for client/server authentication. Describe both stages.

2. One of the key concepts necessary to properly understand VPN connectivity is the step-by-step method of VPN tunnel establishment. List the steps in order of completion.

3. Describe Xauth and why it is beneficial in VPN connections.

4. Why is the RRI important to the VPN connection?

5. Describe the options available for Group Authorization configuration of an Easy VPN Server.

6. In the selection of a transform set for a given VPN connection, by what process is the transform set chosen?

7. List the modes of operation for Easy VPN Remote and provide a brief description of each.

8. To ensure secure tunnel connections, the Cisco Easy VPN Remote feature does not support certain transform set configurations. In what circumstance(s) would this be the case?

Exam Topic List

This chapter covers the following topics that you need to master for the CCNP ISCW exam:

- **Cisco VPN Client Installation and Configuration Overview**—Describes the purpose of the Cisco VPN Client and provides an overview of the installation and configuration process.

- **Cisco VPN Client Installation**—Describes the process of installing the Cisco VPN Client on a client PC.

- **Cisco VPN Client Configuration**— Describes the necessary configuration steps for the Cisco VPN Client.

CHAPTER 17

Implementing the Cisco VPN Client

A core piece of the teleworker or road warrior battle chest is certainly the ability to connect back to the corporate network to access company resources such as e-mail, file shares, documents, and other resources.

The Cisco VPN Client allows Microsoft Windows-based PCs, Apple Macintosh OS X computers, and Linux clients to connect remotely over any IP-based network connection in order to create a secure connection over Internet or dialup infrastructure.

"Do I Know This Already?" Quiz

The purpose of the "Do I Know This Already?" quiz is to help you decide whether you really need to read the entire chapter. If you already intend to read the entire chapter, you do not necessarily need to answer these questions now.

The 6-question quiz, derived from the major sections in the "Foundation Topics" portion of the chapter, helps you to determine how to spend your limited study time.

Table 17-1 outlines the major topics discussed in this chapter and the "Do I Know This Already?" quiz questions that correspond to those topics.

Table 17-1   *"Do I Know This Already?" Foundation Topics Section-to-Question Mapping*

Foundation Topics Section	Questions Covered in This Section	Score
Cisco VPN Client Installation and Configuration Overview	1	
Cisco VPN Client Installation	2	
Cisco VPN Client Configuration	3–6	
Total Score		

> **CAUTION**   The goal of self-assessment is to gauge your mastery of the topics in this chapter. If you do not know the answer to a question or are only partially sure of the answer, you should mark this question wrong for purposes of self-assessment. Giving yourself credit for an answer that you correctly guess skews your self-assessment results and might provide you with a false sense of security.

1.   From which source is the Cisco VPN Client Software obtained?

   a.   Cisco.com with a CCO ID

   b.   CD shipped with VPN devices

   c.   Local software retailer

   d.   Bundled with client PC

2.   Which of the following is the default installation location of the Cisco VPN Client Software?

   a.   C:\Cisco\VPN Client

   b.   C:\Program Files\Cisco Systems\VPN Client

   c.   C:\Cisco VPN Client

   d.   C:\Cisco Systems\VPN Client

3.   To use Group Authentication for a connection entry, which of the following is required?

   a.   Root certificate

   b.   IPsec over UDP

   c.   TCP transport

   d.   VPN dialup

4.   Which is the default transport for a new connection entry?

   a.   IPsec over TCP port 10000

   b.   IPsec over UDP port 10000

   c.   IPsec over TCP port 4500

   d.   IPsec over UDP port 4500

5. To provide for VPN server resilience, which is typically provided by network administrators to the VPN Clients?

    a. Authentication mechanism

    b. Backup server name or address

    c. Transport mechanism

    d. Personal firewall

6. Which of the following connection entry options allows the use of a PSTN connection to provide VPN access?

    a. Mutual group authentication

    b. IPsec over TCP transport

    c. Dial-Up tab configuration options

    d. Backup server configuration

The answers to the "Do I Know This Already?" quiz are found in Appendix A, "Answers to the 'Do I Know This Already?' Quizzes and Q&A Sections." The suggested choices for your next step are as follows:

■ **2 or fewer overall score**—Read the entire chapter. This includes the "Foundation Topics," "Foundation Summary," and "Q&A" sections.

■ **3 or 4 overall score**—Begin with the "Foundation Summary" section, and then go to the "Q&A" section.

■ **5 or more overall score**—If you want more review on these topics, skip to the "Foundation Summary" section, and then go to the "Q&A" section. Otherwise, move to the next chapter.

Foundation Topics

Cisco VPN Client Installation and Configuration Overview

The installation of the Cisco VPN Client Software is a very straightforward process. A number of tasks must be completed to establish connectivity to a VPN head-end, which can consist of a VPN Concentrator or IOS Router. These include

- Installation of the Cisco VPN Client on a user PC

- Creation of a new connection entry in the software

- Configuration of the client authentication properties

- Configuration of transparent tunneling

- Enabling and adding of backup servers

- Configuration of a connection to the Internet via dialup networking

The Cisco VPN Client Software can be downloaded from Cisco.com. A registered Cisco Connection Online (CCO) ID is required to access the software download area on Cisco.com. Cisco recommends that users maintain an up-to-date version of the software. In the absence of a CCO ID, it is possible to use the Microsoft IPsec client that is bundled with Microsoft Windows.

Before installing a new version of the software, it is recommended that existing connection entries (profiles) be exported to a temporary directory and the software be uninstalled. Once the setup process has begun, an installation wizard will step through the entire process to its completion.

After the software is installed, it should be launched so that connection entries can be imported back into the client or new connection entries can be created. Any created connections should be tested for functionality and reconfigured as needed to establish the needed connectivity.

Cisco VPN Client Installation

After the Cisco VPN Client Software has been downloaded from Cisco.com and saved to a working directory on the target hard disk, double-click the self-extracting executable file to begin the installation process. This initial step simply extracts the included files to the same working directory on the PC's hard disk (the extraction location depends on the WinZip settings). Once all files are extracted, double-click the setup.exe file in the directory where all the files have been extracted to begin the installation process. Figure 17-1 lists the files extracted from the downloaded archive file.

Figure 17-1 *Cisco VPN Client Files*

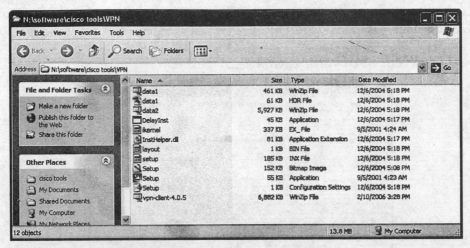

The bottom file in the listing is the one that was actually downloaded from Cisco.com. When the file extraction occurred, the additional files were placed in the same directory.

The installation wizard is launched by double-clicking the setup.exe file. This process first checks to see whether an older version of the Cisco VPN Client is already installed. If a previous version is already installed, the existing software must first be uninstalled. Click the **OK** button on the warning screen to exit the installation. Uninstall the previous version either from the Windows **Settings > Control Panel > Add or Remove Programs**, or by navigating to **Start > All Programs > Cisco System VPN Client > Uninstall VPN Client**. Once the older version has been removed, the machine will require a reboot. If no previous version of the VPN Client is detected, the Welcome screen will be presented, as shown in Figure 17-2.

Figure 17-2 *Cisco VPN Client Welcome Screen*

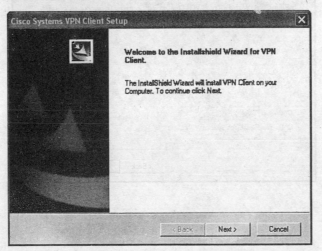

Click **Next** on the Welcome screen to progress the installation wizard to the License Agreement screen, shown in Figure 17-3. If all terms and conditions of the Software Licensing Agreement are acceptable to the user, click **Yes** to continue the installation process.

Figure 17-3 *Cisco VPN Client Licensing Agreement*

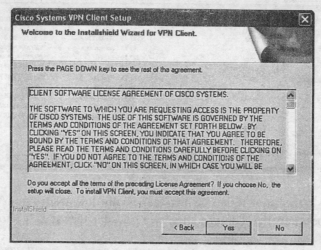

Upon acceptance of the Licensing Agreement, the next screen provides the option of altering or accepting the default program installation directory. As shown in Figure 17-4, the default installation directory is C:\Program Files\Cisco Systems\VPN Client.

Figure 17-4 *Cisco VPN Client Installation Directory*

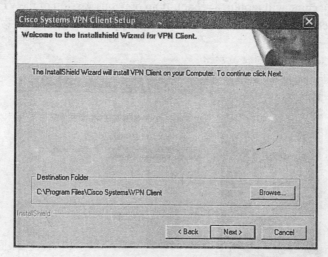

Click **Browse** to select an alternative installation location. Otherwise, click **Next** to move the installation process to the Program Folders screen. This option provides the installer with the choice of how the Cisco VPN Client will be presented under the Windows Start menu. As shown in Figure 17-5, the default setting is to create a subfolder under the Programs folder called Cisco Systems VPN Client.

Figure 17-5 *Cisco VPN Client Program Folder*

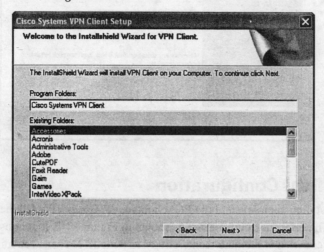

This entry can be deleted entirely to install the Cisco VPN Client Software shortcuts into the Programs folder directly, renamed, or accepted as is. Once the desired folder name is entered in the field, click **Next** to begin the file copy process.

This process is relatively short, and typically lasts less than a minute. While the files are copied and the settings are updated, the user is informed of the file copy process, as well as the installation of a new network adapter for the Cisco VPN Client.

After all the files are copied and settings have been updated and/or added, the installation process is complete. At this point, the PC must be rebooted to put all changes into effect and load the installed drivers. This announcement is shown in Figure 17-6.

Figure 17-6 *Cisco VPN Client Install Complete*

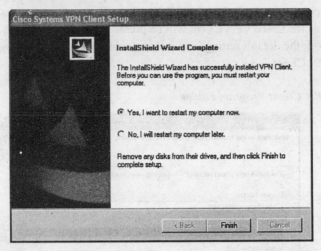

Cisco VPN Client Configuration

With the installation complete and the PC rebooted, the Cisco VPN Client Software can be launched. The interface is quite simple, as shown in Figure 17-7. It consists of a number of connection entries that facilitate connectivity to various VPN sites as might be offered by a large enterprise corporation.

Figure 17-7 *Cisco VPN Client*

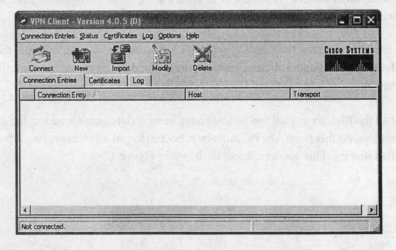

Initially, there are no connection entries, so they must be added to establish a connection via an IP connection to a VPN site.

Connection Entries

The Connection Entries screen is capable of holding multiple entries should multiple access sites and/or methodologies be available. Click the **New** button at the top of the screen to open the Create New VPN Connection Entry dialog box, shown in Figure 17-8.

Figure 17-8 *Cisco VPN Client New Connection Entry Dialog Box*

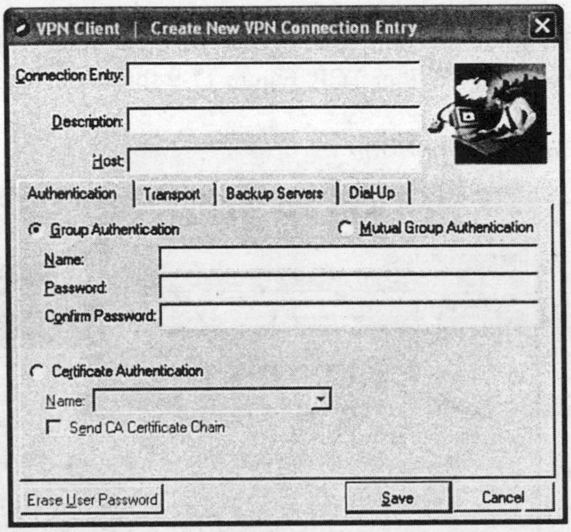

The Connection Entry field is simply a local name for the connection. It should be unique and allow the user to easily identify the site to which it connects. For added clarification, there is a Description field just below it as well.

The Host field is of key importance as it will contain the IP address or the Fully Qualified Domain Name (FQDN) of the host so that a Domain Name System (DNS) lookup can be performed to resolve the IP address of the target VPN device.

Next, the authentication options listed on the tabs in the bottom half of the Create New VPN Connection Entry dialog box must also be configured.

Authentication Tab

The three options (radio buttons) on the Authentication tab are as follows:

- **Group Authentication**—A username and password is necessary to complete the VPN profile. The password must be entered twice for confirmation (typo prevention).

- **Mutual Group Authentication**—A root certificate must be issued that is compatible with the Central Site VPN Concentrator. A network administrator can load root certificates on the system during the VPN Client installation. Such a certificate must be imported in this window when the Mutual Group Authentication radio button is selected.

■ **Certificate Authentication**—After you click the radio button, a drop-down menu allows you to select the certificate to use in this connection. If you choose it and no certificate has been installed, the field reads No Certificates Installed. To use this authentication method, a certificate must be installed.

Transport Tab

The Transport tab allows the configuration of transparent tunneling as well as the choice of whether to use IPsec over UDP or TCP. Figure 17-9 shows the Transport tab.

Figure 17-9 *Cisco VPN Client Transport Tab*

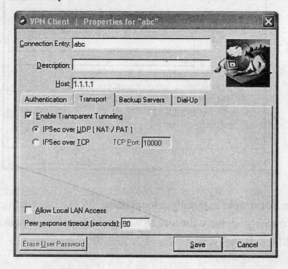

Transparent tunneling allows secure transfer of packets between the VPN Client and a secure gateway through a router running firewall services. Typically, such a gateway is also running either Network Address Translation (NAT) or Port Address Translation (PAT). IPsec endpoints expect the target IP addresses to be globally reachable. In the vast majority of networks today, some form of NAT or PAT is used to extend the number of IP addresses available. Transparent tunneling permits the IPsec end points to operate in such an environment.

Transparent tunneling must use common configuration parameters on both the VPN client and the VPN gateway. Transparent tunneling encapsulates Protocol 50 (Encapsulating Security Payload [ESP]) traffic inside of TCP or UDP datagrams. It can allow both Internet Security Association and Key Management Protocol (ISAKMP) and ESP to be encapsulated inside a transport protocol before being sent through a NAT/PAT device. Virtually every home network sits behind a PAT device, because the home ISP typically gives out only a single IP address. Transparent tunneling is useful when accessing VPN services via a small office/home office (SOHO) router.

The decision to use either IPsec over UDP or IPsec over TCP depends on the configuration of the VPN gateway. Both TCP and UDP can properly deal with PAT environments. TCP tends to work better with multiple connections, and UDP does not operate well through stateful firewalls (because UDP is not connection oriented).

In the VPN Client Software, transparent tunneling is on by default. The Central Site VPN device must be configured to make use of it as well in order to support the connection. Ensure that the Central Site VPN device and the VPN client software are configured identically to ensure proper functionality.

The default Transparent Tunneling mode is IPsec over UDP. It normally uses UDP port 4500 to encapsulate packets before they reach the NAT/PAT device. The actual port number is negotiated during the establishment of the VPN tunnel. This encapsulation allows the VPN client to exist and operate behind a NAT or PAT device.

IPsec over TCP requires that the TCP port number used in VPN connections match on both ends. The default port number is 10000, but it can be changed (typically by policy at the central site). The use of IPsec over TCP also helps with NAT/PAT environments but adds support for stateful firewalls.

The final option on this tab is the Allow Local LAN Access checkbox. The LAN Access parameter provides access to the local network resources such as printers, faxes, shared files, and other resources. Both the client and the Central Site VPN device must be configured to permit this option. The central site informs the client that local LAN access is permitted, and all other traffic travels through the VPN. The client simply checks the Local LAN box. Local LAN is defined as the subnet (or subnets—up to 10) applied to the interface before the VPN connection (and the associated VPN subnet) is established.

For example, if a user initiates a VPN connection from home (where they have their own network-attached printer), this option would be necessary to permit the user to print to their home printer while connected to the VPN. The user could also access other shared resources at home; however, all local communication is possible only with IP addresses, not device names. All name resolution is sent through the VPN, which would not be aware of devices on the home network.

Typically, such configuration is not permitted by the central site because it could permit traffic from an unsecured interface into the VPN. When Local LAN access is not configured, all traffic is sent across the VPN connection and local resources are unreachable.

Backup Servers Tab

To ensure VPN availability, multiple VPN servers can be deployed in a given network model. From an architectural standpoint, this makes good sense if a significant number of employees use the VPN to facilitate their job functions day to day. The VPN client contains a Backup Servers tab to configure a single connection with the capability to connect to multiple servers. Should the primary server configured for the connection entry be unavailable, the client will automatically attempt to contact the servers configured in the Backup Servers tab. The search order for backup servers will be top-down. With this in mind, buttons have been added to this tab to facilitate reordering of Backup Server entries based on preference. Figure 17-10 shows the Backup Servers tab.

Figure 17-10 *Backup Servers Tab*

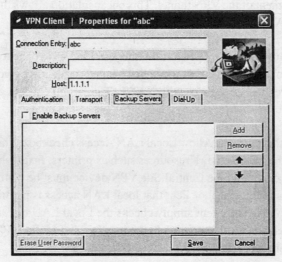

To enable the use of backup servers, check the Enable Backup Servers checkbox. Once checked, the options to add, remove, and reorganize (up/down arrows) become available. Additional servers are added by IP address only. All security parameters for the backup servers are already defined in the authentication tab.

Dial-Up Tab

Not all VPN servers are accessible via the Internet. If access to the central site requires that a dialup connection be made, the connection entry can be configured to do so. To enable the use of dialup, the Connect to Internet via Dial-up checkbox must be checked. This enables the options available on this page. The connection can use the Microsoft Dial-Up Networking phonebook or a specified third-party dialer application. Click the appropriate radio button to configure either option. Figure 17-11 shows the Dial-Up tab options.

Figure 17-11 *Dial-Up Tab*

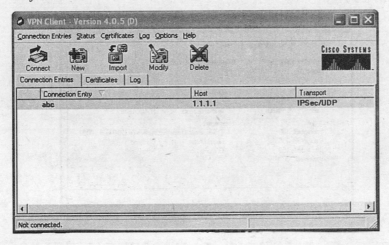

Finish the Connection Configuration

When all required options have been configured, click the **Save** button at the bottom of the Create window. All configurations are saved for this profile, and you are returned to the main VPN Client window. Figure 17-12 shows this window with the new profile added.

Figure 17-12 *New Profile Added*

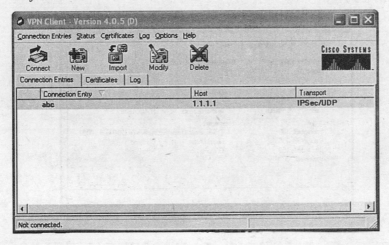

From the main VPN Client window, you can establish a VPN connection by highlighting one of the profiles and clicking the **Connect** button at the top of the window. If the connection parameters were properly configured, the VPN connection is successful. Figure 17-13 shows the VPN Client window with an established VPN tunnel.

Figure 17-13 *Established VPN*

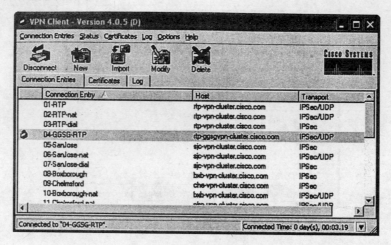

After a VPN connection is established, various statistics about the connection are available. From the Status pull-down menu, select **Statistics**. This launches the Statistics window, as shown in Figure 17-14.

Figure 17-14 *Established VPN*

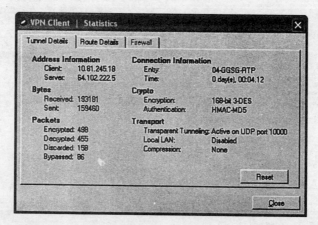

From this window, the Tunnel Details tab shows information about the current VPN connection. The Route Details tab shows which IP traffic is traveling through the VPN tunnel and which is considered local (this assumes that local LAN access was configured earlier).

Foundation Summary

A VPN connection is easily configurable to multiple sites based on geography or access methodology. The connection can be configured to take advantage of various encryption and/or authentication types as well as connectivity options relating to local resource availability, backup servers, and the use of dialup connections in order to establish a VPN session.

Table 17-2 reviews the configuration options available for a given connection entry in the VPN Client Software.

Table 17-2 *Connection Entry Options*

Parameter	Location	Purpose	Description
Connection Entry	Primary Connection Entry page	Specify a connection name	A unique name that will show in the Connection Entries page in the VPN Client
Host	Primary Connection page	Specify primary VPN server address	IP address or FQDN of the VPN server to be used for a given connection
Authentication	Authentication tab	Specify Group or Mutual Group Authentication	Method of authentication to the VPN server as well as name, password, and certificate specification
Transport	Transport tab	Specify transparent tunneling along with TCP- or UDP-based transport	Provide IPsec transport method and port number for a given connection as well as permit or deny local LAN access
Backup Server	Backup Servers tab	Configuration of additional VPN servers	Method of providing fallback server entries for a given connection should a primary VPN server be unavailable
Dial-Up	Dial-Up tab	Allow configuration of dialup parameters	Specify the use of dialup services for a particular connection entry along with Microsoft Dial-Up or third-party dialer application use

Q&A

The questions and scenarios in this book are designed to be challenging and to make sure that you know the answer. Rather than allowing you to derive the answers from clues hidden inside the questions themselves, the questions challenge your understanding and recall of the subject.

Hopefully, mastering these questions will help you limit the number of exam questions on which you narrow your choices to two options, and then guess.

You can find the answers to these questions in Appendix A. For more practice with exam-like question formats, use the exam engine on the CD-ROM.

1. A network administrator has provided the following information:

   ```
   Entry: CorporateVPN
   VPN Host: vpnserver1.mycompany.com
   Connection Options:  Group Authentication, Transparent Tunneling, IPsec over UDP
   Username: RoadWarrior
   Password: cisco
   Backup 1: vpnserver2.mycompany.com
   ```

   Assume that any options not provided herein are to be left disabled and that any necessary certificates have been provided previously.

   Describe the process of configuring the VPN Client to connect to the Central Site via a wired LAN connection.

2. What are the differences between IPsec over UDP and IPsec over TCP?

3. What are the purposes of configuring backup servers in the VPN Client?

4. What is Local LAN Access in the Cisco VPN Client?

5. When either creating or editing a VPN connection profile, which authentication method requires the use of a username and password?

6. Why would the Dial-Up tab be used to establish a VPN?

This part of the book covers the following ISCW exam topics:

Describe network security strategies.

- Describe and mitigate common network attacks (i.e., Reconnaissance, Access, and Denial of Service).
- Describe and mitigate Worm, Virus, and Trojan Horse attacks.
- Describe and mitigate application-layer attacks (e.g., management protocols).

Implement Cisco Device Hardening.

- Describe, configure, and verify AutoSecure/One-Step Lockdown implementations (i.e., CLI and SDM).
- Describe, configure, and verify AAA for Cisco Routers.
- Describe and configure threat and attack mitigation using ACLs.
- Describe and configure IOS secure management features (e.g., SSH, SNMP, SYSLOG, NTP, Role-Based CLI, etc.).

Implement Cisco IOS firewall.

- Describe the functions and operations of Cisco IOS Firewall (e.g., Stateful Firewall, CBAC, etc.).
- Configure Cisco IOS Firewall with SDM.
- Verify Cisco IOS Firewall configurations (i.e., IOS CLI configurations, SDM Monitor).

Describe and configure Cisco IOS IPS.

- Describe the functions and operations of IDS and IPS systems (e.g., IDS/IPS signatures, IPS Alarms, etc.).
- Configure Cisco IOS IPS using SDM.

Part IV: Device Hardening

Exam Topic List

This chapter covers the following topics that you need to master for the CCNP ISCW exam:

- **Router Vulnerability**—Identifies router services and interfaces that are vulnerable to network attack.

- **Using AutoSecure to Secure a Router**—Explains how to automate the process of locking down a Cisco router with the **auto secure** command.

- **Using SDM to Secure a Router**—Explains how to use the SDM web-based utility to configure, monitor, and secure a Cisco router as well as how to use the One-Step Lockdown mode of the Security Audit Wizard.

CHAPTER 18

Cisco Device Hardening

Many network devices have services enabled that create potential vulnerabilities. Such devices include desktop PCs, network servers, routers, and switches. Within an enterprise, most of these devices are protected by a firewall that sits at the perimeter of the network.

The firewall typically has Ethernet ports, and could be the edge device between the provider and the enterprise if an Ethernet service is offered from the provider. However, in many cases, an edge router sits outside of the firewall. This router is typically needed to perform media conversion from Ethernet (which is seen exclusively throughout most enterprises) to some WAN encapsulation for transport through a carrier network.

When a router is the edge device of a network, is it important to disable unnecessary services. Such services may be helpful and even important inside the enterprise, but offer attack vectors when exposed to the Internet. This chapter discusses how to disable unneeded services and secure a perimeter router.

"Do I Know This Already?" Quiz

The purpose of the "Do I Know This Already?" quiz is to help you decide whether you really need to read the entire chapter. If you already intend to read the entire chapter, you do not necessarily need to answer these questions now.

The 10-question quiz, derived from the major sections in the "Foundation Topics" portion of the chapter, helps you to determine how to spend your limited study time.

Table 18-1 outlines the major topics discussed in this chapter and the "Do I Know This Already?" quiz questions that correspond to those topics.

Table 18-1 *"Do I Know This Already?" Foundation Topics Section-to-Question Mapping*

Foundation Topics Section	Questions Covered in This Section	Score
Router Vulnerability	1–3	
Using AutoSecure to Secure a Router	4–7	
Using SDM to Secure a Router	8–10	
Total Score		

> **CAUTION** The goal of self-assessment is to gauge your mastery of the topics in this chapter. If you do not know the answer to a question or are only partially sure of the answer, you should mark this question wrong for purposes of self-assessment. Giving yourself credit for an answer that you correctly guess skews your self-assessment results and might provide you with a false sense of security.

1. Which interfaces should be disabled (shut down) in a router?

   a. Ethernet interfaces

   b. WAN interfaces

   c. Loopback interfaces

   d. Active interfaces

   e. Unconnected interfaces

2. Which of the following services are typically not seen in modern networks (select all that apply)?

   a. MOP

   b. FTP

   c. TFTP

   d. PAD

   e. NTP

3. How can SNMP be secured in a router (select all that apply)?

   a. SNMP is inherently secure.

   b. SNMPv3 offers security features that should be used.

   c. SNMP should be disabled at all times.

   d. Use ACLs to restrict SNMP access to the router.

   e. Wait until SNMPv4 is available.

4. Which of the following Cisco IOS features are enabled by AutoSecure to secure the forwarding plane (select all that apply)?

   a. AAA

   b. CEF

   c. uRPF

   d. SSH

   e. CBAC

5. Which of the following are interface-related security issues that AutoSecure addresses (select all that apply)?

   a. CEF

   b. IP proxy ARP

   c. Banner

   d. IP unreachables

   e. uRPF

6. Which of the following statements are true about the Cisco IOS command **auto secure** (select all that apply)?

   a. **auto secure** is a complete security solution, and no user input is required or possible.

   b. **auto secure** offers both an interactive mode and an automatic mode.

   c. **auto secure** creates a report for the router administrator, who then applies the necessary security configurations.

   d. **auto secure** enables a variety of security features, but only **auto secure** appears in the configuration file.

   e. **auto secure** can perform a complete security adjustment or correct individual portions of the router.

7. Which **auto secure** command option enables automatic mode?

   a. mode-automatic

   b. automatic

   c. no-interact

   d. full

   e. interact

8. Which of the following are security wizards offered by SDM (select all that apply)?

   a. Security Audit

   b. AutoSecure

   c. One-Step Lockdown

   d. Security Lockdown

   e. One-Step AutoSecure

9. Which of the following statements accurately describe the SDM Security Audit (select all that apply)?

   a. The user can define which security features are audited.

   b. The user can determine which security vulnerabilities must be corrected.

   c. SDM uses a predefined list of security settings for audit.

   d. The security audit automatically corrects all vulnerabilities discovered.

   e. The security audit only reports on vulnerabilities discovered and cannot correct issues.

10. Which of the following statements accurately describe the SDM One-Step Lockdown (select all that apply)?

   a. The One-Step Lockdown only secures parameters that are first identified by the user.

   b. A security audit must be run before the One-Step Lockdown to determine current vulnerabilities.

   c. There are no user-configurable options in the One-Step Lockdown.

   d. There are no reports of "vulnerabilities to be corrected" in the One-Step Lockdown.

   e. The One-Step Lockdown process asks the user for confirmation of each corrective measure before execution.

The answers to the "Do I Know This Already?" quiz are found in Appendix A, "Answers to the 'Do I Know This Already?' Quizzes and Q&A Sections." The suggested choices for your next step are as follows:

■ **6 or fewer overall score**—Read the entire chapter. This includes the "Foundation Topics," "Foundation Summary," and "Q&A" sections.

■ **7 or 8 overall score**—Begin with the "Foundation Summary" section, and then go to the "Q&A" section.

■ **9 or more overall score**—If you want more review on these topics, skip to the "Foundation Summary" section, and then go to the "Q&A" section. Otherwise, move to the next chapter.

Foundation Topics

Router Vulnerability

A Cisco IOS router, like many other network devices, has a variety of services enabled by default. Such services help with network management and maintenance. The exposure of such services is normally protected by a perimeter firewall. However, devices that sit outside of the firewall are exposed and vulnerable to attack. Figure 18-1 shows a typical corporate network.

Figure 18-1 *Corporate Network*

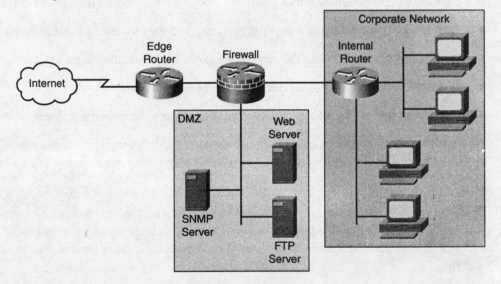

The corporate network and demilitarized zone (DMZ) shown in Figure 18-1 is protected from Internet threats by the firewall. Normally, additional services are permitted onto the DMZ, and access to the corporate network itself is more restricted. Assuming that sufficient policies are configured on the firewall, the corporate network should be sheltered. The internal network contains a multitude of routers, switches, user workstations, and servers.

The DMZ offers services to the public Internet. Devices in the DMZ are behind the firewall, but are purposely more accessible than those in the corporate network. The firewall permits particular ports to specific devices in the DMZ, and additional security is provided by the server/host operating systems.

Although the edge router might be physically similar to any of the internal routers, its location outside of the firewall makes it the first device visible to attackers. Many of the Cisco IOS services that are enabled by default to ease management create vulnerabilities in this circumstance. Such services should be disabled to enhance overall network security.

Vulnerable Router Services

There are a number of router services that are considered security threats. To simplify the list, the services are grouped into categories. Each of these categories is expanded in greater detail later in the chapter.

- **Unnecessary services and interfaces**—Services that are generally not needed

- **Common management services**—Services that assist in network management of the router

- **Path integrity mechanisms**—Services that can affect the forwarding plane in the router

- **Probes and scans**—Services that may return excessive information to an attacker

- **Terminal access security**—Services that help protect the router

- **Gratuitous and proxy ARP**—Services that help identify devices on a segment

Within each of these categories are a number of services. The following sections describe what the services are, how they are normally used, and whether they should remain active in a Cisco IOS router.

Disabling so many services on every network device can be a very tedious process. At a minimum, such services should be disabled on the perimeter routers. Because of the sheer volume of necessary adjustments, such services are typically left enabled on many routers, and the network is at risk.

It is important to realize that most of these services should be disabled to avoid any vulnerabilities. The sections that follow describe each service and how to disable it.

Unnecessary Services and Interfaces

This category of services is by far the largest one. Many services in this category are used to transfer configuration files and Cisco IOS images to the router. As such, these services can be exploited if left unattended. Table 18-2 provides a description of these unnecessary services, their default configuration, and how to disable them.

Table 18-2 *Router Vulnerability: Unnecessary Services and Interfaces*

Service	Description	Default	Disable
Router interfaces	Provide packet access in to and out of the router. It is possible that a connection is severed by removing the cable from an active interface. In this case, it is important to also logically disable the interface. This action prevents the interface from becoming active if a cable is accidentally or maliciously connected.	Disabled (in a Cisco router with no user configuration)	(config-if)# **shutdown**
BOOTP server	This service permits the router to act as a BOOTP server for other network devices. Such a service is rarely needed in modern networks, and should be disabled.	Enabled	(config)# **no ip bootp server**
Cisco Discovery Protocol (CDP)	CDP periodically advertises information between Cisco devices, such as the type of device and Cisco IOS version. Such information could be used to determine vulnerabilities and launch specific attacks. Unless needed inside the network, this service should be disabled globally or disabled on unnecessary interfaces.	Enabled (globally and interface)	(config)# **no cdp run** (config-if)# **no cdp enable**
Configuration auto-loading	This service permits a router to automatically load a configuration file from a network server upon boot. This service should remain disabled when not needed.	Disabled	(config)# **no service config**
FTP server	This service permits the router to act as an FTP server for specific files in flash memory. It should remain disabled when not needed.	Disabled	(config)# **no ftp-server enable**
TFTP server	This service permits the router to act as a TFTP server for specific files in flash memory. It should remain disabled when not in use.	Disabled	(config)# **no tftp-server** *file-sys*:*image-name*
NTP service	This service both receives a time-of-day clock from an NTP server and allows the router to act as an NTP server to NTP clients. Correct time is necessary for accurate time stamps when logging messages. This service should be disabled if not needed, or restricted to only devices that require NTP services.	Disabled	(config)# **no ntp server** *ip-address*

continues

Table 18-2   *Router Vulnerability: Unnecessary Services and Interfaces (Continued)*

Service	Description	Default	Disable
Packet assembler/ disassembler (PAD) service	This service allows access to X.25 PAD commands in an X.25 network. Such a service is rarely needed in modern networks, and should be disabled.	Enabled	(config)# **no service pad**
TCP and UDP minor services	These services execute small servers (daemons) in the router, typically used for diagnostics. They are rarely used and should be disabled.	Enabled (before 11.3) Disabled (11.3 and greater)	(config)# **no service tcp-small-servers** (config)# **no service udp-small-servers**
Maintenance Operation Protocol (MOP) service	This service is a Digital Equipment Corporation (DEC) maintenance protocol. Such a service is rarely needed in modern networks, and should be disabled.	Enabled (most Ethernet interfaces)	(config-if)# **no mop enabled**

Common Management Services

Services in this category are used to transfer configuration files and Cisco IOS images to the router. As such, these services can be exploited if left unattended. Table 18-3 provides a description of these common management services, their default configuration, and how to disable them.

Table 18-3   *Router Vulnerability: Common Management Services*

Service	Description	Default	Disable
Simple Network Management Protocol (SNMP)	This service permits the router to respond to queries and configuration requests. If not used, this service should be disabled. If needed, restrict access to the router via access control lists (ACL), and use SNMPv3 for additional security features.	Enabled	(config)# **no snmp-server enable**
HTTP Configuration and Monitoring	This service allows the router to be monitored and configured from a web browser. SDM uses secure HTTP (HTTPS). If not used, this service should be disabled. If needed, restrict access to the router via ACLs, and use HTTPS for encrypted data transfer.	Device dependent	(config)# **no ip http server** (config)# **no ip http secure-server**
Domain Name Service (DNS)	Cisco routers use 255.255.255.255 as the default address to reach a DNS server for name resolution. If not used, this service should be disabled. If needed, explicitly set the address of the DNS server.	Enabled (client service)	(config)# **no ip domain-lookup**

Path Integrity Mechanisms

Services in this category are used to transfer configuration files and Cisco IOS images to the router. As such, these services can be exploited if left unattended. Table 18-4 provides a description of these path integrity mechanisms, their default configuration, and how to disable them.

Table 18-4   *Router Vulnerability: Path Integrity Mechanisms*

Service	Description	Default	Disable
ICMP Redirects	This service causes the router to send an ICMP redirect message when a packet is forwarded out the interface it arrived on. An attacker can use such information to redirect packets to an untrusted device. This service should be disabled when not needed.	Enabled	(config)# **no ip icmp redirect** (config-if)# **no ip redirects**
IP Source Routing	This service allows the sender to control the route that a packet travels through a network. Such a service can permit an attacker to bypass the normal forwarding path and security mechanisms in a network. Because most network devices should not attempt to dictate their preferred path through the network, this service should be disabled.	Enabled	(config)# **no ip source-route**

Probes and Scans

Services in this category can be used to glean information for reconnaissance attacks. As such, these services can be exploited if left unattended. Table 18-5 provides a description of these probes and scans, their default configuration, and how to disable them.

Table 18-5   *Router Vulnerability: Probes and Scans*

Service	Description	Default	Disable
Finger service	The finger protocol (port 79) retrieves a list of users from a network device, which includes the line number, connection name, idle time, and terminal location. Such information is also seen in the **show users** Cisco IOS command, and can be used for reconnaissance attacks. This service should be disabled when not needed.	Enabled	(config)# **no service finger**
ICMP unreachable notification	This service notifies a sender of invalid destination IP subnets or specific addresses. Such information can be used to map a network. This service should be disabled.	Enabled	(config-if)# **no ip unreachables**

continues

Table 18-5 *Router Vulnerability: Probes and Scans (Continued)*

Service	Description	Default	Disable
ICMP mask reply	This service sends the IP subnet mask when it is requested. Such information can be used to map a network. This service should be disabled on interfaces to untrusted networks.	Disabled	(config-if)# **no ip mask-reply**
IP directed broadcasts	A directed broadcast can be used to probe or deny service to (via a DoS attack) an entire subnet. The directed broadcast packet is unicast until it reaches the router that is responsible for the segment. At that time, the packet becomes a broadcast for the specified segment. This service should be disabled.	Enabled (Cisco IOS Software releases prior to 12.0) Disabled (Cisco IOS Software Release 12.0 and later)	(config-if)# **no ip directed-broadcast**

Terminal Access Security

Services in this category can be used to gather information about router users or to launch DoS attacks. As such, these services can be exploited if left unattended. Table 18-6 provides a description of these terminal access security services, their default configuration, and how to disable them.

Table 18-6 *Router Vulnerability: Terminal Access Security Services*

Service	Description	Default	Disable/Enable
IP identification service	The identification protocol (RFC 1413) reports the identity of the TCP connection initiator. Such information can be used in reconnaissance attacks. This service should be disabled.	Enabled	To disable this service, enter (config)# **no ip identd**.
TCP keepalives	TCP keepalives help clean up TCP connections when a remote host has stopped processing TCP packets (such as after a reboot). This service should be enabled to help prevent certain DoS attacks.	Disabled	To enable this service, enter (config)# **service tcp-keepalives-in**. (config)# **service tcp-keepalives-out**

Gratuitous and Proxy ARP

Services in this category can be used to gather information about router users or to launch DoS attacks. As such, these services can be exploited if left unattended. Table 18-7 provides a description of these gratuitous and proxy ARP services, their default configuration, and how to disable them.

Table 18-7 *Router Vulnerability: Gratuitous and Proxy ARP Services*

Service	Description	Default	Disable
Gratuitous ARP	This service is the primary means used in ARP poisoning attacks. Unless needed, this service should be disabled.	Enabled	(config)# **no ip arp gratuitous**
Proxy ARP	This service permits the router to resolve Layer 2 addresses. This feature is only useful if the router is acting as a Layer 2 bridge. Because this is unlikely in modern networks, this service should be disabled.	Enabled	(config)# **no ip arp proxy**

Using AutoSecure to Secure a Router

Due to the number of CLI commands needed to manually disable services in an attempt to make the router more secure, some routers might not be as protected as they should be. Also, as new features and services become available, additional configurations are necessary to protect against new threats. To combat the mountain of manual configuration statements, Cisco introduced the AutoSecure feature.

AutoSecure helps router administrators secure Cisco IOS Software by automatically performing a variety of functions. AutoSecure is available in Cisco IOS Software Release 12.3 and later. AutoSecure can execute automatically or interactively. In automatic mode, default settings are applied to all security settings. With interactive mode, the user is permitted to select options and features individually.

AutoSecure performs a variety of Cisco IOS router functions. It was shown earlier how to disable many unnecessary features. In addition to disabling unneeded functions, AutoSecure also enables additional Cisco IOS security parameters. The following router functions are performed with AutoSecure:

- **Management plane services and functions**—Include finger, PAD, UDP and TCP small servers, password encryption, TCP keepalives, CDP, BOOTP, HTTP, source routing, gratuitous ARP, proxy ARP, IMCP redirects, ICMP mask replies, directed broadcast, MOP, and banner.

- **Forwarding plane services and functions**—Include CEF and ACLs, which affect every packet flowing through the router.

- **Firewall services and functions**—Include Cisco IOS firewall inspection for common protocols, which permits deep packet inspection on data flows through the IOS router.

- **Logging functions**—Include event logging and password security to keep track of events (attempted attacks) on your network devices.

- **NTP**—Ensures that NTP is securely configured to prevent abuse of the NTP information.

- **SSH access**—Prefer encrypted SSH access compared to clear-text Telnet to prevent packet sniffers from capturing telnet session data.

- **TCP intercept services**—Prevent TCP SYN-flooding attacks, which are a form of DoS attack.

AutoSecure is enabled with the following privileged mode (not configuration mode) Cisco IOS command:

```
Router# auto secure [management | forwarding] [no-interact | full] [login | ntp | ssh |
   firewall | tcp-intercept]
```

full is the default option of this command. This means that the user is prompted (interactively) for input to all security features. **no-interact** induces automatic mode, which applies default configurations to all security parameters without user involvement.

If individual options are selected (**login**, **ntp**, **ssh**, **firewall**, or **tcp-intercept**), only **management** or **forwarding** can be secured at any given time, and only one of **login**, **ntp**, **ssh**, **firewall**, or **tcp-intercept** can be secured at a time. You can run the **auto secure** Cisco IOS command many times to configure a different feature each time, or select the **full** option for all features. Each time the command is executed, the user has the choice of automatic mode (**no-interact**) or interactive mode (no option specified).

When **auto secure full** privileged-mode IOS command is executed, the following steps are performed in sequence:

1. **Identify the outside interface(s)**—Select the Internet-facing interfaces.

2. **Secure the management plane**—Enable and/or disable services and functions mentioned earlier.

3. **Create a security banner**—Configure a message that is displayed when the router is accessed. Remember that a banner is at best a warning, and does not actually prevent an attack.

4. **Configure passwords, AAA, and SSH**—Configure secure modes/features to access the router to include minimum password length, login failure tolerance, AAA, and enable SSH instead of telnet.

5. **Secure the interfaces**—Disable various features mentioned earlier, such as **no ip redirects**, **no ip proxy-arp**, **no ip unreachables**, **no ip directed-broadcast**, **no ip mask-reply**, and **no mop enabled** (on Ethernet interfaces).

6. **Secure the forwarding plane**—Enable CEF, uRFP (if possible), and CBAC (router firewall feature).

The default commands applied by AutoSecure are shown for reference in the "AutoSecure Default Configurations" section at the end of this chapter.

AutoSecure creates a series of Cisco IOS commands and applies them to the running configuration of the router (all "behind the scenes"). As with any configuration opportunity, there is a chance that the procedure could fail before completion. This procedure executes without any notification to the administrator. A failure in the middle of AutoSecure would mean that the router is not as protected as originally thought.

There are two ways to mitigate the failure of the AutoSecure process:

■ As should be done before any configuration modification, manually save the running configuration to either NVRAM, flash, or a network server prior to starting the AutoSecure process. Should AutoSecure only install a partial configuration, you can revert to your copy of the untouched configuration file.

■ Starting with Cisco IOS Software Release 12.3(8)T, AutoSecure creates a copy of the running configuration file for you as part of the AutoSecure process. A snapshot of the running configuration file is saved in flash as pre_autosec.cfg. If this file is needed, it can be restored with the command **configure replace flash:pre_autosec.cfg**.

Using SDM to Secure a Router

As seen in Chapter 13, "Site-to-Site VPN Operations," SDM is a web-based utility used to configure, monitor, and secure a Cisco router. Manually configuring the router to safeguard against many possible threats is an arduous task. In the CLI, the **auto secure** command automates the overall security process of the router.

In SDM, there are two separate wizards that help secure the router. Both are accessed by going to the Configure page and choosing Security Audit in the Tasks bar. Figure 18-2 shows how to access the two different wizards.

Figure 18-2 *SDM Security Audit*

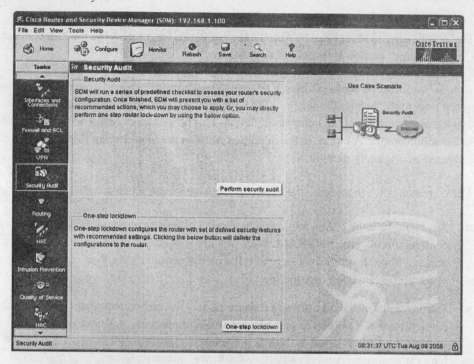

The first wizard is the Security Audit Wizard. This wizard scans the router configuration and reports both good and bad findings. Any or all of the shortcomings can be corrected at the end of the wizard. The second wizard is the One-Step Lockdown. This wizard applies a series of configurations to the router to secure against many vulnerabilities. The execution of this wizard is similar to the **full** option of the **auto secure** CLI command. The sections that follow explore each of these wizards in greater detail.

SDM Security Audit Wizard

As previously described, you access the SDM Security Audit Wizard by choosing the Security Audit task on the Configure page. The upper box on this window (see Figure 18-2) discusses the security audit process. You launch the audit and the wizard by clicking the **Perform Security Audit** button.

The first screen of the Security Audit Wizard is the Welcome to the Security Audit Wizard page. The page explains that the security audit will do the following:

- Check the router's running configuration against a list of predefined security configuration settings

- List identified problems, and then provide recommendations for fixing them

- Allow the user to choose which identified problem(s) to fix, and then display the appropriate user interface for fixing them

- Configure the router with the user-chosen security configuration

At the bottom of this screen, click **Next>** to continue to the wizard, or click **Cancel** to return to the Security Audit Configure page.

The next step in the Security Audit Wizard is the Security Audit Interface Configuration page. This page lists all the active interfaces in the router, and enables you to configure each interface as either an outside (untrusted) or inside (trusted) interface. If an interface is not listed here, you must first enable and configure it by using the Interfaces and Connections Configure task (not detailed in this book).

Figure 18-3 shows the Security Audit Interface Configuration page.

Figure 18-3 *SDM Security Audit Interface Configuration Page*

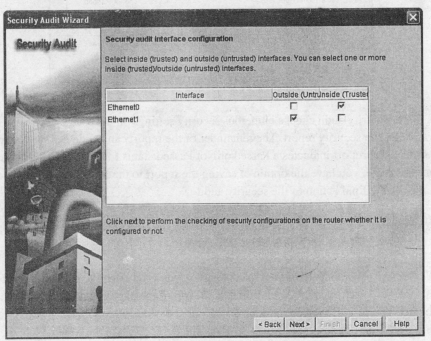

This page starts with all check boxes empty. In Figure 18-3, Ethernet0 has been selected as the Inside (Trusted) interface, and Ethernet1 has been chosen as the Outside (Untrusted) interface. Once all active interfaces of the router have been properly categorized, click **Next>**.

Now that SDM knows which interfaces are Inside and Outside, it compares the current configuration with an extensive list (more than 30 items) of appropriate security configurations. Figure 18-4 shows the results of this interface security validation.

Figure 18-4 *SDM Security Audit Security Report*

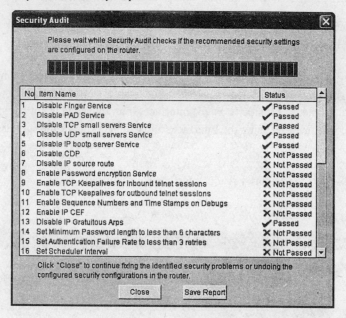

The SDM security audit checks numerous security settings on the router. Figure 18-4 shows only a portion of the security report. The remainder of the report can be viewed by dragging the scroll bar down. The report indicates a Passed or Not Passed status for each of the criteria evaluated. From this page, you have the option of saving the report to the local hard drive. Click **Close** to advance to the final action of the security audit.

The last action in the security audit is to correct the Not Passed issues that were displayed in the security report. Figure 18-5 shows this final page.

If the Security Problems Identified list is lengthy, you might need to use the scroll bar to see all the problems. Clicking the **Fix All** button at the top of the page checks each individual Fix it box in the list. You can also select check boxes individually for correction. Once you have checked the appropriate Fix it boxes, click **Next>** to apply the corrections to the router. Note that the <Back button on this page, although active, does not work. The entire security audit process must be run again to return to the security report.

Figure 18-5   *SDM Security Audit Fix-It Page*

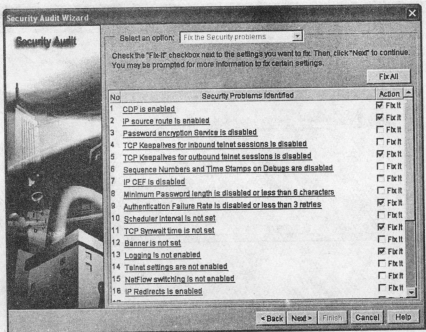

Application of the features is a two-step process. The first screen (after clicking **Next>**) is a summary screen of the features that will be applied. This list corresponds to the Fix it list from the previous screen. It is possible to return to the previous screen with the **<Back** button. This might be necessary to select additional corrective measures or remove selected corrective measures. Click **Finish** to cause SDM to push the appropriate configurations to the router. Click **OK** on the Command Delivery Status window to confirm the corrective actions and exit the Security Audit Wizard.

Once the wizard is finished, you are returned to the Security Audit Configure page, where you can run another security audit or perform the One-Step Lockdown.

SDM One-Step Lockdown Wizard

The SDM One-Step Lockdown Wizard is a web-based solution that works similarly to the **auto secure** Cisco IOS command. To access the wizard, click the **One-step lockdown** button at the bottom of the Security Audit Configure page. Doing so results in the immediate display of a warning, as shown in Figure 18-6.

Figure 18-6 *SDM One-Step Lockdown Wizard*

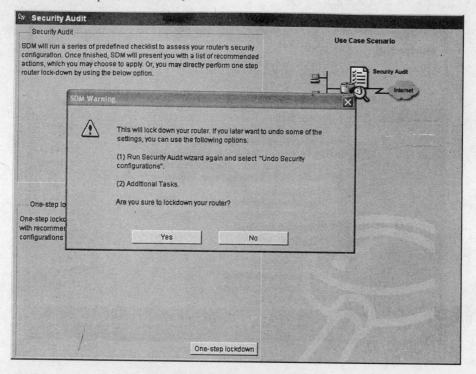

There are no user-configurable options in the One-Step Lockdown Wizard. There are no reminders of what will be secured or what steps will be performed. The One-Step Lockdown Wizard performs every corrective action that was shown in the security report during the security audit. The complete list of correctable actions is shown later in this chapter. The list is not part of the certification test, but you should understand which actions will be taken before you decide to proceed with the lockdown.

AutoSecure Default Configurations

This section shows the default configurations that are applied with the **auto secure full** Cisco IOS command. This list of configuration commands is not part of the certification exam, but serves as a reference as to the scope of the **auto secure** command.

```
! disable several global services
no service finger
no service pad
no service udp-small-servers
no service tcp-small-servers
service password-encryption
service tcp-keepalives-in
service tcp-keepalives-out
no cdp run
```

```
no ip bootp server
no ip http server
no ip finger
no ip source-route
no ip gratuitous-arp
no ip identd

! banner provided by the user
banner # This banner is created by the user #

! log after ten failed login attempts
security authentication failure rate 10 log

! enable passwords provided by the user
enable secret 5 $1$6NpI$ClSvtL5Zs63fPpsQT5Dyq/
enable password 7 09674F04100916

! configure AAA and apply the lines
aaa new-model
aaa authentication login local-auth local
line con 0
 login authentication local-auth
 exec-timeout 5 0
 transport output telnet
line aux 0
 login authentication local-auth
 exec-timeout 10 0
 transport output telnet
line vty 0 4
 login authentication local-auth
 exec-timeout 10 0
 transport input telnet

! login security
login block-for 5 attempts 3 within 5

! hostname and domain-name are needed for key generation
hostname testrouter
ip domain-name company.com
crypto key generate rsa general-keys modulus 1024
ip ssh time-out 60
ip ssh authentication-retries 2

! add ssh to the vty lines
vty line 0 4
 transport input ssh telnet

! logging parameters
service timestamps debug datetime msec localtime show-timezone
service timestamps log datetime msec localtime show-timezone
service sequence-numbers
logging facility local2
logging trap debugging
logging console critical
logging buffered

! disable interface services
interface <something> 0/0
 no ip redirects
 no ip proxy-arp
 no ip unreachables
 no ip directed-broadcast
 no ip mask-reply
 no mop enabled (only on Ethernet interfaces)

! enable CEF
```

```
ip cef

! apply the BOGON ACL (actual ACL not shown) and configure uRPF to the outside interface
interface <outside> 0/0
 ip access-group autosec_complete_bogon in
exit
access-list 100 permit udp any any eq bootpc
interface <outside> 0/0
 ip verify unicast source reachable-via rx allow-default 100

! configure CBAC
ip inspect audit-trail
ip inspect dns-timeout 7
ip inspect tcp idle-time 14400
ip inspect udp idle-time 1800
ip inspect name autosec_inspect cuseeme timeout 3600
ip inspect name autosec_inspect ftp timeout 3600
ip inspect name autosec_inspect http timeout 3600
ip inspect name autosec_inspect rcmd timeout 3600
ip inspect name autosec_inspect realaudio timeout 3600
ip inspect name autosec_inspect smtp timeout 3600
ip inspect name autosec_inspect tftp timeout 30
ip inspect name autosec_inspect udp timeout 15
ip inspect name autosec_inspect tcp timeout 3600

! apply CBAC to the outside interface
ip access-list extended auto_firewall_acl
 permit udp any any eq bootpc
 deny ip any any
interface <outside> 0/0
 ip inspect autosec_inspect out
 ip access-group autosec_firewall_acl in
```

SDM One-Step Lockdown Default Configurations

This section shows the default configurations that are applied with the SDM One-Step Lockdown. This list of configuration features is not part of the certification exam, but serves as a reference as to the scope of the One-Step Lockdown Wizard.

■ Disable:

— Both TCP and UDP small servers service

— CDP

— Finger service

— IP BOOTP server service

— IP directed broadcast

— IP gratuitous ARPs

— IP identification service

— IP mask reply

— IP proxy ARP

- — IP redirects

- — IP source route

- — IP unreachables on all interfaces

- — MOP service

- — PAD service

- — SNMP

- ■ Enable:

    - — Firewall (CBAC) on outside interfaces

    - — IP CEF

    - — Password encryption service

    - — Logging

    - — NetFlow switching

    - — Sequence numbers and time stamps on debugs

    - — SSH for access to the router

    - — TCP keepalives for both inbound and outbound Telnet sessions

    - — Telnet settings

    - — uRPF on outside interfaces

- ■ Set:

    - — Access class on HTTP server service and VTY lines

    - — Authentication failure rate to less than three retries

    - — Banner

    - — Enable secret password

    - — Minimum password length to greater than or equal to six characters

    - — Scheduler interval and allocation

    - — TCP SYN wait time

    - — Users

Foundation Summary

Vulnerable router services include

- **Unnecessary services and interfaces**—Services that are generally not needed

- **Common management services**—Services that assist in network management of the router

- **Path integrity mechanisms**—Services that can affect the forwarding plane in the router

- **Probes and scans**—Services that may return excessive information to an attacker

- **Terminal access security**—Services that help protect the router

- **Gratuitous and proxy ARP**—Services that help identify devices on a segment

The unnecessary services and interfaces that should be disabled include

- Router interfaces

- BOOTP server

- CDP

- Configuration auto-loading

- FTP server

- TFTP server

- NTP server

- PAD

- TCP and UDP minor services

- MOP

The common management services that should be verified include

- SNMP

- HTTP access to the router

- DNS

The path integrity mechanisms that should be verified include

■   ICMP redirects

■   IP source routing

The services that permit probes and scans that should be disabled include

■   Finger

■   ICMP unreachables

■   ICMP mask replies

■   IP directed broadcasts

The terminal access security services that should be verified include

■   IP identification

■   TCP keepalives

The ARP services that should be disabled include

■   Gratuitous ARP

■   Proxy ARP

AutoSecure secures the following router functions:

■   Management plane services and functions

■   Forwarding plane services and functions

■   Firewall services and functions

■   Logging functions

■   NTP protocol

■   SSH access

■   TCP intercept services

Management plane services and functions secured by AutoSecure include

■   Finger

■   PAD

- UDP and TCP small servers

- Password encryption

- TCP keepalives

- CDP

- BOOTP

- HTTP

- Source routing

- Gratuitous ARP

- Proxy ARP

- IMCP redirects

- ICMP mask replies

- Directed broadcast

- MOP

- Banner

Forwarding plane services and functions secured by AutoSecure include

- CEF

- ACLs

The privileged mode command used to invoke the AutoSecure process is

```
Router# auto secure [management | forwarding] [no-interact | full] [login | ntp | ssh |
  firewall | tcp-intercept]
```

full is the default option, which means that the user is prompted (interactively) for all security features.

When **full** mode is executed, the following steps are executed in sequence:

1. **Identify the outside interface(s)**—Select the Internet-facing interfaces.

2. **Secure the management plane**—Enable and/or disable services and functions mentioned earlier.

3. **Create a security banner**—Configure a message that is displayed when the router is accessed. Remember that a banner is at best a warning and does not actually prevent an attack.

4. **Configure passwords, AAA, and SSH**—Configure secure modes/features to access the router, including to include minimum password length, login failure tolerance, AAA, and enable SSH instead of telnet.

5. **Secure the interfaces**—Disable various features mentioned earlier, such as **no ip redirects**, **no ip proxy-arp**, **no ip unreachables**, **no ip directed-broadcast**, **no ip mastmask-reply**, and **no mop enabled** (on Ethernet interfaces).

AutoSecure creates a copy of the running configuration file in flash as pre_autosec.cfg.

The pre-AutoSecure configuration can be restored with the following command:

```
Router# configure replace flash:pre_autosec.cfg
```

In SDM, there are two separate wizards that help secure the router: the Security Audit Wizard and the One-Step Lockdown Wizard.

The SDM security audit does the following:

■ Checks the router's running configuration against a list of predefined security configuration settings

■ Lists identified problems and then provides recommendations for fixing them

■ Allows the user to choose which identified problem(s) to fix and then displays the appropriate user interface for fixing them

■ Configures the router with the user-chosen security configuration

The SDM Security Audit process consists of

■ Determining inside and outside interfaces

■ Performing an audit of various security options in the router

■ Allowing the user to select which shortcomings must be corrected

■ Creating a list of configurations to correct the indicated security vulnerabilities

■ Applying the security configurations

Features of the SDM One-Step Lockdown process include

■ No user-configurable options

■ No reminders of what is secured

■ Automatic security audit to determine vulnerabilities

Q&A

The questions and scenarios in this book are designed to be challenging and to make sure that you know the answer. Rather than allowing you to derive the answers from clues hidden inside the questions themselves, the questions challenge your understanding and recall of the subject.

Hopefully, mastering these questions will help you limit the number of exam questions on which you narrow your choices to two options, and then guess.

You can find the answers to these questions in Appendix A. For more practice with exam-like question formats, use the exam engine on the CD-ROM.

1. How should CDP be treated in a secure router?

2. What are some of the legacy protocols and services that should simply be disabled?

3. What are some of the ICMP features that should be disabled?

4. Which ARP features should be disabled?

5. What is an issue with manually configuring security options and features into a Cisco IOS router?

6. How can AutoSecure help secure a Cisco IOS router?

7. What is the Cisco IOS command to launch AutoSecure to automatically secure all options?

8. What AutoSecure option forces all security parameters to be properly configured?

9. What are the general sequential tasks that AutoSecure performs?

10. How is it possible to recover from a failed AutoSecure process?

11. What are the two security wizards offered by SDM?

12. What type of input does the user have in the Security Audit Wizard?

13. What type of input does the user have in the One-Step Lockdown Wizard?

Exam Topic List

This chapter covers the following topics that you need to master for the CCNP ISCW exam:

- **Router Access**—Examines the various physical and logical ways to access a Cisco router.

- **Password Considerations**—Describes the best way to construct passwords for network devices.

- **Set Login Limitations**—Describes how to limit the number of failed login attempts into the router.

- **Setup Mode**—Covers the script that performs basic router configuration, including passwords.

- **CLI Passwords**—Describes all password options that can be configured in the CLI.

- **Additional Line Protections**—Covers other IOS features to further protect the console, aux, and vty lines.

- **Password Length Restrictions**—Describes how longer passwords are more difficult to guess or break.

- **Password Encryption**—Describes how password encryption prevents password compromise if the configuration is compromised.

- **Create Banners**—Describes how to create banners which are used to warn others that the network is for authorized use only.

- **Provide Individual Logins**—Explains how each administrator can have an individual login to the router rather than a shared password.

- **Create Multiple Privilege Levels**—Describes the various customized privilege levels that can be created to limit access to CLI commands.

- **Role-Based CLI**—Explains how role-based CLI overcomes some of the shortcomings of privilege levels.

- **Prevent Physical Router Compromise**—Covers how physical security is sometimes forgotten.

CHAPTER 19

Securing Administrative Access

A network is only as secure as its weakest link. So far, this book has examined how to create secure paths for user data as it traverses the network. Chapter 18, "Cisco Device Hardening," looked at how to minimize vulnerabilities on an IOS device by eliminating unnecessary services and features; however, it is also important to consider securing permitted access to the router itself.

A compromised router can yield a treasure chest of information to an attacker. The knowledge of internal networks and subnets can be used to create targeted attacks. Privileged-mode access to a router gives the attacker the ability to disable security features that keep the network and the users safe.

It is extremely important that only authorized administrators have access to network infrastructure devices. Additionally, there might be different *levels* of administrative access and configuration responsibilities. Cisco IOS software has a number of tools that permit very granular control of both access to and configuration of an IOS device. This chapter explores many of these features.

"Do I Know This Already?" Quiz

The purpose of the "Do I Know This Already?" quiz is to help you decide whether you really need to read the entire chapter. If you already intend to read the entire chapter, you do not necessarily need to answer these questions now.

The 19-question quiz, derived from the major sections in the "Foundation Topics" portion of the chapter, helps you to determine how to spend your limited study time.

Table 19-1 outlines the major topics discussed in this chapter and the "Do I Know This Already?" quiz questions that correspond to those topics.

Table 19-1 *"Do I Know This Already?" Foundation Topics Section-to-Question Mapping*

Foundation Topics Section	Questions Covered in This Section	Score
Router Access	1	
Password Considerations	2	
Set Login Limitations	3–4	
Setup Mode	5	
CLI Passwords	6	
Additional Line Protections	7–8	
Password Length Restrictions	9	
Password Encryption	10	
Create Banners	11	
Provide Individual Logins	12	
Create Multiple Privilege Levels	13–15	
Role-Based CLI	16–18	
Prevent Physical Router Compromise	19	
Total Score		

CAUTION The goal of self-assessment is to gauge your mastery of the topics in this chapter. If you do not know the answer to a question or are only partially sure of the answer, you should mark this question wrong for purposes of self-assessment. Giving yourself credit for an answer that you correctly guess skews your self-assessment results and might provide you with a false sense of security.

1. Which of the following can be accessed by either HTTP or HTTPS?

   a. CLI

   b. SNMP

   c. SDM

   d. Console port

   e. SSH

2. Which of the following password attributes apply to IOS devices (select all that apply)?

   a. Passwords must be a minimum of eight characters.

   b. Only letters and numbers (alphanumerics) can be used.

   c. Any character, including spaces, is permitted.

    d. "Dictionary" passwords are automatically rejected.

    e. The first character of the password cannot be a number or a space.

3. What actions occur when the threshold rate in the command **security authentication failure rate** *threshold-rate* **log** is exceeded (select all that apply)?

    a. The user is no longer permitted to access this router.

    b. A log message is generated that indicates *threshold-rate* failed login attempts.

    c. Logins are not permitted for 15 seconds.

    d. Logins are not permitted for a configurable amount of time.

    e. The router password is automatically changed.

4. Describe the functions of the three parameters in the command **login block-for** *seconds* **attempts** *failed-attempts* **within** *watch-period* (select all that apply)?

    a. *seconds* defines the login window for the user.

    b. *seconds* defines the window where logins are blocked.

    c. *failed-attempts* defines the number of incorrect logins before action is taken.

    d. *failed-attempts* defines the number of incorrect logins before that user is no longer permitted to access the router.

    e. *watch-period* defines the window of time when a successful login must occur or the router is locked down.

    f. *watch-period* defines the window of time where failed logins are monitored.

5. Which of the following passwords can be configured in setup mode (select all that apply)?

    a. enable secret

    b. enable

    c. console

    d. aux

    e. vty

6. What does the **login** command on the console, aux, or vty ports do?

    a. It enables access to the specific port—without it, users cannot access the port.

    b. It enables password verification—without it, misspelled passwords still grant access.

    c. It permits immediate access to the port without the need for passwords.

    d. It enables password checking—without it, even configured passwords are not used.

    e. It ensures that proper use credentials are used, either from the local database or the AAA server.

7. Which of the following access lists should be used in an access class to permit Telnet connectivity from any host on the 192.168.10.0/24 subnet?

   a. access-list 15 permit 192.168.10.0

   b. access-list 32 permit 192.168.10.0 255.255.255.0

   c. access-list 19 permit subnet 192.168.10.0

   d. access-list 63 permit 192.168.10.0 /24

   e. access-list 44 permit 192.168.10.0 0.0.0.255

8. Which of the following statements describes the behavior of the **exec-timeout** command?

   a. It forces a logout once the prescribed timer expires.

   b. It forces a logout once the line has been idle for the prescribed amount of time.

   c. It causes the user to reauthenticate after the prescribed amount of time.

   d. It enables a count-down timer on the screen so the user knows how long the session will last.

   e. It causes the router to reboot once the prescribed timer expires.

9. What occurs when the command **security passwords min-length *length*** is implemented?

   a. Only future configured passwords must abide by the minimum length set.

   b. The command cannot be executed if any existing passwords do not meet the criteria.

   c. Existing passwords that do not meet the minimum length criteria are erased.

   d. A warning message is displayed about passwords that do not meet the minimum length criteria.

   e. Existing passwords that do not meet the minimum length are automatically adjusted to comply.

10. When the command **service password-encryption** is entered and then removed, what happens to the passwords in the configuration file?

   a. All passwords are encrypted when the command is applied and decrypted when the command is removed.

   b. All plain-text passwords are encrypted when the command is applied and decrypted when the command is removed.

   c. All passwords are encrypted when the command is applied and remain encrypted when the command is removed.

   d. All plain-text passwords are encrypted when the command is applied and remain encrypted when the command is removed.

   e. Only passwords created after the command is entered are encrypted but remain encrypted when the command is removed.

11. What does a user see upon login with the following banner configuration: **banner motd A THIS IS OUR BANNER A**?

   a. No banner is displayed because no delimiting character exists.

   b. THIS IS OUR BANNER.

   c. This is our banner.

   d. THIS IS OUR B.

   e. A THIS IS OUR BANNER.

12. What are some of the benefits of the **username** command in a Cisco router (select all that apply)?

   a. Individual user passwords limit the sharing of a common password.

   b. Individual passwords are more difficult to guess or break.

   c. Shared passwords must be changed when someone leaves the group.

   d. Individual accounts can never be compromised.

   e. Individual passwords can use stronger encryption.

13. How do the 16 different privilege levels compare to each other?

   a. There are 16 user-defined privilege levels (0 through 15), and the numbers have no significance.

   b. Level 0 equates to user mode, level 1 equates to privileged mode, and the user can customize levels 2 through 15.

   c. The higher the privilege level number, the greater the access into the router.

   d. Levels 0–9 are predefined in Cisco IOS Software, while levels 10–15 can be customized by the user.

   e. Level 0 equates to user mode, level 15 equates to privileged mode, and the user can customize levels 1 through 14.

14. What happens if a user attempts to access a privilege level that does not have a password configured?

   a. The user is granted access because no password is configured.

   b. The user must know the enable secret password of the router to access the privilege level.

   c. The user is not allowed to access the privilege level.

   d. The user can use the password of any of the other configured privilege levels.

   e. The user must use their personal username password to access the level.

15. Consider the following privilege level configuration:

```
Router(config)# privilege configure level 2 interface
Router(config)# privilege exec level 2 show ip interfaces
Router(config)# privilege exec level 2 show running-config
Router(config)# privilege exec level 2 show
Router(config)# enable secret level 2 ciscopriv2
```

What is displayed when a user at privilege level 2 executes a **show running-config** command?

   a. Only the interfaces themselves are displayed.

   b. Only the interfaces and the IP information configured on the interfaces are displayed.

   c. All IP-related information is displayed.

   d. All information from all interfaces is displayed.

   e. The entire configuration file is displayed.

16. What are some of the shortcomings of privilege levels that role-based CLI overcome (select all that apply)?

   a. Each IOS command can only be used in one privilege level, but can be used in multiple role-based CLI views.

   b. Each privilege level is bounded by a maximum number of IOS commands, but role-based CLI views have no limit.

   c. Privilege levels can be assigned to a particular interface, which is not possible with role-based CLI views.

   d. Each privilege is unique and separate from others, where role-based CLI views can be grouped together to form superviews.

   e. There are only 14 user-configurable privilege levels, but there are an unlimited number of role-based CLI views possible.

17. What is the first option that must be configured within a role-based CLI view?

   a. The view name

   b. The view password

   c. The root view

   d. The **show** commands

   e. The **configure terminal** command

18.   Which IOS commands can be configured within a role-based CLI superview?

    a.   **configure** commands

    b.   Only **show** commands

    c.   Only user-mode commands

    d.   All commands

    e.   No commands

19.   Which IOS command disables access to ROMMON mode?

    a.   **no service rommon-access**

    b.   **no service password-recovery**

    c.   **no service rommon-recovery**

    d.   **no service rommon**

    e.   **service rommon-protection**

The answers to the "Do I Know This Already?" quiz are found in Appendix A, "Answers to the 'Do I Know This Already?' Quizzes and Q&A Sections." The suggested choices for your next step are as follows:

■   **15 or fewer overall score**—Read the entire chapter. This includes the "Foundation Topics," "Foundation Summary," and "Q&A" sections.

■   **16 or 17 overall score**—Begin with the "Foundation Summary" section, and then go to the "Q&A" section.

■   **18 or more overall score**—If you want more review on these topics, skip to the "Foundation Summary" section, and then go to the "Q&A" section. Otherwise, move to the next chapter.

Foundation Topics

Router Access

Most network users probably cannot accurately describe the function or purpose of a router; however, if the network is inaccessible for any reason, the router is often blamed. The router, like any computing device, is only as good as its programming. Left alone, the router should continue to operate as well as it has in the past. But routers often receive incremental configuration updates to activate a new feature, correct an existing problem, or plan for an upcoming event.

Access to a router can be both physical and logical. You can configure a Cisco IOS router using these three basic methods:

- **CLI**—The CLI is accessed physically via the console or auxiliary ports, or logically via a Telnet or SSH connection.

- **Web interface**—SDM is used to access and configure the router via HTTP or HTTPS.

- **SNMP**—The router can be polled and configured from an SNMP workstation.

Every Cisco router has a console port. Many also have auxiliary ports. Both offer direct physical connectivity and asynchronous connectivity to the router. The auxiliary port is often used to connect a modem to the router for remote access during times of network instability. But both the console and auxiliary ports can be accessed from a directly connected PC with some terminal-emulation software. The user has access to the CLI with either of these connections.

The IP network also offers a variety of means for any user to access any router. Both Telnet and SSH can be used to access the router CLI. Any user can access the router if the network is functional and either Telnet or SSH is permitted. Any web browser can also access the router via SDM. As with Telnet or SSH, network reachability and permission are the only limiting factors. SNMP is another access method delivered across an IP network. As of 2004, SNMPv3 is the current standard. SNMPv3 adds message integrity, authentication, and encryption to SNMP packets that traverse the network. These features are great enhancements over previous versions of SNMP.

Protection against all these access methods is a combination of proper passwords and access restrictions. Password integrity ensures that passwords are both challenging (to guess) and change often. Access restrictions limit the devices or users that are permitted to log into and configure the router.

Password Considerations

The ability to access a router and activate a new feature, correct an existing problem, or plan for an upcoming event is, in most cases, protected by one or more passwords. The use of passwords is typically how all network resources are sheltered. There are a number of best practices for passwords that should be enforced for all network devices, including:

- **Minimum length**—The more characters in a password, the longer it takes to guess it.

- **Mix of characters**—Passwords should contain a mix of upper- and lowercase letters, numbers, and meta-characters (symbols and spaces). More characters translates to a greater number of combinations that an attacker must try.

- **Do not use dictionary words**—Avoid the use of words found in a dictionary to make a dictionary attack less likely to succeed.

- **Change passwords frequently**—A frequently changed password limits the usefulness of a compromised password, and thus reduces overall exposure.

There are actually a number of access points into a router that should be protected by passwords. Figure 19-1 shows how a router can be accessed.

Figure 19-1 *Router Access Points*

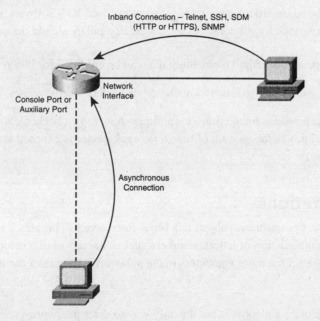

Inband Connection – Telnet, SSH, SDM
(HTTP or HTTPS), SNMP

Network
Interface

Console Port or
Auxiliary Port

Asynchronous
Connection

If a user has direct physical access to a router, an asynchronous connection to the CLI can be established via either the console or auxiliary port. Some routers do not have auxiliary ports, but all have console ports. A terminal-emulation program is needed to establish such a connection.

From the IP network, a user can access the CLI via Telnet or SSH, access the SDM interface via HTTP or HTTPS, or use SNMP to poll/configure a router. As noted earlier, most users likely have no idea what a router is. But for those whose curiosity gets the best of them, the various avenues of approach into the router must be closely guarded.

Every one of the access points mentioned can be protected by passwords, and shielded by access control lists (ACL). The use of ACLs is in the form of access classes, examined later in this chapter. The various passwords in a Cisco device have the following characteristics:

- The password length can be between 1 and 25 characters in length (the longer the better).

- The first character of a password cannot start with a number or a space (leading numbers are illegal, and leading spaces are ignored).

- Within a password, any combination of characters can be used, including alphanumeric characters, upper- and lowercase characters, symbols, and spaces (remember, spaces and numbers cannot be used as the first character of a password).

In addition to the password creation rules inherent in Cisco IOS Software, a password policy should be implemented for all network devices. Such a policy should define criteria such as:

- Minimum password length (something that can be enforced for IOS passwords)

- Password generation tips (such as not using dictionary words, names, and so on)

- Password expiration/change time (to minimize how long a hacker has to crack a password, and/or to minimize the amount of time a network device is exposed after a password compromise)

Set Login Limitations

Even the strongest password is subject to a brute-force attack. This attack simply cycles through every possible combination of letters, numbers, and characters until it discovers the correct password. Of course, the more characters in the password, the greater the number of possible combinations.

Simply making long passwords is not the only way to deter password-guessing attempts. By default, Cisco IOS offers only three chances to log into the router. After the third failed attempt, the connection is reset. However, there is nothing that stops the attacker from repeating their password-thwarting exercise, three guesses at a time.

Many network devices enforce a login failure rate mechanism. Typically, after a preset number of failed logins, the system is locked out for a period of time or the user account is frozen until an administrator can reset it. At a minimum, a log message is created that records the repeated failed login attempts. Cisco IOS has a few of these features also.

Starting with Cisco IOS Software Release 12.3(1), IOS can log failed login attempts. Example 19-1 shows how to set up authentication failure logging.

Example 19-1 *Authentication Failure Rate with Logging*

```
Router(config)# aaa new-model
Router(config)# aaa authentication attempts login 5
Router(config)# aaa authentication login local-policy local
!
Router(config)# security authentication failure rate threshold-rate log
Router(config)#
```

The **security authentication** feature works only when AAA is properly configured. By default, Cisco IOS only permits three login attempts. AAA can be used to adjust this parameter. In Example 19-1, AAA:

- Is enabled (**aaa new-model**).

- Increases the number of login attempts to five (the IOS default is three).

- Creates a policy called **local-policy** that uses the local username database to authenticate users who log into the router.

The **security authentication** command has a single parameter: *threshold-rate*. This defines the number of failed login attempts over one minute that causes a syslog message to be generated. The *threshold-rate* can range between 2 and 1024, and 10 is the default. In addition to a syslog message, a 15-second delay is imposed before any login attempts are again permitted.

Note that the *threshold-rate* must be less than or equal to the **aaa authentication attempts login** setting. Otherwise, AAA will disconnect the connection attempt before the **security authentication** command can log the event.

IOS also offers a series of commands to monitor and block failed login attempts. From configuration mode, the **login** command is used to set parameters regarding failed login attempts. Example 19-2 shows the various **login** options available.

Example 19-2 *Login Failure Options*

```
Router(config)# aaa new-model
Router(config)# aaa authentication attempts login 5
Router(config)# aaa authentication login local-policy local
!
Router(config)# login ?
  block-for    Set quiet-mode active time period
  delay        Set delay between successive fail login
  on-failure   Set options for failed login attempt
  on-success   Set options for successful login attempt
  quiet-mode   Set quiet-mode options
Router(config)#
```

As with the **security authentication** command, AAA must be configured for the **login** feature to be operational. The **login** options enable a variety of features for login attempts into the router:

■   The **block-for** option is the most extensive option. There are three parameters within this option:

   login block-for *seconds* **attempts** *failed-attempts* **within** *watch-period*

   where:

   — *seconds* defines the number of seconds that future login attempts are denied (quiet period).

   — *failed-attempts* defines the number of consecutive failed login attempts that causes the timeout period to be invoked.

   — *watch-period* defines the period of time during which the consecutive failed login attempts must occur to invoke the quiet period.

■   The **delay** option enforces a delay timer between failed login attempts. The timer can range between 1 and 10 seconds. A user (or attacker) must wait the defined delay period before another password can be attempted. This can certainly slow down any attempt to guess passwords.

■   The **on-failure** and **on-success** options enable logging options for failed and successful login attempts (respectively).

■   The **quiet-mode** option maps an access class (identical to the access class used to limit access to the vty ports) to the **login** command. Any devices that are permitted by the access class are exempt from the **login** options.

Once these parameters have been configured, they can be displayed with the command **show login**.

Setup Mode

There are a number of ways to configure passwords in a Cisco router. The first exposure that most router administrators have to configuring passwords in Cisco routers is via the setup utility. This tool runs automatically when the router is reloaded with a blank configuration file (either the configuration file has been erased or the router is new and empty). The script steps through a number of simple configuration scenarios to establish basic network connectivity with the router.

The setup utility can also be run with the **setup** command from privileged mode. Either way, setup mode allows the user to configure passwords for Telnet/SSH access to the router, as well as access to privileged mode. Example 19-3 shows the password configuration portion of the setup script.

Example 19-3   *Use Setup to Configure Passwords*

```
  The enable secret is a password used to protect access to privileged EXEC and
configuration modes. This password, after entered, becomes encrypted in the configuration.
  Enter enable secret: cisco
  The enable password is used when you do not specify an enable secret password, with some
older software versions, and some boot images.
  Enter enable password: cisco
% Please choose a password that is different from the enable secret
  Enter enable password: ciscotest
  The virtual terminal password is used to protect access to the router over a network
interface.
  Enter virtual terminal password: testcisco
```

The first configurable password in setup mode is the enable secret password. Since Cisco IOS Software Release 10.3, this has been the password used to reach privileged mode in the router. The router uses an MD5 one-way hash algorithm to encrypt the password, and is considered virtually irreversible.

The second configurable password in setup mode is the enable password. This password was the original means of reaching privileged mode. If an enable secret password is present in the configuration file, the enable password is not used. It remains a configuration option for backward compatibility (in case the router gets downgraded to something earlier than IOS 10.3). This password is stored in clear text by default.

Note that the setup utility does not permit the enable secret and enable passwords to be the same. It is considered a security vulnerability to have both of these passwords the same, because only the enable secret is encrypted by default. If both passwords are the same, and the configuration file is compromised, then the attacker knows the enable secret password (which would otherwise be extremely difficult to decrypt).

The third configurable password in setup mode is the virtual terminal password. This password is used when a user attempts to access the router via Telnet or SSH. Under normal circumstances, this password offers only user-mode access to the router. This password is also stored in clear text by default.

The setup utility does not offer the ability to configure either the console or auxiliary port passwords. For proper router security, all entry points should be protected. The CLI must be used to configure these two latter passwords.

CLI Passwords

Setup mode offers only three password options; however, you can configure all passwords from the CLI. Example 19-4 shows the CLI commands to configure various passwords in a Cisco router. All passwords are set in configuration mode.

Example 19-4   *Use Configure Mode to Configure Passwords*

```
Router(config)# enable password password
Router(config)# enable secret password
Router(config)# line { console 0 ¦ aux 0 ¦ vty 0 4 }
Router(config-line)# password password
Router(config-line)# login
Router(config-line)#
```

The **enable password** and **enable secret** configuration commands correspond to the similar configuration options from setup mode. Both of these passwords provide access to privileged mode. From here, the user has complete access to the router. Privileged-mode access should be reserved for trusted network administrators.

The console, auxiliary, and virtual terminal ports are considered lines in IOS:

- **console 0** maps to the physical console port.

- **aux 0** maps to the physical auxiliary port.

- **vty 0 4** references the five default logical virtual terminal (vty) access ports into the router.

The enable password, console, aux, and vty passwords are all initially stored unencrypted. Only the enable secret password is immediately encrypted upon creation.

Access via the console, auxiliary, and vty ports initially grants access to user mode. From this mode, various statistics can be examined, but no configuration changes can be performed. The user must elevate the login to privileged mode to modify any parameters in the router.

Both the console and aux ports are physical ports into the router. Both offer asynchronous communication to the router via some terminal-emulation program. The aux port can be used to connect a modem for remote CLI access to the router or dial backup if a primary interfaces fails.

The **login** command on the lines (**con 0, aux 0,** and **vty 0 4**) enables password checking. Without this command (**no login**), the configured password is not checked or used upon line activation. However, with this command, any attempt to access the port requires a password. If the password has been removed, or one was never configured, any attempt to access the router via Telnet or SSH is rejected. Example 19-5 shows a Telnet session to a Cisco IOS router.

Example 19-5 *Router Access*

```
Router2# telnet 192.168.11.110
Trying 192.168.11.110 ... Open

User Access Verification


Password:
Router> enable
Password:
Router#
```

In Example 19-5, any IP device can initiate a Telnet session to 192.168.11.110. When the Telnet client connects to the router, the vty password must be entered. No passwords are ever displayed as a user keys them into Cisco IOS. If the password is successfully entered, the user is granted access to user mode. From there, the **enable** command is used to access privileged mode. The enable or enable secret password is needed to gain access to privileged mode.

Additional Line Protections

A password on the vty ports makes it challenging for users to access the router via Telnet or SSH. However, the use of a password does not restrict who actually has the ability to attempt a Telnet or SSH session. Any device with IP reachability to the router can initiate a Telnet session, and reach the password prompt.

Telnet access can be restricted with the **access-class** command. The access class creates a list of authorized IP addresses/subnets that may establish a Telnet session with the router. Any devices that are not explicitly permitted by the access class are implicitly denied. Example 19-6 shows the application of an access class to the vty ports.

Example 19-6 *Use an Access Class to Protect the vty Ports*

```
Router(config)# access-list 16 permit 192.168.1.11
Router(config)# access-list 16 permit 192.168.4.13
Router(config)# line vty 0 4
Router(config-line)# access-class 16 in
Router(config-line)# password cisco
Router(config-line)# login
Router(config-line)#
```

In Example 19-6, standard access list 16 permits IP addresses 192.168.1.11 and 192.168.4.13. Every other IP address is implicitly denied. This access list is then applied to the vty ports as an inbound access class. When the router receives a Telnet or SSH attempt, the access class compares the source IP address of the inbound request. If the IP address is permitted by the access class, the Telnet/SSH session is granted and the user is prompted for the password. If the IP address is denied by the access class, the Telnet/SSH session is rejected.

It is also possible to configure timeout options on the various lines (console, aux, and vty). This option causes unused sessions to be disconnected after a preset amount of time. By default, IOS disconnects any of the lines after 10 minutes of no activity. Example 19-7 shows how to configure timeout options on the lines.

Example 19-7 *Configure Timeout Options*

```
Router(config)# line { console 0 ¦ aux 0 ¦ vty 0 4 }
Router(config-line)# exec-timeout minutes [ seconds ]
Router(config-line)#
```

Once you have access to the console, aux, or vty lines, apply the **exec-timeout** configuration option. The default is 10 minutes and 0 seconds. If a value for *seconds* is not entered, 0 is applied. Normally, the timeout values should be set to less than the default to ensure that an unattended terminal session is quickly logged out.

It is important to remember that if an access port (console, aux, or vty) is not needed, it should be disabled. It is likely that the console port should always stay enabled. The aux port (if present) should be enabled only if is used for remote access or dial backup. Only the necessary number of vty ports should be enabled.

Password Length Restrictions

The more characters in a password, the more difficult it is to guess. Cisco IOS permits virtually any character to be included in a router password. In a Cisco router, the maximum length of any password is 25 characters. However, by default, a password could be a single character long (certainly not recommended).

Administrative policy for the network should dictate the minimum length for any password used to gain access to a network device. This policy can be enforced in Cisco IOS Software Release 12.3(1) and later. Example 19-8 shows how to implement a minimum password length.

Example 19-8   *Minimum Password Length Enforcement*

```
Router(config)# security passwords min-length length
Router(config)#
```

The range for the minimum password length is from 0 through 16 characters. Recommended practice dictates that a router password should be a minimum of 10 characters. When this restriction is enabled, the creation of any future passwords is restricted by this minimum length. Current passwords are not subject to this setting. You should re-create the current passwords (using the IOS commands shown earlier) to ensure that current passwords meet the restriction imposed by this command.

Password Encryption

All passwords (with the exception of the enable secret) are initially stored in plaintext. This means that anyone who has access to the router configuration file can easily extract all unencrypted passwords. The use of the enable secret password ensures that privileged mode is protected (unless the enable and enable secret passwords are the same).

It is possible to encrypt all plaintext passwords in a Cisco router. Cisco uses an encryption algorithm based on the Vigenere cipher. Example 19-9 shows the plaintext passwords, how to enable password encryption, and the resulting encrypted passwords.

Example 19-9   *Password Encryption*

```
Router# show running-config
...
enable password ciscopassword
...
line con 0
 password ciscotest123
 login
line vty 0 4
 password 123testcisco
 login
...
Router# configure terminal
Enter configuration commands, one per line. End with CNTL/Z.
Router(config)# service password-encryption
Router(config)# end
Router# show running-config
```

continues

Example 19-9 *Password Encryption (Continued)*

```
...
enable password 7 14141B180F0B3A2A373B243A3017
...
line con 0
 password 7 00071A1507541F031C351D1C5A
 login
line vty 0 4
 password 7 11584B56031718180723382727
 login
...
Router#
```

The **service password-encryption** routine encrypts all current plaintext passwords, and any plaintext passwords created in the future (as long as the service is not disabled). As shown in Example 19-9, all encrypted passwords are preceded by the number 7, which indicates encryption based on the Vigenere cipher.

NOTE The encryption algorithm used with the **service password-encryption** utility is relatively weak. A variety of online sites offer routines to decrypt these passwords. Unlike the enable secret password, which cannot be recovered, these encrypted passwords take little effort to decrypt.

Once plaintext passwords are encrypted with the **service password-encryption** routine, they cannot be decrypted by IOS. If this service is disabled (**no service password-encryption**), future passwords will not be encrypted. The only way to put plaintext passwords back into the configuration file is to re-create the passwords with password encryption disabled.

Create Banners

A banner is a message that is displayed upon login to the router. For example, this message can warn users that "access to this site is restricted to authorized personnel." Although the banner does not provide any additional security restrictions, it does clearly define the security policy in use at the site. Example 19-10 shows a sample banner.

Example 19-10 *Message of the Day Banner*

```
Router(config)# banner motd #
** Warning ** - Unauthorized access to this site is strictly prohibited"
#
Router(config)#
```

The Message of the Day (motd) banner appears every time the router is accessed via the console, aux, or vty ports. The banner message itself is between two delimiting characters (in this case, the # character). Any character can be used as the delimiting character, as long as it is not used in the actual banner message. If the delimiting character appears in the banner, the banner message is truncated at that point. Other banners include

- **exec**—A banner that is displayed whenever an EXEC process is created

- **incoming**—A banner that is displayed when a Telnet or SSH session starts

- **login**—A banner that is displayed before the username/password login process starts

Any banner that is used should be reviewed by corporate legal counsel before it is used. A banner should never "welcome" anyone into the router or the site. Such wording could be seen as an invitation to use the site. A banner should be generic and not advertise the router or company name that is being accessed. There is no need to help the hacker perform his job.

Provide Individual Logins

All router passwords that have been examined thus far are shared among all users. Initial access into the router is via the two physical ports (console and aux) or via the vty ports (Telnet or SSH). A single password is shared between administrators who are permitted user-mode access to the router. Not all administrators are permitted access to privileged mode. Thus, the privileged-mode password (enable or enable secret) is more strictly controlled.

One problem with a single password for access is the potential for compromise. A single password, regardless of how challenging it is, can be accidentally shared with unworthy personnel. Also, if a single person leaves the group or company, all shared passwords must be changed and relearned by everyone else. This can be quite a burden in a large organization, even with minimal turnover.

One way to avoid a single access password is to assign unique passwords to each person who has access to the router. The **username** command creates a unique local login for each person who is permitted access to the router. Example 19-11 shows how to create unique logins in Cisco IOS.

Example 19-11 *Configure Unique Usernames*

```
Router(config)# username bobsmith password ciscobob123
Router(config)# username karenjones secret ciscokaren123
Router(config)# line vty 0 4
Router(config-line)# login local
Router(config-line)#
```

In Example 19-11, two unique logins are created: one for bobsmith, and the second for karenjones. Each has a different password assigned. Bob's password is stored in plaintext, unless password encryption is enabled. Karen's password uses the MD5 one-way encryption hash to protect the password in the configuration file. It is preferred to assign a username password with the **secret** option. The **login local** command on the vty lines forces the local username database to be used for access. Example 19-12 shows the login process with usernames enabled.

Example 19-12 *Login Attempt with Usernames Configured*

```
Router2# telnet 192.168.11.110
Trying 192.168.11.110 ... Open

User Access Verification

Username: karenjones
Password:
Router>
```

In Example 19-12, user karenjones successfully logs into the router. Only two users have accounts on this router. Any other user attempt to log into this router would receive a **% Login invalid** error.

Create Multiple Privilege Levels

As seen earlier, the enable and enable secret passwords grant access to privileged mode. Individual logins can be created to ensure that a single, shared password does not get compromised. However, the enable or enable secret password is still a single password that grants access to privileged mode.

Cisco IOS allows the creation of multiple privilege levels. A single privilege mode means that all users who have the password are granted access to all privileged options. Multiple privilege levels permit you to define blocks of commands that are available at the various levels.

There are 16 different privilege levels that can be used. Level 0 is user mode. Level 15 is the all-encompassing privileged mode (enable or enable secret password). Levels 1 through 14 are available for customization and use. Example 19-13 shows how to create privilege levels.

Example 19-13 *Create Privilege Levels*

```
Router(config)# privilege mode level level command
Router(config)# enable secret level level password
```

The **privilege** command is used to add authorized IOS commands to each customized level. This command is likely used multiple times for each privilege level. The **enable secret** command defines the secret password needed to access this particular privilege level. Like any other privileged mode password, this one should be protected and shared only with those who are permitted access to this privilege level. The options in the preceding commands are as follows:

■ The *mode* option selects an exec or configuration option that will be included with this privilege level.

■ The *level* option is any number between 1 and 14. Note that the actual number has no meaning or significance. There are simply 14 different levels that can be created.

■ The *command* option is a specific IOS command at the specified *mode* that is included in this privilege level.

Similar to generic privilege mode access, each level must have its own password. The **enable secret** command configures a particular password (hopefully unique) to a specific privilege level. If a privilege level is not assigned a password, then the level cannot be accessed or used.

Example 19-14 shows a sample privilege level configuration.

Example 19-14 *Create Privilege Levels*

```
Router(config)# privilege interface level 2 ip address
Router(config)# privilege interface level 2 ip
Router(config)# privilege configure level 2 interface
Router(config)# privilege exec level 2 configure terminal
Router(config)# privilege exec level 2 configure
Router(config)# privilege exec level 2 show interfaces
Router(config)# privilege exec level 2 show running-config
Router(config)# privilege exec level 2 show
Router(config)# enable secret level 2 ciscopriv2
Router(config)#
```

In this configuration, users with access to level 2 are allowed to perform the following actions:

■ Access configuration mode

■ Access the interfaces

■ Configure IP addresses on the interfaces

■ Display the interfaces

■ Display the running configuration file

Even though the level 2 user can execute the **show running-config** command, only the **configure** commands that are permitted are actually displayed. A level 2 user cannot view the entire configuration file unless all IOS configuration commands are added to level 2 (which would make it level 15). In Example 19-14, the level 2 user would see only IP address information from the interfaces in the running configuration.

There is one thing to keep in mind when using privilege levels. Each Cisco IOS command that is used (for example, **configure terminal**) can be used with only one privilege level. In Example 19-14, if another privilege level (say 10) is created and uses **configure terminal** as a command, the command would be removed from privilege level 2. The most recently configured privilege level "owns" any commands that are configured in two different privilege levels.

To access a particular privilege level, use the command

```
Router> enable level
Password:
Router#
```

where *level* is the privilege level being accessed. With this access option, any user can attempt to gain access to any privilege level. It is important that the passwords to the various privilege levels remain protected, and that each privilege level use a different password. The user should know the password only of the privilege level that the user has access to. It is not possible to access a customized privilege level that does not have a password (although the lack of an enable password or enable secret does permit access to privileged mode [level 15] if the initial connection is via the console or aux ports). Note that the initial login to the router (to reach the user-mode prompt) is via the common password on the line, or an individual username.

Role-Based CLI

So far, this chapter has explored how to limit which physical devices are permitted to connect to a router (access class on the vty ports). It has also showed how to create individual usernames to control exactly who has access to a router. Finally, this chapter has demonstrated how different privilege levels can be used to control access to various privileged-mode commands in the router.

The use of privilege levels creates tiers of users. Remember that the numbers used for the privilege levels do not imply importance. However, it is good practice to assign higher numbers to privilege levels that access more detailed, descriptive commands.

The use of privilege levels has some shortcomings. Remember that each IOS command can be used in only one privilege level. If there were a need for two different privilege levels to access configuration mode (for two different configuration commands), only one of the privilege levels would actually be allowed to view the configuration file. Also, there is no way to restrict a privilege level. For example, one privilege level can configure all interfaces, but not selected interfaces. By having configuration access to all interfaces, no other privilege levels can configure any interfaces.

Role-based CLI overcomes some of the shortcomings encountered with privilege levels. Role-based CLI creates views, each of which contains a list of IOS commands. Unlike privilege levels, IOS commands can be present in multiple views, which can be grouped together to form superviews. Within a view, commands can be more specific than with privilege levels. A view can be assigned to a particular interface, instead of to all interfaces.

Before IOS commands can be added to a role-based CLI view, the view must be created. The creation and modification of CLI views must be done from the root view. Remember that privilege levels are created from configuration mode. Figure 19-2 shows the hierarchy and relationship between role-based CLI views.

Figure 19-2 *Role-Based CLI Hierarchy*

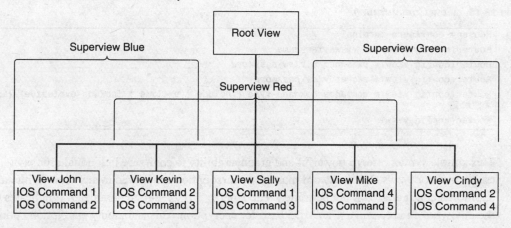

The root view controls access to all other views. Individual views can contain any number of IOS commands. Individual views do not interact with each other, and different views may contain the same IOS commands. The contents of individual views can be collected together in superviews. Creating a superview that combines a few existing views is likely easier than creating a new view with a large number of IOS commands. Plus, the individual views can still be used on their own.

AAA is required to configure role-based CLI views. At a minimum, the command **aaa new-model** must be present in the configuration file. If not, access to views is denied. Example 19-15 shows how to access the root view, and assumes that **aaa new-model** has already been configured.

Example 19-15 *Root View Access*

```
Router> enable view [view-name]
Password:
Router#
```

The optional *view-name* is used to access an individual view. But before an individual view can be accessed, it must be created. **enable view** is used to access the root view. The enable or enable secret password is used to access the root view. Note that the **enable view** command can be issued from either the user-mode or privileged-mode prompt.

Once the root view has been accessed, individual views can be created. There can be a maximum of 15 views in the router (not including the root view). This upper limit also includes superviews, which are explored shortly.

Example 19-16 shows a series of sample commands used to create an individual view. Remember that the root view (**enable view**) must be accessed to configure additional views.

Example 19-16 *View Configuration*

```
Router# configure terminal
Router(config)# parser view view-name
Router(config-view)# password 5 view-password
Router(config-view)# secret view-password
Router(config-view)# commands command-type {include ¦ exclude ¦ include-exclusive} {LINE
  ¦ all}
Router(config-view)#
```

This simple syntax offers a powerful and granular ability to configure individual groups of commands, or views. The password must be the first option configured in any view. Without it, additional configuration is not permitted. The number **5** is a required parameter. It indicates that the password entered will use an MD5 hash for encryption. This is the only encryption option available.

Starting with Cisco IOS 12.4, the **password** option was replaced with the **secret** option. The **secret** option does not need the **5** to indicate an MD5 hash, because the secret is automatically encrypted (unless disabled with the **0** option).

Once the password has been configured, the **commands** option adds IOS commands to the view:

■ The *command-type* selects the command category, such as EXEC, configure, or interface. The actual list is very extensive.

■ You can then decide to **include** commands, **exclude** commands, or **include-exclusive** commands. The latter option means that commands in this view will not be available in other views. This behavior is similar to how privilege levels work.

■ You then select individual commands (**LINE**) or **all** for all commands within the category.

Individual views can be linked together into superviews. The necessary syntax is very similar to what was seen earlier. Example 19-17 shows how to create a superview.

Example 19-17 *Superview Configuration*

```
Router(config)# parser view view-name superview
Router(config-view)# password 5 view-password
Router(config-view)# secret view-password
Router(config-view)# view view-name
Router(config-view)#
```

As with an individual view, a superview also has password protection. Superviews can only link to other views, and cannot contain individual Cisco IOS entries (with the **commands** option). An individual view can be shared among many superviews.

Remember that there can be a maximum of 15 user-defined views (the root view is not included in this count). Resist any temptation to have a large variety of superviews, because that will reduce the number of individual views that can be used. Although superviews link individual views together, only the individual views map to actual Cisco IOS commands.

To access an IOS view, use the following command:

```
Router> enable view view-name
Password:
Router#
```

This is similar to the way to access a privilege level. The user must know which view name they have access to. Unlike privilege levels, view names can be any assortment of letters and numbers, so it is difficult, if not impossible, to simply guess view names. Like privilege levels, each IOS view should have different passwords, and users should know the passwords only to their permitted view.

Note that access to a superview uses the same command, so access to a superview appears no different than access to an individual view.

Prevent Physical Router Compromise

If someone has physical access to the router, then use of the console or aux ports provides a path into the router. If the passwords are not known, it is possible to perform password recovery in an IOS device from the console port (it is not possible to perform this routine from the aux port). Done properly, password recovery reboots the router, accesses ROMMON mode, resets the configuration register, restores the configuration file and network connections, and leaves the router at the privileged-mode prompt.

Network security does start with physical security. If the physical infrastructure is compromised, then routers can be accessed and wires can be tapped. However, Cisco routers offer the option of disabling access to ROMMON mode. To protect ROMMON mode, enter the following:

```
Router(config)# no service password-recovery
```

Every Cisco IOS device has password recovery (ROMMON access) enabled by default. The **no service password-recovery** configuration command prevents access to ROMMON, and thus removes the ability to perform password recovery.

> **CAUTION** Password recovery is an important tool to a network administrator if the passwords have truly been lost. Although there is a minor network outage in the process, administrative access to the router is restored. If password recovery is disabled, there is no way possible to recover lost passwords or gain access to ROMMON mode. ROMMON mode is also useful to load a Flash image if the current one is corrupt or missing. Great care should be taken if password recovery is disabled.

Foundation Summary

There are three basic ways to configure a Cisco IOS router:

- **CLI**—The CLI is accessed physically via the console or auxiliary ports, or logically via a Telnet or SSH connection.

- **Web interface**—SDM is used to access and configure the router via HTTP or HTTPS.

- **SNMP**—The router can be polled and configured from an SNMP workstation.

There are a number of best practices for passwords that should be enforced for all network devices, including

- **Minimum length**—The more characters in a password, the longer it takes to guess it.

- **Mix of characters**—Passwords should contain a mix of upper-and lowercase letters, numbers, and meta-characters (symbols and spaces).

- **Do not use dictionary words**—Using dictionary words as passwords makes a dictionary attack more likely to succeed.

- **Change passwords frequently**—How often a password must change is often decided by policy, but never changing passwords introduces a vulnerability.

There are a number of access points into a router that should be protected by passwords:

- Console port with a terminal-emulation program

- Aux port with a terminal-emulation program

- Any reachable IP address via Telnet, SSH, HTTP, HTTPS, or SNMP

The various passwords in a Cisco device have the following characteristics:

- The password length can be between 1 and 25 characters in length—the longer the better.

- The first character of a password cannot start with a number or a space (leading numbers are illegal, and leading spaces are ignored).

- Within a password, any combination of characters can be used, including alphanumeric characters, upper- and lowercase characters, symbols, and spaces (remember, spaces and numbers cannot be used as the first character of a password).

Cisco IOS can log failed login attempts with the command **security authentication failure rate** *threshold-rate* **log**. AAA must be enabled for this command to have any effect. This command also enforces a 15-second login delay after a failed login attempt.

Cisco IOS also offers a series of **login** commands to monitor and block failed login attempts. As with the **security authentication** command, AAA must first be enabled. The **login block-for** *seconds* **attempts** *failed-attempts* **within** *watch-period* command forces a *seconds* login timeout after *failed-attempts* incorrect logins in *watch-period* seconds.

Setup mode permits the configuration of the enable secret, enable, and vty passwords.

The CLI permits the configuration of all setup passwords, as well as the console and aux passwords.

It is possible to use an access class to restrict the IP addresses that can access the router via Telnet or SSH. An access class is a standard access list that is applied inbound to the vty ports. Only packets permitted through the access list are allowed to access the router.

The command **exec-timeout** *minutes* [*seconds*] is used to force a disconnect from any line after *minutes:seconds* of inactivity. The default behavior is 10:00.

Cisco IOS can enforce minimum password length with the command **security passwords min-length** *length*. This command applies only to new passwords, not existing ones.

Password encryption is enabled with the command **service password-encryption**. Once the router passwords are encrypted, they cannot be reversed. The encryption algorithm used is considered weak, and should not be used to truly safeguard router passwords.

A banner is created with the command **banner motd** *delimiting-character banner-text delimiting-character*. Banners are used to post warning messages, but offer no additional security.

Individual user logins are created with the command **username** *name* **password** *password* or **username** *name* **secret** *password*. The password is stored in plaintext unless password encryption is enabled. The secret is encrypted using an MD5 one-way hash.

The **login** command is required on the lines (console, aux, vty) to enable password checking. Without this command, passwords are not used on the lines.

It is possible to use 16 different privilege levels in a Cisco router. Level 0 is user mode, and level 15 is privileged mode. Levels 1 to 14 are defined by the user. Each IOS command can be used in only one privilege level. Each privilege level should have a unique secret password to prevent unauthorized users from gaining access.

It is possible to have up to 15 different role-based CLI views, including superviews. Each CLI view can have any number of Cisco IOS commands, and Cisco IOS commands can be reused between views. Superviews are collections of individual views, and cannot contain Cisco IOS commands. AAA must be enabled to configure CLI views. CLI views can be configured only from the root view, which must be enabled before trying to access any individual views or superviews. Every view/superview must have a password configured first, or no other configurations are possible.

ROMMON mode can be disabled with the command **no service password-recovery**. Great care should be taken if this command is enabled, because Cisco IOS recovery via ROMMON is not possible.

Q&A

The questions and scenarios in this book are designed to be challenging and to make sure that you know the answer. Rather than allowing you to derive the answers from clues hidden inside the questions themselves, the questions challenge your understanding and recall of the subject.

Hopefully, mastering these questions will help you limit the number of exam questions on which you narrow your choices to two options, and then guess.

You can find the answers to these questions in Appendix A. For more practice with exam-like question formats, use the exam engine on the CD-ROM.

1. What are the different ports on a typical Cisco router?

2. How can a Cisco router be configured?

3. What are some of the password best practices?

4. What are some of the specific characteristics of Cisco IOS passwords?

5. What happens when the *threshold-rate* in the command **security authentication failure rate** *threshold-rate* **log** command is exceeded?

6. Explain the three parameters in the command **login block-for** *seconds* **attempts** *failed-attempts* **within** *watch-period*.

7. What happens in setup mode if both the enable secret and enable passwords are the same?

8. Why is the enable secret password more secure than the enable password?

9. What is the purpose of the **login** command on the console, aux, and vty lines?

10. How does an access class protect the router?

11. How is the Cisco IOS command **exec-timer** used?

12. What happens to current passwords in the router when the command **security passwords min-length 15** is executed?

13. Once passwords have been encrypted with the **service password-encryption** routine, how can the passwords be restored to plaintext?

14. How does a banner provide security to a router?

15. What must be done to have individual logins (usernames) used to log into the router?

16. What are the differences between the 16 different privilege levels?

17. What are some of the shortcomings of privilege levels compared to role-based Cisco IOS views?

18. What is the purpose of a superview?

19. What is a danger of the command **no service password-recovery**?

Exam Topic List

This chapter covers the following topics that you need to master for the CCNP ISCW exam:

- **AAA Components**—Describes the basic functions of AAA and its three components: Authentication, Authorization, and Accounting.

- **AAA Access Modes**—Covers how AAA can use either character or packet mode, depending on the interface used.

- **Understanding the TACACS+ and RADIUS Protocols**—Explores the use of TCP for TACACS+ and UDP for RADIUS, comparing and contrasting the two systems.

- **Configuring AAA Using the CLI**—Explores how to configure AAA using the CLI. A simple five-step process is used to enable you to quickly configure AAA.

- **Configuring AAA Using SDM**—Describes how the SDM provides a graphical interface alternative to the CLI and how to configure AAA using SDM using both the basic and advanced modes of SDM.

- **Using Debugging for AAA**—Describes the debugging tools provided within the CLI to allow the administrator to quickly troubleshoot issues related to AAA.

CHAPTER 20

Using AAA to Scale Access Control

Authentication, authorization, and accounting (AAA) allows the administrator to quickly set security parameters for groups or an individual. These parameters affect the authentication of a user, the user's authorized areas of access, and the maintenance of accounting records. These records can show what the user accessed and for how long the user accessed a network resource.

Using either Remote Authentication Dial-In User Service (RADIUS) or the Terminal Access Controller Access Control System Plus (TACACS+), AAA concepts and implementation are very simple. By the end of this chapter, you will have enough knowledge to quickly configure and maintain a system that uses AAA as part of its security strategy.

"Do I Know This Already?" Quiz

The purpose of the "Do I Know This Already?" quiz is to help you decide whether you really need to read the entire chapter. If you already intend to read the entire chapter, you do not necessarily need to answer these questions now.

The 13-question quiz, derived from the major sections in the "Foundation Topics" portion of the chapter, helps you to determine how to spend your limited study time.

Table 20-1 outlines the major topics discussed in this chapter and the "Do I Know This Already?" quiz questions that correspond to those topics.

Table 20-1 *"Do I Know This Already?" Foundation Topics Section-to-Question Mapping*

Foundation Topics Section	Questions Covered in This Section	Score
AAA Components	1–2	
AAA Access Modes	3	
Understanding the TACACS+ and RADIUS Protocols	4–7	
Configuring AAA Using the CLI	8–9	
Configuring AAA Using SDM	10–11	
Using Debugging for AAA	12–13	
Total Score		

CAUTION The goal of self-assessment is to gauge your mastery of the topics in this chapter. If you do not know the answer to a question or are only partially sure of the answer, you should mark this question wrong for purposes of self-assessment. Giving yourself credit for an answer that you correctly guess skews your self-assessment results and might provide you with a false sense of security.

---

1. What are the three components of AAA?

    a. Accounting, authentication, and ability

    b. Ability, authentication, and accessibility

    c. Authorization, accounting, and authority

    d. Accounting, authentication, and authorization

2. What is accounting in an AAA system designed to do?

    a. Provide a means of charging departments for computer usage

    b. Provide a means to track usage by user or group

    c. Provide a means to secure accounting programs

    d. Provide for new users quickly and efficiently

3. What are the two modes for AAA?

    a. Character and stream

    b. Stream and session

    c. Session and packet

    d. Packet and character

4. Which protocol allows the administrator to use specific ports?

    a. RADIUS

    b. NAT

    c. DHCP

    d. TACACS+

5. Which protocol enables the administrator to specify which users can use a given command on a router?

    a. RADIUS

    b. NAT

    c. DHCP

    d. TACACS+

6. You are required to support NASI. Which protocol is appropriate?

   a. RADIUS

   b. CEF

   c. PAT

   d. TACACS+

7. You want to use Kerberos as an authentication server because of its superior functionality. Which protocol must you use?

   a. RADIUS

   b. TLS

   c. SSL

   d. TACACS+

8. Your RADIUS server with the IP address 10.10.10.5 crashes regularly and must be rebuilt. What single command can you use on the router to stop AAA services without affecting any other parts of your configuration?

   a. **no RADIUS-server host 10.10.10.5**

   b. **no aaa new-model**

   c. **no aaa radius**

   d. **radius pause 10.10.10.5**

9. Which command is used to adjust the number of retries to a server?

   a. **radius-server key**

   b. **tacacs-server key**

   c. **radius-server host**

   d. **tacacs-server host**

10. Which SDM tab is used to change a user password?

    a. User Accounts/View

    b. Personnel

    c. Passwords

    d. Maintenance

11. When first configuring AAA through SDM, which of the following is true?

   a. The console is configured to use only SDM.

   b. The console is configured to authenticate through the TACACS+ or RADIUS server.

   c. The console is configured to authorize through the local database.

   d. The console is configured to authenticate through the local database.

12. Which is the most appropriate **debug** command to display TACACS+ authentication events?

   a. debug aaa

   b. debug authentication

   c. debug tacacs

   d. debug aaa tacacs

13. Which of the following is true about the **debug aaa** command?

   a. You may debug all AAA events with **debug aaa**.

   b. You may debug all authentication events with debug aaa authentication.

   c. You may debug all authentication events with **debug authentication**.

   d. All AAA debugging is enabled with **debug aaa**.

The answers to the "Do I Know This Already?" quiz are found in Appendix A, "Answers to the 'Do I Know This Already?' Quizzes and Q&A Sections." The suggested choices for your next step are as follows:

- **8 or fewer overall score**—Read the entire chapter. This includes the "Foundation Topics," "Foundation Summary," and "Q&A" sections.

- **9 to 11 overall score**—Begin with the "Foundation Summary" section, and then go to the "Q&A" section.

- **11 or more overall score**—If you want more review on these topics, skip to the "Foundation Summary" section and then go to the "Q&A" section. Otherwise, move to the next chapter.

Foundation Topics

AAA Components

AAA stands for authentication, authorization, and accounting. Each of these terms is explored in this section.

Authentication answers the question, "Who are you?." Authentication determines whether the user is whom they claim to be. The combination of a username and a password accomplishes authentication. For example, logging into a router with the username supervisor and the password let_me_in establishes the user's identity.

Authorization answers the question, "What is this user allowed to do?." The user named supervisor might or might not be allowed to access certain hosts or network equipment. Additionally, authorization may assign IP addresses, such as when using a VPN, or assign a specific privilege level, such as when using an EXEC session.

Accounting answers the question, "What have the users been doing on the network?" This can include information such as the length of time a VPN was used, how many times the VPN was used by a specific user, or how many users are actually using a given network resource.

It is important to note that only after authentication is established can authorization and accounting be enabled. There is no requirement for using either authorization or accounting. Either one or both can be deployed, but authentication is required for the other two to work. This provides great flexibility in determining what resources to track and how to track them. Should you simply track which users have accessed the personnel files? Do you need to even track which users have accessed the personnel files? These are questions that only the system administrator can answer; however, AAA provides the flexibility to control the network resources as needed.

AAA Access Modes

AAA has two access modes:

- **Character mode**—Used on the vty, TTY, AUX, and CON ports, which are generally used to configure a device.
- **Packet mode**—Used on the ASYNC, BRI, PRI, and serial ports, as well as on dialer profiles and dialer rotaries, usually when the user is trying to communicate with a different device.

Table 20-2 illustrates the port and its associated mode.

Table 20-2   *AAA Access Modes*

Interface	Mode	Description
AUX	Character	Auxiliary DTE ports
Console	Character	Console port
TTY	Character	Async port
vty	Character	Virtual terminal line
PPP	Packet	PPP on serial or ISDN interface
Arap	Packet	AppleTalk Remote Access (ARA) protocol on serial interfaces
NASI	Packet	NetWare Access Server Interface on serial interfaces

Understanding the TACACS+ and RADIUS Protocols

The TACACS+ and RADIUS protocols perform similar functions, providing AAA services for networks. But, there are also many differences between them. RADIUS, described in RFC 2865, has been supported by Cisco equipment since Cisco IOS Software Release 11.1. Many enhancements and new features have been incorporated into Cisco IOS with each new release.

While Cisco Systems refined its support of RADIUS, it also developed TACACS+ (RFC 1492) because there was a need for greater support to handle increasingly larger networks. The underlying architecture provided by TACACS+ more easily allows for separation of authentication, authorization, and accounting.

The sections that follow explore how using RADIUS and TACACS+ differ on the issues of protocol used, encryption techniques, Authentication and Authorization, protocol support, and interoperability.

UDP Versus TCP

RADIUS relies on UDP, whereas TACACS+ relies on TCP. This has several implications because of the inherent differences between connection-oriented (TCP and TACACS+) and connectionless (UDP and RADIUS) protocols. TCP offers several advantages, some of which include the following:

■   TCP provides an indication that a server has crashed due to a TCP reset (RST) and the TCP keep-alive mechanism. To do this with UDP, extensive additional programming is required.

■   TCP is far more scalable than UDP on large networks, especially on congested networks.

■   TCP allows for multiple simultaneous connections to several servers, automatically sending to only currently active servers. Using UDP, this would require additional programming.

Packet Encryption

TACACS+ allows for encryption of the entire body of the packet while maintaining the standard TACACS+ header. A field inside the header indicates whether encrypted is enabled.

RADIUS encrypts only the password within the access-request packet, leaving the remainder of the packet unencrypted. Information such as the username and the service authorized remain unencrypted, posing a possible security risk.

Authentication and Authorization

TACACS+ completely separates authentication and authorization. For example, it is routine within TACACS+ to use a Kerberos server for authentication and a TACACS+ server for authorization. Additionally, when a new authorization is needed during a TACACS+ session, the access server, before granting or denying the request, first checks with the TACACS+ server to see if the user is allowed to issue the command. This allows great flexibility over which commands can be executed on an access server when it has been disconnected from the authentication server.

RADIUS combines authentication and authorization into a single request. This makes designing a system where authentication and authorization are addressed by separate servers very difficult, and almost impossible if the administrator wishes to use different technologies for authorization and authentication.

Multiprotocol Support

TACACS+ is a multiprotocol tool that supports a wide array of protocols. RADIUS, however, is limited in its understanding and utilization of different protocols. Specifically, RADIUS does not support the following protocols:

- AppleTalk Remote Access (ARA) protocol

- NetBIOS Frames Protocol Control protocol

- Novell Asynchronous Services Interface (NASI)

- X.25 PAD connection

Router Management

RADIUS does not allow users to control which commands can and cannot be executed on a router. RADIUS either allows the user to access the router or does not. For RADIUS, there is no command-specific authorization for a router.

TACACS+ provides two methods to control the authorization of router commands:

■ Specify in the TACACS+ server the commands that are allowable by this user or group.

■ Relying on privilege levels, query the TACACS+ server to determine whether this user or group is authorized to issue a command at this privilege level.

Interoperability

Adherence to standards does not guarantee interoperability between systems. While still complying with the RFC for RADIUS, several vendors have added additional features that do not meld well with the Cisco implementation of RADIUS. If only the standard RADIUS features are used, Cisco equipment works very well. A manufacturer is able to implement features that are outside the scope of the RADIUS standards. In these cases, there may be serious deficiencies in the interoperability of that manufacturer's equipment and Cisco equipment.

Because TACACS+ was designed by Cisco, all TACACS+ features are fully implemented in Cisco equipment.

Configuring AAA Using the CLI

Configuring AAA using the CLI is simple. We will start with a configuration using RADIUS before looking at a TACACS+ example. The examples are followed by an explanation of the commands used. Notice the similarity and slight differences between the two examples.

RADIUS Configuration

Example 20-1 is a general configuration using RADIUS with the AAA command set.

Example 20-1 *RADIUS Configuration*

```
aaa new-model
radius-server host 10.10.1.5
radius-server key TheRADIUSServerKey
username root password MySecretPassword
aaa authentication ppp mydiallist radius local
aaa authorization network radius local
aaa accounting network mynetwork start-stop group radius
```

TACACS+ Configuration

Example 20-2 provides a general configuration using TACACS+ with the AAA command set.

Example 20-2 *TACACS+ Configuration*

```
aaa new-model
tacacs-server host 10.10.1.5
tacacs-server key TheTacacsServerKey
username root password MySecretPassword
aaa authentication ppp mydiallist tacacs+ local
aaa authorization commands 15 tacacs+ if-authenticated none
aaa accounting network start-stop tacacs+
```

AAA-Related Commands

The sections that follow provide an explanation of the commands used in Example 20-1 and Example 20-2, along with the command syntax.

aaa new-model Command

The **aaa new-model** command enables AAA on the router. Use the **no aaa new-model** command to disable AAA. There are no optional parameters for this command.

radius-server host Command

The **radius-server host** command tells the system to look to an IP address for the RADIUS server. This command has a lot of optional parameters. The full version of the command follows:

```
radius-server host {hostname | ip-address} [auth-port port-number] [acct-port port-
number] [timeout seconds] [retransmit retries] [key string] [alias{hostname | ip-
address}]
```

Table 20-3 lists the parameters for the **radius-server host** command.

Table 20-3   radius-server host *Parameters*

Parameter	Description
hostname	Specifies the DNS name of the RADIUS server
ip-address	Specifies the IP address of the RADIUS server
auth-port	Specifies the UDP destination port for authentication requests
port-number	Specifies the port number for authentication requests (0 = no host used; default – port 1645)
acct-port	Specifies the UDP destination port for accounting requests
port-number	Specifies the port number for accounting (0 = no host used; default = port 1646)

continues

Table 20-3 radius-server host *Parameters (Continued)*

Parameter	Description
timeout	Specifies the number of seconds the router waits for a response from the RADIUS server before resending the request
seconds	Specifies the timeout value
retransmit	Specifies the number of times a RADIUS request is retransmitted
retries	Specifies the retransmit value
key	Specifies that an authentication and encryption key will be used by the router and the RADIUS server
string	Specifies the key used for authentication and encryption
alias	Specifies up to eight aliases to be used for a given RADIUS server

tacacs-server host Command

The **tacacs-server host** command tells the system to look to an IP address for the TACACS+ server. This is very similar to the **radius-server host** command, but there are subtle differences within the optional parameters. This command has a lot of optional parameters. The full version of the command follows:

```
tacacs-server host {hostname I ip-address} [key string] [nat] [port [integer]]
   [single-connection] [timeout [integer]]
   no tacacs-server host {host-name I host-ip-address}
```

Table 20-4 lists and describes the parameters for the **tacacs-server host** command.

Table 20-4 tacacs-server host *Parameters*

Option	Description
hostname	DNS name of the RADIUS server
ip-address	IP address of the RADIUS server
key	Specifies the authentication and encryption key used by the router and the TACACS+ server
string	The key used for authentication and encryption
nat	The NAT address of the client that is sent to the TACACS+ server
port	Specifies the TACACS+ server port number (default = 49)
integer	Port number of the TACACS+ server
single-connection	Maintains a single open connection between the router and the TACACS+ server
timeout	Specifies a timeout value
integer	Integer value in seconds for TCP timeout

radius-server key and tacacs-server key Commands

The **radius-server key** and **tacacs-server key** commands are essentially the same, one being used for RADIUS and the other being used for TACACS+. Both commands set the authentication key for communication between the router and the server. In Example 20-1, we are sending TheRADIUSServerKey for the RADIUS key, and in Example 20-2, we are sending TheTacacsServerKey for the TACACS+ key. The full version of each command follows:

```
[no] radius-server key {0 string | 7 string | string}
[no] tacacs-server key {0 string | 7 string | string}
```

Table 20-5 lists and describes the parameters for the **radius-server key** and **tacacs-server key** commands.

Table 20-5 **radius-server key** and **tacacs-server key** *Parameters*

Option	Description
0 *string*	The unencrypted key is entered into the *string* parameter.
7 *string*	A hidden key is entered into the *string* parameter.
string	The unencrypted key is entered into the *string* parameter. This is the same as the "0 string" option.

username root password Command

The **username root password** command is not AAA specific. It specifies a username and password combination.

aaa authentication ppp Command

The **aaa authentication ppp** command specifies the AAA authentication methods for use on serial interfaces running Point-to-Point Protocol (PPP). The full version of the command follows:

```
[no] aaa authentication ppp {default | list-name} method1 [method2...]
```

Table 20-6 lists and describes the parameters for the **aaa authentication ppp** command.

Table 20-6 **aaa authentication ppp** *Command Parameters*

Option	Description
default	Uses the authentication methods following the parameter as the default list when a user logs in
list-name	Character string used to name the list of methods used when the user logs in

continues

Table 20-6   **aaa authentication ppp** *Command Parameters (Continued)*

Option	Description
method1 [method2...]	At least one of the following methods is used:
	if-needed = do not authenticate if the user is already authenticated
	krb5 = use Kerberos 5 for authentication
	local = use the local database
	none = no authentication
	radius = use RADIUS authentication
	tacacs+ = use TACACS+ authentication

aaa authorization Command

The **aaa authorization** command sets parameters that restrict network access for a user. In Example 20-2, we have chosen to check authorization regarding level 15 commands. The full version of the command follows:

```
[no] aaa authorization {network | exec | commands level | reverse-access} {default | list-
name} [method1 [method2...]]
```

Table 20-7 lists and describes the parameters for the **aaa authorization** command.

Table 20-7   **aaa authorization** *Command Parameters*

Option	Description
network	Runs authorization for all network-related service requests
exec	Runs authorization to determine if the user is authorized to run an EXEC shell
commands	Runs authorization for all commands at the specified level
level	Specific command level that should be authorized; level may be from 0 through 15
reverse-access	Runs authorization for reverse access connections (reverse Telnet)
default	Uses the authentication methods following the parameter as the default list when a user logs in
list-name	Character string used to name the list of methods used when the user logs in

Table 20-7   aaa authorization *Command Parameters (Continued)*

Option	Description
method1 [method2...]	At least one of the following methods is used: **if-needed** = do not authenticate if the user is already authenticated **krb5** = use Kerberos 5 for authentication **local** = use the local database **none** = no authentication **radius** = use RADIUS authentication **tacacs+** = use TACACS+ authentication

aaa accounting Command

The **aaa accounting** command enables accounting for requested services. The full version of the command follows:

```
[no] aaa accounting {auth-proxy | system | network | exec | connection | commands level}
    {default | list-name} [vrf vrf-name] {start-stop | stop-only | none} [broadcast] group
    groupname
```

Table 20-8 lists and describes the parameters for the **aaa accounting** command.

Table 20-8   aaa accounting *Command Parameters*

Option	Description
auth-proxy	Performs accounting for all authenticated proxy events
system	Performs accounting for all system-level events not associated with users (reboots and so forth)
network	Performs accounting for all network-related requests
exec	Performs accounting for all EXEC shell sessions
connection	Performs accounting for all outbound connections from the network access server
commands *level*	Performs accounting for all commands at the specified level
default	Uses the listed accounting methods that follow

continues

Table 20-8 **aaa accounting** *Command Parameters* *(Continued)*

Option	Description
list-name	Character string used to name the list; valid options are **group radius** = list of RADIUS servers **group tacacs** = list of TACACS+ servers **group** *group-name* = a subset of RADIUS or TACACS+ servers
vrf *vrf-name*	Specifies a VRF (Virtual Route Forwarding) configuration
start-stop	Sends a "start" notice at the beginning of a process and a "stop" notice at the termination of the process
stop-only	Sends a "stop" notice at the end of a process
broadcast	Enables sending accounting records to multiple AAA servers
group *group-name*	Character string used to name the list; valid options are **group radius** = list of RADIUS servers **group tacacs** = list of TACACS+ servers **group** *group-name* = a subset of RADIUS or TACACS+ servers

Configuring AAA Using SDM

An alternative to using the CLI for configuring AAA is the Security Device Manager (SDM). The use of a graphical interface allows the administrator to configure and modify AAA quickly and easily. This section uses SDM to demonstrate the configuration of AAA.

After you start SDM and connect to the router, click the **Configure** button at the top of the screen. All of AAA is configured through the Additional Tasks list on the Configure page. Choose **AAA** to start the configuration process. The pop-up allows you to start AAA processes by clicking **Yes**. This is the equivalent of the **aaa new-model** CLI command. As Figure 20-1 shows, this enables AAA. Additionally, the vty and console ports become automatically configured for authorization using the local database. Click **Yes** to continue.

Figure 20-1 *Enabling AAA*

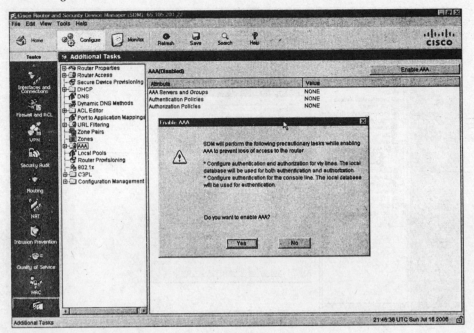

The next task is to add the AAA servers. To do so, choose **AAA Servers** in the Additional Tasks list, as shown in Figure 20-2, and click **Add** to open the Add AAA Server dialog box. The default, as shown in Figure 20-2, is a RADIUS server. When choosing RADIUS, you have the options to specify the authorization and accounting ports, specify the UDP timeout, and configure or change the encryption key. This is the equivalent of the **radius-server host** and **radius-server key** commands in the CLI.

Figure 20-3 shows what the dialog box looks like when you choose a TACACS+ server instead of a RADIUS server. Notice that because TACACS+ uses TCP instead of UDP, you cannot choose the ports for authorization and accounting. While using TCP and TACACS+, you have the option of using a single connection to the server. Using the single connection option, you open only a single connection to the server, as opposed to opening a separate connection each for authentication, authorization, and accounting purposes. As with RADIUS, you are able to configure your timeout and keys. This is the equivalent of the **tacacs-server host** and **tacacs-server key** commands in the CLI.

Figure 20-2 *Adding a RADIUS AAA Server*

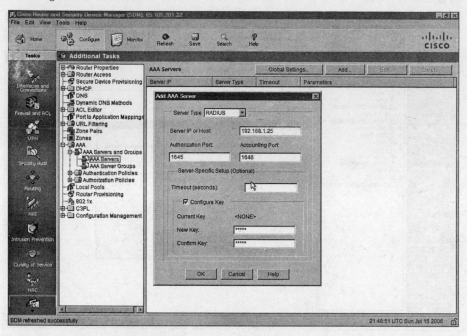

Figure 20-3 *Adding a TACACS+ AAA Server*

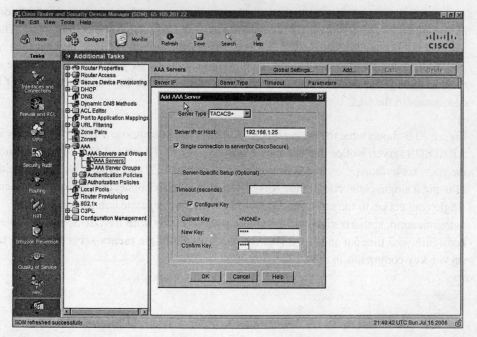

The vty and console ports are automatically configured for authentication and authorization using the local database. You can change these defaults by choosing **Authentication Policies** or **Authorization Policies**, respectively, in the Additional Tasks list. Choosing Authentication Policies gives you options that are equivalent to those that are available with the **aaa authentication** command in the CLI. Figure 20-4 shows how you can change the login authentication.

Figure 20-4 *Changing Login Authentication*

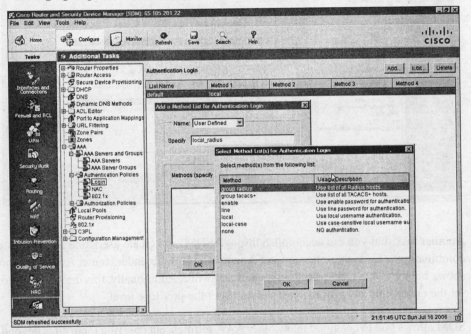

SDM allows you to easily change the authorizations configuration. Figure 20-5 shows how you can modify the EXEC authorization. In this case, the local database is selected for authorization on the EXEC commands. This is equivalent to the **aaa authorization** command in the CLI.

Figure 20-5 *Changing EXEC Authorization*

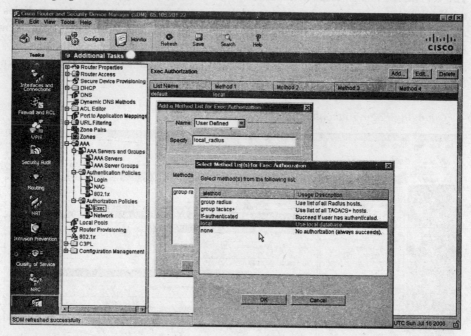

Another task that you can accomplish through SDM is to create username and password combinations. To do this, choose **User Accounts/View** tab under Router Access. Figure 20-6 shows how you can create a username and password. Additionally, this dialog box allows you to set the encryption used for the password and set the privilege level.

SDM allows you to configure many other AAA settings, but covering them all is beyond the scope of this chapter, so we explore only two more items—authentication and authorization of vty lines. Figure 20-7 and Figure 20-8 show how to configure the authentication and authorization, respectively, on vty lines.

Figure 20-6 *Administering Users*

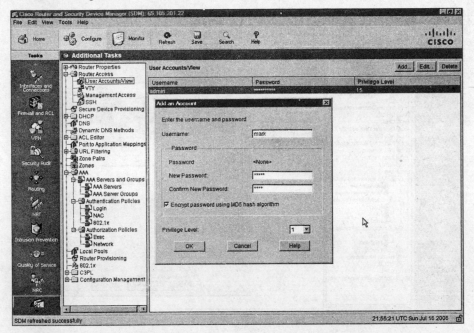

Figure 20-7 *vty Authentication*

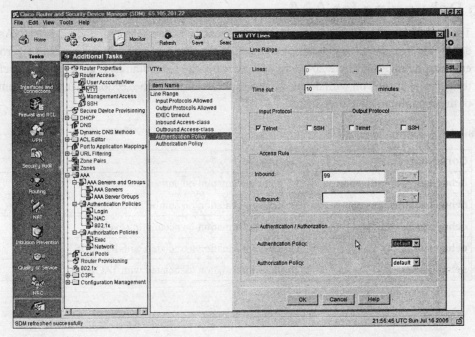

Figure 20-8 *vty Authorization*

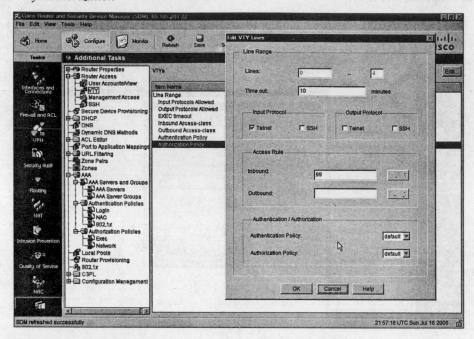

Using Debugging for AAA

There are five debugging commands that you need to be familiar with to debug AAA. As always, debugging can cause huge loads on a router. Make sure that you will not overload the router by enabling debugging. Table 20-9 lists and describes the five commands and their purpose. Each of these can be turned off with the **no** version of the command. The sections that follow examine each of these commands in more detail.

Table 20-9 AAA **debug** *Commands*

Command	Description
debug aaa authentication	Displays information on authentication events
debug aaa authorization	Displays information on authorization events
debug aaa accounting	Displays information on accounting events
debug radius	Displays information associated with RADIUS
debug tacacs	Displays information associated with TACACS+

debug aaa authentication Command

The **debug aaa authentication** command displays information on authentication events. This command does not have any optional parameters. Example 20-3 shows sample output from this command.

Example 20-3   debug aaa authentication *Command Output*

```
Router#debug aaa authentication
4:50:12: AAA/AUTHEN: create_user user='' ruser='' port='tty19' rem_addr='10.10.1.1'
authen_type=1 service=1 priv=1
4:32:10: AAA/AUTHEN/START (0): port='tty19' list='' action=LOGIN service=LOGIN
4:32:10: AAA/AUTHEN/START (0): using "default" list
4:32:10: AAA/AUTHEN/START (42987541): Method=TACACS+
4:32:10: TAC+ (42987541): received authen response status = GETUSER
4:32:10: AAA/AUTHEN (42987541): status = GETUSER
4:32:13: AAA/AUTHEN/CONT (42987541): continue_login
4:32:13: AAA/AUTHEN (42987541): status = GETUSER
4:32:13: AAA/AUTHEN (42987541): Method=TACACS+
4:32:13: TAC+: send AUTHEN/CONT packet
4:32:13: TAC+ (42987541): received authen response status = GETPASS
4:32:13: AAA/AUTHEN (42987541): status = GETPASS
4:32:18: AAA/AUTHEN/CONT (42987541): continue_login
4:32:18: AAA/AUTHEN (42987541): status = GETPASS
4:32:18: AAA/AUTHEN (42987541): Method=TACACS+
4:32:18: TAC+: send AUTHEN/CONT packet
4:32:18: TAC+ (42987541): received authen response status = PASS
4:32:18: AAA/AUTHEN (42987541): status = PASS
```

debug aaa authorization Command

The **debug aaa authorization** command displays information on authorization events. This command does not have any optional parameters. Example 20-4 shows the output of a failed authorization.

Example 20-4   debug aaa authorization *Command Output*

```
Router#debug aaa authorization
5:18:43: AAA/AUTHOR (0): user='carrel'
5:18:43: AAA/AUTHOR (0): send AV service=shell
5:18:43: AAA/AUTHOR (0): send AV cmd*
5:18:43: AAA/AUTHOR (754913891): Method=TACACS+
5:18:43: AAA/AUTHOR/TAC+ (754913891): user=carrel
5:18:43: AAA/AUTHOR/TAC+ (754913891): send AV service=shell
5:18:43: AAA/AUTHOR/TAC+ (754913891): send AV cmd*
5:18:43: AAA/AUTHOR (754913891): Post authorization status = FAIL
```

debug aaa accounting Command

The **debug aaa accounting** command displays information regarding AAA accounting. This command does not have any optional parameters. Example 20-5 shows output from the **debug aaa accounting** command.

Example 20-5 **debug aaa accounting** *Command Output*

```
Router#debug aaa accounting
9:27:28: AAA/ACCT: EXEC acct start, line 10
9:27:40: AAA/ACCT: Connect start, line 10, glare
9:27:54: AAA/ACCT: Connection acct stop:
task_id=80 service=exec port=10 protocol=telnet address=10.10.1.1 cmd=glare bytes_in=340
bytes_out=145 paks_in=65 paks_out=74 elapsed_time=14
```

debug radius Command

The **debug radius** command displays information regarding RADIUS. There are two optional parameters, as the following syntax shows:

> **debug radius [brief | hex]**

The **brief** option displays an abbreviated debug session, while the **hex** option displays the debug information in hexadecimal format. The **hex** option is useful for some debuggers. Example 20-6 shows the debugging of a failed authentication using the **brief** parameter.

Example 20-6 **debug radius brief** *Command Output*

```
Router#debug radius brief
RADIUS protocol debugging is on
RADIUS packet hex dump debugging is off
RADIUS protocol in brief format debugging is on
00:05:21: RADIUS: Initial Transmit ISDN 0:D:23 id 6 10.10.10.1:1824, Accounting-Request,
 len 358
10:05:21: %ISDN-6-CONNECT: Interface Serial0:22 is now connected to 5555551212
10:05:26: RADIUS: Retransmit id 6
10:05:31: RADIUS: Tried all servers.
10:05:31: RADIUS: No valid server found. Trying any viable server
10:05:31: RADIUS: Tried all servers.
10:05:31: RADIUS: No response for id 7
10:05:31: RADIUS: Initial Transmit ISDN 0:D:23 id 8 10.0.0.0:1823, Access-Request, len 171
10:05:36: RADIUS: Retransmit id 8
10:05:36: RADIUS: Received from id 8 1.7.157.1:1823, Access-Accept, len 115
10:05:47: %ISDN-6-DISCONNECT: Interface Serial0:22 disconnected from 5555551212, call
 lasted 26 seconds
10:05:47: RADIUS: Initial Transmit ISDN 0:D:23 id 9 10.0.0.1:1824, Accounting-Request, len
 775
10:05:47: RADIUS: Received from id 9 1.7.157.1:1824, Accounting-response, len 20
```

debug tacacs Command

The **debug tacacs** command displays information about RADIUS. There are no optional parameters. Example 20-7 shows the output of a successful authentication.

Example 20-7   debug tacacs *Command Output*

```
Router#debug tacacs
07:00:09: TAC+: Opening TCP/IP connection to 10.10.10.5 using source 10.10.10.1
07:00:09: TAC+: Sending TCP/IP packet number 383258052-1 to 10.10.10.5 (AUTHEN/START)
07:00:09: TAC+: Receiving TCP/IP packet number 383258052-2 from 10.10.10.5
07:00:09: TAC+ (383258052): received authen response status = GETUSER
07:00:10: TAC+: send AUTHEN/CONT packet
07:00:10: TAC+: Sending TCP/IP packet number 383258052-3 to 10.10.10.5 (AUTHEN/CONT)
07:00:10: TAC+: Receiving TCP/IP packet number 383258052-4 from 10.10.10.5
07:00:10: TAC+ (383258052): received authen response status = GETPASS
07:00:14: TAC+: send AUTHEN/CONT packet
07:00:14: TAC+: Sending TCP/IP packet number 383258052-5 to 10.10.10.5 (AUTHEN/CONT)
07:00:14: TAC+: Receiving TCP/IP packet number 383258052-6 from 10.10.10.5
07:00:14: TAC+ (383258052): received authen response status = PASS
07:00:14: TAC+: Closing TCP/IP connection to 10.10.10.5
```

Foundation Summary

AAA consists of three components, outlined in Table 20-10.

Table 20-10 *AAA*

AAA Component	Answers This Question	Additional
Authentication	Who am I?	Username/password combination
Authorization	Am I allowed to do this?	May assign IP addresses, etc.
Accounting	What have people done?	When was it done and for how long?

AAA has two access modes, character and packet. The mode is determined by the interface. Review Table 20-11 as a guide to the interfaces and their associated modes.

Table 20-11 *AAA Access Modes*

Interface	Mode	Description
Aux	Character	Auxiliary DTE ports
Console	Character	Console port
TTY	Character	Async port
vty	Character	Virtual terminal line
PPP	Packet	PPP on serial or ISDN interface
Arap	Packet	AppleTalk Remote Access protocol on serial interfaces
NASI	Packet	NetWare Access Server Interface on serial interfaces

Table 20-12 outlines the differences between RADIUS and TACACS+.

Table 20-12 *RADIUS and TACACS+ Differences*

RADIUS	TACACS+
UDP	TCP
Password encryption	Packet encryption
Not multiprotocol	Multiprotocol
No individual command control	Individual command control
Supports basic interoperability	Proprietary system

The CLI commands are simple and effective.

1. Turn on AAA using the **aaa new model** command.

2. Set the server addresses using the **radius-server host** or **tacacs-server host** command.

3. Set the server key with the **radius-server key** or **tacacs=server key** command.

4. Set the authentication method with the **aaa authentication** command.

5. Set the Authorization levels with the **aaa authorization** command.

6. Set accounting with the **aaa accounting** command.

Review the following eight commands:

```
aaa new-model
radius-server host {hostname | ip-address} [auth-port port-number] [acct-port port-
   number] [timeout seconds] [retransmit retries] [key string] [alias {hostname | ip-
   address}]
tacacs-server host {hostname | ip-address} [key string] [nat] [port [integer]] [single-
   connection] [timeout [integer]]
radius-server key {0 string | 7 string | string}
tacacs-server key {0 string | 7 string | string}
aaa authentication ppp {default | list-name} method1 [method2...]
aaa authorization {network | exec | commands level | reverse-access} {default | list-name}
   [method1 [method2...]]
aaa accounting {auth-proxy | system | network | exec | connection | commands level}
   {default | list-name} [vrf vrf-name] {start-stop | stop-only | none} [broadcast] group
   groupname
```

SDM provides a graphical alternative to the CLI. You need to become familiar with the layout and usage of SDM. One of the best ways to accomplish this is to download a copy of SDM and use it to configure a spare router.

Table 20-13 lists and describes the five main debugging commands available for AAA.

Table 20-13 AAA **debug** *Commands*

Command	Description
debug aaa authentication	Displays information on authentication events
debug aaa authorization	Displays information on authorization events
debug aaa accounting	Displays information on accounting events
debug radius	Displays information associated with RADIUS
debug tacacs	Displays information associated with TACACS

Q&A

The questions and scenarios in this book are designed to be challenging and to make sure that you know the answer. Rather than allowing you to derive the answers from clues hidden inside the questions themselves, the questions challenge your understanding and recall of the subject.

Hopefully, mastering these questions will help you limit the number of exam questions on which you narrow your choices to two options and then guess.

You can find the answers to these questions in Appendix A. For more practice with exam-like question formats, use the exam engine on the CD-ROM.

1. Name some consequences of using TACACS+ instead of RADIUS for AAA.

2. Your boss tells you to implement accounting for the payroll system, but tells you that authentication is not necessary because the payroll program takes care of authentication itself. Why should you be wary of this approach?

3. You are asked to design the AAA system for a multinational bank with more than 10,000 users. Would you choose RADIUS or TACACS+? Why?

4. You have recently added authentication to the vty lines on your router. A new user is not able to access the router. What is the most likely cause?

5. You have recently added a new user to your system. Her job is to configure routers. She is able to access some commands but not others. What is most likely the problem?

6. You are currently tracking the starting and ending times of access on a certain application. All you really need to track is the last access time. Which command should you use to change this?

7. Your TACACS+ system is not working properly. By using the **debug** commands, you are able to determine that the TACACS+ server takes too long to reply. What command should you be looking at to correct the problem?

Exam Topic List

This chapter covers the following topics that you need to master for the CCNP ISCW exam:

- **Layered Device Structure**—Examines the concepts of a Layered Device Structure. A layered security device provides security on many different IOS layers.

- **Firewall Technology Basics**—Explores the three basic forms of firewall technology: Application Layer Gateway (ALG), stateful filtering, and stateless filtering.

- **Cisco IOS Firewall Feature Set**—Covers the most common features of the Cisco IOS Firewall Feature Set, which is a powerful tool that provides many security options.

- **Cisco IOS Firewall Operation**—Describes how the Cisco IOS Firewall accomplishes packet filtering by using several differing features.

- **Cisco IOS Firewall Packet Inspection and Proxy Firewalls**—Covers how the capabilities of the Cisco IOS Firewall Feature set combine to provide the best possible protection for the network.

CHAPTER 21

Cisco IOS Threat Defense Features

This chapter explores the advantages, concepts, and strategy behind the Cisco IOS Firewall offerings. Using a layered device as part of the overall security strategy allows the administrator great flexibility in access control. Using a demilitarized zone (DMZ) helps to isolate security breaches outside of the internal portion of the corporate network. If a security breach does occur, the rest of the network can remain intact. For example, "hacking" a web server that is positioned in a DMZ will not enable the hacker to penetrate into the internal portion of the network.

In this chapter, you will examine the differences between packet filters, application layer gateways (ALG), and stateful packet filters, learn about the Cisco IOS Firewall feature set, and discover how the Cisco IOS Firewall operates. Chapter 22, "Implementing Cisco IOS Firewall Features," covers how to implement the Cisco IOS Firewall.

"Do I Know This Already?" Quiz

The purpose of the "Do I Know This Already?" quiz is to help you decide whether you really need to read the entire chapter. If you already intend to read the entire chapter, you do not necessarily need to answer these questions now.

The 13-question quiz, derived from the major sections in the "Foundation Topics" portion of the chapter, helps you to determine how to spend your limited study time.

Table 21-1 outlines the major topics discussed in this chapter and the "Do I Know This Already?" quiz questions that correspond to those topics.

Table 21-1 *"Do I Know This Already?" Foundation Topics Section-to-Question Mapping*

Foundation Topics Section	Questions Covered in This Section	Score
Layered Device Structure	1–2	
Firewall Technology Basics	3–8	
Cisco IOS Firewall Feature Set	9–10	
Cisco IOS Firewall Operation	11–12	
Cisco IOS Firewall Packet Inspection and Proxy Firewalls	13	
Total Score		

CAUTION The goal of self-assessment is to gauge your mastery of the topics in this chapter. If you do not know the answer to a question or are only partially sure of the answer, you should mark this question wrong for purposes of self-assessment. Giving yourself credit for an answer that you correctly guess skews your self-assessment results and might provide you with a false sense of security.

---

1. Why is it advised that each server be placed on a separate DMZ?

    a. It forces the administrator to deal with more ACLs, thereby ensuring that there is more security.

    b. It helps prevent one compromised server from becoming a launching platform for more security breaches.

    c. It helps the accounting department by tracking each server independently.

    d. It provides a way of tracking the use of each server.

2. When using multiple DMZs, what equipment is required (select all that apply)?

    a. A Cisco PIX Firewall must be used.

    b. A router with multiple interfaces must be used.

    c. A LAN switch must be used.

    d. A VPN Concentrator must be used.

    e. All these answers are correct.

3. What type of equipment would be employed to prevent the user from any direct access to a server?

    a. Packet filter

    b. Hybrid packet filter

    c. Stateful packet filter

    d. ALG

4. What type of firewall is best used when only UDP is used for access?

    a. Packet filter

    b. Authentication proxy

    c. ALG

    d. Stateful packet filter

5. Which type of equipment is used to provide data from a server while still preventing direct access to that server?

   a. Packet filter

   b. ALG

   c. Stateful packet filter

   d. Hybrid packet filter

6. How does a stateful packet filter's use of access control lists (ACL) differ from a packet filter's use of ACLs?

   a. ACLs are not required in a stateless filter.

   b. ACLs are not required in a stateful filter.

   c. ACLS require a separate database, such as SQL, in a stateful filter.

   d. ACLs are static in a stateless filter.

   e. ACLs are dynamically changed in a stateless filter.

   f. ACLs are dynamically changed in a stateful filter.

7. How does a stateful packet filter handle UDP packets?

   a. Defaults back to packet filter

   b. Allows only FTP UDP packets

   c. Defaults to a stateless firewall

   d. Blocks UDP traffic

   e. Allows UDP traffic

8. What does a stateful packet filter maintain?

   a. A connection database

   b. A session database

   c. A user database

   d. A connection table

   e. A session table

   f. A user table

9. What type of firewall is the Cisco IOS Firewall?

   a. Packet firewall

   b. Application layer gateway

   c. Stateful

   d. Hybrid

10. How does the Cisco IOS Firewall handle streaming video such as VDOLive or Streamworks?

   a. It ignores all streaming video, allowing it to pass.

   b. It ignores all streaming video, blocking it.

   c. It is fully aware of streaming video and blocks or passes as configured.

   d. Streaming video is allowed if the configuration is globally set.

11. What is unique about how the Cisco IOS Firewall handles ACLs?

   a. The Cisco IOS Firewall does not require ACLS.

   b: They are dynamically changed during operation.

   c. They are automatically generated.

   d. They must be applied before the inspection rule is applied.

12. How does the Cisco IOS Firewall handle UDP traffic (select all that apply)?

   a. It ignores all UDP traffic, allowing it to pass.

   b. It defaults to stateless modes.

   c. It uses timeouts for UDP traffic.

   d. It prevents all UDP traffic from passing.

13. Which of the following is not a benefit of the Cisco IOS Firewall?

   a. Allows combinations of proxy, stateless, and stateful firewall technologies

   b. Defaults to stateless when stateful is not practicable

   c. Ignores streaming video

   d. Can provide proxy services

The answers to the "Do I Know This Already?" quiz are found in Appendix A, "Answers to the 'Do I Know This Already?' Quizzes and Q&A Sections." The suggested choices for your next step are as follows:

■ **8 or fewer overall score**—Read the entire chapter. This includes the "Foundation Topics," "Foundation Summary," and "Q&A" sections.

■ **9 to 12 overall score**—Begin with the "Foundation Summary" section, and then go to the "Q&A" section.

■ **12 or more overall score**—If you want more review on these topics, skip to the "Foundation Summary" section and then go to the "Q&A" section. Otherwise, move to the next chapter.

Table 21-2 *Firewall Technologies*

Technology	Description
Packet filtering	Uses IP addresses and/or port numbers with an ACL.
ALG	Works like a proxy server.
Stateful packet filtering	Uses ACLs. Also knows the connection state to determine access.

Packet Filtering

Packet filtering is the simplest technology used on the firewall. The difference between stateful and stateless is merely whether the filter tracks and responds to the context in which protocol requests are given. This technology limits traffic transiting the firewall by using an ACL. The ACL filters by IP address, port, or any other criterion within the assigned access list. Although packet filtering does allow great complexity and ease of use, it does not maintain a database of the current state of connections. Therefore, it is a less secure method than stateful packet filtering.

Figure 21-3 shows how FTP traffic is permitted to enter a single server while other traffic is denied access.

Figure 21-3 *Filtering FTP Traffic to a Specific Server*

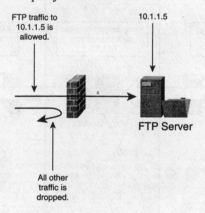

Configuring the ACL can be simple or complex, depending on the requirements. Example 21-1 shows a simple ACL configuration that allows FTP traffic to enter a specific server, as shown in the example in Figure 21-3.

Example 21-1 *Packet Filtering ACL*

```
Router(config)#access-list 100 permit tcp any host 10.1.1.5
Router(config)#access-list 100 deny ip any any log
Router(config)#interface serial 1/1
Router(config-if)#ip access-group 100 in
Router(config-if)#^z
```

Application Layer Gateway

An application layer gateway (ALG) uses a server that provides proxy services. The outside user connects to the ALG. The ALG then makes a connection to the interior server and passes requests between the interior server and the user. This is a very effective method for services such as HTTP, HTTPS, FTP, and e-mail. This method provides a good deal of security because the user connects to the DMZ server and never actually sees the interior server.

Figure 21-4 shows an example of an ALG acting as a proxy server between a user and an internal FTP server.

Figure 21-4 *Application Layer Gateway*

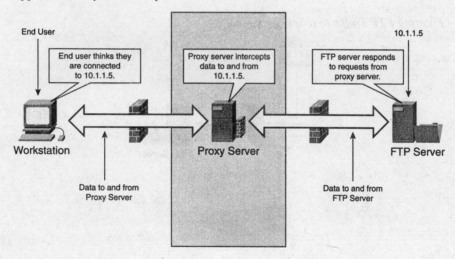

Stateful Packet Filtering

Stateful packet filtering is a refinement of the packet filtering technology that provides additional levels of security. The main advantage of stateful packet filtering is that the firewall understands the "state" of the connection. For example, a stateful packet filter will not allow an TCP ACK packet through unless there has already been a request from the same source to establish an TCP connection and a response from the server allowing the connection to proceed. Because the firewall remembers the state of all connections and inspects every packet, it is able to filter out those packets that are inappropriate.

Additionally, a stateful packet filter understands Layer 7 protocols enough to allow new connections when they are required for the application. For example, FTP data transfers occur over a separate data channel that is negotiated over the original control connection. A stateful packet filter recognizes this negotiation and updates the session table accordingly to allow the traffic through.

Figure 21-5 shows a stateful packet filter in operation.

Figure 21-5 *Stateful Packet Filter Operation*

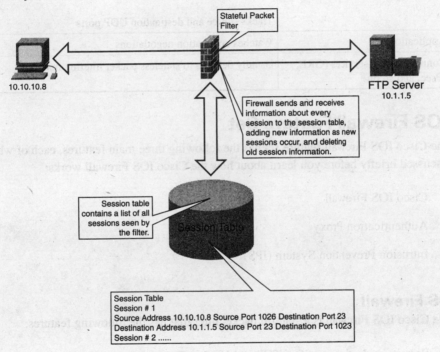

A stateful packet filter treats each protocol in a unique fashion. For example, TCP sequence numbers are checked to ensure they are arriving in a sequential manner. However, UDP does not have a sequence number, so this method cannot be used and the filter reverts to stateless mode for these UDP packets. Table 21-3 describes how a stateful packet filter handles different protocols.

Table 21-3 *Protocol Handling by a Stateful Packet Filter*

Applications	Features
TCP	Checks flow information Tracks sequence numbers
UDP	Hard to track UDP thoroughly No sequence numbers in UDP Checks timeouts Tracks source and destination IP addresses Tracks source and destination UDP ports
Applications	Watches application negotiations
Connectionless services (GRE, IPsec, and so on)	Usually defaults to stateless packet filtering operation

Cisco IOS Firewall Feature Set

The Cisco IOS Firewall feature set has the following three main features, each of which will be discussed briefly before you learn about how the Cisco IOS Firewall works:

- Cisco IOS Firewall

- Authentication Proxy

- Intrusion Prevention System (IPS)

Cisco IOS Firewall

The Cisco IOS Firewall is a stateful packet filter that has the following features:

- Permits or denies specified TCP and UDP traffic

- Maintains a state table

- Modifies ACLs dynamically

- Protects against DoS attacks

- Inspects packets passing through the interface

Authentication Proxy

The Authentication Proxy provides authentication and authorization on a per-user basis through either Remote Authentication Dial-In User Service (RADIUS) or Terminal Access Controller Access Control System Plus (TACACS+) for the following protocols:

- HTTP

- HTTPS

- FTP

- Telnet

Cisco IOS IPS

Cisco IOS IPS is an intrusion detection and response system that identifies and responds to over 700 forms of attack. Identification of an attack initiates one or more of the actions shown in Table 21-4.

Table 21-4 *Cisco IOS IPS Response to Attack*

Action	Description
Drop	Drops the packet
Block	Blocks the sending IP address for a specified period of time
Reset	Terminates a TCP session by sending a TCP reset
Alarm	Sends an alarm to the syslog server or SDM

Cisco IOS Firewall Operation

Before discussing how the Cisco IOS Firewall works, consider the following list of protocols that are fully recognized by the Cisco IOS Firewall:

- BGP

- FTP/FTPS

- HTTP/HTTPS

- ICMP

- Kazaa

- RTSP (Real Networks)

- RADIUS

- Signaling protocols
  - H.323
  - Skinny
  - SIP
- SMTP
- SNMP
- SQL*NET
- TACACS+
- Telnet
- TFTP
- TCP (single channel)
- UDP (single channel)
- UNIX R-commands (rlogin, rexec, and so on)
- Multimedia protocols
  - Microsoft NetShow
  - StreamWorks
  - VDOLive

As stated earlier, the Cisco IOS Firewall modifies ACLs dynamically as data passes through the interface. While this concept might seem strange at first, it is a relatively simple process. The firewall sees permitted traffic and adds a new line within the existing ACL. The Cisco IOS Firewall also allows you to configure real-time audit trails and alerts on a per-protocol basis, using syslog.

Figure 21-6 shows the steps in this process. Notice the state of the ACL before and during the Telnet session. The filter reverts to the original after the Telnet session has ended.

Cisco IOS Firewall Packet Inspection and Proxy Firewalls

The combination of services offered by the Cisco IOS Firewall, providing both power and flexibility, makes the Cisco security offerings an optimal security solution. The administrator has the option to log any or all protocols, and to allow or deny traffic by port, protocol, or IP address.

Figure 21-6 *Cisco IOS Firewall Process*

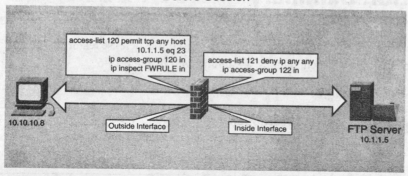

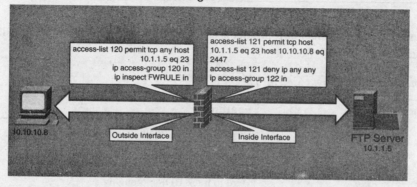

Table 21-5 summarizes the technologies available and the benefit of each to the administrator.

Table 21-5 *Capabilities of the Cisco IOS Firewall*

Capability	Benefit
Layered defense	A breach in one area does not compromise all of the network.
Packet filtering	May block specific types of packets.
ALG	The end user never connects directly to the resource.
Stateful packet filtering	Tracks the state of a connection and drops those packets that are not authorized.
Cisco IOS Firewall	Filters packets based on session and application.
Cisco IOS Authentication Proxy	Enables use of RADIUS or TACACS+.
Cisco IOS IPS	Identifies over 700 common attacks and refutes them.
Logging	Allows real-time logging of any or all events.

Foundation Summary

This chapter has given you an overview of the Cisco IOS defense features. The first area discussed was the three firewall technologies, as summarized in Table 21-6.

Table 21-6 *Firewall Technologies*

Technology	Description
Packet filtering	Uses IP addresses or port numbers with an ACL.
ALG	Works like a proxy server.
Stateful packet filtering	Uses ACLs. Also knows the connection state to determine access.

It is important to remember how protocols are handled within the stateful packet filter, as summarized in Table 21-7.

Table 21-7 *Protocol Handling by a Stateful Packet Filter*

Applications	Features
TCP	Checks flow information
	Tracks sequence numbers
UDP	Hard to track UDP thoroughly
	No sequence numbers in UDP
	Checks timeouts
	Tracks source and destination IP addresses
	Tracks source and destination UDP ports
Applications	Watches application negotiations
Connectionless services (GRE, IPsec, and so on)	Usually defaults to stateless packet filter operation

The Cisco IOS Firewall feature set consists of three systems:

■   Cisco IOS Firewall

— Permits or denies specified TCP and UDP traffic

— Maintains a state table

— Modifies ACLs dynamically

— Protects against DoS attacks

— Inspects packets passing through the interface

■   Authentication Proxy

— Provides AAA authentication

■   IPS

— Provides intrusion detection that allows four actions:

Drop the packet

Block the IP address

Terminate the TCP session

Send an alarm

The Cisco IOS Firewall modifies ACLs dynamically as data passes through the interface, editing the ACLs as data is permitted or denied.

Q&A

The questions and scenarios in this book are designed to be challenging and to make sure that you know the answer. Rather than allowing you to derive the answers from clues hidden inside the questions themselves, the questions challenge your understanding and recall of the subject.

Hopefully, mastering these questions will help you limit the number of exam questions on which you narrow your choices to two options and then guess.

You can find the answers to these questions in Appendix A. For more practice with exam-like question formats, use the exam engine on the CD-ROM.

1. You are designing a network that should have three servers available for access from the Internet, e-mail, FTP, and the web. How should this network be designed?

2. What are the three technologies used in firewalls and what are the main characteristics of each?

3. Which protocols does the Cisco IOS Firewall process recognize?

4. Why does the stateful packet filter not work with UDP?

5. What type of firewall monitors the applications and allows ports to be opened and closed in response to the application protocol negotiation?

6. You have a server that must service two different programs simultaneously. One of these programs contains your company's payroll records; the other program allows external users to browse a list of your employees. How should you design this access?

7. You are notified that a new security risk has been found in your version of BGP. What would you use to see all of the BGP packets on the network?

8. You are looking at an access list on your firewall. This access list has additional **permit** statements that you know, for a fact, are not in the configuration. How do you explain this?

9. What is the purpose of an authentication proxy server?

Exam Topic List

This chapter covers the following topics that you need to master for the CCNP ISCW exam:

- **Configure a Cisco IOS Firewall Using the CLI**—Describes the five steps that enable you to configure a simple firewall using the CLI.

- **Configure a Basic Firewall Using SDM**—Explains how replacing the CLI with a graphical interface, the Basic Firewall Wizard, makes configurations quick, accurate, and intuitive.

- **Configure an Advanced Firewall Using SDM**—Describes how adding a DMZ or configuring multiple untrusted networks through the Advanced Firewall Wizard combines ease of use with multiple options to provide for all your configuration needs.

CHAPTER 22

Implementing Cisco IOS Firewalls

Using a router as a firewall is a viable solution for many networks. This chapter explores how to use Cisco IOS Software features to set up and monitor a firewall. Although this chapter does not go into the design concepts of security, it does show you how to quickly configure the Cisco IOS features to secure your network.

"Do I Know This Already?" Quiz

The purpose of the "Do I Know This Already?" quiz is to help you decide whether you really need to read the entire chapter. If you already intend to read the entire chapter, you do not necessarily need to answer these questions now.

The 9-question quiz, derived from the major sections in the "Foundation Topics" portion of the chapter, helps you to determine how to spend your limited study time.

Table 22-1 outlines the major topics discussed in this chapter and the "Do I Know This Already?" quiz questions that correspond to those topics.

Table 22-1 *"Do I Know This Already?" Foundation Topics Section-to-Question Mapping*

Foundation Topics Section	Questions Covered in This Section	Score
Configure a Cisco IOS Firewall Using the CLI	1–4	
Configure a Basic Firewall Using SDM	5–6	
Configure an Advanced Firewall Using SDM	7–9	
Total Score		

CAUTION The goal of self-assessment is to gauge your mastery of the topics in this chapter. If you do not know the answer to a question or are only partially sure of the answer, you should mark this question wrong for purposes of self-assessment. Giving yourself credit for an answer that you correctly guess skews your self-assessment results and might provide you with a false sense of security.

1. Which of the following is the proper syntax to define an inspection rule named "myrule" that will inspect FTP packets?

   a. **ip inspect name inspection-name myrule protocol alert on timeout 30**

   b. **ip inspect name myrule protocol ftp alert on timeout 30**

   c. **ip inspect name myrule ftp alert on timeout 30**

   d. **ip inspect name inspection-name myrule protocol ftp alert on timeout 30**

2. Which of the following is the correct command to apply the inspection rule named "myrule" to an interface to inspect packets traveling into the interface?

   a. **ip inspect myrule**

   b. **ip inspect in myrule**

   c. **ip inspect inbound myrule**

   d. **ip inspect myrule in**

3. Which of the following is the correct syntax used to enable real-time alerts?

   a. **ip-inspect alert**

   b. **no ip-inspect alert-off**

   c. **ip-inspect alert-on**

   d. **ip-inspect alert-on**

4. What is the default time between alert updates when using IP inspection?

   a. 10 seconds

   b. 20 seconds

   c. 30 seconds

   d. 60 seconds

5. Which of the following is true regarding the Basic Firewall Wizard used in SDM?

   a. The Basic Firewall Wizard allows only two interfaces to be configured.

   b. The Basic Firewall Wizard allows multiple trusted interfaces to be configured.

   c. The Basic Firewall Wizard allows only one DMZ to be configured.

   d. The Basic Firewall Wizard allows multiple untrusted interfaces to be configured.

6. Which of the following is not true regarding the Basic Firewall Wizard used in SDM?

   a. You may edit policies for a specific protocol and interface within the Basic Firewall Wizard.

   b. You must use the CLI or the Advanced Firewall Wizard to edit policies for a specific protocol on an interface.

    c. You may use the Basic Firewall Wizard on a router with more than two trusted interfaces.

    d. You may use the Basic Firewall Wizard on a router with more than one DMZ.

7. Which of the following is true regarding the Advanced Firewall Wizard?

    a. You must already have defined a security policy in order to use it inside the Advanced Firewall Wizard.

    b. There are four default application security policies built into SDM (None, Low, Medium, and High).

    c. There are three default application security policies built into SDM (Low, Medium, and High).

    d. Application security policies are not used in conjunction with the Advanced Firewall Wizard.

8. Which of the following is true regarding the Advanced Firewall Wizard?

    a. Auditing is configured on a global level, affecting all protocols simultaneously.

    b. Auditing is available only if logging is enabled.

    c. Auditing is configured on a per-protocol level.

    d. Logging is available only if auditing has been enabled.

9. Which is true regarding the Advanced Firewall Wizard?

    a. Logging must be configured through the CLI before starting the wizard.

    b. Logging may be configured through the wizard.

    c. The logging hosts must be configured through the CLI before starting the wizard

    d. The wizard allows a maximum of three logging hosts.

The answers to the "Do I Know This Already?" quiz are found in Appendix A, "Answers to the 'Do I Know This Already?' Quizzes and Q&A Sections." The suggested choices for your next step are as follows:

■ **5 or fewer overall score**—Read the entire chapter. This includes the "Foundation Topics," "Foundation Summary," and "Q&A" sections.

■ **6 or 7 overall score**—Begin with the "Foundation Summary" section, and then go to the "Q&A" section.

■ **8 or 9 overall score**—If you want more review on these topics, skip to the "Foundation Summary" section, and then go to the "Q&A" section. Otherwise, move to the next chapter.

Foundation Topics

Configure a Cisco IOS Firewall Using the CLI

Configuring a Cisco IOS firewall using the CLI is simple. You already know how to make and access ACLs. A Cisco IOS firewall allows you to add inspection rules to the interface. An inspection rule is simply another method of ensuring the safety of that interface. The router drops packets that are unsafe in the context of the already established connections. For example, when a TCP inspection rule is added to an interface, a TCP reset (RST) packet is not allowed into the interface unless there has previously been a TCP connection established with the machine sending the reset.

When using inspection rules, you must apply an ACL to the interface. Any packet may be rejected by the inspection rule, the ACL, or both. The packet is first examined by the access list. If the packet passes the access list, then the inspection rule is checked next to determine whether that packet may transition the interface.

There are five simple steps to implementing inspection rules through the CLI:

Step 1   Choose the interface and packet direction to inspect.

Step 2   Configure an IP ACL for the interface.

Step 3   Define the inspection rules.

Step 4   Apply the inspection rules and the ACL to the interface.

Step 5   Verify the configuration.

Step 1: Choose an Interface and Packet Direction to Inspect

Choosing an interface is generally very easy. There are two general guidelines that will help you decide where to apply an ACL and inspection rule. Although every network is different, these two general guidelines will help you decide how and where to apply the ACL and inspection rule:

- On an interface where untrusted traffic originates:

    — Apply the ACL on the inbound direction of the interface so that only traffic allowed by the ACL is inspected.

    — Apply the inspection rule on the inbound direction of the interface so that only traffic considered safe transits the interface.

■   For all other interfaces, apply the ACL on the outbound direction of the interface so that all unwanted traffic is dropped rather than sent over the network.

Step 2: Configure an IP ACL for the Interface

You must use extended access lists when you are also using inspection rules. If you are not familiar with extended access lists or need to review them, you are encouraged to do so now. A full explanation of extended access lists can be found at Cisco.com.

The access list in Example 22-1 would be applied to the outside interface. This access list allows users outside the network to connect to the SMTP server residing at 10.10.1.9 and the HTTP server residing at 10.10.1.15.

Example 22-1 *Extended Access List*

```
ip access-list extended acl_from_outside
 permit tcp any host 10.10.1.9 eq 25
 permit tcp any host 10.10.1.15 eq 80
 deny ip any any log
```

Step 3: Define the Inspection Rules

An inspection rule is defined through the **ip inspect** command, the syntax for which is as follows:

```
[no] ip inspect name inspection-name protocol [alert {on ¦ off}] [timeout seconds]
```

Table 22-2 lists the parameters available for this command.

Table 22-2 **ip inspect** *Command Parameters*

Parameter	Description
inspection-name	Defines the name of the inspection rule.
protocol	Defines the protocol to be inspected. There are more than 170 supported protocols, some of which are as follows: TCP, UDP, ICMP, SMTP, ESMTP, SMTP, EMSTP, CUSEEME, FTP, FTPS, HTTP, H323, NETSHOW, RCMD, RealAudio, RPC, RTSP, SIP, SKINNY, SQLNET, TFTP, VDOLive.
alert {on | off}	Toggles alerts on or off.
timeout *seconds*	Defines the time interval in seconds between alert updates (default is 10 seconds).

Example 22-2 shows how to define the inspection rules for this example.

Example 22-2   *IP Inspection Rules*

```
Router(config)#ip inspect name from_outside ftp alert off audit-trail on timeout 60
Router(config)#ip inspect name from_outside http alert on audit-trail on timeout 30
```

The preceding example sets the timeout for FTP to 60 seconds. No alerts are sent for FTP. The HTTP setting decreases the timeout to 30 seconds and sends alerts regarding HTTP. Both FTP and HTTP in this example use audit trails.

Step 4: Apply the Inspection Rules and the ACL to the Interface

Now that the ACL and inspection rules have been defined, you must apply these to the interface. Audit trails will be used, so your first task is to enable audit trails in the global configuration. Alerts have also been chosen. These are simple to set up with the global commands executed in Example 22-3.

Example 22-3   *Global Configuration for Logging and Alerts*

```
Router(config)#ip inspect audit-trail
! enables the delivery of audit trail messages using syslog
Router(config)#logging on
! turns on logging
Router(config)#logging host 10.10.1.20
! sets out logging server to 10.10.1.20
Router(config)#no ip inspect alert-off
! turns on real-time alerts
```

Now that the global configuration is established, you simply apply the previously defined inspection rules to the individual interface. While you are in the interface configuration mode, you will also apply the ACL to that interface as demonstrated in Example 22-4.

Example 22-4   *Apply Inspection Rules to the Interface*

```
Router(config)#int e0/0
Router(config-if)#ip inspect from_outside in
Router(config-if)#ip access-group acl_from_outside in
Router(config-if)#^z
```

The configuration is now complete. The next step is to verify your configuration.

Step 5: Verify the Configuration

Verification of the setup is very simple. The **show ip inspect** command displays how the inspection rules have been configured. The syntax for the **show ip inspect** command is as follows:

```
show ip inspect [name inspection-name | config | interface | session {detail} |
    statistics | all]
```

A number of options are available with this command, as described in Table 22-3.

Table 22-3 show ip inspect *Command Options*

Parameter	Description
name *inspection-name*	Displays the configured inspection with the defined inspection name
config	Displays the entire IP inspection configuration
interface	Displays the configurations used within the interface mode
session	Displays sessions that are currently being tracked
detail	Displays additional details about current sessions
statistics	Displays statistical information
all	Displays all information

The output from this command is simple to understand, as demonstrated in Example 22-5.

Example 22-5 **show ip inspect session** *Command Output*

```
Router#show ip inspect session
Established Sessions
 Session 70A64274 (172.16.1.12:32956)=>(10.10.1.5:25) tcp SIS_OPEN
   Created 00:00:07, Last heard 00:00:03
   Bytes sent (initiator:responder) [137:319] acl created 2
     Inbound access-list acl_from_outside applied to interface Ethernet0/0
```

Example 22-6 shows the output from a **show ip inspect all** command.

Example 22-6 **show ip inspect all** *Command Output*

```
Router#show ip inspect all
Session audit trail is enabled
one-minute (sampling period) thresholds are [400:500] connections
max-incomplete sessions thresholds are [400:500]
max-incomplete tcp connections per host is 50. Block-time 0 minute.
tcp synwait-time is 30 sec -- tcp finwait-time is 5 sec
tcp idle-time is 3600 sec -- udp idle-time is 30 sec
dns-timeout is 5 sec
Inspection Rule Configuration
 Inspection name inspect_from_outside
```

continues

Example 22-6 **show ip inspect all** *Command Output (Continued)*

```
      tcp timeout 3600
      udp timeout 30
      ftp timeout 3600
Interface Configuration
 Interface Ethernet0
  Inbound inspection rule is inspect_from_outside
      tcp timeout 3600
      udp timeout 30
      ftp timeout 3600
  Outgoing inspection rule is not set
  Inbound access list is acl_from_outside
  Outgoing access list is not set
Established Sessions
 Session 25A6E1C (10.3.0.1:46065)=>(10.1.1.9:25) ftp SIS_OPEN
 Session 25A34A0 (10.1.1.9:20)=>(10.3.0.1:46072) ftp-data SIS_OPEN
```

Although debugging IP inspection is beyond the scope of this book, it can be helpful to know a few of the **debug** commands associated with inspection. Table 22-4 shows the most common **debug** commands associated with IP inspection and describes their purpose.

Table 22-4 **debug ip inspect** *Commands*

Command	Description
debug ip inspect function-trace	Debugs the functions used by **ip inspect**
debug ip inspect object-creation	Debugs the creation of objects used by **ip inspect**
debug ip inspect object-deletion	Debugs the deletion of objects used by **ip inspect**
debug ip inspect events	Debugs events within **ip inspect**
debug ip inspect timers	Debugs timers used in **ip inspect**
debug ip inspect detail	Provides detailed debugging of **ip inspect**

Configure a Basic Firewall Using SDM

SDM provides a graphical interface that allows you to configure security on Cisco routers quickly. The ease of use and automatic features of SDM can be a great benefit to the administrator. When using SDM to configure a basic firewall, you use the same five steps that you used with the CLI, as described in the previous section. However, because you are using a graphical interface, these steps are not easily distinguishable from each other.

This section describes how to use SDM to configure a basic firewall. If you have never used SDM before, you will be amazed by how quickly you can complete a simple configuration. The next section describes how to use SDM to configure an advanced firewall.

After you start SDM, click the **Configure** button at the top of the window. Next, click **Firewall and ACL** in the Tasks bar on the left. As Figure 22-1 shows, the default choice is Basic Firewall. Before you click the Launch the Selected Task button, notice the How do I pull-down menu at the bottom of the window. This menu provides help on the most common tasks when using SDM.

Figure 22-1   *Basic Firewall Creation*

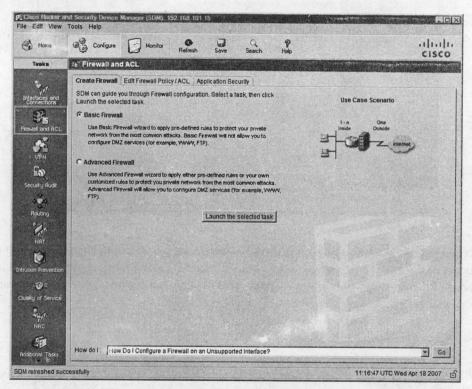

Click the **Launch the selected task** button. You are taken to the Basic Firewall Interface Configuration window, shown in Figure 22-2, where you decide which interfaces are trusted and which are not trusted. Notice that this window also provides you with the option to allow SDM access through the untrusted interface. Assign the trust levels to the interfaces and click the **Next>** button.

Figure 22-2 *Basic Firewall Interface Configuration*

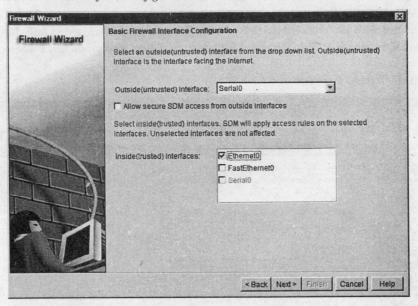

Next, you see the Firewall Configuration Summary window, shown in Figure 22-3. Although this is one of the most basic configurations possible, you can see that many configuration options have been enabled with just a few mouse clicks. These options are converted into CLI commands to be saved in the configuration.

Figure 22-3 *Firewall Configuration Summary*

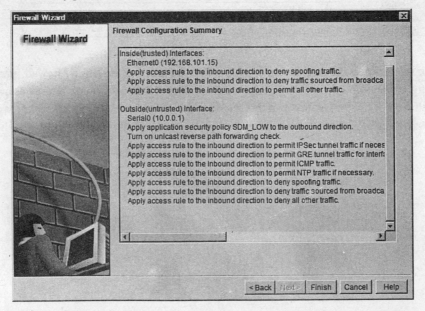

At this point, the basic configuration is complete. However, you might want to adjust some parameters to allow things such as HTTP or FTP access. You so this under the Edit Firewall Policy/ ACL tab. As shown in Figure 22-4, this tab enables you to permit or deny access based on source or destination address, type of service, and application. Although this is still the basic firewall configuration, the flexibility provided is more than adequate for many users' needs. Take a few moments and review this short section before moving on to the advanced configuration using SDM.

Figure 22-4 *Edit Firewall Policy/ACL Tab*

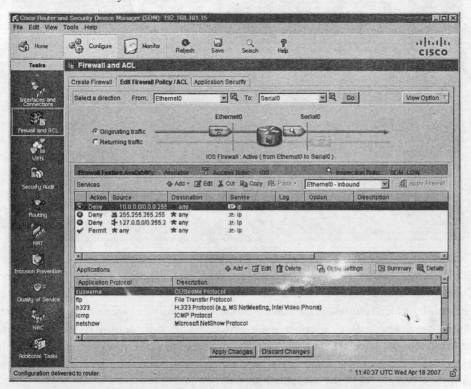

Configure an Advanced Firewall Using SDM

The Advanced Firewall Wizard provides easy access to some features that are not available under the Basic Firewall option. The Advanced Firewall Wizard works similarly to the Basic Firewall Wizard. As shown in Figure 22-5, simply choose **Advanced Firewall** instead of Basic Firewall on the Create Firewall tab of the Firewall and ACL window.

Figure 22-5 *Advanced Firewall Creation*

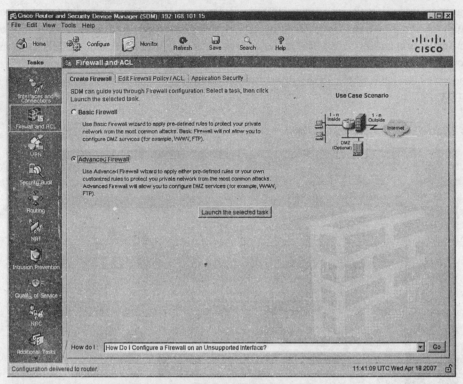

Click **Launch the selected task** and you are presented with the Advanced Firewall Interface Configuration window. The most noticeable differences on this window compared to the Basic Firewall Interface Configuration window (shown previously in Figure 22-2) are that you can choose multiple interfaces as either inside (trusted) or outside (untrusted) and can choose an interface for use as a DMZ. Figure 22-6 shows the Advanced Firewall Interface Configuration window. In this example, Ethernet0 is selected as a trusted (inside) network, Serial0 as an untrusted (outside) network, and FastEthernet0 as a DMZ.

Click the **Next>** button, and you are taken to the Advanced Firewall DMZ Service Configuration window, where you configure aspects of the DMZ. As Figure 22-7 shows, the wizard knows that FastEthernet0 was chosen as the DMZ. Click the **Add** button to continue.

Figure 22-6 *Advanced Firewall Interface Configuration*

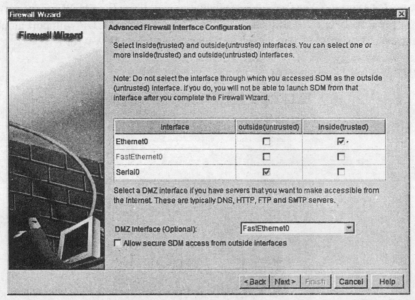

Figure 22-7 *Advanced Firewall DMZ Service Configuration*

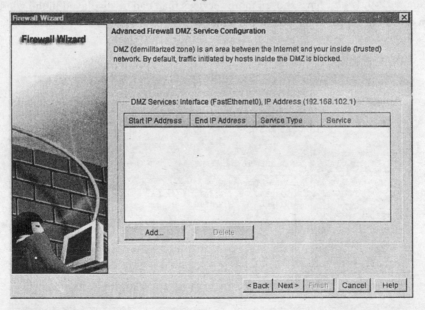

Because you need to add services to the DMZ, you are prompted for the starting and ending IP addresses for a service. You then choose whether you will use IP or UDP and the service associated with the previously entered addresses. Figure 22-8 shows that UDP with port number 500 (IKE) was chosen. Alternatively, you can choose a service such as WWW or FTP.

Figure 22-8 *DMZ Service Configuration*

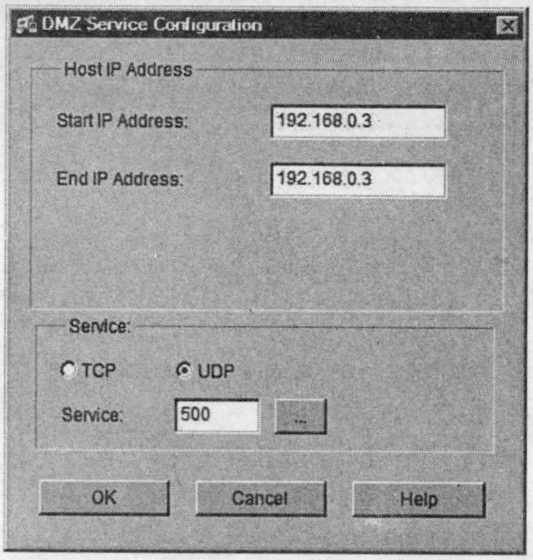

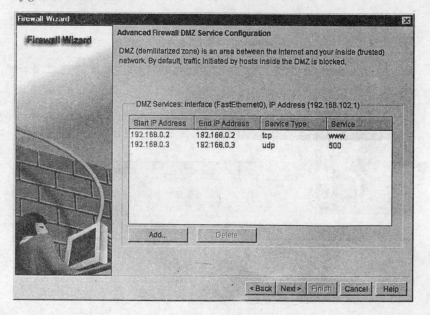

After you have added as many services as you wish to the DMZ, you see a list similar to that shown in Figure 22-9. If you have chosen more services than can be displayed in the window, you will see a scroll bar on the right side of the window.

Figure 22-9 *Configured DMZ Services*

After all the services are configured, click **Next>** to go to the Advanced Firewall Security Configuration window. In this window, you can choose to use one of the three built-in SDM security policies (High Security, Medium Security, or Low Security) or a custom security policy for applications. In Figure 22-10, the option to use a custom policy has been chosen. When you choose this option, you are presented with an additional pull-down menu that allows you to select an existing policy or create a new one.

Figure 22-10   *Advanced Firewall Security Configuration*

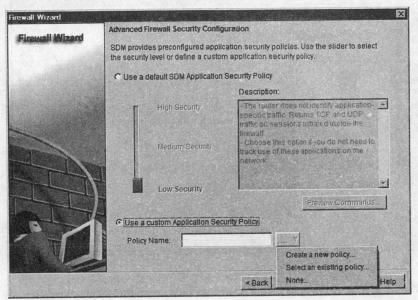

When presented with the Application Security window, you can choose any of the predefined applications from the list on the left. In Figure 22-11, the general parameters for the TCP and UDP protocols have been set up. Clicking the **Next>** button brings up the Application Security Window.

Figure 22-11 *Application Security*

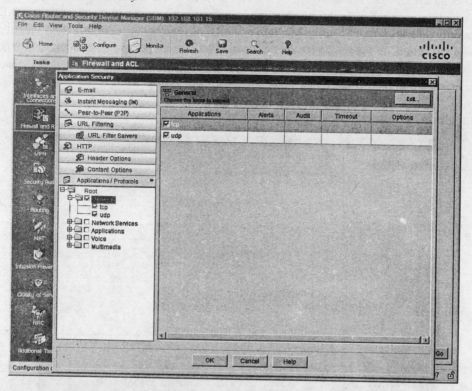

Even after you have configured all the protocols and applications that are required by the network, you can still go back to any given protocol and edit the inspection mode defaults for that protocol within the security policy. As Figure 22-12 shows, you can set alerts, auditing, and timeouts on a per-protocol basis. Clicking **OK** at the bottom of the dialog box takes you back to the Advanced Firewall Security Configuration window (see Figure 22-10), which allows you to save the policy.

Figure 22-12 *Editing the Inspection Mode*

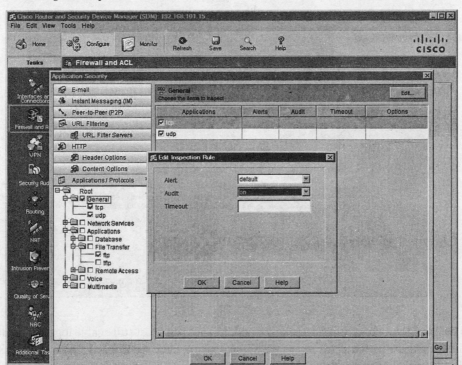

After you have finished configuring the security policy, you need to verify the policy. The Firewall Configuration Summary window shown in Figure 22-13 displays the security policies as configured by interface. Notice that numerous rules have been applied on the outside interface and that HTTP and IKE traffic is allowed to enter the interface bound for specific hosts. Several different protocols have also been filtered.

Figure 22-13 *Firewall Configuration Summary*

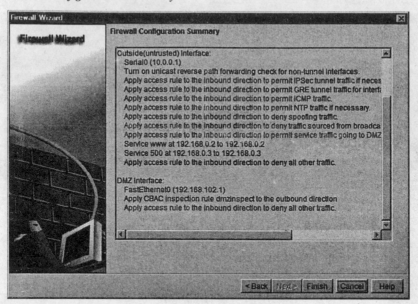

This completes the configuration of the policies, but you must still enable logging. To do so, click the **Configure** button at the top of the SDM window, click **Additional Tasks** in the Tasks bar on the left, expand **Router Properties**, and click **Logging**. Click **Edit** in the upper-right corner of the Logging pane to open the Logging dialog box. As Figure 22-14 shows, you can enable logging, set the logging levels, assign logging hosts, and set the logging buffer.

Figure 22-14 *Setting Logging Options*

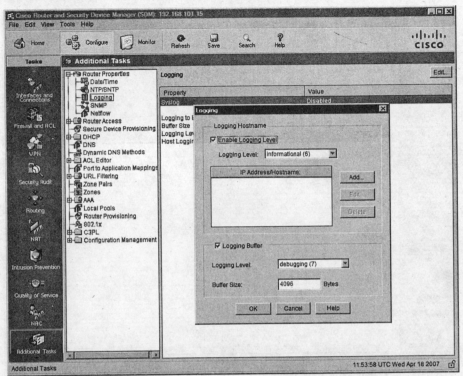

At this point, the security policy configuration has been completed for this router. The final task is to monitor the router. Click the **Monitor** button at the top of the SDM window, and then click **Firewall Status** in the Tasks bar. As shown in Figure 22-15, this allows you to see what packets are flowing through the router.

Figure 22-15 *Monitor Firewall Status*

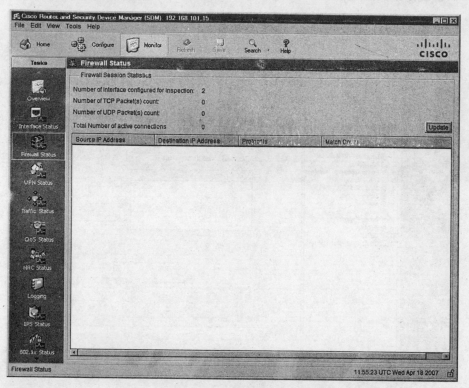

Foundation Summary

Configuring a router as a firewall using either the CLI or one of the wizards is not a difficult task. Take a few moments to review the highlights of this chapter. If you do not understand what is being presented, go back through the text and review.

There are five steps to implementing inspection rules:

Step 1   Choose the interface and packet direction to inspect.

Step 2   Configure an IP ACL for the interface.

Step 3   Define the inspection rules.

Step 4   Apply the inspection rules and the ACL to the interface.

Step 5   Verify the configuration.

To configure an extended access list, enter the following:

```
ip access-list extended acl_from_outside
 permit tcp any host 10.10.1.5 eq 25
 permit tcp any host 10.10.1.10 eq 80
 deny ip any any log
```

To create an inspection rule, enter the following:

```
ip inspect name inspection-name protocol [alert {on ¦ off}] [timeout seconds]
```

Table 22-5 lists and describes the parameters available for the preceding command.

Table 22-5   ip inspect name *Parameters*

Parameter	Description
inspection-name	Defines the name of the inspection rule.
protocol	Defines the protocol to be inspected. The list of supported protocols is as follows: TCP, UDP, ICMP, SMTP, ESMTP, SMTP, EMSTP, CUSEEME, FTP, FTPS, HTTP, H323, NETSHOW, RCMD, RealAudio, RPC, RTSP, SIP, SKINNY, SQLNET, TFTP, VDOLive.
**alert {on	off}**	Toggles alerts on or off.
timeout *seconds*	Defines the time interval in seconds between alert updates (default is 10 seconds).

A sample IP inspection rule is as follows:

```
Router(config)#ip inspect name from_outside ftp alert off audit-trail on timeout 60
Router(config)#ip inspect name from_outside http alert on audit-trail on timeout 30
```

The **show ip inspect** command displays how the inspection rules have been configured. Table 22-6 describes the parameters for this command.

Table 22-6 **show ip inspect** *Command Options*

Parameter	Description
name *inspection-name*	Displays the configured inspection with the defined inspection name
config	Displays the entire IP inspection configuration
interface	Displays the configurations used within the interface mode
session	Displays sessions that are currently being tracked
detail	Displays additional details about current sessions
statistics	Displays statistical information
all	Displays all information

Table 22-7 shows the most common **debug** commands associated with the **ip inspection** command and their purpose.

Table 22-7 **debug ip inspect** *Commands*

Command	Description
debug ip inspect function-trace	Debugs the functions used by **ip inspect**
debug ip inspect object-creation	Debugs the creation of objects used by **ip inspect**
debug ip inspect object-deletion	Debugs the deletion of objects used by **ip inspect**
debug ip inspect events	Debugs events within **ip inspect**
debug ip inspect timers	Debugs timers used in **ip inspect**
debug ip inspect detail	Detailed debugging of **ip inspect**

There are many features available when using either the Basic Firewall Wizard or the Advanced Firewall Wizard. But, there are also a few major differences between the two wizards. Table 22-8 highlights the differences.

Table 22-8 *Basic and Advanced Firewall Wizard Features*

Feature	Basic	Advanced
Configure untrusted network	Yes	Yes
Configure multiple untrusted networks	No	Yes
Configure trusted network	Yes	Yes
Configure multiple trusted networks	Yes	Yes

Table 22-8 *Basic and Advanced Firewall Wizard Features (Continued)*

Feature	Basic	Advanced
Configure DMZ	No	Yes
Configure protocol-specific alerts	Yes	Yes
Configure protocol-specific logging	Yes	Yes
Graphical interface	Yes	Yes
Monitoring capabilities	Yes	Yes

Q&A

The questions and scenarios in this book are designed to be challenging and to make sure that you know the answer. Rather than allowing you to derive the answers from clues hidden inside the questions themselves, the questions challenge your understanding and recall of the subject.

Hopefully, mastering these questions will help you limit the number of exam questions on which you narrow your choices to two options, and then guess.

You can find the answers to these questions in Appendix A. For more practice with exam-like question formats, use the exam engine on the CD-ROM.

1. Name some advantages of using the Advanced Firewall Wizard as opposed to using the CLI.

2. When is it appropriate to use the Basic Firewall Wizard instead of the Advanced Firewall Wizard?

3. What are the steps to configure a firewall using the CLI?

4. Under what circumstances should the default timeouts for alerts be changed?

Exam Topic List

This chapter covers the following topics that you need to master for the CCNP ISCW exam:

- **IDS and IPS Functions and Operations**—Describes the functions and operations of intrusion detection systems (IDS) and intrusion prevention systems (IPS) and the difference between IDS and IPS

- **Categories of IDS and IPS**—Describes the categories of IDS and IPS

- **IDS and IPS Signatures**—Describes the four types of IDS and IPS signatures

- **Signature Reaction**—Describes what happens when a signature is matched

- **IOS Configuration**—Describes how to configure and verify Cisco IOS IPS using the CLI

- **SDM Configuration**—Describes the Cisco IOS IPS tasks that are completed with SDM

CHAPTER 23

Implementing Cisco IDS and IPS

A good network security boundary is designed to prevent unauthorized access by malicious attackers. Although network security has evolved in recent years, so have the attacks. Today, various attacks are actually delivered inside of innocent-looking packets. Consequently, security has advanced well beyond a policy to permit some packets and deny the rest.

Intrusion detection systems (IDS) and intrusion prevention systems (IPS) allow a network to examine packets and decide whether to simply notify an administrator or take some sort of corrective or preventative action. IDS and IPS are often used together to provide additional layers of protection for the network.

This chapter first explains the differences between and unique attributes of IDS and IPS. The different types of IDS and IPS are explored, as well as the various signatures used by the two systems. The chapter then details how to configure IDS and IPS in a Cisco environment.

"Do I Know This Already?" Quiz

The purpose of the "Do I Know This Already?" quiz is to help you decide whether you really need to read the entire chapter. If you already intend to read the entire chapter, you do not necessarily need to answer these questions now.

The 10-question quiz, derived from the major sections in the "Foundation Topics" portion of the chapter, helps you to determine how to spend your limited study time.

Table 23-1 outlines the major topics discussed in this chapter and the "Do I Know This Already?" quiz questions that correspond to those topics.

Table 23-1 *"Do I Know This Already?" Foundation Topics Section-to-Question Mapping*

Foundation Topics Section	Questions Covered in This Section	Score
IDS and IPS Functions and Operations	1–2	
Categories of IDS and IPS	3–4	
IDS and IPS Signatures	5	

continues

Table 23-1 *"Do I Know This Already?" Foundation Topics Section-to-Question Mapping (Continued)*

Foundation Topics Section	Questions Covered in This Section	Score
Signature Reaction	6	
Cisco IOS Configuration	7–8	
SDM Configuration	9–10	
Total Score		

1. Where are IDS and IPS devices located in a network?

   a. An IDS device sits in the path of traffic, while an IPS device sits outside traffic flows.

   b. Both the IDS and IPS devices sit in the path of network traffic.

   c. An IPS device sits in the path of traffic, while an IDS device sits outside of traffic flows.

   d. Both IDS and IPS devices sit outside traffic flowing through the network.

   e. IDS or IPS devices can sit either in the path of traffic or outside the path of traffic. The location determines the functionality.

2. How can an IDS block unsafe network traffic?

   a. An IDS cannot block network traffic.

   b. An IDS can communicate configuration information to other network devices, such as routers and firewalls.

   c. Because the IDS sits in the path of network traffic, it can easily block the traffic itself.

   d. The IDS tells the IPS to block the traffic.

   e. When the IDS sends an alert, other network devices dynamically react according to the alert message.

3. Which of the following are characteristics of NIDS and NIPS (select all that apply)?

   a. Can examine encrypted traffic

   b. Handles additional hosts without additional resources

   c. Can assess the success or failure of an attack

   d. Can detect network reconnaissance attacks

   e. Can detect DoS attacks

   f. Ensures that proper use credentials are used, either from the local database or the AAA server

4. In an anomaly-based system, what is considered statistical information?

   a. Dynamically learned information

   b. Default rules in the IDS and IPS

   c. Statically configured rules in the IDS and IPS

   d. Manually learned information

   e. Information that is transferred into the router via TFTP

5. Which of the following are categories of IDS and IPS signatures (select all that apply)?

   a. Honeypot

   b. Exploit

   c. Anomaly

   d. Connection

   e. String

6. Which of the following actions of an IDS or IPS device is normally not the only action performed?

   a. Send an alarm

   b. Drop the packet

   c. Reset the connection

   d. Block the source IP address

   e. Block the connection

7. What is the purpose of the Cisco IOS command **ip ips name** *ipsname* **list** *ACL#*?

   a. It applies an ACL to all signatures in the IPS indicated, but the IPS must already exist.

   b. It applies an ACL to all signatures in the IPS indicated, and creates the IPS if it does not already exist.

   c. It applies an ACL to a subset of the signatures in the IPS indicated.

   d. It applies an ACL to the interface that the IPS indicated is configured on.

   e. It creates a new ACL for the IPS indicated, and enters ACL configuration mode.

8. Which command is used to display the number of active signatures?

   a. **show ip ips signatures**

   b. **show ip ips signatures active**

   c. **sh ip ips active signatures**

   d. **show ip ips configuration**

   e. **show ip ips configuration active**

9. When creating a new rule in SDM (via the Create IPS tab), what functions are possible (select all that apply)?

    a. Select the interface to which to apply the IPS rule

    b. Create an ACL for use with the IPS rules

    c. Select the traffic flow direction for IPS rule inspection

    d. Merge SDFs together

    e. Specify the location of the SDF

10. In the SDF Locations window, what is the purpose of checking the Use Built-In Signatures (as backup) checkbox?

    a. It adds the default signatures to the SDF.

    b. It causes the IPS to use only the default signatures.

    c. It causes the IPS to use the default signatures only when the selected SDF is unavailable.

    d. It causes the IPS to use the default signatures instead of those in the selected SDF.

    e. It changes the default signature file to be the selected SDF.

The answers to the "Do I Know This Already?" quiz are found in Appendix A, "Answers to the 'Do I Know This Already?' Quizzes and Q&A Sections." The suggested choices for your next step are as follows:

■ **6 or fewer overall score**—Read the entire chapter. This includes the "Foundation Topics," "Foundation Summary," and "Q&A" sections.

■ **7 or 8 overall score**—Begin with the "Foundation Summary" section, and then go to the "Q&A" section.

■ **9 or 10 overall score**—If you want more review on these topics, skip to the "Foundation Summary" section, and then go to the "Q&A" section. Otherwise, move to the next chapter.

Foundation Topics

IDS and IPS Functions and Operations

There are two types of intrusion systems that are typically deployed in networks today: intrusion detection systems (IDS) and intrusion prevention systems (IPS). Each type of system consists of either hardware or software that first detects network anomalies. How a particular system responds to anomalies determines its true role.

An IDS device does not sit in the path of active network traffic. Instead, traffic is copied out to the IDS device for inspection. If the IDS device determines that a series of packets does not have the best of intentions, it sends an alert to a management station for further action. The IDS can also actively configure network devices (such as routers and firewalls) to block or quarantine the mischievous packet flows.

Remember that the IDS itself cannot block any packets, because it does not sit in the data path. So, if the IDS discovers an issue, the first few packets are already in the network. At best, the IDS can block further packets from getting into the network and reaching their target.

An IPS, on the other hand, sits directly in the path of network traffic. All packets must travel through the IPS device as they cross the segment that the IPS lives on. When the IPS detects some sort of anomaly, it can both alert a management station and block the questionable packets. Because all packets are flowing through the IPS, you do not need to configure other network devices to block the bad packets.

An IPS is useful for detecting viruses, worms, malicious applications, and vulnerability exploits, none of which should be permitted into the network at all. Because the IPS can immediately block packets deemed bad, it can shield the network from such exploits.

As a quick review:

- **Virus**—A virus is one type of malicious code that tries to propagate itself across a network. It is normally attached to other programs and executes a particular unwanted function on a user workstation when that program executes. A virus propagates itself by infecting other programs on the same computer. It can do serious damage, such as erasing files or erasing an entire disk. It can also be a simple annoyance, such as popping up a message. A virus cannot spread to a new computer without human assistance, such as opening an infected file in an e-mail attachment or through file sharing.

- **Worm**—A worm is another type of malicious code that executes arbitrary code and installs copies of itself in the memory of the infected computer. It can then spread to and infect other hosts from the infected computer. Like a virus, a worm is also a program that propagates itself. Unlike a virus, a worm can spread itself automatically over the network from one computer to the next. Worms simply take advantage of automatic file sending and receiving features found on many computers, or it uses its own e-mail code to send infected files to mail recipients.

- **Trojan horse**—A general term that refers to a program that appears desirable but actually contains something harmful; for example, a downloaded game that contains code to erase files. The malicious contents could also hold a virus or a worm.

- **Vulnerability exploit**—An attack that specifically targets a known device vulnerability.

The IDS and IPS can be used together to provide tighter network security. An IPS blocks traffic that it considers unsafe. If the traffic in question is legitimate, however, then the IPS could be doing more harm than good. Such traffic is commonly called "gray area" traffic. Instead of forcing the IPS to make a yes or no decision on it, gray area traffic can be sent off to the IDS for further inspection and analysis.

Categories of IDS and IPS

There are two ways to categorize IDS and IPS systems. The first category is the scope of the system. The two IDS and IPS scopes are

- Network

- Host

An IDS or IPS can sit in the network (as a hardware appliance or a software module in an existing network device) and thus provide protection to the entire network or segments of the network. Such systems are called either network intrusion detection systems (NIDS) or network intrusion protection systems (NIPS). One appliance can monitor multiple hosts, and additional hosts can be added without increasing the number of NIDS or NIPS devices. A network-based system can monitor and detect buffer overflows, network reconnaissance, and denial of service (DoS) attacks. The ability to see attacks against the network offers the opportunity to determine the extent of the attack.

As a reminder, consider the following attacks:

- **Denial of Service (DoS)**—Where one device overloads the network access to or CPU utilization of a target system

- **Distributed Denial of Service (DDoS)**—Where multiple devices overload the network access to or CPU utilization of a target system

- **Recon**—An attempt to gather important network information from a device, such as accounts, passwords, host names, other IP addresses in use, and operating systems (to name a few)

Network-based systems can only detect and prevent intrusive activity. If a single packet does sneak through, the network-based system cannot assess the success or failure of the attack. Also, network-based systems cannot inspect encrypted traffic. As networks continue to grow, the need for additional network sensors could become cost prohibitive.

The second scope category of an IDS or IPS is at the host level. Such systems are typically software modules that reside on a workstation or server and provide anomaly detection and prevention services for that single device. These systems are called either host intrusion detection systems (HIDS) or host intrusion prevention systems (HIPS). When encrypted traffic flows across a network, only the HIPS or HIDS can see the plaintext contents of the packets. Virtually all implementations of host-based intrusion systems are HIPS versus HIDS. Cisco Security Agent is an example of a HIPS.

Another way to categorize IDS and IPS systems is the approach they take to identify malicious traffic. The three different identity approach mechanisms are as follows:

- **Signature-based**—Signature-based systems match for a specific byte pattern or content in a packet. Such pattern matching is typically combined with particular IP address, protocol, and/ or port combinations to perform very precise matches. Attacks, such as Trojan horses, tend to change port numbers regularly, which can invalidate a pure signature-based system. Also, because signature patterns are preprogrammed into an IDS and IPS device, day-zero attacks (attacks that exploit a vulnerability in a new system patch) are difficult to defend against.

- **Policy-based**—Policy-based systems use algorithms to examine strings of packets to determine patterns and behavior. For example, such an approach might detect a ping sweep, whereas a signature-based system would see only individual ping packets. Additional restrictions, such as IP addresses, protocols, or ports, can be applied (as can be done with signature-based systems). Some policies, such as restricting the ability to browse certain websites, typically involve communication with some type of blacklist database to ensure up-to-date information.

- **Anomaly-based**—Anomaly-based systems look for behavior that deviates from the "norm." This implies that some definition of "normal" is dynamically learned by (statistical) or preprogrammed into (nonstatistical) the system before it can detect anything abnormal. Such systems tend to work well in small networks, where normal behavior can be easily defined. However, in larger networks, the definition of normal can easily be too expansive and complex to adequately define.

A honeypot is a common term heard in the threat prevention and protection environment. A honeypot is simply a sacrificial network device. Such a machine is left on the network to attract attackers, and thus pull the malicious packets away from important network resources. Packet flows captured on the honeypot device can be used to analyze the attack and construct an appropriate defense. Because the desire is to collect the devious packets, honeypots tend to be considered IDS instead of IPS. It is important to remember that any device that is used as a honeypot is not returned to the general network population, because the honeypot device is quite likely infected with all sorts of interesting malware.

IDS and IPS Signatures

For the purpose of IDS and IPS, a signature is a pattern of data or traffic that should cause a reaction when it passes through the IDS or IPS. As described earlier in this chapter, this action can be either to send some type of alert or to actively block the offending traffic.

An IDS and IPS uses microengines to match signatures against packets and packet flows. In other words, each signature constitutes its own microengine. There are four categories of IDS and IPS signatures:

- **Exploit**—An exploit signature typically identifies malicious traffic by matching a traffic pattern. Usually, each exploit has a unique signature (either packet flows or packet contents). Thus, each attack requires a signature for detection. If the exploit is modified in any way, a new signature is needed to be able to match the modified attack.

- **Connection**—A connection signature is aware of valid network connections and protocols. The behavior of accepted connections and protocols is known in advance, and any actions that occur beyond the normal circumstances are considered suspect. Note that *normal* is also a subjective definition of acceptable network traffic and behavior.

- **String**—String signatures typically use regular expressions to match patterns. This is similar to how exploit signatures work, except a regular expression can be used to match many conditions, whereas an exploit signature usually matches a single exploit.

- **DoS**—DoS signatures examine behavior typical of a DoS attack. Because there are many forms and flavors of DoS attacks, there are a variety of DoS signatures used. As with exploit signatures, a behavioral change in a DoS attack would require an update to the DoS signature engine.

A Cisco IOS router can act as an inline NIPS device. By default, there are 100 signatures embedded in Cisco IOS Software (132 total with all of the subsignatures). Additional signature definition files (SDFs) can be downloaded from Cisco.com. Individual signatures within an SDF can be enabled and disabled.

Signature Reaction

Once a signature is matched, the IDS and IPS device reacts immediately. On a Cisco IDS and IPS device, alert messages can be sent with either syslog or the Security Device Event Exchange (SDEE) protocol. SDEE is considered more secure than syslog. IDS and IPS signature reactions include the following:

- **Send an alarm to a syslog or centralized management server**—Normally, an alarm notification is not the only action.

- **Drop the packet**—This action should not affect a legitimate user if the source IP address is spoofed, as is often the case in DoS attacks.

- **Reset the connection**—This action works only on connection-oriented protocols, such as TCP. This action has no effect on UDP packet flows.

- **Block network traffic from the source IP address for a specified amount of time**—This effectively imposes a penalty on the attacking traffic, and permits time for attack analysis to occur. Blocking traffic should be done only if IP addresses are spoofed; otherwise, legitimate traffic is likely affected.

- **Block network traffic on the connection for a specified amount of time**—This introduces a penalty on the attacking traffic. Connection-oriented attacks typically do not employ IP spoofing, due to the two-way communications needed for such traffic. But if the ability to establish a connection is blocked, the attacker still could use other attack methods, or combinations of attacks.

For fully functional real-time monitoring of IDS and IPS events, the Cisco Security Monitoring, Analysis and Response System (CS-MARS) can be used. CiscoWorks Monitoring Center for Security, which is a component of CiscoWorks VPN/Security Management Solution (VMS), can also be used to collect logs and alert messages.

Cisco IOS IPS Configuration

Only a few steps and Cisco IOS IPS configuration commands are needed to establish a basic Cisco IOS NIPS setup:

Step 1   **Specify the location of the SDF**—Various SDFs can exist in the Cisco IOS device, but only one can be referenced.

Step 2   **Configure the failure parameter**—This tells the Cisco IOS device what to do if the signature microengine (SME) is not available to scan the traffic.

Step 3   **Create an IPS rule**—This creates a name that is later applied to an interface. The rule uses the SDF previously defined. Optionally, an access control list (ACL) can be applied to restrict which traffic is scanned.

Step 4   **Apply the IPS rule to an interface**—Once the rule has been created, it must be applied to an interface to become operational.

Example 23-1 shows a sample Cisco IOS configuration of the four basic IPS setup steps from the preceding list. Comments have been added in the sample output to describe the function of each command. Also, options of each command are shown where appropriate.

Example 23-1   *Cisco IOS IPS Configuration Commands*

```
! step 1 - define the location of the SDF
Router(config)#ip ips sdf ?
  builtin   Use the built in signature definition file
  location  Location of the signature definition file
Router(config)#ip ips sdf builtin
! step 2 - define the behavior if an SME fails
Router(config)#ip ips fail ?
  closed  Do not forward traffic of the failed module.
Router(config)#ip ips fail closed
! step 3 - create an IPS rule, and optionally apply an ACL
Router(config)#ip ips name ?
  WORD  Name of IPS rule
Router(config)#ip ips name testips ?
  list  Specify an access list to match
  <cr>
Router(config)#ip ips name testips list 123
! step 4 - apply the IPS rule to an interface
Router(config)#interface fastethernet 0/0
Router(config-if)#ip ips testips ?
  in   Inbound IPS
  out  Outbound IPS
Router(config-if)#ip ips testips in
Router(config-if)#
```

The **ip ips sdf builtin** command does not appear in the configuration file because this is a default command. This command appears only if a nondefault SDF is used.

The **ip ips fail closed** command instructs the IPS to drop packets if an SME is not available to scan traffic. Use the **no ip ips fail closed** command to forward all traffic that is not scanned.

The **ip ips name testips list 123** command creates an IPS rule called **testips** and applies extended ACL 123 for further scrutiny of scanned packets. The ACL is not shown. A standard access list can also be used if granular packet selection is not desired.

The **ip ips testips in** command applies the IPS rule **testips** to the FastEthernet 0/0 interface. Although an IPS rule can be applied both inbound and outbound, it is best to apply the rules inbound. This ensures that packets are inspected before they enter the router.

Additional IPS configurations are also possible (and desired). Other IPS configuration parameters include the ability to do the following:

- Merge SDFs

- Disable, delete, and filter selected signatures within an SDF

- Change the default location of the SDF

Example 23-2 shows each of these additional configuration parameters. As with Example 23-1, comments and options are shown where applicable.

Example 23-2 *Additional Cisco IOS IPS Configuration Commands*

```
! optional step 1 - merge SDFs
Router#copy flash:attack-drop.sdf ips-sdf
Router#copy ips-sdf flash:newsignatures.sdf
Router#config term
Enter configuration commands, one per line. End with CNTL/Z.
Router(config)#ip ips sdf location ?
  WORD  URL of the signature definition file
Router(config)#ip ips sdf location flash:newsignatures.sdf
! optional step 2 - disable, delete, and filter selected signatures
Router(config)#ip ips signature 1107 ?
  <0-65535>  Sub signature id
  delete     Delete the specified signature
  disable    Disable the specified signature
  list       Specify an access list to match
Router(config)#ip ips signature 5037 0 delete
%IPS Signature 5037:0 is marked for deletion
%IPS The signature will be deleted when signatures are reloaded or saved
Router(config)#ip ips signature 1107 0 disable
%IPS Signature 1107:0 is disabled
Router(config)#ip ips signature 6190 0 list 152
%IPS Signature 6190:0 will use acl 152
! optional step 3 - change the location of the SDF
Router(config)#ip ips name newips list 123
Router(config)#interface fastethernet 0/0
Router(config-if)#ip ips newips in
Router(config-if)#
```

The command **copy flash:attack-drop.sdf ips-sdf** merges the *attack-drop.sdf* file with the default SDF stored in memory. The **copy ips-sdf flash:newsignatures.sdf** command creates a new SDF in flash that can be used when the router boots. Within configuration mode, the location of the SDF that is used by the router is modified with the command **ip ips sdf location flash:newsignatures.sdf**. This location must be changed before any modifications to the SDF can be performed.

The ability to disable, delete, and filter selected signatures is shown in optional step 2 configuration commands. Note that signature 1107 is disabled (but remains in the SDF), while signature 5037 is deleted from the SDF. Signature 6190 has its own ACL applied to it for specific packet scanning.

In optional step 3, a new IPS name is created and applied to the FastEthernet 0/0 interface. The original IPS name from Example 23-1 could be used, but the **ip ips name** command must be executed again to map the new SDF into the IPS. If the original IPS name is remapped, it does not need to be reapplied to the interface.

Once the IPS has been configured in the Cisco IOS device, you can use the **show ip ips configuration** command to examine the IPS configuration, as demonstrated in Example 23-3.

Example 23-3 *Cisco IOS IPS Verification*

```
Router#show ip ips configuration
Configured SDF Locations: none
Builtin signatures are enabled and loaded
Last successful SDF load time: 01:51:57 UTC Sep 22 2006
IDS fail closed is enabled
Fastpath ips is enabled
Quick run mode is enabled
Event notification through syslog is enabled
Event notification through Net Director is disabled
Event notification through SDEE is enabled
Total Active Signatures: 132
Total Inactive Signatures: 0
Signature 1107:0 disable
PostOffice:HostID:0 OrgID:0 Msg dropped:0
         :Curr Event Buf Size:0  Configured:100
Post Office is not enabled - No connections are active
IDS Rule Configuration
 IPS name testips
   acl list 123
Interface Configuration
 Interface FastEthernet0/0
  Inbound IPS rule is testips
    acl list 123
  Outgoing IPS rule is not set
Router#
```

Example 23-3 shows the IPS configuration on the Cisco IOS device using the initial configuration (Example 23-1). At the top of the output, only the built-in signatures are used, and the location is not set (in other words, the default location is used). There are a total of 132 active signatures, which are the 100 default signatures and 32 default subsignatures. And the IPS uses the name testips. Example 23-4 shows the IPS configuration after optional configurations have been applied.

Example 23-4 *Cisco IOS IPS Verification*

```
Router#show ip ips configuration
Configured SDF Locations:
 flash:newsignatures.sdf
Builtin signatures are enabled and loaded
Last successful SDF load time: 02:15:08 UTC Sep 22 2006
IDS fail closed is enabled
Fastpath ips is enabled
Quick run mode is enabled
Event notification through syslog is enabled
Event notification through Net Director is disabled
Event notification through SDEE is enabled
Total Active Signatures: 183
Total Inactive Signatures: 0
Signature 6190:0 list   152
Signature 1107:0 disable
PostOffice:HostID:0 OrgID:0 Msg dropped:0
           :Curr Event Buf Size:0  Configured:100
Post Office is not enabled - No connections are active
IDS Rule Configuration
 IPS name testips
    acl list 123
 IPS name newips
    acl list 123
Interface Configuration
 Interface FastEthernet0/0
  Inbound IPS rule is newips
    acl list 123
  Outgoing IPS rule is not set
Router#
```

In Example 23-4, the SDF location uses the new signature file created in Example 23-2 (*newsignatures.sdf*). The number of active signatures has increased to 183, and the signatures that were modified (1107 and 6190) are shown. At the bottom of the output, the new IPS name is created and applied to FastEthernet 0/0.

SDM Configuration

As has been shown throughout this book, SDM is a powerful web-based tool that permits point-and-click configuration of virtually any Cisco IOS feature. Among its many wizards, SDM provides a useful set of wizards to configure IPS options. To access the IPS configuration wizards in SDM, click the **Configure** button at the top of the window, and then click the **Intrusion Prevention** button in the Tasks bar on the left side of the window. Figure 23-1 shows this initial entry point into IPS configuration within SDM.

Figure 23-1 *SDM IPS Wizard*

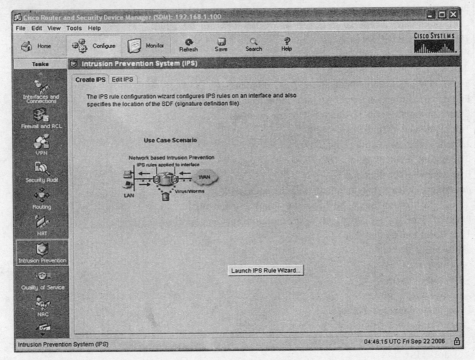

As shown in Figure 23-1, there are two tabs at the top of this window:

- **Create IPS**—Offers the opportunity to launch the IPS Rule Wizard, which permits you to create new IPS rules.

- **Edit IPS**—Grants access to all existing IPS policies, signatures, and interface configurations. This tab is explored later in this section.

To create a new IPS rule, click the **Launch IPS Rule Wizard** button on the Create IPS tab. The wizard starts with a welcome window, which reminds you that the purpose of the wizard is to help you do the following:

- Select the interface to apply the IPS rule to

- Select the traffic flow direction that should be inspected by the IPS rules

- Specify the location of the SDF to be used by the router

Click **Next** at the bottom of the window to continue into the wizard.

The first configuration window in the IPS Wizard is the Select Interfaces window, as shown in Figure 23-2. All interfaces that are not currently configured for IPS operations are displayed. If this is your first IPS configuration in this Cisco IOS device, all interfaces should be displayed.

Figure 23-2   *SDM IPS Wizard Select Interfaces Window*

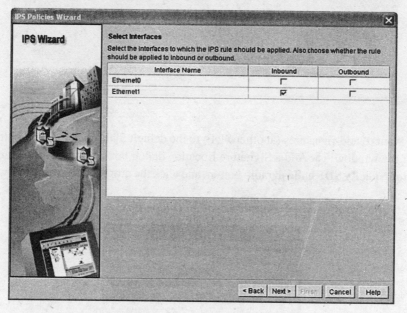

Although both Inbound and Outbound options exist for each interface, it is best to check only the Inbound check box when IPS rules are applied. This triggers the IPS as packets arrive and does not give them access to the router before first being inspected. Notice that the interfaces are listed only by their name and not by their function or role. You must be aware of which interface is attached to which segment (for example, inside or outside) before you continue with this wizard. In Figure 23-2, interface Ethernet1 is selected for IPS operations. Click **Next** to continue.

Next, you must select the SDF location from the wizard. Figure 23-3 shows the SDF Locations window with only the default signature selected.

Figure 23-3 *SDM IPS Wizard SDF Locations Window*

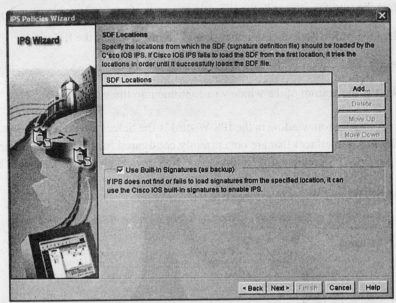

If you want to add signatures (another SDF) to the default SDF, click the **Add** button on the right side of the window. The Add a Signature Location dialog box appears, as shown in Figure 23-4. Click the **Specify SDF onflash** radio button, and click the drop-down arrow to view SDFs in flash.

Figure 23-4 *SDM IPS Wizard Add a Signature Location Dialog Box*

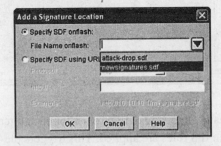

In Figure 23-4, the *newsignatures.sdf* file is highlighted in the drop-down menu. Click the desired SDF in the drop-down menu to enter it in the File Name onflash field. Click **OK** to add the specified file to the SDF locations. It is possible to add multiple SDFs in the SDF Locations window. Simply click the **Add** button again and repeat the process.

In the middle of the SDF Locations window, shown previously in Figure 23-3, is a Use Built-In Signatures (as backup) checkbox, which should be checked. This option allows the IPS to use the default SDF if the specified SDFs are unavailable for any reason (accidentally erased from flash, for example). When the necessary additional files are listed in the SDF Locations window, click **Next>** to continue.

A Summary window appears that simply reminds you of your accomplishments over the last few windows. In Figure 23-2, you selected an interface, and in Figure 23-4, you added a new SDF. Figure 23-5 shows the results of these actions.

Figure 23-5   *SDM IPS Wizard Summary Window*

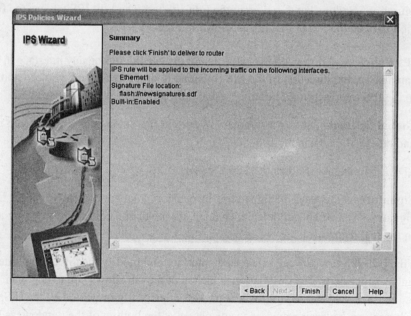

Click **Finish** to complete the creation of a new SDF. SDM then pushes the configuration out to the router and compiles the new signatures into the Cisco IOS IPS. Figure 23-6 shows the results after the new signatures have been added to the Cisco IOS IPS.

Figure 23-6 *SDM IPS Signature Compilation Status*

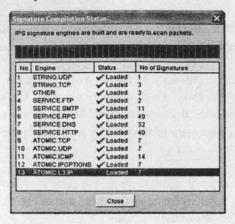

Click **Close** at the bottom of the Signature Compilation Status window. You are returned to the IPS Configuration window, but this time to the Edit IPS tab. The Edit IPS tab has the following four selection bars on the left of the tab, as shown in Figure 23-7:

- **IPS Policies**—Allows you to enable and/or disable the IPS on any interface in the router. You can also set the direction of the IPS (inbound is suggested). And, you can add an access list to the IPS interface configuration so that only certain packets are inspected.

- **Global Settings**—Shows a summary of current IPS settings, and allows you to add SDFs to and delete SDFs from the IPS.

- **SDEE Messages**—Shows the SDEE events.

- **Signatures**—Displays all signatures, by category, that are currently loaded. Individual signatures can be added, deleted, enabled, disabled, and edited (by applying an ACL to an individual signature).

From the Edit IPS tab, you can select each interface and modify the direction of the IPS (although inbound is suggested). The Edit button at the top of the tab allows you to apply an ACL to the IPS on the interface, and thus restrict which packets are actually inspected by the IPS. When there is no ACL applied, a warning message is displayed at the bottom of the window, as Figure 23-7 depicts.

Figure 23-8 shows the Signatures pane of the Edit IPS tab.

Figure 23-7 *SDM IPS Policies*

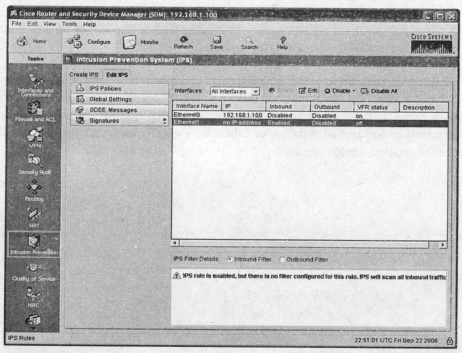

Figure 23-8 *SDM IPS Signatures*

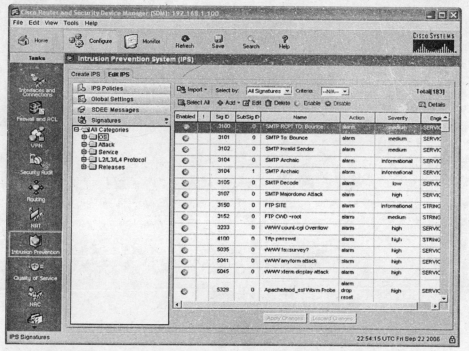

You can view signatures by category (for example, OS or Attack), or you can list all signatures together (All Categories). You can add, delete, enable, and disable individual signatures. Also, you can add an ACL to an individual signature by clicking the Edit button. This enables you to restrict the traffic that is actually scanned by the signature.

Note that once you complete the Create IPS tab (as described earlier), the IPS is operational. There is no need to *apply* the configuration to make it active. All operations performed from the Edit IPS tab are applied to the working configuration. Remember that in SDM, groups of configurations are created offline and applied to the router in batches. Typically, each time you click the OK button in a configuration window, the configuration is pushed out to the router.

Foundation Summary

There are two types of intrusion systems:

- Intrusion Detection System, which is characterized by the following attributes:

  — Does not sit in the path of network traffic

  — Can send alerts when problems are detected

  — Cannot block packets itself

  — Can direct other network devices to block or quarantine mischievous packets

  — Can be used to inspect gray area traffic that the IPS avoids

- Intrusion Prevention System, which is characterized by the following attributes:

  — Sits in the path of network traffic

  — Can send alerts when problems are detected

  — Can block mischievous packets if needed

  — Is useful for detecting viruses, worms, malicious applications, and vulnerability exploits

  — Can send gray area traffic to the IDS for further inspection

There are two ways to categorize an IPS or IPS:

- Scope

- Approach to identify malicious traffic

There are two scopes for IDS and IPS:

- Network

- Host

NIDS and NIPS:

- Sits in the network as a hardware appliance or software module on an existing network device

- Provides protection to an entire network segment, and one appliance can monitor multiple hosts

■ Can monitor and detect buffer overflows, network reconnaissance, and DoS attacks

■ Cannot determine whether an attack is successful or not

■ Cannot inspect encrypted traffic

HIDS and HIPS:

■ Are typically software modules on host systems

■ Can inspect encrypted traffic once it is decrypted on the host

There are three mechanisms to identify malicious traffic:

■ Signature-based:

— Match for specific byte patterns or content in packets

— Combine such pattern matching with IP address, protocol, and port information to perform more precise matches

— Are preprogrammed into IDS and IPS devices

— Are not good at detecting day-zero attacks

■ Policy-based:

— Use algorithms to examine strings of packets to determine patterns and behavior

— Can also restrict by IP address, protocol, and port numbers

— Might require access to databases to ensure up-to-date information

■ Anomaly-based:

— Look for behavior that deviates from the "norm"

— A definition of "normal" must first exist

— Statistical = dynamically learned information

— Nonstatistical = preprogrammed information

— Tend to work better in smaller networks, where normal behavior is better defined and controlled

A honeypot is

■ A sacrificial network device

■ Used to attract attackers away from important network devices

- Captures packet flows for future attack analysis

- Tend to be IDS devices rather than IPS devices

There are four categories of IDS and IPS signatures:

- **Exploit**—An exploit signature typically identifies traffic by matching a traffic pattern. Each attack requires a different signature.

- **Connection**—A connection signature is aware of valid network connections and protocols. Abnormal behavior is considered suspect.

- **String**—String signatures typically use regular expressions to match many patterns.

- **DoS**—DoS signatures examine behavior that is typical of DoS attacks (of which there are many).

When a signature is matched, the IDS and IPS device can react by one or more of the following:

- Sending an alarm

- Dropping the packet

- Resetting the connection

- Blocking traffic from the source IP address

- Blocking traffic on the connection

Cisco IOS IPS configuration commands:

- **ip ips sdf builtin**—Uses the built-in SDF, but does not appear in the configuration file because it is a default command

- **ip ips sdf location** *name*—Uses the SDF *name*

- **ip ips fail closed**—Drops packets if an SME is not available to scan the traffic

- **ip ips name** *name* [**list** *num*]—Creates an IPS rule called *name* and optionally applies ACL *num* to it to refine packet selection

- **ip ips name in** | **out**—Applies the IPS to an interface in either the inbound or outbound direction

- **copy flash:***name1* **ips-sdf**—Merges the file *name1* in flash with the active SDF

- **copy ips-sdf flash:***name2*—Copies the new SDF back into flash so that it is available upon boot

- **show ip ips configuration**—Verifies the entire IPS configuration

SDM offers the IPS Wizard to create and edit IPS rules. The Create IPS tab allows you to

- Select the interface
- Select the traffic direction to inspect
- Specify the SDF

Screens within the Create IPS tab include

- **Select Interfaces window**—Lists all interfaces that are currently not enabled for IPS, and allows you to select inbound or outbound IPS direction.

- **SDF Locations window**—Shows all IPS SDFs. You can add additional SDFs or remove ones from the list displayed. This window also has the Use Built-In Signatures (as backup) check box, which, when checked, permits the default SDF to be used if the selected SDFs are unavailable.

- **Add a Signature Location dialog box**—Used to add another SDF to the IPS rule.

- **IPS Summary window**—Displays all the options configured from the IPS Wizard.

The Edit IPS tab offers access to

- **IPS Policies**—Allows you to edit an existing IPS configuration. You can enable/disable IPS on an interface, and you can add an ACL to IPS to be more selective when scanning packets.

- **Global Settings**—Shows a summary of IPS settings, and allows you to add/delete SDFs.

- **SDEE Messages**—Shows SDEE events.

- **Signatures**—Displays all signatures, and allows you to add, delete, enable, disable, and edit individual signatures.

Q&A

The questions and scenarios in this book are designed to be challenging and to make sure that you know the answer. Rather than allowing you to derive the answers from clues hidden inside the questions themselves, the questions challenge your understanding and recall of the subject.

Hopefully, mastering these questions will help you limit the number of exam questions on which you narrow your choices to two options, and then guess.

You can find the answers to these questions in Appendix A. For more practice with exam-like question formats, use the exam engine on the CD-ROM.

1. What are the two types of intrusion systems deployed in networks today?

2. How does an IDS differ from an IPS?

3. What are the differences between network-based IDS and IPS and host-based IDS and IPS?

4. What are the three mechanisms to identify malicious traffic?

5. Of the identity mechanisms, which one may need access to a blacklist database for further information?

6. What are the four categories of IDS and IPS signatures?

7. What happens when a signature is matched?

8. Which IOS configuration command is used to apply a nondefault SDF?

9. In which direction should an IDS or IPS be applied?

10. What Cisco IOS command is used to display the number of active signatures?

11. What are the two tabs in the SDM IPS Wizard?

Answers to the "Do I Know This Already?" Quizzes and Q&A Sections

Chapter 1

"Do I Know This Already?"

1. A, B, C
2. B
3. B
4. D
5. D
6. A
7. A
8. A, B, C, D

Q&A

1. The Application Layer

2. The network is the essential piece that they all have in common. This applies to all infrastructure (Layers 1, 2, and 3) as well as supplemental services that might be shared additionally.

3. Teleworker architecture

4. Campus, data center, branch, WAN/MAN, enterprise edge, teleworker

5. This is a rather subjective answer as it calls upon the reader to reference a solution from his or her own experiences. To a large degree, the solution will be based on personal networking experiences. A sample solution would include

   ■ Cisco ISR with SRST, VPN, and Content Engine enabled. It may also be prudent to add an AIM-CUE to the ISR to provide a local automated attendant and voice messaging capabilities for some users (up to 25 on an AIM CUE).

- QoS-enabled MPLS WAN connectivity with bandwidth sufficient to support the voice, video, and data needs of those 50 users.

- Cisco IP Phones and IP Communicator Software for user laptops.

6. Voice and collaboration services

   Device mobility services

   Security and identity services

   Storage services

   Computer services

   Application networking services

   Network infrastructure virtualization

   Services management

   Adaptive management services

   Advanced analytics services

   Infrastructure management services

7. Resources to which virtualization capabilities apply include infrastructure components such as VLANs, VRFs, MPLS, virtual firewalls, VPNs, presence information, message routing, load balancing, hard disk space, IO, CPU cycles, and more.

8. SONA is the framework that provides a technological and architectural guide for enterprise networks in the quest to become an IIN. SONA is the path; IIN is the destination.

Chapter 2

"Do I Know This Already?"

1. C
2. C
3. B
4. D
5. A
6. A
7. C
8. A

Q&A

1. IPsec VPNs utilize a CPE router that maintains a nailed-up connection to the central site at all times. A remote-access VPN is a client-initiated connection to the central site.

2. High availability for services and applications, removal of any single point of failure, secure the network infrastructure, implement QoS throughout the entire network, decide on central site VPN solution (IPsec or remote access or both), Internet access, Cisco IP Phone, and Cisco Unified Video Advantage camera solution at teleworker's home.

3. MPLS provides larger sites with Layer 3 connectivity and any-to-any communication capabilities. MPLS also provides for QoS traffic markings to be honored within the provider's network.

   Frame Relay and ATM are traditional Layer 2 WAN technologies. These are useful in providing connectivity to sites that do not require integrated services and applications. Traffic flows are governed by traffic-shaping techniques that do not recognize Layer 3 DSCP markings.

   Site-to-site VPN is useful in connecting to partner or company site networks over the public Internet. Obviously, the nature of the public Internet means that all traffic is best-effort.

4. High-speed Internet access in residences, IP telephony, IP video capabilities, IPsec and remote-access VPNs, service provider network augmentation and service offerings, and QoS traffic classification and protection guarantees.

5. Network administration personnel go to somewhat great lengths to ensure the security of the network through firewall, IPS, IDS, and traffic filtering. This mitigates the effects of day-zero virus outbreaks, exploit exposure, and so on. When an enterprise chooses to support a teleworker solution, they extend the enterprise network presence to the home of the teleworker employee. This adds significant risk and exposure because the company might have a difficult time controlling traffic flow to and/or from the teleworker home. The Internet surfing habits of the teleworker and others in the home pose a potential risk as a point of entry for viruses, spyware, malware, and more. Support for the teleworker home network is also a significant factor. Most homes today have wireless networks that exist in varying degrees of security. Enterprise network administrators do not necessarily wish to dictate wired and/or wireless security practices to individuals in their own homes.

6. There are quite a few ways in which the risks posed to the enterprise by teleworker home networks might be mitigated. The teleworker must agree to the corporate security policy regarding network access, of course. However, some options, such as personal firewalls, anti-spam, anti-spyware, and other related software can assist in mitigating risks. Such software should be dictated and supported by the enterprise network administrators. Disallowing options in the VPN connectivity, such as split-tunneling, might also be considered.

7. Satellite connectivity does offer some degree of connectivity to the teleworker when other access methods are not available. It should be understood that the service levels provided by high-speed, low latency solutions such as DSL, cable, and fiber are more suited to the needs of a converged network. Some services might not function properly via satellite. Other options might include leased lines at the home. A T1 or fractional T1 terminated at a residential premise is not unheard of in the realm of possibilities. Obviously, there is the potential for significantly higher cost in such a solution.

   There are many additional possibilities. Each will come with its own set of challenges and benefits. These must be considered when offering teleworker services to employees.

8. Cisco.com contains a well-documented solution guide, known as an SRND, which contains tested best practices and configuration examples. It can be found at http://www.cisco.com/go/srnd.

Chapter 3

"Do I Know This Already?"

1. C
2. B
3. A
4. B
5. E
6. C
7. D
8. A
9. C
10. A
11. A
12. D
13. A, B, C
14. A
15. B
16. B

17. B

18. C

Q&A

1. As one example, consider a cable provider offering service to a very spread-out subscriber base, such as a rural setting. Fiber optic cable would allow longer distances to be reached and good signal strength to be maintained so that all customers would receive the offered applications and services at similar levels of service.

2. **Antenna site**—A location containing a cable provider's main receiving and satellite dish facilities. This site is chosen based on potential for optimal reception of transmissions over the air, via satellite, and via point-to-point communication.

   Headend—A master facility where signals are received, processed, formatted, and distributed over to the cable network. This includes both the transportation and distribution networks. This facility is typically heavily secured and sometimes "lights-out," meaning it is not regularly staffed.

   Transportation network—The means and media by which remote antenna sites are connected to the headend facility. Alternatively, this could be a headend facility connection to the distribution network. The transmission media may be microwave, coaxial supertrunk, or fiber optic.

   Distribution network—In typical cable system architectures, consists of trunk and feeder cables. The trunk is the backbone cable (usually 0.75-inch diameter) over which the primary connectivity is maintained. In many networks, the distribution network tends to be a hybrid fiber-coaxial network.

   Node—Performs optical-to-RF conversion of CATV signal as needed. Feeder cables (typically 0.5-inch diameter) originate from nodes that branch off into individual communities to provide services to anywhere between 100 and 2000 customers each.

   Subscriber drop—Connects the subscriber to the cable service network via a connection between the feeder portion of a distribution network and the subscriber terminal device (for example, a TV set, VCR, high-definition TV set-top box, or cable modem). The subscriber drop components consist of the physical coaxial cabling, grounding and attachment hardware, passive devices, and a set-top box.

3. From the cable providers' point of view, data over cable has enabled them to offer voice, video, and data services over a common access technology. They can now provide services similar to that of Vonage or other IP-based telephone service providers. From a teleworker perspective, the offerings could be as simple as corporate e-mail service, web services, content filtering and caching, security patches, virus updates, instant video conferencing, remote agent capabilities for call center agents, and more.

Future services might include video content streamed on-demand to the device of one's choosing or multiple devices simultaneously such as video-capable mobile phones, remote or in-car televisions, or devices in other locales.

4. Cable fits into the SONA framework at the networked infrastructure layer under the teleworker architecture. As part of the SONA framework, the teleworker architecture is vital to the evolution of the network into an IIN.

5. The steps defined by DOCSIS are as follows:

- **Step 1: Downstream setup**—At power-on, the cable modem scans and locks the downstream path for the allocated RF data channel in order for physical and data link layers to be established.

- **Step 2: Upstream setup**—The cable modem listens to the management messages arriving via the downstream path. These include information regarding how and when to communicate in the upstream path. These are used to establish the upstream physical and data link layers.

- **Step 3: Layer 1 and 2 establishment**—The connection is established from the CM to the CMTS to build physical and data link layers.

- **Step 4: IP address allocation**—After Layer 1 and 2 are established, Layer 3 can be allocated as well. This is done by the DHCP server.

- **Step 5: Getting DOCSIS configuration**—The CM requests the DOCSIS configuration file from the TFTP server. This is an ASCII file created by DOCSIS editors. A DOCSIS configuration file is a "binary file" that has the parameters for cable modems to come online in accordance to what the ISP is provisioning, such as maximum downstream and upstream rates, maximum upstream burst rate, class of service or baseline privacy, MIBs, and many other parameters. This file can be loaded on the CM via TFTP or the CM can be manually configured.

- **Step 6: Register QoS with CMTS**—The CM negotiates traffic types and QoS settings with the CMTS.

- **Step 7: IP network initialization**—Once Layers 1, 2, and 3 are established and the configuration file is pulled from the TFTP server, the CM provides routing services for hosts on the subscriber side of the CM. It also performs some NAT functions so that multiple hosts might be represented by a single public IP address.

As part of the initialization phase, the CM makes contact with a DHCP server on the provider's network. The DHCP server provides the following information to the CM:

- IP address

- Subnet mask

- Default gateway

- TFTP server

- DHCP relay agent

- The complete name of the DOCSIS configuration file

- Address of ToD server

- Syslog server address

Once this information is obtained, the CM can issue a request to the ToD server to set its clock to the correct time. This facilitates syslog timestamps. At this point, also, it can issue a TFTP request to the TFTP server for its DOCSIS configuration file (discussed in the previous section).

6. Channel bonding capabilities and IPv6 support.

7. Upstream: 120 Mbps; Downstream: 160 Mbps

8. Radio frequency information

- Downstream frequency

- Upstream channel ID

- Network access configuration

Class of service information

- Class of service ID

- Maximum downstream rate

- Maximum upstream rate

- Upstream channel priority

- Minimum upstream rate

- Maximum upstream channel burst

- Class of service privacy enable

Vendor-specific options

- Vendor ID

- Vendor-specific options

SNMP management

- SNMP write-access control and SNMP MIB objects

Baseline privacy interface configuration

- Authorize wait timeout
- Reauthorize wait timeout
- Authorization grace timeout
- Operational wait timeout
- Rekey wait timeout
- TEK grace time
- Authorize reject wait timeout

Customer premises equipment

- Maximum number of CPEs
- CPE Ethernet MAC address

Software upgrade

- TFTP software server IP address
- Software image filename

Miscellaneous

- Concatenation support
- Use RFC 2104 HMAC-MD5
- CMTS authentication

Chapter 4

"Do I Know This Already?"

1. B
2. A
3. C
4. B

5. A
6. B
7. A
8. C
9. B
10. A
11. A
12. B
13. A
14. B
15. B
16. D
17. A, C, D
18. B
19. A and C
20. C
21. A and B

Q&A

1. Loading coils, fiber optic cables, bridge taps

2. Voice: 0–4 kHz; upstream data: 25–160 kHz; downstream data: 240 kHz to 1.5 MHz

3. 256

4. DMT will relocate the signal to another channel.

5. Asymmetric DSL uses mismatched download/upload transfer rates, and symmetric DSL uses matching download/upload transfer rates.

6. 1.5 to 8 Mbps, but newer implementations such as ADSL2, ADSL2+, and ADSL4 promise bandwidths upwards of 20–30 Mbps in the not so distant future.

7. The G.lite standard was specifically developed to meet the "plug-and-play" requirements of the consumer market segment. G.lite is a medium-bandwidth version of ADSL that allows up to 1.5 Mbps downstream and up to 512 kbps upstream. G.lite allows voice and data to coexist

on the wire without the use of splitters. G.lite is a globally standardized (ITU G.992.2) interoperable ADSL system. Typical telco implementations currently provide 1.5 Mbps downstream and 160 kbps upstream.

8. PPP authentication in the form of PAP or CHAP

9. PPP LCP

10. Discovery serves to find the MAC address of the peering device (aggregation router) and obtain a SESSION_ID. It allows the CPE to find all DSLAMs and aggregation routers available to it.

11. The destination MAC is the broadcast address ff.ff.ff.ff.ff.ff.

12. RFC 1483/2684

Chapter 5

"Do I Know This Already?"

1. A

2. C

3. A

4. B and C

5. B and C

6. B

7. A

8. B

9. A and C

10. B

11. A, B, C, D

12. B

Q&A

1. In reality, all the options in this chapter would be relevant. The DSL connection and associated PPPoE session would need to be in place and passing traffic. DHCP may or may not be used on the subscriber-facing side of the connection as many power users make the decision to address their own devices on the home network.

2. Certainly, there is. The use of the static default route is a network administration decision. It may well be that an IT department wishes to use a dynamic protocol to reach every site, regardless of size. Protocols such as OSPF and EIGRP would allow the definition of stub areas, which allow for dynamic protocol connectivity while minimizing impact of convergence events on the stubs.

3. Yes, there are. The purpose of the teleworker architecture is to provide the "in-the-office" experience for remote workers and sites. To provide the same integrated services and applications available to central-site workers, it may be necessary to disable PAT and, at times, NAT. There are still a significant number of applications that do not support use across NAT/PAT boundaries. They are becoming fewer as time progresses, but alas, they are still out there.

    Also of note is the fact that any host that needs to be reached from the outside (for example, an FTP server) would need to use NAT as opposed to PAT.

4. The **import all** option will dynamically populate any DNS server, WINS server, or other options, such as TFTP server, into the database so that they can be provided to hosts on the subscriber network.

5. The dialer interface is a logical interface that will contain parameters necessary for connecting to the provider network. A physical interface is bound to a logical dialer interface through the use of the **pppoe-client dial-pool-number** *number* command. The pool number specified by the **pppoe-client dial-pool-number** *number* command must match the number configured in the **dialer pool** *number* command on the dialer interface to properly bind or associate them.

6. Among the tasks necessary to configure PPPoE are the following:

    ■ Ethernet/ATM interface configuration

    ■ Dialer interface configuration

    ■ PAT configuration

    ■ DHCP server services configuration

    ■ Static default route configuration

    Each of these tasks must be completed before the data connectivity will function properly.

7. **show pppoe session all**

8. When a router receives a DHCP request, it checks all configured DHCP pools for a network match. If one is found, an address will be assigned from the appropriate pool. If no match is found, no DHCP offer is made. To service the request, the router would require an additional pool configuration matching the network in question. Alternatively, if no pool is sharing its subnet, an IP helper address must be configured to forward the DHCP request to the appropriate server or no address will be allocated.

Chapter 6

"Do I Know This Already?"

1. A and B

2. B

3. D

4. B

5. B and D

6. B

7. A

Q&A

1. 32. 0–15 are reserved for use by the ITU and 16–31 are reserved for use by the ATM Forum.

2. The **dsl operating-mode auto** command sets the router to automatically detect the type of DSL modulation in use by the provider.

3. The LLC header provides the ability to transport multiple protocols over a single virtual circuit. It accomplishes this by providing an additional header and a protocol identifier for each CPCS-PDU payload.

4. The AAL5MUX encapsulation would be used. Each Layer 3 routed protocol would require a separate virtual circuit configuration. The following are some of the various reasons why this might be done:

   ■ Policy routing based on protocol. Each protocol can then be routed across the ATM network using different pathways.

   ■ Each protocol can be assigned a differing throughput rate across the ATM network based on protocol priority.

   Certainly there are additional possibilities. These are merely for example and to encourage additional contemplation of the possibilities.

5. The provider-facing interface is interface ATM 0/0, physically. Logically, the virtual-template interface is configured with the necessary Layer 3 component. The virtual-template IP address configuration notes that it should be a negotiated address. That is, the address will be provided via DHCP from the service provider.

6. A dynamic routing protocol must be configured on the router to ensure proper reachability. If no dynamic routing protocol is in use, static routes to all reachable networks must be manually added to the router configuration.

7. Yes, there is. In cases where a default route is critical, even in the event of the loss of reachability via the dynamic routing protocol, a static default route can be added with a high administrative distance. This is called a floating static route and will be used only as a route of last resort.

8. If an inside address does not match a definition of addresses eligible for NAT, according to the access list to which it is associated, the traffic will be forwarded based on an untranslated source address. No attempt will be made to process the address via NAT or PAT.

Chapter 7

"Do I Know This Already?"

1. C
2. B and C
3. A
4. C
5. B
6. D
7. B
8. B
9. A
10. B

Q&A

1. The PMD is the physical medium dependent sublayer. It is part of the physical layer and has the job of interfacing a particular media type, be it copper, fiber, air, or other. Its purpose is to perform physical layer framing functions. The order of the bits is specified by the technology in use. For example, T1 frame types specify a structure containing 24 time slots, each 8 bits in length. The resulting entity is a T1 frame and has an additional bit at the end to specify End of Frame. The structure goes on to specify structures for Superframe and Extended Superframe. This structure is replicated at the far end. Because both ends understand the structure, both can comprehend what is received.

The TC is the transmission convergence sublayer. This is also known as line code. This mechanism specifies the manner in which bits will be transmitted through changes in voltage, amplitude, frequency, polarity, phase, or other characteristics of the electrical or light signal.

2. There are many possible answers to this particular type of scenario. One course of action begins with a discussion with the teleworker.

    Ask probing questions such as, "What were you doing when the connection fell?" "Were any of the physical connections moved?" "Did you experience a power outage?" "Are all devices powered on?" "Have you installed any new software or devices on your PC or on the network itself?"

    All of these will lead to a bigger picture of the nature of the problem and the circumstances surrounding it. Once a state of satisfaction has been reached with all the answers, start simple. Have the user try to ping the local default gateway. If that works, move out one hop or perform a traceroute to the corporate VPN Concentrator and various well-known Internet sites. If no traffic is leaving the local subnet, begin by contacting the local service provider to verify that it is not experiencing an outage. This has the potential to save a great deal of time spent troubleshooting fruitlessly. With that done, begin troubleshooting at the physical layer, moving to the data link layer, and so on. If the DSL connection is training but no connectivity is restored, the provider should be re-engaged in the troubleshooting process.

3. Interface GigabitEthernet0/0 has been placed in a shutdown state as evident by the status administratively down. It has no IP address, a fact which would lead to the idea that the interface is not in use at this time.

4. Interface FastEthernet0/1/1 is in down/down state. Because it is an Ethernet interface, most likely nothing is plugged in to that interface or a bad cable is in use.

    Interface FastEthernet 0/1/8 is in up/down state and requires some further investigation. Because its status is up, it is evident that there is a Layer 1 connection. The line protocol is down, however, indicating a Layer 2 problem. According to the router prompt, this router seems to be a 2821, which is, in fact, the case. It contains an HWICD-9ESW PoE switch that takes up two of the HWIC slots. The ninth port (FastEthernet 0/1/8) is an uplink port that is not in use; however, it maintains up/down status.

    The remaining interfaces show to be up/up and are therefore happily in use and doing their jobs as designed.

5. A typical phone cord will usually suffice; however, twisted-pair cables are often preferred to ensure higher-quality connections. An RJ-11 standard connector is a six-pin connector. A typical phone cord uses only four wires, sometimes only two. The wires on a typical four-wire phone cord use a different color for each wire (red, green, black, and yellow). Typically, red/green are the inner pair and black/yellow are the outer pair.

Each pair of wires has one wire designated as *tip* and one designated as *ring*. The tip and ring wires for xDSL connections are pins 3 and 4, respectively, on the six-pin connector, or 2 and 3 on a four-pin connector.

Chapter 8

"Do I Know This Already?"

1. C
2. B
3. A
4. C
5. D
6. D
7. A
8. C

Q&A

1. When a packet arrives on the ingress interface, the packet destination network is read from the Layer 3 header. A routing table lookup is performed to determine whether or not a next-hop address and egress interface are known. If known, the packet is forwarded out the appropriate interface with the Layer 2 encapsulation appropriate to the media and framing type. It also may be necessary to perform address resolution for the next-hop address, thereby adding additional latency.

2. With process switching, every packet is treated identically with regard to routing table lookups. This is inefficient when considering multiple packets destined for the same destination networks. Fast switching keeps information pertinent to a particular destination, including needed address resolution information, in a cache where it can be queried rather than fully processing a routing table lookup. This allows the bypassing of the routing table and address resolution steps of the process for all but the first packet destined to a particular network. Subsequent packets can be essentially "rubber-stamped" and dispatched.

3. CEF switching information is stored in a FIB. All information in the FIB is copied from the routing table built by the local routing protocol running in the router. CEF updates are triggered by the local routing protocol reaction to convergence events. That is, when the local routing table is changed, CEF copies the changes and updates the FIB. CEF switching need

not maintain address resolution or encapsulation information because it maintains an adjacency table specifically for this purpose. The adjacency table is built at Layer 2 and linked to entries in the FIB.

4. An ordered set of labels attached to a packet header. Each label in the stack is independent of the others.

5. At times, an LSR immediately prior to the destination edge router will pop the label before sending the packet to the final edge LSR or node. This is known as a *penultimate hop pop* of the label. This is advantageous at times, because the final edge device does not need to perform both a label lookup and a network layer routing lookup once it figures out that it is the last hop prior to the destination.

6. Although both provide any-to-any connectivity between WAN sites, the Frame Relay connectivity requires an exponentially increasing number of circuits to accomplish what the MPLS connection can do with a single circuit. With Frame Relay, a 20-site deployment would require 190 circuits, whereas the MPLS equivalent would require only 20.

7. Full routing table lookup is performed only at the ingress edge LSR, at any device that receives an unlabeled packet, or at a device that does not have a label destination for a received labeled packet.

8. CEF-FIB updates are event triggered. There must be a change in the IP routing table for CEF-FIB update to be initiated.

Chapter 9

"Do I Know This Already?"

1. C
2. D
3. A
4. A
5. C
6. B
7. B
8. A
9. C
10. B

11. A and C

12. A

13. A

14. A

Q&A

1. The Control Plane maintains routing information and label information exchange between adjacent devices. Routing protocols such as OSPF, BGP, and others are part of the Control Plane.

2. The Data Plane forwards traffic based on destination addresses or labels. It is also known as the Forwarding Plane. The Data Plane functions based on the information constructed and provided by the Control Plane.

3. When a packet arrives at an LSR, the packet is checked for the inbound label. If no label exists, a label lookup can be performed for the destination. If no label entry exists in the local LFIB, a FIB lookup is done for that destination. The packet is then forwarded on to the next-hop based on FIB information. If no FIB entry exists, the packet is dropped.

If the packet is indeed found to have a label on ingress, an LFIB lookup provides the needed outbound label and next-hop address information. The relabeled packet is forwarded to that next-hop.

If a labeled packet is received and the LFIB shows no label entry for the outbound label, the label is popped and a FIB lookup is performed to determine next-hop information. This inefficiency can be eliminated by the use of PHP.

4. Label stacks are present when multiple labels are imposed on a single packet. The first label added is said to be the level 1 label and has its S-bit set to 1. The next label imposed is the level 2 label and has its S-bit set to 0, as will subsequently added labels.

As a packet traverses the network, the LSR cares only about the highest-level label, ignoring the remainder of the stack.

Additional labels can be added by MPLS-VPN tunnels or MPLS-TE tunnels or both. It is possible to traffic engineer an MPLS-VPN tunnel or route an MPLS-TE tunnel such that it will traverse an MPLS-VPN tunnel. It all comes down to the desired architecture and traffic flow. In such a case, one tunnel will logically ride inside the other, necessitating a label for each. Each tunnel need not ride inside the other to a common end. One may end well ahead of the other.

Each tunnel process will add its respective label to the stack. As the packet reaches the end of the first tunnel, the top label will be popped, thereby allowing the next label to be analyzed and the packet forwarded. Once the packet reaches the end of the next tunnel, the next label is popped. Once the final label is all that exists, the final edge LSR will pop the label and forward the packet based on FIB information, assuming PHP is not in effect.

5. The label itself is a four-octet (32-bit) structure. It includes the following fields:

    ■ Label—20 bits

    ■ Experimental CoS—3 bits

    ■ Bottom of Stack Indicator—1 bit

    ■ Time To Live (TTL)—8 bits

    The Label field itself can contain values between 0 and 1,048,575; however, the values from 0 to 15 are reserved for future use. Therefore, 16 is the first available label value.

    As noted, the second field is currently experimental. Its use is undefined in RFC 3031. Cisco uses this field for CoS using IP Precedence values.

    The Bottom-of-Stack bit is used when multiple MPLS labels are prepended for a single packet. The values for this field are 0 (false) and 1 (true). A value of 1 indicates that this particular label is the last label.

    The TTL field is just what it seems. It has a function identical to that of the TTL field in an IP header.

6. The label value imp-null denotes that this LSR is configured to perform a penultimate hop pop prior to forwarding the packet on to the next LSR, which will be the edge LSR. PHP allows the LSR immediately prior to the edge LSR to pop the label to save some processing resources for the edge LSR.

7. The term *frame mode MPLS* essentially denotes the use of MPLS with Ethernet-encapsulated or other frame-based-encapsulated interfaces. It does not include ATM-encapsulated interfaces. ATM uses cell mode MPLS and has a unique set of requirements due to the lack of a flexible framing structure.

8. A few different scenarios are possible with an edge LSR forwarding decision:

    ■ A received packet can be forwarded as a normal IP packet, based on the destination IP address. In this case, the outbound interface is not MPLS enabled.

    ■ A received packet can be forwarded as an MPLS labeled packet based on a destination IP address. In this case, the outbound interface is MPLS enabled.

■ A received labeled packet is received and forwarded based solely on the label. The inbound label is examined and swapped based on the LFIB so that the packet can be dispatched to the next MPLS hop.

■ A received labeled packet is forwarded based on the label; however, the LFIB shows that this edge LSR is the egress MPLS edge. Therefore, the label is popped and the packet routed normally.

If a received labeled packet is dropped, this is symptomatic of a lack of an LFIB entry, even if the destination exists in the routing table.

Similarly, a received IP packet might be dropped if there is no routing entry in the routing table, even if the entry does exist in the LFIB for the destination.

9. MPLS label switching relies only on labels. While the construction of the label table involves the independent routing tables of various protocols traversing the network, the actual switch process cares only about label-in, label-out, next-hop, and outbound interface. At no time does the MPLS label switching process rely on Layer 3 information.

Chapter 10

"Do I Know This Already?"

1. A

2. B

3. A

4. B

5. B

6. B

Q&A

1. CEF uses the FIB rather than a route cache to eliminate cache maintenance and fast/process switching of packets.

    The FIB and adjacency tables provide the operational base for CEF. CEF uses the FIB to make IP destination switching decisions. The adjacency table keeps a database of Layer 2 information, including Layer 2 next-hop information. CEF uses the adjacency table to prepend Layer 2 information to outbound traffic. This avoids any need for ARP or other Layer 2/3 resolution processes.

2. TDP is a Cisco proprietary label distribution protocol, whereas LDP is a standardized label distribution protocol. A mixed environment might be encountered during times of migration from TDP to LDP or in a multivendor environment.

   In a migration situation, it is prudent to carefully plan the migration from one to the other. Both can be enabled simultaneously or a flash cut from TDP to LDP can be done.

   In cases of multivendor deployments, a simple answer might be to remedy that issue and deploy all Cisco equipment. More realistically, a solution might be to enable both protocols on MPLS interfaces to accommodate both TDP and LDP. Also, a migration strategy could easily be put in place to migrate the Cisco equipment to LDP altogether and eliminate any dependence on TDP.

3. The MTU must be adjusted on all interfaces of all devices in the LSP that will be transporting MPLS traffic, including routers and switches. The size must be set to accommodate the technologies in use. For example, if label stacking is in use, then the MTU must be adjusted to accommodate the entire label stack size at 4 bytes per label.

4. Labels in the range of 0 to 15 are reserved values. The value 3 signifies that the outlabel is implicit null or **imp-null** in **show** command output. This means that the label is to be popped before forwarding the packet to the next-hop device.

Chapter 11

"Do I Know This Already?"

1. A
2. B
3. B
4. A
5. C
6. B
7. C
8. C
9. B
10. C
11. B
12. B

Q&A

1. A Layer 2 overlay VPN is synonymous with what is traditionally known as WAN connectivity. Technologies such as Frame Relay, ATM, SMDS, and more are Layer 2 VPN overlays. The provider has no involvement in the routing processes of a Layer 2 overlay VPN. Typical topologies include full mesh, partial mesh, and hub-and-spoke deployments.

2. A peer-to-peer VPN is Layer 3 aware. The service provider conveys routing information from CE router to CE router. Peer-to-peer VPNs offer optimal routing redundancy and full mesh capabilities with a single connection to the P network.

3. The most overlooked potential issue is a single point of failure between the CE and PE. In many cases, a single access point is available to a particular building. A single fiber cut can reduce even the most ornate redundancy scheme to nothing if all of those fiber strands share a single entry/exit point at the premises.

   Routing loops are also a potential issue. With MPLS VPNs, the provider and customer need to work together to eliminate them. It is necessary to ensure that routes advertised via one circuit are not redistributed out to the PE and then right back in via the redundant circuit to the CE. This will cause a significant routing loop. Split horizon will not stop it, because the update is not received via the interface through which it was initially sent.

4. Router A is running an IGP across the connection to the PE router. The 192.168.1.0/24 prefix is advertised across that link and entered into the VRF in the ingress PE router. That prefix is prepended with an RD to create a VPNv4 prefix and then appended with a VPN-specific export RT prior to being propagated to the egress PE by an MPBGP neighbor relationship between the two PE routers. Upon receipt of the update, the import RT is examined to determine VPN membership. The route is then redistributed into the appropriate VRF and then on to the CE router via the customer IGP.

5. The ICMP packet enters CE-B, where a routing table lookup is performed. The result of the lookup dictates that the interface connected to the PE router is the outbound interface and next-hop address. The packet is encapsulated inside an appropriate frame for the media type and transmitted to the ingress PE.

   The ingress PE performs a routing table lookup in the VRF associated with this customer and determines that the route to the 192.168.1.0/24 network is known as being advertised by the egress PE through MPBGP.

   The PE router imposes a VPN label appropriate to the customer-specific VPN instance. An additional label, an LDP label, specific to the LSP that will get the packet to the egress PE is also imposed.

   Each P router in the LSP performs a label lookup and swap based on only the LDP label (that is, the top label in the stack) to forward the packet.

When the egress PE is reached, a label lookup occurs, resulting in no outbound label entry. Therefore, the top label is popped, revealing the VPN-specific label. This label contains information regarding the VRF containing the customer routes. A routing table lookup is performed in the VRF, finding that the outbound interface is specified. This means that the next-hop device is the CE; therefore the label is popped and the packet is routed to the next-hop address of the CE router and on to the 192.168.1.5 host.

With that accomplished, the path is successfully traced from CE to shining CE.

Chapter 12

"Do I Know This Already?"

1. C, D, E
2. C
3. A, C, D
4. A, E
5. C
6. C, D
7. A, D
8. B
9. B, E
10. E
11. A, B, E
12. C
13. B
14. C

Q&A

1. Data integrity, data confidentiality, anti-replay, and origin authentication are the features of IPsec.

2. IKE, ESP, and AH

3. Data confidentiality is the use of encryption to scramble data as it travels across an insecure media. Data integrity verifies that the data was not modified or altered during transit.

4. Data authentication and data integrity are performed by an HMAC.

5. With IPsec transport mode, the IPsec headers are inserted into the IP packet after the IP header. Thus, the original IP header is exposed during transit. In tunnel mode, a new IP header is applied to the packet. This new header uses the tunnel end points as the source and destination IP addresses. The entire original packet, including the original IP header, is protected in tunnel mode.

6. ESP uses IP protocol 50. AH uses IP protocol 51. And IKE uses TCP port 500.

7. A one-time password is good for only one IPsec session. It is typically implemented as a PIN or a TAN. The discovery of a one-time password would prove useless to anyone.

8. The use of username/password and preshared keys both must be preconfigured into the IPsec endpoints prior to the IPsec tunnel establishment.

9. IKE dynamically exchanges keys for secure communications

10. IKE phase 1.5.

11. IKE uses the bidirectional SA to exchange all IPsec parameters and keys.

12. Main mode uses six messages during IKE phase 2 to exchange security parameters, exchange public keys, and authenticate each end. If main mode is selected, aggressive mode is not used.

Aggressive mode is an abbreviated version of main mode. The six packets of main mode are condensed into three messages. When aggressive mode is used, main mode is not.

Quick mode negotiates the IPsec SAs during IKE phase 2. This mode runs after either main mode or aggressive mode.

13. Dead peer detection (DPD), NAT traversal, mode configuration, and Xauth are additional IKE functions.

14. A single shared secret key is used for bidirectional encryption, and it is best used for bulk encryption requirements.

15. RSA is an asymmetric encryption algorithm, while Diffie-Hellman is an asymmetric key exchange protocol.

16. RA can handle enrollment requests.

17. Digital certificates

18. Both LDAP and HTTP are examples of distribution mechanisms.

Chapter 13

"Do I Know This Already?"

1. C
2. B and C
3. C and E
4. A
5. E
6. A, B, D
7. B
8. C
9. A, B, C, D, E
10. A, C, D
11. B, C, D
12. E
13. A and B
14. B
15. B and C
16. A and D
17. A, B, E
18. C
19. A, B, C
20. D
21. C and D
22. C and E
23. C
24. B

Q&A

1. IKE phase 2

2. An IPsec tunnel is terminated when a preconfigured amount of data has gone through the tunnel or when the tunnel has been operational for a particular amount of time.

3. It is sent out the interface to its intended destination, but not through the VPN.

4. Extended IP ACL

5. Main mode uses the third and fourth packets for Diffie-Hellman, while aggressive mode uses the first two packets.

6. The IPsec process is halted.

7. IKE phase 2

8. Quick mode

9. **crypto ipsec transform-set**

10. **crypto isakmp key**

11. Security Policy Database (SPD)

12. Yes, an IPsec tunnel can expire even if there is traffic flowing through it. In this case, a new tunnel is typically established before the old one is torn down. However, data flow is interrupted until the new IPsec tunnel is established.

13. To prevent weaker sets from being agreed upon between peers

14. IKE phase 1

15. **crypto ipsec transform-set test esp-aes esp-sha-hmac**

16. Remote peer, interesting traffic, and IPsec transform set

17. **access-list 101 permit 172.16.5.0 0.0.0.255 10.1.2.0 0.0.255.255**

18. **crypto map test**

19. Protocol 51

20. Home, Configure, Monitor, Refresh, Save, Search, and Help

21. Site-to-Site VPN, Easy VPN Remote, Easy VPN Server, and Dynamic Multipoint VPN wizards

22. The interface on the local router used to source the IPsec VPN

23. Preshared keys and digital certificates

24. You might choose to send traffic from a single IP address or small subnet in the clear, but send the remainder of the larger subnet through the IPsec VPN.

25. Traffic that does not match the ACL is sent in the clear.

26. The encrypted and decrypted packet counts will be greater than zero, and should increase with successive show screens.

Chapter 14

"Do I Know This Already?"

1. C

2. B, C

3. C

4. B

5. E

6. B, C, E

7. C

8. D

9. A, B

10. A

11. C, D

12. A, B, C

13. A, B, C

14. B, C

15. D

Q&A

1. GRE offers basic encryption, but the encryption key is carried within the packet, which minimizes the effectiveness.

2. Checksum, encryption, and sequencing

3. The key carried in the GRE packet can be used to uniquely identify different tunnels that are set up between the same two sites.

4. The tunnel source at one end is the tunnel destination on the other, and vice versa.

5. Both tunnel and transport modes are possible with GRE over IPsec.

6. GRE provides the ability to exchange dynamic routing information, whereas IPsec alone cannot.

7. Click the **Configure** button, click the **VPN** button, click the **Site-to-Site VPN** option, click the **Create Site to Site VPN** tab, click the **Create a secure GRE tunnel (GRE over IPSec)** radio button, and click **Launch the selected task**.

8. Source interface/IP address, destination IP address, internal IP address/subnet mask, (optional) MTU path discovery

9. Source interface/IP address

10. VPN authentication information (pre-shared keys or digital certificates), IKE proposals, and IPsec transform sets

11. Static routes, RIP, OSPF, and EIGRP

12. 1

13. Either OSPF or EIGRP

14. Go back into the wizard to modify the configuration (click **<Back**), finish the wizard (click **Finish**), and optionally test the GRE over IPsec connection when the wizard is finished

Chapter 15

"Do I Know This Already?"

1. A, C, D, E

2. A, B, D

3. A, B, E

4. B, D, E

5. B

6. D

7. B and C

8. C

9. A

10. B

11. C

12. B and E

13. B and E

Q&A

1. Access link failure, remote peer failure, device failure, and path failure

2. The use of multiple interfaces, multiple interface cards, or multiple endpoint devices

3. DPD, the use of an IGP within GRE over IPsec tunnels, and HSRP

4. On-demand

5. The excessive overhead of encrypting the DPD keepalive messages

6. **crypto isakmp keepalive** *seconds* [*retries*] [**periodic** | **on-demand**]

7. OSPF or EIGRP

8. For a particular HSRP group, the HSRP active router handles all traffic sent to the virtual IP/MAC addresses, while the HSRP standby router only works when the active router fails.

9. The VPN drops and is reestablished to the same virtual IP address.

10. HSRP and SSO

11. The IGP metrics must be configured such that the WAN connection is preferred if it is available.

12. A floating static route is a static route that has a high administrative distance, and is only used if the path is no longer available from dynamic routing updates.

Chapter 16

"Do I Know This Already?"

1. A

2. A

3. B

4. B

5. B

6. B

7. B

8. C

9. B

10. A

11. A

12. C

Q&A

1. Stage 1 is Group Level Authentication, which represents a portion of the channel creation process. During this stage, two types of authentication can be used, either preshared keys or digital certificates.

   Stage 2 of the authentication is known as Extended Authentication, or Xauth. The remote side of the connection submits a username and password to the central site VPN device. This is the same method used when a Cisco VPN Software Client is prompted for a username and password to activate a VPN tunnel. However, in this case, a user is not authenticated to the central site. Instead, the Easy VPN Remote Router itself is authenticated. Although Xauth is optional, it is typically used to improve security. When the Xauth is successfully completed and the VPN tunnel is created, all PCs behind the Easy VPN Remote Router can use the connection.

2. The VPN Client initiates IKE phase 1.

   The VPN Client establishes an ISAKMP SA.

   The Easy VPN Server accepts the SA proposal.

   The Easy VPN Server initiates user authentication.

   Mode configuration begins.

   The Reverse Route Injection (RRI) process begins.

   IPsec quick mode completes the connection.

3. Extended Authentication, or Xauth, allows the remote side of a connection to submit a username and password to the central site VPN device. However, in this case, a user is not authenticated to the central site. Instead, the Easy VPN Remote Router, itself, is authenticated. Although Xauth is optional, it is typically used to improve security. Once the Xauth is successfully completed and the VPN tunnel is created, all PCs behind the Easy VPN Remote Router can use the connection.

4. Reverse Route Injection (RRI) is the process of injecting a static route into the Interior Gateway Protocol (IGP) routing table. This static route points to the client's destination network. This is useful when per-client static IP addressing is used with VPN Clients rather than per-VPN address pools.

   Without the RRI, there would be no path for return traffic to reach the VPN client.

5. Options can be configured for all users within the group membership, including

   Group Name

   Pre-Shared Key

   Pool Information

   DNS/WINS Server

   Split Tunneling

   Backup Servers

   Personal Firewall information

   Local LAN Access while connected

   Maximum Number of Group Connections

   Xauth Options such as Group Lock and Saved Password capability

   Maximum Number of Logins Per User

6. The choice of transform set is made by a progressive trial-and-error method. The configured transform sets are proposed in order of entry until both client and server agrees upon one of them. When a match is made, processing of transform sets ceases. This means that additional transform sets below the one agreed upon will not be processed.

7. **Client**—Specifies that NAT or PAT will be used so that end stations at the remote end of the VPN tunnel do not use IP addresses in the space of the destination server. The needed security associations (SA) are created automatically for IP addresses assigned to remote hosts.

   Network Extension—Specifies that remote-end hosts use IP addresses that are fully routable and reachable by the destination network over the tunnel connection so that they form a single logical network. In such cases, PAT is not used, to allow remote-end PCs direct access to destination network services and applications.

   Network Extension Plus—Identical to Network Extension mode with the additional capability of being able to request an IP address via mode configuration and automatically assign it to an available loopback interface. The IPsec SAs for this IP address are automatically created.

8. Cisco Easy VPN Remote does not support transform sets providing encryption without authentication or those providing authentication without encryption. Both encryption and authentication must be represented.

Chapter 17

"Do I Know This Already?"

1. A
2. B
3. A
4. D
5. B
6. C

Q&A

1. Once the VPN Client has been launched, click the **New** button. This opens the Create New VPN Connection Entry dialog box. This dialog box requires the configuration of the Connection **Entry CorporateVPN** as provided in the scenario given in the question. The entry of a description is optional.

   In the Host field, enter **vpnserver1.mycompany.com**, the specified VPN server.

   The Authentication tab is already active by default when a new connection is created. Under the Name field, enter the username **RoadWarrior**. Enter the password **cisco** and then confirmation of the password **cisco** in the respective fields. Because the certificate has already been provided, no further information is needed on this tab.

   On the Transport tab, check **Enable Transparent Tunneling**, as specified in the scenario. Click the **IPsec over UDP (NAT/PAT)** radio button. No other options need be configured on this tab.

   On the Backup Servers tab, check **Enable Backup Servers** and add an entry for **vpnserver2.mycompany.com** as specified. Because it is the only backup server, no reordering of connections is needed.

   Because there is no information specified in the scenario's parameters, no dialup information needs to be configured on the Dial-Up tab. Click the **Save** button at the bottom of the Create New VPN Connection Entry dialog box to enact all changes. This connection entry is ready for use.

2.   IPsec over UDP typically uses UDP port 4500 to transport IPsec packets through a NAT/PAT device, but the port can be negotiated. IPsec over TCP uses a preconfigured port on both ends and can be used to send IPsec packets through a stateful firewall.

3.   The primary server could be congested or inoperable. If only a single server is configured and it is unavailable, the VPN connection will fail. Backup servers enable the VPN client to step through a list of IP addresses in an attempt to establish a successful VPN connection.

4.   Local LAN Access permits access to network resources on the local subnet. Without this option, all traffic is sent through the VPN to the central site. Local resources, such as printers and file shares, would not be accessible. Both the client and the VPN central server must be configured for Local LAN Access.

5.   The Group Authentication method requires a username and password to be entered. Both Mutual Group Authentication and Certificate Authentication require the use of certificates for authentication.

6.   Although a large majority of devices are accessible via the Internet today, not all are. Some require the use of a dial-up connection to establish connectivity, and thus to create a VPN connection.

Chapter 18

"Do I Know This Already?"

1.   E

2.   A and D

3.   B and D

4.   B, C, E

5.   B and D

6.   B and E

7.   C

8.   A and C

9.   B and C

10. C and D

Q&A

1. CDP should either be completely disabled or disabled where it is not needed, such as external interfaces.

2. BOOTP, MOP, and PAD

3. ICMP redirects, ICMP unreachables, and ICMP mask replies

4. Gratuitous ARP and proxy ARP

5. The sheer volume of Cisco IOS commands makes it easy to miss an important feature and possibly leave the router vulnerable.

6. AutoSecure offers either an automated or interactive means of securing a Cisco IOS router. In automated mode, various features are secured without user input. In interactive mode, the user can select which features need to be secured.

7. **auto secure no-interact**

8. The **full** option causes all options to be examined. This is the default behavior.

9. 1. Identify the outside interface(s). 2. Secure the management plane. 3. Create a security banner. 4. Configure passwords, AAA, and SSH. 5. Secure the interfaces. 6. Secure the forwarding plane.

10. Either restore the manually saved pre-AutoSecure configuration, or execute **configure replace flash:pre_autosec.cfg** if using Cisco IOS Software Release 12.3(8) or later.

11. SDM offers the Security Audit and the One-Step Lockdown wizards.

12. The user first selects the inside/outside interface. Next, the user selects the security parameters to be corrected. Next, the user can create the appropriate configurations to correct the vulnerabilities. And finally, the user can deliver the configurations to the router.

13. The user is only allowed to execute the One-Step Lockdown wizard. There are no user-accessible steps within the wizard.

Chapter 19

"Do I Know This Already?"

1. C

2. C and E

3. B and C

4. B, C, F

5. A, B, E

6. D

7. E

8. B

9. A

10. C

11. D

12. A, C, E

13. E

14. C

15. A

16. A and D

17. B

18. E

19. B

Q&A

1. The console port, the aux port, and the vty ports

2. A Cisco router can be configured via the CLI, which is available on the console and aux ports, and via a Telnet or SSH session. The router can also be configured via SDM via HTTP and HTTPS. SNMP can be used to configure and poll the router.

3. Enforce a minimum length, require a mix of characters, do not permit dictionary words, and force password changes often.

4. Passwords in a Cisco IOS device can be anywhere between 1 and 25 characters (the longer the better), the first character cannot be a space or number, and the password may contain any character (including spaces).

5. IOS imposes a 15-second login delay and logs the failed attempt to access the router.

6. *seconds* defines the login delay. *failed-attempts* defines the number of consecutive login failures. *watch-period* is the time period that *failed-attempts* must occur to impose the *seconds* penalty.

7. Setup does not permit these two passwords to match, and continues to ask for an enable password until a unique one is entered.

8. The enable secret password is encrypted with an MD5 one-way hash, which is considered virtually unbreakable. The enable password is initially stored in plaintext, and at best can be encrypted with the Vigenere cipher, which is known to be very weak.

9. The **login** command enables password checking, which forces the use of the configured password. Without this command, any configured password would be ignored during a login attempt.

10. An access class allows only specific IP addresses or subnets to access the router via Telnet or SSH. This prevents any device on the network from attempting to access the router.

11. The **exec-timer** disconnects a line after a determined amount of time. This prevents an unoccupied terminal from offering access into the router.

12. Nothing. This only forces new passwords to be a minimum of 15 characters.

13. To restore passwords to plaintext, password encryption must be disabled (**no service password-encryption**) and the passwords must be entered again.

14. A banner does not provide any security mechanisms to a router, but it offers warnings to those who connect to the router.

15. The command **login local** must be applied to the lines to use the username database.

16. Level 0 is user mode, level 15 is privileged mode, and levels 1 to 14 are defined by the user.

17. Each IOS command can be used only one time across all privilege levels. The same IOS command can be used in all IOS views. Also, privilege levels do not offer command isolation, such as a particular interface. IOS views offer this level of granularity.

18. A superview is a collection of views. Many individual views can be combined into a superview. However, no individual IOS commands may be configured in a superview.

19. **no service password-recovery** prevents access to ROMMON mode during the router's boot cycle. ROMMON can be used to perform password recovery and access the router without knowing the passwords. But it can also be used to recover a lost Cisco IOS image. Once ROMMON is disabled, there is no way to access the router during boot.

Chapter 20

"Do I Know This Already?"

1. D

2. B

3. D

4. A

5. D

6. D

7. D

8. B

9. C

10. A

11. D

12. C

13. B

Q&A

1. There are many consequences. Among these are

   ■ Scalability

   ■ Ability to see when servers have failed

   ■ Using different servers or technologies for authentication, authorization, and accounting

   ■ Individual command level control

   ■ Multiprotocol support

   ■ Interoperability

2. You must have authentication running before you can enable accounting. It is not possible to track a user until you are sure that the user is who they claim to be.

3. This scenario appears to be perfect for TACACS+. RADIUS is known to suffer, mainly because of its UDP protocol reliance, when deployed in large environments. Although RADIUS has been used successfully in large environments, TACACS+ tends to scale more easily than will RADIUS.

4. This user probably has not been given authority to access the vty lines. Alternatively, the user might not even be in the database.

5. This is almost certainly an issue of privilege level for the command. Check the user's privilege level for the affected commands and change them, if necessary, with the **aaa authorization** command.

6. The **aaa accounting** command allows you to use the **stop** parameter instead of the **start-stop** parameter to track only the last access time.

7. You should look at the **tacacs-server host** command because this allows you to change the default timeout.

Chapter 21

"Do I Know This Already?"

1. B

2. A and B

3. D

4. D

5. B

6. F

7. C

8. E

9. C and D

10. C and D

11. B

12. B and C

13. C

Q&A

1. Place each of the servers on a separate DMZ. This allows for protection of the corporate network and ensures that compromise of a single server does not affect the other servers.

2. Packet filtering, which uses the IP address and/or port number to allow access; application layer gateway, which works as a proxy server, preventing the user from direct access to the server; and stateful packet filtering, which uses dynamic ACLS and tracks the state of connections to determine access

3. The Cisco IOS Firewall recognizes many different protocols, including BGP, FTP, RADIUS, SNMP, and HTTP/HTTPS.

4. UDP is a connectionless protocol. Therefore, there is no "session" as in a connection-oriented protocol such as FTP. Instead of relying on connection status, the firewall uses timeouts to determine whether a session is still active.

5. This is the stateful packet filter.

6. Because you have such sensitive data on this server, you should never allow direct access to the server. We recommend placing this server on its own DMZ and using an ALG for access to the server.

7. Cisco IOS IPS allows you to monitor a single protocol and log all instances of that specific protocol.

8. This server is using stateful packet filtering, which dynamically changes the ACLs.

9. An Authentication Proxy Server is used to provide proxy services related to AAA.

Chapter 22

"Do I Know This Already?"

1. C
2. D
3. B
4. A
5. B
6. B

NOTE The Basic Firewall Wizard may be used on routers with multiple untrusted interfaces. However, the Basic Firewall Wizard will only allow you to configure a single untrusted interface and does not allow you to configure a DMZ.

7. C
8. C
9. B

Q&A

1. There are many advantages, some of which are as follows:

   - Speed of configuration

   - Graphical interface allows you to see what you are doing

   - Less chance of forgetting a critical configuration item

   - No need to remember the CLI syntax

2. Generally, the Basic Firewall Wizard should be used when there is only a single untrusted network and no DMZ. When you have a DMZ or DMZs or multiple untrusted networks, you should use the Advanced version. Some people choose to always use the Advanced version to see all the options that are available.

3. The steps are as follows:

   Step 1   **Choose the interface**—Decide which interface(s) to be protected by the ACL and IP inspection and whether you should apply the ACL and IP inspection going into or out of the interface.

   Step 2   **Configure an IP ACL for that interface**—Create an extended access list.

   Step 3   **Define the inspection rules**—Decide which protocols need to be watched.

   Step 4   **Apply the inspection rules and the ACL to the interface**—Apply the ACL and the rule to the interface.

   Step 5   **Verify**—Use **show** and **debug** commands.

4. The default timeouts are designed for the "average" network. Because no two networks are identical, every one has different requirements. The timeouts may be changed depending on the needs and usage of a network. For example, some networks have a large number of FTP files that can be accessed by the general public. In this case, the time between alerts regarding FTP will be raised because the network could become inundated by the amount of data we receive. Alternatively, we may have a network where the FTP files should be considered secret. In this case, we would lower the time between reports to give us more rapid information.

Chapter 23

"Do I Know This Already?"

1. C

2. B

3. B, D, E

4. A

5. B, D, E

6. A

7. B

8. D

9. A, C, E

10. C

Q&A

1. Intrusion detection and intrusion prevention systems

2. An IDS sits outside the packet flow and examines a copy of network traffic. If it finds a problem, it sends an alert and can configure network devices to stop further packets. An IPS sits in the packet flow, and when it finds a problem, it can stop the offending packets immediately.

3. A single network IDS or IPS can monitor traffic destined for multiple hosts. It cannot inspect encrypted traffic, nor asses the success or failure of an attack. A host-based IDS or IPS monitors behavior on an individual device. Cisco Security Agent is an example of this.

4. Signature-based, policy-based, and anomaly-based,

5. The policy-based mechanism may need access to such a database that keeps up-to-date information.

6. Exploit, connection, string, and DoS

7. The system may send an alarm, drop the packet, reset the connection, block traffic from a particular source IP address, block traffic on the connection in question, or any combination of the these.

8. **ip ips sdf location** *name*

9. Inbound, to scan packets before they enter the network device

10. **show ip ips configuration**

11. The Create IPS tab, which is used to create a new IPS rule from scratch, and the Edit IPS tab, which is used to edit existing IPS configurations

Index

O - P

Q - R

S

W

X - Y - Z